THE WORD BECOMING FLESH

THE WORD
BECOMING FLESH

An Introduction to the Origin, Purpose,
and Meaning of the Old Testament

by HORACE D. HUMMEL

CONCORDIA PUBLISHING HOUSE · SAINT LOUIS

Copyright © 1979 by Concordia Publishing House
St. Louis, Missouri 63118

MANUFACTURED IN THE UNITED STATES OF AMERICA

Library of Congress Cataloging in Publication Data
Hummel, Horace D
    The word becoming flesh.

    Includes index.
    1. Bible.   O.T.—Introductions.   I. Title.
BS1140.2.H85   221.6   78-17095
ISBN 0-570-03273-3

---

08 09 10 11   05 04

To Ruth, Joel, and Eve, who might legitimately
think of this work as a thief of time due them.

PREFACE

One casualty of essaying a book of this sort may be one's peace of mind. In the months since I turned in my manuscript, I have often caught myself agonizing over such questions as: Should I have included this, or omitted that? Should I perhaps have nuanced the argument a bit differently than I did? Such questions surfaced not only when I read parallel literature, but also as I taught isagogics again this year. (And I should stress again that, for better or for worse, this book is intended to be a fair facsimile of what actually goes on in my isagogics classrooms, attended mostly by seminary juniors.) Nevertheless, there comes the point, where somewhat like Pilate, one must simply say, "What I have written, I have written," and leave the ultimate verdict to the tender mercies of the readers.

One difficult decision that had to be made early on was to omit chapters on "general introduction" topics: geography, history, canon, or text-criticism. Their omission implies no disregard whatsoever for their crucial and foundational importance (and, in my judgment, typical seminary curricula often fail in these areas even more consistently than in the "special introduction" to which we have limited ourselves). Hence, these general topics have not failed to receive some discussion when considered necessary in connection with the book-by-book treatment.

Another source of concern is the proper acknowledgment of sources. The early decision not to include footnotes or detailed documentation meant that credit could be given only in general terms or in the rare instances of direct quotations. Even some of what might technically be called plagiarism may have slipped through, because I often depended on my own class-lecture notes, and in many cases I no longer remember precisely what my sources were. Indirectly, however, please allow me to express my indebtedness to all from whom I have learned (sometimes negatively as well as positively) and upon whom I have drawn.

My ultimate concern, however, is that the effort will really succeed in "introducing" and confronting, as I hope, not only in general the special problems the Old Testament poses and the widespread neglect from which it often suffers, but specifically the dominant "higher criticism" of the current academic establishment. To that end this work delineates criticism's intrinsic negativism (from which many often seem to be sheltered) and indicates positive aspects that may be salvaged from it.

"Come, Holy Spirit."

Pentecost 1978

CONTENTS

PART I

Introduction to Introduction

What is "Introduction"? The question might seem superfluous. "Introduction" is not only a common word, but also part of the title of many books on the Bible.

Nevertheless, misunderstandings or ambiguities persist. These seem to be especially two overlapping types: (1) the level of the study, and (2) the amount of theology included.

The first misunderstanding seems to confuse "introduction" with mere "survey" (or *Bibelkunde,* in German idiom). Introduction does not exclude survey of contents, but, in the main, it *assumes* basic Biblical knowledge. On the other hand, it probably will list as one of its subsidiary goals the deepening or extending of that knowledge. On the whole, however, that goal will have to be left to the next stage of study, namely "exegesis" (the detailed exposition of the text on the basis of the original languages, not to be confused normally with mere English language "exposition" either).

"Introduction" thus occupies somewhat of a *middle* position *between* Bible survey and exegesis. Misunderstanding at this point would be greatly lessened if we could revive the more technical term, "isagogics" (derived from the Greek rather than the Latin). "Isagogics" concerns itself primarily with questions of date, authorship, occasion, and purpose of writing. That definition of isagogics does not speak of the level or difficulty of the investigation but only of the nature of the investigation. Neither does it imply anything unique as such about the Bible, because "isagogics" belongs to the study and understanding of all human literature. Nevertheless, both because of the importance we attach to the Bible and because of its antiquity, it deserves not less, but much more isagogical examination than ordinary literature. Within the Bible itself, this is in principle true of the New Testament too, but because of both its cultural and theological greater distance from us, it applies *a fortiori* to the Old Testament.

The second misunderstanding or ambiguity concerns the amount of theology to be included in Introduction. The problem appears in two opposite manifestations. Academic "introductions" tend to do their best simply to prescind from theological questions and to cultivate the "cult of objectivity." In a way this is not surprising, because "historical-critical method" took shape by transferring the major context of the investigation from the church to the secular university (and, in another form, it persists with a vengeance in the present proliferation of departments of "religion" in our tax-supported schools). Hence, one of the most pervasive criticisms of higher criticism has been its irrelevance to the church and to the pastor. Introductions and commentaries explore exhaustively questions of background, date, authorship, development, etc. But just when one expects to hit paydirt—the message, theology—the matter is dropped like a hot potato.

The church, however—pastors, theological students—usually manifest the opposite wing of this misunderstanding by tending to *divorce* exegesis, homiletics, and theology from specifically isagogical issues. As such it's not very preachable—and we're *so* busy! There is an old joke (?) that most pastors suffer through their isagogics courses at the Seminary and do their best to forget about the subject as soon as they graduate. Like most jests, this one obviously contains no little truth, or no one would laugh.

One can only stress that functional neglect of isagogics is in principle *allegorical,* essentially that hermeneutics which was rejected by the Reformation. In practice, it is often indistinguishable from the neo-Orthodox principle of divorcing scientific and religious truth, faith and fact, history and theology. By analogy with Christology, it could be called "docetic," or, at best, "Nestorian." Call it what you will, in practice it often makes conservatives strange bedfellows with those whose theoretical theology they would reject out of hand.

At the same time, if isagogics is to remain isagogics, and if it is remotely as important as we have just insisted, there can be no question about where the *accent* must lie in a work of this sort, namely on "external," historical, literary questions. Indispensable as these are, there is a real sense, however, in which it must not be forgotten that they are only *means* to theological ends.

To use a German distinction, our effort here will be more in the nature of an *Einführung* than an *Einleitung.* Both translate quite indistinguishably into English as "introduction." However, the former implies something more than *mere* questing after date, authorship, etc. It indicates some attempt also to convey some of the theological depth and direction of the contents. Thus, it moves perceptibly in the direction of not only exegesis, but also of "Biblical theology."

This work opts for that alternative because of the conviction that there is an ultimate unity of perspectives here which, like marriage, God has joined together and man should not put asunder. We also hope that option will serve its intended audience better. This we envision as not professional Old Testament scholars, perhaps not even professional theologians (in the narrow sense), but those already with some training in both fields and who have not allowed them to lie fallow, that is, alert, conscientious pastors and teachers. We have tried not to belabor the obvious, and we also hope that we have not taken too much for granted.

Presuppositions (Hermeneutics)

If we include theology, we must also ask about theological standpoint or presuppositions. Precisely since isagogics, like other historical topics, is inseparable from theology, the same standpoint will encompass both. Whatever technical or secular techniques promise to be helpful and do not contradict the theological viewpoint in the study of history will be pressed into service. The basic issue, however, is that of the *theology* of history—or, perhaps even more basically, by what *method* (presuppositions, hermeneutics) one determines that theology. Fortunately, virtually no one any longer defends the possibility of absolute objectivity or presuppositionlessness. This does not mean, of course, that one abandons himself to total arbitrariness or subjectivity. It does mean, however, that the closer we come to the ultimate questions, the more one's basic orientation will inevitably determine the results.

This is not the place to rehearse and defend our basic hermeneutical stance. If we must reach for a label, our preference would probably be something like "confessional Lutheran." Because it is common usage we shall usually substitute "conservative" or "evangelical," which are near-synonyms, though less precise. Suffice it to say that such labels imply such propositions as, "Scripture is its own interpreter," "The Bible *is* the Word of God," and "the canonical books are verbally inspired and inerrant."

Since "historical-critical method" is code for an approach that contradicts those confessions, it is necessarily excluded. This does not mean, however, that either the "historical" or the "critical" is excluded, if one defines those terms in a manner congruent with the starting point. In Lutheran circles, the phrase "historical-grammatical" is commonly urged as an alternative. The point of the substitution of "grammatical" for "critical" is that the "historical" must be defined and evaluated by the "grammar" of the inspired text, not the other way around, that is, not by the critiques of human reason and philosophy.

Let it be stressed that this work represents only *a* "confessional" or "evangelical" viewpoint. Within certain limits, conservatives will often disagree on particulars as much as anyone else, and there is no point in pretending otherwise.

Neither is "confessional" entirely synonymous with "traditional"—although it certainly tends to have much more in common with tradition than liberal, critical viewpoints. Some of the difference is symbolized by the inclusion of "historical" in the label "historical-grammatical." The Reformation tended to speak only of the "grammatical" sense (over against especially allegory). While by no means unknown earlier, the modern accent on "history" is largely a heritage of the Enlightenment. Not even the most conservative have remained uninfluenced by it. No one would deny that, within limits, the accent in history has made—and probably will continue to make—incalculable contributions to Biblical studies. The only question finally is whether the Bible judges "history," or whether "history" (or one's perception and philosophy of it) judges Scripture.

In spite of its general congruence with traditional viewpoints, however, everyone is well aware that in the course of the past century or two, the traditional, confessional stance has been pushed into the corner as a minority viewpoint, and often on the ecclesiastical as well as the academic scene. Whether the current evangelical renaissance will succeed in reversing the field or not remains to be seen. At best, no overnight change can be expected.

The reasons for all this are many and complicated and cannot be discussed in detail here. They are, however, both intrinsic and extrinsic, corresponding to the different natures of the liberal and conservative conceptions of Christianity, as well as to their respective relations to the dominant intellectual culture. For one thing, evangelicalism tends to expend a greater share of its energies on evangelism and the cultivation of personal piety. It is no less "intellectual" however; on the contrary, by reason of its very accent on the reasonableness of faith and the need for intellectual assent to revealed propositions, its theory is in a real sense even more intellectually oriented than that of liberalism.

That understanding of the nature of revelation and faith has not been philosophically fashionable for some two centuries (especially since the work of Immanuel Kant). To the liberal mind, it virtually violates the conscience of our culture to posit any deposit of faith once-for-all delivered to the saints. Hence, the very notion of faith comes to include the idea of a constant "search for truth."

(There may sometimes be truth to complaints that conservatives do not even seriously consider their opponents' arguments. But the reverse is surely even more true. Critics ordinarily consider Mosaic authorship of the Pentateuch and other traditional positions so dated and outmoded that the possibility is not even seriously considered, no matter how many arguments may be adduced in their defense.)

The liberal scholar, thus, is driven by a quest which the conservative does not share (at least in its specifically theological dimensions). To the conservative, it often looks much like a moving target in a shooting gallery. No matter how many ducks you shoot down, an infinite number keep popping up again. If "revelation" is a matter of "encounter" between ever-changing understandings of "God's Word" and ever-changing subjectivities of the interpreter, the result is inevitably a sort of pluralism squared—or, perhaps better, pluralism multiplied exponentially.

It is in that light that the charge of "negativism," frequently leveled against conservative works (and which this one will surely not escape either), must be heard. Critical Biblical scholars often disagree with almost everyone else too, but perhaps because those disagreements are more diffuse and lack the common denominator of conservative ones, they often seem to attract less attention. No one would care to deny that there may be such a thing as sheer "negativism" but given confessionalism's assumption that revelation is also propositional, and that also religious truth is objective in nature, it inevitably follows that antithesis as well as thesis must ordinarily be specified. This is not only the pattern of the church's symbolical literature, but, as this study will remind us again, it is the pattern of virtually every part of the Scriptures themselves.

In a work of this nature, one often must generalize about "critical" positions. The very profusion of individual critical positions, however, makes such generalization both inevitable and risky. No matter what critical position is cited, someone can claim that it does not apply to him or to his colleagues—and, as such, perhaps rightly so. By the same token, however, there is scarcely a conservative argument against typical critical positions which cannot be duplicated somewhere within criticism itself. All of this would suggest no more than a standoff, were it not for the underlying and overarching theological and hermeneutical differences. These are the real differences, the issues behind the issues, never mind the degree of surface agreement or disagreement.

Hence, in this book we have generally adopted the method of a sort of a running commentary of at least highlights of the book, accenting isagogical matters as we state and reject typical critical positions and try to indicate the conservative alternative. We have not attempted to thresh through in minute detail again all the pros and cons. Other works do that admirably, on the evangelical side probably best Archer, Harrison, and Young, from the critical viewpoint perhaps most representatively, Eissfeldt, Fohrer, and Soggin. Further discussion is often a matter of exegesis and of commentaries. If the truth must be told, very often the issues ultimately boil down purely and simply to whether or not one holds to propositional revelation and verbal inspiration. Short of that, the conservative rejoinder to critical arrogance and machismo is often simply: "It ain't *necessarily* so!"

Typology

A few words should be said yet about one major specific theological accent of this book. We shall attempt to summarize it under the rubric of "typology." One might easily cavil at the term. Since it often means different things to different people, let us attempt to summarize briefly what we have in mind.

As such of course, "typology" simply means classification or organization according to types, and is a common part of many endeavors. In the context of theology or Biblical studies, it refers to one method of describing the unity of the two testaments. It is customary to speak of the earlier "type" (prototype, archetype, model, analogy) and the subsequent "antitype." Both the word and the method are found in Biblical usage itself, but subsequent exegesis and theology have often carried the process much further.

We customarily speak of three types of types (!), persons, events, and institutions. For example, Christ is prefigured and anticipated by Moses, the Exodus, and the tabernacle. Conversely, He is the "antitype," the fulfillment (to use Irenaeus' famous categories, the recapitulation and the consummation) of the three.

We may also subdivide between "vertical" and "horizontal" typology. Normally, only the latter is implied. The major difference between most ancient (and much modern) paganism and Biblical theology (as between the former's successor, Platonic philosophy and its child, allegory and typology) is that the former was *primarily* vertically oriented (salvation *from* history), while the Bible's basic orientation is toward the future, (salvation incarnationally through history). It is important to accent that all valid typology is both eschatological and Christological.

Nevertheless, the difference may be overdone as liberalism generally does. It is more a matter of accent than of mutual exclusives. Thus, the earthly tabernacle/temple is also a type of the heavenly temple, its "reflection" or miniature. The holy war of Biblical history is fought *both* and often simultaneously in heaven and on earth. God comes *down* to deal with man, as Christ did climactically. Only eschatologically, at the end of our sinful time, will both the vertical and horizontal types be totally fulfilled or consummated in the "new heavens and a new earth in which righteousness dwells" (2 Peter 3:13).

Typology is often attacked on various grounds. Sometimes it is confused with allegory, as though both dealt with artificial, fanciful meanings without foundation in the original author's intent. That charge often comes from a certain type of liberal (positivist, historicist), who believes that the meaning of a text is entirely limited by its original occasion and audience. Conservatives, too, sometimes make the charge, but with less consistency. Typology *can* degenerate into a sort of matching game of superficial correspondence between the testaments that differs but little from allegory.

It would seem to us that conservatives are more likely to shortchange typology from another perspective. They may rightly insist that, unlike allegory, typological correspondences must be real, and must be rooted in real, genuine history. But the matter dare not end there. Typology, as we understand it, implies much more than *mere* correspondence, analogy, or symbol. Especially Lutherans should have little difficulty with use of the word, "sacramental" in this connection. The external history (or elements) must be real enough, but "in, with, and under" it lies the ultimate meaning. There is an integral, internal connection between type and antitype.

Sometimes typology has been urged in opposition to "prophecy-fulfillment." Let it be clear that there is no such hidden agenda here. The meaning proclaimed at the fulfillment is no more "read into" a genuine prophecy than a genuine antitype finds only superficial parallels in some precedent. In fact, we would argue that typology and prophecy-fulfillment are two sides of the same coin, ultimately two ways of saying the same thing. Hence, we propose and defend the following proportion: prophecy-fulfillment is to type-antitype as Word is to Sacrament. Neither part of the proportion is complete without its mate. Prophecy and preaching would be only words about words, great ideas and ideals, if the "visible Word" did not accompany it. Similarly, mere history or sacramental elements are mute without the inspired word to explain and apply.

That is to say that Old Testament history really is *our* history via Christ. It too was accomplished "for us men and for our salvation," and into it too we were baptized. Since Christ is "Israel reduced to one," and since Israel's inner history was all recapitulated and consummated in Him, the "new Israel," the church, expresses its identity and mission in terms of the promise given the old Israel. The difference between the testaments is not ultimately theological at all, but basically only that the first Israel was *both* "church" and state, while in the age of the antitype or fulfillment the political (and accompanying ceremonial) scaffolding falls away.

This is the real concern with emphasizing "typology" at this point. (We stress it, rather than prophecy, because our topic is more specifically historical, and typology speaks specifically of the fulfillment of the events, personages, and institutions which constitute history.) If "introduction" does not introduce to something like this, we are spinning our wheels. If we cannot finally identify with the history of Israel as our redemptive history, or if we cannot hear God's Word for us as readily in the accents and idioms of the old covenant as those of the new, then it would indeed appear that we are running the risk of abbreviating our canon by one whole testament. Precisely because this is often the *de facto* state of affairs, often even in theoretically the most conservative circles, nothing less than gargantuan efforts are called for to stem the tide. If we shall have made any little contribution to that cause, our efforts in producing yet another "introduction" will not prove otiose.

Once that sense of identity with the people of God in the Old Testament is functional, however, one may (and often must) sit rather loose on specific types and antitypes. Except for those specified in the Bible itself, we may say that all of them are only illustrative of a unity under the Spirit which is finally beyond all articulation in human syllables.

This work's title, *The Word Becoming Flesh,* was chosen to give expression to that deep, organic unity between the testaments, and via Word and Sacrament, also in us. The *logos incarnandus* of the Old Testament, the preexistent Christ in His many manifestations, is the same as He who became flesh of our flesh at Bethlehem. Functionally, the obverse is more important at the moment. Once that fulfillment is clear, we can and will fill the Old Testament with all the fullness of Christ, and His Spirit will illuminate and energize the ancient words for us with all the power and beauty of the Word Incarnate Himself (Luke 24:27).

SUGGESTIONS FOR FURTHER READING

The old classic of P. Fairbairn, *The Typology of Scripture,* 1870 [5], is still helpful, although dated and marred by some postmillennial ideas. Possibly the major classic of modern times (most lamentably never translated into English) is: L. Goppelt, *Typos: die typologische Deutung des Alten Testaments im Neuen,* 1939 (reprinted 1969). More historically focused are J. Daniélou, *From Shadows to Reality: Studies in the Biblical Typology of the Fathers* (1950) and *The Bible and the Liturgy* (1956), the latter especially useful in demonstrating the extent to which traditional liturgies maintained the usages and presuppositions of the Bible in this respect, in spite of some admixture with allegory. The two studies by G. Lampe and K. Woollcombe in *Essays in Typology* (1957) are helpful in considering possible modern (more liberal) appropriation of the ancient method. Two symposia on hermeneutics discuss typology and related issues from various viewpoints: C. Westermann (Ed.), *Essays on Old Testament Interpretation,* 1960, ET 1963 (essays originally published 1949—60); and B. W. Anderson (Ed.), *The Old Testament and Christian Faith,* 1964. Finally must be mentioned the dissertation of D. L. Baker, *Two Testaments: One Bible,* 1976, with almost incredibly exhaustive bibliography.

A Brief History of Higher Criticism

Some in-depth overview of the history of critical investigation in general is necessary, in part merely to understand the terminology involved. The initial concentration will be primarily on the Pentateuch, but it is virtually impossible to limit the survey to the Pentateuch alone, because the critical reconstruction redistributed the date of its various parts over much of the rest of the Old Testament period.

Semler

Our concern at the moment, being "isagogical," is more philosophical than theological. Nevertheless it is almost mandatory to begin with reference to the fateful role of J. S. Semler (d. 1791) in the development of the theological or hermeneutical underpinnings of higher criticism. The paternity of historical-critical method or aspects of it is often disputed, but if by "method" we understand *theological* method (hermeneutical presuppositions, prolegomena), Semler is the one who must be credited (?) with first influentially articulating what to this day defines the parting of the ways between conservative and liberal Bible study.

Two slogans summarize Semler's position. The first is the insistence that the Bible merely *contains* the Word of God, that is, it cannot simply be said to *be* the Word, as conservatives, ancient and modern, confess. That inevitably means that it is up to the critic to judge what is and is not true in the Bible—as well as, ultimately, to define *what* that truth ("Gospel" or "Word of God") actually is.

The other slogan is "Treat the Bible like any other book." Since the Bible is given in history, no one will deny some validity to this maxim. However, to the conservative mind, it loses validity beyond a certain point precisely because the Bible is *not* "like any other book." That means that the method is theologically not appropriate to its subject. It is universalistic *von Haus aus,* and thus lacks empathy with the "scandal of particularity."

Just as rivers do not rise above their source, so the historical-critical method necessarily limits the inspired Scriptures to its own secular level.

Wellhausen

Our main concern at the moment, however, is the particular critical results which ensued from that hermeneutical orientation, beginning in the 18th century, but maturing and triumphing in the 19th century.

It can scarcely be stressed too much at the outset that Wellhausen's reconstruction pertained not only to the Biblical literature but also to the history of Israel's religion which that literature purported to describe. In fact, it is often hard to say which was cause and which effect, and, as a result, one is not infrequently justified in charging "argument in a circle." At any rate, it was especially in the area of the history of religion where the evolutionistic axioms of the early critics found their first and most immediate application. Once that had been fixed, largely according to prior assumptions, the literature reflecting each alleged stage could be fitted in accordingly. The literature was (and is) commonly held to be a valuable source for the *ideas* about religion held at the time of alleged composition, but of minimal value as a source for the actual history of the period described. Furthermore, there has always been the widespread assumption that the Biblical writers were culturally incapable of expressing theology in the abstract, doctrinal form we are accustomed to. Instead, they allegedly must have expressed their theology in story or historical form, and we must understand their products accordingly.

As is common, we have already mentioned the name "Wellhausen" as a sort of summary symbol of the classical critical approach. One must remember that, in one sense, it is only a symbol, but it is an apt one. Wellhausen's accomplishment was not so much an original theory as it was a successful popularization, which "sold" the theory to the vast majority of his contemporaries. When his *Prolegomena* appeared in 1878, a good century of skirmishing and of competing hypotheses had already passed.

Eichhorn, about a century earlier, is often credited with the title, "father of the *old* documentary hypothesis" (the details of which we need not recount here). In the meantime, stiff competition had come from "supplementary," "crystallization," and "fragmentary" hypotheses, as well as from many variations on the main theme. Wellhausen's promulgation of the *"new* documentary hypothesis" incorporated the labors of especially Graf and Kuenen, whose names are often associated with it.

Two features were especially pivotal in the new theory. Most significant of all was the transfer of what critics today know as P, the "priestly code," which structures the Pentateuch as it stands, from its previous position as the earliest source to the latest. What had previously been assumed to be the core to which subsequent additions were made was now viewed as a late (postexilic) construction artificially imposed upon earlier traditions.

Not only was a supposed literary source dated late by this stroke, but most of the "Mosaic" legal and liturgical traditions it contained as well. Individual details may well have been authentically rooted in high antiquity, but the basic conception was supposed to be a product of priestly theorizers after the Exile. As Wellhausen himself commented of the new hypothesis, what had previously been thought to be the foundation turned out to be the roof.

The other new addition was D, the alleged "deuteronomic" school's product, largely coterminous with the Book of Deuteronomy. Its isolation as a separate "source" came first from de Wette in the early 19th century. As we shall note below, it became the kingpin in fixing the relative sequence of the four main sources of the "new" documentary hypothesis. Its pivotal role has remained basically unchanged down to the present day, so much so that even critics have sometimes complained about a "pan-deuteronomism." The other side of the coin is that D remains the Achilles heel of the entire critical construct, and attempts to dislodge the documentary hypothesis from its dominance must concentrate a good share of the attack upon this point.

The Wellhausen reconstruction of the religio-literary history of Israel may be summarized as follows. The picture has been softened and modified in many respects by later criticism, but by no means can it be considered entirely obsolete. The later modifications have mostly to do with earlier roots, not with the date and context of the final form.

Relatively little of Scripture was thought to antedate the Exile, and virtually none of it in its final form. Only about a third of the Pentateuch (that is, not much more than Deuteronomy) had come down in essentially its original shape.

The "Former Prophets" were edited and put into their present form during the Exile. Older sources were used, but these were either unreliable, misunderstood, or else revised and supplemented according to very specific, but largely artificial, conceptions.

Before the conquest, scarcely anything certain historical could be known. The picture painted of the conquest by Joshua was completely idealized and distorted. The real picture was one of the gradual infiltration of individual tribes, who confederated into "Israel" only later, and retrojected that unity even into presettlement times. The books of Judges and Samuel were not much more reliable. Kings fared a little better, but still with great reservations, because of its writer's obvious prejudices.

The religion of Israel's ancestors was polytheistic, and probably animistic, totemistic, and characterized by ancestor worship as well.

Gradually "Yahweh" emerged as the major symbol of personification of the nation and its aspirations. Perhaps especially since the monarchy, Israel's *official* religion had tended in a monolatrous, but not yet a monotheistic direction (worshiping only one deity, but acknowledging the existence of other national gods). Amos in the 8th century was the first to conceive of a sole, universal deity. He, like the best of the prophets in his wake (especially Jeremiah) opposed ritual in favor of ethical service ("ethical monotheism").

Deuteronomy was composed under the influence of the classical prophets, but the work also demonstrated the stubborn hold of older traditions. Ritual still plays a prominent role, and monotheism was not yet entirely triumphant. But the latter did receive a big boost by Deuteronomy's insistence on legitimate sacrifice at only one central altar (where behavior could more easily be monitored and controlled).

Only with the great unknown prophet of the Exile, Deutero-Isaiah, does the breakthrough come to virtually total, theoretical monotheism. In Ezekiel, on the other hand, one also sees the fateful relapse into old cultic patterns that would largely shape the future.

Simultaneously, the priests were developing the idea of a hierocracy to supplant the defunct monarchy, and composed P as the program for it. The latest prophets supinely supported this program, and Ezra and Nehemiah were finally able to establish it.

About this time, the Pentateuch took final shape, its contours largely determined by the needs of the day. While Israel's preexilic faith was popular, natural, and vigorous, the new religion of Judaism was formalistic, harsh, and gloomy, weighed down by a sense of guilt, and morbidly preoccupied with a need to propitiate an angry God of strict justice.

The preexilic prophets had preached almost exclusively doom and judgment. But now their oracles were drastically revised and supplemented with optimistic, eschatological prophecies of divine intervention and restoration of the kingdom at the end of time. When conditions became worse instead of better in Maccabean times, apocalyptic carried this daydreaming even further in various supernaturalistic and Messianic directions. Especially under Zoroastrian influences, this escapist caricature of early prophecy predicted a "new age" after the cataclysmic destruction of the present one.

Before the exile, Israel thought almost exclusively in terms of national cult, expecting only perfunctory commitment by the individual. The shipwreck of national hopes, however, produced a psychological need for individual relationships to God. Not only the welter of sacrifices, but also most of the psalms, proverbs, and Job were developed to meet the new needs of emergent personal piety.

A few of the psalms and proverbs may have been preexilic, at least in root, but, on the other hand, many were demonstrably (!) Maccabean (second century) or even later. Some additions to the prophets dated just as late, and all of this, plus the "obvious" lateness of the pseudo-prophecies of Daniel, combined to "establish" the fact that the Old Testament canon was barely complete even when the New Testament dawned.

Compared with subsequent developments in the history of criticism, the Wellhausen approach is sometimes referred to as *literary criticism*. Because of its ambiguity, however (nearly all types of criticism are dealing with *literature* in some sense), *source criticism* has increasingly come to be the favored term. What both mean to say is that Wellhausen's hypothesis thought almost exclusively in terms of *written* documents, edited (redacted) and assembled in ways very similar to those familiar in the modern West. German university professors tended to see reflections of their own type of work in the Biblical documents. It was this attitude and the extreme atomism of some of the results ("Is the Pentateuch Mosaic or a mosaic?") that led in many quarters to dissatisfaction, and the search for better alternatives.

Form Criticism

Gunkel is the name most closely associated with the alternative, which in English usually goes by the label, *form criticism*. Not only is Gunkel usually dubbed its "father," but it is sometimes asserted, with no little justice, that in many respects, Gunkel is more directly the father of most contemporary practice of Biblical criticism (including that of the New Testament as well) than Wellhausen.

It should be stressed that neither Gunkel nor his successors intended to repudiate or entirely replace the source criticism of Wellhausen. Their program was only to modify and to attempt to determine a more authentic, ultimate *Sitz im Leben* (sociological, cultural, societal setting) than that of, in effect, a professor sitting in his study. A specific type of expression was assumed to be closely associated with each setting.

On the whole, they did not challenge the earlier literary analysis, as such, but tried to penetrate into the preliterary oral traditions allegedly preceding literary fixation. Major "forms" or types, in the case of narrative material, would include "legend," "saga," "myth," "fable," "epic," etc. (Exact definitions and distinctions, however, have eluded scholars to this day!) A basic—and more objective—distinction is that between poetry and prose. Often the assumption was that the purpose of the original tales was primarily etiological—to "explain" why people did this or that, why here and not there, etc.

A word needs to be said about the basic terminology. There is widespread dissatisfaction with "form criticism," but it is doubtful if anything can be done about it. In German, *Formgeschichte* (history of forms) is the usual designation. It is undoubtedly more descriptive of the actual practice. If that be adopted as the umbrella term, form criticism in the strict sense (German *Gattungsforschung,* the investigation of the forms) would follow as one subdivision.

The latter is, on the whole, a much more objective and theologically unobjectionable enterprise than the former. Gunkel himself compared his work to Linnaeus' botanical classifications. Understanding the outline or structure of material, as well as knowing what type of material it is to begin with (poetry or prose, parable, hymn, apocalyptic, etc.), is obviously indispensable for interpretation.

Of course, in practice, various subjectivities intrude here too, perhaps most objectionably the tendency to declare something a nonliteral form in spite of all indications to the contrary, merely because of the antisupernaturalist or other prejudices of the interpreter. Very often, too, classifications are made more on the basis of *content* rather than of structure or "form." A third objection, now often assented to by critics themselves (largely on the basis of archaeological evidence) is to the evolutionistic assumption that shorter units are necessarily earlier than longer, more complex ones.

However, the degree of subjectivity and the possibility for theological mischief is far higher when it comes to the actual *Formgeschichte* ("history of the forms," their presumed development, interaction, reinterpretation, etc.). Perhaps it would not have to be so, but in actual practice the assumption tends to be that the community *invented* many of the individual stories to serve its own needs of self-identification, for example. At very least, it supposedly felt quite free to continue to adapt and refashion (sometimes quite radically) according to changing circumstances. The actual history assumed to have been handed down remained about as minimal as in the case of the Wellhausen brand of criticism.

Although form criticism had risen originally somewhat in a positive attempt at a more synchronic approach than Wellhausen's atomism, it often degenerated into its own type of purely diachronic atomism. Researchers concentrated so much on the alleged individual units in the *Sitz im Leben* of their original nurture that the extended pieces of literature we generally have in the Bible all but became lost in the fog. This weakness probably more than anything else spawned newer approaches, that is, adaptations of form criticism, or, if you will, further adaptations of Wellhausen's source criticism (see below).

There were however, various positive gains in form criticism besides those already mentioned, and some of them conservatism too could appropriate. For one thing, the supposition of a long period of oral transmission tended to imply an earlier date for original composition, closer to that which the Biblical data themselves would indicate. There was also undeniably much greater spiritual appreciation of the material (at least in the sense of aesthetics or the *Geist* of primitive cultures) than the more purely analytical Wellhausen theory had seemed capable of. This was still a far cry from any full-fledged theological sensitivity, but it did overlap with the "art" aspect of all valid exegesis. There was also generally considerable appreciation of the cultic or liturgical aspects of life in the Biblical world. Although theories of this sort often got out of hand, this mood did help correct an oversight (or prejudice) common to much of both conservatism and liberalism.

Unfortunately, the latter accent was also fed by considerable input from "comparative religion," which at times, all but totally lost sight of Israel's uniqueness, externally as well as theologically. Excessive enthusiasm over the results of some new archaeological discoveries led to a "pan-Babylonianism," and later, although to a lesser degree, a "pan-Ugaritism." New anthropological theories, partly fed by the same data, were also eagerly exploited by some Biblical researchers.

In many ways, this problem is still with us, and probably will be for some time. That, humanly speaking, Biblical religion contains many adaptations of forms or motifs current in the surrounding cultures is undeniable. (Just how else could God have communicated to that culture? The indispensable thing is that God be the subject of the adapting process, not man!) That, however, is a far cry from the *theological* "syncretism" which many liberal scholars posit. In theological perspective, the question of Israel's uniqueness is more qualitive than quantitative: not how many "parallels" may validly be established, but of their totally different understanding when "baptized" into Biblical context.

We must also note here the ambivalent role which archaeology has, and probably will continue to play in Biblical studies. It is not totally wrong by any means to play the "archaeology proves the Bible true" refrain, but the theme must be carefully qualified in various ways. Generally, however, it is more accurate to stress that archaeology's value lies primarily in helping us *understand* the Bible better, by providing us with historical and cultural context that was taken for granted by the original audience, but emphatically cannot be by the modern reader.

At least at the hands of liberals, archaeology (with its constant input of new data) must also take the "blame" for providing many of the raw materials for far-out critical theories. But at the same time, archaeology's hard data has also served to call those same wild theories to account, and often to moderate or even demolish them. Sometimes, if the hypotheses seemed to have any basis in fact at all, conservatives, with somewhat more adaptation from their perspective, could also find some of these hypotheses helpful, at least on a provisional basis.

It remains to be noted yet how slowly and grudgingly the newer ideas of Gunkel & Co. were accepted, especially in the German homeland, the bastion of Wellhausen's "critical orthodoxy." Form-critical and cultic hypotheses were pursued far more eagerly on the whole in Scandinavia and Britain than in Germany. To a certain extent this remains true today. Although form criticism has left its mark everywhere, the old-style literary dissection still flourishes in Germany as nowhere else.

Beyond Source and Form Criticism

The next major modification in the history of criticism usually goes by the title of "tradition criticism" or "tradition history" *(Traditionsgeschichte)*. ("Redaction criticism" is a rather parallel term, but is much less used in Old Testament than in New Testament studies, because it implies a "redactor" or "editor" of *written* materials, and in Old Testament scholarship the primary interest remains on the oral period of transmission.) In many respects it is hard to distinguish tradition criticism from its parent, form criticism. Theoretically, however, form criticism concentrates more on the genesis of the unit in its original setting, while its child prefers to theorize about the growth, combination and reinterpretation of those units into larger wholes. In New Testament studies especially, the term "trajectory" is in vogue to describe the history of reinterpretation and recombination of ideas.

In recent years, a new movement labeled "structuralism" has somewhat overlapped with the concerns of tradition criticism. As is so often the case in these matters, the term is not easy to define, and it sometimes appears as though each scholar writes his own dictionary. In the strict sense structuralism has roots in the linguistic philosophy of de Saussure, and the anthropological theories of Levi-Strauss. There appear to be ultimate connections with the Freudian and Marxist dogmas on the role of literature. The concern, then, is not with what the author meant, but with the signification allegedly imposed upon him, on deeper meanings of which he was likely unaware as he wrote. Critics have pointed out that this appears to be a neo-allegorical search for universals underneath the historical particulars.

Fortunately, however, it appears that very often structuralism is used in a much more relaxed and nonphilosophical sense. Then it merely signals a primary concern for synchronic investigation of the structure of an entire pericope as it now stands, never mind what or how many building blocks may have originally gone into the structure. In either event the older diachronic investigations are not in principle repudiated in this latest twist of critical theory.

Whatever the label, one welcome upshot of these current trends is their tendency to refrain from common critical inclinations to evaluate the material *qualitatively* (genuine or ungenuine), according to alleged earliness or lateness. The current tendency is to see *each* stage of reworking of the material as reflecting valid revelatory encounter at that time, and hence offering the possibility of a helpful model for faithful response also to the modern reader. All of this, of course, presupposes liberal notions of the nature of inspiration and revelation. However, at least when applied to the completed units as we now have them in the Bible, this mentality often produces commentaries that accord far more with traditional exegesis than most traditional critical products, and sometimes they can be used by conservatives with relatively little adaptation.

"Biblical Theology"

Our survey would be incomplete without a word about the Biblical theology movement. We may well begin with one of its major monuments, the Old Testament theology of von Rad, built specifically on the foundations of the tradition criticism we have just been discussing. Von Rad's two volumes carry the subtitle, "The Theology of the Historical/Prophetic Traditions of Israel." There are two major implications of the title: (1) von Rad prescinds from the question of the actual historicity of these "traditions" (and, in actual fact, is often quite skeptical of them); and (2) he insists that one can only write a theology of each tradition by itself; any attempt at further synthesis into a Biblical theology is considered invalid. Conservatism, of course, can accept neither of those assumptions, but, up to a point, von Rad remains one of the most insightful and penetrating of all the modern, critical writers on the subject of the Old Testament theology.

Most Biblical theologians attempted more synthesis than von Rad. It must be recalled that the entire movement was closely allied with the "neo-Orthodox" revolt after World War I, associated especially with the name of Karl Barth. Much that had characterized the classical liberalism of the preceding period was strongly repudiated: the atomism of Biblical studies, the almost exclusive concern with the human origins and development of the Biblical literature with scarcely a word about its divine authority, its preoccupation with *religionsgeschichtliche* parallels, etc. In many ways that reaction wrote the agenda for the Biblical theology movement, and concern for the authority and unity of the Scriptures (often of *both* testaments as well) was often high on the list of priorities.

The problem was that no consensus could ever be reached as to how properly to express the unity of Scripture. One of the most famous (and possibly most successful) attempts was that of Eichrodt to structure all of his material around the concept of the "covenant." Others, in effect, employed the traditional tripartite topical outline of systematic theology: theology proper, anthropology, soteriology. And there was always the nagging issue of what attention, if any, should be paid to the theme of the fulfillment of the Old Testament in the New.

Along around 1960 the entire Biblical theology movement sputtered out, and with it major concern about the unity and authority of the Bible. Whether the underlying cause was frustration at earlier attempts to reach consensus, or the massive influence of von Rad, or simply the different *Zeitgeist,* or a combination of all three, is hard to say. Since then, however, it is safe to say that critical scholarship has often been united only in its almost reflexive rejection of any attempt at harmonization into an overarching unity (often dismissing the concern as a sure symptom of fundamentalism). Even the more holistic accents of structuralism have not usually been applied beyond individual traditions or pericopes.

Lutheranism and "Biblical Theology"

Lutheranism, at least in any self-conscious confessional sense, has scarcely been represented at all in this Biblical theology endeavor. Confessionalism by definition puts great accent on *dogmatic* theology, both in terms of necessary prolegomena which must precede Biblical research, and as the final synthesis for the church's use on the basis of the total canonical message. There is, however, no theoretical reason why dogmatics need crowd out Biblical theology. If this is the result, it would appear to be more the case that the conservative church's energies have been largely exhausted after the defense and presentation of its dogmatic tradition, in an age and culture that has few antennae for that accent.

Procksch's early ("All theology is Christology") endeavor presumed a fairly radical criticism and hence was at least as reductive as other endeavors; it was never translated into English. Many subsequent efforts were heavily influenced by covenant accents, which probably further contributed to confessional Lutheranism's coolness. The extent to which even much *Heilsgeschichte* accent roots in Reformed covenant background (especially Cocceius' "Federal theology") is easily overlooked.

At times, there has been an overreaction, however. Law-Gospel can redefine and effect a thoroughly compatible brand of *Heilsgeschichte.* It is even more urgent that covenant and Law-Gospel not be viewed antithetically, because of the prominence of both terms in the Bible itself. Covenant is featured most in the Old Testament, of course, and Lutheranism's neglect of the concept has surely contributed to neglect of much of the Old Testament itself; sometimes, again, it is hard to say which is cause and which is effect.

Lutheranism's coolness toward covenant goes back to Luther himself, who tended to think of a rather legal dispensation in that connection. He much preferred the term "testament," which he thought accented the pure grace of a dying Savior much more clearly (forgetting, perhaps, that testament derives from the world of law just as much as covenant). (It is not unlikely that a mutation of this dislike of covenant is evident even in the tendency of Wellhausen and many of his heirs to date covenant theology relatively late, a deuteronomistic beginning of a slow but sure drift into the full-blown legalism of postexilic Judaism.)

Inevitably, deep-seated differences in accent between Luther and Calvin, and even more so in many of their heirs, on the relation between Law and Gospel (especially on the "third use of the Law" and its political applicability) are involved. One will dismiss the legitimacy of those concerns only if he dismisses in general the validity of confessional hermeneutics as one legitimate expression of the "hermeneutical circle" within which an interpreter always operates.

There may be another, even more subliminal, dimension. If on the one hand it sometimes appears to Lutherans that the Reformed accent on covenant represents an insufficient emancipation from the Old Testament, easily leading into legalism and historicism, Lutherans should also probe their own potential weaknesses in the direction of irrelevant spiritualization, pure interiorization and fideism. If Moltmann and process theology represent a sort of hyper-Calvinism, Bultmann (whose existentialist eschatology found little place for the Old Testament) must at least be credited with a sort of hyper-Lutheranism. Similar points could be made with respect to sacramentology, where Lutherans have often been only formally aware of Reformed differences. This author has often argued that a genuinely Lutheran Biblical theology might better organize itself around the concept of glory than covenant. But a prior task would be to thoroughly comprehend both terms in their full, original Biblical dimensions.

Recent Developments

It is difficult to recount what the course of most Biblical scholarship in the last decade or so has actually been. In many respects the scene would often almost appear to be a reversion to the *status quo ante*, before the entire neo-Orthodox and Biblical theology reaction. Most of the great leaders of those latter movements are deceased too, and there are no obvious heirs apparent. Frenetic activity continues on most fronts, but it is as difficult to discern a center in it all as contemporary critics usually aver it is to discern any center in the Biblical message.

Some of the more extreme expressions in the "wild sixties" appeared all but ready to jettison the Bible altogether. Even the more moderate sometimes appeared primarily concerned only to find models for "liberation," for political and social action of whatever brand. The cliche "revelation in history" increasingly took on an immanentalistic and secularistic coloration. The basically political and sociological paradigm which was applied to the Bible was a far cry from the dominant *heilsgeschichtliche* one of the Biblical theology epoch, and even further removed from the traditional soteriological one, based on "Scripture as its own interpreter."

We conclude on a positive note: the "evangelical renaissance" of the seventies. Its impact on many areas of church life is well documented, but what its long-range influence on Biblical studies will be remains to be seen. A number of important solid commentaries (especially the "Tyndale" and "New International" series) and other studies augur well. (Again, it is regrettable that specifically Lutheran confessionalism has scarcely been able to get off the ground in this respect.) In any event, at best the swimming is going to be upstream, given the solid entrenchment of the liberal "establishment" in most pivotal ecclesiastical and academic circles.

SUGGESTIONS FOR FURTHER READING

The major current reference in this area is undoubtedly H.-J. Kraus, *Geschichte der historisch-kritisch Erforschung des Alten Testaments* (1970²), like Goppelt (above) regrettably never translated into English. H. Hahn, *The Old Testament in Modern Research* (1954, with 1966 and 1970 updates by Horace D. Hummel) contains much useful information. Lutherans will be especially interested in two penetrating studies of Luther on the subject: H. Bornkamm, *Luther and the Old Testament;* and S. Preus, *From Shadow to Promise.* More strictly bibliographical, but indispensable for the more-than-casual reader, are the book lists (with very brief characterization and evaluation) of the British Society for Old Testament Study, issued annually, especially since World War II. As a sort of centennial thankoffering for Wellhausen's work, Ronald Clements has recently (1976) produced the less penetrating but handy *One Hundred Years of Old Testament Interpretation.* Finally may be mentioned: John Hayes (Ed.), *Old Testament Form Criticism* (1974), somewhat more narrowly focused, but at center stage of much recent critical research.

Beyond this, of course, are articles and chapters "which no man could number." And their number continues to multiply, especially as higher criticism's earlier, more unanimous self-confidence fades or, at least, becomes more diffuse, and it tries to reorient itself by exploring its roots.

Pentateuchal Criticism

By friend and foe alike, the documentary hypothesis of the Pentateuch, displacing the traditional assumption of literal Mosaic authorship, has always been regarded as one of the major results of Old Testament higher criticism. By no measure is that judgment unwarranted, seeing that its adoption involves, as we have noted, a total reshuffling of Israel's entire history, literary, religious, and perhaps political as well.

Probably we should add "assured result" as well (at least from the critics' own standpoint). The hypothesis has undergone major revisions and mutations; repeated (usually short-lived) attempts have been made to transcend its intrinsic atomism and centrifugality; even some critics from within have pronounced it passe and dead; but for all practical purposes Wellhausen's reconstruction is still very much alive and kicking. Assertions to the contrary are either wishful thinking, or else confuse minor surgery with lethal blows.

Types of Critical Argument

To a large extent, the main *types* of critical argumentation are the same, whether the subject is the Pentateuch or some other Biblical book. These may be summarized under three headings: historical, religious, and linguistic. These three inquire respectively about the historical circumstances which occasioned the composition of the pericope, about the stage represented in the history of religious thought, and about the phase in the development of the language into which the document fits.

Let it be stressed that, if we were reasonably fully informed about those cirumstances in ancient Israel, and if the Biblical data which we do have were credited with being basically true on its face, those would be extremely useful criteria. In principle, matters would differ little in this respect, at least up to a point, from any historian's study of his sources. In actual practice, however, in the application of these criteria, the critic often does *not* "treat the Bible like any other book" (a major historical-critical slogan).

All three criteria are forced into the Procrustean bed of how things *must* have developed according to the researcher's preferred developmental hypothesis (usually some version of the Wellhausen hypothesis, as we have noted). Hence the conservative argument that much of the critical case is a classical "argument in a circle," proving only the critic's presuppositions.

Especially in the case of the third main type of argument, that from history of the language, sufficient archaeological evidence has come in to drastically undermine much of the earlier assuredness, but not enough to eliminate its use. Many critics will also concede *relatively* earlier origin of many religious ideas, but this does not usually imply any change in the date they assume for final literary fixation. And the basic Wellhausen postulate that most of the Pentateuch in its present form could not possibly find plausible occasion until just before, during, and after the crisis of the Exile, still continues, in effect, to be copied from book to book with scarcely a second thought. Except in very conservative circles, it has simply become *unthinkable* that Moses could have actually written the Pentateuch! Critics never even seriously investigate the possibility.

Even those who mounted radical challenges from within the critical camp itself to the Wellhausen synthesis or school (Cassuto, Eerdmans, Kaufmann, etc.) never proposed literal Mosaic authorship again. Hence, conservatives should take care not to exult prematurely or excessively about their strictures.

Arguments Against Mosaic Authorship

Let us now turn specifically to the Pentateuch. We shall attempt to summarize the major specific arguments which first led to the abandonment of belief in Mosaic authorship, and which to a large extent would still be adduced today. Among the first clues to be noticed and interpreted as indicating different sources were variations in vocabulary and style within the Pentateuch, especially the use of different names for the same person or place. Critics usually give the honor of first (c.1750) calling any widespread attention to such variations to a French physician, Jean Astruc, who also dabbled in the literary analysis of the Bible. (A German pastor, H. Witter, had apparently made similar observations a bit earlier.) Astruc noted especially the different names used for the deity in the opening chapters of Genesis, the generic name *Elohim* in Gen. 1, and the proper noun, *Yahweh,* in Gen. 2.

For a long time, that criterion would play a prominent role in sleuthing for sources, and would even provide names for two of the major sources, J and E, the "Yahwist" and the "Elohist." The latter was eventually subdivided into the "first Elohist" and the "second Elohist," today known as E and P, respectively.

Important as it was as a first clue at the outset, the importance of this criterion in a developed defense of the developed documentary hypothesis can be overstated, because often other criteria override the witness of the divine names, or the evidence is ambivalent. After Genesis, the criterion is of very minimal value, because also E and P are supposed to start using Yahweh thereafter, as J had been doing all along. And critics are by no means above conjuring up as a sort of *deus ex machina* some later redactor or scribe who is supposed to have added, subtracted, or substituted a troublesome name which does not fit their hypothesis! The conservative sees no good reason why any good writer would not alternate divine names simply for the sake of variety (cf. our "Jesus," "Christ," "Lord," etc.), and in addition we now have countless extra-Biblical examples from antiquity of just that type of variety.

Other examples of alleged differences in vocabulary preferences would include J's use of "Sinai" for the sacred mountain in contrast to E's "Horeb"; J's "Canaanite" for the original inhabitants of the land vs. E's "Amorite"; J's predilection for "Reuel" as the name of Moses' father-in-law over E's "Jethro"; etc. In many cases, the usages attributed to E would apply to D as well. This leads many scholars to assume a common geographical locale behind both of those traditions—a northern one, in contrast to J who should represent Judah or the Southern Kingdom.

Further examples could be multiplied almost ad infinitum, but soon overlap with other very subjective critical judgments about thematic and theoretical variations among the sources. For that reason, the variations in vocabulary are often difficult to evaluate or respond to apart from careful scrutiny of individual pericopes.

The criterion of alternate vocabulary is especially intertwined with judgments about *style*. Possibly few of the standards are so subjective as this one, and rarely would it carry independent weight. J is commonly credited with the best narrative style: sprightly, vivid, concrete, excelling in personal characterizations, etc. E is thought to be more abstract and ponderous, partly because of his more specifically theological and cultic interests replacing J's political and nationalistic ones. Other criteria plainly intrude in this judgment (cf. below), and we probably have little more than argument in a circle at this point.

P is supposed to have a sort of nonstyle of narration via the dry-bones procedure of amassing genealogies, chronologies, liturgical specifications, and other statistical material. That there is considerable material of that nature in the Pentateuch is undeniable, but that it characterizes a separate source is something else again.

Finally, there is D, largely limited to the Book of Deuteronomy, but often thought to have left its mark elsewhere in the Pentateuch. It is supposed to be evidenced by its expansive, homiletical style, and telltale phrases such as "with all your heart and mind," "as it is unto this day," "that it may be well with you," "to go after other gods," etc. Again, as we shall note below, those observations are, as such, indisputable, but they also accord well with the Biblical description of the circumstances as an actual Mosaic sermon!

Many other features besides possible differences in style and vocabulary were taken to indicate lack of single authorship. Prominent among these were alleged "doublets," two (or more) versions of the same story, sometimes supposedly with inner contradictions. Of course, Gen. 1 and 2 would be a parade example, each with its own sequence of creative activity according to this interpretation: Gen. 1(P) ending and climaxing with the creation of man, in contrast to Gen. 2 (J) beginning with man. The conventional critical wisdom was also thought to be able to distinguish two versions of the Deluge (in this case interwoven by some later editor rather than placed side by side), allegedly differing on its duration, the number of animals taken into the ark, etc. Ex. 3 and 6 (E and P respectively) are thought to duplicate the revelation of the divine name to Moses (and, of course, to contradict J's account of its antiquity in Gen. 4).

A "triplet" is usually hailed in the three accounts of patriarchs attempting to save their own skins by describing their wives as sisters (twice of Abraham and Sarah in Gen. 12 and 20, and once of Isaac and Rebekkah in Gen. 26). In the Joseph story, the uncertainty whether it was Reuben or Judah who attempted to defend the younger brother, and whether it was the Ishmaelites or the Midianites to whom Joseph was actually sold, were, among other clues, taken to indicate an interweaving of disparate sources there too (although be it noted that this interpretation is currently no longer in much favor among critics themselves!).

The conservative rejoinder to this type of argumentation has found much ammunition in archaeological discoveries. Assuming there really *is* a repetition, we now know that repetitions and recapitulations were typical of ancient Near Eastern literature, especially of epic type, and possible oral backgrounds make it even more plausible. In many other respects, ancient writers obviously used devices and procedures that are quite alien to the modern Occident.

A "contradiction" that played a key role in first distinguishing the sources was the supposedly conflicting accounts of the date of introduction of the name "Yahweh." According to J in Gen. 4:26, the "cult" of Yahweh began shortly after the expulsion from Paradise, whereas P in Ex. 6:2 seems to indicate that it was first revealed to Moses, similarly E in Ex. 3:14.

Conservatives usually countered by asserting that the latter passage spoke of the *full*, Sinaitic revelation of the sacred name and its significance, not its mere knowledge and reverence as such (which J attributes many times already to the patriarchs in Genesis).

There are other possible indications too of earlier knowledge of Yahweh, but the clincher may well now have come from the new archaeological finds at Ebla in northern Syria from well before patriarchal times. There we apparently find Yahweh commonly used as the theophoric element in names, often replacing compounds of "El" during the reign of Eber, the same name and possibly the same person as one of the ancestors of the Hebrews, listed in Gen. 10:21 ff. and 11:14.

Not only different theories about the history of the divine name were thought to be involved. Fundamentally different notions of the *entire* history of Israel's cult on the part of J and P (the latter probably anticipated somewhat here by E) were supposed to be in evidence in the same connection. Isolation of these different theories was used further to try to distinguish the sources. The theory went that J assumed continuity between the patriarchal and later periods also in other respects. He speaks of legitimate priests, altars, and sacrifices well before Sinai, in contrast to P who refuses to recognize their existence until that time. E first introduces a sort of covenantal periodization into Israel's religious history, which P later amplified. Likewise, J is supposed to be quite relaxed about the Canaanites and their cult, in contrast to the harsh proscriptions of later times, as a rigid and exclusive monotheism takes hold. J has no problem in locating the patriarchs at some of the major Canaanite shrines (Bethel, Shechem, etc.), worship at which is strictly forbidden in other sources.

A couple of other examples of such alleged discrepancies should be mentioned because of their importance in other evolutionistic reconstructions. (We return to both of these examples below.) Ex. 33 and Num. 11 are thought to describe a very simple "tent of meeting" in contrast to the elaborate "tabernacle" or miniature Solomonic temple described in the surrounding chapters. Critics generally doubt that the latter ever really existed, except in the fantasies of postexilic priests, who retrojected the developed cult into Mosaic times in order to enhance their own position and authority. Sometimes the "tent" traditions are thought to have been fostered by anti-temple circles, probably especially those who opposed its rebuilding after the Exile.

Deuteronomy is understood to contradict other legislation in many pivotal respects. Deut. 12 is seen to permit legitimate sacrifice of only *one* central sanctuary, while Ex. 20:24 (like the historical books) presupposes many legitimate shrines. Deut. 12:13 ff. is thought to "secularize" for the first time all non-sacrificial slaughter of animals; i.e., no longer requiring its performance at local sanctuaries (now first allegedly outlawed). Deut. 18 is taken to permit all Levites to perform priestly functions, thus contradicting the limitation of this privilege in Ex. 28 to only Aaronides (one Levitical family).

Finally, we note a third main type of argumentation against Mosaic authorship: passages which seem to imply a much later age. Already the medieval Jewish exegete Ibn Ezra had discreetly observed that the explanatory note in Gen. 12:6 ("the Canaanites were then in the land") indicated a time of composition when the Canaanites were *no longer* in the land, at least not in the same sense. Later critics pointed out that Gen. 14 refers to the Danites' homeland in the far north, which according to Judges 17 ff., they did not acquire until much later. Gen. 36:31 refers to the existence of Edomite kings "before any king reigned over the Israelites"— indicating at least a monarchical standpoint, if not later. The repeated refrain, "until this day," suggests a later age than an eyewitness. Of Moses it is specifically remarked that no other prophet like him has arisen "since" (Deut. 34:10—although by all accounts the last chapter of Deuteronomy is a special case). Sometimes the later (Babylonian instead of Canaanite) names for months are used (e.g., 12:2). In Deuteronomy, Transjordan (the *east* bank) is repeatedly referred to as "the *other* side of the Jordan," indicating a vantage point on the *west* bank *after* Moses' death.

Not all of these can be answered in detail here, but they undeniably do mandate a certain post-Mosaic touching-up and contemporization. Conservatives have rarely denied that. However, close analysis clearly indicates that they usually concern only relatively peripheral adjustments for the sake of better communication to later audiences. In no way do they make a case for post-Mosaic composition of the substance of the narratives. A good modern example might be our common reference to Columbus' discovery of "America," even though at the time the continent was not yet known by that designation. Theologically, we should have no difficulty in including such minor adaptations to later usages before final textual fixation in the Holy Spirit's "verbal inspiration." That, of course, would be something quite different from the open-ended "community inspiration," commonly posited by liberals.

One trump argument often adduced as a clear indication of later, post-Mosaic authorship of the Pentateuch is the fact that Moses is usually referred to in the *third* person. There are, however, ample parallels for such practices, where the writer's intent is not simply autobiographical. One thinks, for example, of Xenophon or of Julius Caesar, not to speak of papal or other "editorial we" usages of more formal, elevated style in our own day. (On the other hand, the notice in Num. 12:3 about Moses' "meekness" might well be a later observation, included in the inspired text.)

Arguments for the "JEDP" Sequence

Given the interpretation of all of this cumulative "evidence" as indicating various non-Mosaic sources, how shall they be dated, and in what sequence? Or, to pose the question in terms of the history of higher criticism, why did the "*new* documentary hypothesis" finally dislodge its competitors, and why does it still rule the roost? Previously, P had been commonly thought to be the earliest source, because it appeared to provide the foundation or framework for the entire narrative. (Hence, it was often referred to as G for *Grundschrift*—not to be confused with Noth's later, popular use of the same siglum in an entirely different sense.) Gradually, however, and climaxing in Wellhausen, sentiment shifted toward dating the "second Elohist," or P, as the latest of all the sources. Involved, as we cannot stress too much, was not only pure literary criticism, but philosophically based criticism of the traditional course of Israel's entire religious history as well.

The kingpin in the new chronological scheme was D, with the other sources arrayed in evolutionary order before or after it. And the theoretical anchor of the entire scheme was the identification of D, or Deuteronomy, with the law book found during the reign of Josiah and used as the basis of the subsequent reformation (2 Kings 22). Hardly anyone disputes the likelihood of some connection between the two because of the similarity in the reform program of Josiah and Deuteronomy, and especially the sense of urgency exuded in both. Already Jerome and Chrysostom in the early church had noted the parallelism. (The parallel account in 2 Chron. 34, however, does indicate at least earlier roots of the reform.) What was new now was that Deuteronomy was no longer viewed as part of the Mosaic Pentateuch, but as an essentially *new* composition, destined to play a fateful role in the history of Israelite religion.

How new? De Wette, who originally proposed D as a source, had proposed that it was a "pious fraud" perpetrated by priestly circles and planted in the temple in order to gain power and influence. Few, if any, critics would any longer accept that construction. Most today would probably posit somewhat older roots in the Northern Kingdom (many would follow von Rad in specifying Levitical "country preachers"), whence it (or some version of it) had been brought to Jerusalem after the fall of Samaria a century earlier. Many would even trace its roots back further into the ceremonies of the hypothetical periodic "covenant renewal festivals" of Israel's early history, possibly even with some literal Mosaic input.

None of those variations, however, significantly affect our concern at the moment. Deuteronomy's association with Josiah's reformation in the seventh century retains its pivotal significance for the specific historical and literary reconstruction implicit in the "new documentary hypothesis," regardless of how ancient some of its roots. By the same token, this identification is the Achilles heel of the entire orthodox-critical theory. By so slender a thread hangs virtually all Pentateuchal criticism since the time of Wellhausen!

Possibly *two arguments* are central in defense of the usual JEDP order. The first one builds on Deuteronomy's alleged requirement of worship at only the one central sanctuary. It is *assumed* that Jerusalem is the one meant! Such a restriction is allegedly unknown in J and E, as well as in the early historical narratives, which appear to sanction a multiplicity of legitimate altars. For example, both Samuel and Elijah offer sacrifice, and even erect altars in various parts of the country. In P, however, it is argued, this restriction is not only no longer prescribed, but tacitly assumed, as though it is now a well-established usage. P, possibly not even knowing the actual origin of the restriction, retrojects it to wilderness (Mosaic) times by means of the tabernacle fiction.

Much of the cogency of this argument stands or falls with the assumption that Deuteronomy's program is actually to limit legitimate worship to the temple in Jerusalem. It must be noted that Jerusalem is never even so much as mentioned! The only place-name to appear in such a connection is *Gerizim,* the later sacred mountain of the Samaritans above Shechem. (No wonder the Samaritans later argued that Jerusalem was a usurper, as even some critics agree!)

The actual phrase repeatedly used in Deuteronomy (and elsewhere too!) is "where I shall cause My name to dwell," or variations of it. That is, *wherever* Yahweh legitimates worship by His real presence. Geographical location is obviously a secondary matter, as is also the number of locations. The antithesis is pagan, Canaanite altars. The concern is with their *character.* In the wilderness, legitimate worship was limited to the tabernacle, but by very definition, it was a portable shrine, not a central sanctuary to which Israel periodically had to return.

Initially, after the conquest of Canaan, matters did not change drastically. The exact locations of tabernacle and ark are often hard to keep track of (and has spawned no little critical speculation); Shiloh was obviously one of the main ones, but not the sole one, until both tabernacle and ark finally debouched in Jerusalem. Once the temple was built as the successor of the wilderness shrine, Yahweh did apparently "cause His name to dwell" only there (as emphasized in Solomon's dedicatory sermon, 1 Kings 8), but that by no means precludes earlier mobility or special circumstances in the North after the schism.

That there were outlying *pagan* or semipagan shrines in Judah as well as in the North is apparent both from Biblical indications and increasing archaeological evidence. As the Book of Kings makes plain, this was not the only departure from the norm during that period! Our concern, however, is with the *normative* Biblical tradition or with "orthodoxy," not with the totality of the "history of Israel's religion." (The latter, the usual critical subject, will often not even honor any concept of a normative Israelite "orthodoxy" until well after the Exile.) The sum of all this: the Biblical data makes perfect sense as it stands, *if* we do not begin with the assumption that Deuteronomy was largely a propaganda text of Josiah's reformation.

A second key argument for the JEDP sequence proceeds along similar lines. It argues that in D (the seventh century) the legitimate priesthood (at Jerusalem) is for the first time *limited* to Levites. That is, "priest" and "Levite" are allegedly used synonymously. In contrast, it is said, in the earlier historical narratives, no such limitation of the priesthood is known; for example the Micah of Judges 17:5 installs one of his own sons as priest, and similarly David his own sons (2 Sam. 8:18). Earlier, it is said, we find no distinction at all between clergy and laity, but everyone apparently may sacrifice; at most there was perhaps a certain preference for "Levites." P, however, not only takes D's limitation for granted, but carries it further. He limits the priesthood to the Aaronides, and demotes other Levites to the status of helpers, as minor clergy or the like (Ex. 28, Num. 3, etc). (Ezek. 40—48, allegedly written *before* P, had attempted even a further limitation to the Zadokites, but without success.)

It is not possible to answer aspects of this second main critical argument in short compass, touching as it does on one of the thorniest problems in all of Old Testament exegesis, and one for which no one pretends to have a total, definitive answer. For one thing, critics have never been able to come up with any more plausible explanation than the Biblical one for the mutation of the Levites from an ordinary, secular tribe (Gen. 34, etc.) to one set apart for sacerdotal service. (A few cut the Gordian knot by simply denying there ever was such a secular tribe!) Ex. 32 suggests that this followed from the faithfulness of the Levites over against the Golden Calf apostasy to which even Aaron had succumbed (even though he had already been designated "high-priest," Ex. 28). Subsequent Pentateuchal legislation then spells out the precise priestly role.

The period of the Judges was such a time of chaos and anarchy that one can scarcely prove anything from it concerning *normative* Israelite practice. The brief and cryptic notice about David's sons cannot be answered definitively. Is "sons" here used in a more metaphorical sense?

Should we think of some sort of "adoption" into Levitical families, of which there are other possible indications?

There are many questions about the entire relationship between king and high priest throughout the period of the monarchy. It is not impossible that we already have in David (who was otherwise not totally righteous!) some of the royal usurpation of priestly right, which is evident later on (e.g., Ahaz in 2 Kings 16), and in accordance with common Oriental analogy.

What is not acceptable (on either Biblical or archaeological basis) is the common critical construction that Israel really had no high priesthood at all until *after* the Exile, when it appropriated royal privileges, vestments, etc., for itself.

The deuteronomic phrase in question is literally, "the priests, the Levites." Since Hebrew idiom commonly coordinates where English subordinates or uses an adjective, the ordinary, idiomatic translation of the phrase would be: "the levitical priests." All priests *were* Levites, and, as such, the phrase says no more. The expression appears to be of a piece with the general concern that Moses evinces for the Levites, concern lest the priesthood (in the narrow sense) forget about its brethren after the settlement and the establishment of the Sinaitic legislation in the Promised Land. (This, of course, rejects the critical interpretation that Deuteronomy's concern arises from its own program of centralization of worship, which had put many Levites, previously employed at country shrines, out of work.)

There are clear instances in Deuteronomy where "Levite" and "priest" are *not* simply synonymous, e.g., 18:3 ff., where priestly and levitical portions are distinguished, and 2 Kings 23:9 plainly knows of a Levitical subordination to the priests. By extension, then, the same principle would apply throughout the book. This alone, it would appear, seriously undermines, if it does not simply demolish, the entire critical thesis at this crucial point.

Ezek. 40—48 is throughout an ideal, visionary reconstruction of circumstances after the return. There is no more justification for using Ezekiel's notice about the Zadokites in an evolutionary argument than in appealing to his vision of ideal boundaries of the twelve tribes in relation to those of "prince" and temple, when the latter plainly never corresponded with any empirical reality. The lists in Ezra indicate a fairly poor response by the Levites to the return, and if that lukewarmness was already apparent in the Exile, much of the occasion for Ezekiel's strictures might be accounted for. The *high* priesthood plainly was Zadokite (by descent from Aaron's son and successor, Eleazar) until its usurpation in Maccabean times, and hence Ezekiel may, by common Hebrew idiom, imply by "sons of Zadok" no more than those loyal to their master.

J

Let us now turn to a brief characterization of the main sources themselves according to critical lights. J or the Yahwist is generally the darling of critical writers, partly because he is thought to be the earliest and most "original," partly also because he is the most "person-centered" and least theological and liturgical of the four. Throughout, it is often difficult to discern precisely on what basis judgments about the provenance and contents of the source are actually made. Often it appears that J is merely assigned what does not fit the other sources.

The circular nature of much of the argumentation is especially apparent in the geographical location of J in Judah. (Sometimes J is even made to stand for "Judahite.") This argument is based on the alleged preference for southern locations and for personages closely associated with those locations (Abraham, Hebron, Judah), but that assumption also often helps determine which passages are assigned to J to begin with!

There has been less unanimity about the *date* of the source. Even critics concede that there are no clear internal indications when J may have been written, just as there is no betrayal of who J himself was. If D belongs to the seventh century, and E intervenes before we come to the earliest source, the *ninth* century would appear to be a likely guess. That is precisely where Wellhausen and most early critics did locate it (c. 850—800 B.C.). J was thought to have written under the first stirrings of the prophetic movement more or less contemporaneous with Elijah and Elisha in the north. (Earlier critics often referred to it as the "prophetic" source or narrative of the Pentateuch.) Evidence of this was found not only in J's Yahwistic "monotheism," but also in the strong *ethical* tone of his narrative (over against the allegedly more amoral, ritualistic character of earlier Israelite pluralism).

Contemporary scholars are more inclined to date J at least a century earlier (the *tenth* century) and to view him less as a mouthpiece of the prophetic movement than as an apologist for the *united* monarchy of David and Solomon later. He is no longer seen as being very militant at all about Canaanite religious practices—as Solomon was not.

The net result is about the same: J's purpose was as much political as it was religious. J above all wanted to demonstrate that Jerusalem and David represented the culmination of all divine activity in Palestine since days of yore, yes, for that matter, even since the creation of the world. The welfare and destiny of all other nations depended on their attitude toward the chosen people. The kingdom of David was the legitimate heir of all the various hopes and dreams of Canaan, yes, a veritable "kingdom of God" on earth, and, who knows, perhaps the springboard for an even larger kingdom that might some day control the entire world!

If so, why did J stop where he did? Where did he in fact stop? With that question, we reach another conundrum for the critics, which to conservatives, however, looks more like another fatal flaw in the entire house of cards. If we stop where the Pentateuch does, J would have to end with the death of Moses. Since that seems rather anticlimactic, early criticism often preferred to speak of a "Hexateuch," and tried to trace a continuation of the J source at least into Joshua. Thus, a fulfillment of the promise could at least be included, as well as something concrete that would at least point toward David and his empire.

That particular solution is no longer in much favor, but the problem does not go away. Perhaps most critics would simply assert that J's original ending became lost somewhere in the complexities of later literary history, and let it go at that. Some would explain it in connection with Noth's popular hypothesis of a "Tetrateuch" as the original unit, with Deuteronomy at the *head* of the *following* "deuteronomic history" instead of concluding that which precedes. Some think a fragment of J's account of the conquest may have survived in Judges 1 (understood as conflicting with the picture of the conquest given in most of Joshua). To some of these problems we shall return below, but let it be noted that the entire documentary hypothesis all but suffers shipwreck on this issue alone!

J is ordinarily thought of as having *created* most of the "history" which he reports. This, of course, is the reverse side of the usual massive critical skepticism of Biblical reports about events before the time of the monarchy. (Of course, the "primeval history" of Gen. 1—11 scarcely counts at all as "history" by those lights!) Form criticism generally had the effect of multiplying the number of individual, isolated tales about persons, shrines, and popular etiologies that allegedly floated about before the Yahwist bent their original intent to his own purposes and incorporated them into a connected and coherent narrative. (For example, Gen. 3:14 f. and 11:1 ff. were supposedly little more than popular etiological explanations of why snakes crawl on their bellies, and why people speak different languages, respectively, until J wove them into his grand judgment-salvation scheme.)

The patriarchal stories are commonly thought to reflect group or clan history more than of individuals. Even the canonical Abraham-Isaac-Jacob sequence is widely viewed as a literary artifice. Congruent with the usual assumption that the "conquest" was more a matter of slow, gradual infiltration and of the uprising of many dispossessed, landless elements against their masters, not of a swift, unified campaign under Joshua, the stories of "Jacob's twelve sons" are taken to reflect a host of originally quite independent tribal movements, united under one "father" by the stroke of a pen to symbolize the unity of all under the Davidides.

Especially von Rad's version of how the Yahwist operated has been highly influential. Von Rad believed that the original models for the Yahwist's effort could be found in what he interprets as little cultic "credos" or creeds, such as those of Deut. 6:20-24; 26:5-9; Josh. 24:2-13. These little creeds (it is debatable, at best, if they can really even be called that) contained the story of the Exodus and conquest in a nutshell (never mind even at this stage whether or not the historical memory was accurate).

Von Rad saw the Yahwistic work as basically only an expansion and supplementation of these liturgical formulae. The Yahwist's procedure was to work backward in something like three stages. First, he expanded the "Mosaic tradition" with a variety of material. The most important of these was the entire "Sinaitic tradition." Von Rad argues on the basis of its absence in Deut. 26 and its apparent interpolation between Ex. 19 and Num. 10 (Israel's arrival and departure from Sinai) that it was originally an entirely independent tradition from that of the Exodus. That is, it was said to have been originally experienced (whatever empirical experience actually did underlie it!) by an entirely different component of later Israel than had experienced the Exodus. (Massive critical debate, too extensive to recount here, has swirled around this thesis.)

Second, the Yahwist unified the welter of patriarchal traditions and prefixed them to his narrative, thus giving it much of its "promise-fulfillment" theological structure (fulfillment, of course, seen in the Davidic empire).

Finally, the Yahwist is supposed to have prefixed the "primeval history," now found in portions of Gen. 1—11. Perhaps it was the Yahwist himself who cleaned up these originally polytheistic accounts and gave them their present theological coloration, perhaps this had already been done before this time at some shrine or the other. In any event, all critics agree that it was especially in this section that the Yahwist's theological aims and abilities became most prominent.

By beginning with the creation, he gave his entire story a universal (or even universalistic) signature. Israel's calling was of significance for the entire world and the "moral law" applied to all men everywhere. Through David, as the heir of the patriarchs, Israel had been elected in order that through it "all the nations of the earth would be blessed" (Gen. 12:2, etc.).

Conservatives would have little difficulty with such statements as such, but would scarcely understand them in the critical manner. At best, critics would concede that they received an eschatological-Messianic interpretation only much later, probably well after the Exile, when the political-cultural imperialism originally intended had run aground on the realities of history.

The Yahwist was also well aware of ingrained human perversity, and of the tendency to substitute other goals for God's, but basically he is supposed to express optimism that man's self-sufficiency and stubbornness cannot ultimately obstruct the divinely ordained course of fulfillment of promise. Even when human behavior leaves God no alternative but to punish, He is quite able to turn it into ultimate blessing. A "remnant" always survives to carry the torch, as the line of the elect is constantly narrowed to lead directly to the Davidic throne.

E

Popular handbooks of the critical history of Israel often leave the impression that the case for E is as cut and dried as for J (by critical standards, that is). As a matter of fact, that is by no means the case, so much so that even some have denied its very existence. Others believe that it has been so fragmentarily preserved that they despair of ever being able to say anything for certain about its extent or its emphases. Especially in recent years as the jaunty confidence of earlier literary dissection has waned a bit, many have taken to speaking only of JE, and letting it go at that.

Because of their great similarity, Noth's suggestion that a G (*Grundschrift*) originally underlay both J and E has found many adherents. Others, usually thinking more of a common oral background, speak of an S (for "Source") or a T (for "Tradition"). But this is indeed hypothesis upon hypothesis!

The conventional wisdom, however, remains that E is the northern counterpart of J. It is called E because of the writer's alleged preference for Elohim, the generic name for deity. At times the E is also made to do double duty for "Ephraimite," after the largest and most influential of the northern tribes. This source is assumed to be a northern version of essentially the same history recorded by J, but meeting northern needs, especially after Jeroboam's schism.

Its date is usually estimated about a century after J, that is, ninth or early eighth century, depending on when J is dated. On what basis? Really none, except evolutionary considerations! E is read as being a notch down the line toward the unfortunate particularism and legalism that would triumph with D (a sort of "proto-D") and climax with P.

E's narrower perspective is usually thought to be evidenced already by his starting point. There really would be no way to tell what E originally contained if a later redactor did not see fit to retain it in order to supplement the Yahwistic narrative which he supposedly otherwise preferred. Nevertheless, it is usually confidently stated that the Elohist never did include a creation story, but began with the patriarchal narratives (usually: Gen. 15). That omission is supposed to signal a backing away from J's universalism in favor of a much more narrow particularistic and exclusivistic position.

Instead of J's relaxed spontaneity and lively political interest, there are supposed to be many more signs of theological reflection and of specifically religious and cultic interest in E (that, of course, taken as a retrograde step). No longer is God described simply in J's naive anthropomorphism, but the theologians have begun to view Him in more remote transcendent fashion (a process that allegedly escalated as time went on). God no longer relates so directly to man, but speaks through angels, dreams, or "prophets" (as Abraham is called in Gen. 20:7). Stories about the heroes are allegedly "cleaned up," and the miraculous element begins to be highlighted (again to be continued).

Above all, there is supposed to be much greater accent on law and covenant. (Some would voguishly assert that E was more interested in events, J in people!) Here in the North was thought to have survived in a sort of "underground," unofficial way much more of premonarchical Israel's legal and covenantal traditions than in the South, where they had been all but smothered by accent on kingship and its attendant syncretisms. Presumably reflecting the prophetic struggle itself, E sharply rejects the Canaanite religion and begins to accent God's exclusive "covenant" with Israel. (If so, his preference for the generic "Elohim" over the specific "Yahweh" is anomalous!) This accent, too, triumphed under D, and climaxed in a radically different ambience with postexilic P.

Hence, E is also thought to have preserved far more detailed traditions about the work and character of Moses, the archetypal lawgiver. (Possibly even E's absence of a creation narrative is thought to conservatively reflect earlier forms of the tradition before J added a "First Article"!)

Much of the "early" legal material of Ex. 20—24 was thought to be either E's composition or incorporated into his work: the Decalogue, the so-called Book of the Covenant, and the account of Ex. 24 of the sealing of the covenant.

The Book of the Covenant is still commonly thought to be the earliest of Israel's various law codes, containing the simplest and most "natural" cultic prescriptions, probably dating from the early settlement period. The "Ritual Decalogue" (or "Dodecalogue") of Ex. 34:10-26 is sometimes explained as J's counterpart to E's legal material, but even many critics concede that there are formidable difficulties in such a view, not the least of them being that it is possible to extract a "decalogue" of any sort from the present text only through considerable editing. Form criticism, as usual, tended to bypass "literary" sources like E and J. For a long time, theories tracing the origins of the legal collections back to cultic (especially "covenant renewal") settings prevailed (Alt, Mowinckel), but more recent studies (Richter, Gerstenberger) have instead accented "secular" settings in family and clan contexts.

D

At some point, it is generally theorized, J and E were fused by some redactor (sometimes designated R^{JE}, or the like). Perhaps about the same time the "deuteronomic" movement enters the picture. We sketched above the classical Wellhausen argumentation (stemming from de Wette) for the pivotal date of Deuteronomy at this juncture. We also noted that, at least as far as final, literary form is concerned, for all practical purposes that date still holds quite firm in contemporary criticism.

Not, of course, that there have never been challenges, even to this cornerstone of the critical edifice. Major arguments were launched in defense of an earlier date—not Mosaic—but usually about the time of Samuel or David (tenth or eleventh century). We can do little more than mention names: Robertson, Welch, Brinker. Others argued for a postexilic date (Kennett, Hölscher), pointing to features which most, however, would understand as indicating merely a second edition, expanding on the "proto-Deuteronomy" of Josiah's time.

Most influential has been the form-critically based work of von Rad (perhaps, some have suggested, because von Rad's own theology follows a "deuteronomic" pattern). Picking up suggestions of earlier students, he argues that Deuteronomy is a product of Levitical "country-preachers" in the North who had preserved and adapted ancient traditions. They were heavily supported by laymen, and von Rad stresses the lay character of the movement. Having fled to the South after the fall of Samaria, they were offended by the syncretism they found in Jerusalem. On the basis of their cherished, ancient traditions, they spearheaded the reform movement, and our Deuteronomy is largely the product of that confrontation.

As the ultimate source of the deuteronomic tradition, however, von Rad proposed a "covenant renewal festival," originally celebrated in amphictyonic times (the time of the "Judges") in the sanctuary at Shechem. A similar festival at Gilgal allegedly featured the Exodus and the conquest, and much of our present Pentateuch is the result of the fusion of those two liturgies. In fact, much of von Rad's argumentation for the original independence of the Exodus and the Sinai traditions was a literary one: in the present structure of the Pentateuch Israel supposedly arrives in the vicinity of Kadesh in Ex. 18 and does not leave until Num. 10, with the Sinai material "interpolated" between those chapters.

Much of the above is, at best, purely hypothetical. However, one of its happy results was a renewed consideration of the essential unity of Deuteronomy, based on the covenant renewal ceremony, which von Rad thought he could still reconstruct on the basis of the present book. This has clear exegetical merit, even if the rest of von Rad's hypotheses are jettisoned.

The fourfold pattern von Rad proposed basically follows the outline of the book: (1) Historical and homiletical review of basic principles (chaps. 1—11); (2) Reading of the law in its detailed stipulations (chaps. 12—26); (3) Reminder of the covenant sanctions, blessings and curses (chaps. 27—28); and (4) The ceremonial renewal of the covenant (chap. 29—although the outline does not work out so neatly here). Von Rad even saw this scheme as the pattern of a typical farewell speech when one "covenant mediator" was replaced by another!

It is worth noting that von Rad detected the same basic liturgical pattern behind the "E" material in Exodus, reporting the Sinai events. His reconstruction of the same four liturgical acts there is as follows: (1) "History" of the Sinai events and parenesis (chap. 19); (2) Recitation of the Law—the Decalogue and Book of the Covenant (20—23:19); (3) Blessings or curses (23:20 ff.); and (4) A sacramental rite concluding the covenant (24). Again von Rad's observation is fruitful, if "cultic creativity" does not supplant historicity. At most the conservative might concede on a hypothetical basis some very secondary shaping of the historical material to align it with later liturgical representations, but the priority must remain with the historical event, not some theology or liturgy detached from it. (A fruitful comparison may be made with the evangelists' accounts of the institution of the Lord's Supper.)

The next major impetus to Deuteronomy studies (with repercussions throughout the Old Testament) came with the thesis of Mendenhall and others that the ancient pattern of the Hittite suzerainty treaties could be seen reflected at many points in the Old Testament's covenant formularies. That, of course, would strongly support the Biblical tradition of the antiquity of the covenant theme. Many of the details of what von Rad had taken to be a liturgical pattern were capable of being assimilated to this new suzerainty-treaty thesis. Its details are perhaps still fresh enough and are recounted in enough contemporary literature that we need not repeat them here. We probably should call attention, however, to the admirable studies of M. Kline who argues convincingly on this suzerainty-treaty basis for the authenticity of the Biblical tradition of actual Mosaic authorship of Deuteronomy. Other conservative scholars since have ably seconded him.

In liberal criticism, however, a considerable reaction developed, fed partly by the more secular *Zeitgeist* of recent times. In the wake of the arguments of McCarthy and others that the suzerainty-treaty pattern was still alive and flourishing in the first millennium (Assyrian treaties), not limited to the second, the old Wellhausen tendency to assume that "covenant" in the Bible originated in later (largely seventh-century) literary endeavors has strongly reasserted itself.

Finally, in our survey of the never-ending swirl of critical interest in Deuteronomy, we may mention the works of M. Weinfeld. Riding the crest of the recent interest in "wisdom," Weinfeld argues that the seventh-century compilation by priests or scribes we know as Deuteronomy was also heavily influenced by the wisdom movement (supposedly evidenced especially in Deuteronomy's strongly didactic character).

Assuming, then, with what is still the preponderance of critical opinion that Deuteronomy is basically a seventh-century product (whatever the date or nature of its antecedents), we should next note the decisive role which the deuteronomic reformation allegedly played in the evolution of Israel's religion. The usual verdict is a very mixed one.

On the one hand, the theological importance of Deuteronomy in giving almost classical articulation to Old Testament covenant theology is recognized. Conservatives can readily agree because we are dealing with what plainly *is* a separate unit in the Bible. This is in line with the prominence of the book in New Testament quotation, in Luther's regard, and even, in spite of himself, in the determinedly diachronic theology of the modern critic, von Rad. And, no doubt, in many respects, Deuteronomy is an epitome of Biblical theology. Nor is there any better antidote for those who are still victimized by the stubborn canards that Old Testament theology is somehow fundamentally different from that of the New, knows less of God's love, has less concern for the individual, or whatever.

Deuteronomy is simply pervaded by the theme of God's unmerited love for His people as evidenced especially in their election and the gracious covenant made with them. Almost monotonously we hear the refrain: the people should be motivated to faithfulness out of sheer gratitude. The structure of the book is such that the "deuteronomic code" itself (chaps. 12—26) is framed by "parenesis" (sermonic exhortation and encourage-ment on the basis of that theme). Hence, even the laws themselves, especially in comparison with other "codes," are suffused with a "humanitarianism," a concern for people transcending legalism (even though the term is anachronistic and secularistic). But love is not unprincipled sentimentalism; Deuteronomy is also keenly aware of the divine judgment, of the "covenant curses" instead of promised blessings, which are sure to overtake the people if they are unfaithful.

Also very characteristic is Deuteronomy's "name" theology. God effects His real, personal presence amongst His people, especially in the sanctuary, by means of His "name." Only places of worship where He "causes His name to dwell" are licit. Since in Biblical usage, a "name" is not merely an I.D., but is a sort of extension of the person, this implies a very effective divine presence in grace or judgment. As argued above, the phrase is apparently not primarily concerned with the location or even the number of sanctuaries, but with their *character,* that is, whether their theology and praxis really reflects His "name."

Above all, the sermonic character of Deuteronomy is one of its most prominent characteristics. Like all effective sermons, it does not merely recount history and doctrine, but contemporizes it. The "Were you there?" of the famous Negro spiritual rings throughout this sermon, applied especially to the Exodus and Sinai themes. The hearers must put themselves in the shoes of earlier generations, who actually experienced the events. Hence, the eternal, existential "now" and "today" are repeatedly emphasized: *You* must choose, decide, respond, obey, before it is too late.

For the conservative, the value of these simply descriptive observations is not ultimately invalidated by the critics' denial of Mosaic authorship, nor by their persistent penchant to force the themes into a development framework. There certainly is massive accent on the oneness of the true God and His ethical nature, even if we disagree that such insights first began to triumph in Israel's religious thought in the seventh century. And Deuteronomy's classical expression of Biblical "name" theology stands, even if we cannot regard it as a sort of correction and spiritualization of the allegedly more primitive and magical theology (unfortunately reaffirmed in the priestly code) that had expressed God's presence in terms of His "glory."

This brings us to the negative aspect of the common critical evolution of the deuteronomic movement, which, of course conservatives cannot share. (Here many of the fundamental differences, both in hermeneutics and exegesis, between conservatism and modern liberalism become apparent.)

For one thing, Deuteronomy is often viewed as the beginning of the fateful compromise (to be climaxed in P) between priestly and prophetic impulses, between ceremonial and ethical religion—read also between "Catholic" and "Protestant" preferences. Liberal and Protestant tastes still often converge in preferring "deuteronomic"-type themes such as "covenant renewal" over more sacrificial and ceremonial ones (sometimes even in evangelical circles where the theory would disallow accenting one part of Biblical theology at the expense of another).

Even more serious charges are often laid at Deuteronomy's door. Deuteronomy's very accent on "monotheism" and a "jealous God" is often scored for the intolerance of all other religious outlooks that the book expresses so forcefully. Deuteronomy is deplored as another fateful step beyond E into not only "ritualism," but also "legalism," the notion that God can be pleased by conformity to externals (as though Deuteronomy itself is not one of the strongest Biblical condemnations of that).

Perhaps most seriously, Deuteronomy is regularly presented as the father of "biblicism," "bibliolatry," or the like, because of the accent the Josiah reformation put on a *book.* And not only a book, but here are commonly thought to lie the seeds of the idea of a *canon,* of a closed collection of books which purport to fix the perimeters of God's Word for all time!

All of these strictures are commonly summarized under the caption of "incipient Judaism" or the like. Here another (more parenthetical, but just as important) correction of a common misrepresentation must be insisted upon. In no way is the religion of the Old Testament to be equated with "Judaism," nor its adherents carelessly referred to as "Jews." The religion we know today as Judaism is constituted by more than the Old Testament, just as Christianity is. Judaism supplements and reads the Old Testament in the light of the oral tradition or the Talmud in a manner very comparable to Christianity's employment of the New Testament to interpret the Old. If we want a strictly historical term for the common heritage of both, "Yahwism" is perhaps the best candidate, and its adherents are "Yahwists" or "Israelites," not "Jews" (in the modern sense). Confusion of "Yahwism" and "Judaism" is likely to encourage misunderstandings of both.

P

The "priestly code" (as it is often referred to, as though it were only a collection of rules or regulations) is easily the *bête noire* of most modern criticism, as we have already indicated. The not unrelated judgment that it represents the last stage of a literary-theological process rather than its foundation was the cornerstone of the entire Wellhausen edifice, as we have also stressed.

In the main, that judgment still holds, although there has been no lack of powerful voices (Jepsen, Kaufmann, Cross, Speiser, etc.) challenging it, either dating P earlier, or arguing that it was used only to *supplement* the narrative framework of JE. Hence, its position in the critical reconstruction must be viewed as considerably less secure than the date and role of D are (although, as we have seen, critical challenges are not unknown there either).

Wellhausen, of course, readily conceded, too, that many components of P may well have been extremely ancient. Yet in its totality he insisted it was a product of exilic and postexilic priestly circles, in order to legitimize and adapt Israel to its new circumstances as a "theocratic" community, without political self-determination and existing only by the sufferance of the Persian authorities. Its habit of self-description in literally Mosaic terms, following the precedent of the deuteronomists, lacked virtually all basis in fact.

There has always been general agreement that P's history is largely a history of the *cult* that climaxes in the theophany at Sinai and its subsequent regulations. Wellhausen thought he could subdivide that history into a sort of fourfold dispensationalist scheme (hence his frequent reference to it as "Q," for *Quattuor*). That understanding has today generally been replaced by a two-covenant interpretation, the Abrahamic and Mosaic dispensations in a sort of prophecy-fulfillment relationship.

Yet Wellhausen's observations are still accepted in a different framework: at least three, if not four periods, each with its characteristic ordinances or rites and name for the deity are thought to be discernible. First, the Sabbath may represent God's (Elohim's) "covenant" with *all* creation, even the inanimate world (although the word "covenant" is never used). The Noachitic covenant (sealed by the sign of the rainbow) in the second place, still used the name "Elohim" because it should apply to all men, but prescribed only the first dietary laws (Gen. 9; cf. Acts 15). In the patriarchal period, the name "El Shaddai" is revealed, together with the obligation of circumcision (Gen. 17; JE allegedly knew nothing of such an antiquity of the rite; cf. Ex. 4; Josh. 5). God's true name, Yahweh, is revealed in Ex. 6, and after Sinai God graciously allows men to approach Him through sacrifice and the rest of the cultic apparatus. (Passover, Ex. 12, represents a sort of anticipatory exception.)

The conservative, of course, can recognize a considerable element of truth in this picture, if it is itself regarded as factual truth, and if it is integrated with the rest of the Biblical data, that is, not largely attributed to P's fancy.

The major issues raised are those of the nature of patriarchal religion, which is really beyond the scope of the present discussion. The Biblical data are very sparse, but leave the general impression of a simpler, incipient form of Mosaic Yahwism (of which Passover seems to be a good example). The Bible itself is more concerned with the theological history of the promise, and to that extent Wellhausen is on target. It is really doubtful if Alt's influential "God of the Fathers" hypothesis (or its later development by Cross and others) really helps, even to the extent that it is compatible with the Bible to begin with. No satisfactory explanation of the divine epithet "Shaddai" has been found. Albright's "mountaineer" is widely followed, although most popular translations seem to continue the traditional, "Almighty." In any event, it is plain from the Biblical witness that the name "Yahweh" was at least known in patriarchal times.

In general, P was thought to be readily discernible by its dry, formal, precise style—at the furthest possible remove from J. Lists, genealogies, rubrics, exact measurements, and specifications were thought to be its stock in trade. Any real narrative was constructed only when it illustrated cultic interests (e.g., Gen. 17 on the circumcision), and P's entire historical structure served only as a scaffolding for the eternal law. Hence, the entire block of cultic and legal material for Ex. 25—Num. 10 could readily be recognized as P's handiwork.

Elsewhere too P played his hand at all pivotal turning points in imposing his artificial chronology on the material. Especially in Genesis, a typical term was "*toledoth*" (usually translated, "generations," although "family tree" or "genealogical history" might be better). It seems to introduce major sections of Genesis, and some scholars have followed Wellhausen in thinking of a "*toledoth* book" as one of P's own sources (cf. below).

P was thought to have an equally distinctive vocabulary. In Gen. 1 there is *bara',* the technical term for "create," instead of J's more casual "make" or "form" in Gen. 2. Instead of the older, idiomatic "cut" a covenant, P, for similar motives, substitutes "make" or "establish" a covenant. He speaks of God's effective power and presence in terms of His glory (*kabod*) instead of the indwelling of His "name" as in D, and the even more immediate theophanies of J and E.

Distinct style and vocabulary corresponded to distinct theology: a massive accent on God's universal, omnipotent transcendence (in the supernaturalistic sense). Hence, He could be approached only through sacerdotal and sacrificial mediation. Laws of all sorts multiplied in order to forestall even accidental infractions of His terrible majesty.

To liberal, Protestant critics, of course, all this was almost an apotheosis of everything that true religion should *not* be! One must also seriously ask whether much of P's special vocabulary and accent is not simply another way of saying that the subject matter is largely cultic or liturgical. In our own day, too, liturgics has its own specialized language, like any other subject. In any context this language is about as conservative and unchanging as anything on earth, hence it is an unusually mute datum for dating. Scores of other lists of various sorts have nothing whatsoever to do with cult, and it seems arbitrary to bring them all together and construct a P source out of them.

With that, a body blow is also struck at the entire evolutionistic dogma of the lateness of P. There certainly is the accent in the P passages on a transcendent God, graciously making Himself available to man through the mediation of the priesthood, tabernacle, sacrifices, and other rituals. But that implies necessary lateness only because of a priori assumptions that early Israel *could* not have entertained such ideas of God and religion.

If P was originally a self-contained unit, one of the biggest puzzles is the total absence of any Fall account in a source so concerned with holiness and the forgiveness of sin! Increasingly, archaeology has provided us with rough pagan parallels, *mutatis mutandis,* to such P accents as priestly hierarchies, sacrifice, cultic paraphernalia, etc., and often from periods *far earlier* than Moses! Hence, except for evolutionistic biases, the burden of *proof* would seem clearly to lie upon those who will not accept the Biblical report of the Mosaic authorship of the material.

The isolation of P from its native context also causes theological problems. If read by itself, P readily comes off as theologically quite weak. It easily leaves the impression, indeed, of some mere ritualist or "liturgical nut," who believes that rubrics and externals are the end-all and catch-all of religious existence. Held within *total* Pentateuchal context, however, P reads entirely differently. Particularly Lutherans should have little difficulty in grasping the accent here on (in effect) sacramentology, on the "visible Word" as an indissoluble unity with the "spoken Word." Or, put otherwise, the message of the P sections is that Israel's (and the church's) whole life is to be "liturgy" or "service." In Biblical context, service of God and service of man go together as inseparably as deeds and creeds. In Hebrew, as in English, the same word is used for both kinds of "service."

Finally, as especially Kaufmann has argued, the overall impression left by the P material, even if isolated from its context, is not the critical one of an ecclesiastical community under foreign (Persian) domination, finding its identity and *raison d'être* almost exclusively in religious exercises. Rather the ultimate picture is that of the military camp of the "hosts" of Israel, bent upon the conquest of a promised homeland. If P invented that too out of whole cloth, the fraud at the heart of the Pentateuch almost staggers the imagination! Furthermore, in addition to significant differences in structural detail between tabernacle and temple, liturgical features such as the Levitical choirs (of which especially Chronicles makes so much) are nowhere heard of. If P were trying to pull the wool over people's eyes and simply retroject, he surely would have covered his tracks better than that!

Nevertheless, scholarship on the whole still avers that P took shape sometime in the Exile or shortly thereafter (that is, fifth-fourth centuries). Greater precision is usually not attempted. There is some critical debate as to the nature of the law-book which Ezra brought with him in 458. At the least, it is usually assumed to be basically what critics know as P (that is, with only insignificant changes, if any, made later). Others argue for the more or less completed Pentateuch already at that time, with the assumption that the alleged amalgam of all the sources was now substantially complete. (Conservatism, of course, views the question itself as misbegotten!)

ADDITIONAL SOURCES?

The history of Pentateuchal source-criticism has been bedeviled both by pericopes which, by common consent, do not fit into the four main groupings, as well as by various attempts to isolate additional sources behind the sources. We are not speaking here of form-criticism's attempt to trace earlier oral traditions back to their inception; but of presumed literary sources—although all would agree it might not always be possible to make so neat a distinction.

Of those which do not readily fit into JEDP, even according to critical procedures, especially two pericopes are noteworthy: (1) Gen. 14 (Abraham and Melchizedek), on which critics have reached no consensus whatsoever, neither as concerns literary origins or historicity (cf. below); and (2) Gen. 23 (Abraham's purchase of the Machpelah cave), most often assigned to P, but really minus the usual identification marks.

In addition, critical scholarship has long puzzled over the real origins of the poems or songs preserved in the Pentateuch. Four longer ones stand out: Gen. 49 (Jacob's Testament), Ex. 15 (Song of the Sea), Deut. 32 (Song of Moses), and Deut. 33 (Blessing of Moses). There are also a number of shorter snatches of poetry. Since the line between poetry and prose is sometimes indistinct and debatable, some scholars theorize that much of the Pentateuch (especially while still being transmitted orally) was originally in poetic or epic form. For some reason, these poems allegedly resisted reduction to prose, and were preserved in essentially their original form. Since they generally retain more archaic forms of the Hebrew language, they have often attracted special attention by philologists, especially in the light of comparative linguistic data now provided by archaeology.

In this connection, the various "law codes" should be mentioned again, which, all critics now agree, had independent origin before their incorporation into either the sources or directly into the final editions of the Pentateuch itself. ("Code" is misleading in the Bible as in the ancient Near East in general: these do not attempt to achieve comprehensiveness, or to present a series of legal precedents, but instead intend to be only *illustrative* of the application of theological principles. Theological terminology like "sanctification" or "third use of the Law" is really more accurate.)

As already noted, the earliest "code" is commonly held to be the "Book of the Covenant" in Ex. 20—23 (sometimes designated either by the siglum B or by C). Because it appears to envision a sedentary society, it is argued that it could not really be Mosaic or from the presettlement, wilderness period. (Similar arguments are often presented about the origins of Israel's three main festivals, with their agricultural orientation.) Even humanly speaking, however, the problem with that argument is that, as we now know, the Israelites were not, like some modern Bedouin, pure nomads (camel nomads) with little knowledge of agriculture. Rather, they were only semi-nomads (ass nomads), largely limited in their wanderings to the margin between the desert and the sown, and normally engaging in limited agriculture themselves. In addition, generations of life in Egypt would not have left the Israelites entirely unacquainted with either agriculture or with other aspects of sedentary life!

Between the deuteronomic and the priestly code is usually fitted the "Holiness Code" (Lev. 17—26), commonly referred to as H, and so called because of its explicit overriding concern for Israel's holiness, "as I the LORD, your God, am holy." (It should also be noted that the Second Table of the Law is found in this context—Lev. 19:18.) There are various critical puzzlements over its date, because of affinities with both D and P. One clear example of the former is its peroration or conclusion in chap. 26, setting either blessing or curse before the people, very redolent of Deut. 27—28 at the end of the D code (not to speak of the conclusion of C, Ex. 23). Form critics argue with some plausibility that the feature roots in covenant-renewal ceremonies or the like, with ultimate formal roots perhaps in the political suzerainty treaties of Israel's neighbors.

On the other side is H's puzzling contravention (Lev. 17) of the permission granted for nonsacrificial slaughter of animals away from sanctuaries in Deut. 12:13-28—or so it seems if H is dated later than D. As a matter of fact, all D is doing is reaffirming the prohibition of Gen. 9 of eating blood. Both passages use the Hebrew word *zabah,* but D is not speaking of "sacrifice" in the strict sense. There is no *Biblical* evidence that *ordinary* slaughter was *ever* limited to sanctuaries.

In spite of the difficulties, H is usually dated slightly earlier than P (i.e., exilic times), partly because of affinities with Ezekiel (although Ezekiel has affinities with both). The affinities are, as such, undeniable, but the conservative sees no compelling reason why the Biblical picture of Ezekiel, the priest-prophet, as dependent on both P and H (understood as Mosaic) should not be accepted, rather than treating all three as basically contemporaneous because of preconceived evolutionary assumptions.

With much less success, other critics have attempted to locate subordinate strands in J, E, D, and P. The hope was to explain problems which the earlier quadruple division had not solved, and which not even the invocation of a redactor or redactors seemed to clear up. These efforts have probably met with more favor in Germany than elsewhere, but, on the whole, outside of their proponents (and their Ph.D. candidates) they have never achieved any widespread following. Carried very far, this pursuit would mean the abandonment of a "documentary" for a "fragmentary" hypothesis.

The understanding that some J passages early in Genesis (Gen. 4:16-24; 5:1-4) seemed to be ignorant of the Flood Story led especially earlier critics to distinguish a J^1 and a J^2. Somewhat similarly, Smend, followed by Eichrodt and Eissfeldt, interpreted many J passages as championing a primitive "nomadic ideal." Eissfeldt labels them L (Lay source, because they lack cultic interest and thus are seen as the furthest removed from P); these correspond somewhat to the earlier J^1. Fohrer uses the symbol N ("Nomadic") for these sections. Pfeiffer assigned some of the same passages to a putative Edomite source of the tenth century, and styled them "S" (for Southern or Seir). Other critics have made similar or related proposals.

Von Rad championed a subdivision of P into P^A and P^B, depending on how much historical interest (as contrasted with the purely legal) it exhibited. Various German researchers have in principle followed him in this respect, especially Elliger in his P^g and P^s divisions.

Finally, following especially Steuernagel, there have been various attempts to subdivide D, especially according to whether the address is in the second person singular or plural ("thou" or "you"), according to whether the laws allegedly involve centralization of worship or not, or other criteria. This line of investigation still continues in some critical circles.

Most idiosyncratic of all was Procksch's attempt to subdivide E into an E^1 and E^2 (while others were despairing of the possibility of isolating E to begin with).

At the opposite extreme can be mentioned the proposals of certain Scandinavian scholars, led by Engnell of Uppsala. The "Uppsala school" believed that oral tradition remained dominant until the crisis of the Exile, and hence scoffed at the bookish presuppositions of most criticism. Like Noth, it eliminated Deuteronomy at this point, and considered only the Tetrateuch. At its core, it believed, was the Passover "legend," an expansion of a liturgical text used in the celebration of the festival (following Pedersen). This expanded core was called the P-work (roughly coterminous with the P of other critics), which in the course of time was combined or supplemented with other material (roughly equal to JE). Further dissection was resisted, thus distinguishing this school from many form critics, in spite of their common emphasis on oral tradition.

Contemporaneously, these scholars believed, a D-work (Deut.—2 Kings) was built up by combining material of various origins. Both the P-work and the D-work reached final form in the age of Ezra-Nehemiah.

Virtually no scholars today would subscribe to this precise form of Engnell's reconstruction nor to its overstatement on the role of oral tradition. However, in many ways it proved a harbinger of certain common contemporary attitudes, especially the reaction to the excesses of much source criticism, and its vision of two comprehensive histories of Israel (to which Chronicles is often added as a later third). Its programmatic distinction between the date of contents and the date of writing down would find near universal acceptance today.

Summary Evaluation

Certain other critical hypotheses we shall look at briefly in our survey of contents below. However, first let us attempt an overall conservative, evangelical or confessional evaluation. With Harrison (p. 536, utilizing the research of especially Kitchen) we would counter the entire critical enterprise with a confessionally based "inductive holism."

It almost goes without saying that both the literary and the historical reconstructions of higher criticism conflict so drastically with the Bible's own presentation that "ne'er the twain shall meet." To be blunt, really no one denies that, except certain administrators at times when higher criticism is first invading an institution, and the *hoi polloi* need to be mollified. Far more, of course, is involved than merely reshuffling dates and authors, because, within limits, that by itself, could be a quite innocuous matter theologically. Nothing less than a fundamentally different version of the Christian faith is entailed, beginning with radically different understandings of the nature of revelation and of Biblical inspiration and authority.

Point by point, the individual critical arguments can at very least be checkmated. Virtually all of the conservative refutations can be duplicated somewhere within criticism itself! It is not our purpose to rehearse all of those arguments here. Some we have sampled already; some others will appear in connection with the survey of contents below.

The pivotal argument for Mosaic authorship (considering *only* that one issue here) is at once Biblical and Christological. Not only do both testaments repeatedly refer to the Pentateuch as Mosaic, but Christ Himself does. A few of these might by themselves legitimately be considered mere traditional usages, with "Moses" becoming a cipher for "Pentateuch." The cumulative evidence makes plain that real Mosaic authorship was meant, however. That testimony can be disregarded only by conceding serious error on this point to the Biblical writers—and, as we have repeatedly stressed, even more serious errors throughout the Bible are necessarily implied. And we argue a fortiori when it is Christ who speaks: considering all that hung on "Moses" in the Jewish tradition of his day, it is inconceivable that, in the course of his running debates with the "scribes and Pharisees" our Lord would not have challenged the erroneous notions of His adversaries in this respect—as He certainly did in others! Spurious appeals to His "true humanity" or to some sort of kenotic Christology are not acceptable.

If the critical and confessional stances are ultimately incompatible, where do we go from there? Are fatal compromise or internecine warfare the only alternatives? The air is cleared, and probably everyone is happier, if we *do* admit that such *ultimately is* the case and go on from there. Hard as it often is to turn the other cheek to constant jibes about fundamentalism, *et al.,* there is no future in accentuating the negative or fanning the flames of conflict. But is that all?

Without minimizing the seriousness of the issues involved, let us then ask what, if anything, can be "salvaged" from the entire vast critical enterprise. We are not speaking, of course, of the vast amount of objective historical, archaeological, and strictly exegetical substance which "*critics*" have also contributed.

Often the question comes, in effect, "Why bother?" Sometimes, indeed, the point of diminishing returns may be reached very soon, but the responsible pastor still cannot bury his head in the sand. At very least, we must know the enemy to defend ourselves. But people often learn things from their enemies too! As long as the "establishment" remains liberal and critical, most Biblical commentaries and other literature will continue to be written from that viewpoint, and we might as well learn to make the best of it.

First of all, on the more theoretical level: can we have anything to do with "sources?" If in answer we think of *Moses' own* sources, there would be no problem (assuming, of course, that these are construed as compatible and not contradictory). As elsewhere in Scripture, the Pentateuch sometimes indicates a few of its sources, and there is no reason to doubt that there may be many more. We could scarcely ever advance beyond the stage of hypotheses, but hypotheses may sometimes be very fruitful. We will, of course, insist that the inspired, authoritative text is the final product, not some earlier draft or individual component. All the same, knowledge of or theories about the latter may be exegetically stimulating and helpful.

As we have noted, D is largely limited to the Book of Deuteronomy, so that we may put it to the side in consideration of the remaining four books (that, of course, does not imply acceptance of any original Tetrateuch, as many scholars conceive it). J and E are often so indistinguishable, even by critical lights, that many speak only of JE, or a "narrative source." That leaves us with really only two "sources" for most of the Pentateuch, JE and P. The latter is so largely liturgical in nature, that it is easy to think of a separate "source" of that sort, often using its own specialized vocabulary and idioms. Apart from apriorism, there is nothing implausbile about

Moses often being dependent on two such streams of tradition, which had already taken on a sort of "canonical" shape before him. This might well account for many of the changes in style we observe. If one thinks it fruitful, the conservative may—up to the point of contradiction in terms—pursue possible oral sources even further back, somewhat along form-critical lines.

In the nature of the case, however, such endeavors will never hold the attraction for the conservative that they do for the liberal, precisely because for him the Word of God is to be found *in* the final text, not somewhere beside or behind it. Hence, if the conservative does pursue such options, the vast *ultimate* difference separating him from liberal parallels must also be stressed. Thus, the game occasionally played by compromisers or dissimulators is declared forfeit, namely that a conservative brand of this type of investigation has anything other than coincidental connection with the "documentary hypothesis" or with "historical-critical method," as those terms are universally understood.

Can we entertain any development of the material, possibly along independent lines, *after* Mosaic composition? If we define our terms carefully and proceed cautiously enough, we probably can, and at least up to a point, perhaps must. We have already noted a few undeniable, but marginal signs of updating or modernization for the sake of communication. The same appears to be true linguistically: in the Pentateuch, as in other Biblical books there are signs of modernization of the *language* as it developed (perhaps comparable to the updating of the King James translation). In contrast to some of the poems of the Pentateuch written in an archaic Hebrew, much of the Pentateuch is written in ordinary, classical Hebrew, which, at least in the light of present knowledge, means the David-Solomonic Golden Age of Hebrew literature, some centuries after Moses.

In addition, it is especially apparent in the prophetic books, as we shall see later, that there was some rearrangement or transmission of the oracles for specific literary purposes, whether by the prophet or by disciples, and something analogous is quite possible, perhaps imperative, in the case of the Pentateuch. Certain stylistic differences, in accord with the customary usages of the traditors, might easily have arisen in that connection.

In all this, there would appear to be no reason why conservatives could not often use symbols such as P, H, etc., as a convenient shorthand, precisely because they have become such common currency, whether we like it or not. It goes without saying that it will then also have to be said loudly and clearly that we are referring only to certain blocks of material, and in no way beginning to capitulate to any version of the documentary hypothesis.

Thus, Mosaic authorship need not be taken in so narrow a sense as to attribute every contour to Moses himself. Theologically, the important thing is that also the extensions be brought under the umbrella of *verbal* inspiration, and not be viewed in liberal fashion as the constant process of community reinterpretation in the light of new "inspired" experience and "encounter." The amount of such later refashioning would surely be minimal compared with liberal versions, where at times the "historical Moses" gets lost in the shuffle. But the quantity is not, as such, the significant question. Conservatism might well add to its agenda the investigation of the legitimate perimeters.

The Pentateuch Book by Book

The name "Pentateuch," meaning "five-volumed" or the like, is technically Greek, of course, and hence of Septuagintal derivation. But the idea plainly has Hebraic roots. In the rabbinical tradition we hear of the "five-fifths of the Law." Furthermore the five books are plainly delimited in the Masoretic tradition, although there they receive their name from the opening words of the books (technically *"incipits"*), following ancient Oriental usage. It is quite possible that the division is not original—indeed, on critical premises it cannot be. In any event, it is not possible to determine for certain how ancient it actually is.

"Torah"

The Hebrew name for the totality is *"Torah,"* instead of Pentateuch, a more functional title than the purely formal "Pentateuch." The conventional translation of "Torah" with "Law" is most lamentable, however. If it were possible to turn back the clock and expunge fateful and misleading renditions from our Bibles, this would surely be the place to start. It indisputably is one of the major culprits in reenforcing the stubborn prejudice that somehow the Old Testament is more "legalistic" than the New, or at least contains proportionally far more "Law" than "Gospel."

If it were possible, it might be better not to translate, but simply to transliterate "Torah," as is the common Jewish practice. Short of that, it must be shouted from the housetops that, to the extent that we must settle for a single-word translation, "Gospel" would be far more accurate than "Law." But that must be immediately qualified: Torah means "Gospel," not in its narrow sense of the obverse of "Law," but in its broad sense of *both* Law and Gospel. (For the less theologically sophisticated, the substitution of "judgment" and "salvation" might often be helpful.) It relates both the impossible demand of God upon fallen man as well as the good news of God's own meeting of His demand in the covenant—and in the promises attached to it. Of course, it also *includes* "law" in its more popular political ("first use") and ethical sense ("third use," "sanctification").

Alternatively, "Word of God" would often be a superb "dynamic equivalent" of Torah, because God's Word always confronts us in both Law and Gospel. The synonymity of the two is evidenced by their occasional parallelism in Hebrew poetry (e.g., Is. 2:3 = Micah 4:2, and *passim* in Ps. 119 and in Deuteronomy).

More technically and perhaps etymologically, the root meaning of the word appears to be "instruction," both in individual instances as well as in a more comprehensive sense. From there it is a short step to the sense of "revelation," which again can be a very comprehensive concept.

These passages are also important *sedes* for the proposition that "the Bible *is* the Word of God." Hence "Torah" comes to be applied to the inscripturated Word, especially the Pentateuch, but sometimes by extension to the whole Old Testament. In one sense, the Pentateuch is the *heart,* the quintessence, of the Old Testament, and all the rest is a sort of commentary on it. Jewish synagogal liturgy gives expression to this by the primacy accorded readings from the Torah (the *parashah*).

All of this is very parallel to the derived Christian use of "Gospel," applied to the accounts of the four evangelists and the major liturgical pericopes excerpted from them. If the reading of Old Testament lessons in Lutheran services ever becomes common again, the parallelism of "Torah" and "Gospel" would constantly be expressed in the very liturgical structure of our worship and might more readily be expounded by the alert and conscientious shepherd.

GENESIS

The broad outline of the book is very simple. Chaps. 1—11 report the primeval history of the entire human race, and chaps. 12—50 the beginning of the history of election in the patriarchs. The latter may be subdivided into: chaps. 12—26, Abraham and Isaac; 27—36, Jacob and Esau; 37—50, Joseph. Chaps. 1—11 set the stage for the patriarchal covenant and promise, as chaps. 12—50 lead up to an initial fulfillment in the Exodus and Sinaitic covenant. Hence the title of the book is appropriate in many respects: "Genesis" or "beginning" in various aspects.

Genesis 1—11

We, of course, believe and confess that Gen. 1—11 reports real, empirical history, just as much as the rest of the Bible. Yet it is also pre-empirical in the sense that we are generally not yet able to investigate its history as readily as later epochs. However, the difference is one of degree, not of kind, and in two respects. History always retains its "mystery," both empirically (which is still very much true of the patriarchs), and theologically, because *divine* work in history as well as nature is ultimately a matter of revelation and faith.

Factual though it is, its significance is not limited to its facticity. It is also "protology," the counterpart of "eschatology." These are not human projections in opposite directions and universalizations of Israel's *present,* historical experience of having been "created out of nothing," as liberal theology holds. Yet the present is never Biblically comprehensible without them. Neither are the accounts adaptations of older Near Eastern legends and myths. The many undeniable formal parallels point in the opposite direction: the extra-Biblical tales are garbled reflections of the Biblical accounts.

In the sense of "providence" we may also speak of "continued creation," but the latter has virtually become a code-phrase for a purely existential or immanentalistic interpretation of protology. In fact, in spite of itself, it appears to relapse into pagan type of thinking, where "creation" (which necessarily implies a literal, *personal* eternal deity) is really impossible, and where we have instead the eternity of matter, only personi*fied* as gods. The Biblical God is no mythological construct because He is a real "person."

Even "theistic evolution" fails to break with paganism at the point of *ultimate* beginnings, no matter how far back the date is pushed. Exegetically or grammatically it is invalid to accent "In the beginning God" without its predicate, but theologically it articulates the uniquely Biblical assumption: the Creator alone is eternal. On that premise the Bible explicitly bases not only creation itself, but also judgment and salvation. In a way, evolutionism founders more on the Fall than on creation itself. Either God was not in full control, or He is somehow responsible for the appearance of evil. Also the entire "second Adam" typology of especially Rom. 5 founders apart from the facticity of the first Adam.

Grammatically, it is impossible to try to calculate a date for creation on the basis of the meaning of "day" (*yom*). The word is undeniably used in Hebrew as in English in a variety of extended senses. Yet in the context of Gen. 1, its ordinary 24-hour sense is certainly the most natural or "literal" sense, if external criteria are not invalidly introduced. The problem of Gen. 1—11 is not primarily exegetical, but hermeneutical (philosophical and epistemological starting points).

Most conservatives, however, are prepared to concede a *somewhat* older earth than the traditional 4,004. In general, we are bound by the clear Biblical impression of a relatively *young* earth, but we are in no position to attempt to fix a precise date, nor, in a fully Biblical context, is it an important matter. It is not a question of *whether* the Bible is true, or of letting extra-Biblical evidence overrule the Bible's testimony, but of *what* the Bible's truth at this point is. The uncertainties arise primarily with respect to the Biblical numbers, especially in the genealogies and chronologies. Not only does the Bible *sometimes* use numbers symbolically more than we are wont, but especially "son" is often used in derivative senses of "descendant," or of cultural and political connections, etc.

There is no compelling reason why Gen. 1 and 2 need be read as two disparate creation accounts, as the critical dogma goes. One of its major supporting arguments is that Gen. 1 *ends* and climaxes with man (male *and* female) while chap. 2 *begins* with man (male only). But the two dovetail perfectly if we understand Gen. 1 as a "wide-angle" introduction to *all* of creation, while Gen. 2 zooms in for a "close-up" of the Bible's primary interest. Even otherwise, the small amount of repetition need not bother us: ancient Near Eastern examples galore illustrate that such procedure was common usage, especially in "epic" material (this with countless applications in the Bible, where the critical reflex is to postulate different sources). Many things could account for the difference in style—"sources," properly understood, among them, as we noted above. But a more likely explanation is the deliberate use in chap. 1 of an elevated, measured style to introduce so exalted a subject, before adopting more ordinary narrative idiom in chap. 2.

In 2:4a we meet for the first of ten times in Genesis the word *toledoth,* usually, although questionably, translated "generations." A vast amount of ink has been spilled on this subject, and the last word has by no means been spoken yet. Critics quite unanimously read 2:4a as the conclusion of P's creation account—the problem being, however, that everywhere else *"toledoth" introduces* a section instead of concluding it. Certainly, the expression plays some structural role in Genesis (and not only in P or his predecessors). If so, it presumably plays the same role here as elsewhere. Perhaps the best solution, then, is to understand it as consistently *both* concluding and introducing. It appears to signal major points where the line of election or the "scandal of particularity" is narrowed down still further enroute to *the* Elect One, David, and especially the second David. At this point, then, it would signal the first narrowing of the line, from all of nature to man. So understood, it also helps fuse chaps. 1 and 2 into a structural unity.

It is possibly correct in a technical sense that chap. 3 (the Fall) is never alluded to elsewhere in the Old Testament. But, if so, it is plainly only a technicality, because the subject matter is assumed all over the place, beginning with chap. 4. The point is well made also that we too easily leapfrog over chaps. 4—11 to chap. 12 (and sometimes virtually over the whole Old Testament directly to the "new creation"). The Flood and Tower of Babel stories are important sequels to and confirmations of chap. 3, all of them confirming the "necessity" of the election of Abraham.

Heilsgeschichte (the term *may* be used very positively) does not first begin with Gen. 12, as critics commonly hold, but at Gen. 3:15, the "Protevangelium." The immediate context alone would suffice to refute von Rad's influential interpretation of the passage as presaging nothing more than unending, relentless struggle between two "seeds." Neither does its brief, formulaic expression necessarily imply a similarly limited comprehension at the time of its vast salvific import. At few points is the dictum, "Scripture interprets Scripture" more important. The prophecy of salvation here must be integrated with other themes in the Book of Genesis: promise, blessing, election—and probably, as noted, *"toledoth"* as well.

Critics characteristically view the genealogies of chap. 4:17 ff. and of chap. 5 as originally those of J and P respectively, but even they must concede that the redactor did a good job of welding. As the material stands, chap. 4 introduces Seth as the replacement of Cain, while chap. 5 (the "antedeluvian patriarchs") carries us on to Noah. Chap. 5 may provide us with a parade example of the heavily symbolic and selective component of many genealogies. Here we have 10 names matched by another 10 from Noah to Abraham in 11:10 ff. (cf. the 10 *toledoth* in Genesis and the three fourteens in Matt. 1). Caricatured echoes of these data are found in memories of long-lived ancestors in many parts of the world, most pertinently in the Sumerian king-lists. These, however, describe their subjects as semi-divine, and reigning an average of about 30,000 years apiece.

Many scholars, including some recent critical ones using structuralist premises, have demonstrated that the Flood Story may easily be read as a coherent unit, not necessarily an interweaving of disparate J and P accounts. We may note that many evangelical scholars are now willing to concede that the Bible envisions only a *localized* Deluge, but still with radically different hermeneutical deployment than when liberals give superficially similar explanations. Nevertheless, it is difficult to see how any such interpretation can be called *literal* exegesis.

Chap. 10 is the famous "Table of Nations." We are still far from being able to relate its statistics to known extra-Biblical history. Quite a few of the *place*-names are locatable, however, and now the Ebla discoveries appear to have given us a handle on one of the personal names. The "Eber" of 10:21 ff. (again in 11:14 ff.) appears to be the same as one of the major kings of Ebla (c. 2300 B.C.), and not merely an artificial eponym of "Hebrew," as critics have assumed. When the genealogy is continued in 11:10 ff., it is only the line of Eber and Peleg which is picked up to lead us into the world of the patriarchs.

Patriarchal History (Genesis 12—50)

The transition from primeval to patriarchal history is easily and often exaggerated, especially by critics who disallow any historicity in the earlier section. We have noted the themes of the Messianic promise and the narrowing of the line of the "seed" already in the preceding chapters. Nevertheless, it is correct that the "scandal of particularity" does intensify here, as the history of the promise reaches a first major plateau or "fulfillment" (which, as so often, is the springboard for further prophecy).

The problems of historical confirmation continue, too, with only slight amelioration. Technically, patriarchal history remains "prehistorical" in the sense that we are still unable to make any *definite* connections or synchronisms with extra-Biblical history (of which, by now, we know quite a bit, thanks to archaeological discoveries). From the cultural history of the times (especially the findings at Mari and Nuzi) we can document names and customs, which appear to parallel or illuminate those recorded of the patriarchs. The fact that some of these are different from the standard Israelite laws or customs later on is a sort of confirmation of their historicity, because later invention would scarcely have portrayed the forefathers in that light—or even known of the existence of such usages.

At least, until recently, under the tutelage of more conservative, archaeologically oriented scholars like Albright, Wright, and Glueck, a scholarly consensus along the above lines had nearly been achieved. This synthesis dated the patriarchs either in the Middle Bronze I or MB II eras (c. 2100—1700 B.C.), and associated their migrations with the massive Amorite movements of the times.

In more recent years, however, as more radical winds blow in academe, that synthesis has come unstuck: Israeli scholars (Mazar, Aharoni, etc.), partly on the basis of their view of the archaeological evidence, favor dating the patriarchal stories to the *Late* Bronze period, the time of the main Israelite settlement. Much more radical voices are prominently heard again also, more or less returning to the earlier liberal posture that the stories are basically products of the exilic or early postexilic eras, intended to establish a "divine right" for the Jewish claim to the land at that time (more or less what Ezek. 33:23 ff. condemns).

The final resolution of all these problems is not in sight, but the current relapse is a good reminder that, occasional conservative spells to the contrary notwithstanding, we lean on a broken reed, if we must, hat in hand, go repeatedly to critics to determine what parts of the Bible can still be believed!

As noted above, Gen. 14 remains a historical and literary puzzle. Earlier attempts to associate "Amraphel" with Hammurabi cannot be sustained. A previous tendency amongst critics to accept linguistic arguments for the

chapter's antiquity has tended to give way to interpretations viewing it as a
mere etiology of Jerusalem's later importance, and perhaps especially of
Zadok's displacement of Abiathar as high priest. One notes especially the
designation of God as El Elyon ("God Most High"), an epithet which can
be formally paralleled at Ugarit ("Aliyan," applied to Baal). It seems to
have been especially common in patriarchal times (alongside of "Shaddai,"
often translated the same way, but so far unparalleled).

The dual episodes of covenant-making with Abraham in chaps. 15 and
17 are classical examples of doublets in critical eyes. The two chapters are
usually attributed to E (often thought to begin here) and P respectively.
Again, in addition to marked differences in style and vocabulary, there is
the contrast between the vivid, almost eerie, narrative of chap. 15 with its
accent on Abraham's faith (esp. the famous "Pauline" passage in v. 6), and
the more terse, formulaic account of chap. 17, accenting the name, "El
Shaddai," and interested above all in the rite of circumcision. Nevertheless,
there is no difficulty in reading the two chapters as complementary, the first
accenting the necessary foundation in *sola gratia* and personal faith, the
second reaffirming the first and concerned with its "sacramental" sign, with
the cultic continuation and representation of the promise through the ages.

Gen. 22 is widely understood in criticism as originally concerned to
polemicize against child sacrifice, a rite sometimes thought to have
remained common among the Israelites until much later. However, there is
not a hint of anything like that in the text. Its point is plainly the successful
testing of Abraham, the "father of the faithful." However, knowledge of the
practice of child sacrifice in Canaan is probably assumed, and we should
recall the later legislation substituting the Levites for the firstborn (Ex.
13:11 ff., Num. 3). The "Akedah" (the "binding," after the *hapax* used in v.
8), as especially Judaism knows the pericope, has played a prominent role
in the history of Jewish thought. In the New Testament too, it is probably a
basic type, underlying *"vicarious* atonement" (perhaps most clearly in
Rom. 8:32).

Isaac is a much less distinct figure than either father or son. The
narrative hastens on to Jacob and his twelve sons. Critical scholarship
generally reads this history, like that of the three patriarchs themselves, as
more tribal than personal history (conservatives would prefer to reverse
that). The personal names are understood as eponyms, symbolic ancestors
merely personifying the tribe's legendary origins, aspirations, etc. It is
commonly held that J or tradition preceding him artificially united all these
originally independent tribal histories as "sons" of one father in order to
express the unification of all of Israel under the monarchy. Critical
hypotheses about the nature of the conquest are very much involved too.
As we shall note below, the Biblical account of a unified conquest under

Joshua is usually rejected in favor of a slow infiltration of various tribes. Especially Noth has popularized the custom of speaking of "Leah tribes," "Rachel tribes," etc.

A comment is also in order concerning the Biblical explanations of names, usually at birth. These have often provided critics with ample "evidence" of the popular, saga-type folk character of much of the patriarchal material. Some of the explanations do appear to be "popular etymologies" rather than modern "scientific" ones (although the difficulties and disagreements in connection with the latter should not be minimized either). Some of them could even be called "puns," if we did not tend to hear that word disparagingly. The usual Biblical significance attached to a name, including its sounds and rhymes, is very much involved here, however. It is not a matter of the veracity of Scripture, unless one puts the wrong question to it. "Scientific" etymologies of names apparently played about as minimal a role among them as they do among us.

Especially significant is the change of Jacob's name to "Israel" at the Jabbok ford (32:22-32). Not totally unlike Gen. 2—3, this narrative is probably to be read *both* on the personal and on the corporate level, because "Israel" ever after remains the covenant people's major self-designation (or "sons of Israel"), even typologically of the Christian church. It is the "baptismal name," the *"Christian* name" of the people, and its major exposition should probably be along those lines. Yet the people remain "Jacob," which in prophetic address often alternates with the new name (*simul iustus et peccator*).

Gen. 34 contains a tantalizing glimpse, both of Levi as a secular tribe, and of patriarchal advance settlement in general. The chapter may help explain some of the importance of Shechem later on when the main group of invaders linked up with relatives (?), but modern scholarship appears often to have made more of it than the Biblical evidence will sustain.

The Joseph cycle begins in chap. 37, only to be interrupted promptly by the Judah and Tamar episode in chap. 38. Obviously, some of the reason is interest in the tribe of Judah, whence David—and the Messiah. We may also have an example here of literary devices which were common in antiquity, but alien to us: Joseph temporarily disappears from the reader's sight at the same time that in the narrative itself he disappears from his father and brothers!

As we noted above, the earlier critical tradition of dissecting the Joseph stories into J and E components has fallen upon hard times. At least until recent challenges, von Rad's suggestion carried more weight, namely, that we have here a *novella* of doubtful historicity, produced in wisdom circles, illustrating many of the ideals for which they strove. One may suggest, however, that the clear wisdom flavor of the narrative corresponds to actual fact. "Wisdom," of course, was ancient in Egypt by this time (the Hyksos?). The Joseph cycle contains many other examples of Egyptian "local color" as well.

"Jacob's Blessing" in Gen. 49 is important linguistically because of its many archaic poetic features, and even more so theologically because of the Davidic-Messianic reference in connection with the blessing given Judah (although "Shiloh" itself remains uncertain). Because of this accent, which is missing in the rather parallel "Blessing of Moses" in Deut. 33, the two poems are often regarded as competing northern and southern versions. The form was common enough, however (also evident somewhat extra-Biblically) that we need not be surprised by two such relatively close parallels.

The closing words of Genesis, "in Egypt" (the typological significance of which is powerfully highlighted in the traditional Tenebrae service), sets the stage for the Book of Exodus. Historically, however, there ensues a long interval, a veritable "Dark Age" in our knowledge of the Israelites.

EXODUS

The contents of Exodus divide almost equally into historical and legal material (the latter predominating in the rest of the Pentateuch, and most of it, until Deuteronomy, attributed by critics to P). Chaps. 1—19 brings us through the exodus to Mt. Sinai, and chaps. 20—40 begin the legislation revealed at Sinai.

The book, of course, gets its name from one of the major events it records—a matter of only a chapter (14) or so statistically, but of such towering significance theologically that the extension of the name to the entire book is entirely justified. The book plays a role in the Old Testament comparable to the gospels in the New. The exodus event is the heart of the Old Testament "gospel," and the word "redeem" comes to be forever bound to it. It becomes a major type of, and hence is recapitulatively incorporated into our Lord's "way out" on Easter morning.

The latter antitype must be accented against liberalism: Biblical typology or the analogy of Scripture will not honor popular, liberal use today of the exodus as a model or paradigm for political or sociological "liberation." In both testaments, concerns of that sort on the "left hand" of God follow *from* the Gospel but are in no way to be accounted part of the Gospel itself.

Exodus 1—18

The book first records the phenomenal growth of the Israelites from the mere seventy who had first migrated to Goshen, and then the conflict this occasioned, especially with the rise of a hostile dynasty (presumably to be associated with the expulsion of the Hyksos by native Egyptian forces, c. 1550 B.C.).

Ex. 3, the story of Moses' call, is supposed to reflect E's interest in Moses, in "Horeb," in prophecy, in covenants, etc. (Later form critics often preferred more to accent its composition as an archetypal prophetic-call type.) Curiously, however, the source which prefers to speak of "Elohim" then gives us our only full account of the origins (?) or full meaning of the Tetragrammaton! "I am who I am" probably highlights omnipotence more than pure being. That understanding at least coincides with the most common academic explanation (Albright) of the name, Yahweh (as it almost certainly was originally pronounced, before later misunderstandings led to the artificial, "Jehovah") as a Hiphil (causative) form meaning, "He will cause to be," that is, "bring into being; create, save," etc. Sometimes it is also theorized that originally, before it was isolated as a proper name, it was part of a liturgical phrase something like, "El [God] who brings into being hosts." Since "hosts" translates "Sebaoth," this explanation *could* also account for that common phrase (at least in later times; nowhere does it appear in the Pentateuch). Whatever the correct technical explanation, much of this debate appears to be beside the point: as elsewhere, words and especially names get their meaning from *usage* (in this case, also revelation), regardless of technical etymology.

Before we proceed, the parenthetical observation is in order that expositors at all levels need to make much more of both "Yahweh" and "Sebaoth" than is usually done. At stake is not only the important Biblical-theological accent on the "name" in general, but also the uniquely Biblical accent on a *personal* God (and thence creation, incarnation, Holy Spirit, etc.). One may even argue that this accent better expresses the heart of Biblical uniqueness than mere "monotheism" (of which there are other forms, ancient as well as modern). For that reason this writer personally prefers that the Tetragrammaton simply be translated (or transliterated) "Yahweh." Worshipers might be temporarily jarred a bit, but the gains would be infinitely greater. However, the dead hand of tradition weighing against that, as it does, at very least there must be repeated instruction on the meaning and significance, both of the conventional typography, "LORD," signifying "Yahweh" in most modern translations, and of the "Sebaoth" ["hosts"] when left untranslated in many of our hymns and liturgies.

Ex. 6:2 ff. bolsters Moses' courage by reaffirming God's promise after the initial encounter with Pharaoh. Criticism, however, has quite unanimously viewed it as P's account of Moses' call, originally parallel to E's in chap. 3. As we have noted, much has always been made of v. 3, which seems to report the replacement of the earlier name, El Shaddai, with

Yahweh (cf. at Gen. 14 and 15), in apparent "contradiction" of Gen. 4. Again, however, it is anomalous, in the context of critical theory, that the "Elohist" makes more of the name "Yahweh" than either J or P!

The plague stories are usually explained as a compilation from J, E, and P versions. Earlier rationalistic attempts usually viewed them as supernaturalistic blowups of natural catastrophes. There may be a partial truth there, but it is probably more to the point to approach these struggles as a protracted struggle between the personal God, Yahweh, and the gods of Egypt, mere personifications of nature. The tenth and final plague strikes at the head of the pantheon, the Pharaoh himself, whom the Egyptians viewed as literally divine, and in the Exodus he is definitively bested. We, of course, do not view the final plague as simply narrative expression of the theological conviction that Egypt was punished for not having paid a redemption price for God's firstborn son, Israel. It is much more fruitful to relate the entire account typologically to the "final judgment" motif throughout the Bible.

Interspersed with reports of these climactic events are ritual instructions (naturally, largely attributed to P) concerning Passover, Unleavened Bread, and sanctification of the firstborn, all of which shall commemorate and actualize the events for later Israel. Critical wisdom has it that all of these originally had independent histories, none of them originally associated with the exodus, except possibly an early version of Passover.

Passover is usually thought to have been some sort of nomadic shepherd's festival before its later "historification" in being associated, possibly artificially, with the exodus. If there is no denial of the Biblical reports, some earlier form of Passover is not unthinkable. But, if so, it merely illustrates the principle that pre-Biblical meanings have little relevance for canonical meaning and Biblical theology. More helpfully, however, we may note that Passover is celebrated originally without benefit of clergy within the household and is thus no regular "sacrifice." Thus it may well illustrate older (patriarchal?) usages before the Sinaitic legislation.

Unleavened Bread (Azymes or Matsoth) is thought to have been a *farmer's* festival, which the Israelites could not and did not observe, until after the settlement. (We have argued above that as *semi*nomads with sedentary roots in Egypt the argument does not necessarily apply to the Israelites). Passover and Unleavened Bread are thought to have been merged sometime later, perhaps as late as the deuteronomic reformation. At some later time, too, Passover supposedly ceased being primarily a family observance (as it became again after A.D. 70) and became one of the three great "pilgrimage festivals," associated with the temple in Jerusalem.

Some think this feature too originated in Unleavened Bread, or began under deuteronomic aegis. If Deuteronomy is genuinely Mosaic, this adaptation must have begun shortly after the settlement, however, presumably at first wherever the tabernacle and ark happened to be.

The theological importance of Passover-Unleavened Bread for Yahwism, Judaism, and typologically for Christianity can scarcely be overstated. The latter climaxes at Holy Week and Easter (the Christian Pasch when the "Lamb of God" is sacrificed, but also leads His people out of Egypt). The traditional Easter epistle (1 Cor. 5:6-8) also applies the Unleavened Bread theme. Yet these major Easter motifs appear to be grossly underused, and perhaps it is as good a token of the general neglect of the Old Testament as any.

Corresponding to the importance of the Exodus otherwise, the usual critical tripartite dissection of the crossing narrative (13:17 ff.) has become somewhat of a *cause célèbre,* for both friend and foe. In this case it classically illustrates the use of the criterion of ever-increasing supernaturalization: J allegedly knows only of a fortuitous combination of natural circumstances attributable to Yahweh, while in P we have that blown up into the legend of the dry ground between walls of water on either side.

The "Song of the Sea" in chap. 15 (the *"Te Deum* of the Old Testament") gives a poetic version of the same events, where some critical literalists profess to find still other versions of what actually happened! Many have also thought that its core was originally Miriam's (vs. 20-21), with later expansion attributed to Moses, and hence they speak of the "Song of Miriam." Once dated much later than the event itself (J or later), increased linguistic knowledge has generally forced much earlier dating, a few critics even conceding that it may actually stem from an eyewitness. Most reservations have lingered about verses 13 ff., which have appeared to presuppose the later events of the conquest and even possession of Zion, but Ras Shamra parallels make actual Mosaic authorship perfectly plausible for also this part of the poem. (Note the typological reference to the song in Rev. 15:3.)

As the wilderness journeys begin, we note the gift of the Massah-Meribah grumbling, and the Amalekite attack, all of which reverberate in later Scripture. The command to *write* in 17:14 is of more than passing interest, not least in connection with Mosaic authorship of the Pentateuch.

Jethro's aid in Moses' institution of an order of judges in chap. 18 has been one of the mainstays of the "Kenite hypothesis," which attributes not only this feature but most of Moses' inspiration for his new religion to his father-in-law and/or the Midianites. V. 10, however, indicates that the significant traffic was in the other direction. Other scholars understand the

narrative as merely an etiology by E to give Mosaic authority to a
jurisprudential aspect of Israelite society.

Exodus 19—24

With chap. 19, three months after the exodus, we arrive at Sinai (where
we stay literarily until Num. 10:33). It accents the theophany character of
the revelation, associated especially with natural phenomena, as elsewhere
in Scripture. (This has led to many critical speculations that some natural
convulsions underlie the theologification of our accounts. More plausible
are hypotheses that Israel's worship regularly featured some sort of
symbolic or sacramental "theophany," actualizing the historical event.) At
19:5 (cf. the Christian antitype in 1 Peter 2:9, etc.) it bears notice that the
"universal priesthood" is not a New Testament novelty. The idea is that the
"special priesthood" was God's "consequent will" until that eschatological
time when all believers could actually function as their redemption would
signify (cf. somewhat similarly the Levitical substitution for the firstborn).
The major accent throughout this section, however, is the mediatorship of
Moses, who typifies Christ by combining all offices in one person.

If Ex. 20 is not taken as literally Mosaic, one must ask about the date of
the Decalogue, and, predictably enough, critical answers have varied
widely. Alt and other critical scholars have defended a possible Mosaic
date for at least its original form. (Generally quite a few expansions are
assumed, especially of those commandments now in longer form.) The
once popular form-critical hypothesis of an original *Sitz im Leben* in some
covenant ceremony has recently faded in the face of hypotheses offering
more secular explanations (family, clan, etc., with later, secondary
religious associations). Similarly, Alt's distinction between "apodictic"
(categorical) laws like the Decalogue as uniquely Israelite, in contrast to
"casuistic" (case) laws adapted from the Oriental environment, has proved
simplistic (but the labels remain useful to distinguish types of legal
formulations).

Especially to fend off suspicions of Old Testament "legalism," it is of
utmost importance to underscore the fact that grammatically the
Decalogue is in *indicative,* not imperative form. (The negative is *lo',* not
'al). These are statements of what the believer who has experienced God's
grace *will* voluntarily do, not commands of what he *must* do to deserve or
earn God's love. They represent the perimeters or boundaries of God's
kingship, beyond which the believer will not stray, but *within* which He is
essentially free to respond joyfully and voluntarily, as illustrated by the
rest of the "laws" or "codes" of the Old Testament.

At the same time, because no believer ever measures up to that standard
but remains sinner as well as saint, the Decalogue is also *"second* use of the

Law," summarizing God's case against us, in some of the most stringent prohibitions of all. (We have formal parallels to such "prohibitive laws" in Mesopotamia.)

Two later Jewish usages underscore the same general point: (1) continuing the Biblical usage of speaking of ten *"words,"* not "commandments"; and (2) counting v. 2., which plainly is indicative, as "word" #1.

The Book of the Covenant (so-called after the reference in 24:8) follows hard upon the Decalogue (20:22—23:19). The critical dating is usually somewhere between the settlement and the monarchy, because the latter is unmentioned while the former is taken for granted (cf. above). It ends with a sort of parenetic peroration (23:20-33), which is standard in the codes, as we shall note below in connection with H and D, and hence there is no reason to view it as an editorial (deuteronomic?) addition. Most of the laws themselves in the Covenant Code are "casuistic" in form, with numerous undeniable parallels in the ancient Near East. Theologically, it is more important that these (like most of the subsequent legislation) be seen in proper perspective. Here too it is no case of "legalism," but rather "*third* use of the law." We could partly describe them as *illustrations* or examples of faithful response to redemption, which would also account for some of the minor variations in different codes. That they did have binding, "legal" force in the Old Testament, however, does not imply theological difference from the New Testament, but only corresponds to the fact that Old Testament Israel was a *political* as well as an ecclesiastical unit.

Special comment seems mandatory only in the case of the so-called "*lex talionis*," the "eye for an eye" law governing retaliation in 21:24. Times without number, it is irresponsibly cited as representative of the Old Testament's low morality and spirit of vengeance, in alleged contrast to the New Testament's law of love. The context makes plain, however, that the law enjoins *restraint,* not cold-blooded retribution. We here see ancient Israel in its "left-hand" aspect as a state rather than a church, and the law's intent is to safeguard as much "love" as is possible in that realm. When in the world of power, retributive justice must operate, the law insists that the punishment must not be excessive, but must correspond to the severity of the infraction. The same is true of the parallel in H (Lev. 24:19-20). Deut. 19:21, it is true, speaks to the other side of the coin, the particularly heinous crime of perjury or false witness (which is also blasphemy), but only to that one circumstance. Our Lord's "But I say to you" in Matt. 5:38 ff. is not drawing *any* contrast in the kingdom of power or of earthly politics, but, like the rest of the Sermon on the Mount, must be heard as "eschatological ethics." Somewhat like the Decalogue, it speaks of what believers *will* do in the kingdom of grace, as well as (as Lutherans have especially accented) radically condemning our best efforts as *simul peccator.*

The first phase of the Sinaitic revelation climaxes in the impressive covenant ratification ceremony of chap. 24. We have here (in the very presence of God!) both a sacred meal and a sacrifice with a unique blood ceremony, both elements fulfilled as Christ establishes His Supper, the Eucharist, as the "new covenant in My blood" (Matt. 26:28; cf. Heb. 9:18-21). We note also the reading of a *book* (v. 7) and the first inscription of the Decalogue on stone tablets.

Exodus 25—40

Understandably from critical premises, most of the rest of the Pentateuch, except for a few narrative interludes and Deuteronomy, is attributed to P. In alleged contrast to especially J, it views Sinai as the fulfillment of the Abrahamic covenant and expresses itself predominantly in ritual legislation.

Both liberal and Protestant prejudices against such topics have again combined to make it probably the most unfamiliar and seemingly "irrelevant" portion of the Pentateuch. Before those erosions, however, it was widely viewed, with the New Testament, as of paramount typological significance, and this perspective needs to be recovered. We have here major "sacramental" objectifications of the covenant, of God's saving will and redemptive presence for His people, fulfilled in Christ, whose significance we better grasp in their light. These were not just spiritual ideas, but matters of Sacrament as well as of Word. From the standpoint of the fulfillment, the types are indeed only symbols or "shadows" (Col. 2:17), but from within the Old Testament itself they must be seen as veritable "sacraments" (the strict use of the term must be reserved for the new covenant, but the principle is the same). Specific ceremonial statutes went along with ancient Israel's status as a state, as was the case with most political units before modern times; Yahwism was the "established religion," if you will. That God in the New Testament no longer stipulates *how* to worship Him ritually does not mean that these pericopes are now only of antiquarian interest. "Typology" also implies that via Christ they continue to have great Spiritual and exemplary value for *our* worship.

Theologically very important for all the following material is the word "pattern" (*tabnith* or "type") at the beginning of the section (25:9). The reference here is to "*vertical* typology," not primarily to the horizontal or eschatological typology, which the term usually implies (although the two can never be strictly separated). The tabernacle and its ritual are a "reflection," a miniature, a copy of the heavenly temple. There is God's eternal throne (ultimately the entire universe), but God must become "incarnate" in a special dwellingplace among mankind because of its alienation in sin. The same language and conceptuality is applied to the tabernacle's successor, the temple (and by extension to the entire holy city, Zion) as well as to Christ, both His incarnation, and the fulfillment in Him of God's eternal purpose for the temple of the entire cosmos (Hebrews, Revelation, etc.).

In chaps. 25—31 we have God's instructions concerning the tabernacle ("prescriptive"), and in 35—40 the report of how they were carried out to the letter ("descriptive"). The latter is slightly abbreviated, but otherwise the texts are virtually identical, except for tense. This type of almost verbatim rehearsal is common in ancient texts and sometimes accounts for the "doublets" of the critics. Included are specifications, not only for the construction of the tabernacle and its various appurtenances but also for the priestly vestments (chaps. 28 and 39). The latter climaxes in the ritual for the consecration or installation of the priests in chap. 29 (not carried out until Lev. 8).

Pace the critics, we see no contradiction between the fact that here all the priests are anointed in contrast to Lev. 8:4-16, where only Aaron and the high priests are so described. Neither do we have to suspect some complicated literary history because of the hiatus in the main narrative until Lev. 8.

Between the prescriptive and descriptive texts looms the golden calf apostasy and its aftermath (chaps. 32—34). Critics disagree about the source, and some think of a special one. Others find various hidden agendas behind the "tale": pro-Levite and anti-Aaronide propaganda, polemic against the calves of the later Northern Kingdom, etc. The plural, "gods" in 32:4 (the same as 1 Kings 12:28-29) could possibly intend to draw the parallel with Jeroboam's schism, but more likely simply reflects the inevitably polytheistic implications of the act.

Many scholars agree that compromisers, both at this time and later, may have intended the calves as steeds or mounts of the invisible *Yahweh,* instead of the cherubim (Ex. 25:22) above the ark (i.e., not out and out apostasy). But, if so, it was a fatal compromise, because as both this narrative and the history of the Northern Kingdom made plain, the bull (a better translation) was inextricably associated with the fertility rites of Baalism. The "blessing" promised the Levites for their faithfulness (32:29) probably refers to their subsequent consecration as a priestly caste.

In context, this apostasy represents a breaking of the first covenant (and the tablets on which it was inscribed). Only after intense intercessory efforts by Moses in Ex. 33 is God stayed from abandoning the people, and a "new covenant" instituted in Ex. 34. This is symbolized by another illustrative collection of laws in 34:17 ff. Critics once widely viewed the entire chapter as originally J's tradition of the giving of the covenant and the ten commandments, parallel to E's in chap. 20, a "ritual decalogue" (or "dodecalogue") instead of E's "ethical decalogue" (although only by some legerdemain can one find any decalogue of any sort). In fact, however, it is simply a liturgical calendar, similar to one portion of the Book of the Covenant (23:14-19) as well as a much more detailed one in Lev. 23.

Ex. 33:7-11 requires comment yet because of the pivotal role it plays in critical evolutionary theory. The "Tent of Presence" here (and in a few similar passages) is usually thought to be the only *real* "tabernacle" which Israel had in the wilderness period, before P artificially reconstructed one on the model of Solomon's temple. (The phrase, "tent of meeting," is also applied to the full tabernacle in other passages, alongside more technical terminology, but this is considered part of the artifice.) Here, it is argued, we have only a very simple tent for divine communication, situated *outside* the camp (in contrast to the tabernacle's position at the very center), and with only a single attendant, Joshua (a dynamic "theology of manifestation" here instead of later, static "theology of presence"). One should note, however, that the text does not represent the tabernacle as already built. In Biblical context, the only possible interpretation appears to be that this is Moses' *private* tent, used as a sort of makeshift until the full tabernacle was finished.

The ark of the covenant is also unmentioned, and many scholars postulate still a third originally independent tradition. Archaeologically, many near parallels can be adduced among other migratory groups to something like an ark with its tent-covering, especially the old Arabic *qubbah.* No direct ones can yet be cited to support the historicity of the full tabernacle, but a "tabernacle principle" of sacral construction is well documented in antiquity. It can easily be established that the materials and technology for such a structure would have been no problem for the Israelites because of their Egyptian experience. In addition, there are general parallels to its floor plan and to many ritual details long before the age of Moses (not to speak of Solomon).

Exodus ends with the consecration of the tabernacle by the descent of the same "glory" (*kabod,* God's "incarnational" presence) which had led them from Egypt, now to take up permanent residence above the mercy seat in the Holy of Holies.

This conclusion of the book highlights the "theology of the tabernacle" throughout the Bible, as also of its successor, the temple. The "Word becoming flesh" message of the Old Testament is especially evident in God's incarnational and sacramental "real presence" in the sanctuary, centering above the mercy seat in the Holy of Holies. Hence, the prime significance of the temple as a major type of the incarnation, with a consummation still awaiting us at the end of time, must constantly be underscored.

Very important and central vocabulary conveys this message. "Glory" (*kabod* or *doxa*) often carries such incarnational freight, and this needs to be accented by the modern expositor. Especially in Deuteronomy, God's personal presence is expressed via His "name," but the usual critical antithesis between the "name" and "glory" (allegedly D and P respectively) is to be regarded as wrongheaded. In close connection with both nouns the verb *sh-k-n* is often used semitechnically to describe God's incarnational "indwelling." When God is the subject of the verb, it is carefully distinguished from the root *y-sh-b,* which describes God's "sitting" or enthronement in heaven.

From the former root comes one of the Old Testament's major terms for the tabernacle, *mishkan* (the other being *miqdash* or "sanctuary"). The later noun, "Shekinah," so important in Judaism especially, is not used in the Old Testament itself, but there is no reason why it could not have been. The major New Testament text applying this vocabulary to Christ is John 1:14.

Finally, the cloud and pillar of fire seem to be objectifications of these concepts, and the prominence of incense in the ritual seems to have had as one of its major purposes to "own a deity nigh."

LEVITICUS

The theocratic nation has been organized, the covenant ratified (justification) and the tabernacle erected, but before Israel continues its journey to the promised land, it also needs regulations regarding worship in the tabernacle and the ensuing holiness of life. That need Leviticus supplies.

The book has an impressive simplicity of outline, all of it concerned with the sanctification requisite to serve the holy God. Lev. 1—16 mostly record laws concerning the *removal* of the defilement (unholiness or uncleanness) separating man and God, and chaps. 17—26 again summarize and illustrate the behavior appropriate to the purified people of God (the so-called Holiness Code). Chap. 27 is an independent appendix.

The first section of the book may be subdivided as follows: Lev. 1—7: Regulations for sacrifice; 8—10: Record of the institution of the Aaronic Priesthood; and 11—16: The Laws of Purification, climaxing in the Day of Atonement.

Sacrifice (Leviticus 1—7)

Chaps. 1—7 contain the major sacrificial legislation of the Bible. There is no cogent, extracritical reason to regard it as late, neither in substance nor in present literary form. In chaps. 1—5 the main types of sacrifice are introduced seriatim, followed by miscellaneous, supplementary regulations especially for the priests, in chaps. 6—7. Chap. 1 treats the *Whole Burnt-Offering* or "holocaust," where virtually everything was consumed on the altar; chap. 2, the *Grain-Offering* (probably preferable to meat, meal, or cereal-offering), where only the *azkarah* or "memorial portion" was burned, the rest becoming part of the priestly emolument; chap. 3, the *Communion Offering* (again probably better than *Peace Offering),* where part was burned, part went to the priests, and part in this case reverted to the worshiper for the subsequent "communion meal" in the temple precincts (cf. 7:11-36); chaps. 4—5 the *Sin-Offering* and *Guilt Offering.* The latter two are not easily distinguishable, but apparently the latter pertained more to "*criminal* trespass," to the political than to the ecclesiastical aspect of ancient Israel. Hence, monetary restitution was usually required, in addition to the animal sacrifice. The sin-offering was distinguished from all others, both by its prominent use of blood (varying with both offense and offender), and by the burning of the carcass outside the camp (cf. Heb. 13:12). (Our clearest statement of the role of blood as the bearer of life, offered in sacrifice vicariously for human life, appears in Lev. 17:11.)

Few texts tend to be as opaque and forbidding to the modern reader as these. Both liberal (spiritualistic) and protestantizing prejudices continue to take their toll. The ethical reductionism of the former and the anti-sacramentalism and fideism of the latter have equal difficulty comprehending the holistic assumptions of Biblical theology: sin has corrupted the whole man, body as well as spirit, and the remedy must correspond. The fact that the texts themselves contain little explicit theology, but are almost exclusively rubrical, readily confirm in such minds the suspicion that their "theology" is purely ritualistic; if not quasi-magical.

We have space here for only a few corrective comments. Of course, in one sense, the prominent typological use of the subject in the New Testament should suffice to veto any such sentiments. "Vicarious satisfaction," "lamb of God," etc., are scarcely comprehensible apart from this context. The typological connection would be impossible if Old Testament worship were informed by any fundamentally different type of theology, that is, works rather than grace.

Our initial concern must be to try to understand Old Testament sacrifice on its own terms. At the same time, if Biblical theology is a unity also in this respect, we must approach it in essentially the same way as the New Testament teaches us to regard *our* "sacrifices" of money, time, etc. On the one hand, it had a "eucharistic" aspect; it was a sort of objectified prayer of thanksgiving accompanying and confirming, as it were, the verbal prayers thanking God for His covenant gifts. (Hence, the laudable dictum that we will misunderstand both the Psalter and Leviticus, if we divorce them.) On the other hand, these same gifts were God-ordained means of grace for "expiating" sin and "propitiating" His righteous wrath. Both results must be carefully distinguished from their pagan parallels.

Externally Israel's sacrifices have much in common with sacrifices all over the world, but *functionally (coram Deo)* they are "*sacraments.*" From God's side they belong to the realm of justification (ultimately by virtue of their unity with Christ's one, supreme sacrifice); the human input belongs totally to the realm of sanctification. (We speak of the orthodox theory; as the prophets make plain, Israel often confused the two at least as much as Christendom has.) One major evidence of all this is the fact that *no* sacrifices were valid for willful, deliberate sins (committed "with a high hand"); these, if repented of, were apparently covered only by the comprehensive atonement of the Day of Atonement.

Three sacrificial motifs may be helpfully distinguished: (1) gift (of thanksgiving); (2) communion; and (3) expiation and/or propitiation. Conspicuous by its absence is a motif that usually took pride of place in surrounding paganism: "alimentation" or feeding of the gods. Sometimes the Bible even explicitly polemicizes against such notions (Ps. 50; Micah 6; e.g.).

Each of the three Biblical motifs is especially prominent in certain sacrifices: gift in the whole-burnt and grain offerings; communion in the communion or peace offerings, and forgiveness in the sin and guilt offerings. All three motifs, however, also interpenetrate: all of the concepts seem to be present in all sacrifices.

We pass over here the totemistic and other anthropological theories by which critics once attempted to explain Biblical sacrifices as only one species of a worldwide genus. Also the evolutionistic dogma of Wellhausen on sacrifice is no longer so widely accepted, although still reflected in handbooks and commentaries. The assumption was that the original type of sacrifice was the communion or peace-offering, because it was "natural," "celebrative," etc. Latest, of course, at least in anything like its ultimate prominence in the Bible, was allegedly the sin-offering, which was thought to reflect the degenerate, morbid sense of guilt of postexilic times, and of a priestcraft geared to cash in on that state of mind. No doubt, the communion sacrifices are far and away the most commonly mentioned outside Leviticus, both in the Psalter and in the historical books. The reason for that, however, appears to be that those books, written from a layman's perspective, naturally feature those sacrifices in which laymen and their families and friends were most prominently associated.

Leviticus 8—10

Lev. 8—10, in contrast to the surrounding chapters, is largely narrative in form, relating the consecration and installation of Aaron and the priests, as prescribed in Ex. 29. The ceremonies include a "baptism" or ritual washing, formal investiture, anointing, and various sacrifices. Various irregularities among Aaron's sons (and possible successors) appear almost immediately and are punished, underscoring the need for priestly scrupulosity. The irreverence of Nadab and Abihu is punished by death, but Eleazar and Abiathar draw only a reprimand. The legitimate priesthood is subsequently descended from only these two. (There is no call for second-guessing the text, as critics are wont to do, about what obscure priestly infighting may underlie such narratives.)

Purity and Atonement (Leviticus 11—16)

Lev. 11—16 contains the "Law of Purity," the complex laws governing "cleanness" and "uncleanness," purification from "defilement," or the like. We use quotes because there is no adequate translation of the Hebrew *tamé*. The concept is closely related to "holiness," which we still use, but tend to misconstrue as well by spiritualizing (cf. below). The Biblical concepts are at once physical or material and spiritual, at once envisioning a sort of force or power as well as the resultant state, referring both to the underlying incompleteness and imperfection ("original sin") as well as to the "actual sin" resulting from it. Since the underlying problem is simply sin in its deepest dimensions, both objective and subjective, both ethical and ritual, the "purification" must ultimately be related again to the covenant, that is to God's declaratory verdict of "justified." In this connection we find that verdict reflected in the "declaratory formulae" of the priests, pronouncing one clean. (A similar usage appears in connection with sacrifice, which the priest declares acceptable to God or meeting with His favor.) Only when sin has been comprehensively removed in the cross of the new covenant will it be possible to lift these cumbersome restrictions (Acts 10, etc.).

When it comes to the details, modern explanations of hygiene, psychological revulsion, or the like, are ultimately as irrelevant as many anthropological attempts to classify them together with primitive notions of "tabu," "mana," and the like. Rejection of Canaanite customs may explain a little, but certainly not all. The text itself offers no explanations whatsoever except Yahweh's will. The proscriptions represent Israel's separation from contemporary heathendom, while the "clean" serve as types of the "new creation," the "redemption of our *bodies*" (Rom. 8:23). Purification of women after childbirth (chap. 12) and of both sexes after emissions from sexual organs (chap. 15) are apparently included because of their connection with the generation of life—something again very physical as well as spiritual. "Leprosy" in chaps. 13—14 is basically a mistranslation. "Hansen's disease" is surely included, but also a great variety of fungus infections—including even "leprosy" of clothes and houses, that is, mildew and dry rot! All are unclean or "sinful," because they reflect an imperfect, fallen world, no longer "very good," as originally created.

The laws concerning defilement peak in what is also a peak for the Old Testament in general, the Day of Atonement ritual of chap. 16. Predictably, critics argue again that, while components might be early, its present prominence reflects the guilt-ridden complex of the postexilic community. Also, the ritual is mentioned clearly nowhere else in the Old Testament, but that is an argument from silence. (It is the only *prescribed* fast in the Old Testament, although there were many voluntary ones.) Especially Hebrews expounds the Christological antitype of the ceremony.

Really, three purifications are interwoven in the chapter—not, however, in the neat sequence we might expect, and hence various literary sleuthings. First the high priest makes a sin-offering of a bull for himself, and as he carries some of the blood into the Holy of Holies (thus bringing it into the very presence of God Himself), he also cleanses (expiates) the temple and especially the altar. Next follows the ritual of the two goats, selected by lot: one "for Yahweh," sacrificed for the sins of all the people; the other "for Azazel," released to die in the wilderness—after all the sins of the community have been confessed over it and transferred to it. ("Scapegoat" represents one traditional etymology and explanation of "Azazel"; it seems, however, rather to be the proper name for the devil or one of his demons. Sin and uncleanness is thus returned to its source, the father of lies.) In all of this, there plainly is a poignant witness to utter, "total depravity"—and, backhandedly, as the New Testament points out, an acknowledgment that the entire vast, ordinary sacrificial ritual was barely adequate to stave off pervasive, satanic antiholiness.

Holiness (Leviticus 17—26)

Hence, the transition to chaps. 17—26 is easy. Klostermann in 1877 first labeled them "Holiness Code" ("H"; the symbol remains useful regardless of isagogical position). If cleanness and/or holiness is not *only* ethical, it certainly *is* ethical, exemplification of which is the major burden of the rest of Leviticus. Although the transition from chap. 16 should not be exaggerated, there is enough that is distinctive about these chapters to make plausible the theory that they originally had somewhat of an independent history; that as such need not clash with a high view of inspiration. The statement that H is—at least in present recension—an exilic product and was later incorporated into the Pentateuch, is a conclusion solely based on evolutionistic premises. The work has clear affinities with P, but, considering the common concern and common subject matter, that is scarcely surprising. The relationship with Ezekiel seems to be even closer, so much so that Ezekiel has even been thought of as its author. However, steeped in priestly lore as Ezekiel plainly was, and concerned as he also was with the surfeit of uncleanness which had finally occasioned the Exile, there is nothing whatsoever unlikely about him expressing himself in traditional priestly and Pentateuchal language.

Two quotations from these chapters are famous. Lev. 19:18 is the Second Table of the Law, and it bears emphasis that it, like the First Table, stems from the *Old* Testament! Yet immediately following it are more ritual stipulations illustrating again to what an extent the ritual and ethical, the physical and spiritual, are holistically intertwined in Biblical theology. The same unity is apparent in chap. 18's prohibited degrees of consanguinity in marriage; hence, in practice the facile distinction between "moral" and "ceremonial" laws is often difficult to apply. The obverse of the same point could often be made of the "Liturgical Calendar of the Old Testament" in chap. 23.

The other familiar quotation, Lev. 25:10, is inscribed on the American "Liberty Bell": "Proclaim liberty throughout all the land unto all the inhabitants thereof." The context, however, is that of sabbatical years and specifically the Jubilee year. Hence, as Is. 61:1 also intimates, its fulfillment is found in the great "sabbatical" Christ achieved for us (esp. Hebrews), not as such in any political, sociological, or psychological "liberation."

H, like B and D, ends with a parenetic exhortation in Lev. 26, and the book of Leviticus closes with an appendix on commutation of certain vows and tithes (the latter perhaps so treated because of the voluntary, yet binding, nature of vows).

Understanding the Biblical Vocabulary

Before we leave this subject, further word is in order about both of the concepts which dominate the last half of Leviticus, "expiation" (*k-ph-r*) and "holiness" (*q-d-sh*). In both we meet the same holism of the physical and the spiritual, the ritual and the ethical, which we encountered in connection with "uncleanness," and which the modern mind finds so difficult. Possibly the term "sacramental" is the best adjective for describing the intrinsic unity of internal and external exhibited in all three of these semantic complexes.

Thus "expiation" is not simply synonymous with "forgive," but implies a decontamination, a cleansing of a physical as well as a spiritual order.

This, of course, implies a "sin" which is not only mental and volitional, but a miasma, a negative "charge" or force which invades all parts of the material world as well. Hence also something as physical as blood is necessary to effect expiation.

"Propitiation" must be included in the concept and translation of *k-ph-r* as well as "expiation." Sometimes even well-meaning evangelicals follow especially Dodd and Driver in trying to eliminate "propitiation" from Biblical thought—or at least from the supposedly acceptable aspect of it. The only bit of truth in that objection is that *both* terms must be defined and understood on a fully Biblical basis. Outside of the Bible, of course, "propitiation" often applies to *man's* attempt to appease an angry god by his sacrifices. The solution is not to eliminate the Biblical themes of the wrath of God and of divine retribution from our theology, which is evidently often the liberal hidden agenda in this connection. Rather we must give full weight to the Biblical emphasis that the true God *Himself* graciously provides the means by which His righteous wrath may be allayed. In a way, this was the point of the entire covenant, old as well as new. Thus seen, "expiation" and "propitiation" become virtual synonyms, but *both* are likely to be misunderstood without the corrective emphasis supplied by the other.

Similarly with "holiness." Our common definition of the term, "without sin," is acceptable only if accompanied by a comprehensive, despiritualizing definition of "sin." Plainly objects and bodies are "holy" or "unholy" in the Bible as well as minds and wills. The "wholly other," separating from the "common" or "secular," applies equally to both realms. Because this is most true of the most holy, God Himself, "holiness" comes as close as any Biblical concept to describing God's abstract essence or aseity; in that sense, it certainly is not merely *one* of His "attributes." Sometimes the Bible reserves the idea of "holiness" entirely for God and describes its gracious communication to man under the rubric of His "glory" (the incarnational and holistic import of which we have already discussed). An old apothegm summarizes it aptly: "God's glory is His holiness revealed, His holiness is His glory concealed."

Much of this vocabulary of sanctity was also common in Canaanite religion, as it is in the world of religion in general. What is unique about the Biblical usage? One may summarize it with the "personhood" and ethicality of the true God. Because Yahweh possessed both qualities, His holiness was always dynamic in an ethically purposive way, and His adherents had to be "holy" also in a moral way, corresponding to the radically different holiness of their God. In contrast, pagan deities were mere personifications of faceless natural forces, and basically as amoral as the laws of nature. Hence, pagan "holiness" was purely objective and without clear moral concern (best illustrated in the common description of sacral prostitutes, both male and female, as "holy ones").

However, we need not tilt with ancient windmills. If "objectivism" or pagan magic was the major antithesis then, ours is certainly the reverse: a "subjectivism," which at best (often in "orthodoxy") reduces holiness to sinlessness (understood largely in voluntaristic perspective), and at worst, at the hands of secularists, arbitrarily defines it in terms of whatever ultimates or great causes are currently in vogue. Somewhat as we must stress with the similarly misunderstood "faith," however, the Biblical understanding of holiness is "sacramental": the power and the substance are objectively present whether one knows and believes it or not, but only he who subjectively appropriates can benefit.

NUMBERS

The book received its Septuagintal and Western label from the two censuses recorded in chaps. 1 and 26. Yet in this case the Hebrew name (derived, as usual, from one of the opening words), "In the wilderness," is more descriptive. In some respects the book is a miscellany and quite innocent of an outline, although, upon deeper inspection, it is clear that it continues a pattern established at least as early as Ex. 12. Its structure is basically historical, interspersed with further legislation along the way (to critics, JE and P material respectively). The Israelite itinerary it records may be subdivided into three sections (unfortunately, not coinciding with our chapter divisions): 1:1—10:10—Preparations for leaving Sinai (where we have been since Ex. 19); 10:11—21:9—The journey from Sinai to the Plains of Moab; and 21:10-36—On the Plains of Moab.

The symbolism of the arrangement of the camp in Num. 2 is theologically significant as well as historically and militarily plausible (with archaeological parallels): the tabernacle at the center, and three tribes encamped on each side, with Judah (Messianically) stationed in the center of the east side, opposite the entrance. Chaps. 3—4 describe the division of labor among the Levitical families of Gershon, Kohath, and Merari. The stipulation of a trial by ordeal for a wife suspected of adultery (5:11-13) is easily dismissed as a relic of primitivism, especially because of the many extra-Biblical parallels. Even externally, however, the Bible compares favorably with the latter. Unfortunately, the text does not clarify exactly how the process worked, except to indicate Yahweh's guidance (v. 21).

The voluntary Nazirite status (chap. 6) represented a sort of exemplary ideal of holiness, not totally unlike the monastic ideal of non-Protestant Christendom (although without the objectionable theology of the latter). Its features need not be read as representing a "nomadic ideal," a protest against later sedentary life as in the case of the Rechabites (Jer. 35).

It is to be noted that only the priests were permitted to utter the Aaronic Blessing (6:24-26), as the name itself indicates. "Blessing," like "holiness," in Biblical usage has much more physical, dynamic, and "sacramental" content than our reductionistic idiom would tend to admit.

At 10:11 we finally break camp and leave Sinai. At 21:9 we already arrive in Moab. That means that most of the 40 years in the wilderness is compressed into these few chapters. The majority of the 40 years apparently were spent at and around the oasis of the Kadesh (-barnea) (probably the modern Ain Qudeis). The name means "holy," perhaps suggesting sacral associations even before the Israelite sojourn there.

The procession's leadership by the Ark (an "incarnation" of Yahweh) is depicted by two snatches of poetry in Num. 10:35-36, often referred to as the "Song of the Ark." It is one of many reminders that Israel in the wilderness was a "church militant." (Cf. echoes of the song in the Psalter, esp. Ps. 68:1 and 92:9.) One puzzling question for which we lack clear Biblical answer is that of the relation between the ark in repose in the Holy of Holies and leading the Israelite column. Critics, of course, reflexively, claim conflicting sources and traditions. We will meet this problem again in the Psalter, where many cultic hypotheses (not impossible as such) conceive of periodic processions featuring the ark's return to the temple (a type of the goal of all redemptive history).

The account in Num. 11:16 ff. of the sharing of Moses' "spirit" with 70 elders (for Judaism, an archetype of the Sanhedrin) and the excessive spirit evidenced in the ecstasy of Eldad and Medad is interesting on at least two counts: (1) possible origins or first manifestations of prophecy, often closely associated with ecstasy; and (2) "varieties of gifts, but the same Spirit" (1 Cor. 12:4) in the inevitable tension, but interrelation, of the institutional and the "charismatic."

In Num. 13—14, the reconnaissance of Canaan by the twelve spies, critics revert to type by dividing the material between J and P. Hormah (which apparently means "banned," "placed under the sacral anathema") can probably be identified with one of the tells between Arad and Beersheba, either Tell Masos or Tell Malhata.

The entire narrative is punctuated by other rebellions, especially against Moses and his authority. In Num. 12 Miriam and Aaron object to his marriage to a "Cushite," which can easily be translated "negress," but may here signify "Midianite." (Is this Zipporah, or someone else?) In chap. 16 the agitators are Korah, Dathan, and Abiram (thought by critics to be a telescoping of two or possibly even three rebellions). The tragic anticlimax is Moses' own rebellion at Meribah (20:7 ff.), often explained by critics as simply manufactured by P to explain why Moses did not make it to the Promised Land, and usually placed in opposition to D's allegedly conflicting theory (Deut. 1:37) that it was merely *vicarious* punishment for the sins of the people.

We cannot bypass the difficult pericope of the "red heifer" (Num. 19). The water prepared from its ashes was to be used especially to remove defilement caused by contact with a dead body. Both detailed allegorical interpretations and obsessions with its "magical" parallels miscarry. It is simply one more gracious means of grace (externally not unusual in that culture) for deliverance from the realm and power of death, the antipode of life, of holiness and wholeness. Heb. 9:13-14 expounds its typological significance.

At 20:14 the community sets out from Kadesh and, after Aaron's death (succeeded by Eleazar) and a reversal of the earlier defeat at Hormah, first bypasses Edom and later enters that land. Note the two poetic quotations on chap. 21, one from the otherwise unknown "Book of the Wars of Yahweh," and the other usually simply called "The Song of the Well."

The trek is marred by another rebellion, that climaxed by salvation through the Bronze Serpent (explicitly typologized in John 3:14— introducing the "Gospel in a nutshell"). Critics treat the story as an etiology devised to offer a Mosaic origin of and justification for "Nehushtan," the bronze serpent in the temple destroyed by Hezekiah (2 Kings 18:4). It is usually understood, then, as a syncretistic remnant of the widespread and ancient snake cult of antiquity, also well documented by archaeology. Perhaps we should turn that on end: it represents God's "baptismal" adaptation of a common pagan cult symbol now ultimately representing that "he [the devil] who by a tree [in Eden] once overcame might likewise by a tree [the cross] be overcome."

The third section of Numbers (21:10-36) continues the miscellaneous character of the earlier chapters. Most of the material deals with the conquest of future Israelite territory on the East Bank of the Jordan and with initial administrative moves in consolidating the conquest. We have largely historical narrative until chap. 26, very little after that.

Num. 21—25 relate clashes with the three East Bank powers of the time. The information given is scanty, but there are many echoes of all three victories down through the corridors of Biblical history. It is the beginning of the fulfillment of a major plank in the patriarchal promises. The two redoubtable "Amorite" kings are vanquished, Sihon of Heshbon at Jahaz (his territory assigned to Reuben and Gad), and Og of Ashtaroth at Edrei (displaced by half of the tribe of Manasseh). Quailing Balak of Moab falls next, in spite of his desperate attempt to enlist the aid of the famed diviner or seer; Balaam (now also known extra-Biblically) is compelled to bless Israel in spite of himself. The poetic oracles of Balaam in chaps. 23 and 24 have attracted interest on many counts. The language again is archaic, but most critics persist in transmuting the Messianic prophecy of a "star" smiting Moab and Edom into a confident boast of Davidic times, artificially placed here in Balaam's mouth.

True to character, even within sight of the Promised Land, one of our last historical scenes before the crossing of the Jordan is the massive apostasy at Shittim (Num. 25). Balaam has all but won the day after all, by encouraging the nomadic Midianites to seduce Israel into the licentious fertility rites of the Baal of Peor. The immorality penetrates even into the Holy of Holies (v. 8), where Phinehas, Aaron's grandson, courageously stems the tide. The entire narrative is almost a "prophecy" of Israel's behavior throughout her history in Canaan. (The sequel of this narrative, the defeat of Midian and death of Balaam, comes in chap. 31).

Beginning with the second census of chap. 26, Numbers concludes with mostly statistical material, much of it anticipating the conquest of the West Bank as well. Chaps. 27:1-11 and 30 safeguard "women's rights." In chap. 27:12 ff. Joshua is appointed as Moses' successor (not pursued until Deut. 31 ff.). Chaps. 28—29 contain the Old Testament's fullest tariff of sacrifices, hence by critical reflex considered one of the latest strata of the Pentateuch. The war with Midian in chap. 30 occasions the rules of "holy war" and of the *herem,* the sacral ban, which will also be featured prominently in Deuteronomy and Judges.

Num. 32 anticipates portions of Joshua 12 ff. in describing the apportionment of the land among the trans-Jordanic tribes. It is commonly considered J's last appearance in Numbers (representing, allegedly, a different theory of the conquest, with the main thrust being Judah's from the South). The lists may well have been updated at some later date like other portions of the Pentateuch. Also anticipating Joshua (20 and 21) are the lists of the 48 Levitical cities, six of which are also cities of refuge (asylum). Once dismissed as totally ideal or utopian, there is increasing disposition to concede at least some historicity, going back at least to the time of Josiah, if not of David and Solomon.

Intervening in Num. 33 is a summary of the itinerary from Egypt, assigned to P or even later by critics. By any measure it is not easy to harmonize with preceding accounts, stylized as it appears to be into 40 stages, including some 16 names not met previously (esp. vs. 18-30).

Moses' actual command to invade cis-Jordan comes at the end of Num. 33, followed in chap. 34 by an outline of maximal territorial claims (entirely irrelevant to issues of modern "Zionism").

DEUTERONOMY

Let us remember that in critical thinking we do not with Deuteronomy come to the end of a "Pentateuch," at least not as concerns presumed original literary connections. In earlier criticism, the favored reconstruction was a "Hexateuch," with the original narrative (and JEDP) continuing through Joshua. (Some scholars even attempted to pursue the same literary sources through the following historical books.) In that way the original authors would have also recorded the fulfillment (the conquest of Canaan) as well as the promise. In recent years, Noth's theory of a "Tetrateuch" has come to be favored, viewing Deuteronomy as a theological introduction to the subsequent "deuteronomic history" (cf. below).

In either event, critics generally assume that our "Pentateuch" was not constructed until the Exile or after, when the concern with Moses and Torah rode roughshod over earlier history. If the original were a "Hexateuch," the rearrangement was also supposed to have reminded the Exiles that they again were outside the Promised Land, which had to be repossessed. Spiritually they were where their ancestors had been at Moses' death. The literary rearrangement might also have allayed the suspicions of the Persian authorities about possible Jewish irredentism.

Critics have never found a satisfactory answer to the question of "deuteronomistic" passages elsewhere in the Pentateuch. Early critics tended to note a fair number of these, e.g., Ex. 13:5 and 11; 32:9-14, etc. More recent critics have tended to see in such passages mere reflections of the same ancient liturgical or homiletical usages employed in Deuteronomy itself. If the latter is true, the conservative can hardly but see a concession in the direction of the literal Mosaic authorship of Deuteronomy.

Technically, "Deuteronomy" is a misnomer, based on the Septuagint's mistranslation of a construct chain in 17:18. The Hebrew there commands the king to prepare "a copy of this law," but the Greek translators mistakenly rendered it "this second law" (*deuteronomion touto*). For those who understand Greek that would imply that the book consists mostly of *repetition* of laws already encountered in previous books. Even apart from the Greek, that misapprehension still appears to be widespread—or at least it is a charitable explanation for the common neglect, even by some conservatives, of what is theologically one of the most important books in the Old Testament. There is some repetition of previous laws here, no doubt, but the book's major thrust is the *theology* of Torah ("Law"), that is, the good news of the *Gospel,* which empowers and motivates all valid obedience before God. The frequency of its citation in the New Testament is no accident!

We have spoken above of the theological importance of Deuteronomy, as well as its pivotal role in both the literary and historical reconstructions of higher criticism. We shall concentrate here more on the literary and isagogical issues pertinent to the Book of Deuteronomy itself.

So why should the book *not* be accepted as actually Moses' "farewell sermon," as it presents itself? Studies of the Hittite suzerainty treaties have certainly demolished the critical theory that "covenant" *must* represent a later, incipiently "legalistic," development in Israel (although especially German scholars still cling tenaciously to the argument).

The language is distinctive enough in many respects, e.g., syntaxis instead of classical parataxis, that is, many subordinate clauses in contrast to the "and—and" coordination of most Hebrew narrative. Likewise the style is often expansive, if not at first glance rambling and repetitious. But is not the latter rather characteristic of sermons in all ages? Many similar hortatory passages appear elsewhere in the Pentateuch as we just noted.

The critical penchant again is to construct an evolutionary pattern, with Deuteronomy representing the language of the Josianic "Silver Age," in contrast to the classical "Golden Age" prose of JE of Solomonic date. But do we really have sufficient evidence or controls for such a construct, other than arguments in a circle? The extra-Biblical Lachish letters, sometimes adduced, are too brief to prove anything in this respect. From about the same date are the prose sections of the Book of Jeremiah, which are often considered major evidence. Less certainly, there are the homiletical sections of the historical books of uncertain date (often considered a "deuteronomic history," of a piece with Deuteronomy originally, and hence yielding another argument in a circle). But, if Moses, the great pioneer, had set the pace, is it so unlikely that prophets and other writers would sometimes continue to use the same idiom for centuries, especially when dealing with similar topics? One would have little difficulty adducing parallels in various homiletical traditions of the West.

All of this does not mean that our present Book of Deuteronomy has no literary history. There is no reason why all of it need have fallen from Moses' lips at one time, but like the prophetic oracles, may well have been edited and shaped later, in language possibly as well as arrangement, either by Moses or by others. Two recent evangelical commentaries make the same point: Craigie (*NICOT*) thinks of a final form after the ceremony at Shechem of Joshua 8, while Thompson (*Tyndale*) extends the time to the eleventh or even tenth century, about the same time as championed also by a minority of critics (Welch, Robertson, Brinker).

Very few would care to argue that the final chapter (Moses' death and burial) stems from Moses (not theologically impossible, but historically unlikely). That, plus other concluding material, makes plain that the bulk of Deuteronomy was welded into the entire Pentateuch at some later date, presumably after—but not too long after—Moses' death. Little more can be said with any certainty, but such assumptions are entirely compatible both with the Biblical data and with the dogma of verbal inspiration.

Outline

In contrast to the rather shapeless variety of Numbers, Deuteronomy's overall structure is clear and simple: the "Deuteronomic Code" (12—26), preceded and followed by homiletical material. This holds, even if we reject the critical notion (especially from Steuernagel on) of a slow historical genesis outwards from the core (itself allegedly with an inner history of deuteronomic adaptation).

The profound theological import of this structure must not elude us. Deuteronomy's main point is the proper *motivation* for obedience, the spontaneity of love ("Torah") in contrast to legalism. By the repeated recital of God's grace in spite of the people's perfidy, the congregation is, as it were, almost shamed into grateful response.

Two sermons (discourses, prefaces) precede the code, Deut. 1—4 and 5—11, with antiphonies of blessing and cursing (27—28) and a "third sermon" (29—30) following it. Chaps. 31—34 are miscellaneous appendixes or conclusions, both to Deuteronomy itself and to the entire Pentateuch.

Deuteronomy 1—4

Many critical scholars today follow Noth's suggestion that chaps. 1—4 were composed more as the introduction to the entire (hypothetical) deuteronomic history (resumed, it is thought, at Joshua 1) rather than to Deuteronomy as such. No doubt, this "first sermon" is characterized by more detailed historical survey than the second (rehearsing much of Num. 10 ff.) but that can scarcely be called inappropriate to literal Mosaic circumstances. Also in archaeological light, it rings true as original if viewed as an expanded "historical prologue," such as commonly introduced suzerainty treaties. The point of the extensive historical survey is made in the conclusion in 4:1-40: *therefore* the people are to cling faithfully to Yahweh and resist idolatry.

The chapter divisions may be misleading at this point; after a brief interlude on the cities of refuge (vs. 41-43), the "second sermon" seems better to begin at 4:44 than at 5:1, although the point is debatable. Hence, it also serves admirably as a transitional device. A new title at v. 44 need not imply that the book proper once began at this point, as criticism generally assumes. It seems entirely natural when now, after a break, Moses almost begins anew with the actual exposition of Torah, first in general (chaps. 5—11), then in specifics (12—26).

Deuteronomy 5—11

In many respects, chaps. 5—11 are the heart of the book, at least from the viewpoint of theological articulation. The theme of homiletical contemporization of the covenant is sounded immediately in v. 3: "Not with our fathers—but with us." Hence, chap. 5 reiterates the Decalogue, the epitome of the covenant (with only minor variations from Ex. 20), followed by a commentary stressing, as Moses does elsewhere in the book, that God had delegated the task of communicating His revelation to Moses (as "covenant mediator") at the people's own fearful request.

Deut. 6 is virtually a commentary on the First "Commandment," and reminds us of Luther's theme that the entire Decalogue is really comprehended in it. In fact, v. 5 is the "first and great commandment," cited by our Lord alongside Lev. 19:18 as the summary of the entire Torah. (Jesus and the New Testament speak of "commandments" as the Old Testament does not at this point, because in the new covenant obedience will follow spontaneously from the new heart [Jer. 31], and no imperative is so irresistible as what one really *wants* to do.) Preceding it (6:4) is the *"Shema"* ("Hear"), virtually the creed of later and modern Judaism. While grammatically no airtight case can be made for monotheistic doctrine on its basis (as is also true of the First Commandment), functionally the statement certainly has that import (and the quibbles are probably evolutionistically motivated, to begin with).

V. 6 ff. also gives classical expression to another main theme of Deuteronomy, as certainly befits the historical occasion: the high priority that must be given to "Christian education." (This theme certainly reverberates further in the subsequent "deuteronomic history," whatever the actual relation with the Book of Deuteronomy.) As Moses had ample opportunity to observe, pious parents by no means automatically insure pious children—sometimes, it would almost appear, more the opposite! The church is always only one generation away from extinction, except by the grace of God! Vs. 8-9 are usually assumed by Christian scholars to have been meant metaphorically, but it is by no means self-evident that their literal application by Judaism to phylacteries and mezuzoth is entirely a later bit of literalism.

Deut. 7—9 accents another of the book's major themes: the complementary necessity of exterminating Canaanite paganism, if their best efforts are not to prove abortive. The themes of the *herem* and holy war surface, as before in Num. 30 and later especially in Deut. 20. Deuteronomy gives classical expression to the theme of the centrality of love in Biblical theology, but plainly that is not meant in the universalistic sense by which modern, liberal thought tends to dilute and neutralize it; Biblical "love" is not one species of a universal genus! No doubt, the battle with idolatry continued through the centuries, but never was the message more apropos than on the plains of Moab—all the more so after the tragic events of Baalpeor (Num. 25)!

Deut. 11 is a peroration, summarizing the second sermon (as 4:1-40 had the first), existentially setting before Israel the choice of life and death, curse and blessing—associated specifically, be it noted, with Mts. Ebal and Gerizim (near Shechem); cf. chap. 27. This quintessential homiletical theme reappears prominently again after the "code."

Deuteronomy 12—28

In the Deuteronomic Code (chaps. 12—26) Moses turns to *specific* examples or illustrations of what covenant faithfulness means ("*third* use of the Law," as we stressed in connection with other codes). In general the concerns exemplified are less civic and more specifically religious than in the other "codes" (especially the expurgation of all heathen contamination). It is an anachronistic, secularistic misnomer to speak of the "humanitarian" flavor of this collection of laws. Neither is there any developmentalistic need to attribute this accent to prior prophetic influence—as though Moses or Israelite religion of an earlier era were incapable of such profound thoughts. Rather the laws continue the strong accent on *love* in the preceding sermons; there it was more love of God, now it is virtually assumed that love of fellowman follows as a matter of course. The refrain to remember that once *they* were aliens and slaves in Egypt is constantly repeated. Examples of the so-called humanitarianism would include the concern about women captured in war (21:10 ff.), the requirement of a parapet around flat roofs to prevent falls (22:8), the year's exemption of a newlywed from military conscription (24:5), etc.

Two themes in the "code" are especially held to betray undeniable post-Mosaic circumstances. These are the discussions of prophecy in Deut. 13 and 18, and the "Law of the Kingdom" in chap. 17:14-20. The latter is potentially more damaging than the first. It is the only passage in the Pentateuch that even broaches the subject of kingship (itself a major argument for pre-kingship origins).

Even humanly speaking, however, there is no clear reason why Moses should have been less aware of both the attraction and the dangers of kingship than Samuel obviously was a short time later. In Egypt he had learned firsthand about absolute monarchies, and contact had already been made with lesser kinglets in Transjordan (Sihon, Og, Balak), of the sort that were surely known to thrive also across the Jordan. The story of Gideon (Judges 8:22 ff.) demonstrates how early the problem arose, and how timely this warning was. Vs. 18-20 stress that Israel's kings were to be "constitutional monarchs," that is, subject to the covenant, as the prophets would later never let them forget.

The appearance of the theme of prophecy in a speech by Moses poses less problems. The origins and development of prophecy is a complex problem (cf. below), but both the archaeological and the Biblical evidence massively demonstrates that "prophecy" of some sort was an institution far older than Moses. Inevitably, the problem of "true" and "false" was just as ancient; Balaam was probably the example freshest in the hearer's minds! In Deut. 18:16 the origin and legitimation of *Biblical* prophecy are again rooted in the people's request at Sinai for Moses to mediate between themselves and God. The preceding verse stresses that Israel will never *need* to have recourse to pagan "prophets," because God will never leave them in the lurch, but will continually raise up "covenant mediators" to succeed Moses. If the passage then, as is commonly agreed on all sides, refers primarily to a *succession* of faithful prophets, this is no way precludes ultimate and climactic fulfillment of the prophecy in Him who is prophet and mediator in the fullest sense (Acts 3 and 7).

Many of the themes of the book are summarized in the little historical confession which the worshiper is to make in connection with his offering of firstfruits (Deut. 26, esp. vs. 5-9). We have already noted the almost incredible influence exerted on recent critical scholarship by von Rad's hypothesis that a "credo" of this type was the point of departure for J's literary work and ultimately for the whole history of the Pentateuch.

The "code" concludes (Deut. 27—28) following the ancient suzerainty treaty pattern, with a list of blessings and curses that may befall the people, depending upon their response. At first blush, chap. 28 appears to fill that bill much more naturally than chap. 27, which seems intrusive. Many critics readily conclude just that, and even conservatives may conclude that a literary seam is evident. At any rate, chap. 28 can be read easily as following directly upon chap. 26. The preponderance of curses over blessings is not due to any legalistic negativism, but reproduces the standard suzerainty-treaty tradition (based, no doubt, also on keen insight into human nature, also of believers). Neither is some mechanical, automatic principle of retribution envisioned (of which the wisdom writers are also often indicted), but rather of the *ultimate* outcome *sub specie aeternitatis.*

Chaps. 27 and 28 together reiterate the themes of chap. 11, just before the code, and that may explain the presence of chap. 27 here. In both cases, not only is the present, existential response to the sermon envisioned, but also a one-time climactic ceremony at Shechem (in the pass between Mts. Ebal and Gerizim), where vivid dramatic expression will be given to the theme. Joshua 8:30-35 explicitly records the fulfillment of this stipulation after the conquest was well begun. Chap. 27 first stipulates the erection of stones inscribed with the law (Decalogue) and of an altar on Mt. Ebal. In vs. 15 ff. there follow a series of curses, which again predominate as in chap. 28. Perhaps this also explains why the stones and altar are unexpectedly erected on Mt. Ebal, the mountain of cursing (v. 12, etc.) Since the Samaritan text does read "Gerizim," many critics are ready to assume that it was original, only later changed by "Zionists" to "Ebal" for polemical purposes! (Let it also be shouted from the housetops again that the references to Shechem in chaps. 11 and 27 are virtually fatal to the keystone of the critical hypothesis that D's major program was to admit only *Jerusalem* as a legitimate shrine—*except* by excision of embarrassing evidence to the contrary!)

Deuteronomy 29—30

There is no more reason to assume with many critics that the "original Deuteronomy" ended with chap. 28 than that it began with chap. 5. Chaps. 29—30 are then thought to have been added in the Exile, but, no doubt, in these chapters we have a sort of third, concluding sermon. In many respects it is, like the two sermons that precede the code, setting the choice of life and death before the people. However, as one might expect, it also seems to reflect the antiphonies of chaps. 27—28 more directly. Chap. 29 paints in vivid, homiletical pictures the possible implementation of the curses, while chap. 30 (again more briefly) presents the opposite alternative.

Deuteronomy 31—34

The final chapters are still concerned with the continuity of the covenant, both immediately with Joshua's preparation to assume Moses' mantle (31:1-8, 14-23; cf. Num.27:12 ff.), and more long range, both with provision for its periodic reading (31:9-13; 24-29) and the stipulation that what Moses had written (*sic!* 31:9 and 24, whatever the extent of this specific reference) be deposited in the ark (31:24-29). All three themes again have suzerainty treaty parallels. Deuteronomy's pervasive concern for religious instruction is also apparent in all these provisions. The periodic reading may possibly have been intimated already in 30:10 ff. In any case, in 31:10 ff., it is prescribed for the feast of booths ("tabernacles") each sabbatical year (i.e., every seventh year), "in the place which He will choose." This plainly is a "covenant renewal festival" of sorts, but, at best, scholarly speculation has magnified its importance beyond the clear evidence. Particularly, the theory's frequent association of the ceremony with Shechem has little, if any, certain foundation; the Biblical support cited (Deut. 27, Joshua 8 and 24, etc.) apparently speaks of a different event, a one-time event, not a periodically repeated one.

The "Song of Moses" in Deut. 32 has spawned a vast literature. In a way the debate begins already with 31:16-22, where the introduction to the song appears to be premature or misplaced (another introduction ends chap. 31). Since v. 23 follows easily and naturally after v. 15, it is possible that the introduction was inserted here, both to link the two events, and to underscore the major theme of the song (thoroughly consonant with Deuteronomy as a whole), viz., God's faithfulness in contrast to Israel's unfaithfulness.

Critics generally view both the "song" and the succeeding blessing as thoroughly independent units, only artifically connected with both Moses and Deuteronomy. A tremendous debate still rages about the date of the song—and since it is not considered Mosaic, also about the catastrophe that would have served as its *Sitz im Leben*. Earlier critical opinion usually favored an exilic date, partly because of presumed affinities with Ezekiel and "Second Isaiah." Many still defend that judgment, but other scholars are impressed by the linguistic archaism of the poetry and date it much earlier—but still usually no earlier than about the time of Samuel (e.g., Albright after the fall of Shiloh, c. 1025). Recent form-critical studies have emphasized the song's dependence on the *Gattung* known in Hebrew as a *rib,* a "covenant lawsuit," often employed by the prophets (Is. 1:2 ff; Micah 6:1 ff., etc.), but also again with a secular prototype in the suzerainty treaties.

The latter circumstance will be a major leg of the defense of Mosaic authorship. Moses will not only have been acquainted with a form far older than himself, but also with its theological theme: "pessimism" about Israel's historical future, but "optimism" in God's "justification" of His people nonethless. Esp. v. 36 rings true as rooted in Moses' historical experience, and was often anticipated in the preceding chapters of the book.

The "Blessing of Moses" (chap. 33) will usually more readily be dated somewhat earlier than the Song, but with that all agreement stops. By any standard, there are far more internal exegetical difficulties than in the case of the Song. Many view it as the northern version of the same tradition ascribed to Jacob in Gen. 49 (e.g., the major attention paid to Joseph here in contrast to Judah). However that interpretation assumes that the genre of the material is ultimately *vaticinium ex eventu* (a "prophecy" after the event). The theophanic picture at the outset and the reference to an assembly in v. 3 has led others to postulate an original cultic setting, but there is even less evidence in its favor (cf. also clear affinities with other archaic poems, Hab. 3, Ps. 68, Judges 5).

Simeon is not mentioned, and Dan's apparent association with its later northern home (context, and "Bashan," v. 22) have been major arguments for a date in the period of the Judges. Some post-Mosaic updating is not unthinkable (also not theologically). However, the problem with Dan, at least, has been undercut by recent arguments, on the basis of a Ugaritic cognate, that "Bashan" really should be translated "viper," as the parallel with Gen. 49:17 might suggest (although a different Hebrew word is used there). All in all, no convincing case exists to deny this poem to Moses either. The idea appears to be that Moses figuratively acts here like a father, blessing his "sons." That would also explain why the poem begins with the Sinaitic theophany.

The Book of Deuteronomy (and the Pentateuch) closes, of course, with the account of Moses' death in chap. 34. The subject had been anticipated already in 32:48-52, intervening between the two poems. Critical opinion usually attributes the pericope to P at the time when the Pentateuch was finished (i.e., when P allegedly divorced Deuteronomy from what followed (Tetrateuch or Hexateuch). The attribution to P is made largely on the basis of the assumption that it explains Moses' personal failure to reach Canaan as due to his own personal sin (Num. 20:12, etc.). This is supposed to conflict with D's view that it was because of his *vicarious* suffering for the sins of the people (cf. Deut. 1:37). Are the two explanations necessarily incompatible? The only grain of truth in all this is that the Holy Spirit evidently inspired someone else (like Moses' grave, only God knows the details) to compose at least this final chapter, and thus to conclude the "Book of Moses."

PART II

The Former Prophets

With this caption, the arrangement and classification of books in the Hebrew Bible begins to differ from that of the Septuagint.

The Hebrew arrangement achieves a lovely symmetry: *four each* of "former" and "latter" prophets. It is possible to count four "latter" prophets for two reasons: because Daniel is classified among the "Writings," the third section of the canon (cf. below); and because all twelve of the minor prophets are subsumed under the single heading of "the Twelve" ("Dodekapropheton" in Greek), yielding a unit which is roughly the same size as the three preceding prophetical books. It has been suggested, not implausibly, that this arrangement arose partly from the ease with which all twelve minor prophets could be written on one scroll.

Four "former" prophets could be counted because Samuel and Kings were considered single units (cf. below). To a large extent, this classification coincides, of course, with our "historical books." The major exception is Ezra-Nehemiah-Chronicles (often referred to as simply the "Chronicler's History"). It, like Ruth and Esther (and Daniel), appears among the "Writings."

It is not entirely clear how or why Joshua, Judges, Samuel, and Kings came to be called "prophets." The explanation is commonly offered that the designation was only formal, that is, that it arose merely from early Jewish traditions of prophetic authorship of these works, as we shall note below. This is not impossible, but, at best, does not appear to suffice.

It is certainly more helpful, and perhaps also more accurate, if we understand the appellation as *material* rather than merely formal, that is, as characterizing the *contents* of the books as well. Then these works are understood as exhibiting prophetic *theology,* as the "sermon illustrations" preceding the "sermons" of the prophets themselves.

It may even be argued that "former prophets" is a much better and more accurate designation than our "historical books." For better or for worse, "history" for us has come to imply certain standards of "objectivity," comprehensiveness, and usually also secularity, to which these Biblical products do not correspond. When they, then, diverge from our notion of "history," the stage is set for doubts and questions of various sorts. This is not only true of historical-critical method, which programmatically uses alien yardsticks, but comparable difficulties may easily arise also for the more ordinary reader.

Accordingly, it must be accented that these "histories" are unabashedly "tendentious," or have "an axe to grind." They select and present only as it serves their purposes. The fact that we can scarcely hear such language except in a negative sense only illustrates the problem. Possibly the recent realization that complete objectivity is an impossibility in such matters has mitigated the difficulty for modern audiences, but probably not a lot.

When we stress that the "history" presented here is not of the same genre as the modern type, it is not at all with the implication that what is presented is somehow less than true. Rather, the presupposition is that whatever is asserted is entirely true, factually as well as theologically, even though many questions we might raise remain unanswered. By hypothesis, or on the basis of external archaeological evidence, the believing scholar is free to supplement the Biblical account, but not to supplant it. When we stress that the Biblical writer's concern is *more* theological than "historical," this must not be heard in the dichotomous sense of much critical scholarship. What the Holy Spirit offers us is not *less* than "history," but infinitely more. The *ultimate* concern is with *inner* history, but perhaps again "sacramental" would be a better adjective to forestall dichotomous misunderstanding.

The basic pattern illustrated throughout the "former prophets" is that of reward for obedience or faithfulness, and retribution or punishment for unfaithfulness. That scheme is commonly criticized as, at best, hopelessly simplistic, and probably mechanistic and legalistic as well. Some critics condescendingly concede only a certain long-range, pragmatic truth to the principle, and many are motivated by a universalistic aversion to the entire idea of divine retribution. We shall encounter the same principle— and the same objections—in wisdom literature (classically in Ps. 1), and in more recent scholarship this similarity is often cited as evidence of wisdom influence on the historiography.

The correct understanding commends itself readily, even humanly speaking, if we remain aware of the theological scopus of the material: it was not that the writer was especially naive, or even less that he artificially arranged his material to score homiletical points. Rather, instead of judging externally (politically, sociologically, psychologically), the viewpoint is *sub specie aeternitatis,* concerned with what is *ultimately* true, even if empirical observation does not always seem to bear it out. As the latter prophets preached tirelessly, the Word of God is always operative in either blessing or cursing, Law or Gospel. What we have is not so much a "philosophy of history" as a "theology of history," and in a very real sense the "former prophets" classically enunciated the latter.

Modern discussion of the "former prophets" in almost any aspect is virtually impossible without reference to Noth's widely followed hypothesis of a "deuteronomic history" (often abbreviated Dtr). As we have noted already, this theory proposes that a second edition of the Book of Deuteronomy (adding chaps. 1—4 there) continued with the "sermon illustrations" of the former prophets. There is less agreement about the date of this alleged endeavor. Probably most would think of the Josianic reformation as the major occasion, but with at least one major revision in the Exile (where 2 Kings concludes—with the favor shown King Jehoiachin).

Is there anything in this hypothesis for the conservative? Of course, many aspects of the total historical-theological reconstruction are out of the question. The non-Mosaic authorship of Deuteronomy is not acceptable, neither is the skeptical assumption that the intent was not to write a "history," but to offer a theological rationale for coming to terms with the destruction of Jerusalem and subsequent Exile. Nevertheless, something may be salvaged, at least provisionally, and in both theological and historical respects.

Theologically, there is much that can be congenial about the label "deuteronomic" in this connection. There simply is no denying that the "former prophets" *do* apply and illustrate the same basic principles that inform the Book of Deuteronomy. The theme of "blessing" or "cursing," contingent upon obedience or disobedience, which Deuteronomy constantly inculcates, is precisely the organizing principle of the subsequent historiography. And, no doubt, Deuteronomy itself looks forward as well as backward.

However, if the conservatives says "deuteronomic" in this connection, it implies later and deliberate modeling upon a literally Mosaic Deuteronomy. If Moses had even a fraction of the status and reputation which the Bible attributes to him, it would be easy to understand that later writers would often emulate him. This is just as possible of style as of theological substance. When in the later histories we often meet "deuteronomic" sermons or commentaries at key junctures, these need not be attributed to an editorial hand (the same one which supposedly composed Deuteronomy) that thus stitches together originally disparate materials. Moses' reputation and influence being what it was, it is entirely plausible that later speakers would couch their "deuteronomic" ideas in "deuteronomic" phraseology as well.

If the adjective "deuteronomic" does not prejudice the questions of date and authorship, the idea of a *single* "deuteronomic history" might be useful historically or isagogically as well. The fact is that we simply do not know for sure whether the four "former prophets" were originally discrete units, or whether this division is secondary. As we shall note below, there are internal indications of somewhat later compositions of *all* four units (at least after the fall of Samaria). Thus, it is by no means impossible that all four were composed or completed at essentially the same time. That would mean that the reference to Jehoiachin in captivity (c. 562) would set a *terminus a quo* for earliest possible composition of the entire history. Beyond that, as we shall note, we scarcely have a single further certain clue for either date or authorship of the material.

The weakest link in the hypothesis of one unified history (for that matter, whether the critical "deuteronomic history" or a conservative adaptation of it) is Samuel, where there is far less theological framework and commentary than in the other three present units. The "weakness," however, is mostly an argument from silence, and by no means suffices to demolish any hypothesis of original unity.

A final decision might hinge on the nature of the present headings. The question is not, as such, merely the historical one of their antiquity, but also the theological one of whether or not they are part of the inspired text. If the latter question could certainly be answered affirmatively, the odds against unified composition would rise considerably, although the possibility would still be there. In a way, the question is not seriously different from that of the five books within the Pentateuch, and in that case there is no doubt that we are dealing with an essentially unified composition. (The problem of titles or superscriptions will continue to haunt us, all the more so when we turn to the "latter prophets" and the psalms.)

Whether the present subdivisions are original or not, the conservative is not confronted with the critical problem of explaining how and why Joshua ever became separated from Deuteronomy. The problem is essentially the same for the modern critic with his "deuteronomic history" hypothesis as it was for the older scholar's "Hexateuch" assumption. (In a few cases, it was not only a matter of a "Hexateuch," but of a "Heptateuch," "Octateuch," or even an "Enneateuch" as well— however far beyond Deuteronomy the Pentateuchal sources were thought to continue.

One of the major historical arguments for the original separation of

Joshua from the Pentateuch is found in the fact that the Samaritan sect preserved only a *Pentateuch,* in spite of the fact that Joshua contains passages highlighting Shechem and Mt. Gerizim, which they would have found congenial. This argument, of course, is based on the assumption that the Samaritan schism roots in *pre*-exilic circumstances, and its embarrassment to critical theories may explain the tendency in some critical circles to postpone a final separation to as late as the second century B.C.

The critical explanation for the sundering of Joshua and Deuteronomy is usually sought in the circumstances of the exilic and/or postexilic periods when both the Pentateuch and the Former Prophets are presumed to have assumed their final and present shape. Both the magnitude of the "Moses legend" by this time and possible Persian suspicions that the original climax in taking possession of the land might conceal revolutionary designs for doing the same thing again are thought to have dictated the resultant disjunction.

Mutatis mutandis, there is truth in both assertions. Both the end of Deuteronomy and the beginning of Joshua highlight the incomparable stature of Moses. Furthermore, the stress that the land was no permanent possession, but a gift of grace which could be—and was—lost through infidelity, the theme that in a real sense the people of God always remain pilgrims, has left its impress upon not only both Deuteronomy and the "deuteronomic history," but also upon all of Scripture and Christian theology.

JOSHUA

Few books in the Bible are better named (at least if contents or chief figure is the criterion), because Joshua is the subject of virtually the entire book, from beginning to end. This title, however, whatever its provenance, tells us nothing whatsoever about authorship or date of composition of the book.

Theology

Regardless of isagogical questions about the relationship between the books of Joshua and Deuteronomy, the former follows the latter naturally as simple historical sequel, continuing the narrative line from the death of Moses to the death of Joshua. In slightly more theological perspective, the contents of Joshua must be construed as a fulfillment of the promise so often reiterated in the Pentateuch. We say *"a"* fulfillment, not "the," because in broader Biblical perspective this fulfillment is only a first plateau or "landing" for *the* ultimate fulfillment in Jesus Christ.

Even after Christ's advent, our language remains inadequate to describe the complexities of the situation. We too live simultaneously and dialectically in the time of the "not yet" that is, in a sense, still in the old testament. We too still wait and hope for *the* fulfillment—although now we often prefer the term "consummation," so as not to demote Christ to merely one in a series. After Christ, there can no longer be "fulfillment" in the strict sense, but only an "end" or "climax" of His fulfillment in the eternal Kingdom.

Expressed typologically, we have both the figure of Joshua himself as a type of Christ and the "promised land"-"crossing the Jordan" complex as a type of His benefits. Another expression of the same theme is "rest," used so repeatedly in both Testaments (e.g., Deut. 3:20; Joshua 1:15; Ps. 95:11; Matt. 11:28; Heb. 3:11 ff.). By baptismal incorporation into His body, we already now share in His "kingdom of grace," and dialectically await the consummation in the "kingdom of glory." Etymology facilitates the Joshua typology, because "Joshua" and "Jesus" are one and the same names (Hebrew and Aramaic respectively), both meaning "salvation, victory," etc.

Particularly in Christ, the antitype, it becomes clear that the typologies of Joshua and of the land converge (much as, when using sacrificial types, we speak of Christ as both priest and victim). Not that the Joshua typology has been overworked, but it would seem that the "land" motif has almost been spiritualized into nonexistence, so much so that many Christians experience special difficulty in appropriating this major Old Testament theme.

Contents

The Book of Joshua can easily be outlined into three major sections: (1) Chaps. 1—12: the conquest of cis-Jordan (the conquest of Transjordan being already recorded in Num. 21 ff.); (2) Chaps. 13—22: the apportionment of the conquered land among the twelve tribes; and (3) Chaps. 23—24: Joshua's last words and death. Many of the narratives in the first section of the book are probably about as familiar to many Bible readers as the more statistical second section is not.

After Moses' death, Joshua immediately assumes command, and all the tribes pledge fealty. From Shittim, the last trans-Jordanic encampment (exact site disputed), Joshua sends spies to Rahab's brothel in Jericho (chap. 2). This Rahab should not be confused with the name of a mythological monster sometimes applied to Egypt (Is. 30:7; 51:9; Ps. 89:10, etc.) In Hebrew the two names are spelled differently, the woman's name with a hard "h" or "cheth" instead of the ordinary "h." Hence, the older Catholic transcription of the prostitute's name as "Rachab" is both technically more accurate and also less confusing. One often also rightly makes much of the fact that the harlot's name appears in the genealogy of Jesus (Matt. 1:5; cf. Heb. 11:31; James 2:25).

Joshua 3—4 describe the crossing of the Jordan itself. The "holy war" military formation is not to be overlooked, with the Levites carrying the ark at the head of the column. "Incarnate" in the ark, Yahweh himself was the real commander-in-chief of the "hosts" of Israel, a point underscored by a personal theophany just before the fall of Jericho (5:13-15).

Critics commonly see considerable conflation or confusion of the Crossing and the Exodus accounts, possibly under liturgical auspices. The details of their theories, however, differ markedly. The "Adam" of 3:16 (the modern Damiyeh), where the waters heaped up, is also known in modern times to have been the scene of collapse of the river banks, with resultant temporary stoppage of the river's flow. This may be partly analogous to the Biblical event—as long as the strictly miraculous element is not entirely eliminated as a result.

The site of Gilgal remains unknown, and perhaps none of the many tells in the Jericho area are to be associated with it. Etymologically the name implies something circular, possible a temporary encampment marked by a circle of sacred stones. Such sites are known elsewhere archaeologically (cf. even Stonehenge). There may be a connection here between the name and the twelve stones brought up out of the river, although the text does not make that explicit. It is not impossible that the site was sacred by pagan associations long before the Israelite arrival. Not only the name, but also the observance of the rites of circumcision and passover at Gilgal, and the liturgical cast of the crossing narrative and the circumambulation of Jericho have spawned many critical theories about "cult legends" having shaped, if not invented, much of this material.

We have no space to discuss the grievous problem of the date of the conquest. Obviously, it is dependent on the dating of the Exodus, as well as relations with many other events. The traditional date would be shortly before 1400 B.C., and it is still defended by many conservatives, partly because, at least on the surface, it readily accords with some Biblical chronological data. Critics quite unanimously and, increasingly, even many conservatives, prefer a date around 1240. The issue, of course, will not be Biblical veracity, but the correct exegesis of the pertinent Biblical statements in the light of all the evidence.

There follow (Joshua 6—9) the well-known stories of the capture of Jericho, Ai, and Gibeon (the latter peacefully because of the inhabitants' ruse). These three sites are all basically in a straight east-west line, into which Joshua's sudden appearance at Shechem (8:30-35) to the north, in order to fulfill the command of Deut. 27 to read the law antiphonally, does not readily fit. Has the account of the conquest of the heartland of later

"Israel" (the ten tribes) simply fallen out? Can Gen. 34 be taken to mean that some advance guard of "Hebrews" was already ensconced at Shechem, with which Joshua needed only link up peaceably? It is one of the many puzzles about the details of the conquest which the Biblical writer did not see fit to record. We have noted von Rad's theories (pp. 47-48; include Kraus and others too) about ancient liturgies of conquest and covenant, centering at Gilgal and Shechem respectively, which should have produced much of our Biblical material. For critics of that mind Joshua 8:30 ff. is often pointed to as a suture which later traditions never succeeded very well in concealing.

Joshua 10 continues the story line of chap. 9 with no difficulty. The Gibeonite defection provokes retaliation by a five-king Canaanite league, led by Adonizedek ("The lord is righteous" or "Zedek is my lord"). Their defeat, partly due to miraculous intervention, in the Bethhoron pass west of Gibeon and in the valley of Aijalon below it, leads into a summary account of the conquest of all of southwestern Canaan and the Negev. This account is often construed as conflicting with Joshua 15 and Judges 1, read as implying a separate invasion of that territory from the south under Caleb. More likely, however, as with other "contradictions" in the conquest narratives, it is a matter of Joshua's rapid *Blitzkrieg,* followed by various reversals, mop-up operations, consolidations, etc.

In Joshua 10:12 we have a snatch of poetry quoted from the "Book of Jashar." The critical "explanation" of the signal miracle of the sun standing still is that some later theologian misunderstood the poetic expression literalistically. Some in both the liberal and the conservative camps, however, seek an explanation in terms of a prolongation of the night's darkness through a hailstorm (v. 11) or the like, thus enabling a surprise attack.

Joshua 11, again in summary fashion, describes the conquest of northern Canaan, essentially the territory known as "Galilee" in later times. Only Hazor, "the head of all those kingdoms" (11:10) is razed—of which we now have superb archaeological illumination. Beginning with a recapitulative retrospect at 11:16, and continuing in chap. 12, we have a summary of the territory conquered, described by means of lists of the defeated Canaanite kinglets.

This makes a natural transition to the second part of Joshua (chaps. 13—22), depicting the allotments of land and other administrative decisions after the conquest. If we understand considerable fighting as still continuing while these arrangments are being made, Joshua's conquest of Canaan would by no means be the only example in world history. In fact, Joshua 13 begins with a recognition that "very much land remains to be possessed!"

Joshua 14 takes pains to include Eleazar the priest in the castings of lots for apportionment, thus underscoring the sacrality of the proceedings. The mention of the assembly at the "tent of meeting" at Shiloh in 18:1 (in the midst of the proceedings) further underlines the sacral atmosphere.

The allotments to the two and one-half trans-Jordanic tribes in Joshua 13 is in confirmation of arrangements already made by Moses (Num. 32). Formal taking possession had been left contingent upon these tribes aiding the other tribes' conquest of cis-Jordan. Joshua 22 records their return to their allotments after also the West Bank is secure. Civil war almost erupts because of their erection of a commemorative altar and is stayed only upon acceptance of their explanation that the altar does not signify apostasy from Yahwism but is only a "Witness" to their total unity with the other tribes under Yahweh.

Critics can scarcely refrain from second-guessing the incident further, usually viewing it as a precipitate of tribal rivalries especially of some border shrine. No doubt, it does presage the alienation of Transjordan during much of the subsequent history, especially as Ammonite, Edomite, and Moabite kingdoms soon established themselves in this territory. (The cleft, of course, is partly geographically determined by the great Jordan rift and continues in modern Arab history.)

The bulk of the allotments to the nine and one-half cis-Jordanic tribes is recorded in Joshua 15—19, followed by the establishment of the six cities of asylum and the 48 Levitical cities in 20—21 (the latter two items largely anticipated in Num. 35). Two types of material are used to describe the new possessions: city lists and boundary lists. Both types bristle with difficulties when it comes to precise locations. Critics commonly view both types as much later. At one time they were even considered exilic, but in more recent times the date is often pushed back to the Josianic period, and increasingly even to the united monarchy. As long as their basic acuracy is not called into question, it is a parade example for the possibility of considerable later updating in the light of subsequent settlements and other population shifts. The precise boundaries may often have been fluid and adjusted according to demographic realities.

The final two chapters of the book consist of two parallel addresses by Joshua. Critics commonly view them as two versions of the same event, chap. 23 often being considered merely a deuteronomic meditation on the events recorded more objectively in chap. 24. The first (chap. 23), couched in classical "deuteronomic" language, is an impassioned warning against apostasy. The second in chap. 24, Joshua's farewell address at Shechem and also in good deuteronomic idiom, reviews past *Heilsgeschichte* and drives harder toward renewed commitment: "Choose this day whom you will serve." The Biblical text indicates no more than a onetime occasion, but it does not totally veto some critical hypotheses of repeated ceremonies connected with covenant renewal, possibly also at Shechem.

Perhaps by a sort of editorial principle of attraction, the book closes with a record of three burials, not only Joshua's but those of Joseph (at Shechem) and Eleazar as well.

Date and Authorship

Jewish tradition consistently understands the "Joshua" heading to refer to authorship of the book as well as of contents. The situation *could* be quite comparable to Moses' authorship of the Pentateuch, even with respect to the burial notices at the end. Unlike the Pentateuch, however, we have no later *Scriptural* notices attributing the book to Joshua, nor are there compelling internal indications in that direction. Exceptions would include the various references to Sidon instead of Tyre as the major Phoenician city, the absence of the Philistines as a threat and the "we" notices in 5:1 (KJV), 6, 13; etc., indicating direct Joshuanic input at least at those points.

It may well be, as we have already noted, that isagogically Joshua is not to be considered independently apart from the other "former prophets." But by the same token, there is nothing objectionable about considering the book by itself.

There are, however, indications of post-Joshuanic composition, unless these are to be regarded again as relatively peripheral editorial additions. These include not only the burials at the close of the book and the repeated "until this day," but also the reference to the later Danite migration to the north in 19:47, and the citation of the "Book of Jashar" in 10:12 (which also includes David's lament over Jonathan and can scarcely have been intact until after the latter event). Probably latest of all is the apparent distinction between the two kingdoms of Israel and Judah in 11:21. None of this evidence would, however, *necessarily* imply a later date than the united monarchy, or possibly the early divided monarchy.

Critics instinctively go on to cite numerous alleged repetitions and inconsistencies, which should indicate late compilations from multiple sources. These include: two supposed versions of the crossing of the Jordan (3:17 and 4:10 f.); two versions of the placing of the twelve memorial stones (4:8 and 4:9), and two versions of the capture of *both* Jericho and Ai. Above all, as we have noted, there is usually cited the alleged conflict between the general impression in the book of a swift, unified campaign during Joshua's lifetime, in contrast to telltale notices elsewhere in the book and especially in Judg. 1, which should indicate a long, protracted struggle against stubborn Canaanite resistance.

Classical Wellhausenianism was confident that Joshua, as the final member of the "Hexateuch," had the same literary history as the preceding five books. The resulting picture was one of a composite JE for the first 12 chapters, a D revision, and finally a P revision, which contributed most of the rest of the book (the paraneses and the statistical material, respectively). Joshua 24, however, was usually considered E because of its locale at Shechem. E was sometimes held responsible for the fiction of a unified campaign in contrast to J's better historical memory.

This approach has largely fallen out of favor today, especially with the preference for Noth's "deuteronomic history" hypothesis. It is debatable, however, whether much has really changed besides nomenclature. Noth and his followers simply think of a collection of a great variety of independent materials (some of it possibly even contemporary with the events), organized within a deuteronomic framework. If construed a little differently, the conservative would have little remaining difficulty with the latter construction.

Form criticism, however, has again tried to move behind the written sources, with results that are not generally very congenial. "Cult-legends" are thought to account for the heavy liturgical cast of much of the material, regardless of how much actual history may be involved. Especially Gilgal and Shechem figure prominently in these speculations, as we have noted. "Hero-legends," especially of Joshua, and various etiologies ("explaining" ruins and rites especially to pilgrims), are also thought to have contributed. The fact that detailed narratives of conquest are preserved only in the Gilgal-Jericho-Ai-Gibeon series suggests to many critics that only tales from the "Rachel tribes" (or maybe only the tribe of Benjamin) were preserved in later times, and that Joshua had originally spearheaded the conquests of only these groups. Allegedly, then, the quasi-historical Benjaminite tradition became normative for all of Canaan, and a local hero, Joshua, became the conquistador of the entire land. (The real course of the invasion of Canaan is often thought to have been three-pronged, Judah from the South, Benjamin from the East, and "Joseph" from the North, but that plainly flies in the face of the Biblical data.)

Probably to be included here is the explanation commonly given for the book's allegedly grossly oversimplified account of the conquest: "deuteronomic history" at critical hands implies postexilic homiletical license, which subordinates facts (presuming they were even known) to making a theological point: the land was a gift of grace, which Israel had lost through its own fault, and must now repossess and retain through answering faithfulness. Obviously, a half-truth is enunciated here, if it is not pitted against historicity. All the more in later retrospect it could be stressed that God *had* given His people their land, never mind for the moment the fine points!

Historical Problems

Space prohibits adding much more to the discussion of the historical problems of the conquest beyond what has already been said. The topic provides a parade example of the frequent ambiguity of the archaeological evidence at best ("*Who* is responsible for this destruction layer?") It must also be conceded that, at least at the present, the accumulated archaeological evidence is not only often ambiguous, but seems most non-confirmatory of the Scriptural accounts, precisely in the cases of Jericho, Ai, and Gibeon where the most Biblical detail has been preserved.

The very location of Ai (the name means "Ruin") is debated; certainly the traditional site had lain in ruins for centuries already at the time of Joshua. On the basis of early, imperfected archaeological method (and probably also out of overeagerness to "prove the Bible true") Garstang originally claimed to have produced confirmation of Joshua's capture of Jericho. Most of the "evidence" (by no means all of it, however) has evaporated in the face of Kenyon's more recent and more scientific excavations. Evidence of Late Bronze occupation is also meager at Gibeon. There are various expedients for explaining these current archaeological difficulties, which we cannot discuss here, but we should not pretend as though the difficulties are not there.

Ironically, much better evidence of Late Bronze destructions, presumably by the Israelites, is evidenced in the excavations of sites which the Bible mentions more in passing: Hazor, Lachish, Debir, Eglon, etc. It is worth noting that there is no archaeological evidence of a destruction of Shechem at this time, just as Joshua 8:30 indicates. As noted above, the absence of the Philistines in the wars of Joshua also appears to fit the archaeological evidence: there would appear to be no reason why Joshua should not have swept all the way to the Mediterranean coast (and assign Simeon and Dan territory there), but with the Philistines sweeping down from the North and displacing Israel, perhaps only a very short time later.

Earlier critics, partly in the absence of archaeological evidence, quite unanimously presumed that the picture of the Book of Joshua was artificial, the reality being rather a slow protracted infiltration with much independent guerilla activity. The favored German term, *"Landnahme,"* was a sort of code word for that reconstruction. For a long time, especially the American "Albright school" was able to maintain a massive counterattack on the prevailing critical skepticism, and to persuade many to believe at least the "substantial historicity" of the Biblical accounts.

In recent times, not only has that counterthrust from within criticism weakened considerably, but Mendenhall, an Albright student, has been one of the most influential in leading a sort of return to the *status quo ante.* As one major part of his basically sociological reconstruction, Mendenhall thinks not only of a variety of tribal infiltrations, but of a linking up of a great variety of dispossessed and disaffected elements, both native Canaanites and newcomers, against the aristocratic oppression of the Canaanite city-states (the Israelites at most serving as a catalyst for a peasant revolt). Such a thesis is not *totally* incompatible with the Biblical data, but, at best, it is not the aspect of things which Biblical theologians care to emphasize.

"Holy" War?

One other problem which often arises for modern readers must be considered before we leave the Book of Joshua. That is the problem of a war of conquest, even a "holy" war explicitly commanded by Yahweh, including the *cherem* or sacral ban calling for the total extermination of the enemy. Some critics seek to evade the issue by viewing it as largely just later deuteronomic rhetoric, intended only to stir the audience to uncompromising opposition to Canaanite *religion,* but that is scarcely a solution.

External evidence indicates that such usages were common in antiquity, when there was no such thing as nonsacral warfare. Hence, no doubt, an element of historical aspects of the *"scandal* of particularity" is involved.

However, the real "scandal," here as always, is precisely that of "particularity," that is, the real problem is universalism and spiritualism. Unless one, *a priori,* regards Biblical history and the Israelite conquest, as *special,* unique history, of a piece with God's eternal warfare against evil, the Israelite conquest is, indeed, only one more example of a sordid "war of liberation" (of course with God and justice in its corner) of which also modern history reeks, and really no example at all for us. In a way, the whole point of the Book of Joshua is that the conquest of the land was in accordance with the divine purpose, and to reject this is virtually to reject the entire book in its theological dimension.

Liberal failure to distinguish church and state, both in Biblical and modern applications, compounds the problems. If we remember that Old Testament Israel was a political as well as a spiritual unit, we will neither think that it can be used as a direct model for the political action of the *"church* militant," nor will we spiritualistically imagine that it would have been possible for Israel to conquer Canaan only in some realm of the Spirit.

Nor will we forget that ultimately the warfare is total, involving bodies as well as souls, the physical real estate of this planet as well as "the spiritual hosts of wickedness in the heavenly places" (Eph. 6:12). And only human fatuity could imagine that there could ever, in any real world, spiritual or material, be a "victory" or "salvation" without corresponding "defeat" and "damnation."

Finally, we easily overlook the unique thrust of the Book of Joshua's account in another respect. The entire story might easily have been told as an epic of national achievement—and that would have countless parallels! Or the conquest could have been covered with a thin theological veneer by means of some mythology of "manifest destiny" or of high-sounding platitudes about justice, liberation, etc. Again the parallels are legion, whether in the modern secular guise of nationalism, or in ancient mythologies, where the god was little more than a personification of the ideals and claims of a people or nation. Contrast all that with the Biblical theology of an independent, personal Creator, who had freely *elected* to give His people a land, but which land could also easily be forfeited by infidelity.

JUDGES

The second of the "former prophets" recounts the troublous history of God's people in the aftermath of the conquest. Not only the pockets of unconquered Canaanite city-states, and the emergence of the Philistines as a major threat, but also the recurrent apostasy and disunity of the tribes themselves (the latter facilitated by Palestinian geography) contributed to making the period anything but tranquil.

Historical Reconstruction

Until recently, Noth's proposal that the tribal structure in this period be considered an "amphictyony" (after Greek analogies) had attained nearly universal acceptance. This hypothesis envisioned a purely religious league centered around some central shrine, with each tribe retaining full internal and political independence. It was often combined with a "covenant renewal festival" hypothesis, which purported to describe periodic meetings of the tribes or their representatives at the amphictyonic center. Amphictyonic officials were supposedly limited to religious functions, such as "covenant mediator" or major preacher at the festivals.

Plausible though it was in many respects (and accepted by many scholars who otherwise distanced themselves radically from Noth), it has increasingly come under sharp attack, and it remains to be seen if it will survive. Some of the dispute may be semantic (the Hebrew federation was not exactly like the Greek amphictyonies), but a good measure of hypothesis is involved in any event. No other hypothesis has won acceptance in its place, and many today would not care to venture beyond the sorry picture Judges itself paints: a clear memory of Moses and

Sinaitic covenant, but honored more in the breach than in the observance, and precious little unity, political, religious, or otherwise.

In connection with these hypotheses, it should be noted that much modern critical scholarship envisions the liturgies of this period as the first major creative incubator of many of Israel's later traditions, religious as well as literary. While this does represent a somewhat earlier verdict on the date of the material than that rendered by most previous criticism, the conservative must note that it envisions positive, creative formations in precisely that period which the Bible itself remembers as characterized by massive and recurrent backslidings. A more fundamental clash between the Biblical record and critical hypothesis is scarcely conceivable!

In general, it appears to be relatively easy to date the period of the Judges to roughly the two centuries between 1250 and 1050 B.C. From archaeological data we know that the period that followed the invasion of the "Sea Peoples" (the Philistines are the best known representatives), which had prostrated or annihilated all the great political powers of the area, was a time of greatest possible ferment throughout the ancient Near East. Into the vacuum swept many of the nomadic desert tribes of which the Israelites themselves had partly been harbingers, but who themselves suffer from similar incursions once they have settled down.

Typically, however, the Biblical writer is interested in that broader picture, only as it impinges on Israel's history, and specifically as God employs one or the other of those historical agents as instruments of His wrath upon a perfidious people. This leads to two especially severe problems in the historical interpretation of the book.

Meaning of "Judge"

The first of these is the precise meaning of "judge" *(shophet)* itself. Already on the Sunday school level it is regularly pointed out that the Biblical "judge" does not have the same, almost exclusively courtroom, associations as the modern term. Increasingly it becomes plain that the Biblical usage is ancient, also outside of the Bible, but also that the Biblical writer uses the term in a broader, almost double, sense.

On the one hand, we have evidence from Ugarit, Mari, Ebla, and even Carthage (a Phoenician colony) for the term's use as a virtual synonym for "king"—or at least "ruler." That the Biblical figures certainly were, although not by any principle of dynastic or other regular, institutional succession or appointment. In sociological terms they were "charismatic leaders," men of the hour who proved themselves and won acceptance by their success. (The distinction is useful even if Max Weber did grossly overstate the distinction.) The Biblical attribution of their calls to the "Spirit" is not instrinsically contradictory of the sociological explana-

tion, but by no means synonymous with it either! Once the deliverance
had been won, many of them apparently continued to wield some
authority. The latter is particularly in line with the extra-Biblical usage,
where, as modern scholarship rightly stresses, "judge" implies not so
much unique acts of deliverance as a sustained series of acts of
government (ideally at least), maintaining justice by means of righteous
judgments. Thus the Hebrew term for such ordered rule, *mishpat* (often
translated "justice" or "judgment") is derived from the same root as
shophet.

At the same time, the Biblical writer is plainly interested in a broader
sense of the term, almost derived, as it were, by a pun on the common
inner-Biblical usage (especially in the psalter) of "judge" in the sense of
"save, vindicate, deliver." Both kings and judges (in the narrow sense)
make many "judgments," implying either acquittal or condemnation.
When God is the subject in relation to His faithful, covenant people, the
ordinary assumption is that His "judgment" will be one of acquittal or
salvation, in faithfulness to His promises. (Neither dare the ultimate
connection of this usage with the forensic picture of "justification" be
overlooked, that vicarious verdict of "not guilty" for Christ's sake, which
will be publicly declared at the final "judgment.") Perhaps the implication
here already is that God is the real "judge" of His people; certainly it is a
point of the book as a whole. The Biblical writer helps bring out this
nuance of "judge" by often paralleling it (cf. 2:16) with the very term
"saviors" or "deliverers" (*moshi'im,* derived from the same Semitic root as
the names Joshua and Jesus). Possibly it is significant that the *noun,*
"judge" is never used directly of an individual in the book.

The problem is complicated slightly by the appearance of both
"major" and "minor" judges in the book. The latter term is often applied
to the same six figures (Shamgar, Tola, Jair, Ibzan, Elon, and Abdon),
about which very little information has been preserved. Possibly it is only
an argument from silence to try to make something out of their cases. It
may simply have not served the writer's overriding theological concerns to
include more information at those points. Possibly these six were more
the ordinary Semitic type of "judge" (in the sense of "ruler") with few
charismatic attainments, and were included only for the sake of
completeness.

Nevertheless, critical theory is rife with speculations in other
directions. Isagogically, some version of a hypothesis that an original
"savior book" was transformed into a "judge book," perhaps on the
model of especially these figures, has often been proposed. Alt argued
that the "minor judges" first propounded casuistic-type law to the settling
Israelites, while Noth viewed them as garbled derivatives of the office of

the amphictyonic "covenant mediator," but both proposals are entirely speculative. It should be noted in passing that especially in Numbers (hence often considered P's alternative to D's "judge") we meet a tribal functionary called a *nasi'* ("prince"). His precise role is also unclear, but apparently some, first-level regular administrative machinery is reflected there, in contrast to the apparent rise of the *shophet* or "judge" in times of great emergency and possible continuing authority on a second level.

Chronology

The other major problem in the Book of Judges is its chronology. For the liberal it is a parade example of the "errancy" of the Scriptures, and even the conservative must concede that it is probably a clear instance of a symbolic use of numbers (here for theological purposes), far more congenial to the Orient than to the Occident. If the writer's symbolic procedure is understood, the issue of his veracity is not even legitimately raised.

The total of all the figures in the book (times of oppression and periods of judgeship) is 410 years. That in itself is patently too high, because, at most, there can be an interval of only some 400 years between the Exodus (high date in the 15th century) and the establishment of the monarchy in the 11th century. If Judges itself consumed 400 years, where would we find space for all the other events which must be fitted into our period?

The figure is just as difficult to reconcile with the datum of 1 Kings 6:1, that 480 years intervened between the Exodus and the founding of Solomon's temple. Assuming that 480 is not also symbolic (a multiple of 40), the 70 years' difference between 480 and 410 is again much too small to accommodate all the other events (which often have their own Biblical notices on duration) which must be fitted in.

Various expedients have been proposed to reconcile the various figures on a more literal level (probably better: "literalistic"), but none have commanded much acceptance, not even among conservatives. It is almost universally recognized that many of the judges were relatively contemporaneous, and that most, if not all, of them, delivered and ruled over only portions of the land. In a certain sense all of them *did* represent "all Israel," but not in simple sequence. Likewise, the "sum" of the recurrent apostasies and deliverances did add up to a composite portrait of the "*massa perditionis*" of this period, more than matched, however, by the magnitude of God's forgiving grace for all the people, whenever His judgments aroused sincere repentance. The situation is not unlike that which often confronts us in the gospels of the New Testament, where strict chronological considerations often yield to topical ones. There are many examples in antiquity, both in the Bible and outside it, of stories being stitched together in a cycle by means of "afterward," "then," etc., which often imply not chronology, but simply the narrator's chosen sequence.

Of course, a sermonic or pedagogical interest is very much in evidence, but from that follows neither "errancy" nor the radical disjunction of theology and history, so characteristic of liberalism. What begins as a grievous historical problem thus ends as a great exegetical bonus, highlighting some of the main themes of the book (as of the "deuteronomic" corpus in general): the fragility of faithfulness, the high priority of "Christian education," all the more so in the face of the propensity of children to rebel against parents, and of parents to be remiss in both example and instruction.

Contents

Contentwise, the bulk of the book appears in the middle section of 2:6—16:31, narrating the history of the "judges." This is followed by a sort of appendix (chaps. 17—21), recounting two isolated stories of the period, and preceded (1:1—2:5) by an introduction, summarizing the internal political state of affairs at the beginning of the period. Many problems shrink or disappear if we understand the "After the death of Joshua" at the beginning of the book as a title of the *whole* book, not merely an introduction to the events of chap. 1, and, if so, those events, or some of them, may well have occurred *before* Joshua's death.

As we have noted, Judges 1 is the key plank in critical argumentation against the reliability of the picture of the conquest presented in Joshua. However, we have also stressed that Joshua includes notices to remind us that behind the main scenes everything did not go so smoothly—or that initial conquests were not always permanent. In fact, some verses in Judges 1 are almost verbatim parallels of some in Joshua (e.g., 1:21 and 15:63; 1:29 and 16:10 etc.)

Hence, we must understand these "minority reports," not as contradictions of the main picture, but as indicating its complexity. Much data indicates that, in many respects, the "conquest" could not be said to have been consolidated until the time of David. Especially, many of the large, fortified and walled cities held out until that time.

After a few initial anecdotes, the rest of Judges 1 (vs. 27 ff.) simply lists the natives who had not yet been subjugated. The Adonibezek of Judges 1 is very similar in name to the Adonizedek of Jerusalem in Joshua 10, but that type of name is so common that there is no justification for suspicions about confused traditions. In Judges, furthermore, the tribe of Simeon is involved. As we have noted, Simeon may well have initially occupied the later Philistine territory, only to be quickly expelled and then virtually to become a "lost tribe." The atrocities requited upon Adonibezek probably well characterize the frontier type of situation in the entire period.

The fortunes of Jerusalem in these narratives probably illustrate the see-saw nature of the fighting as well as anything. In Joshua 10, at least the king of Jerusalem had been slain by Joshua; in Judges 1:8 Judah razes the city (or its environs?), while in 1:21 Benjamin does *not* expel the Jebusites who live there. Apparently, early successes there could not be capitalized on until David took it for his capital (2 Sam. 5).

The notice in Judges 1:22 ff. of the capture of Bethel is redolent of the account of the capture of Ai ("Ruin") in Joshua 7—8. Especially since the archaeological evidence appears to be confirmatory for Bethel, but not for Ai, some scholars have proposed some confusion, interchangeability or migration of the names of the two cities as a solution. That is not utterly impossible, but, at best, remains only one hypothetical possibility.

Judges 2 begins the main section of the book with a "deuteronomic" retrospect and prospect setting the theological stage for proper reading of the following accounts.

The dramatic appearance of the Angel of the LORD at Bochim ("weepers") introduces the tripartite framework into which most of the subsequent accounts in this section are structured: (1) the chronological scheme; (2) the national perspective, which for purposes of theological relevancy is given to events which technically were largely local or tribal; and (3) the theological interpretation of the events in terms of the "deuteronomic" principle of grace or judgment, depending on the people's behavior. (The two stories in the third section of the book differ on all counts: they tell of no judge, they are not fitted into the same chronological scheme, and explicit theological commentary is largely absent.)

Judges 2:11—3:6 spells out the recurring theme and pattern of that theological interpretation: (a) Israel's apostasy; (b) divine punishment in the form of foreign oppression; (c) Israel's repentance and cry to Yahweh for deliverance; (d) Yahweh's compassion on His people, shown by raising up a "savior" for them.

Judges 2:6-10 is very parallel to Joshua 24:28-31. It need not be considered a doublet, or even the original continuation of Joshua before the insertion of the miscellaneous material intervening. We can readily understand it as another retrospective glance before the narrative proceeds.

The "Cushanrishathaim, king of Mesopotamia," from whom Othniel, the first judge, delivers Israel (3:7-11), remains unidentified. Since the name of the adversary appears to mean "Cushan of double wickedness," many critics suspect that the entire account is an invention (perhaps to make Othniel a "judge"), all the more so since it is short on specifics. A more congenial attempt at historical explanation suggests a scribal confusion of "r" and "d" (the Hebrew letters are very similar), situating the enemy more plausibly in E*d*om than in A*r*am (translated "Mesopotamia" here).

Ehud's semihumorous assassination of Eglon, king of Moab (3:12-30) is, in a way, only another chapter in the almost incessant friction between these two neighbors. Not long after this, however, Moab must have expelled the tribes of Reuben and Gad permanently from that territory.

Shamgar's exploit, described in a single verse (3:31; cf. 5:6) reminds one of Samson, and his own non-Semitic (apparently Hurrian) name, plus a father apparently named after one of the major Canaanite sex-goddesses (Anath), raise all kinds of unanswerable questions.

In Judges 4 and 5, we have two parallel accounts, in prose and poetry respectively, of the victory engineered by the prophetess Deborah, with the assistance of Barak (not to speak of the gory, but courageous, action of "Jael, the wife of Heber the Kenite"). The parallelism of prose and poetry here corresponds almost exactly to the situation in Ex. 14 and 15, which both describe the Exodus event. Like Ex. 15, the "Song of Deborah" in Judges 5 swarms with linguistic archaisms, and is widely accepted as very possibly contemporaneous with the event itself (c. 1125 B.C.). At least in linguistic form it is commonly agreed to be the oldest or second oldest (depending on how the critics date Ex. 15) piece of literature in the Bible. (This is certainly reflected in the text of the poem; ancient copyists apparently often no longer understood it!)

Precisely what happened at this "Battle of the Kishon" or "Battle of Taanach" is disputed: critics often profess to find a contradiction between the poetic and prose versions. Since only Sisera is mentioned in the poem, the inclusion of Jabin of Hazor in chap. 4 is commonly thought to reflect either a conflation of two separate battles, or else a confusion with the events of Joshua 11. However, "Jabin" is probably a dynastic name, and the other difficulties probably reflect hypercriticism.

The participation in the battle of the "stars from their courses" (5:20) may imply the common vertical typology of the heavenly "hosts" alongside Israel's, although it may refer more specifically to the torrential rainfall which secured the victory (cf. the miracle at Aijalon in Joshua 10).

Many duplicates and contradictions are also commonly "discovered" in the Gideon narratives (Judges 6—8). These include the variation in name between "Gideon" and "Jerubbaal" (once attributed to J and E respectively), but since the latter is compounded out of "Baal," a later disinclination to continue its use is readily understandable (even if it originally referred to Yahweh in its neutral meaning of "lord"). Gideon's rout of the raiding Midianites well illustrates the procedures and presumptions of "holy war." The pursuit and execution of the princes, Oreb and Zeeb, and of the kings, Zebah and Zalmunna, is echoed in later Scripture (Ps. 83 and Is. 10). The touchy jealousy of the Ephraimites, because Gideon had not called them to action at the beginning of the campaign (8:1-3), anticipates not only similar difficulties by Jephthah but probably much of the history of the divided monarchy as well.

Gideon's semi-apostasy and refusal to be crowned king (8:22 ff.) are harbingers of things to come. Abimelech, Gideon's son by a concubine, has no such scruples, however! He scarcely rates as a "judge" *except* in the old Canaanite sense of "king." In thoroughly Canaanite fashion he follows up his coronation at Shechem with a massacre of his 70 half-brothers. Only Jotham escapes, whose famous fable (9:7-15) anticipates the subsequent disaffection of the Shechemites with Abimelech, and his ignominious death at Thebez. (Cf. also Jehoash's fable told to Amaziah in 2 Kings 14).

Jephthah (most of Judges 10—12), originally expelled as an illegitimate child, is welcomed back by the Gileadites to repulse Ammonite pressure. The Ammonites are a new power in northern Transjordan. We soon hear much more of them, so apparently Jephthah's victory over them was impermanent. That is also indicated by the fact that the tribes which previously occupied its territory (Gad and half of Manasseh) soon disappear from the Biblical scene. The tribe of Reuben, to the South, had perhaps already been displaced by Moab, whose role in the early history is also recounted in Jephthah's message to Ammon (11:12 ff.). The inclusion of Moab does not necessitate the two strands critics are wont to see.

Whether or not Jephthah actually sacrificed his own daughter (11:34 ff.) is an old *crux*. The apparent implication of the text is that he did, but there are many who argue that he only "devoted" her somehow, and hence she bewails only her *virginity*. The incident does not indicate that human sacrifice was common in "primitive" Isreal—the very opposite; nor does it conceal some etiology of a Gileadite mourning custom or fertility rite, as form critics often opine.

Jephthah is far less indulgent of Ephraimite jealousy than Gideon had been (8:1 ff), and initiates a slaughter of all who, speaking a different dialect, could not pronounce "Shibboleth" (whence the Hebrew word's inclusion in English).

Samson's escapades mirror the rising Philistine threat on Israel's southwestern flank. Gone is the day when many critics seriously thought that his name was related to "Shemesh" (Hebrew for "sun") and reflected some kind of solar myth (all the more so, allegedly, since his home, Zorah, was close to Bethshemesh, which means "Shrine of the Sun"). But the Samson cycle is still commonly viewed as a heavily folkloristic genre, a Biblical example of worldwide tales about the brave village wit and trickster, a sort of Biblical Puck or Till Eulenspiegel. And, no doubt, in some respects Samson is the strangest "judge" of all: moved mightily by the Spirit, under Nazirite vows from conception, and yet with a fatal weakness for women (dare we say, *simul iustus et peccator?*). The story can be read as a negative example of abuse of a high calling, but it is more than passing strange that the author of the Book of Judges makes little of that.

The two narratives in Judges 17—21 are rightly labeled a sort of "appendix" because the structure and commentary found in most of the rest of the book are absent, as we noted above. They are two detached stories, apparently from the end of the period (c.1100), among other things illustrating the quality of life in those days when "there was no king in Israel, and every man did what was right in his own eyes."

The first appendix (Judges 17—18) relates how one, Micah, makes his own idol, and hires a Levite by the name of Jonathan as priest. When the Danites (who had been expelled from their allotment by the Philistines) come through in search of a new homeland, they offer Jonathan more money to become their priest, and he eagerly accepts. It is not at all unlikely that the story was preserved (not concocted) as part of Jerusalem's polemic against the later Israelite shrine at Dan. Jonathan apparently had better credentials than merely "Levite"; in 18:30 we learn that he was also a grandson (descendant?) of Moses, and in one of the most interesting bits of Hebrew textual history, some later scribe inserted a *nun* in the name in some manuscript, making Jonathan "really" a descendant of the hated king Manasseh!

The second appendix (Judges 19—21) begins with the grim tale of the gang-rape and murder of a Levite's estranged concubine in Gibeah of Benjamin. There are a few parallels to the scene in Sodom (Gen. 19), but that scarcely requires literary influence! The tribe's intransigence leads to an "amphictyonic" assembly at nearby Mizpah, and Benjamin's decimation in battle (two traditions, according to many critics), concluded with a common vow not to allow the Benjaminites any daughters of the other tribes for purposes of repopulation. Later second thoughts about this harsh vow led to the adoption of two artifices to circumvent it: (1) when Jabeshgilead is destroyed for not joining the attack, its virgins will be spared and given to Benjamin; (2) the still wifeless Benjaminites will be allowed to kidnap dancing girls at "the yearly feast of Yahweh at Shiloh"

(21:19). (This mention of Shiloh anticipates the shrine's importance in the opening chapters of Samuel.)

Obviously, this final account is not narrated for our edification or example any more than many of the other stories in the book (not the proper hermeneutical criterion for the Bible to begin with, of course!). Among other things, however, it probably is not entirely mistaken to recognize a certain anti-Saul animus involved (humanly speaking) in its retention. Saul was not only a Benjaminite, but Gibeah, just north of Jerusalem, was his capital, and his entire career was closely related to Jabeshgilead.

Date and Authorship

Isagogically, the situation with Judges is very similar to that in Joshua. The Talmud attributes authorship to Samuel—an opinion which is by no means impossible, and which does not lack for defenders today (at least among conservatives). On the other hand, there is the strong "deuteronomic" tone of much of the book (cf. above), and various indications suggest that the book might have been put together much later. Most of these, like the apparently pro-monarchical "no king in Israel" refrain, would not necessarily point to a date later than the united kingdom. However, in 18:30 we read that Jonathan's descendants were priests in Dan "until the day of the captivity of the land," which almost certainly brings us down to the time of the fall of the Northern Kingdom in the eighth century. It must always be conceded, however, that these rather marginal comments might have been updates made long after the composition of the main work itself.

The introduction to Judges (1:1—2:5) was once often viewed as, in essence at least, the original conclusion of the "Hexateuch," and many contemporary critics would only reformulate that judgment. It is also widely viewed as originally the continuation or conclusion of the J source. Others would view the section as only a miscellany of memories of the conquest—which, as such, we can readily agree with.

Few would disagree with the observation that the heart of the book is characterized by a variety of stories organized around a "deuteronomic" framework. (As already noted, such a description can also be understood in a manner acceptable to orthodoxy.) The problem is the absence of that "deuteronomic" comment not only in the final chapters of the book, but also in the case of Abimelech and the "minor judges," plus the fact that it occurs twice with Samson (15:20 and 16:30). This has led to a curious theory about a "pre-deuteronomic Judges" containing much of the present book, with the deuteronomic editor omitting sections that were offensive to him, which, however, were restored by some later editor in their original form minus the D comment. Such a "subtraction and addition" theory seems unlikely on its face, neither does it explain why certain pericopes did not offend "Dtr" as much as others are supposed to have.

The theory, already mentioned, of an earlier, popular "savior book" transformed into a later "judge book" may have greater plausibility, but, at best, really explains very little. It suffers shipwreck on the fact that "savior" language is least in evidence precisely in those stories where one might most easily see popular memories at work. There was a time when many critics indulged in a further dissection of the presumed pre-deuteronomic Judges into J and E sources, but that finds little current favor. Form criticism generally prefers to speak of a congeries of sundry legends of tribal wars, sagas about heroes, etiologies, etc., which was eventually gathered into a sort of coherent order for religious purposes.

Text

A note is necessary finally about the text-critical problem of Judges (somewhat similar to the one we will meet in Kings). The Hebrew text poses no serious problems, but we have two different recensions reflected in the Septuagint. Qumran evidence makes likely what was usually assumed previously: both Greek versions were probably based on variations already in *Hebrew* textual tradition. Hence, the variations cannot be attributed to slippage in the process of translation.

What is usually considered the earlier of the Greek uncials (Alexandrinus, representing the "Lucianic" recension) also offered the translation which is found in the majority of LXX manuscripts. But it is precisely these which diverge most from the Masoretic text. The other recension, best represented by Vaticanus (B), is much closer to MT, but, at least from the Greek textual standpoint, would not ordinarily be accorded the same weight. It remains to be seen precisely how Cross' theory that these recensions represent successive revisions of the Greek text on the basis of a Hebrew text will affect matters in Judges.

The degree of the differences involved should not be exaggerated. As usual with textual variations, matters of great substance are rarely implicated, and doctrinal matters even less so. At the same time, the variations dare not be glossed over (for details and examples see the commentaries). The believer in verbal inspiration is naturally interested in what the autograph said, and the fact that we often cannot be sure about that does not mean that there never was an autograph!

SAMUEL

There are various ancient traditions about this book's name, how or whether to divide it, and how to relate it to what we know as Kings.

In the Hebrew canon, at least as far back as we can trace it, the books of Samuel and Kings are distinguished from each other by the names we know, but neither one is internally subdivided into "First" and "Second." Only thus, of course, was it possible to count *four* "former prophets," balancing the four "major prophets."

The internal subdivisions for each book apparently were a Septuagintal innovation. On the other hand, the Septuagint does not distinguish "Samuel" and "Kings" from each other by title. Rather it presents both together as one unified history of the united and divided kingdoms, with the title, "Books of the Kingdoms" *(basileiōn)*, but still with essentially our four divisions. Essentially the same fourfold arrangement was bequeathed to the Vulgate, where Jerome, however, substituted "Kings" for "Kingdoms" (perhaps partly reflecting his Hebrew influences). Hence, at least until very recently, Roman Catholic literature has referred to "I-IV Kings."

About the time of the Reformation, the Septuagint's internal subdivisions were introduced into editions of the Hebrew text, each pair of books, however, retaining its original title in the Masoretic tradition. Thence, this sort of a compromise of Greek and Hebrew nomenclature entered into Protestant Bibles.

Nothing depends on it, of course, but in many ways the consistent Greek use of "Kingdoms" instead of an initial "Samuel" is more appropriate to the contents, since Samuel plays a trivial role after 1 Sam. 15. Already 1 and 2 Sam. are divided by a monarchical event—the death of Saul.

Contents

A convenient outline for Samuel is: (1) 1 Sam. 1—7: Samuel; (2) 1 Sam. 8—15: Samuel and Saul; (3) 1 Sam. 16—31: Saul and David; (4) 2 Sam. 1—8: David's triumph over the house of Saul; (5) 2 Sam. 9—20: "David's Court History" or the "History of the Court Succession"; and (6) 2 Sam. 21—24: Miscellaneous Appendixes.

It is to be noted that in the eyes of many critics the "Court History" is artificially interrupted by the appendixes and is continued in 1 Kings 1—2. One need not buy that precise theory to see here probable evidence *both* of the original unity of "Samuel" and "Kings," as well as of a complex transmissional history that made it possible for the appendixes to be inserted where they are.

The figure of Samuel certainly dominates the first half of 1 Sam., beginning with the familiar stories of his birth and tutelage under Eli at Shiloh. The Dead Sea Scrolls appear to confirm explicitly what had often been suspected, viz., that Samuel had been dedicated by his mother as a

Nazirite. On the other hand, there is no call for the common critical
negativism to the effect that some of these stories were originally told of
Saul and later transferred to Samuel. Hannah's explanation of her child's
name, "Asked for the Lord" (1 Sam. 1:20), may etymologically fit Saul
better than Samuel; but the meaning of Samuel, "God has *heard*," is only
the obverse of "asked," and certainly fits the context.

Hannah's song, psalm, or prayer in 1 Sam. 2:1-10 is clearly the
prototype and Old Testament counterpart of Mary's Magnificat (which
itself, in both form and content, could easily be only another Old
Testament psalm). In form, Hannah's song is a quite typical "individual
thanksgiving" (cf. on the Psalter).

There is no need to regard the poem as a purely literary flourish,
originally having no connection at all with Hannah. On the other hand,
some later expansion or modification is not unthinkable—not
theologically, either. The RSV typography suggests that only v. 1 is
literally Hannah's—which, however, is venturesome, to put it mildly.
Most concern centers on the reference to the king in v. 10. However, there
is no absolute need for it to postdate establishment of the monarchy. It
may well be a more private expression of the hope which all the people
would soon articulate in a demand to Samuel (1 Sam. 8). At the same
time, Hannah exemplarily views her private situation in the perspective of
God's public redemptive activity. It is to be noted that this is the first Old
Testament reference to the king as "anointed" (the root from which the
technical term, "Messiah," would eventually arise).

The weakness and perversion of the family of Eli leads to a curse on
their house by an unnamed "man of God" (1 Sam. 2:27) and the prophecy
that it will be replaced by another line of priests, fulfilled when Zadok
supplants Abiathar upon Solomon's accession. Complex issues of the
history of the Israelite priesthood are involved, which cannot be discussed
here. The ascendancy of a Jerusalemite line over that of a northern shrine
is obviously part of the picture, but there is no need to question the
Biblical reports on the detail.

At the battle of Aphek or Ebenezer, the ark is captured, and its
fortunes are the dominant interest in 1 Sam. 4—6. The name given her
child by the dying widow of Phinehas reflects the trauma: "Ichabod," that
is, "Where is the glory?" or "Inglorious" (*kabod* or "glory" being a
common epithet for the ark and God's "incarnational" presence in it).
Commentators are probably right in noting a certain wry humor in some
of these ark narratives: Dagon must fall on his face in homage to Yahweh
(the ark) even while He is, in a sense, in captivity; the Philistines are
inflicted with an embarrassing disease (apparently hemorrhoids); etc.
Strangely enough—or maybe significantly—nothing is said of the fall of

Shiloh, but Jeremiah later alludes to it (chaps. 7 and 26), and there is no doubt now about its archaeological confirmation.

In chap. 7, Samuel comes into his own, sparking a great religious revival and a temporary reversal of Israel's fortunes vis-a-vis the Philistines, who are trounced at Ebenezer, the scene of their original triumph. The reversal is commemorated in the erection of the great "Ebenezer" stone (7:12).

In 1 Sam. 9, Saul makes his debut, first only as a searcher for his father's lost asses, who catches the contagion of epidemic "prophecy" before he returns home, giving rise to the saying (useful for expressing any incredulity), "Is Saul also among the prophets?" (10:11). The saying is reinforced by a similar incident later in Saul's life while pursuing David (19:24). True to form, the critics usually cry "Doublet," etc., and, in fact, throughout 1 Samuel they profess to find a great number of them.

There is obviously very interesting information here and in the context about the origins and rise of prophecy in Israel (cf. below), but we scarcely know what to make of it. It seems clear that a much more ecstatic, *glossolalia*-type of "prophecy" is implied here than was common later—although reams have been devoted to that issue. In 1 Sam 9:9 we have an "antiquarian" note about the previous change of terminology from "seer" *(roeh)* to "prophet" *(nabi)*, although the former root and an apparent synonym *(chazah)* continue in use.

The narratives of Saul's election and acclamation are usually thought to be a confusion of a number of traditions or sources. The Bible reports—and there is nothing intrinsically unlikely about it—that Saul is privately anointed, then publicly chosen by lot, but acclaimed as the charismatic choice of the populace only after he courageously rescues Jabeshgilead from the outrageous threat of Nahash, the Ammonite (1 Sam. 11; cf. various parallels with Judges 20).

In 1 Sam. 12, Samuel makes a sort of "deuteronomic" farewell speech, similar to the oration in chap. 8 when the people first requested a king, but he obviously does not retire when Saul ascends his throne (chap. 13).

Samuel's Significance

Samuel has always been a difficult figure to classify, but that probably answers to his position on the threshold of one of the major transitions in Israel's political and theological history, namely from theocracy to monarchy. In many ways he is the last and greatest of the "judges," and even his venal sons, Joel and Abijah (8:2) are so described.

Presumably he was also a priest, because he was Eli's successor, and his conflict with Saul (1 Sam. 13:13) implies that he alone had the right to sacrifice. Conversely, Saul's behavior may presage much later interference in cultic affairs by the monarchy.

In many respects, he must also be understood as the first of the great prophets (cf. Acts 13:20), and from here on we meet many of them also in the historical books. Chap. 9 indicates that he has the clairvoyant powers of a "seer," yet his "prophecy" towers head and shoulders above the ecstatics among whom Saul fell. As the great prophets of later times spearheaded a "back to Moses" reformation after the devastations of Baalism, so Samuel can be understood as leading Israel's first great religious revival after her "first love" had failed in the period of the Judges (cf. esp. chap. 7). His famous "Behold, to obey is better than sacrifice" oracle against Saul in chap. 15 is in many respects almost the quintessence of the prophetic message.

Thus, Samuel is a veritable "second Moses," representing virtually all offices in Israel as no one had since Moses. It is no accident that Jer. 15:1 views Moses and Samuel together as great mediators and intercessors for Israel. In this, as in other respects, Samuel anticipates both Elijah and Christ. Typologically, not as much is usually made of Samuel as many other figures, but there appears to be no good reason for that neglect.

In many respects, Moses had functioned as a "king," and likewise with Samuel, also in his apparent capacity as a "judge." (Note the reaction of the Bethlehemites at his coming in 16:4.) No doubt, that accounts partly for his coolness toward the idea of kingship in the more formal sense. But it will not do to attribute it all to personal insecurity or pique!

Samuel tends to get a very "bad press" in much critical scholarship. Conversely, sympathy is often expressed for Saul (sometimes compared to the protagonists of Greek tragedies), partly on the basis of a "winners write history" presupposition. No one would care to deny that altogether. The Bible certainly judges Saul from the viewpoint of Samuel and, later, David. There may well have been another side to it from a purely historical standpoint. It is not hard to view Saul as the unfortunate victim of circumstances beyond his control, especially in contrast to the consummate (and sometimes unscrupulous) politician, David. But the ultimate question is whether or not we norm ourselves according to the Bible's theological criteria!

Samuel certainly is nothing if not ambivalent about kingship. He strenuously resists the people's request, but then accedes to it (1 Sam 8—9). He anoints Saul but is also his undoing. Source critics have usually "solved" this "contradiction" by distributing Samuel's various attitudes among various sources, each of which allegedly tried to get Samuel in its corner by making him a mouthpiece of its own pro- or anti-monarchical sentiments. But, among other things, it should be noted that Samuel's attitude is typical of the whole "deuteronomic" corpus (*in germine* already in Deut. 17:44 ff.): kingship is recognized as one of God's great gifts to His people, alongside of a realistic awareness of the extent to which it could also be a magnet for syncretism and a focus of apostasy.

Much is often made of the fact, and apparently rightly so, that Samuel does not anoint Saul (or David) as *melek* ("king," in the proper sense), but only as *nagid,* usually translated "prince" (9:16; 10:1, 13:14, although *melek* is used in other passages in the context, apparently in a more popular sense). Apparently, Samuel thus hoped to satisfy the people's demand for centralized authority, without opening the floodgates to the pagan, Canaanite ideology, that almost necessarily came with *melek.* Samuel did not really succeed, and Saul's failure, too, can probably be laid in part to his inability to synthesize two worlds of thought. First with David (and Nathan) is kingship grafted successfully into native Israelite stock, and *nagid* and *melek* come to be virtual synonyms, as we often meet them in later literature.

Finally, it should be stressed, as Samuel clearly illustrates, that "prophecy," humanly speaking, arises in Israel largely as a counterpoise to kingship. One of prophecy's major and standing tasks is to call the throne to account, especially to remind it that the absolutist, mythological, and "divine right" models of paganism are inappropriate for the covenant society of Israel. And when kings fade after the Exile, prophets soon disappear from the scene too.

1 Samuel 13—31

The account of the beginning of Saul's reign in 1 Sam. 13 is marked by two famous textual corruptions in the main Masoretic tradition. Possibly it was deliberate by some anti-Saul copyist. Saul's age at accession is entirely missing and hard to estimate. Only the digit "two" appears for the length of his reign. Noth thinks it the total, but that is unlikely. Acts 13:21 says "forty," apparently a round figure.

The note in 13:19 ff. on the Philistine monopoly on iron is interesting. It reveals much about the economic realities of the period, alongside the religious ones. Apparently the Philistines had brought the new technology along with them from the defeated Hittites in Asia Minor. Archaeologically, the "Iron Age" replaces the "Bronze Age" in this part of the world at about this time. Conventionally the date for its inception is given as 1200 B.C.

Saul's strange behavior over against Jonathan's inadvertent transgression after his daring exploit at Michmash first reveals facets of his personality and character, which grow progressively worse (1 Sam. 14). The final break with Samuel comes fast, after Saul's disobedience of the *cherem* laws of "holy war" in the battle against the Amalekites, Israel's ancestral enemy (Ex. 17). Only in that light can one understand and justify that "Samuel hewed Agag in pieces before Yahweh" (15:33).

David is secretly anointed instead, while also joining Saul's entourage to assuage his "evil spirit" (1 Sam. 16). David distinguishes himself in the famous "battle of Socoh" in the valley of Elah against Goliath (chap. 17). The statement in 2 Sam. 21:19 that one Elhanan of Bethlehem slew Goliath appears at first blush to be in flat contradiction to the narrative of chap. 17. Many critics are only too happy to jump to precisely that conclusion, arguing that the tale was transferred to David after he became famous on other grounds, Others have offered various explanations, but the most likely one appears to be that Elhanan slew the *brother* of Goliath, as 1 Chron. 20:5 has it. (Critics generally distrust Chronicles and think it added "brother" to harmonize with 2 Sam. 21.) A much less likely possibility is that Elhanan was David's personal name, which his famous "throne name" eventually all but displaced.

Another "contradiction" is sniffed out in David's introduction and service to Saul in 1 Sam. 16, yet Saul's unfamiliarity with him before the battle at Socoh. It does not seem difficult to explain that a harried king, especially one of Saul's disposition (if not simple mental illness), might not recognize someone who had often been in his presence previously. The troublesome passage in chap. 17:55-58 is missing in the Septuagint's Codex Vaticanus (which could be harmonistic), and also the Qumran text of this chapter is markedly shorter (by 17 verses) than MT.

In spite of his friendship with Jonathan and marriage to Michal, David is eventually forced to become a fugitive and guerilla in the mountains and caves of southern Judea. The priests at Nob (Mt. Scopus just north of Jersualem?), except for David's future priest, Abiathar, are massacred for aiding him (cf. Matt. 12:4, etc.). David flees to Achish, the Philistine king of Gath, for refuge, but still fearing for his life, feigns madness in order to keep on the move (chap. 21). David fares better with Achish in chap. 27, when he is welcomed as an enemy of Saul. The Philistines were not yet aware of the breach the first time (v. 11), so that, again, critical talk of a contradictory doublet evaporates. Adullam (cf. Micah 1:15), Keilah, Ziph, and Engedi are among the names of David's bases during this period.

That David twice spared Saul's life under similar (although by no means identical) circumstances (1 Sam. 24 and 26), or that the Ziphites twice betrayed him to Saul (23 and 26) need not imply "doublets" either. If such things happened once, there is no improbability, especially under the circumstances, that they might happen twice.

In the wilderness, David marries Ahinoam and Abigail, widow of the churlish Nabal (1 Sam. 25). They join him at Gath with Achish, who now welcomes David as "the enemy of my enemy" and eventually gives him

Ziklag as a sort of fief. While pretending to be fighting Achish's enemies, David is really shrewdly engaging the Amalekites and other enemies of the Judahites, thus laying a groundwork of goodwill on which he can capitalize later (chaps. 27 and 30).

The suspicion of the other Philistines spares David the dilemma of being invited to join in the showdown battle with Saul (chap. 29). As Samuel had predicted through the witch at Endor, the now pathetic king Saul is ignominiously defeated in the "Battle of Gilboa" and commits suicide. His body is displayed on the temple walls in Bethshan, but the Jabeshgileadites repay an old debt by giving him a decent burial (chap. 31).

2 Samuel 1—8

2 Sam. opens with David's execution of the thief who hopes for a reward by claiming to have killed Saul. (Critics often claim he really did and cite a "contradiction.") David laments Saul and Jonathan in a famous and moving elegy (1:17-27), which even some critics concede may be genuine. Its source is cited as "the Book of Jashar" (cf. Joshua 10:13).

For seven and a half years the land is divided (no doubt, in a sense paralleling the later rift between Israel and Judah). David establishes his capital at Hebron, initially, no doubt with the encouragement of the Philistines who hoped to use David to finish off Saul's heirs. Ishbosheth, Saul's son, rules at Mahanaim—east of the Jordan, out of Philistine reach—but the real power behind the throne is obviously Abner, the commander-in-chief.

Parallels in 1 Chron. 8:33 and 9:39 make plain that Saul's son and successor was really named Eshbaal, not Ishbosheth—"A man [devotee] of the Lord," not "A man of shame." On its face, it is hard to imagine any loving mother naming her son the latter! It is rather an opprobrious pun on the real name, either by contemporary enemies, or by later scribes. The "baal" or "lord" originally implied is surely Yahweh, not the pagan Hadad whom we better know as "Baal" (there is no indication that Saul was not a Yahwist), but in the heat of later polemics this earlier usage easily became obscured. We have a similar circumstance with the name of another of Saul's sons: Mephibosheth (2 Sam. 9 ff.) vs. Meribaal (1 Chron. 8:34 and 9:40). Likewise for Gideon's earlier name: Jerubbesheth (2 Sam. 11:21) instead of the usual Jerubbaal (Judges 6 ff.).

A famous sort of gladiatorial contest between the two armies by the pool of Gibeon (which excavations have probably uncovered) led to a massacre (2 Sam. 2). Especially fateful was Abner's (reluctant) slaying of Joab's brother Asahel, avenged when Abner later defected to David in a falling out with Ishbosheth over Saul's concubine, Rizpah. Without

Abner, Ishbosheth is soon murdered, but David deals as harshly with his murderers as he had with those who claimed to have killed Saul (chap. 4).

In 2 Sam. 5 all the (ten) tribes of Israel come to Hebron, to "make a covenant" with David as king over the whole land. The voluntary nature of the act must be remembered, because it undoubtedly was invoked at the Disruption after Solomon's death. Joab's daring capture of Jerusalem from the Jebusites can probably be fully illuminated now from Kenyon's archaeological work. Since it had previously belonged to neither North nor South, Jerusalem quite literally became the "city of David," ideal for symbolizing neutrality, and ideally located on the old border.

Perhaps only now do the Philistines realize that their protege has double-crossed them, but it is too late. The epochal defeat of the Philistines in the valley of Rephaim (on the southwestern outskirts of Jerusalem) is reported with surprising brevity (2 Sam. 5:17-25).

David fetches the ark from Kirjathjearim, planning to install it in a temple, but Nathan intervenes in his famous oracle (2 Sam. 6—7). Many form critics treat chap. 6 as merely the reflex of an annual ark-festival or the like, but that seems fatuous. Pfeiffer (quoting Arnold) once dismissed chap. 7 as "monkish drivel," but its theological importance can scarcely be overstated. 2 Chron. 7 and Ps. 89 are closely related but allusions to it are legion. It is often regarded as the key Messianic (in the narrow, royal sense of the term) oracle of the Old Testament. The promise to uphold David's "house" in perpetuity (instead of a destructible temple) could only be fulfilled eschatologically in Christ (Heb. 1:5).

Relatively formulaically, 2 Sam. 8 records David's victories on all sides. His unusual harshness with the Moabites (v. 2) after earlier friendship is not explained, but one suspects unrecorded treachery. His victories over the Aramean kingdoms to the north (while Mesopotamia still lies prostrate) gives him a sphere of influence, if not an actual empire, that reaches to the banks of the Euphrates. No wonder it became a type of the universal "empire" of another order, led by the second David.

2 Samuel 9—20

With 2 Sam. 9 begins what is widely regarded as originally an independent source, detailing the "History of the Court Succession." It is usually thought to continue through 1 Kings 2, except for the extraneous interpolations sometime of the appendixes in 2 Sam. 21—24. Because of its intimate, detailed knowledge of often relatively private affairs, it is often thought to have been written by an eyewitness and participant in the events it records. Ahimaaz, the son of Zadok, is probably the favored candidate for authorship, but Abiathar, or Abiathar's son, Jonathan, are also frequently mentioned.

There is nothing intrinsically objectionable about that reconstruction. That the entire section is very much concerned to illustrate divine recompense, however, is remarkably similar to the general "deuteronomic" thesis. It is a considerably different matter when its author is sometimes effusively praised as the "father of history" (allegedly antedating Herodotus), or when its "secular," nonmiraculous, immanentalistic view of history (ordinary cause and effect, in which faith merely "discerns" God), allegedly reflecting the new court "Enlightenment," is highly lauded. Obviously, the modern critical view of "history" is being used to judge and evaluate the Bible here, and the judgment almost summarizes all that is objectionable about the historical-critical method. In another context, however, the observations might be acceptable enough: obviously miracles cluster at certain pivotal points in the Bible, and God, at His pleasure, rules the world through "providence," working "in, with and under" ordinary events, just as effectively as through overt miracles.

Nahash's abuse of David's envoys leads to a major Aramean revolt and ultimately to Joab's siege of the Ammonite capital, Rabbah (the citadel of modern Amman—the ancient name preserved in the name of the capital of modern Jordan). David's adultery with Bathsheba sets in motion a train of retribution which the rest of the "Court History" records just as unflinchingly. Not only does the "love-child" die shortly after birth, but David's oldest son, Amnon, rapes his half-sister, Tamar, leading to the retaliatory murder of Amnon by her brother Absalom (2 Sam. 13). Absalom is exiled, but Joab engineers his return by means of a clever tale told by the wise woman of Tekoa. Absalom's revolt is joined by David's counselor, Ahithophel, but thwarted by another counselor, Hushai, who is also in contact with the spies, Jonathan and Ahimaaz. David flees to Barzillai in Gilead, and after Joab has dispatched Absalom, Ahimaaz and Cushi race to inform David. And 2 Sam. breaks off the account of the "Court History" in chap. 20 with report of still another unsuccessful revolt, this time led by Sheba.

2 Samuel 21—24 (Appendixes)

The appendixes are basically six in number. (1) A famine (probably early in David's reign) is attributed to Saul's breach of Joshua's ancient covenant with the Gibeonites in putting some of them to death. They claim their right of retaliation in the execution of some of Saul's descendants. Rizpah's eerie vigil over the bodies of her sons leads David to retrieve the bones of Saul and Jonathan from Jabeshgilead and rebury them in the family tomb.

(2) In 2 Sam. 21:15 are listed miscellaneous exploits of David's

warriors against the Philistines, including Elhanan's (!) slaughter of
Goliath (cf. above).

(3) Chap. 22 is a psalm of thanksgiving by David, virtually identical
with Ps. 18. In beautiful theophanic language it describes *God's* victory in
David. Its archaisms make literal Davidic authorship plausible even to
some critics. It is one of the undeniable "doublets" in the Bible, but not
with the usual critical implications of that label.

(4) The "last words of David" (23:1-7) is similar, though apparently
intended as a sort of testament.

(5) In 23:8 are more exploits of David's warriors, arranged apparently
in lists of the "three" and the "thirty." Joab is conspicuous by his absence.

(6) A census taken by David, apparently in pride at the height of his
power, provokes God's wrath. Through the prophet Gad, David chooses
the lesser of three evils, a pestilence, but it too is stayed through the
purchase of Araunah's threshing floor (probably to be identified with the
future temple site, perhaps specifically the rock at the center of the present
"Dome of the Rock"). The parallel passage in 1 Chron. 21 attributes
David's presumption to Satan's instigation. Evolutionary critics inevitably think of greater theological sophistication and growing
"dualism" in the rise of Satanology. There is no need to harmonize,
however, because the two passages express the same thing in different
ways: precisely because Biblical theology is not dualistic, also evil
through Satan must ultimately be attributed to God, even if only in a
permissive sense.

The six appendixes so clearly interrupt the sequence of thought, that it
seems futile even to try to deny that they were apparently placed in their
present position sometime after Samuel and Kings had been separated
(possibly by the capacity of scrolls). Furthermore, the six sections appear
clearly to be arranged chiastically: (1) and (6), both natural catastrophes,
corresponding; (2) and (5), both exploits of David's warriors; and likewise
(3) and (4) the two poems in the middle. It would seem likely that (1) and
(6) were added first, then (2) and (5) inserted between them as a unity,
only to be sundered later by the insertion of (3) and (4). Possibly such a
collection of miscellanies had taken shape independently before being
added at the end of 2 Sam. If such a procedure seems strange to us, it is an
excellent reminder of the different procedures of ancient Oriental scribes,
and there is no reason why the Holy Spirit should not accommodate
Himself to them. (The general principle has many other applications to
Biblical study, sometimes for conservatives as well as for liberal critics.)

Isagogics

Isagogically, the situation in Samuel is very similar to that in Joshua and Judges, and it probably should not be considered independently of Kings either. Jewish tradition attributed the first part of the book to Samuel and the rest to Gad and Nathan, but that seems artificial, at best. There are apparent evidences of later composition, possibly pointing again to the period after the fall of Samaria, although quite certainly to the early divided monarchy for at least the major sources.

It is to be noted that Samuel is the weak link in the "deuteronomic history" hypothesis, or anything like it. The deuteronomic commentary which is so prominent in the other three "former prophets," at least in their frameworks, is almost totally absent here. This, of course, is not necessarily fatal to some version of the thesis. The material may already have been in relatively complete or protocanonical shape when the author worked. Or perhaps the final compiler viewed it as a period of transition and growth, whose lessons largely spoke for themselves—all the more so, when framed by the surrounding books.

We have already called attention to some of the major doublets or other inconcinnities which critics profess to find throughout much of the book, and have attempted to answer them briefly. Older scholars often tried to divide the material along J and E lines, the Yahwist as a Judahite often thought to be favorable to the monarchy, while the Elohist was not. Eissfeldt still finds evidence of three strands.

With the general abandonment of that approach, however, most scholars have contented themselves with merely attempting to isolate and enumerate the various early sources or traditions which the "deuteronomist" allegedly utilized. In slight mutation, many of their results would not be intrinsically objectionable to a conservative.

As noted, the "Court History" hypothesis (mainly Rost's) has found as wide acceptance as any critical hypothesis ever does. The unity and homogeneity of this section (2 Sam. 9—20) is often contrasted with greater unevenness in much of the rest of the book. Other original sources which are often located include: some originally independent Ark narrative, a biography of Samuel, especially his infancy; royal archives, etc.

Finally, a text-critical note again. Unlike Judges and Kings on either side, the major difficulties do not come primarily from the Greek, but from the Hebrew—for reasons which entirely elude us. The Greek sometimes follows a different recension too, but the *Hebrew* of Samuel has the dubious honor of exhibiting the most poorly preserved text of all the historical books, with only Ezekiel and Hosea possibly worse in the whole Old Testament. The amount of textual corruption can be—and sometimes has been—exaggerated, but there is no responsible denying that much of it exists (we noted one egregious example at 1 Sam. 13:1).

Sometimes parallels in Chronicles, the Septuagint, and now the Qumran scrolls are helpful in attempting a reconstruction of the original. See the commentaries for details.

KINGS

As we noted at the beginning of Samuel, the Hebrew had one book of "Kings" until the Reformation, while the Septuagint included Samuel in four books of "Kingdoms." Artificial and unoriginal though its separation from Samuel appears to be, the name, "Kings" or "Kingdoms" is quite appropriate, for the book(s) narrate(s) the history of the kingdom(s) from David's last days until after the Babylonian Exile. The internal subdivision of Kings (at the death of Ahab) appears to be as arbitrary as that at the end of 2 Sam. We surmise that it was made mostly on the basis of equality of contents (22 chapters in 1 Kings, 25 in 2 Kings), probably determined by the space available on scrolls at some point in the history of transmission.

1 Kings 1—2

The first two chapters narrate David's sad final days and Solomon's succession. As noted above, the proposal that they form the original conclusion to an original, discrete "History of the Succession" or the like, beginning at 2 Sam. 7, is not at all implausible. They read like a tale of typical Oriental cabal. If Solomon believed that he was both God's and his father's choice as successor, he certainly scrupled at nothing to help make it come true!

While attempts are made to stimulate and vivify the senile David through the ministrations of youthful Abishag, the court is awash with intrigue. Adonijah, supported especially by Joab and Abiathar, attempts a *coup d'etat* and has himself sworn in at the spring of Enrogel, a short distance down the Kidron valley. But his efforts are foiled by the counterplot of Nathan, Bathsheba, Zadok, and Benaiah, who support Solomon and install him at the spring Gihon, at the foot of ancient Jerusalem.

Solomon finds a "show of right" to eliminate all competition as soon as possible. He is only too happy to find reasons to carry out David's deathbed request to even old scores with Joab and Shimei. Adonijah makes a fatal request to marry Abishag, which was at least interpreted as a continuing claim on David's throne. Abiathar, the priest, alone of the principals opposing Solomon, escapes death, but is banished to Anathoth (also Jeremiah's home), thus fulfilling the ancient curse on the house of Eli (1 Kings 2:27). Zadok replaces him. "So the Kingdom was established in the hand of Solomon" (2:46).

Outline

The remainder of Kings is handily divisible into three main sections:
(1) 1 Kings 3—11: The United Kingdom under Solomon; (2) 1 Kings 12—
2 Kings 17: The Divided Kingdoms (931/922—722/1); (3) 2 Kings 18—
25: The Kingdom of Judah from 722/1 to 587/6. It is a history
supplemented in the Bible by Chronicles and by the prophetic books of
the period, especially Jeremiah, which records events in Judah after the
sack of Jerusalem, which we would otherwise not know. Outside of the
Bible, we now have extensive and sometimes rich sources as a result of
archaeological excavation, some of which we will allude to below.

During most of this period, even the secular historian feels basically
"out of the woods." (That, of course, by no means implies the absence of
problems!) After the Exile, our sources often rapidly fail us again, and we
are sometimes more in the dark than in the very early periods.

It is important to remind ourselves again of the special, religious
viewpoint of the Biblical writer, which is often labeled "deuteronomic."
As a matter of hermeneutical principle, we confess that what he reports is
wholly true, but it almost goes without saying that many things he does
not report at all, and what he does report he makes no effort to examine
"objectively" from every possible angle. As always, "external evidence" is
ever welcome to illuminate the Bible's testimony, but it cannot be allowed
to cross-examine Scripture's self-interpretation.

1 Kings 3—11 (Solomon and the Temple)

1 Kings 3 opens on an ominous note: "Solomon made a marriage
alliance with Pharaoh king of Egypt." There is no reason, then, to be
cynical or even skeptical about the famous dream at Gibeon which
follows, nor about other acts and expressions of piety by Solomon,
especially the construction of the temple. Nor need we distribute the
varying portraits among different sources. Solomon, as a very complex
person, with multiple motivations, and sometimes less consistent in living
his religion than at other times, is no less credible in that respect than
David—or, any human being, for that matter. Solomon's internationalism was a two-edged sword, to be wielded for either good or
evil—and it was for both.

Research indicates that Solomon's administration, described in 1
Kings 4, was heavily dependent on Egyptian models—there were few
native models to follow. In v. 4 we hear for the first time of the system of
corvee or "forced labor" (cf. 5:13 ff.), which would ultimately be the
empire's undoing. Solomon's "twelve officers" (v. 7) apparently oversee
districts which no longer correspond exactly to the ancient tribal

boundaries. Reasons of efficiency may have been involved, but one also suspects a deliberate attempt to break up old centrifugal loyalties.

Solomon's vaunted "wisdom" (1 Kings 4:29 ff.) was also an international phenomenon, thriving at this time especially in Egypt. The term does not quite mean what the Western ear hears in it; cf. below on the "Wisdom Literature." Among other things it was often a court phenomenon, concerned with training in statecraft, diplomacy, and the like. On that count too, the introduction of formal "wisdom" to Israel under Solomon rings true.

What does seem misguided, however, is the common critical interpretation of the movement as a semi-secular "Solomonic Enlightenment" after the benighted previous period of cult, legend, etc. The Yahwist, the writer of the "Court History," and others are supposed to have labored in its wake. At best, the construction is anachronistic and speculative, and probably reflects critical wishful thinking as much as anything.

Internationalism is certainly not absent in the construction of the temple either. This is apparent from the Biblical reports themselves of massive Lebanese influence, not least in the employment of the half-Tyrian Hiram as its chief architect (1 Kings 7:13-14). Both in general architectural plan as well as in numerous details, there are many ancient Near Eastern parallels to Solomon's temple. The parallelism may be exaggerated as well as unduly minimized.

Critics, however, generally reject the plain Biblical implication that the temple is patterned after the wilderness tabernacle: exactly twice its size in basic dimensions (60 x 20 x 30 cubits), although with more than twice as many of certain items. The skepticism is misguided, however, because many of the parallels antedate even the tabernacle. Corroborative influence from contemporary structures is not thereby precluded, especially when it comes to details.

Other variations from the tabernacle include: the cherubim in the Holy of Holies facing out towards the nave instead of facing each other over the Mercy Seat; the addition of a porch or vestibule in front of the structure with the two freestanding (?) pillars, Jachin and Boaz, in front of that; the various side chambers around the other three sides, presumably for storage; the great "Bronze Sea" in the courtyard, etc. In spite of the great detail with which certain aspects of temple construction are narrated, the description (like that of the tabernacle) is often more impressionistic than a blueprint. Hence, grave problems abound on many details, which cannot be discussed here.

Critics also tend to exaggerate the largely pagan interpretation of the temple. There is a half-truth here, however, because much of its

symbolism (like most symbolism) was susceptible to various interpretations, and the Bible itself unblushingly reports how the rankest
paganism often did center in its precincts. Some argue that it was
originally only a private, royal chapel on the palace grounds with later
"democratization," but that flies in the face of the Biblical evidence.

As we stressed in connection with the tabernacle, temple typology is
both vertical (natural) and horizontal (historical), whereas pagan
counterparts were only vertical. The temple was indeed a miniature, a
reflection, a microcosm of the heavenly temple (ultimately the universe),
and what was done there was, as it were, also done in heaven. At the same
time, the uniquely Biblical accent is on the horizontal connection with
Heilsgeschichte: God temporarily and "incarnationally" takes up
residence with His elect people, as He guides them, together with all of
nature and history, to the temple not made with hands, the new
Jerusalem, yes, the "new heavens and a new earth in which righteousness
dwells" (2 Peter 3:13), which, under God, is the eschatological goal of all
of history. Both the vertical and horizontal typologies must be expounded
as ultimately Christological in substance.

This dual significance of the temple—and also potential for
paganization when the duality is forgotten—is also apparent in various
details. The import (and even the structure) of the free standing pillars in
front of the temple remains a mystery (cf. 1 Kings 7:15-22). Especially in
pagan context, they could represent the pillars upholding the earth—
which was also thought to be upheld by the magical rites of the shrine,
repeating and imitating the primeval creation (really, of course,
cosmogony and/or theogony). A more congenial explanation for at least
the "orthodox" segment of Jerusalem would understand them as huge
cressets for eternal flames, representing the now more permanent
presence of God in the same cloud and pillar of fire which had led them in
the wilderness. The significance of their names, "Jachin" and "Boaz" ("He
establishes" and "Strength," respectively?) is equally obscure, but they are
often thought to be the opening words of some dynastic formula, possibly
used at royal coronations (cf. 2 Kings 11:14). If so, the intimate
connection of kingship and temple would also be expressed by the pillars.

Similarly, with the huge molten Bronze Sea (1 Kings 7:23-26). The
twelve oxen facing the four points of the compass suggest cosmic (proto-
zodiacal?), fertility motifs. The sea itself suggests "Yam," the embodiment
of chaos and enemy of Baal in Canaanite mythology. The parallel
pericope in 2 Chron. 4:2 ff. suggests, however, that in normative, Israelite
understanding, the "sea" was demythologized into nothing more than an
ornate reservoir of water for the many ablutions in the ten lavers of the
temple. It surely had this function in any event, because adequate water

supply must always have been a major concern, especially during the rainless summer.

Much of the theological significance of the temple is given classical expression in Solomon's great prayer at its dedication or, better, consecration (1 Kings 8). It is couched in classical "deuteronomic" language and conceptuality; hence, according to the evolutionary canons of criticism, it cannot be in any sense literally Solomonic, but must be a "Thucydidean speech" or the like (literarily put in the mouth of the speaker, after the manner of the Greek historian). Obviously, however, if Deuteronomy is literally Mosaic, the difficulty evaporates.

One of the topics included in the prayer is the mystery of the omnipresent God's "real presence" in an earthly structure (1 Kings 8:12-13, 27 ff.). It once was often argued that until the deuteronomic "name" theology was developed some two centuries later, Israel would have been too primitive for so exalted a paradox. To a large extent, history-of-religions research has now shown that not even paganism was that naive, and long before Solomon. Possibly there were simpletons then, as there may be today, who thought in crasser terms. Today, certainly, the infinitely greater problem is a spiritualistic nominalism that has no antennae for Biblical realism.

In Old Testament theology, as in the piety and religion of Israel viewed more historically, the importance of the temple can scarcely be exaggerated. It overlaps to a large extent with theologies (and typologies) of the holy city (Jerusalem-Zion) and of the holy land. In fact, a sort of picture of concentric circles is helpful: from His real presence in the Most Holy Place, God's holiness "radiates" outward into all the world; from there, as from His heavenly throne, He judges and rules all that is, and His conquest of the entire world looking toward the eschaton also follows that pattern. Christianity uses the same language to describe typologically the same procedure in the Incarnate One.

It is especially important to emphasize the intimate interconnection of the temple-Zion complex with Davidic-Messianic themes and types. For all practical purposes, David and the Messiah cannot be discussed apart from the temple and Zion, any more than Christ can be considered apart from His body, the church.

One curious fact is that, for all its supreme theological importance, the temple texts in Kings itself are almost exclusively statistical. Nor is there any direct command from God to Solomon to construct the temple. In the broader context in Kings, this is surely without significance. But it apparently bothered someone in the Qumran community. The "Temple Scroll" sets out to remedy the problem by "writing up" the story "properly," even by writing it in a hand normally preserved for canonical literature.

1 Kings 11 signals the beginning of the end of the David-Solomonic empire as a result of Solomon's increasing apostasy. Rezon cultivates old grudges in Damascus (11:23-25), indicating the resurgence of the Aramean states, which would bedevil the Northern Kingdom throughout its history. David's other two adversaries, Jeroboam and Hadad the Edomite, are given asylum and obviously encouraged by Egypt (vs. 14-22 and 26-40). The Pharaoh involved is probably the same Shishak who invaded both North and South after the schism. It signals both the revival of the great powers in general after long dormancy, and specifically the beginning of Egypt's meddling pretensions which continue in one form or the other down to the time of Christ.

It is no accident that Jeroboam had been in charge of forced labor (v. 28) before his disaffection and flight to Egypt. Nor, probably, is it accidental, that the prophet Ahijah, who encouraged him by a dramatic "symbolism" and prophecy (that is, both action and verbal prophecy), hailed from Shiloh. Ahijah probably represented the old, conservative northern religious order; that order found it even harder than did the loyal circles in the South to stomach Solomon's innovations.

It is to be noted that Ahijah's prophecy with respect to Jeroboam does not imply endorsement of all his policies. It is no contradiction when other Yahwistic spokesmen condemn him and his policies. (Cf. similarly with Hazael, Jehu, etc.) In addition to this alleged "contradiction," critics often fault the writer of "Kings" for his mechanical or "legalistic" construction of what the prophets had actually intended as only *possibilities!*

1 Kings 12—22

When Rehoboam journeys to Shechem to be crowned king of Israel as well as of Judah (1 Kings 12), we are not surprised that the Northern grievances turn on the hated *corvee* or forced labor. Rehoboam not only rudely rebuffs them but pours salt in the wounds by dispatching Adoram to enforce it. Adoram pays for it with his life (v. 18), and only Shemaiah the prophet dissuades Rehoboam from further armed misadventure (vs. 21-24). The disruption is permanent (c. 922 or 931).

It was not until the reign of Omri about a half-century later that the northern capital became fixed in Samaria (1 Kings 16:24), which thereafter is often used by synecdoche of the entire country (as also Ephraim, its largest tribe, often is). Jeroboam first situated the capital in the ancient religious center of Shechem, and possibly even for a time across the Jordan in Penuel (12:25), but about 900 it was apparently moved to Tirzah (15:21, 33).

No such indecision attends Jeroboam's religious measures in establishing a countercult to Jerusalem at Dan and Bethel (1 Kings 12:26 ff.) There are no grounds for suspecting with some critics that Jeroboam preserved a more authentic version of early Yahwistic religion than Jerusalem, but the liturgical refrain of v. 28 clearly indicates that he presented himself as "orthodox" and traditional enough (like most heretics). Ex. 32 may well reflect its *claim* to have been founded by Aaron, and, as we noted, Judges 18:30 indicates that the priesthood of Dan claimed to be descended from Moses. It is, however, possible that Jeroboam did not intend the calves as simple idols, but only as steeds or pedestals for the invisible Yahweh (comparable to the cherubim in Jerusalem). But, if so, the Canaanite use of calves or bulls as fertility symbols, soon took precedence. Jeroboam's retention of the ancient covenant name "Israel" probably also indicates his attempts to attach to tradition. To the eternal confusion of Bible students, it is henceforth used both of a political unit (the ten northern tribes) as well as of all the people of God, whatever their location—as by extension also of Christians.

The prophet's specification of Josiah as the one who would demolish the altar at Bethel (1 Kings 13:2) some three centuries later is noteworthy as perhaps the only prophecy of its type, besides Isaiah's prophecies of Cyrus, which is so explicit. Critics usually dismiss the entire narrative as "midrash" (edifying fiction on a historical theme).

1 Kings 14:25 ff. records Shishak's invasion and plunder of Jerusalem. His own inscriptions make plain that he did not stop with Judah, but also raided the territory of his former protege, Jeroboam, who presumably now showed a mind of his own.

War erupts between Judah and Israel under Asa and Baasha (1 Kings 15:16 ff.). The latter, commanding the greater resources, would have prevailed, had Asa not bribed Benhadad of Damascus to intervene. A tragic precedent was thus established, and the triangle pattern continues in one form or another as long as the kingdoms last.

The chaos ensuing after Baasha's death is finally checked by Omri, one of Israel's ablest kings, who not only built Samaria as its capital, but also brought it to the height of its power and influence. But we know this primarily from Assyrian sources that refer to Israel as *Bit Humri* (House of Omri) even long after Omri's dynasty. The Bible dismisses Omri with relatively few words, as only one of the more evil of the Israelite kings (16:23 ff.). It is often cited as a parade example of the almost exclusively religious concerns of the Biblical historian, who is characteristically silent on the political importance of kings, often praising highly those who were politically not so successful (e.g., Hezekiah and Josiah), while panning those like Omri and Ahab whom the secular historian would rate very highly. We also know from Assyrian records that the beginning of Assyria's empire period pretty well coincides with the rise of Omri. Omri's son, Ahab, in 853 at the battle of Qarqar is even the major contributor to a coalition which temporarily halts an Assyrian advance.

The Biblical writer, in contrast, beginning with 1 Kings 17 turns his attention to Elijah, the advance guard of the great prophetic movement which a century later would also bequeath us many literary products. Not only is this major prophetic figure a northerner, but he also hails from Tishbe in Gilead across the Jordan, more isolated from the syncretism and internationalism of the centers of power. Elijah's major target is Ahab (c. 869—850), and even more so, his Tyrian wife, Jezebel, who as a fanatical devotee of Melqart, the Tyrian Baal, symbolized all that Elijah opposed.

Nowhere is the infinite gulf between the two worlds of Israel and Canaan, Yahweh and Baal, better illustrated than in the famous story of Naboth's vineyard (1 Kings 21). Two fundamentally different conceptions of kingship are illustrated: the absolutist, "god-man" concept of paganism self-evident to Jezebel, versus the elected, but responsible, incorporation of the promises of God championed by Elijah (and obviously not unknown to Ahab). Also different concepts of "land" are exhibited: in this case not so much between Yahwism and Baalism as between the sacral views of antiquity and modern secularism. Yahweh was the real owner of all land, and it was only "rented out to His elect people"; conversely, real estate was part of the covenant relationship, of the "inheritance," the "blessings," of the "promise" (cf. above).

Elijah's flight to Sinai after the dramatic contest on Mt. Carmel (1 Kings 18—19) is often thought by critics to conceal a tradition of pilgrimage to the holy mountain or an etiology of how an old pagan shrine came to be replaced by a Yahwistic one. The former is not entirely impossible, but is, at best, beside the point of the narrative as it stands.

Many other fancies have clustered about Yahweh's dialog with Elijah at the mountain, especially the "still small voice" (19:12). ("The sound of a thin/gentle silence" is a better translation, evidently implying on the surface something like "a silence so deep you could hear it.") Liberal, neo-Kantian Protestants have long been inclined to read into it the instruction of "conscience" as the organ and arbiter of revelation, and an implied rebuke of Elijah's violent measures at Carmel. Allegedly, this was the great insight of "prophetic religion" over against the externalism and particularism of "priestly religion." This interpretation was enforced by evident linguistic echoes of the "tent of meeting" pericope in Ex. 33, which is usually interpreted as a "prophetic" contrast to the complicated, priestly tabernacle-religion in the surrounding chapters. (Indeed, it is not unlikely that the "cave" of 1 Kings 19:9 is identical with the "cleft of the rock" of Ex. 33:22, where Yahweh appeared to Moses.)

Possibly the major argument against that interpretation is the fact that only three verses later (1 Kings 19:15 ff.) Elijah is ordered to instigate the revolts of Hazael and Jehu in Syria and Israel, respectively (as well as to anoint Elisha as his successor). Part of the import of the "still small voice" appears to be God's internal buoying of Elijah's courage, as an answer to Elijah's implied criticism. Somewhat like Jesus' parables of the leaven and the mustard seed, the progress of the kingdom cannot be measured by external criteria. The point is not that God is *never* "in" natural phenomena, but, as independent Creator, He is not mechanically linked to them after the fashion of paganism.

The great historical and theological significance of Elijah must be underscored. To no little extent he can be characterized as embodying the very spirit of prophecy—a veritable "Mr. Prophecy." Much as Samuel had some two centuries earlier, he sparks a major revival of genuine Yahwism at a time when the fires were burning very low—and one which would continue and grow into the great prophetic movement, beginning with Amos, a century later.

Especially noteworthy is the way Elijah is implicitly presented as a "second Moses," personifying the "back to Moses" character of the entire prophetic revival. (The most striking expression of the parallelism, of course, is Yahweh's theophany to him on Mt. Sinai, probably at the very spot where He had allowed Moses to see only His back.) Thus, as "Mr. Prophecy," Elijah personifies Messianic expectation (Mal. 4:5, and the gospels), and, together with Moses, he witnesses to the fulfillment and antitype of both on the Mount of Transfiguration (Matt. 17; etc.).

1 Kings 20 and 22 are concerned with Ahab's battles with Damascus, at one of which (on a favorite battlefield, Ramothgilead) Ahab loses his life in fulfillment of prophecy. Chap. 22 is of unusual value for understanding prophecy. When Ahab is trying to convince the reluctant Jehoshaphat of Judah to join him in battle against Syria, Ahab's "kept prophets" dutifully prophesy what he wanted to hear (certain victory). The one prophet, Micaiah ben Imlah, who might counsel otherwise, Ahab is not eager to hear (vs. 7 ff.). At first, Micaiah, too, mockingly forecasts success, but eventually predicts not only defeat, but Ahab's death. Most revealing of prophetic self-understanding is Micaiah's articulation of his vision in terms of Yahweh's heavenly throne-room, to which the prophets are given access, and the decisions of which they must herald (esp. v. 19). (Cf. further on prophetism below.)

Jehoshaphat's deference to Ahab in the above pericope is often understood to imply that Judah virtually became a dependency of Israel under the able and powerful Omrides. There is no indication, however, that any such relationship was not entered into voluntarily—even if, perhaps, mistakenly. Future events certainly did prove it a mistake for Jehoshaphat to allow his son Jehoram to marry Ahab's daughter, Athaliah. We learn much more of Jehoshaphat's internal policies from 2 Chron. 17—20. Among his major accomplishments was a reform of the Judahite judiciary.

2 Kings 1—17

2 Kings moves quickly into the ministry of Elisha (the stories of which do not always appear in strict chronological order). Critics have been quick to note that the "Elisha cycle" highlights the miraculous element far more than the Elijah narratives (e.g., the poisoned pottage, 4:38-41; the floating axe head, 6:1-7; even the vivifying power of Elisha's bones when a corpse accidently touches them, 13:20-21). Furthermore, at least at first reading, much of the theological profundity of the Elijah narratives appears to be missing. The critical explanation is that these "legends" took shape in more popular circles, which described their hero more as a shaman or village medicine man than as a theological leader. Comparisons with medieval hagiography are also often attempted. Far more to the point is the parallelism between many of Elisha's and Jesus' miracles: raising the dead, multiplying food, controlling nature, etc. In both cases miracles cluster about signal interventions of Yahweh in the life of His people.

Elisha's involvement in a campaign against Moab (2 Kings 3) is instructive of prophetic methods, especially the use of a minstrel (vs. 15 ff.). As so often the uniqueness in comparison with pagan practices is not external, but only in theological context. Mesha, king of Moab, here is the same one who boasts, apparently a little later than our narrative, on the famous "Mesha Stone," one of the earliest great archaeological finds, of his victories over Israel. In this narrative, Mesha apparently is satisfied to repulse Israel's attack; apparently, at least, that is the meaning of the "great wrath" that comes upon Israel after his desperate act of sacrificing his own son (3:27).

Nowhere is prophetic involvement in politics, even of foreign nations (remember that Israel was a church-state, as Christianity is not) clearer than in Elisha's role in fomenting the revolts of Hazael and Jehu (continuing Elijah's charge). We have few particulars about Hazael's coming to power, but Jehu's is a veritable bloodbath (2 Kings 9—10). Above all, with one fell swoop, he is able to liquidate both Joram of Israel (son of Ahab) and Ahaziah of Judah (Joram's nephew through his sister Athaliah); see 8:25-29. After the gory murder of Jezebel in fulfillment of Elijah's prophecy (9:30-37) and the treacherous massacre of Ahab's 70 other sons, the Omride dynasty had been exterminated and the slate wiped clean. As Hosea's prophecy makes plain later on (Hosea 1:4-5), God made use of Jehu's savagery but did not condone it or leave it unrequited.

No doubt, Jehu's revolt does represent a victory of the Yahwistic over the Baalistic prophets in the North (cf. 2 Kings 10:18 ff.) and revival of Yahwism, at least after a fashion. Its conservative tenor is underscored by the commendation given the revolt even by the Rechabites (a sort of Amish-like movement in Yahwism, reactionary socially as well as religiously; cf. Jer. 35).

If it was a plus religiously, there is no doubt that Jehu's victory was a minus politically, however. It is doubtful if Israel ever again had the power that she wielded under the Omrides (not even half a century later under Jeroboam II, when the Assyrians were temporarily weak). 2 Kings 10 closes with a notice of Damascus' increasing encroachments on Israelite territory. And on the famous "Black Obelisk" of archaeological discovery, we see Jehu prostrate before the same Shalmaneser III of Assyria, whom Ahab had once stopped in his tracks at Qarqar (a step taken by Jehu in part probably to halt Hazael's depradations).

In 2 Kings 11 ff., almost for the first time since the Disruption, the Biblical historian begins to devote major attention to affairs in Judah. Athaliah, a true daughter of her mother, Jezebel, seeing that her son, Ahaziah, has also been slaughtered by Jehu, attempts to extirpate the whole Judahite royal family and usurp all power by herself. Only the infant Joash is rescued and secretly cared for by his nurse. In his seventh year Athaliah's assassination in a revolt led by Jehoiada the priest brings Joash to power, leading to a Yahwistic reformation also in Judah (including a restoration of the temple financed by private contributions). The Book of Kings fails to mention it, but in 2 Chron. 24 we learn that in his later years, Joash, like Solomon, relapsed and even executed Zechariah, the son of Jehoiada, his benefactor, for reproving him. Christ refers to Zechariah's innocent blood as still seeking requital (Matt. 23:35 = Luke 11:51).

Israel turns the tables on Syria under Jehoash (or Joash, one of several times the kings of Israel and Judah confusingly bear the same names). Amaziah of Judah apparently does not get the message, because he foolhardily launches an invasion of the North, in spite of Jehoash's attempt to dissuade him through a fable (very redolent of the one Jotham told Abimelech in Judges 9). Amaziah is not only trounced but eventually loses his life in a revolt, apparently by his disgruntled subjects.

Jeroboam II (786—746; 2 Kings 14:23 ff.) is able to take advantage of both Aramean and Assyrian weakness and regain much of the territory to the North that David had once controlled. His contemporary Uzziah (Azariah) is able to do the same to the Southeast, so that, between them, one may almost speak of a neo-Davidic empire. Sometimes the halcyon period is referred to as Israel's "Indian summer." The respite is brief, and when the Assyrian lion stirs again, Israel's days are strictly numbered.

With Jeroboam II we also enter in the period contemporary with the great literary prophets. Jonah is mentioned in 2 Kings 14:25, but only his prediction of Jeroboam's successes. Amos, who was far more critical, must have been active later in Jeroboam's reign but is not mentioned here at all.

In fact, Jonah's mention is very much the exception, even though writing prophets come fast and furious hereafter. It is one of those curiosities for which we have no good explanation, that, although both Kings and Chronicles mention scores of prophets, the great literary figures virtually never appear on their pages!

The Biblical historian moves rapidly over the chaotic final quarter-century of Israel's existence after Jeroboam's death, as Assyria relentlessly tightens the screws. Judah is inevitably threatened too, but by accepting vassalage manages to stave off destruction for nearly a century and a half. Ahaz of Judah's overtures to Assyria for "protection" from Rezin of Syria and Pekah of Israel, which Isaiah (chap. 7) opposed so strenuously, is mentioned here in only a few verses (2 Kings 16:5-9). The religious syncretism which ensued is not slighted, however (vs. 10 ff.).

2 Kings 17 brings us to the end of the Northern Kingdom, after one too many flirtations with Egypt's vain promises. Just as would be true later of Judah, Israel's final years were wracked by conflict between pro-Egyptian and anti-Egyptian factions. The chapter describes the application to Israel of the ruthless Assyrian imperial policy of shuffling populations to break further resistance, and the subsequent rise of the Samaritans. (It is widely doubted by critics that the sect's history began this early.) Primarily, though, the "deuteronomist" seizes the occasion for a religious meditation on the theological principles illustrated in the catastrophe.

2 Kings 18—25

All along, the writer had kept reminding us that God had spared Judah because of his promise to David. Now only Judah is left. Ahaz had been subservient, both politically and religiously, but with Hezekiah it is different. Critics are commonly skeptical of the account of Hezekiah's reformation, but there are no real grounds for that skepticism. From Assyrian records, we know that Hezekiah also headed a local anti-Assyrian coalition, which Sennacherib could not let go unchallenged for long. But, for once, Assyria did not have her way. Whether the "angel of the LORD" in 2 Kings 19:35 implies strictly miraculous intervention, or in this instance is simply a theologoumenon for a more "natural" debacle (Herodotus may suggest an epidemic of the plague in the Assyrian army) has long been debated, also by conservatives.

Also interesting is the role which the Aramaic language plays (2 Kings 18:26 ff.). It has not yet displaced Hebrew, as it would all but do after the Exile, but plainly Jerusalem's leaders already understand fully this *lingua franca* of the Assyrian (and Babylonian and Persian) empires.

A major historical and literary question arises about the relation of the material on either side of 2 Kings 19:8-9, which we can only broach here. Were there *two* campaigns by Sennacherib against Jerusalem (so Albright, Bright, etc.), or did the "Rabshakeh" (a title, not a name) make two visits to Jerusalem on the same campaign? As the Biblical narrative stands, the latter must be the case. However, there are enough difficulties with that view, that it is possible that our *text* is in disorder, although with present evidence that cannot be demonstrated. (Literary critics often solve the problem by positing at least two conflicting versions of the same campaign.)

Isaiah plays a prominent role in 2 Kings 18:13—20:19 too. That is the major exception to the little mention of the literary prophets in the Biblical histories on which we commented above. But there is more that is unusual about this section: it is one of the undeniable "doublets" in the Bible. For the most part, except for minor exceptions, it is identical with Is. 36—39. The only major exception is that the "Song of Hezekiah" (the *"Ego Dixi"* canticle; Is. 38:10-20) is not included in 2 Kings. Isaiah's highly poetic taunt-song against Assyria, delivered in answer to Hezekiah's prayer, is, however, included in both versions (2 Kings 19:21-28 = Is. 37:22-29). It is really impossible even to guess what accounts for the parallelism, whether a common source lies behind both, or one was dependent on the other. Critics generally feel that it is more likely secondary in Isaiah. Certainly, as a long piece of historical narrative in the middle of a collection of oracles, it is more anomalous there.

We have little hard information on the religious dark age of Manasseh (2 Kings 21:1-18). The Chronicler reports (2 Chron. 33:11 ff.) that at one time he was imprisoned in Babylon (because of a revolt?), but after a prayer of repentance he was allowed to return. If any genuine repentance was involved, it must have been very fleeting, and Kings certainly knows nothing of it. It is usually presumed that Yahwistic prophecy simply went underground during this period. It may well be that some Biblical literature, especially the oracles of the earlier prophets, was collected and put in present shape during this period, but scarcely to the degree required by critical speculations.

Shortly after Josiah came to power (2 Kings 22:1—23:30), Assyria collapsed and disappeared precipitously. Josiah plainly had hopes even to annex the lost territories of Israel to the North and to rule over another united empire. In defending that dream, however, he lost his life at the Megiddo pass in 609 while trying to prevent Pharaoh Necho from consolidating his power as he marched north to meet Nebuchadnezzar coming from the other direction to fill the Assyrian vacuum.

The Bible, of course, is far more interested in Josiah's famous religious reformation than in his political assertions. We cannot help but wonder why it is Huldah, rather than Jeremiah, who is called to authenticate the "book of the law" found while repairing the temple. The reaction and the measures taken make it not at all unlikely that the find was Deuteronomy (or even the entire Pentateuch with its Deuteronomic conclusion). As we have noted, however, critics commonly make this find the axis of their entire evolutionistic reconstruction of the history of Israel's religion and of Biblical literature.

With Josiah's death, his reformation collapsed too, to be followed by Jehoiakim's malevolence of which we hear so much in Jeremiah. His rebellion after three years' reign (c. 605) is evidently related to Nebuchadnezzar's definitive defeat of Pharaoh Necho at Carchemish in 605, when the brief Egyptian hegemony of Palestine was replaced by Babylonian power. At least a token deportation of Jerusalemites seems to have ensued, including probably the prophet Daniel.

A few years later Jehoiakim apparently listened to the blandishments of Egypt again, bringing swift retaliation from Nebuchadnezzar. Jehoiakim is dead before he arrives, however, whether from natural causes or a local insurrection we do not know. His young son, Jehoiachin, is left to bear the brunt of Nebuchadnezzar's wrath; the latter carries Jehoiachin into Exile together with others, including the prophet Ezekiel.

We know for sure from Babylonian records that the conquerors still considered Jehoiachin as the legitimate king of Judah. Left in charge of Jerusalem as the Babylonian puppet is the hapless Zedekiah, Jehoiachin's uncle (Josiah's youngest son). A more pitiable figure scarcely appears on the pages of the Bible. Finally assenting to still another revolt against Babylon, the pathetic Zedekiah is captured in flight, and forced to watch the execution of his sons before being blinded and carried away in chains. Jerusalem is razed to the ground in 587/6 B.C., almost certainly in August.

Gedaliah is appointed governor of the now Babylonian province, only soon to be assassinated by the fanatical Ishmael, who then flees to Ammon, whose king, Baalis, had instigated that action. Babylonian records indicate that this was part of still another substantial rebellion, necessitating still another Babylonian campaign about 582.

The Book of Kings is entirely silent on Jeremiah's role in all of this fateful history, although 24:18—25:30 is essentially identical with the final chapter of Jeremiah, where it appears almost as an appendix. The literary question is thus very similar to that of Is. 36—39 vs. 2 Kings 18—20, except that Jeremiah himself is nowhere named in the pericope. We know, of course (Jer. 39 ff.) that Jeremiah elected to remain in Jerusalem after 587 but was forced to join Ishmael in his flight to Egypt, where we soon lose sight of him.

2 Kings (25:27-30), and possibly the entire "deuteronomic history," closes on the upbeat notice that after Nebuchadnezzar's death, his successor, Evil-merodach ("A devotee of Marduk") elevated King Jehoiachin from ordinary detention to a sort of preferential house arrest (c. 562). In the light of the book's constant accent on God's mercy to Judah on account of His promises to David, it can only be read as saying that the Messianic promise has by no means been abandoned by the necessary judgment His people are presently experiencing.

Date and Authorship

Isagogically, the situation of Kings is very similar again to that of the other "Former Prophets." The Talmud attributes the book to Jeremiah. In the light of the history we have just reviewed, it will be evident that this is by no means impossible, except possibly for the closing verses. Its likelihood is enhanced by the strongly "deuteronomic" diction of much of the prose of the Book of Jeremiah. If we do finally judge it to be another of tradition's overly neat simplifications, it remains undeniable that the author(s) must have belonged to circles of very much the same mind as Jeremiah.

When that was cannot be exactly determined either. The notice of Jehoiachin's release gives us a *terminus a quo* of c. 562, while the total absence of any allusion to the fall of Babylon in 539 or the other momentous events under Cyrus seems to give us a *terminus ad quem* too. If so, the completion of not only Kings, but possibly of the entire "deuteronomic history" may be dated to within those two decades. The majority critical view probably favors the location of this work in Canaan, among the survivors of the debacle rather than in Babylon among the exiles, but there are no real grounds for deciding between the two views.

There are some other passages in Kings, however, which can be read as stemming from a date earlier than the fall of Jerusalem (1 Kings 8:8; 11:36; 2 Kings 8:19) or even than the death of Josiah (2 Kings 22:20). As a result, most critics assume a double "deuteronomic redaction," with a first edition of the book appearing in connection with the Josianic reformation. (Noth is a major exception, but many do follow Noth in supposing that the first four chapters of Deuteronomy were added to that book when it was incorporated into the entire historical work.) The many critical overtones of that assumption are to be rejected, of course, but, in proper context, it is not impossible.

Sources

The author of Kings himself mentions many of his sources, and there is no reason why, with the critics, many others should not be hypothesized. In the first part of the book, "the Book of the Acts of Solomon" is referred to in 1 Kings 11:41, and thereafter we have repeated mention of "the Book of the Chronicles of the Kings of Israel" (17 times) and "the Book of the Chronicles of the Kings of Judah" (15 times). The Hebrew phrase translated "Chronicles" is the same as the title of the canonical book, but it is usually assumed that more official archives and annals are implied here than the material found in the heavily theological Biblical book by that name. By those references, the author reminds his readers that he is not interested in any exhaustive history or biography, but only in what serves his theological purposes. If the reader is interested in more details, he is, in effect, advised to "go look it up in the library." (Would to God they were available to us as they were to the original readers.)

Besides the sources explicitly cited in the Hebrew text of Kings, the Septuagint attributes Solomon's great prayer at the consecration of the temple (1 Kings 8) to a "Book of the Song" (and, if so, some critics are magnanimously willing to concede some historical substance in the "deuteronomist's" record of the prayer, possibly limited to vs. 12-13). Some opine that this is really the same "Book of Jashar" that is cited elsewhere (Joshua 10 and 2 Sam. 1), since a Hebrew *yodh* could easily have fallen out (*yashar* becoming *shir*).

It is not unlikely on its face that temple archives were available for the book's description of that edifice. Likewise with the possibility of earlier cycles or clusters of prophetic traditions about Elijah and Elisha (although not with the usual critical presuppositions). We have already discussed the puzzle of the relation of 2 Kings 18:13 ff. to Is. 36 ff. and of 2 Kings 24:18 ff. to Jer. 52.

Whatever the number or nature of the sources, the "deuteronomic" hand is very much in evidence throughout Kings, and in a manner very similar to Judges. It shows itself in the overall framework, as well as in theological interpretation and commentary. The latter appears both in

short comments, such as those calling attention to the power and
fulfillment of the prophetic Word, as well as longer sections (e. g., the
concluding meditations on the fall of Israel in 2 Kings 17 and of Judah in
chap. 21).

Framework

The "framework" of Kings, as that of Judges, combines chronology
with religious judgments. However, whereas the material within the
framework of Judges consisted of more disconnected episodes, the
histories of the two kingdoms in most of Kings constitute parallel and
continuous records. The two histories are integrated by the scheme of
narrating the reign of one king to its conclusion, and then describing the
reigns of all the kings who came to the throne in the other kingdom
during that same period. To one who is basically familiar already with the
history (as the original audience surely was), the scheme is simple and
effective.

An invariable pattern, with only very minor modifications, is
consistently used to describe the kings of Judah: (1) "In the —th year of N,
the king of Israel, began N, the son of N, the king of Judah to reign" (that is,
a synchronism of the king's accession with the regnal year of the
contemporary king of Israel); (2) "He was—years old when he began to
reign"; (3) "and he reigned—years in Jerusalem"; (4) "and his mother's
name was N"; (5) The history of his reign, varying considerably in length
and character, (6) The "deuteronomic" verdict on the religious quality of
his reign (cf. below); (7) (the beginning of the conclusion) "and the rest of
his acts, and all that he did, are they not written in the book of the
chronicles of the kings of Judah?"; (8) "So he slept with his fathers, and they
buried him with his fathers in the city of David"; and (9) "and N, his son,
reigned in his stead."

The framework to the histories of the kings of Israel is slightly shorter:
we are told neither the names of their mothers nor their age at accession,
and in the conclusion the phrase, "was buried with his fathers," is never
used. The abbreviation in itself undoubtedly constitutes an implicit
censure of the northern kings.

In both forms of the framework, however, very explicit religious
judgments are made on the reigns of each king, and these differ drastically
in the two kingdoms. The standard obviously is that of Deuteronomy—or
of the "law of Moses" generally. The major concern is about the sole
legitimacy of the Jerusalem cult, but even more basically the sole deity of
Yahweh (vs. any and all idolatry). No doubt, this was the *articulus stantis
et cadentis ecclesiae* in terms of the writer's subject.

Thus, not all deviations are placed in the same category. The kings of
Judah who champion true Yahwism at Jerusalem, but tolerate worship at

high places (outlying shrines, some of which were probably at times relatively Yahwistic themselves) are only slightly censured. Those who openly encourage or patronize paganism receive no commendations whatsoever, of course. Of all the kings of Judah, only Hezekiah and Josiah receive unconditional praise, and five others receive conditional approbation.

By this same criterion, *all* the kings of Israel are said to have done evil (except for Shallum, who reigned only a month), even when, as in the case of Jehu, power came on the coattails of a Yahwistic revival. The recurrent refrain is that "they did not depart from the sins of Jeroboam the son of Nebat with which he made Israel to sin."

Chronology

One of the most vexing problems in Biblical study is the chronology of the framework of Kings. The situation is not dissimilar to that in Judges, but probably even more difficult of definitive solution. In the case of Judges, we thought of the use of symbolic numbers and/or of a theological schematism as likely possibilities. Those same factors may be involved in the case of Kings, but the main solutions are not usually sought along those lines.

The framework uses a double system of dates (nothing like our modern systems was apparently in use anywhere). It gives both *absolute* dates of the total regnal years of each monarch, and *synchronisms* in terms of the regnal year of the king of one kingdom at the time of the accession of a new king in the other (the latter only between the Disruption and the fall of Samaria, of course).

The problem consists in the serious discrepancies between the totals of the two systems. Jehu's simultaneous slaughter of the kings of both Israel and Judah provides a handy midpoint for calculations. Between that event in 842 and the Disruption about 931—922 (there is this much variation in the date in systems commonly in use) we have a total of roughly 80—90 years in both kingdoms. Instead, the Biblical sums are 95—98 for Judah and Israel respectively. Similarly, between 842 and the fall of Samaria in 722 we should have a total of 120 years in contrast to the Biblical figures of 172 and 143 for Judah and Israel.

There is no commonly agreed upon solution to the problem at all. Wellhausen and earlier scholars tended simply to reject the synchronisms as later and purely artificial systematizations. Knowledge now of even earlier Assyrian and Babylonian synchronisms of a similar sort has made that stance difficult to maintain.

German critics (Begrich, *et al.*) still tend to favor a largely literary solution, however, thinking of a combination and confusion of a number of independent chronological systems by the deuteronomic compilers. American scholars especially tend to trust the text more and to seek solutions more on the basis of archaeologically based data.

We have space here only to mention some of the major factors apparently involved. Possible copyists' slips must surely head the list, and the varying figures we sometimes encounter in Chronicles, the Septuagint, and Josephus indicate that it is more than a possibility. We know that sometimes scribes, when confronted with conflicting figures in different manuscripts were wont to choose the higher of the two figures—or even to add the two numbers together! Sometimes round numbers were also substituted, although these can be original.

Second, the possibility of coregencies (overlapping reigns) and of interregna (gaps between reigns) must be considered. The latter seems a possibility especially in the case of revolutions or other disorders. One coregency of which we know for sure is that of Jotham, who became regent before the death of his father, Uzziah, because of the latter's leprosy. Coregencies seem to have been more common in Judah than in Israel.

Third, there is the question of the use of different calendars at different times and places, although that issue is rife with uncertainties itself. (That all of them were *lunar* calendars is not in debate.) The major issue is whether New Year began in the spring (Nisan, as it is called on the current Jewish calendar) or in autumn (Tishri). It is often argued that in Judah the year was counted from the first of Tishri (= September-October), while Jeroboam introduced into Israel the ancient Mesopotamian tradition of commencing the year with Nisan (March-April). The custom may have changed in each nation however, and, in addition, one may have to reckon with a liturgical calendar distinct from the civic one.

Fourth, there is the question of when a king's "first year" began to be reckoned. This problem overlaps with the previous ones because of the importance of the New Year in ancient Near Eastern religious thought— and, of course, kingship was sacral or "divine" too. The period of time between a king's technical accession and the following New Year's observance when he was formally crowned is known as the "accession year." The question is whether that interval shall be counted as year one of the new king's reign, or whether the counting begins first with the following new year. If the "accession year" is counted, there is the possibility that the other part of the year had also been included as the final year of his predecessor's rule. In that case, one year would have to be subtracted in dead reckoning. If the counting began at new year, however, we have no problem at this point.

We know that both systems were in common use in the ancient Near

East. Mesopotamia generally used the "accession year" system, or "postdating," as it is called, in which part of a year or the "accession year" of a new king is *not* counted, but calculations wait until New Year's. On the other hand, in Egypt, the "non-accession" year system or "antedating" was in vogue, which means that we must subtract one year per pharaoh in our calculations.

Which system was employed in Judah and Israel, and when in each? There is no unanimity in answering. One theory has antedating as the usual practice in both Israel and Judah (reflecting Egyptian influence at least from Solomonic normalizations), with postdating beginning in Judah only after the reign of Hezekiah, when Mesopotamian influence dominated. Others argue that Judah usually employed postdating and Israel antedating, but each with occasional shifts to the opposite method.

We can only summarize by saying that, especially in America, two major solutions are usually employed: (1) the more "conservative" one of Thiele, which assumes a phenomenally accurate Hebrew text, and a complicated, but consistent, system of coregencies and shifts in calendric systems and methods of computation in the two kingdoms; (2) that of Albright, who assumes few changes in systems until postdating began under Manasseh, but who is forced to assume many textual errors when things do not otherwise work out.

When it comes to *absolute* chronology, our major anchor, of course, is the Assyrian king lists, with occasional reference to eclipses or the like, which can be astronomically determined. When there are synchronisms of Mesopotamian and Biblical events, we can often, then, determine the Biblical date very accurately. Hence, for many events in the period of the monarchy, scholarly computations often differ by only a year or less (often depending on when New Year's is believed to have been observed). A major pivot is Jehu's accession in 842/1, with calculations forward and backward.

Text

Finally, we have more than normal textual problems with Kings. Again the problem is more like Judges than Samuel: the issues do not immediately arise so much out of corruptions in the transmission of the Hebrew text, as from Septuagintal variations from it—and variations within Septuagintal traditions themselves, all of which may be based on Hebrew prototypes. (There are also variations at times in parallel passages in Chronicles—and, among other things, some version of Kings may well have been among its sources.)

Sometimes the LXX text is shorter, at other times it contains material not in MT. Two of the additions are noteworthy. After 1 Kings 2:35 and 2:46 in the Septuagint we encounter the "Miscellanies," which do not correspond at all with MT at this point. As the name indicates, it is a heterogeneous collection of data especially about Solomon's reign, and its insertion here strongly suggests that at some stage of Greek transmission, the book of "Kingdoms" was divided at this point. A longer addition appears after 1 Kings 12:24, containing various traditions about the life and career of Jeroboam I. Some scholars argue that it represents a second and different recension of the story of the Disruption, but that is unlikely. Some of these additions appear elsewhere in MT, dispersed throughout 1 Kings 2—11.

Finally, of course, the recent theories of Frank Cross must be taken into account, who argues that in Kings, as elsewhere, the "Vaticanus" and "Lucianic" traditions of the Septuagint are not independent translations of different Hebrew texts but represent rather successive revisions of the Septuagint to bring it into conformity with the Hebrew tradition represented by MT. For details see the commentaries and periodical literature.

The Latter Prophets

As we noted above, the Hebrew canon reckons four of these, matching the four "former prophets" (many of our historical books). Four can be counted because Daniel is not included (but classified among the "Writings," the third part of the canon) and because the "Twelve" (what we know as the "minor prophets") are considered one. Thus, with the exception of Daniel, "latter prophets" corresponds to what are usually simply referred to as the "prophets" or prophetical books.

GENERAL INTRODUCTION TO THE PROPHETS

No one disputes the importance of the prophets. Precisely how and why they are important, however, will draw widely varying explanations. Perhaps it is true to say that Christianity rates them higher than Judaism, and that this is one of the historic differences between the two religions, but one must be cautious. In one sense, as we noted earlier, Judaism does accord the Pentateuch (Torah) a certain priority, and regards the prophets as only commentary on it (a view to which, as such, also the Christian can readily assent). However, the danger lurks that Christians prematurely hear such statements as implying Jewish "legalism" or disfavor toward the prophets. That would be as much of a misrepresentation as to assert that Christian regard for the prophets implies disregard for the Pentateuch.

But even within Christianity, expositions of the significance of the prophets will vary drastically. To a fair extent, the major differences will follow liberal-conservative lines. No doubt, much of the traditional Christian importance attached to the prophets arose from their interpretation as primarily predictors and heralds of Christ. Even in this respect, however (as an analysis of New Testament citations of the Old will readily demonstrate) prophecies and/or typologies are usually adduced with equal ease from virtually all the rest of the Old Testament.

Classical Critical Views

Almost simultaneously with the rise of liberalism and higher criticism came a radical change in the estimation of the prophets. They continued to be regarded every bit as highly—possibly even more highly. The prophets (or remnants of them, after criticism) virtually became a canon within the canon, the quintessence of Biblical religion. "Prophetic religion" became the precursor or model of *liberal* religion, as liberalism thus sought to authenticate itself Biblically.

The new synthesis had many dimensions, most of which still retain their influence, although usually in tempered form. The label "Wellhausenian" is once again handy for symbolizing its classical expression. Wellhausen himself, however, never concentrated in this area, leaving others, especially Duhm, to work out the applications of principles he had enunciated.

The first dimension is historical, because the prophets provide the pivot for the entire critical reconstruction of the history of Israel's religion. In "orthodox" critical thought it is no exaggeration to label the prophets the *originators* or inventors of Biblical religion. With Amos in the 8th century had allegedly first come the breakthrough into ethical monotheism, rising above more primitive notions of religion (ritualistic, legalistic—and worse).

The true prophets were allegedly nearly all antiliturgical, and preachers of judgment on those who failed to live righteously according to the newly evolved standards of morality. The prophetic books had to be—and were—edited according to such criteria, and it is only slight hyperbole to assert that, as a result, "prophets" was (and sometimes still is) in practice reduced to only *two* prophets, Amos and Jeremiah—and expurgated editions of those. (A check of the curricular offerings of most liberal theological seminaries will usually readily confirm this!)

Some of the insights of the early prophets were thought to have been refined and advanced as time went on, but all too often there were fatal relapses and compromises with priestly, "legalistic," and institutional forces. As we noted, the deuteronomistic movement usually gets major blame for first accomodating such regressive forces. The relapse worsened and hardened after the Exile as the hierocracy took over. At the same time, people succumbed to pie-in-the-sky, wishful thinking about divine intervention, and these optimistic oracles were added to the genuine prophetic material. All this eventually institutionalized in "Judaism" and its closed canon. Thus, as the "greatest of the prophets," Jesus' work was cut out for Him—only to have the regression repeat itself in Christianity. However, there were occasional heirs of the prophets to transcend the main drift, such as Luther—and the liberal heirs of the Enlightenment, the critics themselves.

The other major dimension is theological, or quasi-theological. The entire supernaturalist orientation implicit in the "Messianic prophecy" concentration was rejected on philosophical grounds, or drastically watered down. Rarely was it absolutely denied that predictive prophecy, Messianic or otherwise, *could* happen, but since it apparently never did (in the traditional sense, at least), that was the upshot nonetheless. Much of the prophecy of the Bible was regarded as *vaticinium ex/post eventu,* prophecy after the event, artificially placed in the mouths of earlier figures to express the theological conviction that whatever had happened must have been according to God's will. At most, the prophets were "inspired" to see what ineluctably *had* to happen sooner or later according to the moral principles allegedly implicit in the universe. What they originally expressed in terms of probabilities or very long range necessities were misunderstood or altered by later generations to imply literalistic, detailed prediction.

In what became a major slogan, the prophets were not "foretellers," but "forthtellers," that is, proclaimers or preachers primarily of social and moral reform. In other words, the focus shifted from that of supernaturalist prediction to naturalist commentary on current events, albeit of a moral and religious sort. The basic frame of reference was no longer so much theological as sociological, psychological, and political.

As a result, and at the heart of classical historical-critical research, an incredible amount of effort was devoted to the attempt to pinpoint the precise historical occasion on which virtually every syllable was spoken or written. It was this ideal which motivated what often appeared to be only atomism, as chapters and even verses were divided and subdivided and distributed among who knows how many prophets, disciples, editors, or redactors. By thus eliminating the "ungenuine" additions, the idea was to recreate as closely as possible exactly what the original stimulus to the prophetic Word was, so that the modern "prophet" could do his best to enter into the same situation, evaluate it and proceed according to his best lights.

As indicated already, the new "hermeneutical circle" envisioned as student and beneficiary of this new research, not the traditional preacher of supernaturalistic salvation through a Messiah now come but a prophetic ministry which would use the great Biblical figures as models of their own efforts toward a better life for all. The social Gospel and its political and social relevance and activism followed as a matter of course. The early liberals were too optimistic about human progress to find revolution very necessary, as some of their later heirs did, but the point of departure was not dissimilar.

"Prophetic," of course, to a large extent meant "Protestant." To be prophetic meant to subscribe to the "Protestant principle" that absolutely nothing but "God" was absolute, final, sacred; no institution, no dogma, not even the canon. It was to be a "spiritual" religion of inwardness, or, in radical caricature of a Reformation slogan, a religion of the "Word." And what did "spiritual" mean?

The not-so-hidden antitheses were not only Protestant Orthodoxy, but, even more ultimately, Catholicism and Judaism—all of them allegedly embodiments of "static" religious institutionalism. All of them, of course, suffered from supernaturalistic "biblicism." In addition, Catholicism represented priestly religion, authoritarian, sacramental, and sacerdotal, a veritable incarnation of all that prophets in all ages oppose. Surpassing all of them in legalism, perhaps, was Judaism, at least of the orthodox variety (and, sad to say, with that criticism very often a clear anti-Semitism as well, sometimes explicit in Lagarde, G. Kittel, and even Wellhausen on occasion, but more often subtle and probably often not even diagnosed).

Philosophical Bases

One must be aware of some of the philosophic underpinnings of this entire stance. Only in this way will the conservative reader not be taken for a simple sucker and assume that liberal criticism uses words and phrases with traditional meanings. "Ethical monotheism" is perhaps the chief example, but the entire vocabulary is involved. The philosophic situation is far too complex to survey in detail, but possibly brief attention to three key names will suffice: Kant, Hegel, and Schleiermacher. (Their influence is just as great elsewhere in Biblical studies, but it is especially evident and determinative in the case of the prophets—precisely because that was the major focus of critical Biblical study. Sometimes the vocabulary we shall use to describe them derives technically from their heirs, but the gist is the same, regardless of vocabulary.)

With Kant comes a definitive denial of any certain "revelation" in the traditional supernaturalist, propositional sense. Instead religious knowledge and certainty is allegedly possible only on the basis of individual, subjective "encounter" with the numinous and of the constructs of his own mind, as it attempts to order and classify its sensations. In a word: "conscience" and the entire liberal, Protestant accent on ethics as the essence of religion. Conscience and the moral law, in principle, then had to be universalistic, that is, available to all men by "creation," albeit with various dispensable mythic scaffoldings.

Simultaneously and just as necessarily came the liberal, Protestant culture-accent on individual subjectivity, "freedom," and creativity (to which "faith" tended to be reduced, nothing but a sort of *"fides qua,"* never mind what rational content, if any).

Especially Schleiermacher gave a sort of classical expression to the latter accent on subjectivity. In more recent times existentialism in its many forms has been its bearer ("existence," that is "I-Thou," person-centered relationships, rather than "essence" or doctrinal and metaphysical substance). Not even neo-Orthodoxy, for all its frequent surface conservatism, ever repudiated this subjectivistic epistemology or hermeneutics (hence the "neo"), as became especially evident in its demise in the 1960s.

The other wing of post-Kantian philosophy is summarized in German "idealism," especially Hegel. His direct influence on Wellhausen (via Vatke) may have been overstated at times, but it appears ultimately to have been massive nonetheless. "God" is now no longer a literal supernaturalistic being, but a religious name for the "Idea," the life-force or "eternal spirit" (cf. Freemasonry) that somehow motors and drives all of history. *Just* how varies with the philosophy, of course, but the "Hegelian waltz" or "dialectic" of thesis-antithesis-synthesis is probably the most famous—or should we give the Marxist inversion of it into "dialectical *materialism"* as our major example? Process theology, with many congeners, has also recently given very explicit expression to these motifs. Since God is totally immanent in the historical process, "transcendence" can only mean the individual's (or culture's) ability to transcend selfish self-interest and "prophetically" descry where "God" is going.

The better we can by historical-critical research stop the clock, as it were, and study individual frames of the prophets' "moments before God," the more they will be available to us as models for our activism. "Spirituality" then means to attune my "spirit" or historicality to the universal "Spirit" (the course of universal history) by means of constant and repeated "vertical" encounter. The cliche "revelation in history" implied both the vertical encounter of the individual with the ultimate as well as the immanental movement of the "Word" in the historical process. "Liberation" (not redemption) must proceed simultaneously on the personal and psychological front as well as in the public (political, social, cultural) sector. Jeremiah's emotionalism made him the major darling of the critics in the former respect, Amos usually receiving pride of place in the latter. The understanding of "spiritual" was informed, then, both by anti-Catholic motifs as well as by deep philosophic input.

"Monotheism," of course, means *monism,* one *principle* or "Idea" underlying all of nature, an "Omega point" toward which all existence is tending, not the personal deity of the Bible. God becomes virtually a cipher for "change"; whether heard optimistically and melioristically, as is repeatedly the case in liberalism, or more soberly and cautiously at other times, the immanentalistic and evolutionistic principle remains the same.

We have stressed that in the above survey no effort has been made to keep separate various expressions of this entire "prophetic" ideology by various spokesmen at various times. Nor have we gone out of our way to conceal our ultimate disdain for it, especially when it parades as Biblical. Probably a bit more evaluation is in order before we continue the historical survey and consider form-critical innovations from within criticism.

Recent Developments

Even apart from form criticism, it is exceedingly difficult to say where the majority of scholarship today would situate itself with respect to the above construct. The fissiparous tendencies within criticism itself are so great that all generalizations are risky. Anyone who is *au courant* will not fail to recognize many impulses within the above sketch that are still very powerful, however much they may vary from individual to individual. In the sixties, there was a reaction to the reaction of neo-Orthodoxy—and often with a vengeance! "Radical religion" and quasi-Marxist "liberation theology" not only resuscitated many of the old "prophetic" and social Gospel causes, but often urged them in a revolutionary way that would have thoroughly embarrassed their predecessors. The partially salutary stress that no institution was sacred became at times a very literalistic anti-institutionalism!

No one would deny that there are other differences in the modern mutation, but these are just as hard to get one's fingers on. Most of the same contours are visible, but in much more blurred form, usually expressed more cautiously and variably. If one may generalize at all, one may say that the old ideas still thrive in least adulterated form in their old German *Vaterland.* Furthermore, in the "ecumenical age" many Catholic scholars are as "Protestant" as their counterparts. Except for being a distinguishable subculture otherwise, liberal (Reform) Judaism never had differed in these respects from culture (or counterculture) Protestantism, and as the trauma of the Nazi holocaust faded, many other Jewish scholars warmed up to aspects of it themselves.

Hardly anyone today would credit Amos and the other prophets with pioneering "ethical monotheism" in the crass and simplistic way the dogma was once propounded. As we have stressed, the origins of much of Israel's religion will often now be pushed back several centuries prior to the prophets, but the prophets' importance for, at very least, "getting it all together" and giving classical expression to it will still usually be proclaimed. Few would care to defend the simplistic antiexternalism any longer, and it is widely accepted (and much more congenially) that the prophetic antithesis was rather Baalistic religion with its nature-centered, orgiastic character. The implicit monism is still pervasive, even if often unrecognized (or it is rejected only on the basis of Kantian subjectivity). As we shall see shortly, form criticism tended to undercut the entire accent on individual and historical circumstance in classical criticism, as well as its anticultic prejudices, but it remains to be seen how in the long run the dust will settle in all these respects.

Orthodox Response

How shall confessionalism or orthodoxy respond? To accentuate the postive first, there is no denying that classical criticism made contributions in the area of study of the prophets too. (From a sheer quantitative standpoint alone there would be bound to be valuable spinoff from such intense concentration!) Not surprisingly, the contributions that conservatism can salvage are in the two areas of critical strength: historical occasion and social consciousness. No doubt, tradition did at times accent the supernatural aspect of prophetism so much that there was truth in the liberal caricature of "verbal inspiration" as a mechanical, dictation theory. The futuristic or predictive aspect of prophecy was so highlighted that its date and circumstances were, at best, coincidental. The concerns of private, individual piety and the promise of eternal life received such accent that it all but crowded off stage the prophet's obvious concern for public, social justice in this life. At least by default, ecclesiastical tradition often did uncritically second the mores and ideals of the mass culture as much as liberal criticism did that of the intelligentsia and avant-garde. To the extent that those blind spots still exist, conservatism still stands to profit from its competition.

But even where much can and should be learned, one cannot forget the vast amount that must be unlearned at the same time. At best, the concentration on historical circumstance was disproportionate to the results achieved, all the more so because the researchers could rarely agree beyond a few broad lines. Obviously, the Bible itself never paid *that* much attention to the topic! It is scarcely accidental that no *precise* dates or circumstances were preserved for the vast majority of *individual* prophetic oracles (although that scarcely means that they are anonymous either, the products of a faceless community inspiration). The situation is not unlike the *logia* of Jesus in the gospels. Theologically, in a way everything depends upon their historicity as communications of Him, who was both "historical Jesus" and incarnate Son of God. But the same cannot be said of the precise location and occasion for each *logion* (where, of course, criticism has commonly indulged in the same "wild goose chase"). In general, the more such isagogical information we have, the easier it is to understand and apply, but one must recognize where the point of diminishing returns begins.

One could laud the critical recovery of the prophetic concern with ethics much more heartily if one more often met it in an acceptable hermeneutical framework. Very often liberal concern for this life waxed in direct proportion to the waning of interest in eternal life (often not so much denied as quietly ignored). The "Messianic prophecy" accent wore its own blinders, to be sure, but it did give high visibility to the soteriological and christological center of not only the prophets, but all of Scripture. Sometimes the conservative accent seemed unwilling or unable to read or utilize much of the Old Testament except a few traditional prophecies (and then only in Advent), so isolated from their historical context had they become, but, then, liberalism was highly selective too! Sometimes it was almost guilty of "reading into" the Old Testament ideas that were not there—or at least of failing to understand and employ the Old Testament's own vocabulary and conceptuality, but it did not lose sight of "Scripture as its own interpreter," without which, in a sense, the "Old Testament" ceases to live up to its Christian label, and is returned to the synagogue.

In less radical guise, the liberal accent on prophetic ethics continued in one form or the other, the traditional Reformed confusion of the two kingdoms (i.e., of Law-Gospel), and of inordinate stress on the third use of the Law. The prophets may well be salutary reminders to traditional Lutheranism that the alternative to political and social action (as usually conceived) is not some quasi-existentialist pietism and quietism. At the same time, it can scarcely be underlined too much that "two kingdoms" is not only Lutheran "social theory," but an essential part of Lutheran hermeneutics, especially of the prophets. Lutheranism orders and articulates its life of sanctification also according to its reading of the prophets—and vice versa.

Form Criticism

Let us move on to form criticism and tradition criticism. As noted earlier, it would more often define the particulars of scholarly investigation today than the literary dissections of earlier criticism (although the latter still flourishes, especially in Germany). As Wellhausen largely left it to Duhm to pursue his insights in the study of the prophets, so it was especially Gressmann who pioneered in applying form criticism to prophecy. As elsewhere, the dominant concern was to penetrate behind the literary products to the preceding oral tradition. The erstwhile search for the *ipsissima verba* of the prophets was abandoned as abortive. The distinction between "genuine" and "non-genuine" was no longer appropriate; rather it should be a matter of the organic growth of smaller into longer units. The prophets were viewed as speakers rather than writers. In this field too, "form criticism" was beholden to a host of anthropological and *religionsgeschichtliche* theories. Gressmann and Co. thought it possible to find ancient Oriental analogues especially to prophetic (and thence Biblical) Messianism and eschatology. Over against Wellhausenianism, this did usually carry the implication that short, futuristic—even Messianic—sayings were genuine and primary, but at the same time the Biblical variety was departicularized, made only one example of a universal genius. If earlier criticism tended to make the Bible "relevant" by trying to skim some "timeless" cream or "values" off the time-bound historical particularity, form criticism now unflinchingly accented the Bible's external uniqueness and ancient Oriental strangeness, generally without a care for "relevance" or the like.

A good example of this would be the "Gentile oracles": since they embarrassed the early critics as unworthy of "prophets," ancient or modern, they were usually bypassed in one way or the other; Gunkel and many form critics, on the other hand, were convinced that the genre represented some of the earliest and most original prophetic sayings— never mind what the modern consequences might be.

Gunkel's *Urzeit gleicht Endzeit* ("Primordial time equals end-time") provides a major example and is widely quoted. However, while it aptly summarizes the circular "myth of the eternal return" of paganism, it applies at best in only broken form to the Bible, and we would want to insist that the direction of influence is not from ancient Orient to Israel but from revelation to fragmentary human memory and perversion. Biblical typology is not simply an adaptation of mythology's cyclicism— let alone an unassimilated remnant of it, as more radical critics would have it. The Bible, indeed, often describes eschatology in terms of protology or the "new" in terms of the "old" (alternate ways of saying typology or prophecy-fulfillment), but, in this respect at least, the classical critics were more on target in stressing the radical uniqueness of the Bible's accent on "history."

Similar examples could be cited of the parallelism attempted between nearly universal expressions of yearnings for peace (found in ancient Sumer in our earliest known human literature) and the Biblical variety, between legends of a paradise or "good old days" and/or of a divine hero who would messianically deliver mankind from its woes.

Subsequent scholarship was often able to concede more uniqueness to the Biblical expressions of these topics, but the "parallelomania" was endemic. Each new wave of archaeological discovery seemed destined to spawn a host of attempts to explain nearly everything in terms of the new horizons. "Pan-Babylonianism," a major school of thought of this sort, need not detain us because it seems largely behind us, with the exception of certain cultic reconstructions, particularly "cultic prophets." We have also survived a lesser surge of "pan-Ugaritism," but one fears we are now in for a round of "pan-Eblaitism" or the like. However, as we shall note, discovery and documentation of undeniable external parallels to prophecy was slow to come, so that the repercussions in the area of our concern at the moment were often less than elsewhere in the Bible.

Prophecy and Cult

It was especially with respect to "cultic prophecy," however, that much initial form criticism clashed most frontally with much that earlier criticism held dear. The earlier portrait was essentially that of an anti-establishmentarian individualist, a loner, raising his voice *contra mundum*. Now, all of a sudden, prophets became functionaries and mouthpieces of the official, institutional apparatus, sometimes almost indistinguishable from the priest. Joel, Nahum, and Habakkuk became prime examples. There was external evidence from surrounding cultures in that direction, no doubt, but the argument proceeded at least as much *ex hypothesi*. The Biblical evidence, too, supported the idea that there were such figures as "cultic prophets" (perhaps especially Chronicles—but critics generally discounted its historical value).

In general, it is agreed on all sides today that in this respect the form critics greatly overstated their case, but they did establish that cult and prophecy often operated in tandem. Nevertheless, the corrective to the sometimes almost virulent anti-priestly and anti-institutional motivation of much classical criticism was overdue and welcome. If the normative Israelite cult was Mosaic, and if prophecy was reformatory, the prophets could scarcely have been at total loggerheads with priestdom. The prophets themselves reprove false prophets in far harsher terms than they do faithless priests. Subsequent research has confirmed that the prophets certainly speak in the temple in cultic contexts even if they held no office there, and often the very vocabulary the prophets employed was derived from the cult with which most of their audience was perfectly familiar. (We may only note in passing here that in more recent times, as one manifestation of the revival of interest in Wisdom, it has seemed to many critics to provide more fruitful background than cult.

One cannot ignore, of course, the vast amount of anti-cultic language in the prophets, to which classical liberals have often loved to appeal. One must, however, distinguish, for example, between ritual and ritual*ism*. The prophets are forever condemning the Israelite tendencies to relapse into the magical, *ex opere operato* understandings of cult which characterized paganism. But there is no evidence that they ever rejected externals as such in favor of some specious, spiritualistic "religion of the heart" (although the critics were by no means above excising embarrassing evidence to the contrary). If one reads the prophets literalistically at this point, we would even have Isaiah condemning prayer (1:15) as much as other acts of worship!

Sometimes the prophets do express themselves very strongly (here as elsewhere) on the point of hypocritical worship, of creeds without deeds. Sometimes they indulge in hyperbole, and specifically in what has been called dialectical negation, that is, saying "not" when "not only" is meant. Thus, classically Hosea 6:6 (and reiterated by our Lord, Matt. 9:13; 12:7; etc.): "I desire mercy [*chesedh*] and *not* sacrifice"—but note the explanatory parallel "the knowledge of God, *rather than* burnt offerings."

If pressed, of course, such statements would flatly contradict much of the Pentateuch—and by no accident were they prominent in Wellhausen's argumentation that the priestly legislation was not ancient and "Mosaic" at all. Especially two famous rhetorical questions in the prophetic literature can be read as explicitly asserting that God had never given sacrificial legislation in the wilderness: Amos 5:25 and Jer. 7:22. Fortunately, one may safely generalize and say that even most of criticism which never bought the form-critical "cultic prophecy" has by now tended to agree that the prophets are speaking of abuses of the cult, not calling into question its ultimate divine authorization.

Possibly classical criticism's most damaging riposte came in the charge that "cultic prophets," if there were such, were "false prophets," mindless echoes of the establishment in contrast to the faithful witness of genuine prophecy, or who at most had simply criticized a few malingerers. (Form criticism itself had typically tended to try to prescind from such value judgments one way or the other.) The Micaiah pericope (1 Kings 22) and some of the canonical prophet's broadsides against false prophets would indicate some truth in the claim. However, sometimes the riposte went even further to claim that some of the *canonical* prophets would have originally been classified among those "false prophets!" Nahum and Obadiah would be prominent examples. Why? Because they preached only salvation for Israel (largely in the form of denunciation of Israel's enemies), *ergo* they must have been jingoistic spokesmen of the establishment. Obviously, we have here a recrudescence of classical liberal-critical prejudices—and with a vengeance!

Tradition–Historical Correctives

The atomistic bent of form criticism, that is, its tendency to concentrate on small, allegedly original discrete units to the neglect of the whole was often also evident in study of the prophets. Gunkel himself had thought of the primary prophetic communications as largely terse, ejaculatory, and often cryptic. Even though the idea of distinguishing "genuine" and "non-genuine" tended to be abandoned, as we noted, the subsequent editor of the books became little more than a collector of beads on a string, and literary context counted for little. At points, as we shall note, there may have been a little truth in the latter viewpoint, because of the apparently different notions in antiquity about how to arrange and present such material. The evolutionism implicit in this atomism, especially in early form criticism, should not escape us—not a philosophico-theological developmentalism a la Wellhausen, but a simplistic dogma of necessary movement from simple to complex nonetheless. Today, in the light of archaeological evidence, Gunkel's notion that early, original units were necessarily short and pristine, with length and complexity an indication of a culture's senility, looks simply laughable.

One corrective counterthrust came from especially the Swedish "Uppsala School," which went its own way in study of the prophets as elsewhere (cf. above). It put strong accent on "oral transmission"—but by almost common consent overaccented it. It did stress the phenomenal accuracy of memory in cultures where writing had not yet become a crutch—a welcome alternative to the consummate skepticism of much early literary criticism. However, it also argued that writing was little used or a least largely inoperative in Israel outside of priestly circles until about the time of the Exile, when ancient traditions were allegedly first written down for fear of total loss in the catastrophe. That, however, flies in the face of Biblical testimony.

However, Uppsala probably had a point. There is no reason, theological or otherwise, to question at least the possibility that oral transmission played some role in the development of some Biblical literature. In fact, certain features such as "catchwords" (cf. below) seem to be more readily explainable in this way than in others. More speculative, but having possibilities, was Engnell's further attempt at classification of types of oral tradition. He distinguished between: (a) a "liturgy type," where sacred cult material, largely impersonal in type, had been handed down partly in written form (e.g., Nahum, Joel, Habakkuk); and (b) a *"diwan*-type" (after Arabic parallels), where the personality of the prophet and his historical situation still shine through after later adaptation and remolding. Engnell's distinction is curiously similar to other current form-critical distinctions along similar lines, cultic and non-cultic call settings, "covenant lawsuits," etc. Since such an hypothesis overlaps with others such as "cultic prophecy," the various presuppositions would have to be carefully examined.

When we speak of tradition-*history,* it is often oral transmission which we have in mind, in contrast to tradition-*criticism,* which more often implies texts. Before we leave the subject, the very influential classification of types of traditional material made by Mowinckel should be noted. The proposal was originally made of the Book of Jeremiah, but it is often applied elsewhere in the prophetic literature. Mowinckel distinguished three types of material: (A) Various sayings, poems and/or oracles in the first person, representing God's direct discourse through the prophet, and usually poetic in form and usually regarded as genuine; (B) Narratives about Jeremiah (the "Baruch Biography") concerned especially with the occasions for speeches and prophecies, and thought to be influenced by "legend"; and (C) Speeches or sermons by Jeremiah, prose in form and in his case often characterized by "deuteronomic" diction presumed to reflect the preaching interests of the exilic community. Sometimes a fourth (D) type was included: hopeful prophecies, such as in Jer. 31 and 33, but this material was usually considered ungenuine. Mowinckel himself used the designations A, B, C, and D, respectively, and has been followed by many scholars. They appear to be useful, neutral, descriptive labels, regardless of isagogical or theological stance.

In addition to all these movements, more recently structuralism has arisen to redress form criticism's atomism. We sketched it above and need not repeat it here. Similar, but much less philosophically based was Muilenburg's call for "rhetorical criticism." He stressed strongly that the important thing was the way a prophet *used* a form, the way it appears in the text as we have it. His primary application was to the prophets, but it has applications across the board in Biblical studies.

Conservative Evaluation

Perhaps the theological underpinnings of nearly all this sort of scholarship (when there are such concerns) should be emphasized: the rationale again is that of a sort of "community inspiration" (so much so that sometimes any distinct prophetic personality behind the "tradition" gets lost in the fog), as the church under the guidance of the Spirit continues to reflect on the original encounter and to expand, contract, or adapt according to ever-changing circumstances. Obviously, then, the modern church in its use of Scripture must "go and do likewise!" Allegedly later additions are not now thrown out as "ungenuine," but the *church's* tradition assumes an importance nearly as great as the "Biblical tradition."

The conservative should not overreact, however. As already Luther observed, few of the prophetic books are put together in the type of logical order we should expect. Obviously, the original sermons have often been drastically condensed. We really know so little about practices of the time that, within limits, we should not try to tie the Holy Spirit's hands, as it were. Tradition and conservatism have usually assumed that the prophet himself was responsible for the final form of his book. We would scarcely care to deny that, but there is no theological reason why the role of disciples or other traditors should not also be considered. Their own input and the amount of time presumably involved would, however, almost perforce be much abbreviated over that commonly envisioned by critics.

A few connective devices in the prophetic literature do indisputably appear to be purely formal. One of these is the "catchword" principle, where the closing word or phrase of one unit provides a sort of "cue" to the beginning of the next one. One thinks especially of oral transmission in such instances, but, of course, we really do not know. A good example of the possibility of such a "catchword principle" is the transition from Micah 3 to Micah 4 provided by the nearly contiguous "mountain of the house" phrases.

At the same time, Micah 3 and 4 are also a good illustration of another principle for joining oracles together. This type is both more common and theologically more fruitful. It illustrates that, no matter who put our prophetic books together, it was not simply some mechanical process which the exegete or preacher can safely ignore. This one sometimes goes by the name "alternation of weal and woe," that is, the juxtaposition of oracles of judgment with those of salvation. Surely more is involved than mere psychological relief—such as the depiction of the eschatological oracles of promise at the conclusion of many prophetic books as "euphemistic liturgical appendixes." And even if liturgies are involved here too (as some seriously propose—and which is surely not to be dismissed out of hand), it surely is more than a purely formal matter of choral antiphonies.

The antiphonies of blessing and cursing in Deut. 27 = Joshua 8 might well suggest the precedent for this common pattern in the prophetic literature. At any rate, the import of the pattern appears to be essentially "Law-Gospel," the simultaneity of God's confrontation of the believer in both judgment and salvation. Either topic will be caricatured, if not perverted, without constant reference to the other.

Sometimes more complicated expressions of the same theological principle are found, e.g., the use of an "inclusio," as in Is. 2:1—4:6, where a number of oracles of judgment are "included" or framed in two beautiful oracles of promise.

But perhaps the most all-encompassing application of the principle is found in what appears to have been a sort of classical or traditional outline for prophetic books. One can illustrate it in almost pure form in the Book of Zephaniah, in the Septuagint sequence in Jeremiah, and less clearly many other places. It takes a simple tripartite form: (1) Oracles against Judah (and/or Israel), (2) Oracles against Gentiles or foreign nations, (3) Promise of salvation to all, both Jew and Gentile, who repent. Here we obviously have our "Law-Gospel" or "judgment-salvation" principle again, only with the first part divided into two. The idea can be summarized by two New Testament passages: (1) judgment begins with the household of God (1 Peter 4:17), and (2) there is ultimately "no difference" (Rom. 3:22) between Jew and Gentile when it comes to the judgment and the grace of God. (Perhaps, in passing, the very prominent universal perspective of the Old Testament, as illustrated in the very structure of many prophetic books, should be accented again, over against persistent ignorance and/or misunderstanding.)

This theological context may help to "salvage" the Gentile oracles for us, which bulk so large in the prophetic corpus. Early critics scorned them as unworthy of the great prophets (chauvinistic, particularistic, etc.), and even conservatives, it is feared, usually give them about as wide a berth as anything in the Old Testament. The universality of God's moral law, to which they give forceful expression, may be especially apropos today. If one uses a proper, Biblical hermeneutics (typology), it is these oracles which apply most immediately to America (and all modern nations, since "Israel" became only a church in the new covenant), not the judgment-oracles against Israel and Jerusalem, as in the false hermeneutics of the liberal activists.

Individual "Forms"

We turn finally to what was the most neutral and often helpful aspect of the whole form-critical enterprise: "form-criticism" in the strict sense of the term, the analysis of the genres and structures in which the prophets expressed themselves. In this area, the conservative often needs register no a priori misgivings and is sometimes as "free" as the confessionally uncommitted scholar to pursue the evidence. Tremendous logomachies have often been waged in this area, and radical disagreements on nomenclature often suggest far more subjectivity and belaboring of the obvious than the researchers would care to admit. Some useful observations have been forthcoming nonetheless.

Only a few illustrations are possible. Gunkel had originally thought that the threats were the original prophetic unit, with the condemnation (alias invective, reproach, diatribe, etc.) a later expansion. That position has largely been abandoned, and, as at many points, Westermann has given classical expression to a plateau of thought, currently subscribed to by many. He isolates two major types of *"Botenspruch"* or "messenger speech": judgment speeches against individuals and against the nation. The form or outline is similar in both cases: (1) an initial, "Hear," plus vocative, on the like; (2) The Speech of Reproach (Accusation, Indictment), (3) The Messenger-Formula ("Thus says Yahweh," etc.), often introduced by its transitional, "Therefore," and (4) The Proclamation of Doom. Similar, but less structured, probably, are the prophecies of salvation; Begrich's thesis that a "priestly oracle of assurance" was the model for many of them has commanded wide acceptance.

Very congenial also is the proposed *Gattung* of a "covenant lawsuit" (*"rib"* in Hebrew): the prophet is a herald of the case which the heavenly court has filed against Israel for breach of covenant (e.g., Is. 1, Micah 6, Hos. 4, Jer. 2, Deut. 32). Here, as elsewhere, the lines between God and His spokesman, the prophet, often become very indistinct—as similarly in the New Testament, especially in the Gospel of John. God Himself often plays almost simultaneously the roles of judge, plaintiff, and prosecuting attorney. Some have gone on to try to reconstruct a specific "form" for prophetic calls, but these seem to be more speculative and often carry the intimation of non-historicity, or at least a pure subjectivity on the prophet's part.

The central form-critical understanding of much of the prophet's self-understanding as one who has been permitted to stand in Yahweh's heavenly council (where history is really made), and who now must herald what he has heard on earth, appears to be a valid and helpful insight (cf. 1 Kings 22:19; Amos 3:8; Jer. 23:18). Not, of course, that that construction has gone unchallenged! In addition to challenges, many have suggested such things as calls to arms (presumably derived from holy war traditions) and many cultic settings, but the "covenant renewal festival" still remains the favorite *Sitz im Leben*.

Beyond this, form critics observe that the prophets apparently in many cases adapted "secular" or everyday forms for their purposes: love songs (Is. 4), funeral dirges (Is. 14), taunt songs (Is. 47), hymns and psalms and proverbs. Sometimes the detail may be debatable, but there is nothing surprising about this, and often the observation does little more than belabor the obvious.

One note of disapproval must be added. When prophetic material, as we have it, frequently fails to appear in the neat, simple form the theory demands, the temptation is great to wield the literary-critical scalpel and peel away layers allegedly added by later tradition. At best, the degree of subjectivity in such an endeavor is about as high as possible. But, even presuming the critical theory is sound to begin with, there is no reason, even humanly speaking, why the prophets themselves should have been bound that rigidly to any traditional "form," or not have used it creatively, as circumstance required. Form critics are, no doubt, largely correct in stressing that Israel, like most ancient ones, was a "traditional society," where novelty tended to be guilty until proved innocent, but the insight dare not be driven into the ground.

Definition of "Prophet"

So what was "prophecy" really? Perhaps the first thing to stress is that the Bible itself answers the question from a fundamentally different standpoint than most modern scholarship. The modern question and attempt at answer is primarily sociological, while the Bible's is theological. Of course, the two are not mutually exclusive, but it is important that the approaches be carefully distinguished.

The Bible's own understanding of a "prophet" is something like "spokesman, interpreter, mediator of God's will" —and in about the most comprehensive sense possible, regardless of the political, sociological, or psychological circumstances which the historical-critical researcher tends to inquire about first. In this sense, Abraham is a "prophet" (Gen. 20:7) because he intercedes with God for the welfare of Abimelech, although it is doubtful if he externally had much else in common with the great figures of the eighth century. Similarly, Aaron is to be a "prophet" to Moses (Ex. 7:2) in the sense of Moses' spokesman.

And, as we have stressed, Moses is *the* prophet *par excellence* because of his unique role as representative and mediator of the primary, Sinaitic revelation. Moses' functions or behavior may well have coincided externally somewhat with the classical prophets, but the association is more theological: the great prophets were reformers, calling Israel back to its Mosaic roots. It is no accident that one of the few Biblical passages that even approaches a theoretical discussion on prophecy is Deut. 18:15-19, which emphasizes "Mosaicity" as the standard of true prophecy.

Christians would scarcely care to discuss this topic long without also invoking the name of Christ as the greatest, the Incarnation, the fulfillment, and the antitype of all true prophecy. But then we are well aware that our language is primarily theological—although that by no means precludes actions by Jesus which might also externally classify him among the prophets.

Perhaps it should also be stressed that only in this theological sense, is it safe to generalize about "prophetism." Sometimes that usage may be a semantic convenience, but it may easily obscure the rich variety of prophetic accent and expression. It is probably even riskier to speak of "prophetic religion/theology"; classical liberalism meant the phrase in its thoroughly evolutionistic sense, and if it has any validity at all, care must be taken to clarify its essential synonymity with the theology of the *entire* Bible, of which the prophets are one classical expression.

Externals of Prophecy

The Bible, of course, in passing preserves no little information which may be useful in a "scientific" reconstruction of the externals of prophecy. These overlap somewhat with questions of the origin and rise of the movement, to which we turn shortly. Especially in its earlier reaches, as the Books of Samuel make plain, Israelite prophetism was very much characterized by ecstaticism (apparently not totally dissimilar from the *glossolalia* of Corinth). Hence, a vast percentage of scholarly discussion of the externals of prophecy has turned on the question of whether the later, great prophets continued to be ecstatic. To make a long story short, the Biblical evidence would indicate that ecstaticism played, at most, a very minimal role among the later prophets (depending partly on how we define the term). That may, however, be largely due to lack of evidence, because the collectors and transmitters of the prophetic messages were almost exclusively interested in just that—in the prophet's words, not in externals of their accompanying behavior. There are instances, however, even in later times when at least the verb *n-b-'* appears to be used in a sense implying ecstatic behavior, e.g., 1 Kings 22:8, and even in Jeremiah's (29:26) day, it is readily equated with madness, lunacy, or fanaticism *(meshugga').*

Such a debate raged on the issue, however, largely because of the hidden agendas involved. It forms almost a classical example of the confusion of external and theological criteria in evaluating prophecy— and sometimes among conservatives as well as liberals. Both often assumed that there was something degrading about ecstatic behavior, and hence at all cost it was not to be attributed to the great prophets. In addition, classical criticism tended to view the classical prophets as cool, rational analysts of the current scene, and orthodoxy has a comparable commitment to the rationality (or propositionality) of revelation. Since both tended to view ecstaticism as a species of mysticism and to hear the latter *in malem partem,* it was not to be ascribed to the great prophetic figures if at all possible.

Within liberalism, it was mostly certain form critics, especially Hölscher, who dissented, appealing partly to extra-Biblical parallels, and, as usual, not very concerned with its implications for prophetic "authority." The conservatives too ran the risk of introducing alien criteria: "mysticism" may, at least, be heard *in bonam partem* (cf. Luther), as describing the suprarational, transcendental, even supernatural component of inspiration—nor even excluding the valid emotional and volitional component! As far as external behavior patterns are concerned, it is one of those areas where we must remember that it was the ancient Orient, not the modern West, where God saw fit to reveal Himself and become incarnate! Certainly, ecstaticism is never as such censured in the Bible.

Assuming that ecstaticism is not a misleading term to begin with, Lindblom's distinction between "absorption" and "concentration" ecstasy may be useful to prevent initial misconceptions. The former, following the etymology of "ecstasy" (literally a state of standing outside oneself), implied some sort of fusion of the divine and human personality. It seems to have been typical of pagan ecstasy, but was incompatible with the Biblical sense of the infinite gulf between creature and Creator. On the other hand, "concentration ecstasy" or "possession" might, if we do not press them, come about as close as possible to an external, psychological description of "inspiration."

One should stress that the Biblical-theological definition must be as carefully distinguished from the psychological one in the case of "inspiration" as with "prophet." Again the Bible drops information about the former only in passing. Obviously, the "uniqueness" of Biblical inspiration did not inhere in any externals. One wing of criticism did pass through a phase of virtually trying to psychoanalyze the prophets (a field day was had with especially Hosea and Ezekiel), but fortunately that is now almost totally behind us.

Besides ecstaticism, there also appear some external parallels between Israelite prophets and the clairvoyants of surrounding cultures. Biblical prophets, or at least some of them, were originally called "seers" (1 Sam. 9:9). There the ordinary Hebrew root for "see" is used (presumably for "second sight"), but even later another root (*chozeh*) is regularly used, apparently in a more specialized way, for the prophetic "vision" (presumably implying "inspiration"). Whatever the similarity in particulars, it appears that the Bible vocabulary itself takes pains to underscore the *theological* chasm between Israelite and pagan clairvoyance. Hebrew has two common words *(q-s-m* and *'-n-n,* usually translated "diviner" and "sorcerer," or the like, and always used pejoratively (one possible exception in Prov. 16:10).

Development of Prophecy in Israel

We turn, then, to the question of the origins and rise of the phenomenon of prophecy in Israel. Here, then, we speak primarily phenomenologically, not theologically. For a long time, it appeared that prophecy was one Israelite institution which was really unique externally as well as theologically (in contrast to kingship, priesthood, wise men, etc.). Of course, the two types of uniqueness overlap somewhat (the theological type at least determining perimeters of the other), but it is the externals of the situation that primarily concern us at the moment.

Gradually, however, the frontiers of our knowledge of the issue are being pushed back by new discoveries, and increasingly it appears that, externally at least, the idea of "prophecy" was not at all unique in Israel. In fact, the Biblical descriptions of the "false prophets" and the difficulty in distinguishing them from the genuine variety would indicate as much. Some of the issue is complicated, however, by questions of terminology (both in the Bible and outside of it), of the validity of "parallels," and of the course of prophetism within Israel (where evolutionary dogmas again sometimes obtrude).

At one time, parallels were sought quite far afield, namely in Egypt and the major Mesopotamian cultures, but these appear to be of minimal pertinence, at best. Discoveries closer to home—not surprisingly—have been more fruitful. It remains to be seen how revolutionary the new finds at Ebla in northern Syria will be, but at this writing it is already known that the major Hebrew word for "prophet" *(nabi')* also figured prominently there.

Mari, to the east, on the middle Euphrates, was one of the major Amorite cultures, and illuminates the history of the patriarchs and of early Israel in many ways. The prominence of prophetic activity there suggests that it may well have been familiar to the patriarchs already. One common term at Mari is the *apilu,* an "answerer," apparently related to specific deities. Here we also meet the *muhhu,* a sort of "ecstatic," but also associated with the cult. (The latter also appear elsewhere in Mesopotamia, alongside the *baru,* a "diviner" or "seer.") The terms are often used of both men and women.

More significant is a certain similarity in the setting and content of the Mari oracles with the Biblical ones. Oracles came from and were delivered in temples and had more "secular" impetuses as well. The Mari prophets, like their Biblical counterparts, were very much involved in political and military affairs. There are both rebukes of the throne as well as oracles of assurance. Often a "messenger formula" ("Thus says N") is used, just as in the Bible. However, we find little comparable to the profound ethical and eschatological concerns of the Biblical prophets.

How much difference, if any, there was in this respect in Bible times between Mesopotamia and the Mediterranean littoral is hard to say. Outside of the Bible itself we have little information. The Bible is usually speaking of "false prophecy," but the same vocabulary is often used as of the canonical figures. That ecstaticism was known, however, is confirmed by the famous Wen-Amon text, where an Egyptian fugitive encounters such behavior at Byblos in Phoenicia. Evidence from Asia Minor and the Aegean regions may be just as helpful. (It may well illustrate Gordon's thesis of the many cultural continuities between Greece and Canaan.) Ecstaticism, often epidemic, can be documented there from the prophetess Cassandra of Homeric fame through the Montanist heresy of the early Christian church.

When did the phenomenon of prophecy surface among the Hebrews? As we have noted, the Bible is not concerned to answer those kinds of questions. However, the virtual ubiquity of some kind of "prophecy" makes it very likely that it was present from the outset. Possibly Israel's only problem was to domesticate it or "baptize" it, if you will. Thus, when the Bible speaks of "prophets" in the theological sense (cf. above) already in the earliest times, it may just be conveying some phenomenological information as well.

Before archaeology demonstrated that ecstaticism was common in the ancient Orient also outside of Canaan, it was common to explain the Eldad and Medad pericope (Num. 11:26 ff.) as illustrating Israel's first contact with ecstaticism as she approached Canaanite territory. The names certainly do not appear to be Israelite, but it now seems doubtful that the explanation can be so simple. What is significant is that Moses not only refuses to prohibit the pair's activity, but exclaims, "Would that all the LORD's people were prophets . . ."! It is not explicitly stated, but perhaps implicit already here is the idea later enunciated by Joel (2:28), and similar to what we saw earlier (Ex. 19) with respect to priesthood, that a special order of prophets is only for the interim after the Fall, while in the eschaton everyone will receive the Spirit.

The figure of Balaam (from Pethor in northern Syria) in Num. 22 ff. illustrates how familiar Israel must have been with a "prophet" or that sort. It is interesting to note that we now have a very similar characterization of Balaam from the excavations at Deir Allah in the lower Jordan valley.

Miriam, Moses' sister, is called a "prophetess" in Ex. 15:20. The context of singing suggests, however, that we may have here a usage, similar to that found especially in 1 Chron. 25:1, where the word often implies to sing or play an instrument (at least etymologically perhaps because inspiration by the same spirit as that in prophecy was thought of). Elisha's call for a minstrel to stimulate prophecy (2 Kings 3:15) may also illustrate the intimate connection of music and prophecy in ancient thought.

Prophecy appears to be well established by the time of the Judges, although the evidence is elusive. Deborah, who is also a judge, is specifically styled a "prophetess" (Judges 4:4), and an unnamed "prophet" anticipates the call of Gideon (6:7 ff.). One wonders, however, if the prominence of the Spirit throughout the Book of Judges does not describe essentially the same activity, albeit in different vocabulary. It may well be, as some have suggested, that in the subsequent period the office of "judge" was divided among the "prophet" and the "king."

In any event, by the time of Samuel, "prophecy," at least of the ecstatic, epidemic sort, is obviously well established at the same time that kingship is fast taking root. The surprise at Saul's participation suggests, however, that the activity tended to be scorned as a rather plebeian activity. We have already underlined Samuel's towering importance as concerns the theological aspects of prophecy, but his possible influence on its phenomenological aspects cannot be ascertained. Critical scholarship may oversimplify a bit in accenting the novelty of prophetic activity in Samuel's time, but this is one place where, *mirabile dictu,* most contemporary critics would essentially agree with the Biblical picture. As one critical scholar himself has commented: being "deprived of one of the secret pleasures of critical scholarship, namely, arguing that the traditional picture is altogether wrong," in this area there is little left to do but fill out background and details.

As noted, 1 Sam. 9:9 records a change in usual vocabulary from "seer" to "prophet," but we lack context to assess its significance. It may imply a shift of accent from clairvoyance to ecstaticism, but again the difference may be only semantic. Neither is it clear what the expression "man of God" or the various words translated "oracle," "saith," e.g., tell us, or whether they are merely alternate vocabulary. Various detailed evolutionary schemes of the further rise of prophecy in Israel, especially its presumed emancipation from early ecstaticism have been worked out, but they all appear to tell us more about the prepossessions of the writer than about the actual course of events.

We continue to hear of "sons" and "schools" of the prophets in the 9th century in the time of Elijah and Elisha, but are little better off for the knowledge. Thereafter, we lose clear sight of such phenomena, but are not sure whether or not the Biblical silence implies absence. Especially Elijah's theological importance is massive again, but we cannot say more. Why, humanly speaking, "writing prophets" (that is, whose oracles were preserved in separate books) first appear in the eighth century, we cannot say either. If there is any connection between that and the decline of ecstaticism, as is often surmised, it cannot be established. Much has sometimes been made of Amos' disassocation of himself from the "prophets" *(nebiim)* in 7:14 in this connection, as though he is making a clean break with ecstaticism, but it is doubtful if he is saying anything more than that he had been no *professional* prophet or otherwise engaged in prophetic activity until God had said, "Go, prophesy . . ." (v. 15).

The traditional designation of "writing prophet" is totally misleading. At best, it describes the fate or transmission of their precise oracles, not the nature of their public activity. It flew totally in the face of the form-critical stress that the prophets were orators, not writers, which in this respect was probably basically correct, *pace* both tradition and earlier criticism. At any rate, there is no indication that they were any less primarily *oral* preachers than their ninth-century predecessors. The major difference is rather their eschatological accent: the impending judgment, but salvation for a "remnant" beyond and through the judgment. Humanly speaking, it may be the impact of that eschatological accent on the survivors of the catastrophe who identified themselves with the remnant which caused these oracles to be written down, preserved, and canonized for the first time.

As we noted earlier, Israelite prophecy, at least in its full theological dimensions, arose and operated largely as a counterweight to kingship and its paganizing proclivities. After the Exile, when the monarchy fails to reestablish itself, prophets quickly fade from the scene too. The revival of prophecy as well as of kingship are plainly not expected until the Messianic era—and, of course, the New Testament prominently proclaims the fulfillment of both of those hopes and promises. Phenomenologically, however, it is "apocalyptic" on which the mantle of prophecy falls within the Old Testament aeon itself.

True Versus False Prophecy

How then were true and false prophecy distinguished? The truth question arises almost everywhere in Scripture where the topic of prophecy appears. If we remember, however, that the Bible's own definition of prophecy is a theological one, we will not be surprised to discover that the criterion of truth is also primarily a matter of revelation and faith.

As noted before, there was a certain tendency among some scholars to posit ecstasy as a clear, external sign of false prophecy, but the argument can be sustained only by playing rather fast and loose with the Biblical text. Especially Mowinckel championed the idea that the true prophets, in conscious self-distancing from false prophets, thought of themselves and set themselves forth as motivated and empowered by the "Word," not by the "Spirit." Allegedly, only in and after the Exile, when the old confrontation was past, did appeal to the "Spirit" become common (Ezekiel, Joel, Zechariah), and often compositions really of that date found their way into earlier books (Micah 3:8; Is. 11:3, etc.). There is truth, of course, in the observation that the great prophets most characteristically express themselves as spokesmen of the "Word," neither can it be denied that explicit accent on the "Spirit" (especially as a major agent of the eschaton) becomes more prominent in later times. However, it may be doubted if there was ever that much difference between the two hypostases to begin with, and there is no sign at all that it was ever understood as a qualitative yardstick. (And, of course, the difference between exegetical and dogmatic idiom must be noted: even if the prophets do not technically speak of themselves as led by the "Spirit," it does not follow that they were not "inspired!")

Not that external touchstones were totally lacking. Sometimes we hear of the venality of the false prophets (e.g., Micah 3:5), but there is no indication that was a characteristic of the entire class. Many indications, however, that the false prohets tended to be sycophants, adept at prophesying what their audiences wanted to hear, is probably closer to the mark. The Micaiah pericope (1 Kings 22) is very instructive here, as is Jeremiah's repeated complaint about his opposition, which proclaims "peace, peace, when there is no peace." Conversely, Jeremiah describes "war, famine, and pestilence" (28:8; cf. 34:17) as characteristic of the tradition of true prophecy, and the scroll which Ezekiel is to eat has written on it "words of lamentation and mourning and woe" (2:10).

It was partly passages such as that which induced classical Wellhausenianism to set up preachment of judgment as a nearly infallible sign of "genuine" prophecy and excise most other passages as ameliorative additions from later times. That there was *some* truth in the observation is beyond denying, but it would be lovely, indeed, if matters were that simple! The preponderance of judgment-oracles in the preexilic prophets corresponds to the preponderant needs of the hour. Together with the social decay, probably hastened by the Aramean wars, had come a total collapse of the ethos of traditional Yahwism. And, no doubt, the great prophets were convinced that *coram Deo* Israel had passed the point of no return; God would no longer limit Himself to judging only the wicked within Israel, but now had no alternative but to bring a "final judgment" upon all Israel. The use of that phrase indicates the great typological significance of the oracles of judgment, which bulk so large in the prophets, but whose contemporary theological significance eludes even many Christian readers. It is imperative that we assimilate them typologically to Christ's death and resurrection (cf. Ezek. 37) and thence via Baptism to *our* death and resurrection—or to "Law-Gospel" in general.

However, in their very preaching of judgment, the preexilic prophets looked forward also to God's new eschatological act of redemption. And when the circumstances change after the judgment (even in prospect as especially in Is. 40—55), the prophets themselves are quick to change the dominant note of their preaching to hope and promise. The same explanation is undoubtedly to be given for the many positive and promissory oracles which are interspersed throughout the books of the preexilic prophets. Critics have commonly objected that it is quite unlikely that the prophets would preach scathing judgment and "cheap grace" with one breath, as it were, almost out of both sides of their mouths. But who would disagree with that? Juxtaposition of oracles in the prophetic books in no way implies chronological proximity of delivery—as the most cursory study can often establish when the oracles are dated (especially Jeremiah). It is useful to remind ourselves again that, whatever motives dominated in giving final shape to our prophetic books, chronological sequence is rarely an overriding one!

We have usually assumed that the Messianic and similar oracles were delivered to different audiences entirely, perhaps primarily in private to the prophet's own disciples or other circles of the faithful. From any inner Biblical standpoint, the burden of proof would clearly lie on him who wishes to argue otherwise! One thing is crystal clear: the oracles of comfort and promise cannot be sundered from the rest of the prophetic corpus except by the most drastic surgery, and, indeed, except by recourse to developmental assumptions that are not even remotely compatible with the Bible's own testimony.

The most important two criteria for distinguishing true and false prophecy are enunciated in two important passages in Deuteronomy. Not surprisingly, the critieria are theological, and the pericopes are about as close as we ever come to a theoretical discussion of the subject in the Bible.

The first of these, Deut. 13:1-5, propounds what may unhesitatingly be called a *doctrinal or confessional* criterion. The test is in what the prophet teaches and preaches, whether or not it harmonizes with the rest of revelation, not in accidents of behavior as such. The rest of Deuteronomy, of course, is one of our major sources for spelling out the major articles of that doctrinal or confessional standard. Jeremiah's running battles with the false prophets of his day are good collateral reading, perhaps especially chap. 23. Jeremiah expresses himself in somewhat more transcendental language ("Who among them has stood in the council of the LORD?"), but the upshot is the same.

The second, Deut. 18:21-22, sets forth as a standard the fulfillment or nonfulfillment of prophecy. Here plainly "prophecy" is used in a sense largely synonymous with "prediction" or *"fore*telling," and we enter into that entire question. The "truth question" here was ultimately just as theological as in the case of the other criterion, but it obviously was intended to be empirical as well. Here at the very heart of Biblical theology we have none of the dichotomy of "historical truth" and "religious truth," which is virtually synonymous with liberal method. Biblical prophecy was not externally unique by reason of placing less emphasis on prediction than pagan counterparts, but what kept the former from becoming mantic, mechanical, and magical was precisely its saturation with a *theology* of a living, personal God. The distinction between "foretelling" and "forthtelling" is entirely artificial; even when proclaiming. Perhaps it is worth noting that the dual sense of "prophecy" continues even into the New Testament, where we meet the term not only in the sense of past predictors, but of present proclaimers (often apparently also of a charismatic sort).

Nor is Deuteronomy by any means alone in its stress on fulfillment of prediction as a major touchstone. It can be overstated, of course: prophecy was far more than mere foretelling, as fulfillment was far more than mere correspondence to prediction. But in our empiricist day and age, the danger is far greater that it be understated—if not simply denied. The concept of predictive prophecy so suffuses Biblical literature from one end to the other that it almost seems redundant to cite further examples. Perhaps we need note only the prominence of the apologetic argument from fulfillment of prophecy in Is. 40—66, or quote the familiar refrain of Ezekiel: "When this comes to pass, then they shall know that a prophet has been among them." In fact, humanly speaking, the prophets were honored (and their writings received into the canon) after the Exile—as they emphatically often had not been before—precisely because their predictions of destruction and captivity had proved crashingly true.

How this more empirical criterion worked in practice is not always clear. It obviously must often have been more useful in retrospect than it was for contemporaries. The distinction between short-range and long-range (more explicitly eschatological and Messianic) prophecy may be helpful. The first type of prediction was apparently more precise (not the studied ambivalence of many pagan oracles), and its accuracy could be determined in relatively short order. The long-range prophecies, on the other hand, were often couched in more general, illustrative terms, and, in any event, only future generations could evaluate them empirically.

The concept of the "contingency" or conditionality of much prophecy is an important one to bear in mind in this connection. Very often prophecies are explicitly introduced by an "if" clause (e.g., Is. 1:19-20). In accordance with the ancient covenant formula (cf. Deut. 27), whether blessing or cursing would come, depended on the response (not, of course, in the sense of meriting God's favor, but in the sense of being able to thwart it by unfaithfulness). If the people repented, God might "repent" and a prophecy of doom be suspended or revoked. If they rebelled, a prophecy of salvation might be set aside until God had, as it were, raised up children to Abraham from the stones (Matt. 3:9, etc.). God illustrates this principle to Jeremiah through a potter's shaping of a vessel (chap. 18), and it was one of the lessons God had to teach the pouting Jonah.

In this sense, that is, from a short-range empirical perspective one might even speak of "unfulfilled prophecies," and we shall note some of the problematic ones below. (And we ought to remind ourselves that apart from Christ very few of the prophetic oracles of hope, often appearing to announce imminent salvation, ever came true; all we have is pretty poetry, a poem of the invincible *human* spirit!) But, obviously, the Bible does not invoke the judgment of "false prophecy" when the fulfillment is not immediately apparent. "God's mills grind very slowly," and if it was not the matter of contingency, it may have been a matter of symbolic speech, or that the time of fulfillment—or all of it—is not yet. Typically, with long-range prediction the *entire* future stands before the prophet's eye as it were, and the various periods or stages of fulfillment are not distinguished (cf. even in the New Testament the telescoping of prophecies of the destruction of Jerusalem and of the end of the world).

Obviously, if everything were "contingent" or relative, as it were, we would have no real prediction left at all. This one valid qualification should not be overstated either. If pressed onesidedly, it would leave us with little more than the liberal construct of impassioned oratory about what "must" happen instead of prophecies of what "will" come to past. On the other hand, "contingency" accentuates that the LORD of prophecy is neither some magical cipher nor an impersonal, quasi-deterministic principle immanent in the universe, but a personal God of both justice and love.

But the main point here is the limited value for contemporaries of the criterion of fulfillment of prophecy. (In a broader sense, of course, it must be stressed, that as with all apologetic "proofs," it could not ultimately coerce or even found faith, but could only be corroborative of a conviction which the Holy Spirit had already worked.) In a very real sense, the problem of discerning true prophecy in Bible times must have been very similar to the one confronting believers today. In the welter of claims and counterclaims, how does one decide? The various churches are externally very similar, and often even use much of the same language. Then as now, the criterion can finally only be the Spirit's objective and inscripturated revelation, matched by the subjective and personal *testimonium Spiritus Sancti internum.*

Something must be said about the confusion of terminology, especially in critical literature (although sometimes in conservative circles too). The first confusion, with respect to "eschatological," is of a piece with the chaos of opinions in liberalism in general, often rooting in various evolutionary or other philosophical notions. Sometimes "eschatological" and "apocalyptic" appear to be virtually synonymous, especially under the sway of prejudices that such otherworldly escapism was a product of the postexilic period. At other times, the two terms are quite carefully distinguished, usually in some evolutionary manner; either apocalyptic is considered a late outgrowth of classical prophetic eschatology or, more commonly, is considered a regressive perversion of it (cf. below). Nothing inheres in the semantic question as such, but a certain "evolution *outward*" (like the opening of a bud) is discernible in many of the oracles in question, and a sequence such as teleological-eschatological-apocalyptic might be useful, but would have to be used with due caution.

There is also great variety in use of the term "messianic." Even conservatives often use it in a sense virtually synonymous with "eschatological"; at other times, it is used only of passages which specify an eschatological *person.* The distinction is exegetically useful, but it must be recognized that theologically, or from the standpoint of the fulfillment, it is virtually a distinction without a difference: there is no *eschaton* that is not ushered in and presided over by a personal messiah. In Jewish and liberal circles there is a certain disinclination to speak of a personal messiah, but one often hears of "messianism" or of the "messianic age." Often a radically different hermeneutic is concealed under those terms, but, if Biblically defined, they are not objectionable. A very common limitation of "messiah" is to prophecies only of a *royal* figure (excluding then "Servant," "Son of Man," etc.). From the vantage point of the fulfillment, no such delimitation will pass muster, or course, but, again, from a strictly exegetical-descriptive standpoint, it may be useful. Critics commonly go on to argue that there were very few of such "messianic" texts (perhaps only four or five) and that these originally applied only to the imminent future (the immediate history of the Davidic dynasty), with only later transposition into an eschatological and messianic key—and that, of course, is an entirely different matter. Finally, it should be noted that a few scholars refuse the label "messianic" to Old Testament texts altogether on the technicality that the Hebrew "anointed" never became a technical title until the intertestamental period. There is truth in the technicality, but observing it appears to hinder more than help. The moral of this story of migrant meanings is twofold: the student had better check what dictionary his source is using, and, second, must determine whether the issue is only semasiological, or whether all types of theological and hermeneutical hidden agendas lurk behind the scenes as well.

A final word is in order about the "symbolic actions" of the prophets. The label, however, is a misnomer. "Sacramental" might again be a better adjective than "symbolic." These were not *mere* "illustrations" of prophetic points, as we usually hear the word "symbol" (although prophetic speech teems with those too). They were themselves actual prophecies, albeit in dramatic rather than verbal form. Neither were they at all externally unique either (cf. Jeremiah vs. Hananiah in Jer. 28), but their validity was guaranteed only by the Validator of all actions.

Theologically, it is also very instructive to bring them into relation with the entire concept of typology. One might well regard them as miniature types, in this case not performed directly by the Lord of history Himself, but mediately through His servants, the prophets. They are a salutary reminder of the interpenetration of typology and prophecy, whether one comes at the matter empirically or discusses it hermeneutically. As we stressed earlier, there dare be no hidden agenda here of demoting predictive prophecy or of sidling in more immanentalistic directions. Rather the concern is to bring out the full dimensions of Biblical prophecy in historical context and with cosmic implications, as well as to forestall verbalistic and fideistic reductionisms. The prophetic Word was constantly accompanied by the "Sacrament," either in the form of their own actions or by pointing to the concurrent action of God "in, with, and under" history. The Word was becoming incarnate.

ISAIAH

Isaiah is such a protean figure that one hardly knows where to begin. Both in variety and forcefulness he excels, whether one measures from literary or from theological standpoints. Only a few of the early critics ever seriously disputed that evaluation, either because Isaiah allegedly was not "original" enough for their developmental scheme, or because his social action accent was less prominent than in some other prophets. For tradition and conservatism, of course, Isaiah towers especially because of his prominent Messianic pronouncements.

All of this is true enough even if one divides the book into the two parts (at least), so self-evident to higher criticism. Obviously, if one dissents from that posture, the magnitude of Isaiah's work is easily doubled.

Unity of the Book

Criticism has long since (beginning with Doederlein in 1775) become accustomed to distinguish "I Isaiah" or "Isaiah of Jerusalem" (chaps. 1—39) from some unknown anonymous "II Isaiah" or "Deutero-Isaiah" (chaps. 40—66). Perhaps only the non-Mosaicity of the Pentateuch may be said to be as secure an "assured result" in critical minds. An extremely small number of critical dissenters may lend a little comfort to conservatives, but, critically speaking, they are scarcely a drop in the bucket. Gesenius in the early nineteenth century, like a few recent scholars (Brownlee, etc.) have argued for some kind of *non*-Isaianic unity to the book. Many will concede the likelihood of some authentically Isaianic material in chaps. 56—66, but the fundamental theological problems remain untouched by these variations. Conversely, then, rejection of any dichotomy of the book is widely regarded as a major touchstone of conservatism or orthodoxy.

Neither side really listens to the other at all, not so much out of mutual intransigence, as because of the fundamentally different presuppositions or "hermeneutical circle" involved, of which the position on Isaiah will be only the tip of the iceberg. As we shall see, far more is involved than merely the question of authorship of a portion of Scripture, which in and of itself might be theologically a matter of indifference.

One should stress, however, the frequent utility of the critical labels, also for conservatives, as a very convenient shorthand, if it is clear that they are being used neutrally. We too may employ designations such as "Isaiah I" and "Isaiah II", or even, on occasion, "Second Isaiah." But let it be clear that no hidden agenda lurks there. The reference is purely *literary*, to sections of the book, not to authorship. By the same token, because the accents and contents of the two parts of the book do undeniably differ sufficiently, we shall largely treat them separately below.

But first to the isagogical issue itself (we make no attempt to treat it exhaustively). It must be stressed again that far more is at stake than merely whether or not there are "two Isaiahs." As a matter of fact, virtually no one of critical mind thinks any longer of only "two Isaiahs." As we shall detail shortly, both parts of the book are further dissected, much as the traditional unities of other Biblical books are. That is, for critics "I Isaiah" and "II Isaiah" are only tags of convenience. Much material within chaps. 1—39 is dated later than the eighth-century figure, some of it even later than the bulk of chaps. 40—66. Similarly, chaps.

56—66 are usually considered separately as a "III Isaiah" or "Trito-Isaiah." However, the unity of those chapters is widely questioned too, as is also true to a lesser extent of chaps. 40—55.

Furthermore, the "unity of Isaiah" is fraught with significance not only for the particulars of the entire Book of Isaiah but for the study of all the prophetic books. The same principles used for the dismemberment of Isaiah are also employed elsewhere, as will be obvious in our discussions of the other "latter prophets." The resultant critical picture of the course and development of prophecy differs about as much from the traditional one as the critical reconstruction of Israel's early history does from the canonical, Pentateuchal record. The shift centers not only on the question of prediction as such, but especially on eschatology in the broader sense. The old Wellhausen inclination to regard *Heilsprophetie* as somehow late, "ungenuine," hence inferior, still lingers, no matter how nuanced. Even recent, more holistic approaches, which shrink from the value judgments traditionally associated with talk of "genuineness," still tend to retain the technical isagogical conclusions of classical criticism.

Philosophical *a prioris* about the possibility of predictive prophecy are very much involved, of course. Probably nowhere in the Old Testament is this issue so prominent and so inescapable as here. It is not only a question of the prominent and famous Messianic oracles of Isaiah, where many critics today would concede genuine prophecy, at least of a sort. Even more to the point at the moment is the fact that nowhere in Scripture do we have so extensive and so sustained a prophecy of the future as we find in Is. 40—66. Shorter pericopes of the same sort appear also in chaps. 1—39 and in other prophetic books, where, as we noted, the critical treatment is generally the same as here.

In Is. 40—66 we have not only a single prediction or two, but a sustained projection of the prophet's vision into the future, to which he speaks *in extenso* as though he were contemporary with the Exile, with Babylon, not with Assyria, as the enemy. The message can be extremely precise, as he brings comfort and promise to the exiles whose ordeal is about over. The major example is the specification twice by name of Cyrus (44:28 and 45:1), although the figure of Cyrus is plainly implied elsewhere in the context. As noted earlier, the only real parallel in the Old Testament is the specification of Josiah in 1 Kings 13 some three centuries before his historical appearance. Since there is no evidence whatsoever of textual tampering at these points, the entire issue of the unity of Isaiah pivots to no little extent on these Cyrus passages. For liberals, they clinch the case for a contemporary, sixth-century date of these chapters, while for most conservatives they represent the pinnacle of the predictive material in the entire context. Allis, in particular, has demonstrated that the parallelistic and climactic structure of 44:26-28 would be destroyed if *Koresh* (Cyrus) were removed.

The issue is ultimately decided on a dogmatic basis, but a certain historically based apologetic is also in order. If the prophets ever engaged in such projection at all, the question becomes a matter of degree rather than of kind. (Some critics will concede that a lesser amount of it is indeed found among the "genuine" oracles of Isaiah I!). Furthermore, some such projection seems almost synonymous with the idea of "prophecy," of seeing "visions," and so on. Isaiah's call (chap. 6) reflects the usual vertical vantage point of the prophets, standing as it were, in God's throne, from which height they can readily "see" horizontally far into the future, and in which standpoint the temporal distinctions of ordinary humanity faded behind the eternal "now," and all of time became, as it were, one day as much as for God Himself (cf. 2 Peter 3:8).

It has traditionally been assumed that Isaiah had the visions of chaps. 40 ff. in his later years, but there is no need for such an assumption, and we simply have no way of knowing. The fact that they appear last in Isaiah's book does not imply that they occurred last, precisely because much similar material is scattered throughout the first part of the book. The hypothesis of later composition is thought to account for the "mellowed" viewpoint and for the shift in vocabulary (cf. below), but, even humanly speaking, both the different subject matter and Isaiah's unrivaled literary abilities render the assumption moot. If such oracles were ever delivered publicly at all, it would seem likely, under those circumstances that the occasion was private, and among a closed circle of the faithful.

One must be aware of the extent to which the integrity of *all* of Scripture is implicated at this point, because the pattern of restoration through and after judgment, that is of Law-Gospel, forms a sort of substructure to the entire Bible. It is given overt expression not only in the judgment-salvation polarity of the two halves of Isaiah, but in virtually every other prophetic book. And not only other prophetic books, but elsewhere in Scripture: classically in Deuteronomy, but also at other points in the Pentateuch. Assuming they really are Mosaic, the concept was established and traditional long before Isaiah picked it up. In a sense above all, this constant Old Testament pattern finds its antitype and ultimate validity in the death and resurrection of Christ. Thus, to question the basic structural unity of Isaiah is to strike a body blow at the coherence of the entire Bible, isagogically as well as theologically. A theologically literate mind which looked at the inner meaning of all of salvation-history in that light would find such a message meaningful already in advance of the historical Exile, just as we, who historically also have no experience of it, find it spiritually and typologically pertinent to our circumstances via its eschatological consummation on Good Friday and Easter.

The crowning and decisive argument for the unity of Isaiah for conservatives, of course, is ultimately rooted in dogma. That critics reject out of hand such appeal to dogma (that is, conservative presuppositions) as "unscientific," as though they had none, summarizes as well as anything the almost infinite gulf separating the two camps. The dogmas involved here, as also with respect to Mosaic authorship of the Pentateuch, are at once Christological and Scriptural. Not only the New Testament in general, but also our Lord specifically and repeatedly refers to both halves of the book as equally Isaianic. Many of these references are not only to the book, but to the person of Isaiah. In John 12:38-41 quotations from both parts of the book are attributed to the man Isaiah in one breath. The cumulative evidence and the nature of the argumentation on the basis of the citations is such that it will not be dismissed as mere casual, popular reference by anyone who takes Christ's and the New Testament's testimony seriously. See further, e.g., Young, pp. 202—203 for a handy summary of the evidence in this respect.

The critical case for a "II Isaiah" is a classical example of the convergence of the three main *types* of arguments characteristic of the historical-critical method: historical, history of religions, and literary. The first type of argument, that from historical background, is again the primary one. The point of departure is the dogma that the prophet must speak to his *own times,* in other words that he is a "forthteller" rather than a "foreteller." (Cf. the previous chapter.) Conservatives would not care to challenge the general value of this principle, both for understanding Biblical prophecy and for distinguishing it from its pagan counterparts. However, again the distinction is artificial: there is no reason why in a broader sense a prophet cannot be said to be speaking to his own time even when speaking (and *in extenso)* to the future, or, for that matter, of eternity.

Even meeting critics on their own turf, the conservative has no trouble detecting serious weaknesses in the critical application of the historical principle. One would certainly be the very anonymity of such a towering figure as the putative "II Isaiah," something entirely unprecedented, and contrary to the fact that often the "tradition" preserved *only* the prophet's name, and the known circumstance that apparently considerations of authorship were significant in debates about canonicity. Another problem is the radical difference between the preaching of Ezekiel and "II Isaiah," who on the critical theory would be contemporaries. (Many critics, of course, unconcerned about the unity of Scripture, would see in these two prophets the fountainheads of the contradictory "utopian" and hierocratic accents which would allegedly be at each other's throats in the rest of the Old Testament, e.g., Hanson.)

Furthermore, Biblical usage in general does not warrant such massive accent on precise, historical occasion. The Bible's concern is more with History or with Time in the broad, sacramental sense, than with, as such, empirical, datable occasion—although the two, of course, dare not be severed or even dichotomized into two entirely different types of history. It is also interesting to note that more recent form criticism, especially with its frequent accents on cultic setting, has moved in somewhat the same direction: worship in all times is more concerned with what is valid for all time, rather than, as such, with what happened at one time. It is thoroughly hypothetical, but there is no reason why conservatives should not entertain the possibility that such worship interests played a role, under God, in the final canonical form of much prophetic literature.

If such oracles were delivered in private to disciples (or only written down), we can understand that they were not precisely dated, precisely because their scopus was God's Time, whenever and however in the future their ultimate Author would see fit to fulfill them. But to the faithful who believed that the prophet's thundering oracles of doom would come true first, and that the route of salvation for the remnant was only via that cross (for Christians typical of the Cross), it simply cannot be said that the oracles of restoration would be meaningless to those of the prophets' own time.

In any event, there is no debate about the historical circumstances to which Isaiah II is addressed. The only issue is *when* that address was made. Plainly the previously predicted Exile has already come to pass. Jerusalem and the temple appear to lie in ruins. But the "great reversal," so prominent also in earlier oracles, is also about to take place. Given that ancient theological pattern in the prophets—and earlier—and given the "foreshortening" (telescoping) of periods of time characteristic of eschatological vision, it seems entirely in character that one of the grandest of the prophets should have given grandest expression to a keystone of prophetic and Biblical theology.

The second main type of critical defense of a sixth-century date for Is. 40 ff. is based on the correspondence of the material to a presumed stage in the history of Israel's religious development (in earlier years often styled misleadingly, "progressive revelation"). As the language indicated, however, this type of argumentation is so bound up with the evolutionism and isagogical fruit-basket-upset of the remainder of the critical approach to the Old Testament, that the conservative is constrained to reject it almost *in toto*.

It once was commonly asserted that monotheism, having first surfaced in the eighth-century prophets, received its classical expression by "Deutero-Isaiah" (or at least came as close to a theoretical, philosophical monotheism as anywhere in the Old Testament). Few today would make the assertion in so unguarded a form, but the pattern remains (what was previously a mere "faith" now becoming a "certainty" or the like, with *theoretical* polemic against idolatry, etc.). Given that assumption, parallel assertions in Scripture, no matter what their present literary context (especially those attributed to Moses in the Pentateuch) must be dated to about the time of the Exile too.

The "evidence" from monotheism overlaps both with the previous historical type of argumentation as well as with other aspects of the religious argument. Allegedly, it was the shock of the Exile, when Yahweh plainly could no longer be thought of as a mere national god, bound to a people and their land, which first produced the historical content requisite for a full and virtually explicit monotheism. The inevitable corollary was supposed to be the simultaneous climactic expression of Biblical universalism, based on clear enunciations for the first time of "creation" or "protology" and "eschatology." The God of Israel's history had now graduated into the status of sole universal Creator-Judge of heaven and earth, as the people's historical experience of *creatio ex nihilo* in the return was extrapolated into eternity.

No doubt, the theme of creation, with its implication of a universal Creator of heaven and earth engaged in judging and redeeming in a "new creation," is extremely prominent in Isaiah II. Also the semitechnical vocable *bara'* is prominent, as in Gen. 1 (which critics commonly assume was dependent on Isaiah II in this respect). But that any of this is in any real sense novel in Isaiah II is defensible only in connection with an evolutionary redistribution of much of the rest of the Old Testament. On the other hand, it would seem to be precisely the accent required also in oracles dealing with the source and scope of all history. In principle, it differs little from the theme of God's holiness or ineffable transcendence prominent in Isaiah I.

Similarly, with Isaiah II's eschatology, the obverse of protology. The future now envisioned is, indeed, *somewhat* more consistently concerned with the entire universe than in Isaiah I (or at least the "authentically Isaianic" parts of it by critical lights), but, except for heightened accent and specific accent, the Biblical evidence would indicate that the idea was no more novel to the faithful then that it is to orthodoxy today. As befits the times, the specific *expression* of the eschatology varies also: the "remnant" motif of Isaiah I mutates into "Suffering Servant" language, and the specifically *royal* Messianism of the earlier chapters is almost totally submerged under the broader version of the restoration of Zion, but the latter two are the obverse sides of the same coin, as we noted earlier. Only a critical mind, which almost on principle seeks to *de*unify and *de*harmonize Scripture, will have difficulty recognizing the ultimate unity of only slightly different articulations. In fact, the accent on Zion is one theme which emphatically unites the two parts of the book, as well as accents on holiness and faith.

A developmental pattern is also commonly detected in connection with the *"Suffering* Servant" theme. Here, it is stated, suffering is no longer viewed as *punishment* for one's own sins, as in Wisdom and the "deuteronomic" corpus, or a cause for lament as in the psalms and Jeremiah, but is presented as vicariously redemptive and expiatory. One might concede a bit of this if it were presented as an *accent* of "Isaiah of Jerusalem," but the strong piacular concern of the entire sacrificial system, plus certain accents on Moses' substitutionary death (in a sense) show that the basic idea had been around in Israel for a long time.

The third type of critical argumentation is literary, based on both vocabulary and stylistic differences. Recent computerized studies have only basically confirmed what we knew previously. To no little extent, the differences between the parts of the book in this respect are as undeniable as the shift in the historical circumstances envisioned, or in the correspondingly different theological accents. The only question again is why or whence the differences. Like the previous types of argument, the literary ones can easily be overstated, however, and often are in critical literature. The more hymnic style of Isaiah II, so evident even in translation, also appears frequently in Isaiah I—which means that an ultimate disjunction of the two halves can be sustained again only in conjunction with considerable surgery on chaps. 1—39. The shifts in style as well as vocabulary are easily credible in the case of a past master of the Hebrew language like Isaiah. Change of vocabulary inevitably also attends change in style and subject-matter. We shall not cite statistics here, but actual counts indicate a substantial continuity in vocabulary as well as variations. One of the most obvious of these is the frequent use of the favorite Isaianic epithet for the deity in all parts of the book: "the Holy One of Israel." Others would include the "highway," the "banner" *(nes)*, etc.

At one time, absolute datings on the basis of vocabulary differences were in vogue (largely determined, to begin with, by arguments in a circle based on the dating of literature in which the words occurred), but archaeological evidence has so undercut that approach that one finds it employed today only very sparingly, e.g., *bara'* in conjunction with the religious evolutionism we noted above. Today, the literary argument would, as such, normally be carried no further than notice of the differences, and an attempt to interpret them as corroborative of the other types of argument. The linguistic argument always was conceded to be the weakest of the three types, and its cogency is today as minimal as ever. Furthermore, if the other two types of argument are shown to have feet of clay, the independent value of the literary argument is virtually nil.

Isaiah's Life and Times

There is not the slightest debate about the historical circumstances of "Isaiah of Jerusalem," and if we take the book as a unity, they ultimately apply to all the oracles in it, even when further precision is impossible. The superscription of the book specifies the reigns of Uzziah, Jotham, Ahaz, and Hezekiah, and in this case not even critics challenge its applicability to Isaiah. Chap. 6, if presumed to record Isaiah's call, as is usually done, would pinpoint the beginning of his prophetic activity "in the year that King Uzziah died," i.e., about 742. Whether or not he outlived Hezekiah (d. 687) is not entirely certain, but the reference in 2 Chron. 32:32 to a sort of biography of Hezekiah written by Isaiah, as he had earlier written one of Uzziah (2 Chron. 26:22), would suggest as much. If so, however, there was apparently no later prophetic activity. There is no way to test the reliability of the ancient tradition of his martyrdom under Manasseh by being sawn asunder within a hollow log. The story is thoroughly credible, and perhaps we should invoke the ancient, *In dubito pro traditio* in its favor. If the reference in Heb. 11:37 is to Isaiah, its historicity is established, but the precise allusion there is uncertain.

In any case, Isaiah lived through, witnessed, and commented on one of the major turning points in Israel's history—from the halcyon days of empire and independence under Uzziah through the fall of Samaria and the semi-escape of Judah only by accepting colonial status under the relentless pressure of the Assyrian colossus. Fortunately, we know the events of that period about as well as any era in Old Testament history, thanks to copious Biblical as well as extra-Biblical evidence. Some of Isaiah's oracles are precisely dated in connection with specific historical events, and, within limits, even conservatives will legitimately theorize about the exact historical location of many of the others.

Partly on the basis of the dated oracles, it is common to see two main phases of Isaiah's ministry, each concluded by a retirement or period of silence after rejection. The first would peak under the reign of Ahaz, ending in a withdrawal to a nucleus of faithful disciples, according to a common understanding of Is. 8:16 ff. Upon Hezekiah's accession, Isaiah would take heart and become vocal once more, only to retire again to an inner circle in the latter years of Hezekiah—or so 30:8 ff. can be construed. The picture is somewhat hypothetical, but not incompatible with the Biblical data. In fact, much of the undated material in the Book of Isaiah, especially that focused on future time or almost on Time itself (e.g., chaps. 40—66) may congenially be thought of as having been delivered to the faithful during those periods out of the public eye.

The name "Isaiah" means "Yahweh is salvation" or the like (essentially synonymous with the names Hosea, Joshua and Jesus). The name is not only fortuitously appropriate to the contents of the book, but Isaiah explicitly makes the name and his life which embodied it, a "sign" or a "type" (so in a semitechnical sense) of his entire message, and thus also of the Antitype, who in both name and life brought that message to fruition.

Of further precise details of Isaiah's life we know very little, although probably more than of any other prophet except Jeremiah. (That circumstance is itself a major illustration of the Bible's own somewhat different accent on history than modern criticism's historicism.) Of his father Amoz (not to be confused with Amos), we know only the name (the Biblical counterpart of the modern cognomen or family name). If Isaiah was not a native of Jerusalem, he certainly was thoroughly at home there, and apparently spent his entire ministry there. Humanly speaking, that context helps account for the literary elegance, exalted ideas, and general patrician bearing of the book. It also explains Isaiah's intimate involvement in the local and international politics of the period, as well as his theological concentration on Zion and its Davidic throne.

Whatever secular calling the prophet also pursued, if any, eludes us, but, as often, hypotheses proliferate in inverse ratio to hard evidence. The suggestion that he was a member of the ruling aristocracy, a court official, official advisor, and confidant of kings, conceivably of royal blood himself, is not uncongenial, but neither is it required by the evidence. The recent accent on wisdom has popularized an understanding of Isaiah as a wisdom teacher (especially Fichtner), not only because of the cast of some of his oracles, but also because of his court associations, which we know was often characteristic of the "Wise," as the ancient Orient heard that term. Many have explained him as a priest or at least a temple official because of his apparent presence inside the temple, where only priests had access, at the time of his call. However, it is risky to extract certain information of that sort from a vision, or there could be other explanations for a layman's presence in the Holy Place. Most obviously grasping at straws is the tradition that makes Isaiah a physician by original profession because of his "medical" advice to Hezekiah (38:21).

As regards personal life, we know that Isaiah was married (Is. 8:3, where his wife is not named, but called only "the prophetess," probably not meant in a professional sense, but as in the German idiom which makes the professor's wife *Frau Professor*). Two sons were both given "symbolic names," thus becoming walking prophecies or types (Isaiah explicitly includes them with himself as "signs and portents" in 8:18). The first was named Shearjashub (7:3), "A remnant shall return," embodying one of Isaiah's chief themes. It is debated whether the name was primarily promise ("A remnant shall *certainly* return") or doom ("*Only* a remnant shall return"); probably it was both at once. The name of the second son, however, is pure, unrelieved doom: Mahershalalhashbaz (8:1), "The spoil speeds, the prey hastes." Many scholars, also including some conservative ones, believe that Immanuel ("God with us") was a third child of Isaiah's, but the position is fraught with considerable difficulty (cf. below).

Outline and Structure

Is. 1—39 may be outlined as follows: (1) Chaps. 1—12: Largely oracles of judgment or doom against Judah and Jerusalem (often considered to come from the first period of Isaiah's ministry under Ahaz), although balanced by considerable promissory and Messianic material; (2) Chaps. 13—23: Largely "Gentile oracles"; (3) Chaps. 24—27: Cosmic judgment and final deliverance of Israel (in criticism commonly known as the "Isaiah Apocalypse," hence a handy label regardless of exegetical and isagogical judgments); (4) Chaps. 28—33: More oracles of judgment against Judah and Jerusalem, apparently deriving largely from the latter part of Isaiah's ministry under Hezekiah; (5) Chaps. 34—35: Contrasting oracles on the future of Israel and Edom (with especially close parallels to Isaiah II); and Chaps. 36—39: The historical narrative of Isaiah's and Hezekiah's successful confrontation with Sennacherib (almost identical with 2 Kings 18:13—20:19). Duhm may well have been partially correct in viewing these sections as preliminary collections of Isaianic material; that little authentic material was recognized outside of 1—12 and 28—33, however, was a consequence of the dogma that early true prophets preached only doom.

Already the many qualifiers one has to add to any attempt at a simple outline indicates how highly variegated are the contents of the first part of the book alone. It is not easy to discern rhyme or reason in the overall outline. However, it appears likely that we can make out a *double* use of the classical prophetic outline sketched above: (1) Judgment on Judah/Jerusalem (1—12 and 28—33); (2) Judgment on Foreign Nations (13—23 and 34—35): and (3) Salvation for all who repent (24—27 and 36—39). If so, the profound "Law-Gospel" message of the prophet is conveyed also by the structure of his book. The scheme does not work out neatly, however, so it apparently was used relaxedly. Since other schemes, such as "alternation of weal and woe" are discernible within some of the major sections, it is possible that some of these had already assumed semifixed form before being incorporated into the larger pattern. The tripartite scheme does not work as well the second time as the first, especially with respect to chaps. 36—39. Here it would appear considerations of the unity of the entire book took precedence: the chapters appear to be in their present position partly to effect a transition to chaps. 40 ff., and, if so, at least by association they suggest the motif of salvation available to all.

Considering the great variety and rapid alternation of themes in the Book of Isaiah (at this point also including Isaiah II), it is readily understandable why critics commonly refer to the entire book as an "anthology" or a "library" of diverse materials. Up to a point the conservatives can readily concur in that judgment; at any rate, it certainly does not follow from insistence on the unity of Isaiah that it had no transmissional history. In that sense, much of the Biblical literature is anthological.

It is a somewhat different matter, however, when liberalism goes on to think of an "Isaianic school" of anonymous disciples or traditors who not only collected and arranged the master's material, but also composed freely, as they supposed Isaiah would have spoken, had he lived in their later times. That construction contradicts not only Biblical testimony about Isaianic authorship of the entire book, but is obviously also beholden to liberal concepts of open-minded "community inspiration," etc. In much more modest form, however, there is no necessary clash with "verbal inspiration" in thinking of a sort of a "school" of disciples, who collected their mentor's oracles into their present canonical form not too long after his death. With all due caution, neither is it entirely unthinkable that some of the stylistic variation or some of the connective pericopes are attributable to followers. Isagogically, those can never be more than mere possibilities; and theologically it is a *sine qua non* that such possibilities remain subsumed under the presuppositions of *special* inspiration and revelation. (Budde's "accident theory," to the effect that the two halves of the book had no kind of original connection, but were placed together to fill up a scroll about the same size as the other three "latter prophets," no longer has much of a following.)

Of course, modern students of the Bible were not the first to spy out the problem. Luther's observation in his preface is worth quoting (and similar ones precede many of the other prophetic books). Luther first observes that Isaiah treats three topics in the book: (a) sermons against sin and predicting Christ; (b) prophecies against Assyria; and (c) prophecies about Babylon. Luther then continues:

> [Isaiah] does not treat them in order, and give each of these subjects its own place, and put it into its own chapters and pages; but they are so mixed up together that much of the first matter is brought in along with the second and third, and the third subject is discussed somewhat earlier than the second. But whether this was done by those who collected and wrote down prophecies (as is thought to have happened with the Psalter), or whether he himself arranged it this way according as time, occasion, and persons suggested, and these times and occasions were not always alike, and had no order—this I do not know.

(A few Lutherans have tried to make hay out of Luther's prefaces such as this, as though we have here some incipient higher criticism. It plainly is nothing of the sort. Luther evinces awareness of the non-chronological arrangement of the material and suggests that others besides Isaiah might be responsible for that. However, the common critical value judgments are totally lacking: disparagement of the manner of compilation, alleged misunderstandings, errors, contradictions, etc.)

Text

A word is in order about textual criticism of Isaiah (and again this applies to the entire book). In this case, the Masoretic text is in good shape, occasioning only a few, relatively routine, problems. The Septuagint, however, is so free, sometimes almost as periphrastic as a Targum, that its value as a witness to the original text is sharply reduced. In recent years, interest has focused on the phenomenal finds of Qumran, which yielded two manuscripts of Isaiah. One (usually referred to as IQIs[b]) was preserved only fragmentarily, but was virtually identical with the Masoretic text, thus establishing the antiquity of that textual tradition. The other Qumran copy (IQIs[a]) was complete, but differed somewhat at points, although still not significantly. Enthusiasm sometimes caused the differences to be overrated initially (also in the RSV), but equilibrium has generally been restored.

Style

Isaiah's style is so exceptional that it can scarcely be passed by without comment. Rarely have "inspiration" in the poetic and the theological senses been wed so beautifully. Different styles are adopted in different parts of the book, but the same peerless ability is evident throughout— and it is one argument against a "school," because committees rarely exhibit such qualities! Commentators commonly vie with each other in reaching for superlatives or even comparisons: Demosthenes (so Jerome),

Homer, or even Mozart with his classical sense of *peras,* never too much, never too little. Some features of the style come through even in translation, many others are untranslatable. It is a feature which the conscientious exegete cannot ignore, and in the original context it must have contributed inestimably to the impact of Isaiah's preaching. Paranomasia and startling simile are the order of the day. Isaiah has an almost uncanny ability to find an apt figure or illustration to clinch his point (e.g., the hut in a cucumber field, Is. 1:8, or a child in a forest of few trees, 10:19). More technically, he is a master of all the formal devices of Hebrew poetry. And, as the novice in Hebrew often discovers to his dismay, we find in the Book of Isaiah a richness of vocabulary and synonyms unparalleled elsewhere in the Bible (someone has counted a total of 2,186 words).

There are many variations also within Isaiah I, but esp. in chaps. 40—55, the style is often called lyric or "hymnic," because there are close connections with the style of especially the so-called Enthronement psalms or hymns. (Scholars have debated in which direction the dependence lay, but it seems to this writer far and away the more likely that Isaiah adapted a familiar liturgical pattern both in applying its theme to current events and in projecting it upon the screen of eschatological fulfillment.) The eloquence in the second part of the book is more cumulative rather than the sharp contours favored in the earlier chapters, and natural imagery tends to give way to human figures, especially personification. Triads, imperatives, rhetorical questions are also much in evidence. (See especially Muilenburg's commentary.)

Theology

Finally, because of Isaiah's overwhelming importance, an initial word should be said in a more systematic way about his major theological emphases. It is scarcely excessive to label him "*the* theologian of the Old Testament," although, of course, without prejudice to the other Biblical literature, and minus the abstract scholastic form the West associates with "theology." At this point we concentrate more on Isaiah I, but the division from Isaiah II is fluid. Possibly six captions will do initial justice to Isaiah's almost unfathomable depths.

Perhaps above all towers the theme of God's "holiness" or absolute transcendence, His being and status as wholly other, "God and not man." It receives classical expression in the Trisagion of the call (Is. 6:3) and in the favorite epithet, "Holy One of Israel," but also appears in a hundred and one other formulations. Especially earlier critics thought of prophetic pioneering in the ethicizing of holiness (or accent on the ultimate inseparability of justification and sanctification, if you will), but, if we are not evolutionists, we plainly have here a major instance of the prophetic "reformation," underscoring ancient Mosaic teaching. Just as in the "Holiness Code" (Lev. 17—26), the gift of the covenant means for Isaiah that Israel must be holy as her God is Holy. That must be evident in political stance as well as in social demeanor. Sin in Isaiah's thought is preeminently "rebellion" *(pesha')*, unwillingness to recognize God's sovereignty over all aspects of life, whether in the public or private sector (let us not forget that Israel, unlike modern states, was church and state at once).

The obverse of God's holiness, His "glory" (His holiness revealed) is obviously present by implication too, but receives explicit expression more in Isaiah II (and Ezekiel). These themes are so prominent also in Israel's cult, that one might well think of massive cultic influence in this connection (and also Is. 6 might point in that direction). In any event, God supplies the means for His people to assume His character, if they will accept, but, if not, that same energic holiness requires damnation. It was such themes that especially classical Calvinism found congenial, and much of the Reformed tradition's affinity with the Old Testament centers in those Isaianic accents.

Traditional Lutheranism would probably be disposed to put proportionately somewhat more stress on a second Isaianic refrain, that of "faith." In this respect Isaiah shares with Habakkuk the epithet, "the St. Paul of the Old Testament." The only faithful response to God's holiness and the "cornerstone" (Is. 28:16) of Israel's survival is "returning and rest, . . . quietness and trust" (30:15). The meaning of "faith" in Isaiah should not simply be equated with Paul's but neither should it be disjoined from it. On the surface it has much more the popular sense of "trust" *(fides qua)* or "firmness" *('emunah*; 7:9b). But in contrast to the popular, modern paganization of the term, in Isaianic context it plainly implies also the corresponding object of the trust and its content *(fides quae)*, that is, ultimately the same divine work of judgment and salvation which Paul highlights so emphatically.

Third, the motif of the "day of the LORD" is very prominent in Isaiah, perhaps climactically in Is. 2:6 ff. We need not enter here into the fruitless academic debate about the ultimate origins of the concept, holy war or cult (probably both). Neither can it be true that Amos first deployed it as a theme of judgment instead of certain redemption, on whom Isaiah should be dependent. Also futile is any attempt to distinguish historical and eschatological accents in connection with the phrase: as throughout the Bible, *today* is judgment day and/or the day of salvation, but today also participates in the ultimate, eschatological action of God. ("Apocalyptic" would change the emphasis, but not the formula.)

Fourth, the concept of the "remnant" runs throughout. Much of Isaiah's judgment-salvation or Law-Gospel message centers at this point. "The blood of the martyrs is the seed of the church." There is no other way for the eschatological people of God, the "holy seed" (Is. 6:13), to be formed than in the crucible of exile and restoration, death and resurrection. The theme is present in the bleak terms of Isaiah's call (6:11-13), and the main vocable expressing it appears in the name of his first son, Shearjashub (7:3). It is debatable, but highly possible, that many scholars are right in understanding Isaiah as viewing the nucleus of the remnant already present in a circle of faithful disciples clustered about him. Not palatable, however, is the evolutionistic construction that Isaiah first viewed Judah as the remnant, then narrowed it to Jerusalem or Zion, and finally came around to a purely spiritual understanding. Even though the term "remnant" is little used in Isaiah II, one must note the obvious parallelism of this formulation in Isaiah I with the clear distinction between the physical and the true Israel in chaps. 40—66.

Finally, the twin motifs of Zion and the Messiah are nowhere so prominently displayed as in Isaiah. In fact, many critics want to make Isaiah the major spokesman of those uniquely Judahite "traditions" and pit them against the allegedly more ancient traditions (supposedly preserved underground in the North until the fall of Samaria) of Mosaic covenant, Exodus, etc. As usual, there is no denying the variation in accent, but they need not be construed as disjunctive. Even humanly speaking, it stands to reason that the North would not cherish traditions of the election of David and Zion as a citizen of the South would. There is even less justification for construing the latter motifs as essentially pagan in character, allegedly only later and rather unsuccessfully grafted into the trunk of ancient Israelite religion.

Accents in Isaiah I and II also differ somewhat in these respects. "Zion" themes are prominent enough in both halves, but in Isaiah II specifically *royal* Messianism is almost completely submerged by an eschatology stressing the universal kingship of God, and by the Servant themes. Also eschatological and typological use of Exodus and general covenant motifs appears more prominently in Isaiah II. The least that one can say is that such variety is at least as attributable to one unusually resourceful poet, varying his figures with the topic, as it is to some faceless "schools" or other figure of unparalleled anonymity.

It is important that "Zion" (the eschatological city of God, already proleptically and sacramentally "incarnate" on earth) be distinguished (although not divorced) from the earthly Jerusalem, or Isaiah and other prophets will soon be embroiled in the crassest contradictions. The theme of the "inviolability of Zion" is close to constitutive of Isaiah's message, but, of course, the earthly Jerusalem is doomed to destruction. The "gates of hell" cannot prevail against Zion (the church), and after the earthly holocaust it will rise as the center of the eschatological, Messianic kingdom, the joy and desire of all the earth (cf. Is. 2:1-4). Isaiah II descries and celebrates the beginning of the realization of those promises, and the New Testament proclaims their fulfillment in Christ's kingdom (yet with a consummation in the kingdom of glory still awaited).

Last and climactically there is the theme of the Messiah, of the son of David enthroned in the city of David, the personal embodiment and type of the fulfillment of all election and covenant *Heilsgeschichte*. The distinction between Messianism and the more general eschatology is ultimately artificial, as we noted earlier, but at the moment we pinpoint the former. Both atomistic critics and well-meaning conservatives are often guilty of isolating these oracles from their total Isaianic context. Involved are not only some of the best known prophecies in the Old Testament (Is. 7; 9; 11), but others that are not so well known (e.g., chaps. 32 and 33). It is especially nugatory to try to distinguish historical and eschatological content in these pericopes.

Before we conclude our brief survey of Isaianic theology, the phenomenal similarity of many of these motifs with three "Isaianic psalms" (Is. 46—48) must be noted, most famously in the refrains of Immanuel, of faith, of God's transcendence, and of the "inviolability of Zion," in Ps. 46, the Reformation psalm. Close connections between Isaiah and the Psalter also surface in the "hymns of Zion" in general, as in the enthronement and royal psalms. We need not join the chicken-or-egg enigma of debating priority, but it seems quite undeniable that here we see some of the literary sources of Isaiah's theological accent on those same themes.

Isaiah 1—12

Is. 1, since the days of Ewald in the nineteenth century, has often been known as the "Great Arraignment," and more recent scholars will often cite it as a parade example of "covenant lawsuit." What historical devastation occasioned v. 7 ff. is unspecified, as so often. The aftermath of the "Syro-Ephraimitic war" under Ahaz is a possibility, but Sennacherib's depredations under Hezekiah seems more likely. In any event, chronological considerations do not seem to have determined its position, but rather its suitability as an epitome of and introduction to the entire book. If so, the superscription of Is. 1:1, which is surely intended for the entire book, may well have been put in place at the same time. In v.

4 for the first time we encounter Isaiah's favorite divine epithet, "Holy One of Israel." In v. 10 ff. is the first of many denunciations of worship without accompanying ethics. Famous v. 18 depicts Yahweh as offering judicial, forensic pardon (justification) if the people will only repent, and thus vs. 18-19 are classical formulations of the "contingency" of prophecy. V. 21 introduces Isaiah's central focus on Zion, but it and the chapter conclude (v. 24 ff.) with promises of eschatological restoration of the *civitas Dei*. This oracle was presumably not delivered by Isaiah on the same occasion, but appended here to denote the Gospel intent of the Law.

Is. 2:1 certainly appears to be another "superscription," and the frequent supposition that it indicates some preliminary subcollection of Isaianic oracles may be construed acceptably. If so, it was apparently adjudged suitable even in its subsequent, larger context—as, indeed, it is. The collection it originally headed might have included an extended section of the present book, or only chaps. 2—4. In any case, those three chapters form an artfully constructed unit in their final form, framed by an "inclusion" of eschatological oracles at beginning and end, with perhaps three judgmental oracles in the middle.

The first oracle, of the eschatological Zion, is another of the obvious doublets in the Bible. Is. 2:2-4 is virtually identical with Micah 4:1-3, although each prophet adds his own conclusion. (Critics quite universally regard it as an "ungenuine," probably late, addition in both Isaiah and Micah.) Debate has raged back and forth again about the direction of dependence, or whether both had a common source. The latter would seem the most likely supposition to us—perhaps an ancient hymn or liturgy. In fact, it probably illustrates the apparently frequent prophetic procedure of utilizing and adapting familiar, traditional material. Vs. 2-3 attach to the originally mythological notion of the *Weltberg* (=Paradise) or "mountain of the gods" (cf. Mt. Olympus), which we frequently meet in demythologized form to describe the universal and transcendental significance of Mt. Zion (cf. Is. 11:9; Ps. 48:1-2; etc.). The utter inappropriateness of the appearance of v. 4 on the UN cornerstone must be accented; the peace envisioned is not within the reach of any human maneuvers, but can and will be ultimately established only by supernatural, eschatological intervention. In the context of Isaiah particularly, that would almost appear to be too obvious to require mention!

The balancing oracle of Is. 4:2-6 is at least proto-Messianic because of its mention of a "branch." It describes the eschatological triumph of God's holiness, that is, the ultimate "incarnation" in the heavenly Zion of the same "glory" which led Israel in the wilderness.

Intervening are less familiar oracles, but some of Isaiah's most powerful ones. Is. 2:6 ff. features the "day"—a day *against* every human conceit, a day in which the LORD alone will be exalted—quintessential Isaiah! In 3:16—4:1 (cf. 32:9 ff.) Isaiah even takes on Jerusalem's vain and indulgent women (Isaiah and Amos share the distinction of including the distaff side in their fulminations).

Without transition Is. 5:1-7 continues with the famous "Song (Parable) of the Vineyard," the *tertium* for that figure, as so often, being Israel. Jesus' parable of the wicked husbandmen (Matt. 21:33 ff., etc.) is obviously a restatement of it. It is widely supposed that Isaiah played the role of a troubador or the like, singing a sort of love song in order to first attract attention for his judgmental punchline, and that certainly would not be out of character for all that we know of prophetic behavior. A forceful double pun in the Hebrew conclusion (7b) cannot be reproduced in translation.

The following sections show at least two signs of transmissional displacements. Conservatives are often loath to admit as much, but, strange as it may seem to us, negative evaluations need not follow, even if we are unable to say exactly why the apparent shuffling of original unities took place. Not that we lack attempts at explanations, but none seem definitively convincing.

Is. 5:8-24 is often labeled "Seven Woes," but we get seven (a likely symbol of completeness) only if we include 10:1-4, which appears to have become displaced for unknown reasons. (There also is no telling whether the seven were an original sermonic unity, or represent a collecting device.)

An almost balancing (is the symmetry deliberate?) displacement begins with Is. 5:24-25 and its refrain, "His hand is stretched out still." The original unit appears to continue and conclude in 9:8—10:4. The prophet's point is Israel's stubborn refusal to heed preliminary judgments and repent.

In matchless poetry Is. 5:26-30 describes the relentless, invincible advance of the Assyrian army—at Yahweh's "signal" or "whistle," a veritable prelude to the eschatological day. Possibly it too formed an original unity with 10:27b-32, describing Assyria's itinerary up to Jerusalem's very doorstep.

How does one possibly do justice to Is. 6, even with unlimited space? The infinite dimensions of eternity itself open up before the prophet, and before us. Christendom has no difficulty at this point in sensing its undiminished applicability to the time of the fulfillment—as witness the *Sanctus* of the liturgy, Luther's powerful hymnic paraphrase, *Jesaja dem Propheten das geschah,* and countless more. A few dissent, but the common understanding of the pericope as Isaiah's call seems thoroughly justifiable. The pattern of the call is not exactly that of Moses or Jeremiah—but neither is much of the rest of Isaiah's individuality, and the chapter certainly is an "Isaiah in minature." Some also dispute the apparently clear *Sitz im Leben* of a sort of transfiguration of the earthly liturgy as Isaiah worships in the temple, and suddenly finds himself transported to the counterpart heavenly temple "together with angels and archangels . . . ." The plural, "us" in v. 8 indicates that the vision overlaps with that of the council chambers of the heavenly King, so basic to prophetic ideology. If the pericope is a call, the question arises why it appears as chapter *six,* but that appears to be of a piece with the transmissional puzzles of the entire book. (We have a possible parallel in the Book of Amos, if his visions in chaps. 7—8 are to be related to his call.)

One should enter an energetic protest against the common homiletic practice of concluding the text with v. 8. The entire *Law*-Gospel theme of the chapter commonly gets lost as a result, and the clear connection with prophetic judgment oracles in general forgotten. Isaiah's bleak commission is relieved only by the picture of a remnant, a "holy seed" in v. 13. We cannot, however, overlook the severe textual problems there, and the LXX and Qumran variants raise the possibility that the original text spoke *only* of *total* destruction of a trunk as perverted as a pagan pillar. Such a conclusion would not fit so well for a "call," but the ultimate Gospel-import would still be amply documented in the total Isaianic context.

The theme of the divine obduration in Is. 6:9-10 summarizes much of the prophetic conviction that most of Israel has passed the point of no return and *can* no longer repent because God's longsuffering is exhausted (cf. the Pharaoh of the Exodus). This is not "double predestination" or impersonal determinism, of course, nor does it exempt anyone from further judgment. Critics often assume that Isaiah reached this defeatist conclusion only *ex post facto* after his rejection by the populace, but even humanly speaking there is no reason why it should not literally have been present already at his call. Note Jesus' antitypical appropriation of the theme, especially in explanation of the multitudes' inability to understand His parables (Matt. 13; etc.).

If possible, Is. 7 is still more famous—and certainly more controverted! The clear historical context—often neglected—is Isaiah's futile attempt to dissuade Ahaz from appealing to Assyria for "protection" from the threats of Rezin and Pekah (Damascus and Samaria) to invade if he refused to join them in an anti-Assyrian coalition. As always, Isaiah's counsel is to "believe" (v. 9), to let the Lord of history run history. Thus, the suprahistorical dimension of the pericope is inseparable from the "historical" (in our secular sense). The "sign" will seal and sacramentalize that unity.

What is that "sign?" The Matthean citation (1:23) makes clear Messianic import beyond cavil, but the *fides quaerens intellectum* still explores the empirical dimensions of the miraculous prediction. Both context and the analogy of prophecy indicate that here too we should avoid any false prediction-typology antithesis. Both "house of David" in Is. 7:13 and the apostrophe to "Immanuel" in 8:8 confirm a royal-Messianic import. It would seem likely that, as in the contiguous prophecies of Is. 9 and 11, the prophet points to a Davidide or Davidides of the near future (Hezekiah?) as a type and illustration accompanying his prediction of the further and ultimate fulfillment in Immanuel incarnate. If the total Biblical context is not critically truncated, there is no reason why Ahaz too should not have fully perceived that eschatological-Messianic import. Particularly in Isaiah, the prayer, "*Thy* kingdom come" (which Isaiah commends to Ahaz) is unthinkable apart from the King.

For all the often tumultuous debate, the Hebrew *'almah* appears technically to mean only "young woman" of marriageable age, who as such may or may not be virginal, but (at least in that culture) normally would be (Hebrew has no word with the precise, technical meaning of *virgo intacta*.) Nevertheless, the translation "virgin" is to be preferred, not only because of its thorough exegetical compatibility with this pericope, but especially because of its fulfillment and antitype in the Virgin Mary and in our Lord's virgin birth. (Also many conservatives prefer to explain the immediate application of the passage to Isaiah's own (future?) wife and son; in a narrowly exegetical sense that is perhaps not impossible, but the hermeneutical difficulties are certainly compounded.)

Immanuel-related messages reverberate throughout the rest of this section of Isaiah. Precisely how Is. 7:15 ff. relates to v. 14, especially in their Christological dimensions, is difficult to say—and often the problem is not even faced. The "curds and honey" (vs. 15 and 22) are enigmatic. In this context they must be primarily another of the descriptions of the depopulation and devastation of the land before Immanuel is grown. Yet especially in v. 22 the phrase appears to include overtones of an ambrosial food in paradisiacal plenty (based on a desert dweller's perspective). Perhaps the best solution is to assume both meanings, with both the Law and the Gospel dimensions of the Immanuel sign adumbrated in the remainder of chap. 7. This would correspond to the prominent judgment-salvation duality of the succeeding chapters, and typologically would find its fulfillment in Christ's death and resurrection.

The relation between the Immanuel sign and the symbolic name of

Isaiah's son Mahershalalhashbaz ("The spoil speeds, the prey hastes") appears to be that the totally dire import of the latter will be fulfilled within only a couple of years, in contrast to the more ambivalent and more ultimate import of Immanuel (8:1-4).

"Shiloah" (Is. 8:5) is the Hebrew original of the Greek form "Siloam," which we also meet in the New Testament. It means "sender," conduit, aqueduct, or the like, and here the reference is probably to a predecessor of Hezekiah's famous tunnel of archaeological discovery, which the modern tourist can still wade through. In this context it symbolizes Zion and the quietness of trust in Yahweh, which the people have rejected. Therefore says Isaiah sarcastically, "*the* River," that is, the Euphrates (as often in Hebrew idiom), symbolizing Assyria, will offer them the rashness and worldly politics which they seem to prefer. In the final verse (8) Isaiah shifts to direct address to "Immanuel," apparently here the royal house and/or its present incumbent—but also antitypically the King of kings.

In Is. 8:10, the name "Immanuel" is translated as part of an alternating word of judgment on Israel's foes, but in vs. 11-15 we return to judgment upon Israel. God and His requirement of trust will be salvation for the faithful, but "a stone of offense and a rock of stumbling" to the others, a concept the New Testament could readily apply to God incarnate (Rom. 9:32-33; 1 Peter 2:8).

Finally, in this chapter loaded with symbolic names, Isaiah tosses into the ring once more, as it were, his own name and those of his sons. As we noted, many interpret Is. 8:16 as implying Isaiah's temporary retirement from public life, committing his teaching to the faithful disciples until God can vindicate his testimony. There is no way to test that hypothesis, but it is plausible, and it would provide occasion for a preliminary collection of the prophet's public preaching into what eventually became the Book of Isaiah. The picture Isaiah paints of an accursed, superstition-ridden land, ripe for judgment, does not make the hypothesis less attractive!

Where does the famous Messianic prophecy of Is. 9 begin? Note that the chapter division is different in the Hebrew than in English. Our 9:1 is the last verse of chap. 8 in the Masoretic text, describing the great reversal in contrast to the sorry picture preceding. In the English text, as in its citation in the New Testament, it is linked more directly to the Messianic portrait which follows. (In practice, one fears that Christians usually revert to the Hebrew usage of ignoring historical context.) Maybe we ultimately come out the same place, but the New Testament linkage helps remind us that the prophecy had contemporary, historical as well as eschatological-Messianic import (the latter, by itself easily dehistoricized and treated spiritualistically). Our versification will also support the tendency of more recent critics to regard the oracle as genuine (presumably delivered in private) over against the consensus of most classical liberalism to judge it necessarily late and inauthentic. Isaiah says that Zebulun and Naphtali (captured by Assyria shortly after Isaiah's meeting with Ahaz) which first experienced the darkness of judgment will be the first also to experience the light of salvation and of eschatological peace after the final battle, a light which will then encompass the entire earth, as God's kingdom replaces the kingdoms. The immediate New Testament application is to Jesus' Galilean origins and early ministry.

This oracle concentrates on the Messianic king as much as on the kingdom, especially his deity. Liberals are not totally wrong in seeing some reference to the historical bearers of the Davidic promise but are wrong in limiting its original meaning to that. The epithets did apply to the heirs of David in a lesser, metaphorical sense as "sons" of God by election and adoption—not radically different from the sense in which all true Israelites, then and now, are "sons of God." Thus again we see typological illustration inextricably bound up with verbal prediction. The full, intended, literal import of both aspects of the prophecy can only be to Him who was literally Son of God—and God.

Is. 10:5, describing Assyria as "the rod of my anger," is often cited as an apt summary of Isaiah's "philosophy of history." It must be taken in context with vs. 12 ff., where Assyria too receives its comeuppance after God has made use of its arrogance for His purposes. Then the "remnant" concept surfaces explicitly in vs. 20 ff., followed by typological allusion to Gideon's victory over Midian (v. 26, as in 9:4).

The Messianic prophecy of Is. 11:1-9 picks up the image of the stump encountered in 6:13. We also met the "branch" in 4:2, but here we have a different Hebrew word: *netser*. It is similar in sound to "Nazarene," and as Israel often did in bringing out the symbolism or significance of names, it is probably Matthew's reference in 2:23. We are accustomed to expound Is. 11:2 as the "sevenfold gifts of the Spirit" (especially at ordinations and installations, where the Messiah's ministry is extended), but grammatically it is here a threefold spirit resulting from the Spirit which first empowered the King (as at Jesus' baptism). In vs. 6 ff., as commonly in eschatological oracles, the vision of the Kingdom merges with that of new creation and Paradise Restored. The redemption is spiritual, but not spiritualistic (limited only to men's hearts). The location of Paradise is described as a "holy mountain," a *Weltberg*, of which earthly Zion, like the church, is anticipation, type, and prophecy. Parts of vs. 6-9 are paralleled in 65:25 and Hab. 2:14, the latter perhaps a quotation from Isaiah.

The picture of new creation continues in Is. 11:10-16 with somewhat more historification. Many of Isaiah's favorite symbols cluster here: ensign, remnant, highway.

The first section of the book concludes with a doxology or hymn of thanksgiving. Its location here may well be redactional (cf. the conclusions of the books of the Psalter), and it may even represent worship influences in transmission, but such possibilities need not preclude Isaianic authorship and/or adaptation of a familiar hymn. Perhaps especially significant is the parallelism of 2b with Ex. 15:2a (Song of the Sea). It might be coincidental, but more likely we have here a typology of the "second Exodus." Since that motif is prominent in "II Isaiah" and not in Isaiah I, critics commonly date the piece to exilic times or later. However, there is no reason under the sun why also "Isaiah of Jerusalem" should not have known and employed the Exodus motif on occasion.

Isaiah 13—23

In Is. 13—23 we clearly have a distinct section of the Book of Isaiah, which might also have once formed a subcollection. Most of its contents are "Gentile oracles," but other types of Isaianic material are included. Sometimes it is referred to as the "*Massah* collection" because of the tenfold repetition of that Hebrew word (translated either "oracle" or "burden") at the beginning of passages.

See our discussion (chaps. 9—12) of the theological import of this genre of material, often among the most opaque to the modern reader. Again we see commentary on specific history of the time, but obviously as a sort of transparency of metahistory and eschatology. All of the specific nations mentioned are examples of "*all* the kingdoms of this world." Increasingly, the names of certain nations were singled out for that broader significance (especially Edom and Babylon), and thus lose some of their immediate historical specificity. Critics inevitably want to fit that development into a neat evolutionistic scheme of movement from particular to general (the latter, then proto-apocalyptic). However, the role of Babylon in these oracles (as Edom later in the book) both forbids such rigidity of scheme, and indicates the inner unity of prophetic and apocalyptic forms.

Is. 13—14:23 consists of two oracles, both targeted against Babylon. Intervening (14:1-3) is a brief "alternation of weal." Erlandsson has recently proved decisively the verisimilitude of these oracles for Isaiah's own day, but whether that will ever make a dent in the critical orthodoxy of dating them to the time of the neo-Babylonian empire—we will believe it when we see it. Comparing the two oracles, one may say that the first speaks more to Babylon in an empirical, historical sense, while the second is addressed more to transhistorical Babylon, a type of the kingdom of

Satan. In form the latter is a taunt-song sung *after* the people of God has received its eschatological rest. Incredulously it comments on the descent of the tyrant, who thought to become God Himself, to Sheol (the grave), like any other mortal. To bring out the typical, transhistorical aspect of the message, Isaiah uses as illustration a former myth, built on observation of the fading of the Day Star before the rising sun. The Hebrew *helel* was rendered "Lucifer" (light-bearer) by Jerome, whence one of our epithets of Satan. Not only is "Babylon" in this context the kingdom of Satan, but we might also have here a poetic allusion to Satan's primordial rebellion and fall. By God's sufferance, that primordial pattern repeats itself and constitutes "Babylon," but Satan's ultimate eschatological defeat is also implied. It is reported that also in modern times this chapter has been a favorite pericope (read without comment) for churches under both fascist and Communist tyrannies. The application is good, as long as it retains contact with *Heilsgeschichte*, and is not reduced to merely another timeless myth with the moral, *Sic semper tyrannis.*

Is. 14:24-27 (naturally considered authentic by critics in contrast to the preceding material) follows with a far briefer oracle against Assyria than one would expect, probably because so much of Isaiah's commentary on Assyria appears elsewhere in the book. Vs. 26-27 are about as close as the prophets ever come to a *theoretical* statement of Yahweh's transcendent guidance of universal history.

The oracle against Philistia (Is. 14:28-31) is dated (715). The word translated "serpent" (v. 29; cf. 30:6) is the same as "seraph" in chap. 6. What desert creature is in mind we cannot say, and it is not utterly impossible that some of the heavenly denizens were pictured on its analogy. More likely, however, in Biblical thought the connection is only etymological—or coincidental. The oracle concludes with another brief "alternation of weal" (v. 32).

Two chapters, Is. 15 and 16, are devoted to Moab. They contain little historical particularity, however, and two close parallels with Jeremiah's oracle against Moab (15:2-7=48:34-38, and 16:6-11=48:29-33) indicate that here Isaiah is quoting or adapting ancient, traditional material. Note the Messianic prophecy of 16:5; Isaiah says that since the Moabite refugees are too proud to seek shelter in the "tent of David," the judgment must run its course.

Is. 17 is more varied. Beginning with a brief oracle against Damascus (1-3), it proceeds (4-6) against "Jacob"—either the Northern Kingdom (then a very early oracle of Isaiah), or more likely "Israel" in the more theological sense. The rest of the chapter describes the great reversal, climaxing (12-14) in the beautiful, near-apocalyptic defeat of "many peoples," depicted in the originally mythological language of "many waters."

Ethiopia (not that modern territory, but really ancient Nubia, modern Sudan) is labeled a "land of whirring wings" (18:1) because of the flurry of diplomatic activity from the Nubian rulers of Egypt's twenty-fifth dynasty, urging Hezekiah to join them in an anti-Assyrian coalition. Isaiah responds, typically, with incomparable portraits of Yahweh's sublimity and unchallenged mastery of history.

Is. 19 is directed against Egypt proper. But especially in vs. 18 ff. Isaiah shifts to universal restoration after the final judgment, when Egypt and Assyria will join the tribes of Israel in a new aeon. Critics have often thought they could detect late, postexilic allusions in these "prophecies," especially v. 19 which was thought to reflect the Oniad temple of Leontopolis in Hasmonean times. Certain conservatives have also been too sure of the precise fulfillment of these prophecies. Rather, in these more general visions, we have a structural anticipation within the book of chaps. 24—27, and of the universal restoration concluding the classical prophetic outline.

Is. 20 is a Gentile oracle in the form of an "action prophecy," one of the few we have of Isaiah. Walking "naked" means clad in only a loincloth, as Isaiah typifies the taking of Egyptian and Ethiopian captives by Assyria (also a familiar scene in Assyrian monuments uncovered by archaeologists). Archaeology has also given us far more background to Sargon's campaign against Ashdod which occasioned this prophecy (v. 1). Its fulfillment, however, did not come until nearly a half-century later.

Is. 21 is highly visionary, allusive and elusive. "Wilderness of the sea" (v. 1) appears to describe the desert as an "ocean of nothingness." In one panoramic sweep Isaiah sees the fall of all the tribes and kingdoms to the East. The recurring themes of the watchman and his watchtower anticipate Habakkuk and Ezekiel, and Rev. 18 takes up the refrain of v. 9, "Fallen, fallen is Babylon." Vs. 11-12 also use "Edom" in universal application; Seir is an alternate name, and Dumah one of its oasis outposts (the latter perhaps also punningly suggests the "silence" of death).

But even among the Gentile oracles, Isaiah must remind Jerusalem that neither is it, even though it is "the valley of vision" (Is. 22:1), the home of prophecy, exempt from judgment. The occasion appears to be some fickle, bacchanalian (v. 13) revelry after a victory or deliverance (possibly even the famous one from Sennacherib in 701), giving credit to armaments and human defenses (8-11) instead of to the LORD of hosts.

The rest of the chapter (22:15-25) is unique in its concern with leading individuals, who, however, exemplify the pride of Judah. It is possible that archaeologists have discovered the very tomb for which Shebna is condemned. The name is missing, but "over the household" (v. 15) does appear; unfortunately, that was a fairly common title. Eliakim will be invested with full authority instead (in the light of Rev. 3:7 we may even view him as a sort of a type of Christ), but, in the end, he too will be unequal to the responsibility.

Isaiah's Gentile oracles conclude with the great emporium Tyre. After "seventy years" (vs. 15, 17), however, the "forgotten harlot" (v. 16) will return to her ways. Man's greed and lust will flourish until the end, but God will know how to turn even that to His advantage (vs. 17-18).

Isaiah 24—27

With Is. 24—27 we come to a sort of climax of the first round of Isaiah's prophecies, describing salvation for all the redeemed. It is widely referred to in criticism as the "Isaiah Apocalypse," and even for conservatives this is a handy label. Critics debate both the aptness of the title and the date of the material. By no stretch of the imagination is it "apocalyptic" in the fully developed sense of detailed imagery, etc. It can possibly qualify as apocalyptic only because of its indeterminacy and universalism. Hence, some speak of "proto-apocalyptic" or the like, allegedly comparable to Ezek. 38—39 or Zech. 9—14. The earlier critical inclination to date it in the second century and to make it one of the latest components of the Book of Isaiah has given way somewhat to a slightly earlier date in the Persian or even exilic period.

We have noted this type of universal perspective earlier in the Book of Isaiah, and, indeed, it is implicit in the Bible's failure to share the usual critical obsession with precise date and circumstance of each part. If one refuses to buy the critical dogma of evolution from prophetic particularity and more immanental salvation *within* the historical process toward apocalyptic generality, universalism and supernaturalistic salvation from beyond history, there is no reason at all why we should be surprised to find a number of Isaiah's more general oracles brought together in one collection. In fact, Isaianic authorship of these chapters is fatal to the critical schematism.

Is. 24 opens, indeed, with a vision of imminent *world*-catastrophe, not, as such, any simply historical catastrophe of local import. In 24:10 we are also introduced to some proud tyrannical city now fallen. It probably is "Babylon" in the typical sense, even if unnamed, but critical attempts to pinpoint an occasion such as Babylon's fall to Xerxes in 485 or to Alexander in 331 are, at best, beside the point. In v. 21 the judgment becomes explicitly cosmic as well; also the "host of heaven," the celestial partners of the "kings of the earth," will be cast down. (The first phrase is so ancient and traditional that by no means need it imply the developed angelology of later times, which critics appeal to in defense of a later date.) The mirth of the "city of chaos" [*tohu;* cf. Gen. 1:2] (vs. 8-11) is contrasted with the supernal joy of the city of God, beginning with v. 14, and many hymns of the redeemed punctuate the remainder of the section (cf. Revelation). In fact, the entire "apocalypse" has been styled a "festival cantata" of the redeemed as they see God's "glory" coming from the East to Zion (vs. 15, 23). There are other cultic echoes in the pericope, and it is not at all far-fetched to hypothesize it taking shape in or under the influence of Israel's liturgy, where that eschatological triumph was regularly experienced and celebrated sacramentally.

Is. 25 proleptically sees the city as already fallen, and the Kingdom established once for all. Hence the songs of vs. 1-5 and v. 9. "On this mountain" (Zion, Paradise Restored; cf. 2:2, 11:9, etc.) the Victor will host the "Messianic banquet," the Eucharist of eternal life, which earthly ceremonies and sacraments can only present to faith (cf. Rev. 7 and 21). Vs. 6-9 are often used most appropriately as the Old Testament lesson for Easter, the "*Feast* of the Resurrection of our Lord."

In almost grotesque contrast is the picture of Moab (v. 10) drowning in a latrine, wallowing to death in its own filth. "Moab" is here surely used typically of the depraved world, but it is a reminder that Isaiah has not generalized us entirely out of this world, as the label "apocalyptic" might imply.

Is. 26 is another hymn of thanksgiving, closing (vs. 20-21) with the central Isaianic admonition to "hide yourselves for a little while until the wrath is past." Evolutionists find ample evidence of lateness in the chapter, and, indeed, it features two themes which became much more prominent and central later. In v. 17 we encounter the *dolores Messiae,* the birth-pangs or labor pains preceding the delivery/deliverance of the Messianic age.

Even more significantly, in vs. 14 and 19 we meet the theme of resurrection of at least the righteous dead under the figure of dew. Critical handbooks commonly assert that only in Dan. 12 do we find this theme elsewhere in the Old Testament. Other critics, however, prefer to think of only the nation's "resurrection," as in Ezek. 37. The Old Testament plainly does not understand the grave as ending all, as liberalism often teaches, but neither is life after death as prominent or central as it became after Christ's death, at least not in any explicit way. Perhaps we can summarize by saying that the Old Testament simply assumes immortality (though not in the Greek sense) rather than resurrection—but no ultimate cleft should be made between the two.

In a single verse Is. 27:1 depicts the defeat of Satan and his empire under the ancient mythological pictures of a snake, Leviathan, and "the dragon that is in the sea." Both images were greatly exploited and expanded in later apocalyptic, including the Apocalypse of the New Testament. From Ras Shamra (Ugarit) we now have verbatim parallels to some of the language of the verse. That does not mean that Isaiah is consciously quoting mythological literature (although that need not be excluded on principle); it may mean only that this phrase was traditional in the ancient Levant, ready to be understood and applied in many ways, depending on the hermeneutics. As often in mythology, Yam (Sea) and Leviathan, the serpent and/or dragon, both personify chaos or the monstrosity of evil and cannot be clearly distinguished.

The "apocalypse of Isaiah" concludes with a final hymn (27:2-5) and sundry descriptions of the restoration of Yahweh's people to "the holy mountain at Jerusalem" (v. 13).

Isaiah 28—33

In Is. 28—33 we return, as it were, to the book's starting point: oracles of judgment on Judah and Jerusalem. It does seem to represent an independent collection, which after Delitzsch is often called the "Book of Woe," because its six main prophecies are introduced by that word (28:1; 29:1; 29:15; 30:1; 31:1; 33:1). (Cf. the "seven woes" of chap. 5.) Interspersed, however, are a number of alternating oracles of comfort and salvation—whether original to the collection, or added later by Isaiah or another, who can say!

The contents for the most part also seem to stem from the latter period of Isaiah's ministry, whether or not there may have been an intervening period of silence or retirement. Sometimes the section is called the "Assyrian Collection," but not too helpfully because Assyria was also featured prominently in Is. 1—12. The king is now Hezekiah instead of Ahaz, but the problem is the same, and Isaiah's counsel remains the same: avoid entangling alliances, and simply wait, trust, believe.

Since Is. 28 excoriates Ephraim or Samaria, some think the oracle was originally uttered before 722 and later adapted to Judah. Certainly the chapter is vintage Isaiah. In vs. 9 ff. Isaiah answers his mocking critics: if they compare his teaching to nursery instruction, God will teach them "by men of alien tongue" (v. 11) and "it will be sheer terror to understand the message" (v. 19). They have rejected His offer of rest (v. 12) and of a solid cornerstone inscribed, "He who believes will not be in haste" (v. 16; cf. 8:14), a Gospel promise incarnated and fulfilled in Christ (Rom 9:33; 10:11; 1 Pet. 2:4-6). Instead they have preferred a "covenant with death" (v. 5, 18), the annulment of which Isaiah depicts in unforgettable imagery.

Is. 28:21 alludes to David's defeat of the Philistines on the outskirts of

Jerusalem (1 Chron. 14:11 ff.) as a type of God's eschatological judgment—indeed, also of His *opus alienum* ("strange work") of judgment throughout history. That favorite phrase of Luther's to describe the Law (second use) derives from this verse. Similarly the concept of the *"opus proprium,"* God's "proper work" or Gospel, was suggested by 29:14, though not so directly.

In Is. 28:23-29 the prophet uses the example of a farmer's planning and doing everything in its appropriate time to describe God's supervision and control of history. The section does have a wisdom aura (cf. v. 29), and it is even possible that here Isaiah adopts a professional wisdom-teacher's pose, but especially the recent flurry of critical interest in wisdom has made more of it than the text will bear.

The "Ariel" of Is. 29 is an old conundrum. The traditional guess, "lion of God," derived by dividing the word in two, is no longer followed. The reference is obviously to Jerusalem, but the question is how. Our best clue is Ezek. 43:15 f., where the same word means the hearth of the altar. In alternate spelling the vocable also can mean "mountain of God," attaching to the frequent cosmological significance of altars, as miniature temples or universes with the mountain pictured as situated directly above the underworld (v. 4). The altar was also central to the various festivals with their processions and circumambulations. But now God Himself threatens to encamp about the city and bring it down to the dust.

Suddenly, however, in Is. 29:5, we have the "great reversal": the multitude of nations investing Zion will find their prize forever out of reach (a frequent theme also in the psalms of Zion and in apocalyptic). In v. 9 we return just as precipitously to judgment upon Judah, spiritually blind, drunk, illiterate, arrogant, even though very "religious" in a rote way. But weal breaks through the woe again in vs. 14 and 17 ff.

Much of Is. 30 is directed squarely against the pro-Egyptian politics of the court, condemned as "a plan, but not mine" (v. 1), and Egypt is ridiculed as "Rahab who sits still." "Rahab" (a different Hebrew spelling from the Jericho prostitute, Joshua 2) means "arrogant" or the like and is an alternate name or epithet for Leviathan or the satanic monster of chaos (cf. Ps. 89:10; Is 51:9). Apparently pictured something like a crocodile, it was often applied to Egypt (cf. Ps. 87:4 and Ezek. 29)—but more the typical than the historical Egypt, and very possibly with Exodus overtones. The picture is that of the clumsy, lumbering beast on land, threatening but unable to help herself, let alone others; "one little word can fell him."

As noted earlier, Is. 30:8 is often interpreted as a second "retirement" of the prophet, as perhaps earlier in 8:16. Perhaps more congenially, it may tell us a little about the beginning of the writing down of the prophet's oracles in the face of massive rejection. Their preference for activism instead of "quietness and trust" (v. 15) must eventuate in shattering devastation (the vivid pictures of vs. 13, 14, and 17).

The chapter ends (vs. 29-33) with another eschatological projection of liturgical rites. The "holy feast" is most likely Succoth ("Tabernacles") with its final-judgment themes. This time the joyful procession to the "mountain" will be the final one; "Assyria," now a type of all unbelievers, will be defeated in the final theophanic intervention in "holy war" and will itself be the sacrifice.

Is. 31 uses fresh figures for similar themes. Isaiah's idiom in calling Egypt "flesh and not spirit" must be distinguished from the Pauline use of those terms (esp. Gal. 5).

Is. 32 is one of the little known Messianic oracles of Isaiah. The kingdom will be characterized especially by "righteousness," the new life consequent upon God's acquittal. As in Is. 3, the women too are berated, but the overall picture soon merges with "new creation."

Is. 33 concludes this section of the book with a sort of doxology or hymn, comparable to chap. 12. It too contains Messianic and Zion themes, but many others are also found. Gunkel is often followed in styling it a "prophetic liturgy," a prophetic imitation of liturgical antiphonies of priests, choirs, prayers, sermons, etc. If we do not date it in postexilic times, as is also commonly done, the hypothesis is not unattractive.

Isaiah 34—35

Is. 34—35, an independent section of the book, certainly are a sort of "antiphony": contrasted pictures of the futures of Edom and Israel. But "Edom" is plainly typical and universal, while chap. 35 is as eschatological as anything in the book. Since there are many parallels with "II Isaiah," many critics think of a displaced fragment of that prophet, or a circle close to him; it is certainly a major illustration of the dissection of the *entire* book which follows from any Deutero-Isaianic hypothesis. In another direction within the criticism of the book, others think of a "second apocalypse" approaching the "Isaiah Apocalypse" (Is. 24—27), especially because of language such as 34:4. The oracle against Edom is redolent of Is. 63:1-6, Obadiah, etc., so that some think of a reworking of an old tribal oracle—not impossible concepts, as such. In chap. 35, eschatological redemption is described on all three levels, psychological, historical, and cosmological—little wonder that it is quoted messianically in the New Testament, and plays a prominent role in pericopal systems.

Isaiah 36—39

Is. 36—39 is substantially identical with 2 Kings 18:13—20:19 (see our

214 THE WORD BECOMING FLESH

discussion there). The Isaianic version here adds the "Song/Psalm of Hezekiah" (Is. 39:9-20), but otherwise it appears to represent a slight abridgment of the Kings text. What the pericope is doing here, and how (humanly speaking) it got here is hard to say. It plainly is about Isaiah, but one would scarcely think of direct Isaianic authorship of a third-person narrative. Possibly, however, it was written under Isaianic supervision or by disciples, which would help account for its presence. Again, whether Kings quotes Isaiah or vice versa or both use a common source is anyone's guess.

One frequent and attractive hypothesis is that the chapters were placed here to help fuse the two main halves of the book. (If so, however, we must also recall the repeated prophecies of Assyrian invasion with their implications of the usual Assyrian policy of deportation in the preceding chapters, even in Is. 6.) Is. 39 tells of Isaiah's denunciation of Hezekiah's welcome of and apparent complicity in Merodach-baladan's plots against Assyria (which we know well from archaeological sources), ending (vs. 6-7) in a prophecy of captivity in the land of Babylon, whence the envoys had come. That, of course, leads easily into chaps. 40 ff. with their visionary setting in the Babylonian exile. Similarly, the account of the miraculous destruction of Sennacherib's forces may be read typologically, i.e., anticipating the ultimate defeat of all the enemies of God's people, which theme figures prominently in the latter chapters of the book. We may put aside critical developments of these observations, which unite them with theories about how the two halves of the book ever came to be conjoined in the first place (Budde, Pfeiffer, Brownlee, etc.).

We may note that a *leitmotiv* of Isaiah's preaching also informs these chapters: adamant opposition to human attempts by that "church-state" to make history through politics, and its obverse emphasis, the "inviolability of Zion," classically in 37:22-38. Hezekiah's psalm (38:9-20) is a very typical "individual thanksgiving," but that is no warrant for doubt of his authorship. While he may well have employed traditional material, the point of the typicality (as regularly in the Psalter) is its applicability to any and all in comparable circumstances.

CHAPTERS 40—55 (ISAIAH II)

We discussed the isagogical question briefly above and need not repeat. However, the reader and exegete must shift gears corresponding to the substantially different milieu, historical (in vision), theological, and stylistic.

Because of the spiral, repetitive (cf. the Johannine literature) style, it is all but impossible to outline—or every verse or two becomes a separate point of the outline. For that reason too, much form criticism of these chapters was wildly atomistic, alleging only fragments connected by catchwords or the like, and excesses here played a prominent role in provoking critical reaction to some aspects of the approach. In contrast, conservatives prefer to speak of the "symphonic structure" of the book or the like: themes are first introduced almost in passing, gradually to be developed as the composition proceeds. One may illustrate that principle in two major respects: (1) the problem of sin as the real issue behind the Exile, first broached in Is. 40:2; and (2) the identify of the Servant, who is first mentioned almost in passing in 41:8. Both themes are resolved in Is. 53, with the following two chapters describing the results of the Servant's atonement. Chap. 40 can also be viewed in this light as a sort of "overture," not only as a miniature of much of the book, but also beginning at the end of the total development ("comfort"), as is common with overtures.

Earlier, Duhm played a fateful role in subsequent critical study of the section by further subdividing it in especially two respects, which are still largely with us: (1) the hypothesis of Is. 56—66 as deriving from still a third figure, "Trito-Isaiah," allegedly living a good century later than II Isaiah, i.e., about 520, the time of Nehemiah (cf. below); and (2) because of their individual portrayal and a possible logical progression if taken by themselves, the isolation of the four "Servant Songs" from the context, understanding them as either composed by someone else entirely, or if by "II Isaiah" himself, then independently, and later inserted somewhat clumsily into their present contexts. (We return to this problem shortly too.)

Theologically, the overarching motif to note is the eschatology of the book: no longer much on the person of a royal Messiah (although certainly not repudiated; cf. Is. 55:3), but celebrating the restoration of Zion throughout. The historical return to Jerusalem after the Edict of Cyrus (538) is not only *depicted* in eschatological and cosmological colors, but the two are totally fused: the historical event is a type, "sacrament," anticipation and proleptic realization of the "restoration of all things." Neither has the preceding judgment and suffering been only a bad dream, but in the light of, and in connection with the cross, it too was eschatologically redemptive. The exile, far from a defeat by Yahweh, represented a victory and a vindication of His revelations to the earlier prophets. Similarly Christ *reigns* from the cross; especially John describes His death as His "glorification."

As noted earlier, critics often find occasion in this connection to vent their developmental presuppositions. Deutero-Isaiah is supposed to have carried Israel's "philosophy of history" further in the direction of apocalyptic by its periodicity, by its clear contrast between the calamitous present and a future era of bliss. Strong as those accents are in Isaiah II, however, they are scarcely *all* that different from even those oracles of Isaiah I which critics allow to be "genuine," and certainly the contrast fades almost completely if one does not use a mutilated text as evidence!

If any outline at all can be offered, a slight break at the end of Is. 48 can probably be detected. Chap. 48 itself appears to be somewhat transitional. Chaps. 40—48 are incandescent with expectation of God's imminent coming, as typified in the release from captivity, while chaps. 49—55 appear to envision a slightly later moment, perhaps the earliest return to Palestine. The argumentative tone of the earlier chapters wane, the earlier prominence of Cyrus is displaced by increasing accent on the Suffering Servant, as well as other shifts to be noted below.

Some conservatives (e.g., Archer) prefer a more theologically than historically oriented outline and build upon the repetition of the phrase, "No peace to the wicked" at the end of both Is. 48 and 57. That is, the first division comes at the same point, but not the second. Archer is thus able to find a major doctrinal emphasis in the three parts (theology, soteriology, and eschatology), but that type of systemization seems to least fit Isaiah of all the prophets, neither is there clear evidence that repetition of the refrain has structural significance.

The prophetico-historical setting of Is. 40—48 appears to be between Cyrus' first startling victories (especially over Croesus of Lydia in 546) and the fall of Babylon in 539, when the disgusted inhabitants hailed him as a liberator from Nabonidus' neglect. The prophet, however, not only prophesies the political events but explains them as God's instrumentality for the people's release, just as Assyria had earlier been the rod of His anger.

Two audiences among the exiles are addressed (and, in principle, Isaiah was already full acquainted with them among contemporaries): (1) those who have apostasized to worship the false gods and rely on their ability to foretell the future (we know that divination was very prominent in Babylonian religion, especially in the sixth century); and (2) those who still confess the true God, but have inadequate trust in His power and grace. The former Isaiah scathingly condemns, and poetically summons to debate with the true God (a sort of "covenant lawsuit"), who alone can foretell events since He creates and controls them. For the latter, Isaiah marshalls various arguments to demonstrate Yahweh's power and ability to fulfill His promises. Apologetic from fulfillment of former prophecy plays a prominent role (in fact, more than anywhere else in the Bible): because the "former things" have come to pass as predicted, there is no reason to doubt that the "new" (eschatological) prophecies of restoration will also be fulfilled.

It is as impossible to do justice to the opening pericope (Is 40:1-11) as it is to chap. 6, even with unlimited space. The two sections are parallel in many ways. While these verses cannot represent II Isaiah's call, as many critics aver, if the book is one, we may take it as a sort of reiteration of the call at a crucial juncture in the prophet's preaching. Again we have a setting in the heavenly council ("a voice"), and essentially the same accent on God's transcendent, eternal omnipotence in contrast to man's frail ephemerality ("All flesh is grass," indeed a requiem). But now God's "glory" (v. 5) comes in universal, cosmic redemption—an Advent fulfilled antitypically and climactically in the incarnation, but also not yet, to which the church's prominent liturgical use eloquently testifies.

The Septuagint and the New Testament punctuate differently from the requirements of the Hebrew poetic parallelism ("a voice crying in the wilderness," applied to John the Baptizer) but the difference is ultimately inconsequential. The theme of the "highway" is familiar from Isaiah's previous oracles, but the accent on the "word" as a quasi-incarnate, semi-hypostatic guide of history is somewhat new (cf. Is. 55 and the "deuteronomic" literature).

In Is. 40:9-11, Zion the redeemed community is apostrophized and exhorted to evangelize (the semitechnical root, b-s-r, is used) all in the environs. The theme of retribution is still strong (v. 10) as in the earlier chapters, but here the accent is on the "reward of grace," in fulfillment of the covenant oath.

The rest of Is. 40 (12 ff.) reminds us of the theophany to Job: a cosmological argument for Yahweh's ineffable incomparability (a prominent motif throughout the book).

Is. 41 introduces us to the prominent *Gattung* in Isaiah II of the "trial of the nations" (or really more their gods than the nations as such, and, in effect, a final judgment scene, part of the forensic picture of "justification," and intimately related to the theme of God's "righteousness," so prominent in these chapters). The accent is much more on Israel's vindication than on the condemnation of the nations, but that does not add up to the "universalism" with which critics usually credit "II Isaiah." The very condemnation of the idols implies the condemnation of the nations whom they personify. The "coastlands" are probably technically the Levant and the Aegean regions, but they plainly represent all nations.

The first (rhetorical) question of the heavenly judge introduces us to Cyrus, who is not yet named but who dominates these chapters (here Is. 41:2-3 and 25). A favorite critical interpretation in many variants understands Deutero-Isaiah as initially captivated by the figure of Cyrus, but later becoming disillusioned and remolding many earlier Cyrus oracles into Servant themes, that is, retreating into hopes of spiritual deliverance after the political deliverance failed to meet his high expectations. The hypothesis, so typical in a way of historical-critical method, scarcely even deserves refutation on conservative premises. The disappearance of Cyrus in the later chapters proves only that after Isaiah has hailed the chief historical agent in God's work of deliverance, he proceeds to concentrate on the special calling of the redeemed. The text here is emphasizing Yahweh's superiority because He alone could have "stirred up" Cyrus (vs. 2 and 25), as, in general, He alone knows and can predict the future (vs. 21-29).

In Is. 41:8-9 Israel is comforted by being called Yahweh's elect "servant," "the offspring of Abraham, my friend," whom God will never abandon. It is the first time the "servant" motif appears in the book, and we note that the identification with Israel is explicit! The point here is that Israel need not fear Cyrus' advent as the nations do.

In Is. 42:1-4 the portrait of "my servant" is far more individual. This was the first of the separate "Servant Songs" isolated by Duhm. Others want to include vs. 5-9 within the song, but the impossibility of deciding, as well as the continued duality of individual and collective portraits of the figure, indicate how misleading and ultimately counterproductive Duhm's notions were. Nevertheless, if one proceeds more synchronically, the four "Servant Songs" do stand out somewhat from the context, especially because of their individual portraiture, so the designation remains useful.

Since Is. 42:1 is quoted at Jesus' baptism (in conflation with Ps. 2:7), and other verses of the pericope are also prominently featured messianically in the New Testament, we obviously must regard Christ as the fulfillment and ultimate embodiment of the prophecy. Here His task is described as establishing "justice" *(mishpat)*, that is the total redemptive "order" resulting from God's judgeship. Furthermore, He is *personally* (v. 6) (incarnately) to be "a covenant to the people, a light to the nations" (cf. the *Nunc Dimittis)*. Perhaps the debate is only semantic whether missionary work to evangelize the Gentiles is implied by these words (cf. 49:6, etc.). The universal implications of the Servant's mission are plainly set forth, but, as far as we know, the corollary of aggressive missionary witness was never drawn until Pentecost (in whose light *we are* obligated to read them, of course). The Old Testament view by itself was more that, merely by existing faithfully, the light of Israel would attract Gentiles, especially in the eschaton (with the beginning of which the Gospel identifies itself).

This initial Song should also correct at the outset the frequent misreading of "servant" *('ebed)* as somehow implying servility, denigration, perhaps even slavery. Old Testamental and Oriental usage in general, however, make plain that it was a title of great honor and status, something like "right-hand man," plenipotentiary, "minister" in a government, etc. (Cf. Ebedmelech—"servant of the king" in Jer. 38—39; Eliakim in Is. 22:20; etc.)

In Is. 42:10 ff. we hear the eschatological "new song," as in the "apocalypse" and in some of the psalms (esp. 96 and 98). In great contrast to the gentle, "Gospel" work of the Servant (v. 3), Yahweh intervenes "like a man of war (v. 13) and "like a woman in travail" (v. 14) when the "Law" must be invoked.

In Is. 42:18 ff. the "servant" returns (never having really left us, and surfacing constantly in the following chapters). The "servant of the LORD" (or various synonymns), here quite obviously Israel, had been "blind" or "deaf" in not responding to God's largesse, leaving Him no alternative but judgment.

But beyond the judgment is the great reversal (Is. 43:1-7), when God will once more call His people by name, and Egypt, Ethiopia and Seba will exchange places with Israel. The exchange and the return are described again in terms of trial of the nations (43:8 ff.). In contrast to the impotence of the gods, Israel, though blind and deaf, is also Yahweh's servant and witness (v. 10) to His sole power to save, to effect a new Exodus (v. 16) and to a new creation (v. 19) in spite of its purely ritualistic "gratitude" (vs. 22-24; cf. chap 1). In 44:1-2 Israel/Jacob is once again explicitly labeled "my servant," and, after an interval, this oracle concludes with essentially the same language in vs. 21-23.

Intervening is one of Isaiah's major satires on idols (44:9-20), especially idol manufacture out of the same wood used for baking and heating. Really the idol should be thankful it did not suffer the same fate (esp. vs. 15-17)! It is debatable whether this section is really prose, but that typography in most modern versions does serve to set it off from the context. In a purely formal sense, there is no doubt that it is intrusive in the context. The only reason one can see for its insertion at this point is to point up the inanity of those who, unlike the prophet, believe there is another "Rock" besides Yahweh (v. 8), but it apparently could just as easily have been inserted many other places in the book. Technically, it is true that paganism made a theoretical distinction between the image and the numen or divinity itself, but that is quite beside the point here, and it does not mean that Isaiah did not even understand what paganism was all about.

In Is. 44:24-28 we have a major Cyrus pericope—all of it one sentence (rare in Isaiah), in Hebrew nine participles modifying "I am the LORD," climaxing in the explicit designation of Cyrus as "my shepherd," for the rebuilding of Jerusalem and its temple. Is. 45:1 ff. continues the theme, again naming Cyrus, and even more boldly calling him God's "Messiah" ("anointed," of course, in a more general sense). The purpose is indeed universal: that all, beginning with Cyrus, may acknowledge Yahweh as sole Creator, who unlike pagan dualisms, alone "make weal and create woe" (v. 7). (In dogmatic language, God is not the "author" of evil, but in a permissive sense He is still responsible for it.)

The climax comes in the new creation poetry of v. 8: "righteousness" (God's right order) and "salvation" (victory) are to suffuse nature as well as men's hearts. We should not overlook the prominence of Is. 45:1-8 in lessons and other liturgical contexts in the Advent and Christmas seasons; their resuscitation might help to desentimentalize the occasion and reanchor it thoroughly in the universal scope of *Heilsgeschichte*. We should note v. 15 in passing as part of the inspiration of the *Deus absconditus* theme, prominent in Luther's theology. Finally in v. 20 ff. the nations are put on trial once more and challenged to present their case.

Is. 46 and 47 both contemplate the imminent fall of Babylon. The first satirizes the humiliated idols, Bel and Nebo (the first an alternate spelling of Baal, "Lord," here applied to Marduk, Babylon's chief god, the second, the Babylonian "Mercury," especially popular in this period, and appearing in many names, such as *Neb*uchadnezzar). Chap. 47 is a sort of "Gentile oracle," a taunt of the "virgin daughter of Babylon," who must now relinquish her power and forego her luxuries.

Is. 48 is an apt summary of this part of the book: the "former things" replaced by the "new things," the trial of the nations and the final reference to Cyrus (Vs. 14-16), etc. In spite of the strong promise of sure deliverance in this chapter, it is uttered in the same breath with sharp rebuke for Israel's sin (instead of rapid transition from one to the other) - in fact, almost for the first time Israel is directly accused of idolatry and hypocrisy (v. 1). It concludes with a command to "go forth from Babylon." Here, as often in prophecy, the imperative is little more than a stylistic variant of similar predictions. It is similar to 52:11 f. as v. 22 here is parallel to 57:21, reminders of the continued repetition in the rest of the book and the indissoluble unity of the whole. V. 22 seems out of place but really exemplifies the traditional pattern of "alternation of weal and woe."

Isaiah 49—53

Nevertheless, as noted earlier, a clear turning point is discernible beginning with Is. 49. The units tend to be longer, and the "symphonic structure" of the earlier chapters is not so obvious. The controversial tone of Yahweh vs. the idols, God's ability to predict the future, and the themes of Cyrus' capture of Babylon and liberation of the exiles all fade away. With the latter already accomplished in the prophet's vision, the emphasis shifts to the restoration of national life in the homeland, to the plight of Jerusalem more than that of the exiles as such. Critics often think of a second phase of Deutero-Isaiah's ministry, presumably now among the repatriated exiles. On the other hand, the clear knowledge of Palestinian geography, etc., provides conservatives with another argument for the material's origin in "Isaiah of Jerusalem."

The section opens (Is. 49:1-6) with what is usually regarded as the second "Servant poem." Here the Servant certainly speaks as an individual (a sort of soliloquy) as perhaps he already did briefly in 48:16— if so a remarkable adumbration of the Trinity! We also note the explicit parallelism of "servant" and "Israel" in v. 3. At the same time, he has been called like a prophet (vs. 1 and 5; cf. Jer. 1) with a commission *to* Israel as well as to be a "light to the nations" (v. 6). Here, then, both the individual and the collective aspects of the Servant are clearly enunciated, although it has been implicit all along.

The third Song is usually considered as following shortly in Is. 50:4-11. The intervening verses (49:7—50:3) are simply miscellaneous reassurances of God's undying, unmerited love. 49:8 is quoted by Paul in 2 Cor 6:2 in antitypical application to Christ. The "Sinim" of 49:12 is usually understood as Syene (Aswan) on the upper Nile by modern scholars, but the traditional interpretation of "China" should not be dismissed out of hand. Note the two striking pictures in 49:15-16, and the argument of 50:1 that since Zion has no "bill of divorce" in hand, the separation (Exile) cannot have been permanent, but only a temporary disciplinary measure. As in chap. 54 and elsewhere, it is accented that Israel's election has not been abrogated, but only suspended (cf. Paul in Rom. 9—11). The third Song, then, highlights the Servant's total faithfulness to his commission, in spite of great suffering under most adverse circumstances. The speaker, the Servant, is clearly distinguished from the rest of Israel (vs. 10-11). The language reminds us of Jeremiah, Lamentations, and many of the psalms of lament. The *vicarious* nature of the suffering is not yet so clear, but plainly we have an anticipation of and preparation for the climactic Song of 52:13 ff.

The intervening material, Is. 51:1—52:12, devoted entirely to reassurance, contemplates the coming salvation and the establishment of Yahweh's kingship. The prophet's jubilation is reflected in triplication of a double "Awake/Rouse yourself," the first time addressed to the "arm of the LORD," the second and third times to Zion. God's arm is reminded how it once "cut Rahab in pieces" and "pierced the dragon," another use of originally mythological imagery (cf. 30:7; 27:1) to describe the Exodus—and especially the current second Exodus from Babylon. Is. 52:7-8 ff., reminiscent of Is. 40, sees the heralds of good tidings (of Cyrus' edict?) arriving in Jerusalem to the exultant response of the city's watchmen. Both 51:1 and 11 evince a "priestly" concern for "cleanness" and purification, and for the return of the sacred vessels to the rebuilt temple. 52:4 contains the only reference to Assyria in Isaiah II (versus over thirty in Is. I), but in the past tense, consistent with the viewpoint of this part of the book.

The fourth and climactic "Servant Song" begins at Is. 52:13, and the delay of the chapter division for three verses must be one of the most inept and unfortunate in the entire Bible (some of the verse divisions are probably mistaken too). Nevertheless, "Isaiah 53" remains common and convenient shorthand for the pericope. It is also somewhat misleading to speak of it as "climactic." At any rate, it is not the *final* appearance of the Servant theme in the book. At least Is. 61:1-3 picks it up again, albeit in different nuance. We are reminded again of the ultimate artificiality of discussing the four songs apart from the total context.

The Song is structured by an "inclusio": in prologue and epilogue God speaks in the first person describing the Servant's future exaltation, while in the body of the poem the congregation mediates on his present ignominy. It is possible to see liturgical influences on this structure; in any event, we should note two other cultic (sacrificial) themes in the poem: "sprinkle" in 52:15, and "offering" *(asham)* in 53:10. The contrast between humiliation and exaltation dominates the entire poem. There have been many relatively sterile form-critical debates about the genre of the poem's middle section (vs. 1-9), but, as in the case of the third Song, its closest formal relations appear to be the psalmic laments, Jeremiah's so-called "confessions" and Lamentations. As in the royal Messianic oracles of Isaiah I, the entire pericope swarms with unique or rare words, perhaps deliberately to connote the *magnum mysterium,* but leading to an unusual number of textual and exegetical difficulties.

As we noted, already the third Song (50:4-11) had described the Servant's vindication by God in spite of severe suffering, but the reasons for the suffering had not been spelled out. The new thing here is twofold: the suffering eventuates in death (before resurrection), and the meaning of it all is vicarious.

Who Is the "Servant"?

Nearly everyone agrees that in many ways Isaiah II peaks here, both poetically and theologically. The hermeneutical question is the crucial one again, and to that we must now turn before proceeding. The four main types of interpretation may be labeled: (1) autobiographical, (2) biographical or historical, (3) collective or corporate, and (4) Messianic or Christological. The first may be peremptorily dismissed, because the New

Testament does so (Acts 8:34), and the second almost as quickly. That need not be construed, however, to imply that, humanly speaking none of Isaiah's personal experience, or of other great Old Testament figures often suggested (especially Moses, in connection with the "second Exodus" themes) could have flowed into the portrait. On the same principle, it does not take long to decide that the fourth alternative is ultimately the only one compatible with the New Testament. There is still, however, the totality of the Old Testament evidence to reckon with, and the *fides quaerens intellectum* still has the task of exploring the precise connections. The result is a Messianic interpretation that does not totally exclude the corporate and other dimensions. As frequently, the wrong interpretations retain a grain of truth. The analogy of prophecy also reminds us that the predictive and typological aspects of prophecy must be held together as two aspects of an indissoluble whole.

While traditional Christian understandings have been quite un-animously Messianic, it is interesting to note that both traditional Jewish (at least since Rashi in the Middle Ages) and modern liberal-critical exegesis has been predominantly corporate or collective, identifying the Servant with the Israelite community. Even apart from the New Testament witness, however, there is the problem of how the Servant can then have a mission to Israel. Another way to try to solve the problem is by distinguishing the true, spiritual Israel from the external confines of the community; the responsibility for the mission rests with the community as a whole, but the accomplishment is possible only for an individual. As an Israelite, he represents Israel in fulfilling its responsibility, yet he possesses characteristics that could not possibly be attributed to the entire nation. Yet even if we concede that, we still flounder on the vicariousness of the action (unless it happens quite automatically and universalistically) and on the massive *sola gratia* context. How can the experience of even "true" Israel be ultimately redemptive of sin? That would utterly contradict not only much of the rest of the Old Testament, but especially the prophetic vision, which, at best, never put that kind of hope in *Israel!*

On the other hand, we have noted that at points the "Servant" is *explicitly* identified with Israel! How do we reconcile the two? H. W. Robinson's theory of "corporate personality" (though not as popular in scholarship as it once was) is helpful: the Servant is "Israel reduced to one"—not only metaphorically, but in a real "incarnational" sense. Some of this type of thought was already present in the general Biblical understanding of kingship and priesthood. However, Engnell's influential theory that "servant" originally referred to a king and his Babylonian-like participation in New Year's rites of humiliation and renewed exaltation goes far beyond the evidence (at best), although it would have the merit of justifying a Messianic (in the narrow royal sense) import for the servant concept from its very roots.

All of that helps, however, only if we continue to identify that "Israel reduced to one" with Jesus Christ, who both antitypically and in fulfillment of prophecy, not only recapitulated but also consummated Israel's history—as the New Testament is often at pains to point out. Jesus *is* Israel, true man, but also radically distinct from Israel, true God. Thus, "in Christ," by submersion under and identification with Him—and only then—can Israel's suffering be said to have any salvific value. We are speaking of sanctification here, not justification. The principle applies backwards to Israel and the Old Testament, but also forward to the New Testament church. Only as baptized into Him is it theologically meaningful to speak of the "suffering/caring community," etc. Sometimes Isaiah seems to point in this direction by distinguishing the Servant from the "servants" (e.g., eight such in Is. 65—66 alone). In neither testament is it functionally possible to consider the body apart from the Head, but the accents vary in different texts, and theoretically it is of prime importance that the two be most carefully distinguished.

We, of course, are following Delitzsch's classical three-dimensional or pyramidal exposition of the Servant, as do most conservative scholars. At the base of the pyramid is the elect Hebrew nation as a whole, the church-state which God had charged with responsibility for the mission. At the middle level is the true, spiritual Israel, the faithful remnant, who fulfill that exalted calling. But at the apex stands a single individual, who is Israel and without whose vicarious atonement there could be no true Israel.

One may well go even further and place *two* isosceles triangles on the horizontal, with their apexes meeting in Christ. That would well represent the universal sweep of all Biblical *Heilsgeschichte* centering in the Servant, with obverses on either side of His advent. As history began with universal "salvation," so the eschatological intent of the entire redemptive design is universal. As the Fall necessitated the repeated narrowing of the line of election until it rested in the one Elect of God, so in Him and after Him through the witness of the church it must again be broadened until all the elect have been saved.

Isaiah 54—66 and "Trito-Isaiah"

The following Isaiah chapters, 54 and 55, are almost equally famous, but the transition is as abrupt as ever in Isaiah II. Perhaps the best one can offer is that the following exultation and invitation are based on the event of chap. 53—as in a broader sense they emphatically are! Is. 54 uses predominantly marital imagery: the "desolate" woman will have more children than the "married" one (cf. Paul's famous, explicit typology comparing the Old and New Testament congregations in Gal. 4). V. 5 is even bolder: "your Maker is your husband," anticipating both themes in "Isaiah III" and various accents on the church as the bride of Christ.

This renewed "covenant of peace" is even compared with the Noachitic covenant (Is. 54:9-10). (Critics commonly believe that this reference, like the one to Abraham and Sarah in 51:2, indicates the initial stages of acceptance of those stories into the exilic community, while to the conservative they are interesting confirmation of their common knowledge already in the eighth century.) The picture of the "new Jerusalem" (54:11-12) anticipates apocalyptic (cf. Rev. 21:2, 19).

This section of the book concludes with an invitation to "every one who thirsts" to a free Messianic banquet (cf. 25:6). (Yet in the afterglow of chap. 53 we do not forget that it was very costly to the Giver!) In v. 3 we have the only explicit allusion in Isaiah II to the everlasting, *Davidic* covenant (in contrast to, but also in unity with, its prominence in Isaiah I). This is not to say that the prophet's own thought made no connection between that promise and the Servant, but it was apparently made only very tenuously, if at all, in the rest of the Old Testament, and in Judaism till this day. The unity of those themes was thus understandably a major stumbling block also for Jesus' disciples (Matt 16:21 ff., etc.), even after His death (Acts 1:6). It will not quite square with the Biblical evidence to assert that Jesus (let alone the later church) first unified the two prophetic streams, but it obviously was a key element in His preaching about Himself (probably most evident in the Gospel of John). Like Is. 40, 55:10 f. accents the power of the Word to accomplish God's will, *usque ad* a new creation.

CHAPTERS 56—66 (ISAIAH III)

Somewhere around the beginning of Is. 56 we have an unusually sharp transition, and not only with a single chapter. Precisely where to place the major break is moot, however—a scarcely surprising circumstance in the Book of Isaiah. The usual caesura is made at the end of chap. 55, but a good case can be made for linking 56:1-2 with chap. 55: even in "the freedom of the Gospel" the "third use of the Law" retains its validity for the believer, and he needs God's power to obey it. Similarly, 56:3-8 fits at least as well with what precedes as with what follows (which on the whole has greater affinity with Isaiah I than with chaps. 40—55). If so, it stresses in conclusion that the glorious promise is ultimately open to all people, regardless of background (even to eunuchs and bastards, which Deut. 23 excluded in the old covenant.) As we noted above, Archer and others, appealing to the repetition of the refrain, "No peace for the wicked," at the end of both chaps. 48 and 57, locate the beginning of the third division of the book at chap. 58. Then Isaiah II concludes with condemnation of Israel's wicked rulers (56:9—57:21), while the "program for peace" in part III begins with a "contrast between false and true worship" (58:1-14). One can scarcely view such a division as inappropriate either, and perhaps it all only proves how subjective *all* such conclusions are—particularly the facile critical divisions into "Deutero-" and "Trito-Isaiah."

Regardless of where we find the major transition, the use of "Isaiah III" or even "III Isaiah" is thus justifiable, even if one disassociates himself altogether from the critical reasoning behind those labels, which have been common since Duhm. Duhm thought of a discrete prophetic figure behind chapters 56—66 allegedly addressing the Restoration, not the Exile. Others have thought of a late or third stage in "Isaiah's" ministry, as he allegedly discovered to his regret that the parousia had not arrived with the return, but that all the old problems and perversities were still at hand as much as ever. The bulk of critical opinion, however, has clearly shifted away from any understanding of the chapters as a unity. Rather they are usually considered as anthological as the rest of the Book of Isaiah, deriving from various figures and periods of the "school of Isaiah." Most of them are considered exilic or later in date, although many critics are prepared to admit some material here from "Isaiah of Jerusalem."

The conservative most readily views the chapters as a third shift in Isaiah's own vision, as he corrects possible enthusiastic misunderstandings of his own eschatological exuberance. At the same time, one may see here a sort of wedding of some of the language and themes of Isaiah II with the realism and ethical concern of Isaiah I. The contrast must not be overstated, however; a unified perspective of the book will note many anticipations of, if not parallels to, Isaiah III already in Isaiah I.

Certainly, beginning with Is. 56:9 we find ourselves in an almost entirely different world than the second part of the book. How serious the problem is, no matter what the precise historical reference, becomes evident in the description of avaricious rulers as "dumb dogs" (56:9—57:2), and even more so of the strange, licentious heathen rites, which are flourishing (57:3-13; cf. 65:3 ff.; Ezek. 6—8). But Yahweh's condescending grace persists nonetheless too (57:14-21). Chap. 58 contrasts the false, purely ritualistic fast with the true "fast" of unselfishness, helpfulness, etc. (cf. chap. 1). If the people keep that fast together with the Sabbath, blessing will ensue.

After an excoriating rebuke (Is. 59:1-8), which Paul applies to the total depravity of all mankind (Rom. 3:15-17), at least some of the community is moved to confess its desperate sinfulness in moving terms (9-15). Since, however, the people are unable to extricate themselves, Yahweh Himself must don His spiritual armor (cf. Eph. 6:14, 17; 1 Thess. 5:8) and go to war on their behalf (cf. 63:1-6).

In Is. 60—62, there are stronger contacts again with Isaiah II and eschatological material in Isaiah I. The famous Epiphany pericope (60:1-7) exhorts the congregation to rise and witness the epiphany of Yahweh's "glory": while darkness still envelopes the rest of the earth, the longed-for light (59:9; cf. 9:2) rises over Jerusalem, and not only the diaspora, but all nations with their wealth pour in (cf. Haggai). The rest of the chapter develops these themes, stressing especially that the supernatural light will be eternal (esp. 19-20; cf. Rev. 21), and many of them continue in 61:5-11.

The term "servant" is not used in the intervening part, 61:1-4, but the speaker's commission and empowerment by the Spirit to effect the new era plainly connects the pericope with the earlier Servant Songs, and Jesus' explicit application of the prophecy to Himself (Matt. 11:5, etc.) underscores it. The Jubilee year (Lev. 25) appears to be the dominant figure for the Messianic restoration.

The special feature of Is. 62's description of the felicity of the Messianic people is the series of symbolic names, esp. v. 4 ("Hephzibah" and "Beulah") and 12. We need to recall that Biblical names usually are not just ID's, but partake of and help establish the circumstances they describe.

Is. 63:1-6 is in the form of a dialogue between the prophet and Yahweh, described as a blood-spattered Victor returning victoriously from His eschatological "day/year of vengeance/redemption" over "Edom" (plainly a type), where He has "trodden the wine press alone." It is an important pericope for getting Biblical "universalism" in proper perspective: no victory without defeat, no salvation without damnation, etc!

Is. 63:7—64:12 is more or less a unit. It appears to be a litany (liturgy of repentance and supplication and /or intercessory prayer), apparently spoken by the prophet on behalf of the congregation. It has many parallels elsewhere in Scripture: recital of God's theophanies and redemptive acts, and prayer that they will again become manifest, in spite of the congregation's unworthiness. The comparison in 64:6 of even human "righteousness" as but a "menstrual rag" before God is one of the stoutest in Scripture.

Is. 65 speaks, in effect of a "new remnant" of the faithful out of all the Exiles who often thought of themselves *en bloc* in the light of those prophecies. Salvation must still come through and out of judgment (Law-Gospel), but the attraction of the strange pagan rites to many will not lead to the rejection of the faithful. Instead, they will be given a new name (v. 15) and a new blessing (v. 16) which will ultimately lead into the creation of "new heavens and a new earth" (v. 17) with a radically new order of existence. And we do not overlook the apparently deliberate allusion in v. 25 to the Messianic oracle of 11:6-9 (cf. Hab. 2:14).

Is. 66:1-4 reminds Israel, as Solomon had in 1 Kings 8, that no earthly temple can contain or control God (the old paganizing conception) because the whole earth (not merely the Ark in the Holy of Holies) is His "footstool." This has always been a favorite passage for those who wish to view the prophets as spiritualistic champions of a religion solely of the "heart," but, as we stressed earlier, that is very wide of the mark.

Is. 66:5-24 concludes the book of the greatest of the prophets with contrasted portraits of the glorious blessedness in prospect for the new Jerusalem, and the terrible, eternal punishment impending on her foes. The final verse of the book describes that damnation in language very close to the New Testament's "Gehenna" and "hell." That the book closes on such a horrendous note is not out of line with much of its contents, but it is interesting to note the ancient custom of the synagogue to repeat part of v. 23 after v. 24, so that the lection may "close with words of comfort."

JEREMIAH

We are better informed about the details of Jeremiah's life than of any other prophet, thanks mostly to copious information found within his book itself. There is no prophet where detailed knowledge of the tortuous history of the period is as important for understanding as in the case of Jeremiah. Although very precise historical data are sometimes given, the problem is complicated by the often completely unchronological order in which the oracles occur—another reminder that "history" in Biblical thought is not identical with the modern, secularist construct.

Jeremiah's Life and Background

The superscription (which even critics in this case find no cause to question) identifies Jeremiah as "the son of Hilkiah, of the priests who were in Anathoth in the land of Benjamin." Of the father, we know nothing (unless, as seems very unlikely, he was the same priest who discovered the "book of the Law" in the temple), but Anathoth (still bearing essentially the same Arabic name, 'Anata) lies on the second ridge of hills, a few miles NNE of Jerusalem. Mention of priestly descent makes it not at all unlikely that Jeremiah was descended from David's priest, Abiathar, whom Solomon had banished to his home city, Anathoth, in favor of Zadok (1 Kings 2:35). That would also mean Jeremianic roots in Shiloh (Abiathar was descended from Eli) and thus in the heartland of the

North, whose traditions might well be very much alive a century after the fall of Samaria. That would explain Jeremiah's affinity with Hosea, another northern prophet, as well as with the "deuteronomic" traditions; criticism has often developed these connections in a way unacceptable to conservatism, but a certain degree of likelihood remains.

Among the Jeremianic accents which at least appear to be especially "northern" in type are: (1) the degree of accent on the Mosaic covenant and the Exodus; (2) the use of the marriage metaphor to describe the covenant relation with God (cf. Hosea); and (3) the related portrait of Israel's wilderness days, not as a period of rebellion, but a "honeymoon" period of complete and blissful faithfulness to her "husband." The "deuteronomic" style of many of Jeremiah's sermons is a related issue, to which we return below. Finally, Jeremiah's northern background might also explain the plot against Jeremiah's life by his own countrymen (Jer. 11:18—12:6), who perhaps disapproved of his close connections with certain ruling circles in Jerusalem.

The superscription goes on (Jer. 1:2) to date Jeremiah's call in the thirteenth year of the reign of Josiah (cf. 25:3), that is, about 627. How old he was at the time, we do not know, but in his autobiographical account of his call which follows, he describes himself as a *na'ar,* that is (usually) a "youth" of marriageable age, probably not older than twenty. His last recorded words (chap. 44) were spoken in Egypt, whither he had been kidnapped by Johanan after Ishmael's assassination of Gedaliah, sometime after 587. Thus, Jeremiah exercised a ministry of at least forty years, perhaps somewhat more. Presumably, that length of activity is also reflected in the length of the book, second only to Isaiah among the prophets.

The detailed information we have of the intervening years (often attributed to Baruch, his scribe and presumed biographer) will be reviewed in our survey of contents below. Suffice it to say here that Jeremiah lived out his entire life in that chaotic and fateful period a century after the fall of Samaria (and the activities of the great eighth-century prophets) when we have almost a rerun of the earlier history, only this time with Judah as the victim. In the three-cornered contest for world supremacy between Assyria, Babylon, and Egypt, Judah's mercurial foreign policy was largely based on expediency instead of principle, and Jeremiah is usually obliged to oppose it as uncompromisingly as Isaiah had Judah's a century earlier. After Babylonian supremacy has largely been established, pro-Egyptian and anti-Egyptian factions wrack the court at Jerusalem as they had Samaria's in its final days (cf. Hosea).

Among the epochal events of which Jeremiah was a contemporary, we may mention: the death of the great Assyrian king Ashurbanipal, the subsequent swift decline and fall of Nineveh (612) and of the entire Assyrian empire, the battle of Megiddo (609) in which Josiah lost his life, Nebuchadnezzar's subsequent defeat of Egypt at the battle of Carchemish (605), the rapid change of imperialist occupier of Judah, from Assyria to Egypt to Babylonia and two or three deportations from Jerusalem, the last one accompanying its destruction. Jeremiah is, indeed, "the prophet of the decline and fall of the Hebrew monarchy."

Many other prophets were active during Jeremiah's lifetime, but, as with all the prophets, none are ever mentioned. Among these were Ezekiel, Daniel, Nahum, Habakkuk, and possibly Obadiah and Zephaniah. Of contemporaries, the false prophet Hananiah is featured prominently (Jer. 28) because of his clashes with Jeremiah, as is the faithful prophet, Uriah, who had been extradited from Egypt and executed by Jehoiakim (26:20-23). In the same connection we do, however, have mention of Micah (26:26-39), active a century earlier—the *only* time a prophetic book mentions another "writing prophet" by name!

Tradition and Jeremiah

Later ages were much impressed by Jeremiah's life, all of which was a sort of martyrdom, and with that, especially in certain ages, the faithful could easily identify. They readily saw in his sufferings a type of themselves, and drew from his constancy courage to endure. Many critics would cite as a first example, "Deutero-Isaiah's" portrait of the "Suffering Servant," and, while that will not wash, there is no reason to doubt that the two reinforced each other to a certain extent, and that Jesus may well have thought of himself as an antitype of and successor to Jeremiah. In Matt. 16:14 at Caesarea Philippi we certainly see in the popular identification of Jesus as *Jeremiah redivivus* an echo of the role he played in the eschatological hopes of the day; Jesus does not so much reject it as establish its inadequacy to describe His person.

Fascination with the figure of Jeremiah is also reflected in the legend of 2 Macc. 2, depicting the prophet's instrumentality in preserving the ark and the sacred fire of the temple from extinction at the time of Jerusalem's fall. Jewish traditions attributed authorship of various Old Testament books to Jeremiah (Kings, perhaps Lamentations, etc.), and his popularity is also reflected in the Qumran literature.

Later tradition attempted especially to compensate for the Biblical silence in the circumstances of his death. One has it that he was ultimately stoned to death in Egypt by his infuriated countrymen (Jerome; probably a deduction from Jer. 44). We have pseudepigraphical letters purporting to have been written by Jeremiah from Egypt to the other exiles in Babylon, and still other traditions (especially Josephus) have it that he ultimately found his way to Babylon, where he died. We may also mention in this connection the somewhat more respectable "Letter of Jeremiah," usually classified among the apocrypha (sometimes treated as the final chapter of the also apocryphal book of Baruch), which purports to be a letter Jeremiah sent to the exiles in Babylon, similar to the canonical one recorded in Jer. 29, although in fact it appears more to be an expansion of the Aramaic counsel against idolatry in Jer. 10:11 (cf. below).

Liberalism and Jeremiah

Modern liberal "tradition" has also been very much taken by the figure of Jeremiah, although for different reasons. As we noted earlier, classical liberal chatter about "prophetic ministry" or the like tends to have Jeremiah and Amos as its two real models—and edited editions of them, of course! Jeremiah cannot be appealed to so much for his ethical activism, but he more than makes up for it by his frank, "person centered" religion. Skinner's classically liberal commentary on Jeremiah is titled, *Prophecy and Religion;* and similarly Hertzberg's *Prophet und Gott.* Bentzen observed that "a book on prophecy will always be, to a great extent, a book on Jeremiah." One more quote (Davidson): "Prophecy had already taught its truths; its last effort was to reveal itself in a life."

By early liberals, Jeremiah was lionized for allegedly having pioneered in liberating religion from its previously largely corporate, cultic, and group expressions and developing it into a matter of "inwardness," of "me and my God." True religion could be practiced just as easily in distant Babylon as in the temple of Jerusalem. Jeremiah was the "prophet of the heart," almost for the first time a champion of *individual* responsibility, or personal accountability before God. Some even tried to make him the first precursor of Luther's accents on *Anfechtung* and "faith." Cf. Wellhausen: "Jeremiah is the father of true prayer.... The Psalms would not have been written without Jeremiah. . . . Through sorrow and woe there arose within him the certainty of personal fellowship with God, the truest essence of piety."

In later, slightly different version, to existentialists for whom God has long since been banished to the inner life, and for whom the essence of "revelation" is personal encounter (*not* intellectual assent to propositions) the fascination with Jeremiah centers on the extent to which he carried his heart on his sleeve, as it were, and bared his inner soul. This is especially apparent in his laments (inappropriately often called "confessions"), but his inner conflicts are frequently exhibited also in his public preaching. Of course, his "anti-cultic" profile and social action declamations have not usually hurt his "liberal image" here either.

In another hermeneutical context, the topic of Jeremiah's inner life is a legitimate one, of course, and required by the book itself. Some details we shall consider below. It must be conceded that sometimes tradition and conservatism have represented the other extreme of the spectrum in their relative neglect of the topic, and of the Book of Jeremiah in general, preferring others with more explicit Messianic and other doctrinal expression. We may note here Jeremiah's unmarried state and frequent unsociability (Jer. 16)—at God's own command as an "action prophecy" of the Exile. He apparently regarded it as an unusual burden, however, as he did in general the ignominy and calumny which followed from his call. Thus, although his communion with God was in many respects exemplary, at other times he lashes out even at God, whom he accuses of having tricked him into becoming a prophet (20:7 ff). That is, although his public utterances betray no sign of it, his laments reveal an inward blanching at the possibility that his call and inspiration were false. Although he can even speak of dissolving in tears on occasion (9:1; 13:17), it is entirely misleading to refer to him as "the weeping prophet": the record shows that, far from being a brooding recluse, Jeremiah was as intimately involved in the public events of the day as Isaiah, and absolutely adamant in his counsel. All in all, even humanly speaking, a thoroughly credible figure, and certainly one from whom, as with other Biblical characters, the Christian can and should learn both positively and negatively. Cf. below also on Jeremiah as a type of Christ.

Jeremiah and Josiah's Reformation

The question of Jeremiah's attitude towards Josiah's reformation is an important one in the study of the book. Surprisingly (?), Jeremiah makes no clear reference to it whatsoever, although he apparently was a staunch supporter of Josiah in general. Higher criticism, of course, attaches supreme importance to the issue, because of the pivotal role which Deuteronomy and the "deuteronomic reformation" plays in its entire reconstruction of the history of Israel's religion. As we noted earlier, conservatives would not necessarily find the label, *"Deuteronomic* reformation," entirely inaccurate, and the question is an inevitable and important one, even on radically different premises.

Critics have given contradictory answers to the question, partly depending on their presuppositions. Duhm argued from the classically liberal viewpoint that Jeremiah could not possibly have countenanced the deuteronomistic sanction of sacrifice, externalist, biblicism, etc. A favorite proof text for those of that mind has always been Jer. 8:8, condemning the "false pen of the scribes" and those who trust in the "law of the LORD," but there is no clear indication of any specific target, only the usual prophetic ones of insincerity, venality, etc. (A few suggested pique that Huldah's advice was sought, not his, but that scarcely merits reply.) An opposite extreme, though a tiny minority, even argued for the dependence of Deuteronomy on Jeremiah!

Many however, argue for Jeremiah's dependence on "D," pointing especially to the discussion in 11:1-17, where Jeremiah stoutly exhorts his audience to "hear the words of this covenant" (but again the text lacks particulars, and some would attribute the text to later deuteronomic editions, to begin with). This camp argues that Jeremiah not only approved of D's theology, particularly its alleged program of centralization of worship, but also adopted its characteristic style in many of his homilies. The latter point attaches to the undeniably "deuteronomic" character of many of the Jeremianic sermons in their present form, but other explanations are possible, of course, and we return to the issue below.

A very popular middle—and sort of compromising—position argues that Jeremiah at first welcomed the reform, but later became disillusioned at some of its unfortunate developments and came to the realization that real regeneration would have to come from within rather than by law or statute. A few have tried to explain Jeremiah's famous "new covenant" discourse (31:31-34) as Jeremiah's later alternative to the deuteronomistic quasi-legalism.

This debate may be illuminated by comparing the major phases of Jeremiah's ministry with what appears to be a very rough overall chronological order of the main sections of his book. Jer. 1—6 may stem largely from the beginning of Jeremiah's career, from his call to Josiah's reform (c. 627—620). The second period of his ministry would be concurrent with the latter part of Josiah's reign, from the beginning of the reform until his death at Megiddo in 609. It is certainly striking that relatively few passages in the book can certainly be ascribed to this period. Jeremiah's "silent period," of course, may be construed as implying either approval or disapproval. Since, at best, it is an argument from silence, other scholars interpret it in still others ways, or even question if there ever was any "silent period," and reject the entire chronological schematism supposedly present in the book. The pattern does work out better in the latter two periods, but it proves little because we are dealing with largely historical narrative in the Book of Jeremiah, not with oracles. Some question the dating of the early oracles to Josianic times and believe that Jeremiah was not very active at all (or perhaps not even called) until around 609. Chapters 7—39 of the book (after the "silent period"?) do seem to report primarily on events in a "third phase," between Megiddo in 609 and the sack of Jerusalem in 587. Likewise, chapters 40—45 describe events involving Jeremiah after the catastrophe.

The truth is that we have no direct information on the subject of Jeremiah's attitude toward Josiah's reform. Given conservative premises that the *Josianic* reformation was based on a *Mosaic* Deuteronomy (or its equivalent), every likelihood would indicate that Jeremiah was in thorough sympathy with the movement. The relative paucity of oracles certainly datable to the period can just as easily imply approval as disapproval. Again the lack of specific mention may be for the same puzzling reason as the failure to mention other contemporary canonical prophets—perhaps a desire to avoid duplication.

What is often overlooked in this entire issue is its political dimension, perhaps because we so easily forget that ancient Israel was state as well as "church." The account of Jeremiah's near arrest and execution or lynching in Jer. 26 concludes with the significant statement: "But the hand of Ahikam the son of Shaphan was with Jeremiah so that he was not given over to the people to be put to death." Careful reading of various references makes plain that Jeremiah had the closest association with some three generations of this influential family, which was also one of the mainstays of Josiah's throne. The father, Shaphan, had been something like state-secretary to Josiah in charge of temple renovation, and when the book of the law was found, it was to him that Hilkah first reported it. Shaphan, in turn read from the book to Josiah, and on the king's instructions, it is he and his son, Ahikam, who seek validation of its message from Huldah the prophetess. (Why not Jeremiah? Was it because Jeremiah was of northern priestly descent, and thus somewhat an outsider? The incident does at least suggest that Jeremiah's later cordiality with the family of Shaphan was solely a matter of coincidence of religious convictions. Of course, if as seems entirely unlikely, this Hilkiah was also Jeremiah's father, the incident appears in much different light!)

After Josiah's death at Megiddo and the collapse of his policies (including, no doubt, his religious reform), the family, like Jeremiah, apparently continued in firm support of that direction and in opposition to the policies of Josiah's various relatives who succeeded him. Two of Ahikam's brothers also appear beside Jeremiah: Elasah, one of the two couriers who bore Jeremiah's letters to the exiles in Babylonia (Jer. 29:3), and Gemariah, from whose house Baruch read Jeremiah's scroll in Jehoiakim's reign, and who vainly tried to prevent the king from burning it (chap. 36). To the Babylonians, the Shaphan family and Jeremiah both appeared "pro-Babylonian," so after the fall of Jerusalem and Jeremiah declines to journey to Babylon, we are not surprised that the Babylonians commend him to the care of Ahikam's son, Gedaliah, whom they had appointed governor of the captured province (39:14).

Jeremiah and the Lachish Ostraca

Another topic relating to Jeremiah's lifetime is his possible mention in some of the eighteen letters found by archaeologists in 1935 in the guardroom of Lachish, southwest of Jerusalem, which fell just before Jerusalem (cf. Jer. 34:7, where it is mentioned as still standing). Two mentions of prophets once led to intense speculation that Jeremiah (or even Uriah) was meant, and while that is unlikely, the texts do shed important extra-Biblical light on the Hebrew language and prophetic activity in that period. Ostracon XVI is broken and refers only to " . . . iah the prophet" (unfortunately thousands of names besides Jeremiah concluded with that theophoric). Letter III mentions some unnamed prophet who had sent a warning of some sort, perhaps of possible sedition. Letter VI is also interesting in its complaint that some princes were "weakening the hands" (discouraging, demoralizing) the people— precisely the same accusation made by the princes of Jerusalem against Jeremiah (38:4).

Form Criticism

In sum, although we know considerable about Jeremiah's life and lifetime, many hiatuses remain. However, our relative ease at that point is more than compensated for by the problems raised by the text of Jeremiah and its transmission, to which we must now turn. The questions posed by textual criticism and by "tradition-history" (the formation of the Book of Jeremiah) must be considered in tandem, because textual (written) variations *may* simply continue oral variations before anything was written down, or at least before there was any kind of canonical stabilization. Critical vagaries are very much in evidence in studies of the subject, but often the right questions have been raised, even if the hypotheses offered in answer are not totally acceptable.

Let us first repeat the results of Mowinckel's influential form-critical classification of types of prophetic literature, which he first worked out on the basis of Jeremiah, but which is often applied to other books as well, and which, as we have noted, has clear *formal* merit, regardless of the isagogical and theological milieu. Mowinckel and others use the first four letters of the alphabet as follows: (A) oracles, couched in poetic form, and often in the first person, that is, God speaking directly through the prophet (this often thought to be the original form of most prophetic discourse)—and Duhm applied the principle ruthlessly to Jeremiah; (B) historical narratives or "legends," especially concerned with recording the occasions of prophetic speeches or actions; (C) prose discourses or sermons; and (D) prophecies of hope (often dismissed as ungenuine).

Applied to the Book of Jeremiah, type A, which can readily be spotted by its poetic format in most versions, seems to cluster especially in chaps. 1—25. Type D is especially represented in chaps. 30—31. The Gentile oracles (chaps. 46—51) are not immediately covered by Mowinckel's scheme, and may be set aside for the moment. (Also the monologues or laments and some other materials do not readily fit one or the other of the above classifications, one of its weaknesses.) That leaves the middle twenty chapters as the major concentration of B and C types, but unfortunately the material is not arranged that neatly either. It is, however, these two types which are most characteristic of Jeremiah, and as a result scholarly speculations have focused especially on them.

Type B, the historical narratives, in Jeremiah are often referred to as the "Baruch Biography," on the assumption that they stemmed from the prophet's constant companion and confidant. The supposition is by no means impossible or even unlikely, but it must be stressed that the Bible itself never makes such an assertion, and in criticism too it has come under increasing attack. All we are told is that "Baruch wrote upon a scroll all the words of the LORD which He had spoken to him" (Jer. 36:4), and after Jehoiakim had destroyed the first one, "many similar words were added" (36:32) to the replacement.

With only that to go on, almost incredible critical energies have been devoted to debates about the nature and contents of the original scrolls. One debate turned on the question of whether the contents were primarily of the A or C type. Even more of a will-o'-the-wisp was the goal of determining the precise limits of Baruch's scroll (sometimes even the materials first added in the expanded, second edition!) Fortunately, even criticism has largely abandoned both pursuits.

Type C, the prose sermons usually in the first person, and sometimes apparently related to A or B passages, are scattered throughout the book. This type is not only more extensive in Jeremiah than in any other prophetic book, but Jeremiah's prose is remarkable "deuteronomic." Inevitably, that too has spawned a host of speculations, mostly asking whether Jeremiah ever originally used that idiom, or whether their present form represents a later "deuteronomization" of prophetic traditions by later traditors. Tradition-critics have tended to assume the latter, but we really have no way of knowing. Theologically, too, conservatives might assent, although within a different hermeneutical context (of verbal, not community inspiration).

However, on no cogent grounds does it appear possible to make out a case for the unlikelihood of Jeremiah's own employment of that style. Only arbitrary form-critical dogma can argue for the supposed originality or priority of the poetic or A type (and Reventlow has argued strongly for the artificiality of the distinction). Not only its extensive use in the "former prophets," but also the Lachish Letters indicate that the idiom was very popular in that period.

The issue also inevitably overlaps with the question of the Mosaicity of the Book of Deuteronomy. Critics who assume the book's production or composition in this same period use that supposition both to support actual Jeremianic use of the D style, and to argue from its current popularity for the near-inevitability of some traditional reworking of Jeremiah under that influence (perhaps all the more so if he is assumed to have supported the "deuteronomic reformation"). Conservatives would like to argue that its very antiquity as a traditional sermonic idiom, plus its historic association with Moses and the Torah, would make it not at all unlikely that Jeremiah would, on occasion, adopt that form of communication. However, as noted, the issue need not, as such, be theological.

Tradition-Criticism

How did all the material in the Book of Jeremiah get put together in its present form? Inevitably, we are reduced to hypothesis, but hypothesize we almost must. First of all again, the theological implications of the question: there is no *a priori* reason why we must assume Jeremianic writing of all the *ipsissima verba* in the book, as long as whatever subsequent development is assumed is held under the umbrella of objective revelation. Unlike liberal "tradition-criticism" one would generally assume that the period of traditioning was relatively short, much of it perhaps even taking place under Jeremiah's own supervision. That Baruch, the master's *alter ego,* played a prominent role, and that his scroll formed the core of the ultimate product also appears likely, but one can only guess. Whether or not the oracles fell from the master's lips in essentially that form or not, a plausible supposition would be that Mowinckel's four types somewhat correspond to independent patterns of collecting or remembering the prophet's life and speeches until subsequent combination. Since the beginning of the series of Gentile oracles (46:1) speaks of *all* "the nations" before the individual targets are enumerated, it may be read as an original superscription to an erstwhile separate collection of that type of material.

Beyond that, however, conclusions become very subjective. Possibly some of the procedure of the compiler (?) can be cautiously reconstructed as follows: to each group of poetic (type A) utterances, he began by adding a suitable selection from the prose collection (type C). When the latter were nearly exhausted, he began (around Jer. 19) to use B type of material (historical narrative), which after chap. 25 became dominant. At the end of the book were appended the Gentile oracles and chap. 52. Both thematic and chronological classifications are in evidence, as are the other devices such as "inclusio." Perhaps the best one can say is that if anyone dislikes that modest attempt to "track through the snow" the process of compilation, let him propose an alternative! The results are less than satisfactory to the Western mind, but we are reminded again that the Holy Ghost did not originally give the Bible to the Occident. The dogma of the "perfection" of Holy Scripture does not purport to answer isagogical questions of this sort.

Text-Criticism

The Septuagint text, however, throws a "monkey-wrench" into the entire works and must be considered in conjunction with the above considerations. We have at this point easily one of the most grievous text-critical problems in the entire Old Testament. The problem is twofold, concerning both the length and the arrangement of the material. As concerns length, the LXX text is roughly one-eighth (some 2,700 words) shorter than MT. Most of the lacunae consist of single verses or parts of verses, but sometimes longer portions are missing too. Some of the variations are readily explainable on normal text-critical principles (homoioteleuton, etc.), others not. Some of the metrical regularity of MT seems to be missing, but that is a frequent casualty of translation, at best. Usually the variations are ultimately no more serious than alternate, usually abbreviated, ways of saying the same thing. In any event, the variations are often of such a nature that no number of translational vicissitudes suffice to account for them, but one must simply assume that the Greek translator(s) worked from a different Hebrew *Vorlage* or exemplar from that represented by MT. Now the Qumran discoveries have given us some *Hebrew* manuscripts of that same type, demonstrating beyond all reasonable doubt that the textual divergence antedated the LXX, probably by a considerable period of time. All of this, almost certainly takes us out of the realm of mere *text*-criticism, back also into the period of *oral* transmission before there was any fixed, written text, that is, into the realm of *tradition*-criticism.

Not only is the LXX considerably shorter, but the material is arranged in entirely different sequence. Let us place the two outlines side by side. In the Hebrew (and English) versions we have the following (if it can really be called an outline): (1) Chap. 1: the prophet's call; (2) Chaps 2—25: various oracles, mostly of doom (A) with some supplementation of C (prose sermon) types, and, toward the end, also of biographical narratives (B); (3) Chaps. 26—45: mostly biographical material (B), but containing a little A and D, but no C; (4) Chaps. 46—51: Gentile oracles; and (5) Chap. 52: an appendix relating Jerusalem's fall and immediately subsequent history (essentially parallel to 2 Kings 24:18—25:30).

In the Septuagint, in contrast, we have essentially the same blocs of material, but in different sequence (we give the rough Hebrew chapter and verse equivalences for the sake of convenience): (1) the prophet's call (chap. 1); (2) oracles of doom in Jerusalem and Judah (chaps. 2:1— 25:13); (3) Gentile oracles (chaps. 46—51+25:15-38); (4) oracles of deliverance (chaps. 26—35); (5) Jeremiah's sufferings (chaps. 36—45).

If we compare the two sequences, it must be said that at least two initial considerations seem to favor the LXX. Any student of prophecy will note at once that the LXX sequence is that of the "classical" prophetic outline of universal judgment followed by universal (offer of) salvation— in this case followed by the "Book of Suffering" which did not fit that outline. That order could, of course, represent a later *re*arrangement of the material, but such a thing appears unlikely and is quite un- precedented. Furthermore, it must be conceded that 25:15-38 has no immediate connection with its MT context (that by itself is scarcely surprising), while it makes a superb conclusion to the Gentile oracles (although one cannot deny the possibility that the association is "redactional" on the part of the LXX translators).

The issue is by no means so clear-cut when it comes to choosing between the two different lengths of text. Evaluation of the differences, especially in this respect have varied widely with the climate of textual criticism in general, especially with respect to the value of LXX relative to MT. Here the swings of the pendulum have sometimes been wide indeed! Early critics tended toward a clear Septuagintal favoritism, often, one suspects, ultimately on no more profound basis than that it was not the traditional stance! In addition in the case of Jeremiah, the evolutionistic equation of "shorter" equals "earlier" clearly favored the briefer LXX version. Others, however, (e.g. Driver) dismissed nearly all the LXX variations as attributable simply to the incompetence and arbitrariness of the Greek translators. Uppsala prejudice, as usual, was strongly in favor of the *hebraica veritas*. The pendulum appeared just about to have settled near the middle when the Qumran finds unsettled everything.

The situation with the text of Jeremiah now appears not to be radically different from what we have noted earlier in the "former prophets," especially Judges and Kings, except that there the divergencies were more between two Septuagintal traditions than between MT and LXX. Possibly one can generalize by asserting that the LXX nearly always exhibits a somewhat different text than MT, but rarely with such dramatic differences as in the case of Jeremiah. In the case of Jeremiah, Cross and students generally prefer the shorter LXX text to the "expansionist" MT, but the objective grounds for the choice are not clear.

That judgment is balanced, however, by the interpretation of the Qumran evidence as evidencing successive revisions of the Greek tradition to conform it more with (what became) MT. If so, that clearly implies a recognition (at least by that time) of the superiority of a given Hebrew text. However, how ancient or objective that superiority is, or whether the decision was made on more subjective grounds, cannot be determined.

How shall the conservative react? Since the differences are not ultimately world-shaking, one need not be unduly concerned, but questions of principles are very much involved. It seems to this writer that conservatives have often prematurely and simply assumed MT to be the inspired text, and largely dismissed the LXX. But that procedure is inconsistent with the text-critical affirmations professed elsewhere; it will scarcely do to welcome text criticism when matters are simple and abjure it when the going gets rough! The priority and superiority of MT may well be established in due time, but it will have to be tested and weighed by the normal text-critical canons. The wide LXX variations at very least seem to suggest that the process of redaction of the Book of Jeremiah was relatively protracted, and the upshot fluid for some time. Text-critical considerations thus legitimately overlap with tradition-critical ones, even with conservative presuppositions. Perhaps the LXX provides us with one example where we have preserved the "first edition" of a Biblical book, before it achieved final, canonical form. If we had full information, we could surely say that at such and such a point we have *the* verbally inspired, canonical, and normative text. That we are unable in the light of present knowledge to pinpoint that moment does not call into question the theological principle.

Style

Finally, a word on Jeremiah's style. We have already noted that there is far more prose in Jeremiah than in any other prophet, and that it generally has a "deuteronomic" flavor. We have also defended the thesis that there are no good reasons why that should not correspond to Jeremiah's own choice, but some transmissional influence need not be excluded. While the prose is relatively easy to render into English, that is never the case with poetry. From a purely literary standpoint, Jeremiah's poetry is not quite the exquisite piece of art we beheld in Isaiah, but it is of the first order nonetheless. The ancient, classical canons of Canaanite poetry are obviously still alive with Jeremiah, but perhaps employed more flexibly and spontaneously than in earlier writers. Whether that is a reflex of Jeremiah's apparently more emotional temperament, or whether it signals the beginning of the end for the ancient cultural patterns, is hard to say. At any rate, already in Jeremiah's contemporary, Ezekiel, and increasingly thereafter, they appear to fall by the wayside or to be repeated without real mastery or comprehension.

Perhaps even more than Isaiah and Ezekiel, Jeremiah loves to repeat certain pet phrases. We can mention only a few: "Peace, peace, when there is no peace" (e.g., Jer. 8:11); "accept discipline" (2:30; rendition of the Hebrew phrase varies); "early and late" or "persistently" (7:25); "terror on every side" (6:25); "the voice of mirth and the voice of gladness . . ." (7:34); "not to make a full end" (4:27); "sword, pestilence, and famine" (14:12). Three relatively unique patterns of introducing divine oracles in Jeremiah may also be noted: (1) "Thus says Yahweh [often with 'of hosts'], the God of Israel" (common in Kings, but not in the other prophets); (2) "Behold, I am about to bring . . ."; and (3) "The word which came to Jeremiah from Yahweh as follows" (or variations, its Hebrew uniqueness often obscured further by varying translations).

Jeremiah 1—6

Jer. 1:4-19 is indisputably the account of the prophet's call. Jeremiah's protestation of his youthful incompetence (v. 6) has certain formal parallels with Moses' call (Ex. 3), but if one cares to think of one influencing the other at all, Jer. 1 would clearly have to be the dependency. Other elements in the chapter, e.g., prenatal influences (v. 4), touching of the mouth (v. 9), and the assurance of v. 19 may echo both halves of Isaiah (not vice versa). Jeremiah's commission "to destroy and to overthrow, to build and to plant" (v. 10) well summarizes the judgment-salvation, Law-Gospel polarity of the entire book. Although a developed eschatology in one sense is not Jeremiah's "strong suit" (and many critics seek to eliminate what there is), in at least the general sense of a sure future under God after the judgment, it is one of his most consistent and foundational themes. Judgment is never final or for its own sake, but above all is "discipline" (a major motif).

Jeremiah's call is also punctuated by two visions which remind us especially of Amos. The meaning of the first is dependent on a Hebrew pun which cannot be reproduced in English. The second vision points to "the north" as the direction of the impending evil, a refrain which we hereafter meet repeatedly in Jeremiah and later prophets. Some of its significance is simply geographical: except for Egypt, Canaan cannot feasibly be invaded from any other direction than along the eastern Mediterranean littoral. (A once popular theory, championed by Duhm and partly based on Herodotus, that the barbaric Scythians invaded Canaan in this period is today without support.) However, especially in later prophets, the "North" (or even the mysterious Northerner) assumes much more transcendental dimensions as the symbolic home or source of all evil. The ultimate origins of this imagery again appear to be mythological: since the North was regarded in paganism as the home of the gods (the "Mt. Olympus" of the Canaanites, Mt. Casius near Ugarit, was locally even known as Mt. Zaphon or "Mt. North"), it also came to be viewed as the source of divine intervention, especially of the "mystery of iniquity."

Jeremiah's oracles in chaps. 2—6 are distinguished from many of those which follow in at least two respects: (1) their more general tone (at least historical specifics are lacking); and (2) their possibly great affinity with themes we associate with Hosea and the northern kingdom, especially the prominent use of the metaphor of adultery to depict apostasy. Whether the concentration of these features early in the book is transmissional and redactional, or corresponds to Jeremiah's style in the earliest phase of his ministry is debatable.

Perhaps Jer. 3:6—6:30 is to be regarded as one long discourse. Certainly the "north" figures prominently throughout the section: 3:12; 3:18; 4:6; 6:1, apparently following up the call vision (1:13 ff.). In 3:15-18 we encounter our first "alternation of weal" in Jeremiah: the exiles will return from the "north," and all nations will join them at Zion, and the ark of the covenant will be superseded. The first two points are familiar from Isaiah, but the third is unique. Some critics have seized upon it as evidence of Jeremiah's anticultic stance, but it is plain that Jeremiah is speaking of the *eschaton,* when all the "sacraments" of earthly cults will be superseded in the fulfillment! Other critics, however, take the entire section to be late (like the similar promises in Isaiah), but they can't have it both ways! Jer. 4:1-2 states the promise conditionally; and in the phrase "bless themselves" apparently alludes specifically to the great Messianic promise to Abraham (Gen. 12:1-3).

Most of the material in the discourse, as most of Jeremiah, pronounces doom, however. It peaks in the famous "chaos vision" of Jer. 4:23-26, the opposite of "new creation" ("waste and void" in v. 23 translates Hebrew *tohu wa-bohu,* as in Gen. 1:2). Yet note that even this vision of final judgment is tempered by implicit promise of a remnant; "yet I will not make a full end" (v. 27—one of Jeremiah's favorite expressions). Just preceding this vision, in 4:18-22, Jeremiah's "emotionalism" first surfaces; as we said, however, its significance should not be exaggerated. We may note finally the excoriation of rich and poor alike in 5:1-5, possibly related to some emphases in Zephaniah, probably an early contemporary of Jeremiah.

Jeremiah 7—20

The material in Jer. 7—20 is largely undated; it may well stem from the reign of Jehoiakim, as scholars who try to see a chronological sequence in the early part of the book think, but most of the oracles could have been delivered almost anytime in Jeremiah's ministry. The question becomes acute immediately with respect to chap. 7 (perhaps continuing through 8:3), often known as Jeremiah's "temple sermon," after the locale of its delivery. No date is given in chap. 7, but chap. 26, which appears to be somewhat parallel, is specifically dated "in the beginning of the reign of Jehoiakim" (26:1). Do the two chapters really refer to the same occasion and the same sermon? Chap. 7 can be read as a more detailed report of the sermon itself with little information on historical circumstance versus the reverse in chap. 26: only a brief resume of the sermon (vs. 2-6), but considerable historical detail, specifically Jeremiah's near lynching except for the appeal to the preaching of Micah a century earlier and the intervention of Ahikam (cf. above). Relating the two chapters in that way may entail the assumption of different preliminary sources behind the present book, but, if so, the slight repetition would be theologically no more serious than some of the other clear "doublets" in Scripture. After all, some things are worth repeating! Rather than literary duplication, however, conservatives have generally preferred to think of two entirely different occasions (cf. also 19:14) but with essentially the same sermon each time; that would hardly be surprising either.

In any case, note the populace's almost superstitious invocation of "the temple of the LORD" (v. 4), as though it were Jerusalem, not Zion, that had God's promise of inviolability. (Some critics too cannot differentiate, and trumpet a contradiction between Isaiah and Jeremiah!) Jeremiah says the covenant *curses,* as "incarnate" in the temple as the blessings, will come upon the structure, as happened earlier at Shiloh, (v. 14; cf. 26:6) because they have turned it into a "den of robbers" (cf. Jesus' eschatological cleansing of the temple, Matt. 21:13, etc.). 1 Sam. 4 fails to specify a destruction of Shiloh in connection with the capture of the ark, but archaeology has clearly confirmed Jeremiah's "memory."

Liberal reductionists of true religion to sincerity and interiority have found the entire chapter very amenable to their prejudices (as though Jeremiah were opposed to the temple and its forms *per se*). Above all, however, as noted earlier, Jer. 7:21-26 has almost become a *locus classicus,* not only for the same alleged prophetic attitude in general, but specifically as an alleged frontal contradiction of the Pentateuch's ascription of the sacrificial cult to Moses (and thus a major springboard for Pentateuchal criticism). As we noted earlier, however, v. 22 can easily be read as typical prophetic hyperbole: the revelations to Moses were not about sacrifice and cult as such, but about the *totality* of the covenant relationship, external as well as internal, ritual as well as ethical. It is not explicitly stated, but it seems not unlikely that hereafter Jeremiah was forbidden to preach in the temple courts; at any rate that would explain his resource to scrolls, messengers, etc.

Jer. 9:23-24 contrasts human and divine wisdom. The latter is in effect equated with the covenant, "special revelation" validating and clarifying "general revelation" (thus almost summarizing the Biblical hermeneutics of the Wisdom Literature). To stress "wisdom influence" on Jeremiah in such a pericope, as is currently popular, is probably, at best, carrying coals to Newcastle. St. Paul cites the passage in 2 Cor. 10:17, and 1 Cor. 1:31 applies it typologically to Wisdom Incarnate.

Jer. 10:1-16 is a satire on idol manufacture, very similar to Is. 44:9-20 (hence often considered ungenuine by critics). Special interest has always centered on v. 11, which is not only clearly intrusive in the context, but is written in Aramaic, not Hebrew. With the possible exception of an Aramaic name in Gen. 31:47, it is the earliest appearance of that language in the Hebrew Bible (long Aramaic sections appear in Ezra and Daniel). Many scholars believe that it was originally a marginal gloss by a late scribe, which still later crept into the text itself. As a matter of text criticism, that is by no means impossible or even unusual, but since we lack all evidence of such happenstance here, it must remain conjectural. The verse can be understood as genuine, however: as a formulaic reply prepared by Jeremiah, especially for the exiles (in their daily language), to use when tempted or invited by their captors to join in idol-worship. The apocryphal "Letter of Jeremiah," from about 300 B.C., is largely only commentary on or expansion of this single verse, thus testifying to its canonical status at that date.

Jer. 11:18—12:6 seems to revolve around plots on Jeremiah's life, even by those closest to him. In 11:19 Jeremiah describes himself in language similar to Is. 53:8. It could be coincidental, but Jeremiah could also be thinking of himself in terms of the Suffering Servant. (Higher critics, of course, see traffic in the other direction.) Jesus too may have viewed His calling as, in part, antitypical of Jeremiah.

Jer. 13:1-11 records Jeremiah's first action-prophecy, that of burying his waistcloth by the Euphrates (this also symbolically?) and letting it rot, to signify Israel's deterioration. It is followed (13:12 ff.) by what appears to be a parable: Jeremiah sarcastically agrees with the popular optimism that "every jar shall be filled with wine," but its real meaning should be that God will inebriate His faithless people into self-destruction. 13:23 is a famous passage describing their incapacity for repentance. (Cf. 17:1, 9-10, etc.) In fact, the Book of Jeremiah is almost a *locus classicus* for Christian hamartiology; sin is repeatedly presented as not merely wrong acts, but wrongheadedness, sin*ful*ness, an ineradicable part of human nature, a *non posse non peccare.* Technically, of course, Jeremiah applies the relevant passages to only one circumstance, but within a conservative hermeneutics of *tota Scriptura,* they may be used without hesitation as classical proof texts for the doctrine of original sin (with many parallels to this procedure, of course).

In Jer. 14:7-10 the prophet utters a superb prayer on behalf of the remnant, and even when God "forbids" him because of its futility (vs. 11-12), in vs. 19-22 Jeremiah seems to persist. Jer. 15:1 seems to be God's rejoinder: Israel is so far gone that not even the intercession of those two classical mediators, Moses and Samuel, could have any effect.

This, in turn, seems to precipitate the first of Jeremiah's so-called "confessions" (Jer. 15:10-12; 15-18), lamenting Job-like the day of his birth because of the bitterness of his opposition and the hopelessness of his ministry. "Soliloquy," or especially "lament," is a much better label, however (and there are clear parallels with the laments of the Psalter.) Furthermore, the isolation of such passages is somewhat artificial, because they often merge almost imperceptibly with the context. Hence, there is no unanimity even on the number or extent of these "confessions." Among the most commonly cited, however, in addition to this one, are: 17:14-18; 18:19-23 (really an imprecation); and 20:7-18. The latter is the sharpest and most poignant of all; in a weak moment, Jeremiah even accuses God of having taken advantage of his naivete, and of having forced him to prophecy against his own free will (a metaphor of "seduction" perhaps, but scarcely of "rape," as some commentators perfervidly embellish the language).

The close connection in the context between the first lament and God's prohibition to intercede further for Israel is probably important for fully understanding all the "confessions." Reventlow has recently reacted strongly against the traditional critical reading of the "confessions" as solipsistic and autobiographical, arguing instead, on the basis of their clear parallels with the psalmic laments, that these too are liturgical pieces in which Jeremiah speaks in the name of the people as their mediator. Most agree that Reventlow has overstated his case in seeking to eliminate the personal element, but he has surely demonstrated Jeremiah's dependence on cultic forms (hence he is not simply anticultic), and has made a significant theological observation on Jeremiah's mediatorial role.

Chap. 16 reports two commands to Jeremiah, to remain celibate, and to boycott social gatherings of both mirth and mourning. Thus Jeremiah's entire life became an action-prophecy (cf. Is. 8), anticipating the fate that awaited all. (Only a liberal could understand the pericope as subjective, retrospective rationalization; cf. on Is. 6:9 ff.)

Jer. 17:19-27 is really Messianic (esp. v. 25). Critics have difficulties with its genuineness, because the promise is conditional (in a sense) on observance of the sabbath, a "ritualistic" note that ill accords with the liberal image of Jeremiah. As usual, however, the son of David and the city of David are mentioned in the same breath, and the passing horizontal vision of the new Jerusalem here should be read alongside 17:12, a glorious epitome of the "vertical typology" simultaneously informing the theology of Zion and of the temple.

Possibly a "catchword" connection between Jer. 18:1 ff. and 19:1 ff. can be discerned. At least both are action-prophecies related to pottery. The first (with many parallels in prophetic preaching) illustrates from pottery manufacture and in language reminiscent of Jeremiah's call the "contingency of prophecy": God is no determinist, and His word does not operate magically and impersonally or legalistically; rather, like the potter, He creates, destroys, molds or remolds according to need. The second action "symbolizes" Jerusalem's destruction by the shattering of a ceramic vessel. In this case, the ultimate background may even be found in magical practices among Israel's neighbors, as best illustrated by the Egyptian "Execration Texts." Normally, however, it was the enemy who was thus execrated, while here it is Jeremiah's own homeland. Depending on its date, the final rupture with his countrymen and their ostracization of him (at the mildest) may be traced to this drastic, significance-laden act.

Preceding his bitterest lament, chap. 20 then describes how Pashhur, the priest, beats Jeremiah and puts him in the stocks for a day. Upon release, Jeremiah defiantly applies to him as a "symbolic" (i.e., prophetic) name one of his favorite phrases "Terror on every side" (v. 4; cf. v. 10).

Jeremiah 21—29

We probably detect another catchword connection in the mention of a different Pashhur in Jer. 21:1. However, we also have here our first clearly dated oracle in the Book of Jeremiah, but coming from *late* in his ministry. (Both here and in the following chapter, chronology clearly was the least of the compiler's concerns!) The occasion is apparently not long before the fall of Jerusalem in 587, as King Zedekiah anxiously inquires concerning the outcome of the Babylonian siege. As he does consistently, Jeremiah holds out no physical or military hope whatsoever.

Note in Jer. 21:2 for the first time the technically correct "Nebuchad*r*ezzar," instead of the more familiar, "Nebuchad*n*ezzar," which spelling, for some curious reason, appears in the Book of Jeremiah only in chaps. 27—29. The original Akkadian form of the name was, "Nabu-kudurri-utsur," meaning, "May [the god; cf. Is. 46:1] Nabu protect the border." As often happens with foreign languages, the name usually mutated in Hebrew, but in Jeremiah it is usually reproduced in technically more correct form.

Jeremiah concludes (21:11-14) his reply to Zedekiah's inquiry by a sort of punning sermon on his name, which means, "Yahweh is just/righteous." Doom is coming, says Jeremiah, because the king has not lived up to his name by executing Yahweh's justice. If he were really a righteous king, however, the Messianic prophecy of Nathan would be established (22:4), and he would be a type and namesake of the Messianic "righteous Branch" (23:5-6), who would finally establish "justice" and incarnate His name, "the LORD is our righteousness" (i.e., *justify* vicariously in fulfillment of the ancient covenant promise).

That sad, "it might have been" rebuff to Zedekiah leads (22:10—23:40) into a commentary on the other post-Josianic kings of Judah, and gradually into a general contrasting of false "shepherds" (leaders, kings, prophets) with representatives of the truth (the Messianic 23:5-6 again illustrates "alternation of weal" in the context). Certainly, some of the other connection must be editorial, but not all of it need be.

The three other kings are considered in chronological order. First (one notes that Josiah remains unmentioned) is Jehoahaz in Jer. 22:10-12 (called Shallum in v. 11). Upon Josiah's death at Megiddo in 609, he succeeded his father—significantly passing over his older brother, Jehoiakim, who perhaps was simply less popular, but more likely was out of favor with the Shaphan establishment because of his disagreement with Josiah's political and religious policies. Thus, it is probably no accident that Jeremiah does not upbraid him, but simply laments the fact that, after only a three-month reign he has been deposed by Pharaoh Necho (in favor of Jehoiakim, who might be more amenable), never again to see his native land. Here and in 1 Chron. 3:15 he is called "Shallum," apparently his personal name. The name "Jehoahaz" is then a throne name, which is also borne by other kings of the divided kingdoms. We suspect that such a change of name upon accession occurred more often than we are aware (perhaps even David and Solomon), and it surely explains the consistent name changes in the instances of the kings of Judah following Jehoahaz. Since they all ruled at the pleasure of imperial powers, in their cases the change of names might also have been intended to remind who held the *real* power.

Not surprisingly, Jehoiakim (to which Necho had changed his name from Eliakim; almost Jeremiah's *bête noire*) is censured most scathingly (Jer. 22:13-23). Because of his malevolent malfeasance, he shall receive "the burial of an ass" (v. 19; cf. 36:30).

Jehoiachin (elsewhere called "Jeconiah" and here by the hypocoristic "Coniah") comes off a little better (Jer. 22:24-30), being called nothing worse than a "broken pot" (v. 28). The reference is to his deportation to Babylon in 598, the scapegoat of his father's (Jehoiakim) misadventures, who died (or probably more likely, was assassinated) three months earlier. V. 30, predicting that no Davidide would ever occupy the throne again, would be a direct contradiction not only of Nathan's oracle (2 Sam. 7) but of some of Jeremiah's own Messianic prophecies elsewhere, if there were no distinction between Jerusalem and Zion, the visible and the invisible church. Perhaps it is no accident that the series is not concluded by comment on Zedekiah (Jehoiachin's uncle, brother of Jehoahaz and Jehoiakim, originally named Mattaniah) who succeeded Jehoiachin, because it is plain that both the Babylonians and the Israelites continued to regard Jehoiachin as the rightful monarch.

Jer. 23 is one of the most important chapters in the book. As a false versus true shepherd pericope (esp. vs. 1-6), it takes its place alongside Ezek. 34 and John 10. ("Shepherd" as nearly always in the Bible, and as in the whole ancient Near East, when used metaphorically, means *king*—also in Ps. 23!) Cf. our comments above; we note only that when the epithet, "The LORD our righteousness," is repeated in 33:16, it is applied to Zion, not to Messiah. But it is almost a distinction without a difference; we have here a parade example of the near interchangeability of the two themes.

Denunciation of false "shepherds" leads in the remainder of the chapter (23:9 ff.) into denunciation of false prophets, who almost by definition, supported false kings instead of the King of kings. The final, objective touchstone of their falseness is that they never stood in Yahweh's "council" (vs. 18 and 22), that is, that they are unaccredited and unable to speak God's own words. V. 29 is a famous description of the power of the true Word. The chapter concludes (vs. 33-40) with a double play on the Hebrew word *massa'*, which may mean either "oracle" or "burden," literally, a "lifting up" (cf. v. 39) of either one's voice or of a load. When people ask what "burden" (oracle) there is from God, the reply can only be that their faithless lives are the real burden, which God will surely lift up and eliminate.

Chap. 24 enunciates another of Jeremiah's consistent themes, heartily seconded by Ezekiel, that the future of God's people lay in and through the exiles, not in continuity with those who escaped it and remained in the homeland. Here it is only the first major deportation in 598 (headed by Jehoiachin or Jeconiah) which elicits the message, but it is not altered after the sack of Jerusalem in 587. The message is triggered by a vision of two baskets of figs, one good, the other rotten (cf. Amos 8:1). Theologically, this theme is a major expression of the prophetic sense of salvation only through judgment, life only through death, Gospel only through Law, etc.

Jer. 25:1 is dated in Jehoiakim's fourth year, that is, apparently soon after the epochal battle of Carchemish in 605, when Necho is definitively worsted and Nebuchadnezzar heads the neo-Babylonian empire as clear heir of Assyria. Apparently also, soon after, there occurred a token deportation of Jerusalemites, including Daniel (1:1) to signify Nebuchadnezzar's hegemony. In 25:9 (as also in 27:6 and 43:10) the Babylonian king is labeled God's "servant"; cf. Cyrus' designation as God's "shepherd" and "anointed [Messiah]" in Is. 44:28 and 45:1. Jeremiah asserts that the nature of Nebuchadnezzar's "service" to God will be still worse punishment for Judah at his hands—but after "seventy years" (vs. 11-12) the tables will be turned.

From what point did Jeremiah reckon "seventy"? It seems likely that the original intention was at least as much symbolic as literal ("seventy" as seven times ten, that is, doubly complete; cf. Is 40:2). The likelihood is enhanced by the appearance of the same figure in an Assyrian reference to Sennacherib's investment of Babylon (and possibly also by Isaiah's use of the figure on Tyre, Is. 23:15, 17) and by Ezekiel's use of the symbolic figure "forty" to describe the period of divine judgment upon both Israel (Ezek. 4) and Egypt (Ezek. 29:11-13). However, "symbolic" and "literal" are not mutual exclusives. If we calculate from 605, the date of this oracle (as is commonly done, but is not required by it), it is nearly seventy years until Cyrus' edict in 538, close enough for a good round figure. Perhaps this is also the understanding of Dan. 9:2, but the main interest of the chapter is in the typology of "weeks of years" or hebdomads. It is possibly theologically more meaningful, however, if we calculate from the temple's destruction in 587 to the rebuilding of the temple in 516 (at least if we recall the centrality of the "theology of the temple"). The latter calculation not only underlies the reference in Zech. 1:12 and 7:5 (though without mention of this prophecy) but also its application in 2 Chron. 36:21 to the "sabbath" of the land.

We have already alluded to the fundamentally different Septuagintal version and arrangement of the oracles in Jer. 25. Nebuchadnezzar is nowhere directly mentioned in the chapter, and after v. 13a it inserts in modified order the Gentile oracles (MT, chaps. 46—51) and concludes them with vs. 15 ff. (v. 14 is omitted). As MT stands, there is a sort of "catchword" connection between the "many nations" of v. 14 (that is, the Medes and the Persians) and "nations" of vs. 15 ff. with more universal, even proto-apocalyptic reference. Note also in v. 26 the use of the cipher "Sheshach" for Babylon (also in 51:41), a type of procedure very popular in apocalyptic (and some rabbinic) literature. Technically, we know it as "Athbash," the substitution of the last letter of the Hebrew alphabet for the first, the second last for the second, and so on. We thus have in

Jeremiah only a mild dose of apocalypticizing techniques, in contrast to the considerable amount in Ezekiel and the full bloom in Daniel. (Critics often prefer to see an ungenuine intrusion from later times.) (On chap. 26, see on chap. 7 and the introduction above.)

The historical narratives of Jer. 27—29 are really a unit (characterized also by the sole use in Jeremiah of the technically incorrect spelling, "Nebuchad*ne*zzar; cf. on 21:2). Chap. 27 is dated in MT at the beginning of Jehoiakim's reign, but the contents obviously indicate that Zedekiah must be meant. Hence, even though text-critical evidence is entirely lacking, it is unanimously agreed that we must have a scribal slip here.

In Jer. 27, by means of the symbolism of a yoke on his neck (cf. 1 Kings 22), Jeremiah seeks (evidently successfully) to convince Zedekiah of the futility of joining five neighboring nations in an insurrection against Nebuchadnezzar. Much less successfully, he tells Zedekiah, as he did repeatedly, that he might as well have it over with and surrender now! Jer. 28 recounts the counter-symbolic action of the false prophet Hananiah ("Yahweh is gracious"), who breaks the yoke off Jeremiah's neck, to suggest that the Babylonian threat will pass within two years (v. 11), and to that Jeremiah responds quite testily. (One suspects that this type of exchange went on quite regularly in the history of prophecy.) It is fundamentally inaccurate to assert, as is common in the critical literature, that Hananiah is here championing Isaiah's old "inviolability of Zion" doctrine, whereas Jeremiah has departed from it; nevertheless, the superficial similarity probably often made it as hard for some ancients to distinguish as it does many modern critics.

Jer. 29 is parallel. Jeremiah sends his famous letter to the exiles in Babylon, telling them that, contrary to the seductions of the false prophets, they are not destined to be repatriated shortly, and so they might as well "build houses—plant gardens—take wives—seek the welfare of the city" (vs. 5-8). Nevertheless as always, there follows the reassurance that the ultimate purpose of the judgment is salvific, and after "seventy years" God will restore Israel (vs. 10-14). The chapter concludes with condemnations of three specific false prophets, especially one, Shemaiah, who had urged the high priest to put in the stocks "every madman who prophesies" (v. 26).

Jeremiah 30—31

Jer. 30—31 are undated, strangely for this part of the book, and form somewhat of a subunit. Their general gist is that, although the present suffering is grievous, a glorious future certainly lies ahead. Because of their relative uniqueness, Mowinckel classified them as Type "D," and considered them ungenuine. Many critics follow him, but militating against that position is their relative unity with the following two chapters, a unit which many scholars refer to as "the book of consolation" (after mention of a book in 30:2). If one looks for historical circumstances, the most likely setting is again Zedekiah's reign, after the land had already been decimated. In 31:29, Jeremiah, like Ezekiel, quotes and corrects an apparently popular "sour grapes" proverb by which the populace tries to evade its responsibility for the judgment and blame it all on their parents!

The Messianic-eschatological oracles stand out in Jer. 31. The first, 31:15 ff. promises that the "lamentation and bitter weeping" of Rachel for her children will be reversed. In immediate context the primary meaning can be only that the exiles from Ephraim (vs. 18, 20), the Northern Kingdom, will also share in the restoration. (Cf. also Josiah's obvious hopes to regain the territory politically after the Assyrian's collapse, and there are, indeed, critics who want to read the entire chapter as little more than Jeremiah's declaration of support for Josiah's program!) "Rachel's" bitter vigil is thus part of the *dolores Messiae,* one manifestation and fulfillment of which (the massacre of the innocents by Herod) Matt. 2:18 cites at the dawn of the Messianic age.

The prophecy of the "new covenant" (Jer. 31:31-34) is almost structural of the entire Bible, both materially and formally. It is no accident that the New Testament features it so prominently (esp. Heb. 8 and 10 and the Words of Institution)—and, indeed, that the names of the two "testaments" are ultimately derived from this passage. In balance, we have probably lost more than we have gained by the common substitution of "testament" for "covenant" (especially in the Lutheran tradition where the latter term is little used). Basic Biblical literacy is often part of the imperative to compensate for the change. This precise formulation occurs only here in the Old Testament, but in substance is common in the prophets (see already the next chapter, Jer. 32:38-40). Indeed, one must insist that it is implicit in the ideas of "promise," "oath," "blessing," etc., all inextricably linked with the idea of "covenant." After the critical rewrite of the Old Testament, of course, "covenant" *first* becomes prominent in Jeremiah, more or less in conjunction with deuteronomistic influence, with the latter often scored for perverting the promise into merely a new obligation. Debates about the authenticity of the oracle are too bound up with related critical apriorism to merit further review here.

"New" here, as often, is semitechnical for "eschatological fulfillment of prophecy" or the like. The essential contents of the new covenant will be the same as the old, except that now they will be written on the heart. The point is not the pure inwardness and interiority rendering all externals obsolete, as earlier liberals loved to interpret. Rather we have a prophecy of the full, eschatological triumph of the Gospel when even the faithful will no longer be *simul peccator*. The external compulsion of the Law (even the "third use of the Law") will fall away as superfluous in the face of the freedom, joy, and spontaneity of the new creation. The very centrality of the proclamation of its fulfillment in Christ and the Holy Spirit for the Gospel makes more poignant and wrenching its continued "not yet," and should heighten our eschatological consciousness and make us more aware in another sense of the continuing indispensability of the Law until the consummation.

Jeremiah 32—45

Most of the remaining historical narrative in the book takes place in the years immediately before and after the final catastrophe. Come what may, Jeremiah never once wavers in his stance, at least not publicly (cf. on the "confessions"). Jer. 32 is dated in the tenth year of Zedekiah, that is, during the city's siege about a year before its fall, while Jeremiah is under detention in the "court of the guard." It records one of his major action prophecies and is continued in chap. 37. In the presence of witnesses, Jeremiah buys the field of his cousin Hanameel in Anathoth, fulfilling his duty of "redemption" of family property as next of kin (Lev. 25:25), but above all (at a time when real estate values must really have been depressed) as an earnest of his repeated preaching that the inevitable fall of Judah would not be the end. There would be continuity through the Exile, and life would pick up where it had left off. In a way, it is a major exemplification of the "alternation of weal and woe," of prophecy of hope while relentlessly proclaiming doom. An accompanying prayer (32:16-25) and promise of "an everlasting covenant" make explicit the intentionality of the prophet's behavior.

Another oracle while under detention is even more outspoken in its prediction of restoration after the catastrophe (Jer. 33). As often, the near and the remote (eschatological) future telescope in the prophet's vision. The Messianic epithet of Jer. 23:5-6, "The LORD is our righteousness," is here (33:16) applied to Judah and Jerusalem, that is, they will be "justified" by virtue of covenant promises. But in order that the unity of Messiah and Zion not be missed, the following two verses (17-18) proceed to stress both the perpetuity of David's throne (2 Sam. 7) and the eternity of the promises to the "Levitical priests." Critics, predictably, have difficulty imagining such words on Jeremiah's lips, and, indeed, only in Christological light can they be fully and correctly understood. (33:14-26 are absent in the Septuagint, one of its major and surprising omissions.)

Jer. 34 is dated to the very last days of the siege, when only Lachish and Azekah were still also standing (vs. 6-7; perhaps only hours before

Lachish Letter IV, which reports that the fire-signals of Azekah are no longer visible; cf. above). In final desperation, Zedekiah and the nobles even "get religion": they manumit their Hebrew slaves in accordance with the ancient stipulation that they could be held only six years (v. 14; Ex. 21; Deut. 15—probably widely ignored in all periods). However, perhaps when an advance of Pharaoh Hophra forced a temporary lifting of the siege (cf. chap. 37) they reenslave them (cf. Is. 23). This provokes Jeremiah to the sarcastic prediction that they too will ultimately be set at liberty—"to the sword, to pestilence, and to famine" (34:17). Because of such an arrant breach of covenant, the ancient symbolic curse accompanying "cutting" a covenant (the usual Hebrew idiom) will be fulfilled in them: men will halve them and pass between them (cf. Gen 15)!

For some reason, in the next two chapters we have a "flashback" to the reign of Jehoiakim. (Is it a sort of relative "alternation of weal"?) In chap. 35 Jeremiah commends the Amish-like Rechabite sect for their scrupulous faithfulness to their social conservatism, in contrast to Judah's permissiveness. (Note that the Rechabite tenets are not praised as such; Jeremiah does not here champion some "nomadic ideal," as many scholars have held.) Chap. 36 describes Jeremiah's dictation of a scroll to his faithful amanuensis, Baruch, its contemptuous destruction by Jehoiakim as Jehudi reads it, and Jeremiah's dictation of a replacement. We mentioned above the critical "much ado about nothing" excited by this chapter.

Jer. 37—39 almost rudely brings us back to Jerusalem's last hours. Jeremiah takes advantage of a temporary respite in the siege caused by Pharaoh Hophra's advance (cf. chap. 34) to attempt to inspect his newly purchased property outside the walls (chap. 32). But this gives his enemies the opportunity they have been waiting for. The prophet is accused of desertion and cast into the dungeon. Not even when Zedekiah furtively seeks to induce Jeremiah to change his predictions of the city's fall will he relent (vs. 17 ff.). Nevertheless, his request to be returned to the guards' court is honored, until leaders again accuse him of "weakening the hands of the soldiers" (38:4) by constantly urging surrender. This time he is cast into a cistern, where he might well have died, save for the intervention of the Ethiopian eunuch, Ebedmelech (sometimes called "the Good Samaritan of the Old Testament"). Not even when the pathetic Zedekiah pays him yet another clandestine visit will Jeremiah change his counsel (38:17 ff.). When "death" finally comes to the beleaguered city in chap. 39 at the hands of "Nebuzaradan, the captain of the guard," it means Jeremiah's release (and even offer of a "pension" in Babylonia) as a "friend" of the conquerors, but Zedekiah's unspeakably sad fate before Nebuchadnezzar at his headquarters in Riblah (central Syria).

Of the chaotic events in Judah after its fall, we would know next to nothing were it not for the historical narratives in Jer. 40—42. (We do have a seal from this period, inscribed, "Gedaliah who is over the house.") Gedaliah, serving as the Babylonian regent in Mizpah, just north of Jerusalem, disregards Johanan's warnings and is assassinated by Ishmael (for reasons unclear, but Ammonite complicity is noted). For good measure, Ishmael also slaughters seventy pilgrims from the North (!) who had come to worship at the site of the destroyed temple (41:4 ff.)—also revealing to us that cult probably never ceased completely there all during the Exile.

Johanan and his band surprise Ishmael "at the great pool which is in Gibeon" (Jer. 41:12; cf. 2 Sam. 2), but then, fearing Babylonian reprisals, decide to flee to Egypt. First they stop at Bethlehem (where Jeremiah must now be living) to seek a word from God (41:17 ff.). The real issue, of course, is whether or not they really constitute the "remnant" of promise (the word occurs frequently in the context). It does not take Jeremiah long to answer negatively, as, in principle, he always had. God's future lay with the *Babylonian* exiles, and they would only compound their troubles if they fled to Egypt.

Contrary to Jeremiah's advice, and their word, they force Jeremiah and Baruch to accompany them to Egypt (Jer. 43:6 f.), the last known *Sitz im Leben* of the prophet's work. In 43:8 ff. at Tahpanhes (in the Delta) we encounter his final action prophecy: large stones are hidden in the pavement of Pharaoh's palace as a symbolic pedestal for Nebuchadnezzar's future throne there. The same point is underscored in chap. 44, Jeremiah's final known sermon, addressed to Jewish refugees all over Egypt. ("Pathros" is Upper Egypt; in this area, at Elephantine, near the modern Aswan dam, a Jewish colony of mercenaries was established after 587 B.C. It became quite famous.) Disaster will overtake all but a remnant of those who have fled to Egypt, but the reason for the catastrophe is not, as many of them have been saying, because they have stopped worshiping the "queen of heaven" (Asherah, or Ishtar, the fertility goddess; cf. Jer. 7:14). One suspects that that rationalization was often heard after 587!

Chronologically, Jer. 45 belongs with chap. 36, and technically appears here as a sort of appendix. Nevertheless, its fulfillment fits here. Baruch too was human and in one of his depressed moods; Jeremiah assures him that his own life will be spared in the impending catastrophe. "He who loses his life for my sake will find it" (v. 5).

As we lose sight of Jeremiah, it is hard not to meditate typologically on his life. The text never does so—but in a less secular age, that was probably otiose. Especially in connection with the Servant Songs, there is nothing fatuous about viewing his "biography" (and possibly Baruch's too) as *passion history,* ending in Egypt, the ancient embodiment of death, grave, and hell. But his suffering was also closely identified with God's own suffering, and although his mortal eyes never beheld it, his oracles are full of the hope of the future "resurrection" that was available only via the route of exile.

Jeremiah 46—52

Last in the Book of Jeremiah come the Gentile oracles (chaps. 46—51). (To the modern reader, one must add: "Last, but not least!") As noted above, they appear in the Septuagint in altered sequence (Elam first and Babylon third) after 25:13a, and are concluded with 25:15-38. This accords better with the classical prophetic outline, but it does not follow that the Hebrew arrangement is "inferior" (especially not in a book like Jeremiah!). As the Baruch oracle has just indicated, traditors often preferred to defer a certain type of material to avoid interruption of a main sequence, and that explanation would suffice to account for their appearance here.

The first eight of these oracles are probably related to Babylonian victories as the organ of God's judgment, but in Jer. 50—51 (almost as long as chaps. 46—49) we have various oracles predicting Babylon's own day of reckoning. However, the precise historical occasion is often unclear, and perhaps it should not be more clear! The formal inclusion of such oracles almost *de rigueur* expresses the theology of God's universal Judgeship.

The first poem in Jer. 46 (vs. 3-12) is all but an eyewitness account of Pharaoh Necho's defeat at Carchemish in 605 (v. 2). But "alternation of weal" is also operative in this context (God's judgment has salvific intent even for Gentiles): both Egypt (v. 26b) and Israel (vs. 27-28) will eventually be restored. The latter two verses are almost the same as 30:10-11; the repetition is not impossibly redactional, but neither is there any reason why Jeremiah should never repeat himself.

The oracle against Moab (Jer. 48) has clear affinities with Isaiah's in chaps. 15—16 (also with other prophetic material), and likewise that against Edom (49:7-22) has parallels especially with Obadiah. It is scarcely a question of "borrowing" versus "originality" or genuineness, as critics often make it, but rather an indication of the extent to which *all* the prophets dipped into a common pool of traditional material for their special ends.

Of all the oracles against Babylon in Jer. 50—51 (again with parallels to Is. 13—14) much critical opinion will acknowledge only 51:59-64 as genuine. It is an action prophecy dated about 594 (thus chronologically to be related to chap. 29) by which a scroll containing Jeremiah's curses upon Babylon should be tied to a stone and sunk in the Euphrates, to depict Babylon's irreversible submersion. One would scarcely be surprised at a number of even more specific anti-Babylonian oracles in Jeremiah, except for the prophets' own unwavering "pro-Babylonian" posture. Critics cite that and especially his letter advising the exiles to prepare for a lengthy stay there (chap. 29) as incompatible with these impassioned predictions of Babylon's destruction and of the deliverance of God's people from captivity. Certain passages (50:28; 51:11, 51) also clearly envisage the destruction of the temple, which had probably not yet occurred at the time these oracles were delivered. The major reply must not be only on the basis of a sufficiently long historical perspective; the theological myopia is more serious. Not only is the pattern of divine judgment upon the erstwhile agent of judgment long since established (cf. only Isaiah on Assyria), but church and state, Zion and Jerusalem, again fail to be distinguished.

We note only two further instances of "Athbash" in Jer. 51: "Sheshach" for Babylon again at v. 41 (as at 25:26, which see), and "Lebqamai" at v. 1 for Chaldea (the southern section of Babylonia). Since such procedures were supposed to be "apocalyptic" and much later, critics have used them (and other alleged "apocalyptic" influences in the Gentile oracles) as further arguments against their genuineness.

If the Gentile oracles in the Hebrew text are a sort of appendix, Jer. 52 is an appendix to the appendix. It is also another clear "doublet": the chapter is largely identical with 2 Kings 24:18—25:30 (and 2 Chron. 36:11-13). Notices in Kings about Gedaliah are omitted here because Jer. 40—41 has already included them, and the record of the number of captives in vs. 28-30 here is not found in Kings. But both texts (and books) conclude with the favor shown King Jehoiachin in captivity, an act pregnant with promise. This is probably our clue to the reason for the addition of the appendix: as surely as Jeremiah's oracles of judgment had been fulfilled, so surely must all his inspired promises finally be realized. In Christ, we confess both "Already!" and "Not yet."

EZEKIEL

Ezekiel is a late contemporary of Jeremiah, although, as usual, they make no mention of each other. Many aspects of their prophecies, hence, run quite parallel. However, in contrast to Jeremiah who was active in Judah in its last days and even spurned the conquerors' offer to grant him safe conduct to Babylonia, Ezekiel's entire ministry was spent among the exiles there. Both because of the extra-Biblical literature and the record of his own book, we are nearly as well informed about the external circumstances of his life as of Jeremiah's. Ezekiel, however, reveals far less of his inner, personal life than Jeremiah.

Date and Background

In his own "superscription" to the book, Ezekiel relates the date of his call to the "fifth year of the exile of King Jehoiachin" (593). This is nearly always taken to imply that Ezekiel himself was among the aristocracy which was deported by Nebuchadnezzar to Babylon in 598 after Jehoiakim's foolhardy revolt. The preceding reference to the "thirtieth year" is somewhat of a crux, however. Most likely, it refers to the prophet's age at his vocation (the age at which Levites were allowed to commence official functions), but there are other explanations.

The last dated prophecy in Ezekiel (29:17) is in the "twenty-seventh year" (after Jehoiachin's exile, i.e., 571). Thus, Ezekiel has a total recorded ministry of slightly over twenty years.

His father, Buzi (Ezek. 1:3), was a priest, and the sacerdotal coloration of the book (especially the final nine chapters) make it plain that Ezekiel too lived and moved and had his being in that world of thought, whether or not he ever officially functioned in priestly capacity. Although that can be exaggerated, he still differs markedly from Jeremiah, who, though a priest, evinces remarkably little interest in such matters (though not for the reasons or quite to the degree to which many spiritualistic critics would have it). Perhaps the difference itself marks the beginning of a new era, when, after the judgment, the now purged and purified rites and institutions could serve their divinely intended purpose (so especially the import of chaps. 40—48). Certainly, sociologically, sacerdotal rites would be crucial means of identification in the Exile, as they were not in Judah. In either perspective, no basic cleavage dare be driven between Jeremiah and Ezekiel in this respect, as early criticism did almost instinctively. It should also be noted that, whereas Jeremiah's descent was probably from the "disenfranchised" line of Abiathar, Ezekiel's links were with the main sacerdotal line of Zadok, whom Solomon had chosen to replace disloyal Abiathar (1 Kings 2). Thus one is not surprised when Ezekiel himself strongly underscores the divine legitimacy and prerogatives of the Zadokites (40:46; 43:19).

In exile, the prophet lived "in the land of the Chaldeans by the river Chebar," that is, in southern Mesopotamia, whence the neo-Babylonian dynasty of the conquerors hailed, along one of the major irrigation canals, which as we know from cuneiform inscriptions was used to bring water to the ancient city of Nippur, a short distance southeast of Babylon itself. In Ezek. 3:15 he further indicates that the name of the "DP-camp" was "Tel Abib" (the "mound of the flood," also, ultimately, the inspiration for the name of the modern Israeli metropolis, usually spelled more phonetically).

The fact that the prophet had his own house (Ezek. 8:1) would indicate fair living conditions for not only the prophet, but also for most of the rest of the exiles. Both extremes of understanding their physical circumstances have been defended, and both should be avoided. The Babylonians in general were much more benign in their policy of deportation than the Assyrians had been. But the lot of deportees or refugees is never a happy one, and it probably was a long time before many were able to pick up the pieces of their shattered lives. That many had gotten back on their feet a half-century or more later is evidenced by the poor response, especially by the younger generation, to the opportunity to return after Cyrus' edict; a little later we even know from Babylonian records of a fairly well-to-do Jewish business establishment, "Murashu & Sons." It will not do, however, to retroject that later semi-assimilated prosperity and equanimity back into Ezekiel's times.

Perhaps above all, whatever their physical circumstances, subjectively and psychologically they were often simply devastated, as not only the Book of Ezekiel witnesses but also the contemporary Lamentations and Ps. 137. No doubt, humanly speaking, had it not been for the theological interpretation of deserved divine judgment given the cataclysm by Ezekiel and the other prophets, they would have soon joined the countless numbers of others in similar circumstances all through the corridors of history who simply dropped from sight.

In contrast to his predecessors, and especially to his contemporary Jeremiah, Ezekiel is apparently tolerated, possibly even held in some esteem, by his compatriots. He is apparently the first to benefit from the "authentication" that the fulfillment of prophecies of exile lent to prophecy. In spite of the vocabulary of his call, there is not the slightest intimation of anything like persecution. He is consulted by the elders of the Exile (Ezek. 14:1; 20:1), and sometimes even listened to by large crowds. Sometimes apparently it was more in uncomprehending amusement at his antics (20:49 and 33:30-32) than in assent to his message (at least until after the fall of Jerusalem), but even that was a far cry from the reception often accorded the earlier prophets.

Ezekiel's Personality

Much attention was once drawn to Ezekiel's allegedly bizarre personality, especially when psychology was in its heyday. Epilepsy, catalepsy, autohypnosis, schizophrenia, aphasia, levitation, paranoia— you name it, almost all were suggested. Some conservatives overreacted in fear that study of the subject was almost intrinsically irreverent or a denial of inspiration. Fortunately, that furor has abated, and no one is the better for it. Even if it were possible to psychoanalyze Ezekiel, the most that we would learn would be a little about the *form* of his original delivery, but nothing of its contents. The only moral of the story might be that, then as now, God and special inspiration are not bound to "balanced personalities," but employ the entire range of human personality in communicating the message.

Even more, one must ask if the question is properly framed. To label Ezekiel "the strangest figure in the goodly fellowship of the prophets" may only betray cultural insularity. It would seem that a better formulation would be acknowledgment that the ancient prophetic tradition of action-prophecies or "symbolic actions" receives climactic expression in Ezekiel, although we may argue somewhat from the silence of other prophetic books in this respect. At any rate, resort to such behavior was not only encouraged, but virtually mandated by the dumbness which God lay on Ezekiel almost from the moment of his call until the fall of Jerusalem. Thus, like Isaiah and Jeremiah, his entire life becomes an action-prophecy, a "type" or embodiment of his message. His own explanation for his behavior, of course, is simply that the "hand/spirit of Yahweh" had induced it.

Perhaps the same circumstance explains the apparent austerity of Ezekiel's personality. Although he encounters little overt opposition, his consistent refrains, *"Jerusalem delenda est,"* and the possibility of salvation only through that judgment were ultimately little more palatable to his audience than they were to Jeremiah's. The terms of his call say as much: "Like adamant harder than flint have I made your forehead . . ." (Ezek. 3:9). Certainly, that he bares his inner feelings less than Jeremiah should not surprise us; people have varied widely in that respect in all ages. Sometimes it is asserted that one of the few revelations of his humanity is seen when he calls his wife the "desire of his eyes" (24:16), but that this is canceled out by the fact that when his wife dies on the day that the final siege of Jerusalem began, it does not deter him from preaching to the people. It must be countered, however, that the latter was at God's explicit command—and Ezekiel, in contrast to Jeremiah, *was* married, and apparently happily. Beyond this, however, many oracles in the book suggest that Ezekiel was ultimately quite an ordinary mortal: themes of divine compassion and tenderness (e.g. "shepherd" in chap. 34), almost lurid descriptions of sexuality (chaps. 16 and 23), etc.

Outline and Structure

The Book of Ezekiel exhibits a massive, almost architectonic simplicity of structure. In contrast to many other books, it has at least the external appearance of complete unity and orderliness. The overall outline is an almost perfect example of the classical prophetic outline with its Law-Gospel theological import. In the use of Ezekiel, that outline is thoroughly integrated with the book's historical context. Apparently, its indigenousness to Ezekiel is a direct result of the exilic imprint of "death and resurrection" on all the material. Hence, in the eyes of many critics, the original precedent for that classical redactional scheme of prophetic oracles is to be found in Ezekiel. While not impossible, that does not necessarily follow.

The outline is as follows (A) Chaps 1—24: Mostly threats against the Jews, especially those still living in Judah, but also the expatriates to some extent; (B) Chaps. 25—32; Gentile oracles; (C) Chaps. 33—39: Mostly oracles of Israel's future restoration; and (D) (beyond the classical outline) Chaps. 40—48: Detailed vision of the new age, especially the temple and the "new Jerusalem." (A certain "internal outline" or frame formed by the departure and return of the *Kabod* ("glory") to the temple (11:23 and 43:1-2) must also be noted, attaching also to a motif informing the entire book.)

This impressively orderly outline is accompanied not only by a precise dating of a number of oracles but also by the arrangement of most of them in chronological order. (Critics often profess to see here some of the same passion for order and chronology allegedly surfacing in "P," as later in apocalyptic and in Chronicles). Dates appear at fourteen points in the book: Ezek. 1:1; 3:16; 8:1; 20:1; 24:1; 26:1; 29:1; 29:17; 30:20; 31:1; 32:1; 32:17; 33:21; and 40:1. Except for 29:17, which gives the latest date in the whole book, these chronological notices are essentially in proper sequence. The one exception can probably be attributed to the interposition in the overall outline of the Gentile oracles: this prophecy on Egypt is apparently brought forward to follow another oracle on Egypt in 29:1-16.

Higher Criticism

Higher criticism of Ezekiel has swung wildly from one extreme to the other and back again. The atomization of much of the other Biblical literature at the hand of early critics made a wide detour around Ezekiel and left the book almost totally unscathed. It was almost as if they themselves were struck dumb by so repulsive a figure! A prophet who behaved so weirdly, who fatally compromised and contaminated the pure light of prophetism with priestcraft, legalism, apocalypticism, etc., surely deserved to be treated like a pariah! At best, there was nothing "creative" about Ezekiel, and it is to be noted that, to this day, liberal books on "prophecy" virtually always stop short of Ezekiel (sometimes excluding

"Deutero-Isaiah" as well). Pfeiffer, not untypically, could dismiss him as "the first fanatic in the Bible," and even when, more defensibly, he was styled the "father of Judaism," the usual denigrating overtones of that language were an open secret.

Suddenly, around 1920, Ezekiel became a storm center of criticism (and one can almost generalize by asserting that today the majority viewpoint has returned to something approaching the *status quo ante*). Three issues came under intense debate: (1) the unity and composition of the book; (2) the place or places where Ezekiel exercised his ministry; and (3) the date of the prophet's ministry.

First of all, in spite of the impressive, external unity of the book, all kinds of "evidence" began to be found allegedly supporting drastic editorial revision, if not also multiple authorship. Remarkable parallels or doublets were noted, especially Ezek. 3:16-21 = 33:1-9 and 18:21-25 = 33:10-20. The opening vision and call of the prophet (chaps. 1—3) was often thought to conflate two distinct experiences. The last nine chapters were held to be divisible into (a) the narrative of how the heavenly guide interprets Ezekiel's vision, and (b) subsequent additions to the narrative. The old saw of prophecy of doom as a touchstone for original, genuine prophecy was refurbished, in the light of which the juxtaposition of words of promise to some of the denunciations in the earlier part of the book seemed out of place, and virtually all of chaps. 33—48 with its promissory tone became problematic. The strongly apocalyptic atmosphere of chapters 38—39 in particular was judged premature on Ezekiel's lips.

Easily the most extreme practitioner of the new criticism of Ezekiel was Hölscher (1924), who applied to Ezekiel the same radical method which Duhm had exercised on Jeremiah. That is, the major criteria of genuineness were brevity and especially poetic form. That left as "genuine" (that is really written by a real prophet of preexilic tradition) only a few poems, plus a few visions, and a part of the narratives in chaps. 4—6. The remainder (nearly six-sevenths of the whole) allegedly came from a fifth-century editor or editors whose purpose was to present and further the policies of the Zadokite faction in Jerusalem. Their work was supposed to be discernible by its prosaic quality, only not attributable to "deuteronomists" (as in the case of Jeremiah) but to "priestly" or "Aaronitic" tradition (alleged similarities with "P" and "H").

Many other less radical proposals have been made (in a few cases, still are), and we cannot possibly review them all. Very popular is some version of originally parallel recensions (almost a two-document hypothesis), either by the prophet himself or others, and later combined. (Much is made of an obscure statement by Josephus that Ezekiel wrote two books—whatever that may have meant.) Some seek to distinguish along first versus third person lines, others think of a sort of "diary" of dated oracles alongside a more general collection of speeches and poems, etc. Some invent a later (third century?) apocalypticist who retrojected his dreams into Ezekiel's scheme. A "conservative" version has Ezekiel himself revising his records of his career at a late stage of his ministry. Form critics characteristically thought of a congeries of originally small, independent units later assembled by Ezekiel himself or others and given their present artificial unity. The fourteen dates are widely held to refer only to the immediately following pericope, with any further redactional scheme largely fictitious.

Even many critics were never convinced that anything had been demonstrated beyond editorial activity, as in any book, and possibly even by Ezekiel himself. To the conservative mind, many of the above suggestions are within the range of possibility, and perhaps even probability, especially if Ezekiel himself is the subject. Certainly, limitation of his range of choices to poetry seems groundless, and, in fact, as we shall note, his less-than-classical poetry suggests that his main talents did not lie in that direction at all. There are indications in the book of some deliberate alternation of allegories or action-prophecies with sermons perhaps only for the sake of variety (cf. Ezek. 17—22). Just as restrictions on Jeremiah's oral activity may have forced him to resort more to writing than he might otherwise have done, so Ezekiel's seven-year dumbness would tend to make him a "writing prophet" by necessity. In both cases, priestly background and training would enhance the plausibility. Likewise, with "artificial," written quality, but writing may well be more indigenous to that genre than to others. At any rate, beyond a few general considerations of this sort, the point of diminishing returns is reached early on!

Critical speculations about the locale of Ezekiel's activity were, in their very nature, far more radical in terms of tradition than animadversions about its unity. In contrast to the clear statement of the book that Ezekiel exercised his entire ministry in the Exile in Babylon, many began to construe the evidence to indicate that he really spent part (or even all) of it in a Judean ministry. As a famous saw has it, it was not a heavenly hand that brought him to Jerusalem (Ezek. 8:1 ff), but a literary device that transferred him to Babylon!

Thus, Herntrich (1932) argued that Ezekiel spent his *entire* ministry in Jerusalem, and during the Exile some editor enlarged and adapted the oracles to exilic conditions, supplied the descriptions of para-psychological experiences, etc. A little less radically, Bertholet (1936) posited a Jerusalem ministry (initiated by the call of 2:3—3:9) until the fall of the city, whereupon Ezekiel journeyed to Babylon and received a second call (1:4—2:2). An editor later provided a Babylonian background for his earlier oracles.

One must concede that on the surface it is more than passing strange that only some four chapters in the entire book focus on the people of Babylon among whom Ezekiel lived (33, 34, 36, 37). Not only does he address his denunciations in chaps. 3—24 to the Jerusalemites, but also his action-prophecies, requiring witnesses, portray people a thousand miles away. In 11:13 the prince Pelatiah even falls dead upon Ezekiel's distant imprecations. All in all, Ezekiel is phenomenally well informed about events back in Jerusalem.

These bare facts are quite undeniable, of course, but they scarcely add up to the radical-critical construction put on them, and, again, even many critics found such a massive departure from the book's own testimony more than they could swallow. At best, the new hypotheses raised more questions than they answered. The lines of rebuttal are many, even prescinding from any supernaturalist appeal. If the Babylonian setting were really an editorial artifice, one would expect it to be more conspicuous than it is in the book. On the other hand, both language and imagery offer considerable indirect evidence of original Babylonian provenance. It has been characteristic of exiles in all ages to keep themselves well-informed of circumstances and developments "back home," and as Jeremiah's letter indicates, correspondence between the groups will have been regular. Like Jeremiah, Ezekiel's major task, until the lightning itself struck, was to disabuse those still in Jerusalem that there was any future for them or through them, and hence also the direction of the bulk of his oracles. (The great community of themes and accents among Jeremiah and Ezekiel will find the same explanation.) Ezekiel takes the whole of scattered "Israel" as the object of his ministry, not totally dissimilar from the way other prophets included the Northern Kingdom in their audience—even after the fall of Samaria. Visions of events in distant Judea were at least partly a way of saying that even those sins were not hid from God—nor from his messenger. Finally, we may note that the prophetic corpus affords many other examples of both spoken and acted prophecies to distant audiences, most obviously and regularly in the Gentile oracles.

Most of the radical attempts to redate Ezekiel need not detain us, and they never did have much of a following. Even theories of drastic editorial recasting usually dated the final form of the book no later than 516 (consecration of the second temple)—and, as such, maybe that is not very radical to begin with. Some hypotheses took off from the enigmatic "thirtieth year" of Ezek. 1:1, but it is too insecure a base for much of anything!

Before we leave this topic, it may be of some small comfort to remember that the rabbis also had their problems with Ezekiel. The canonicity of the book was under fire at Jamnia, the only work outside the hagiographa of which we have any record of such problems. Objections, especially from the more conservative school of Shammai, are supposed to have been of three sorts: (1) alleged contradictions of the Pentateuch, especially in the laws of chaps. 40—48 and the "creation" context of chap. 28; (2) the alleged immorality of chaps. 16 and 23; and (3) fears of gnostic, theosophic, or other sectarian misuses of the call account and the apocalyptic portions. Some of the fears were eventually met by a proscription of reading the book until the age of thirty (Ezekiel's own age at his call?), but, above all, the difficulties are reported to have been solved by the lavish use of "midnight oil" (300 jars of it) in one Rabbi Hananiah's study, who resolved all problems to the satisfaction of the other rabbis! (In addition there is a Talmudic statement of Ezekiel, as of other books, that the "Great Synagogue" wrote Ezekiel, which, at most, may preserve some authentic memory of compilers' activities.)

Style

From the standpoint of classical Hebrew stylistic canons, Ezekiel rates as noticeably inferior to Jeremiah and, even more so, to Isaiah and Amos. That, of course, has nothing to do with the validity of his inspiration in the theological sense, nor does it imply that Ezekiel's oracles do not have a remarkable impact and power of another sort. It may be a matter of individual ability (though scarcely to be associated with his priestly proclivities!), but it may also signal the massive cultural breakup throughout the ancient Near East as a result of the political convulsions of the time. After Ezekiel, much literary activity appears to have been even more epigonic, or else it charted out entirely new forms for itself.

Ezekiel makes little use of the shorter and more classical forms, and instead composes long literary dissertations, and his prose is often prolix and repetitive to the extreme. (We, of course, do not share the old liberal prejudice that there was something inherently decadent about original dependence on a written idiom!) Even when he writes poetry, the old glory seems often to have departed. In form as well as vocabulary, one may often begin to speak of "post-classical Hebrew." Nevertheless, let it be clear that these are technical, literary judgments. No one who takes the trouble to read Ezekiel will dismiss him in any broader sense as less forceful or less important.

Possibly even more so than Jeremiah, Ezekiel is characterized by many favorite phrases. They should not so much be labeled "stereotyped" as viewed as the repeated blows of a hammer. Among them are: (1) "Son of man," that is "(mere) creature/human being," as God consistently (93 times) addresses the prophet; (2) Israel as a "rebellious house"; (3) the command to "set his face against X"; (4) God's action "for His name's sake"; (5) "They shall know that I am God/a prophet has been among them."

Text

The corrupt state of the Hebrew text of Ezekiel will not lie unnoticed. Critics have often exaggerated that state of affairs to justify their own mischief, but the solution does not lie in desperate justifications of an impossible text. As usual, the general gist remains clear, but obscurities abound in details. Text-critically, the Masoretic text of Ezekiel must be rated as the worst of the major prophets, with only Hosea, Samuel, and some psalms exceeding it in textual difficulties. As though that were not enough, the Septuagint often differs markedly from MT. The general consensus is that the LXX often goes back to a superior prototype, but so far we have little Qumran illumination on the subject, and each instance must continue to be judged on its own merits.

Theology

Finally a word on Ezekiel's importance theologically, and his importance from the standpoint of the history of Israel's religion. Possibly this is more important in Ezekiel's case because he is probably the "sleeper" of the major prophets, and illiteracy of his message is probably here at its height. Consideration of his role in the "development" of Israel's religion will look considerably different in a conservative than in an evolutionistic, critical one. Nevertheless, if we think of an "evolution outward," the topic is a valid one, and there is no denying that Ezekiel presides over the major watershed of Israel's history, in many respects, humanly speaking, determining the shape of the future more than any other prophet. It is no exaggeration to think of him as the first postexilic prophet, perhaps in specific contrast to Jeremiah as the last preexilic prophet. Only he who is so beholden to a "Protestant principle" that he regards the essentially conservative forms of institutional preservation as intrinsically inferior and unexciting will underrate the cruciality of Ezekiel's role.

On *a priori* grounds, the conservative need not address the critical issue of the relation between Ezekiel and "H" or even "P." (Cf. our earlier discussion; a recent hypothesis even tries to factor out a "Deutero-Ezekiel" in the book which is supposed to be closest to "H"!) That there is a community of theme, concern, and expression is obvious, however. There is no good reason why one steeped in priestly lore like Ezekiel should not express himself in the vocabulary characteristic of his own circles. If that usage, furthermore, is genuinely Mosaic, it will also have been familiar and readily comprehensible to the ordinary Israelite, even the lukewarm and apostate.

That specious issue does highlight, however, Ezekiel's overriding concern with God's holiness and/or its correlative, God's glory. If Isaiah can be said to champion more God's transcendence itself, Ezekiel places the greater accent on its "incarnational" presence on earth—but it is almost a distinction without a difference. Jeremiah, by contrast, stresses God's immanence, but all three know of His paradoxical indwelling in the temple. The net effect in any case can only be judgment on the faithless, but the promise and presence of God to the faithful. Contrary to critical evolutionism, this retributional pattern was as old as revelation itself, not a new, mechanistic and corporate doctrine which Jeremiah and Ezekiel must struggle to adjust to individual, personal circumstances. Even the allegedly "deuteronomic" phrase of acting "for My name's sake" is prominent in Ezekiel and with essentially the same import.

In developing the main theme of God's transcendence as well as in all its applications, Ezekiel is the major refutation of any ultimate antithesis of prophet and priest. Yet one fears that it is precisely at this point that most Protestantism, conservative as well as liberal, tends to have the greatest difficulty. If Lutheran sacramentological doctrine is functional, however, Ezekiel will remain a major source and inspiration. One need subscribe to no reductionist ecumenism to agree that he illustrates the intrinsic, necessary union of "Protestant principle" and "Catholic substance," of Pauline and Petrine (Abrahamic and Mosaic) strands in a total Biblical theology. The immediacy and subjectivism of "prophetic religion," of "justification by faith," are inseparably linked with the mediacy and objectivism of the sacraments, of an inscripturated word, of the Word in its broadest sense behind both. Atonement and incarnation, salvation and new creation, form the warp and woof of the Biblical fabric.

Virtually everything else which may be asserted of Ezekiel follows from those two points: transcendence in its dual (verbal and sacramental) dimension. "Sin" is a good first example. If anything, Ezekiel sees "total depravity" in all its heinousness over against divine perfection in even sharper contours than Jeremiah. It is ritual and sacral indeed, but social and moral at the same time—that is, applying to the "whole man," body and soul. Individual accountability also is stressed at least as much as in Jeremiah, yet even more clearly within a corporate, congregational context. Both ruin and revival, when and if they come, will affect the "heart" and "spirit" as much as the "bones" and ultimately also the earthly valley or stage. God's holiness necessarily implies the strict exclusion of the unregenerate, but it also means that His honor, His "name" (reputation) is at stake so that there is also a dynamic toward restoration, in the hope that all may know "that I am the LORD" (more than thirty times in the book).

It emphatically is not that these accents begin to triumph in Ezekiel for the first time. But, no doubt, the times did require a new highlighting of them and sometimes with new accents—and the times were never again as they had been before. God is not now increasingly "kicked upstairs," but heightened awareness of the infinite gulf between Him and His sinful creature brings mediatorial, hypostatic concepts to the fore—a major part of the *praeparatio evangelica.* Angelology (the cherubim, the heavenly guide) is a major example. And, formally, second only to Daniel, the baroque character of Ezekiel's visions and actions ushers in the age of the apocalyptic idiom with all its supernaturalist, eschatological accents that are also structural for the New Testament. Ezekiel is often called, albeit with slight exaggeration, the "father of apocalyptic."

In proclaiming these themes, Ezekiel is not only symbolist and sacramentalist, priest and prophet, but *theologian* as well (about as close as the Old Testament comes to our abstract understanding of the word). Von Rad has well written: "No other prophet feels so great a need to think out problems so thoroughly and to explain them with such complete consistency. . . . He confronted a presumptuous and indeed rebellious generation for which a prophet's preaching was not enough: he had to debate and argue with it." If the Bible is one, none of those issues are new to Ezekiel, but in a time of total collapse, he confronts them with a terrible urgency. Among those worth bearing in mind below are: law and grace, faith and works, promise and fulfillment, the now and the not-yet, eschatology and ethics, immanence and transcendence, election and freedom, the sacred and the secular, institutional and charismatic, individual and society/church, particularism and universalism, etc. And, if, in conclusion, we recall that Ezekiel is supremely concerned to be the pastor, the watchman of the flock, we begin to get the measure of the man and his message.

Ezekiel 1—11

Chaps. 1—3 contain the account of Ezekiel's inaugural vision and call, which has had such tremendous impact on later art and literature, both Biblical and post-Biblical. Its roots are surely in the ancient prophetic tradition of inauguration into the divine throne room, but characteristically it is easily the most "far out" of all such visions. Certainly its point is to assure the prophet that his ministry is accredited by Yahweh himself. It may well reflect to some extent the impact of

Babylonian art and culture upon the prophet, and it surely presages the proto-apocalypticism of some of his message (esp. chaps. 38—39, whose genuineness can also be defended on the basis of the connection). That it first approaches the prophet in a storm cloud may also signal its roots in ancient theophanic traditions, which often nourished apocalyptic.

No precise reconstruction of the vision is possible from Ezekiel's impressionistic account, nor should one be attempted. Ezekiel himself is extremely guarded in his descriptions, and those given are circumscribed by the "appearance/likeness of" and other qualifiers. The overall picture is that of the living creatures with their wheels forming a chariot which serves as a platform for the throne of the incomparably transcendent and invisible God (this the point of departure for the widespread "Merkabah mysticism" of early and medieval, especially qabbalistic, Judaism). The four faces (later applied to the four evangelists) surely indicate God's omnipresence, even in a foreign land. Similarly, the eyes suggest universal intelligence and omniscience, and the "wheels within the wheels" instantaneous mobility in all directions.

More theologically or abstractly expressed, the vision describes God's *Kabod,* "glory" (Ezek. 1:28, 3:12, 23), not only a dazzling brightness, but the "incarnate" revelation of His presence and holiness among men. Normally it resides above the propitiatory (mercy seat) between the cherubim in the Holy of Holies; however (and significantly even in a priestly work like Ezekiel), it is not imprisoned there, but free also to encounter and domicile in men. Since the concept of the *Kabod* virtually structures the book, it dominates the call vision as one might expect.

Ezek. 2 begins the verbal explanation of the vision—the first divine communication to the "son of man" (creature, mortal), the first entrance of God's Spirit into him, the strict command to "speak my words to them, whether they hear or refuse to hear; for they are a rebellious house" (2:7).

The call is not only verbalized, but also "internalized": the son of man is commanded to eat a scroll (probably made of parchment or animal skin) with words written on it of "lamentation and mourning and woe" (2:10; early critics sometimes cited the verse as further evidence of their dogma that genuine prophecy was only negative). The response, unlike Jeremiah's and more like Isaiah's, is eager and joyful: "it was in my mouth as sweet as honey" (3:3). By this initial "action-prophecy," the prophet's entire life becomes a "walking prophecy," a type or living embodiment of his words.

Seven days later, after still another manifestation of the "glory of the LORD," the implications of his call are further expatiated upon (Ezek. 3:16-21). The accents of this section are expanded in 33:1-20 (one of the alleged "doublets" a few critics have tried to make hay of; cf. also 18:1-

32). Ezekiel is called to be a "watchman," a theme also heard in Is. 21 and Habakkuk, but developed much more here. The prophet is to be a pastor, a *Seelsorger,* liable for each individual if he has not warned them. As in Jeremiah, there is indeed a certain accent on "individual responsibility" here, but not in the evolutionistic, solipsistic context of much liberalism: it is not that God did not deal with individuals as moral persons before this time, although the chaos of the catastrophe did highlight the "every man for himself" aspect of also religion. Exegetically, the application is primarily to the fall of Jerusalem, but in proper hermeneutical context we are free to apply it dogmatically to all aspects of the God-man relationship. Words like "righteous" and "wicked" must not be heard moralistically, but within the context of the covenant: basically "justified" or not, as *evidenced* by conduct. "Stumbling block" in v. 20 also introduces a prominent Ezekelian motif. In Greek it was regularly translated *skandalon,* that is, "offense" or "scandal" (often of particularity). Here, as usually in Ezekiel, it is applied to God's probative work (cf. "test" in the Sixth Petition).

After instruction the "hand of the LORD" is again on the prophet (3:22, as repeatedly in Ezekiel), and His *Kabod* ("glory") appears to him a third time. Strangely now the "commission" is to dumbness (a standing "action-prophecy"), lifted only seven years later when Jerusalem is taken (33:22, immediately following the expatiation of the "watchman" theme in the earlier part of that chapter). Both because of the double parallelism of chaps. 3 and 33, and because of the anomaly of a prophet being ordered to silence, all the more so almost immediately after his call, many critical attempts are made to regard this pericope as misplaced, as really occurring much later in the prophet's ministry, or else referring only to one specific occasion. However, such expedients are possible only in connection with mayhem on the book. It may be that dumbness applied only to ordinary intercourse, not to special prophetic utterance. The point of the prophet's malady was to prophesy the shocked speechlessness of the exiles when the judgment fell, and, as we noted, it helps explain his "weird" behavior.

Chaps. 4—5 contain four "charades" designed to hasten the fall of Jerusalem. Ezekiel sketches the city on a brick and uses it to mime the city's siege (4:1-3); lies stationary on his side to symbolize its length (4:9-17); eats siege rations, baked with dung, to depict its horrors (4:9-17); and shaves his head, dividing the hair into three parts, to illustrate the three fates of the captives (chap. 5). Note in 4:6 that Ezekiel describes Judah's captivity as lasting forty instead of seventy years. (Cf. our discussion at Jer. 25; "forty" here as often may be a round figure for a generation, and corresponds roughly to the period 587—536; Ezekiel applies the same figure to Egypt in 28:10-16.)

Chaps. 6—7 are the verbal sequel to the preceding action prophecies: vivid previews of the horrors of the judgment, at points even broadening out to involve the cosmos (cf. Jeremiah's "chaos vision"; 4:23-28). Nevertheless, a remnant will be spared (6:8-10).

In chaps. 8—11 we have Ezekiel's visit to Jerusalem in the Spirit. A supernatural guide points out to him the abominations of the city, crying out for judgment (8:2 ff.). The guide has "the appearance of a man," very similar to the incarnate "glory" of the call vision (1:26 f.), which continues to play a prominent role in these chapters. Apparently, he is not only *an* angel, but *the* "angel of the LORD," a preincarnate form of our Lord Himself. Ezek. 8 is a very instructive picture of the various types of syncretistic paganism flourishing in the first temple in its last days: gross idolatry (the "image of jealousy" (v. 5; cf. Daniel's "abomination of desolation"), worship of various animal deities in some dark, secret chamber (7-13), of Tammuz (i.e., Adonis, god of vegetation and fertility; 14-15; cf. Is. 17:10 f.); and of the sun (16-18).

Ezek. 9 really has an apocalyptic aura and is strongly echoed in the New Testament Apocalypse. The *Kabod* moves from the adytum of the temple to the threshold, where it directs seven angels (one with the heavenly records) to mark the foreheads of the faithful with a *Tau* (the last letter of the Hebrew alphabet, at that period identical in form with our X; cf. the "Tau cross") and ruthlessly to slay the rest, "beginning at my sanctuary" (v. 6; cf. 1 Pet. 4:17). The apparent point of the lengthy repetition of the vision of the *Kabod* in v. 10 is that its fire (v. 7) will destroy the city; that is, God's real presence which was misunderstood as a magical guarantee of the city's security will instead destroy it (cf. Jer. 7). In spite of the leaders' confidence that the city's wall will ultimately protect them as a caldron does flesh from the fire (11:7), they will perish, of which Pelatiah's instantaneous death is the beginning (13). A promise of restoration precedes the stroke of judgment in vs. 14-21: afterwards the people will be restored and given a heart of flesh (cf. chap. 36 and Jeremiah's "new covenant").

So in Ezek. 11:22-25 the *Kabod* abandons the city to its fate and takes its position on the Mt. of Olives, only to return to the purified "new Jerusalem" (43:1 ff.), a major structural bond of the book. Zion is indestructible, but not Jerusalem, and except for God's "incarnational" presence, Jerusalem is only another human structure. The formulation differs from Isaiah, but the underlying theology is obviously identical.

Ezekiel 12—24

Following the preceding extended vision, 12:1-20 records two more action-prophecies introducing a long series (through chap. 24) of sermons and prophecies against Jerusalem. Ezekiel digs through the wall of his home like a refugee and obeys the command to "eat bread with quaking and drink water with trembling." In 12:21-28 the prophet turns against the people a popular proverb which false prophets are encouraging: the "vision" will no longer be delayed, but its content is of catastrophe, not deliverance. This leads into an impassioned denunciation of false prophets and prophetesses and all their magic (chap. 13).

The elders of the exilic community pay their first visit to the prophet in 14:1 ff., and it is obvious that they scarcely grasp even the First Commandment. As part of his instruction (vs. 12-23) the prophet stresses that the presence of a few righteous will not suffice to save a city (perhaps just as it had not in the case of Sodom and Gomorrah). Here the illustrations of the principle of individual accountability before God are "Noah, Daniel, and Job," vs. 14 and 20; (cf. Moses and Samuel in Jer. 15:1-4).

Noah and Job plainly lived long before Ezekiel, but a major crux arises with the mention of Daniel (cf. also 28:3). Mention of the contemporary Biblical prophet in the same breath as the two ancient worthies has seemed strange (not to liberals, of course, who doubt that he ever existed). From Ugarit now we learn of a Dan'el (essentially the same name as "Daniel") of at least 1400 B.C., who is described as a "righteous judge of widows and orphans." Liberals quite unanimously prefer that reference, while conservatives generally continue to prefer the contemporary, Biblical figure. However, the case is not cut and dried: one notes that Noah and Job were non-Hebrew too, and the triad may have had somewhat of a fixed, proverbial character.

Ezek. 15—17 contain allegories, stressing the imminence of an overdue judgment. We say "allegory," not merely "parable," because of the detailed, point-by-point correspondences. They are probably more characteristic of Ezekiel than of any other Biblical writer. Hermeneutically, one must note that when an allegorical sense is intended, it is the *literal* sense. Chap. 15 compares Judah to a vine-branch, of little value as wood at best, now half-burned (the deportation of 598), and soon to be discarded altogether.

Ezek. 16 (roughly parallel to 23) was one of the chapters understandably troublesome to some rabbis at Jamnia (cf. above). At great, almost lurid length, it depicts Jerusalem as a brazen whore, even a nymphomaniac, who insatiably pays for her own customers! All of this in spite of the loving care which Yahweh had lavished on her ever since He first found her, apparently exposed to die after birth, helplessly wallowing in her amniotic fluid. Because of her utter ingratitude and degradation, her restoration can take place only *after* that of her "sisters," Samaria and Sodom (46 ff.)! The references in vs. 3 and 45 to Jerusalem's "Amorite" and "Hittite" mother have excited inordinate debate; the details, however, are surely not to be pressed, but indicate only Israel's "mongrel" status before God apart from election; she has no claim on God by virtue of race.

Ezek. 17 is an elaborate allegory of two "eagles" or vultures (Babylonia and Egypt) contending for a vine (Judah), and condemning Zedekiah's disloyalty to the Babylonians who gave him power. Now he must pay the consequences (except in style, a stance identical with Jeremiah's). Using similar imagery, the chapter closes with a prophecy of the future (Messianic) restoration of the Davidic kingdom on Zion. The great tree which gives shelter to all creatures has many Biblical and extra-Biblical parallels (cf. Ezek. 31 and Dan. 4).

Chap. 18 is Ezekiel's major statement of his common theme of "individual accountability" before God (also especially prominent in the two "watchman" pericopes, chaps. 3 and 33). He begins by attacking the same "sour grapes" saying that Jeremiah (31:29) had, by which the Judahites evaded their responsibility, blaming it all instead on their parents and predecessors. While in Jeremiah the orientation is more toward the future (when they will know firsthand the inapplicability of the saying), Ezekiel scores the proverb as a springboard for a major, almost doctrinal, statement of the principles of God's covenantal justice. The chapter's message is succinctly and classically summarized in v. 20. It must be stressed again that, as in parallel Jeremianic accents, we are not witnessing the triumph of a new stage in the evolution of spirituality, but only a major Biblical exposition of a principle that pervades the Bible from start to finish.

Allegories return in Ezek. 19, specifically two "lamentations" of the fall of Judah: (1) the lioness (the Davidic kingdom) has two whelps (Jehoahaz and Jehoiachin) both of whom are caught and carried into captivity, never again to return (vs. 2-9); and (2) the flourishing vine (Judah), now forcibly uprooted (vs. 10-14).

The elders visit Ezekiel a second time in chap. 20, and in response he justifies his constant preaching of judgment by launching into an exposition of Israel's history as a history of unbroken apostasy all the way from the sojourn in Egypt until the present time. The assertion in 25—26 that "I gave them statutes that were not good and ordinances by which they could not have life" has an almost Pauline, *"lex semper accusat"* tone to it. And, indeed, the Old Testament does not usually express itself in that way. At the same time, there could be no fundamental divergence, or the Bible would massively contradict itself. Cf. our earlier discussion on the semantic problem of "Law" and "Torah," the confusion of which commonly contributes to subliminal feelings that the Old Testament is subevangelical. The principle of the potential "curse of the Law" is prominent throughout the Old Testament, yet Ezekiel's sharpened articulation of it will stand as a striking precursor of Paul's formulation. Significantly, Ezekiel cannot conclude a diatribe of this sort without also proclaiming the Gospel, the ultimate Messianic great reversal "on my holy mountain" (vs. 33-44).

In the Hebrew text, Ezek. 21 begins already at 20:45, a much better division. Another allegory, this time of a great conflagration engulfing the Negeb (20:45-49) leads Ezekiel to confess (in a sort of sigh or lament to God) that the people's general reaction to him is to say, "Is he not a maker of allegories?" (Cf. 33:30-32.)

Ezek. 21:1-17 picturesquely depicts the sword of God's judgment as already drawn, including a poetic snatch (possibly a quotation) in vs. 9-10. Presumably, the occasion is the launching of Nebuchadnezzar's final campaign against rebellious Judah, because in the remainder of the chapter (vs. 18-32) Ezekiel envisions (and mimes) the Babylonian king reaching the crossroads leading to either Judah or Ammon. He casts lots to decide which to attack first, and when the lot falls to Judah, Ezekiel (in a sort of Gentile oracle) assures Ammon that her respite is only temporary.

Chap. 22 is one of the most detailed and impassioned descriptions of the innumerable sins of all classes of Judahite society to be found in all prophetic literature—a veritable *massa perditionis*. It forms a sort of sequel to chap. 20, which cataloged the trespasses of the past.

Again an allegory in Ezek. 23, a recension of chap. 16, and one of the most "sexually explicit" in the Bible (hence again misgivings at Jamnia). Samaria (the Northern Kingdom) is given the symbolic name "Oholah" ("Her [own] tent") and her "sister," Judah, the corresponding "Oholibah" (My tent is in her"). "Tent" probably means "tabernacle" as a place of worship in a god's house; thus Samaria's worship was misguided from the outset, while Judah's had the advantage of God's "Incarnation" in the temple—all the worse foil for her current depravity. Since Judah refused to take warning from the punishment visited upon her sister, but even surpassed her in harlotry, she must share the judgment.

Ezekiel 25—32 (Gentile Oracles)

As the siege of Jerusalem begins in Ezek. 24, the first section of the book concludes (the coincidence is not coincidental). Using the homely allegory of a rusty pot, Ezekiel scoffs at the city's defenses, considering it already "as good as gone." When his wife dies (v. 15 ff.) and, at God's command, he "sighs, but not aloud" and makes no mourning for her, the people are moved to ask "what these things mean for us" (v. 19). It is an action-prophecy, forecasting how they will be stunned into speechlessness at the news of Jerusalem's fall, which Ezekiel treats as a foregone conclusion.

In a superficial sense, then, the Gentile oracles following interrupt the story of Ezekiel's ministry, which picks up again in 33:21 with the news of the city's capitulation. In a more profound sense, however, the shift to preaching primarily Gentile oracles at this point means that the time for preaching judgment or Law is now in principle past. Rather now the primary message shall be Gospel or restoration. The first phase of that must be judgment also upon Israel's enemies, that is, upon *all* competitors with Yahweh's kingship. Only then can salvation be offered to all at Zion, the major message of the third section of the book (chaps. 34 ff.). Let it be stressed that this is not political chauvinism (any more than the prophets *ever* gave simply "political" counsel), the major evidence of which is its precedence by judgment on the people of God. Since Ezekiel's Gentile oracles are often precisely dated, like other oracles in the book, we may be confident that this sequence of themes is not editorial, but stems from the prophet's own activity. (Only the oracle beginning at 29:17 is significantly later, undoubtedly included at that point for topical continuity.)

Ezekiel uses seven (symbolizing completeness?) foreign nations to illustrate the theme of universal jugdment, but five of them only briefly and quite generally, four in chap. 25 (Amnon, Moab, Edom, Philistia), and Sidon in 28:20-23. Multiple oracles, however, are directed at Tyre (three in chaps. 26—28) and at Egypt (seven in chaps. 29—32). In many of them originally mythological illustrations are deployed very effectively, especially considering the original audiences.

The three oracles against Tyre envision Nebuchadnezzar's inevitable reprisal against that city, which had been heavily involved in essentially the same conspiracies as Jerusalem. And, indeed, shortly after Jerusalem's fall (Ezekiel prophecies a year before it) Nebuchadnezzar did begin a thirteen-year siege of Tyre. Tyre's role as the major emporium and mercantile center of the Levant at that time must be in mind to appreciate the oracles.

Ezek. 26: because the rich merchant city exults over Jerusalem's imminent fall, hoping to profit from it, Yahweh will shortly destroy her through Nebuchadnezzar, and the whole world will stand in awe of her collapse. "Capitalism" is thus not pictured as intrinsically evil, but the prophet warns against the temptations to inordinate pride that it offers, or that "the *love* of money is the root of all evil." Vs. 13 and 16-17 are applied to "Babylon" in Rev. 18, illustrating the typical significance of all

Gentile oracles. In highly poetic language in vs. 19-21 Ezekiel pictures the entire city engulfed by "the great waters" (the mythological embodiment of chaos and murky evil) and living a sort of nonexistence in the Pit (Sheol); cf. on Babylon in Is. 14:4-21 and on Egypt in Ezek. 31 and 32.

Ezek. 27 anticipates the fall of Tyre by means of a magnificent elegy, picturing her as a well-constructed ship, which for all her commercial prowess, capsizes on the high seas. Vs. 27-36 are reproduced in Rev. 18:9-19. Also from an archaeological and historical standpoint the chapter is of first-rate importance.

Tyre's "prince" *(nagid)* or ruler must also suffer retribution (Ezek. 28). From an exegetical and theological standpoint it is the most interesting of the three chapters. After an indictment and condemnation of the king in vs. 2-10 we have another threnody in vs. 11-19. Even though the king is "wiser than Daniel" (v. 3; cf. on 14:14), he is condemned for saying "I am a god ..." (v. 2 and 9), and therefore must be cast down into the Pit (v. 8). He had, indeed, been a sort of Adam or *Urmensch* "in Eden, the garden of God" (v. 13) or "on the holy mountain of God" (v. 14, a common figure of Paradise; cf. Is. 11:9), clad in precious stones, (v. 13) like a king or high priest (LXX has a total of twelve stones, the same as the high priest's breastpiece; Ex. 28), but who is now cast out by "the guardian cherub" as a "profane thing" (v. 16).

Liberal literature loves to trumpet the portrait of Ezek. 28 as betraying an alternate tradition of creation, Paradise and the Fall, before later dogmatic standardization exalted Gen. 2—3 to canonical status. It, of course, can be nothing of the sort, but there are undeniable points of contact, and individual symbols are also used elsewhere secondarily to illustrate the Biblical doctrines. Here Ezekiel is apparently employing for his polemical purposes traditions or mythologies which were current in Tyre itself. Besides the historical application, this oracle, like all Gentile oracles, has suprahistorical import, which is especially significant in this case. Even though, like all "powers that be," the king of Tyre had been empowered by God (cf. Ps. 82), he had become a tool or "incarnation" of Satan (or in fulfillment terms, of Antichrist). In other words, as his fall had recapitulated Satan's primordial fall, so his (Tyre's) judgment typifies and anticipates the final judgment on Satan, Antichrist, and all the kingdoms of this world.

Appended to these three oracles against Tyre is a brief malediction of Tyre's neighbor, Sidon (28:20-23), but before continuing against Egypt, the prophet significantly inserts an "alternation of weal," a promise of restoration to Israel (vs. 24-26). Egypt, of course, not only figured prominently in the anti-Babylonian intrigues of this period but had been a prime embodiment of Satanic evil at least since the Exodus. Hence, again historical and suprahistorical (often articulated in originally mythological terms) motifs intertwine.

The first anti-Egyptian oracle (Ezek. 29:1-16), in a manner not too dissimilar from chap. 28 against Tyre, compares Pharaoh (Hophra) to a crocodile in the Nile, who will soon be dragged out of his lair and left to die (2-9). Egypt will be desolate "forty years" (cf. on 4:6), after which she will regain her strength, but never again in the old imperialistic way vis-á-vis Israel. But on the suprahistorical level, the Pharaoh claims that "My Nile is my own" (vs. 3, 9), thus historifying the dragon (v. 3), that is Rahab or Leviathan, the chaos monster (cf. Is. 27:1; 30:7; 51:9; Ps. 89:10), that is, again Satan, Antichrist, etc.

The second oracle, the latest dated one in the book (c. 571), chronologically out of order but topically in order here, attaches directly to the first oracle against Tyre in Ezek. 26. Because Nebuchadnezzar and his troops had been little rewarded by the long siege of Tyre (perhaps because her wealth had been spirited away by sea to Egypt), Ezekiel promises Egypt and her wealth as "consolation prize" for Babylon. Liberal commentaries love to tout both the Tyrian oracle and this one as examples of unfulfilled prophecies! Not all details are clear, but there is little doubt that both Tyre and Egypt did capitulate to Babylon. Tyre was perhaps not plundered in exact accordance with the poetry of chap. 26, but—no one is so *literalistic* as the critics when it serves their purposes!

The fifth oracle (Ezek. 31), another allegory, compares Egypt to a proud cedar of Lebanon, which "all the trees of Eden envied" (v. 9), that is, in exmythological terms, a sort of world-tree or "tree of life" straddling heaven and earth (in 17:22-24 the image is applied to Israel, and in Dan. 4 to Babylon), which must be cast down to Sheol because of its pride. Chap. 32:1-16 expands on the other major demythologized figure of the crocodile-dragon applied to Egypt already in chap. 29, describing in gory detail the rotting of the monster's carcass. Finally, and seventh, 32:17-32 vividly describes the descent of the shades of Egypt into Sheol to join all the others who once diabolically tyrannized the world (cf. on Tyre in 26:19-21 and Babylon in Is. 14)

Ezekiel 33—39

Ezek. 33 is not only the second major turning point of the Book of Ezekiel (preceding prophecies of restoration), but it records the historical axis of the dialectic of judgment and salvation, Law and Gospel of all of prophecy, yes, of the entire Old Testament. The chapter's own pivot is in vs. 21-22, reporting the arrival of a messenger with the tidings that "The city has fallen," after which the prophet is no longer dumb but can begin to proclaim God's "proper work" of salvation. One must read the chapter in its full typological and Christological dimension. Just as Israel's new era began at lowest ebb, so the Gospel proclaims Christ's (and the church's) glorification in His death. So also Bach's *St. John Passion* interrupts the lugubrious aria, "It is finished," with the magnificent paean, "The King of Judah triumphs now!"

Preceding that pivot (Ezek. 33:1-20) is a reiteration and expansion of the same "watchman" theme, stressing the individual accountability of both pastor and people, which we met at the end of the prophet's call (3:16-21; cf. chap. 18). It is no seam in the book's composition (many critics think chap. 3 is a misplaced doublet), but it is a sort of recommissioning of the prophet at this crucial juncture. The same awful responsibility relates to the Gospel as much as to the Law.

But the proclamation of Law does not cease as soon as the Gospel can be proclaimed. Neither does Ezekiel make a clean break with the Gentile oracles of the preceding chapters. A final minatory oracle against Judah concludes chap. 33 (vs. 23-29), directed against the few left in Judah after Nebuchadnezzar's deportation, who cherish the vain hope that the promise to Abraham of many descendants from few in order to inherit the land (Gen. 12:1-3) will be fulfilled in them. Ezekiel's trenchant deflation of those hopes might well have been uttered by Jeremiah!

The note in Ezek 33:30-33 might have applied at any point in the prophet's ministry, the people's frivolous, flippant reaction to his preaching (cf. 20:49). They jest, "Let's hear what God has to say today" and regard him "as one who sings love songs." But in God's good time, "they will know that a prophet has been among them."

Ezek. 34 begins the third section of the book with a major Messianic prophecy, very similar to Jer. 23. False "shepherds" will be deposed, and Yahweh Himself will gather all His scattered sheep and install "one shepherd, my servant David," (v. 23) over them. The two contrasted pictures are expressed in national terms in chaps. 35—36, which might almost be compared with Is. 34-35: Edom will be destroyed (cf. Ezek. 25:12-14) while Judah will be restored. "Edom" here is partly typical and eschatological, but the firm historical rootage of all Ezekiel's Gentile oracles remains. Especially after Judah's third revolt, Edom took advantage and began moving across the Arabah into the Negeb and southern Judea (cf. perhaps Obadiah). After God has "vindicated the holiness of His great name" (36:23), the land will become "like the garden of Eden" (36:35), and God will sprinkle "clean water" on His people, and given them a "new heart" and a "new spirit" (vs. 25-27; cf. Jeremiah's "new covenant").

Ezek. 37:1-14 contains the famous vision of the "valley of dry bones," prophesying Israel's "resurrection" from the death of the Exile. As v. 12

makes explicit, it is a national "resurrection" which is meant, not that of individuals as such. Nevertheless, it provided fertile soil in which God could nurture the latter concept too. Ezek. 37, together with Is. 53, are perhaps the major references in the New Testament and the Nicene Creed to Christ's resurrection "according to the Scriptures."

The last half of Ezek. 37 (vs. 15-28) is more specifically Messianic. By the "symbolism" of joining two sticks, Ezekiel prophesies the future reunification of Judah and Joseph/Ephraim (the counterpart and type of the eschatological ecumenicity of the *Una Sancta*). "My servant David shall be king" (v. 24) over both of them, and the "everlasting covenant" with Abraham (v. 26) will be established. Naturally, the locale is Zion where God will forever set His sanctuary in their midst, sacramentalizing His incarnational presence among them (with parallels all through Scripture from Ex. 25:8 to Rev. 21:3).

That final account of Ezek. 37 makes an excellent transition to the vision of the new Jerusalem in the last nine chapters of the book—in fact, it anticipates them in embryo. But first there intervene some really eschatological, even apocalyptic, "Gentile oracles," describing the manifestation of God's glory to all nations. The earlier Gentile oracles (Ezek. 25—32) had "intruded" in much the same way, but the same Law-Gospel dialectic is proclaimed in both instances. Partly because the book can be climactically concluded with chap. 37, much critical skepticism has been entertained about both of the following blocs of material, none of it very convincingly. More moderate critical positions see later expansion of a genuine core. One popular position understands Josephus' reference to Ezekiel's *two* books as considering chaps. 40—48 separately, and then chaps 1—39 are viewed as the original conclusion of the book. But neither theological logic nor evidence cogently supports that position.

Theological or hermeneutical variations wreak as much havoc among conservatives. The basic picture is simple enough (a typically Ezekelian expansion of the ancient "day of the LORD" motif): a massive, last-ditch invasion of Israel by hordes from the north (!), led by "Gog of the land of Magog." This time, however, the enemies are not God's agents of judgment upon His people, but their incursion turns out to be virtually their self-immolation. It will take seven months to bury the corpses in the Valley of Hamon-gog ("Horde of Gog") in the Dead Sea region (Ezek. 39:11-16), or, alternatively their flesh will become a great "sacrificial feast" for all the earth (vs. 17-20; cf. Rev. 19).

"Gog" and "Magog" have never been suitably identified. Possibly the most attractive identification of Gog still is with Gyges, king of Lydia, the "Gugu" of Assyrian records. "Magog" is mentioned as a son of Japheth in Gen. 10:2, but possibly here it stands for "Babylon" by means of a shuffling of letters similar to "Athbash" (cf. on Jer. 25:26). In any event, it seems plain that, in contrast to Ezekiel's earlier Gentile oracles, *no specific* historical individuals or nations are in mind. Here the *trans*historical is primary, with, however, constant manifestations and anticipations within the course of history. The major focus, however, is eschatological, the final showdown "battle of Armageddon" at the end of time.

At the same time, since the idiom is quasi-apocalyptic, literalistic and allegorical pressing of details must be eschewed. Hence, as in similar passages, Lutheran confessionalism believes no precise eschatological timetable is presented. To the amillennial mind, the fundamentalistic debates about the chronological relation of these events to the "Tribulation" are, at best, beside the point. The easiest reading of Ezek. 38—39, then, in relation to the material on either side is that they describe the final overthrow of the powers of darkness *before,* not after, the dawning of the new age, forecast already in chaps. 34—37 but not described until chaps. 40—48.

Ezekiel 40—48

The final nine chapters pose almost as many problems as all the rest of the book. Spiritualism, both liberal and conservative, has little patience with the ritualistic detail of the section. Literalism, both liberal and conservative, often fails to see the forest for the trees. Baffling textual corruptions betray that the ancient copyists were often not very comprehending either! The rabbis were worried about apparent contradictions of the Pentateuch, and some said only Elijah would explain them all!

Much of Ezekiel's poor image among the liberals as the "father of Judaism," the major initiator of the transformation of the lofty moral ideals of the prophets into legalism, dogmatism, and ritualism, soon to be implemented by "P," Ezra, and other postexilic circles, stems from these chapters. The problem was once (and still often is) "solved" by denying the material to Ezekiel, although it usually is not dated too much later. It certainly must strike one that explicitly ritual concerns are often as prominent elsewhere in Ezekiel as in these chapters. Furthermore, the structure and themes of these chapters are so thoroughly mortised into the rest of the book that only radical rebuilding can eliminate them.

The vision of the restored theocracy is dated (Ezek. 40:1) some thirteen years after the fall of Jerusalem (c. 574), hence, somewhat like Is. 40—55, projects itself into the future *after* the return from the Exile. The same "man" who had led Ezekiel on a tour of the doomed city in chaps. 8—11 now meets him at a "very high moutain" (Zion; Paradise) and directs him about the New Jerusalem (40:2 ff.). The *Kabod* of the call vision which abandoned earthly Jerusalem in 11:22-23 returns and restores "Zion" in 43:1. The same concern for distinguishing the sacred and the secular, the "holy and the common," in all its dimensions pervades both parts of the book (explicitly at 22:26 and 44:23). The land, even all creation, which was earlier included in the judgment is now also caught up in the restoration. Although the vision is still through the filter of the Old Testament, the ultimate concern is not with externals as such, but with the new covenant, not merely with a theological idea or abstraction, but as a "sacramental" manifestation of the basic covenant promise that "The LORD is there" (48:35, the book's climactic conclusion). Chaps. 40—48 may be thought of as representing the institutional realization of the promises of chaps. 33—39—which, as long as the "not yet" remains, will continue to be a valid topic for the "present Jerusalem" (Gal. 4:25).

Again, it is of the essence to remember that we have eschatological, even apocalyptic, copy. (Sometimes one meets the word, "utopian," but it is ultimately as secularistic and inappropriate as it is to speak of Biblical "ideals," "optimism," etc.) Already the rabbis were misguided in worrying about harmonization with the Pentateuch. Some modern scholars too have imagined that the prophet presents a blueprint here which he supposedly could only have written before "P." Actual memories of first-temple features and practices probably entered the priest-prophet's mind, and, used with caution, they have no little historical and archaeological value, but the major import of the section is not along those lines. If one takes the chapters as a unity, as we must, they obviously contain elements which cannot be fulfilled on the earth as we know it (the high mountain of 40:2, the river of life of 47:1 ff., etc.). As Hengstenberg summarized it, we have the words of a prophet, not of an architect. By numerical and other symbolism the chapters seek to evoke all that the temple, "holy land," etc., ultimately signified and sacramentally pointed forward to, in short, Paradise Restored.

Fundamentalist literalism is every bit as misguided, as far as Lutheran confessionalism is concerned. To understand the chapters as predicting a literal rebuilding of the temple and revival of its sacrificial cult in a millennium clashes frontally with the insistence of both gospels and epistles (esp. Hebrews) that Christ's atonement has fulfilled and externally nullified the Old Testament cult once for all. The heirs of the promise are the members of the New Israel by baptismal incorporation into Christ, who is Himself the eschatological temple, the definitive incarnation of God's glory and presence among men.

Ezek. 40—42 depict the rebuilt, eschatological temple itself, the measurements of its various courts and chambers, etc. Led through the same eastern gateways (well illustrated now by archaeological finds at Megiddo, Gezer, Hazor, etc.) by which the *Kabod* will shortly make its reentry, the prophet is escorted through the outer and inner courts up to the vestibule of the temple (chap. 41). After surveying the nave and adytum (only the guide enters the latter) of the sanctuary, the prophet is led back outside for a final survey of the temple area (chap. 42). In contrast to the often irregular dimensions of the historical temples and environs, here everything has perfect symmetrical precision: the entire temple area is a perfect square, etc.

In Ezek. 43 the *Kabod* returns, and a voice from the temple assures the prophet that it will never again forsake the people of Israel, but their bahavior must match its holiness. Vs. 13 ff. describe the altar of burnt offerings at the center of the inner court, its consecration and its ordinances. It is built in stepped fashion like Babylonian ziggurats, probably indicating some of the altar's significance as a miniature temple, a meeting place of heaven and earth (cf. on Is. 28).

Ezek. 44 regulates the priesthood of the new temple. The strictest regulations are enforced to safeguard the sanctity of the temple. Since the *Kabod* had entered via the eastern gateway, it is now permanently closed, except to the "prince" (not the "king," who is God Himself) to eat his sacrificial meal there (vs. 1-3). "Foreigners" (that is, unbelievers) are to be permanently excluded (vs. 6-9). The Levites "who went far from Me" will be limited to the more menial chores of the temple (vs. 9-14), while "the Levitical priests, the sons of Zadok, who kept the charge of My sanctuary when the people of Israel went astray from Me shall come near to Me to minister to Me" (v. 15), that is, for sacrifice itself. Their behavior is regulated (vs. 17-27), and their "inheritance" consists solely in their portion of the offerings (vs. 28-31).

All of this is fundamentally parallel to Pentateuchal regulations, and we need not refute again critical allegations that Ezekiel represents instead the beginnings of such hierarchical arrangements. That is, these regulations are *not* understood as veiled references to power struggles among rival priestly groups, each one concocting fictitious genealogical lines of "apostolic succession" to establish its claim. The poor Levitical response to the return from Babylon (Ezra 2) may correspond, at least in part, to Ezekiel's charge in 44:10; there is no need to feel sympathy for poor, unemployed "country priests" after the alleged deuteronomic centralization of worship. "Sons of Zadok" (44:15) may, according to Hebrew idiom, refer to all descendants of Eleazar, Aaron's oldest son, who remained faithful. The existence of apostate priests no more contradicts Ezekiel's statement than the presence of false prophets neutralizes true prophecy. The descendants of Aaron's other surviving son, Ithamar (Lev. 10) had apparently been in eclipse ever since Abiathar's opposition to Solomon (1 Kings 1—2), although the relations may well have been more complex than that. In any event, we know that the Zadokites did retain the priesthood in Jerusalem until Seleucid interference in Maccabean times. And Biblically, of course, we know of *no* time since the days of Moses when *no* distinctions were made within the tribe of Levi!

Ezek. 45:1-8 continues with an "ideal" distribution of the sacred portion of the land (the other allotments are discussed in 47:13 ff.). A strip is envisioned between the allotments of Judah and Benjamin, with the "prince's" portion contiguous to both the Jordan and the Mediterranean, and the priest's position in the center around the sanctuary, thus further protecting its sanctity. Very specific sacrificial dues, especially at the festivals, are prescribed for the "prince" in 45:13-17; he plainly is only a civic leader of the theocracy, the nation's religious symbol, and dare not arrogate to himself the political and sacerdotal privileges the preexilic monarchy often claimed.

When sundry other regulations have been underscored, and the heavenly guide in 47:1-12 brings Ezekiel back to the door of the temple, the vision becomes even more otherworldly. Water flows out from under the threshold, gradually increasing in depth until it finally sweetens the waters of the Dead Sea and fructifies the entire region. We obviously have here not only a visionary depiction of a "new creation" in general, but specifically of Paradise Restored with its four-streamed river (Gen. 2:10), the river of life. The temple always had sacramentalized that concept (Ps. 46:4; 65:9, etc.) but now it is eschatologized, as often in later prophecy (Joel 3:18; Zech 14:8). Our Lord identifies Himself as its fulfillment (John 4:14; 7:37-38), but the time of the church is still the time of the not-yet (Rev. 22:1-2).

The final vision concludes by continuing the theme of the allotments of the twelve tribes (Ezek. 47:13 ff.), begun in 45:1-5 with discussion of the central, holy portion. In parallel strips, seven tribes are placed north of the portion and five south with the Leah and Rachel tribes closest. No territory in Transjordan is included. Comparison with the historical allotments in Joshua 12 ff. is one of the clearest evidences of the transhistorical character of all the final chapters. The "foursquare city" of Jerusalem will have three gates on each side, named after the twelve tribes.

"And the name of the city henceforth shall be, 'The LORD is there'" (v.35b), the climactic conclusion of the book. Even closer to the consummation is the vision of Rev. 21, which often reworks this chapter and similar prophecies.

The Book of the Twelve

This title to the fourth of the "latter prophets" in the Hebrew canon ("Dodekapropheton" in Greek) is superior to our familiar "minor prophets," which inescapably carries the connotation of a quantitative as well as a qualitative judgment. Of course, no theological judgment is implied, and we have no way of knowing whether their shorter books correspond to shorter ministries or lesser output or neither. In some cases, however, it does seem that they were "one-theme" prophets or nearly so, in contrast to the multiformity of others.

Sometimes the "anthological" character of the Dodekapropheton is used to justify critical theories about the alleged multi-authored composition of the larger books, but the parallel does not hold. The names of the individual "minor prophets" and their discrete literary deposits were always distinguished, in contrast to the speculative anonymity of critical hypotheses. (Cf. also the theory that twelve minor prophets were artifically preserved to correspond to the twelve tribes.)

We still have no good explanation for the sequence of books in the collection of the "Twelve." From Nahum on, the books are in chronological order (except for the slight irregularity of Zephaniah) but before that hardly at all. Thus chronological considerations were plainly a factor, but others also appear to have entered in. The Septuagint has a different order which is even less chronological. Whatever the explanation for the sequence, there is little reason to doubt the hypothesis that they were collected to begin with, because together they filled a scroll of roughly the same size as the three preceding "latter prophets." Just when that might have been done (after the composition of the last book) we have no clue.

HOSEA

Hosea was the only one of the prophets, so far as we know, who was both a native of and active in the North (Amos the latter only). Possibly it is for that reason that he heads the list of the "Twelve." (The proposal that Hosea was placed first because of the use of the word "first" in Hos. 1:2 at best treats the traditionists like dolts). He certainly is not chronologically the earliest, both Jonah and Amos certainly preceding him, and possibly also Joel and Obadiah.

The evidence for Hosea's northern origins is somewhat indirect (depending on how much politics one reads between the lines), but uncontested. The stance appears to be what we associate with the North: covenant, law, God's love, coolness toward kingship, etc. and conversely "southern" accents are in short supply (Zion, temple, cult, Messiah, etc.). Sometimes Hosea is depicted as antimonarchial in principle (perhaps especially Hos. 13:9-11), but that goes beyond the evidence, at best, and appears to be flatly contradicted by 3:5 (which many critics regard as ungenuine). There are many parallels with Deuteronomy and Jeremiah, usually associated especially with the North (although one must avoid critical entrapments in making the association). "Ephraim" is repeatedly referred to, and in 6:8 and 12:11 we find mention of Gilead as part of Israel before Tiglathpileser II annexed it in 732. In 7:5 there is a reference to "our king," apparently in connection with governmental intrigues. Some have tried to be even more precise and locate Hosea in Transjordan, whence Elijah had also hailed. He himself mentions Gilead (cf. above); one of the highest peaks in Gilead is still known in Arabic as *Jebel Osha* (Mt. Hosea), and there is a predominance of rural imagery in the book, but all of this is inconclusive. Neither does it prove that he was originally a farmer, any more than 5:1 ff. makes him a priest (Duhm, etc.) or 9:7-8 an ecstatic prophet.

The superscription is curious. It lists four kings of Judah under which Hosea labored, but only one of Israel (Jeroboam II), and the latter is contemporaneous with only the first of the Judahite kings listed (Uzziah). The total would give Hosea a fairly long ministry of *at least* twenty-seven years (c. 742-715). There is little direct evidence in his book of activity after the fall of Samaria (722), but, then, his book gives relatively little direct evidence of historical occasion of any sort. Hence, there is no good reason to doubt it.

Apparently, the mention of only Jeroboam in the North is meant to be a general reference. Perhaps a disdain for northern kings, especially their short tenure after Jeroboam's death, is implied by omitting mention of the others. That could betray a purely southern viewpoint, but other allusions in the book suggest that Hosea was not particularly enamored of the short-lived northern dynasties. If the superscription stems from well after Samaria's demise, there would be less point in mentioning all the relevant occupants of a now defunct throne.

Critics tend to be entirely skeptical of the superscription, as of all superscriptions. (If there were *text-critical* evidence indicating their later addition, it would be a different matter, but there usually is none, except on minor detail. Until we have such evidence, we have little alternative but to regard them as part of the inspired text.) One typical speculation is that the original superscription mentioned only Jeroboam, with the four Judahite kings added later to try to bring Hosea into Isaiah's orbit. From a more conservative viewpoint, it may also be legitimately argued that the southern kings were listed first and in great detail, even for a northern prophet, because they alone were the bearers of the Messianic promise (cf. also 3:5).

Assuming that Hosea labored in the last years of Israel, one may cautiously align three subdivisions of that history with three sections of the book (cf. below on outline). Hos. 1—3 may reflect the externally halcyon days of Jeroboam's stable reign (some would push its extent up to 5:7); chaps. 4—9 (especially 5:8—6:6, according to Alt's reconstruction) may be taken to reflect the Syro-Ephraimitic alliance against Ahaz (cf. Is. 7) or the anarchic conditions of much of that period in general; and chaps. 10—14 can be read as originating in the last days of Israel under Hoshea. (The king's name is the same as the prophet's—meaning "Yahweh saves"—only conventionally distinguished by different sibilants.) There is no clear indication of events after 722, although the reference in 11:11 to return from Egypt and Assyria has been associated with the Exile.

The problem with all the above associations is that the book's political allusions are cryptic and indirect, at best—presumably corresponding to the posture of the prophet himself. Hosea's major target seems consistently to be the syncretistic cult of the North (so chap. 2 and repeatedly), and hence the high proportion of specifically religious or theological prophecy. If again, however, we recall that Israel was "church" and state, we must take care not to overstate the case. Conservatives have often been as guilty of reducing the material docetically and spiritualistically as liberals and critics have been of onesided pursuit of historical and isagogical occasion.

Of personal information we otherwise know only that Hosea (chap. 1) was the son of one Beeri and that he was married to the prostitute, Gomer, daughter of Diblaim, who bore him three children, two sons and a daughter, to whom he gave the symbolic names of Jezreel (God sows), Lo-ruhamah (Not pitied), and Lo-Ammi (Not my people). (On further interpretation of the names, see below). In chap. 3 we have a further divine command to love an immoral woman (presumably Gomer), so

Hosea buys her (redeems her from slavery?), but keeps her secluded from her former associates.

Interpretation of Hosea's Marriage

The major debate surrounding the Book of Hosea, of course, is whether that account of the prophet's marriage to an adulteress is literal, or symbolic (allegorical, parabolic, or visionary) of the country's faithlessness to its "lord" or husband (following an ancient metaphor; cf. Is. 54; Ezek. 16 and 23). Subsidiary aspects of the issue are whether or not Hosea knew of his wife's character already at marriage, and whether or not chaps. 1 and 3 are to be taken as sequels. Understandably, there is a vast bibliography on the subject.

The old hermeneutical canon of "one *literal* sense" would inevitably tip the scales in favor of taking the story *literally*—and it, no doubt, does so for the majority of both liberals and conservatives. yet there is always the nagging fear that what appears at first blush to be the literal sense may upon closer inspection turn out to be literal*istic,* if that was not the writer's intent. Usually the text gives indications if it wants to be understood in some non-literal fashion, but there are many exceptions (cf. Ezekiel, Canticles, etc.).

It must be stressed that, for once, the issue does not divide along simple conservative-liberal lines, although many conservatives fear that a non-literal interpretation here might be the proverbial "camel's nose in the tent" for similar procedure elsewhere. There are many from both camps on both sides of the fence today, as there have been throughout the history of both church and synagogue. Among the defenders of a literal intent are: Irenaeus, Theodore of Mopsuestia, Augustine, Luther, Laetsch, and probably a majority of modern exegetes, especially in the critical camp. Defenders of an allegorical intent (many of whom one is surprised to find here) include the Targum, Jerome, most medieval commentators, Calvin, Gunkel, Gressmann, von Rad, Young, and many evangelicals. A sort of middle position (really more a subdivision of the allegorical understanding) defends the view that the prophet saw this "marriage" as a vision: Origen, Ibn Ezra, Kimchi, Hengstenberg, Keil, etc. Still others try to ease the problem by treating Hos. 1—3 differently (cf. below).

The major argument for an allegorical, parabolic or other "spiritual" understanding is that a righteous God would never command such a thing, all the more so in the light of laws (Lev. 19:29 and Deut. 23:17) that exclude prostitutes from the theocratic congregation and prescribe stoning for an adulteress (critics might well argue that the laws are later than Hosea). Similarly, then, the argument goes, how could such a prophet have an effective ministry, any more than a modern pastor would under such circumstances? And what kind of an example would that set for God's people? Another line of argument points out that the husband-wife metaphor scarcely appears in the Book of Hosea after chap. 3, being replaced (if any metaphor is used) by the father-son analogy. Von Rad, who defends a non-literal position, is apparently overreacting against the classically liberal effort to extract minute biographical information in precise historical circumstance from the prophetical literature.

The major reply (with which this writer identifies himself) would have to be that the same God who made such commands is free, on exceptional occasion, to suspend them (much as He can with "laws of nature" in the case of miracles). Kline gives it as one example of his principle of "eschatological suspension of ethics." No doubt, this is an extreme, almost repugnant, example, but in principle it differs little from many other bizarre action-prophecies, especially in the case of Ezekiel. Many of the prophets' whole lives were standing action-prophecies, and Hosea fits readily into the pattern. And, no doubt about it, such behavior would highlight in the extreme a major theological point of Hosea himself, namely, God's election and continuing love for a people who had not merited it in the slightest (cf. Deut. 7:7; Ezek. 16). Negatively, one of the major weaknesses of any real allegorical approach is the apparent impossibility of finding any convincing symbolic meaning for the names Gomer and Diblaim.

There is a certain undeniable attractiveness for the centrist position that Hosea was not *aware* of Gomer's propensities at the time of marriage (so Wellhausen, Eichrodt, Bright, Marti, C. J. Pfeiffer, G. W. Anderson, etc.). Either "wife of whoredoms" in Hos. 1:2a is understood as Hosea's own sad, retrospective statement, or, more conservatively, that, of Gomer, it is initially used proleptically but with immediate metaphorical application, "for the land commits great harlotry by forsaking the LORD" (1:2b). 2:2 is then often understood as containing an actual divorce formula after Gomer began her life of sin. But just as God purposed to restore Israel after the "divorce" of the Exile (cf. Is. 50 and 54), so Hosea later reclaims his wife, who, now chastened and repentant, no longer lusts after her former ways but is content to be faithful to her husband ("lord"). (The double application of the Hebrew "baal" to both religious and marital "lords" greatly facilitates this interpretation, and it undeniably is part of the text's *theological* import, regardless of the issue at hand.)

This position inevitably overlaps with the broader issue of the relation between Hosea 1 and 3. The one just described understands the "woman" of 3:1 as identical with the "wife of whoredom" of 1:2. Less conservative positions either posit two entirely different women (but both chapters taken literally), or take chap. 1 as literal and 3 as allegorical (the latter then simply a theological commentary on the state of affairs, much as chap. 2). Grammatically, the issue turns partly on the punctuation of "again" (odh) in 3:1. Is it "Yahweh said, 'Go again . . .' "; or is it "Yahweh said (spoke) again: . . .' "? The majority of translations follow the Masoretic accents and prefer the former, and while we would agree that that is probably correct, we must remember that the Hebrew pointing is not part of the inspired text. Militating against it undeniably is the usual Hebrew word order ("again" precedes "go"). Some commentators have also tried to exploit the fact that chap. 1 is presented in the third person (about Hosea; B type), while chap. 3 is in the first person (A type). The variation could betray entirely unrelated narratives, but transmissional variation or simple stylistic change could also account for it.

Yet, when all is said and done, "unus sensus literalis" still seems to cast a decisive vote in favor of not only taking Hos. 1 and 3 as simple sequels in one literal, historical narrative, but also in favor of the interpretation that Hosea, upon God's explicit command, understood perfectly well at the outset what he was getting into! This implies that after the birth of their third child, however, Gomer either left her husband, or they were separated and/or divorced. She eventually fell into slavery, whence Hosea redeemed her and brought her back to his home, an entirely different woman. The word translated "brought" in 3:2 is unusual, but at least its general meaning seems well established.

This interpretation yields a superb basis for the theological application to Israel's history of deserved Exile but eventual return, which is implicit in both Hos. 1 and 3, and very explicit in the intervening chap. 2. What Hosea then predicts or typifies by his marital life is exactly parallel to the message of virtually all the other preexilic prophets. It is very true that Hosea's theological lesson comes through pellucidly even if the marriage is understood as an allegory, parable, or vision, but then one also runs the risk of indulging in precisely that dichotomy of theology and history, of the "Christ of faith" and "Jesus of history," which is all but synonymous with historical-critical method. However one must concede that the simple antisupernaturalism and disregard of New Testament testimony which often complicates issues of this sort are not necessarily involved here.

Two minor aspects of the issue must be mentioned. The first, fortunately, is now largely behind us. In the days when Freud was all but regarded as among the inspired prophets, various efforts (Allwohn, Oesterley, Sellers) were made to psychoanalyze Hosea. The general line seemed to be that the struggle between his subsconscious obsession with sex and the purity or even prudishness of his conscious thought was finally sublimated in a theological message, where Yahweh's love for a disgusting people receives extraordinarily powerful expression. I suppose one might concede a possible germ of truth here with respect to the purely human aspects of the mystery of divine revelation in Hosea's case, but, at very best, it contributes little or nothing to the interpretation of the message.

A more significant variant suggests that Gomer was no ordinary hooker but a *sacral* prostitute, of the type that we know well from Mesopotamia as well as Canaan, and which even invaded the temple of Jerusalem in its darker days, as Kings does not hesitate to report. Various marital arrangements with such prostitutes are also known from archaeological finds. Hence, it is by no means unthinkable that Gomer too was a hierodule of that sort, and possibly even in the quasi-Yahwistic northern shrines of Bethel or Dan. The theological application would ulltimately be the same, but the specific religious conflict with Baalism would be highlighted. The major weakness of this approach, however, is that Hebrew and Canaanite have a specific word for *"sacral* prostitute" *(qedeshah,* "holy woman" (!) which is *not* used in chaps. 1—3, (although it is later in 4:14). Hence, at best, this possibility must remain hypothetical.

Style and Text

Some have hypothesized that Hosea's style is related to his marital experience, or to his reaction to it. Certainly his style is relatively unique among the prophets and provides about the greatest possible contrast to the elegant, classical Hebrew of an Amos or Isaiah. It is not flowing and regular, but staccatto and jagged. Already Jerome styled it *"commaticus,"* that is, broken up by commas or asyndetic connections into many clauses. A modern commentator describes it as "an artless rhythm of sighs and sobs." At the same time, this need not imply any ultimately negative judgment (cf. on Ezekiel). There is frequent paronomasia, and many striking and effective pictures, although usually indicated by only the bare simile or metaphor and rarely worked out.

Hosea's style in turn may have something to do with the text-critical problem of the book—easily (at least as concerns the Masoretic tradition itself) the worst in the whole Old Testament (followed by Ezekiel and Samuel). As usual, we do not have a clue as to why this is the case. In addition to his style, it has been plausibly suggested that Hosea's northern dialect (the differences from that of Jerusalem we are now able to document somewhat) was less familiar to later copyists, and may have been a contributing factor. Hos. 1—3 are generally in somewhat better shape than the rest of the book, but that is a relative matter. Scarcely a single verse in the entire book has entirely escaped. Of course, many of the problems are trivial and critics have not always been above exaggerating and aggravating the problems. Nevertheless, there is no denying that in many instances the MT as it stands is simple gibberish, and the translator has no alternative but to resort to conjecture. The Septuagint, as so often, frequently goes its own way. The worst corruptions appear to have occurred before the bifurcation of the traditions, which means that the Greek renditions are themselves often conjectural. Even in the case of Hosea, however, only the precise details are ordinarily affected; rarely is the main thrust and message at stake.

Outline and Structure

The extreme difficulty of outlining the Book of Hosea may also be a derivative of Hosea's personality and style and may also have aggravated the textual problem. Beyond Hos. 1—3 it is difficult to say anything but "Varied Oracles." In the total absence of Gentile oracles, one cannot expect to find the classical tripartite prophetic outline. Yet nowhere does the thematic of judgment and grace, Law and Gospel, seem more indigenous, and it may be reflected more relaxedly also in the sequence of oracles. Possibly one can discern a primary accent on Israel's guilt in chaps. 4—8, on Israel's punishment in 9—11, and on both in chaps. 12—14, with an undeniable denouement in promise or hope in chap. 14.

The question inevitably overlaps with that of "tradition-history" in the neutral sense of the term—whether it was Hosea or successors who were responsible for the final shape of the book. Many of the oracles give the impression of being only fragmentarily preserved, or else of having been condensed to the point of ambiguity and obscurity. How much of this reflects Hosea's own style of preaching? Recent form-critical suggestions that the book contains only a string of isolated, kerygmatic units might seem to apply to Hosea as well as anywhere, but the reception has been indifferent. The form-critical proposal, however, that Hosea's frequent *Sitz im Leben* was the licentious festivals of the North may have more merit and would account for the relatively apolitical, religious concentration of the book.

We also noted above a possible threefold chronological division of the book, corresponding to three phases of the last years of the Northern Kingdom. Some profess to find a general accusation-threat-promise movement in all three of those complexes. Catchwords and liturgical influences may be in evidence (e.g., Hos. 5:15—6:3 and chap. 14), and the recent interest in wisdom has not overlooked the clearly proverbial character of the final verse in the book (14:9). Chap. 11 has been understood as opening a fresh collection of oracles emphasizing the apostasy of Yahweh's "son" rather than of His "wife." Bentzen thought to distinguish a special collection of oracles in 9:10—14:10, imitating funeral dirges, and organized around the theme: "Oh, how different things were . . ." (i.e., in the wilderness honeymoon period, before entry into Canaan corrupted Yahweh's relation with His people).

Finally, we may note a proposal to divide Hosea at the end of chap. 2 and to discern a symmetry between the two parts, each arranged according to an "alternation of weal and woe" scheme (this is especially attractive if chaps. 1 and 3 refer to two different marriages). According to this proposal, we would have the first marriage presented in threat (1:1-9) and promise (1:10—2:1), followed by a commentary with the same alternation (2:2-13 and 2:14-23). Likewise, the second marriage (3:1-4 and 3:5) followed by three alternations of threat and promise in commentary (4:1-5, 15a and 5:15b—6:3; 6:4—11:7 and 11:8-11; 13:12-13, 16 and 14:1-9). Perhaps the major weakness of this intriguing suggestion is the gross inequality in size of the two parts.

Perhaps there is a connection between tradition-history's inability to achieve any certain results and the relatively tame behavior of higher criticism of Hosea in general. Kaufmann's idiosyncratic suggestion that Hos. 1—3 and 4—14 have to do with two entirely different Hoseas has found no takers. The mainstream of criticism challenged two types of material in Hosea: the oracles of hope and those referring to Judah.

The latter were often rejected as unlikely on the lips of a northern prophet, and hence probably later additions. Most of them, however, are critical of Judah—not what one would expect of Judahite supplements. If Hosea was active at all in the South after Samaria's fall, as the superscription clearly indicates he was, this minimal deposit of his preaching there would almost be expected. Perhaps, above all, there is no good reason why a northern prophet should not set his sights on "greater Israel" as one people of God any less than the southern prophets obviously did, while the North still stood. Hos. 12:2 appears to be a good example and in the pericope, 5:8—6:6, Judah is intrinsic to the sense. The biggest problem in this connection arises with the mention of "David, their king" at 3:5; cf. below. We must also take note of Swedish critic Nyberg's use of Hosea for a major counterattack upon the usual critical penchant for conjectural divisions into genuine and ungenuine, together with theories of a complicated transmissional history.

A few critics attempted to excise the oracles of hope in Hosea, largely on the basis of the old liberal dogma that true prophets were not supposed to talk that way. This prepossession was extremely difficult to apply to Hosea, however, not only because of the obviously positive outcome of his marriage, whether taken literally or figuratively, but also because of many expressions of undying love all through the rest of the book. Hence, even the critical following was quite restricted at this point. One cannot refrain, however, from observing how nearly fatal the integral accent on promise in Hosea is to the entire liberal-critical presupposition, especially in so early a prophet as Hosea! Many critics simply passed by the embarrassing "exception" on the other side. A few tried to turn it to advantage by arguing that Hosea's hope indicated that he was one of the most radical of all in his expectation of judgment. Others tried to compensate by construing Hosea alongside Jeremiah as a major exemplar of a true prophet's interior struggles, that is of their own "man against the system" notion of what a prophet should be, prototypes of the "liberated" man of the Renaissance, free, uninhibited spirits, unshackled by convention, speaking *ad hoc* to problems as the spirit "listed."

Contents

As concerns content, one must note again the "great reversal" pattern centering about the symbolic names of the children, Hos. 1:1-9 versus 1:10—2:1, and again in 2:2-13 versus 2:14-23. The name, "Not my people" attaches to the fundamental covenant promise that they would *really* be His people and He their God (vs. 8, 10, 23). The fulfillment of the promise in Christ and the Christian church is proclaimed in 1 Peter 2:10. Note also the obvious reference in Hos. 1:10 to the Abrahamic promise of innumerable descendants (cf. St. Paul in Rom. 9:25, 26).

The name "Jezreel," however, receives a double interpretation (to critics sometimes a sign of a seam, as though Hosea himself could not have interpreted it in more than one way). In vs. 4-5 and probably also v. 10, the name is not explained etymologically like the other names, but geographically and historically, with respect to the bloodbath on the site by which Jehu had come to power about a century earlier (2 Kings 9—10). That revolt had occurred with the active encouragement of Elisha, but Hosea's condemnation of it here need not imply some kind of "contradiction," but only that God had not ultimately sanctioned procedures of which He had nevertheless made use (much as with foreign nations, especially Assyria and Babylonia). In 2:22, however, we have an etymological explanation of the name: Jezreel means "God will sow," that is, fructify the entire earth in the "new creation" aspect of the eschatological reversal.

Hos. 2, interposed between the biographical account of chap. 1 and the autobiographical narrative of chap. 3, is almost pure theological application of the marriage to Israel and appears in form to be a speech by Yahweh Himself. The Hebrew text begins Chap. 2 already at 1:10 in most Western versions, which follow the Septuagintal chapter divisions. The difference is not only formal, as evidenced by the way 2:1 in our division seems to belong to chap. 1 and by the unusually abrupt transition (even for Hosea) to 2:2. Critics often assume some displacement in transmission, and offer their own rearrangements, most commonly either, in effect, to insert chap. 3 between 1:9 and 1:10, or to move 1:10—2:1 to the end of chap. 2. One cannot *a priori* exclude such possibilities, but they appear to raise as many questions as they answer.

"Plead" in Hos. 2:2 translates the Hebrew *rib,* which almost unanimously today is interpreted as another example of "covenant lawsuit," that is presupposing the *Sitz im Leben* of Yahweh as judge presiding over the heavenly court, calling His people to account for their infractions. The same *Gattung* appears in 4:1 (translated "controversy"), 4:4 (translated, "contend"), and 12:2 (MT 12:3, translated, "indictment").

In 2:14 ff. Hosea introduces the theme of return to the wilderness (starting over from scratch, as it were, in the new aeon with a new honeymoon), a theme to which he later returns (7:16 and 11:5) to press the "second Exodus" typology even further into a "return to Egypt," which must precede the eschatological reversal. The portrait here and in Jer. 2:2 of the wilderness period, as one of Israelite faithfulness in contrast to the picture in Ezekiel and "P" of that era as one of unbroken apostasy is a major liberal-critical proof text of its dogma of the errancy of Scripture. Yet it should be noted that elsewhere in the book (9:10, 15; 11:2; 13:6) Hosea too refers to the wilderness period negatively, and it is unlikely that Hosea would contradict himself. Obviously, it all depends upon what the theological point of comparison is at the moment!

In a way, the change between calling God "husband" (*'ish*) and "Baal" in Hos. 2:16 is only nominal, because in Hebrew "baal" also meant "lord/husband." Nevertheless, in the struggles to the death between Yahwism and Baalism at the time, the latter usage was so fraught with pagan overtones that mere use of it was virtually compromising. As we have noted, at least in earlier times many apparently orthodox Israelites had applied the epithet "baal" to Yahweh quite innocently (e.g., Gideon, Saul's sons), but Hosea insists that those days are no more (and study of Israelite onomastica does indicate a clear shift away from the earlier usage about this time, especially after the fall of the North).

The covenant which Hosea continues to describe (2:18 ff.) includes the standard prophetic features of "new creation," of a perfect society with eternal peace, etc. In vs. 19-20, Hosea picks up the marital metaphor again, and rather daringly describes the eschatological climax of the covenant promise in terms of the consummation of a human marriage.

The two verses are also almost a catalogue of the most important theological vocabulary in the Old Testament.

After that full eschatological portrait, one should not be surprised that 3:5b is explicitly Messianic, and describes the children of *Israel* as returning to "David their king—in the latter days." Critics quite unanimously excise this half of the verse, as though no northerner would ever have such regard for David—or for the second David. (Often it is explained as a scribal addition from Jer. 30:9) However, plainly *a prioris* are calling the shots in such judgments. Even if Hosea had never been active in the South, there is no reason why he should not have been disgusted with conditions in the North, or why the legitimacy of the Davidic throne before the North's separation should not have been recognized. People in the North presumably longed for reunification as much as many in the South. And in that presecular context, religious hopes inevitably accompanied political ones.

The next pericope of note for our purposes is Hos. 5:15—6:6. Since Alt, many commentators have viewed it in relation to the preceding verses as political commentary in relation to Assyria's first major incursions into Israel in 735 ff. These verses are to express the prophet's hope for a new nonpolitical, quasi-religious national policy. If so, Hosea's "political" commentary would be very similar to Isaiah's. However, the fact that the book itself does not clearly reveal any such occasion is a major illustration of the undue priority which historical criticism attaches to such questions. Even if true, we are little better off for the knowledge, and plainly the book itself invites us to concentrate on the theological message.

What is that message? The different answers in commentaries are illustrative of difficulties the exegete often faces in Hosea. Much depends on where we put quotes (there are none in Hebrew) and how we relate components to each other and to the context. Hos. 6:1 ff. may well be the people's response to God's previous speech, but in what sense? One line of interpretation (omitting the "saying" of RSV, which is not in the Hebrew) sees 6:1-3 as an expression of the people's superficial or even insincere "repentance," which the prophet condemns in vs. 4-6. With that contrast, the confession can indeed be read as a mechanical, ritualistic one, with Yahweh "bound," as though in a nature cult, to respond favorably if they go through the right motions. Efforts have even been made to relate the "resurrection" of v. 2 to the vegetation rites of Tammuz (Adonis, Osiris). However, it should be noted that it is the people, not some god, who rises! "After two days" and "on the third day" are essentially synonymous, a type of synonymous parallelism which we often meet in ancient Oriental poetry, and which here simply means "in a very short time." There is no evidence, however, of its association with the fertility cult and fertility;

"new creation" language is commonly associated with Yahweh's redemption in prophetic literature (e.g., Is 45:8).

It seems preferable then to understand Hos. 6:1-3 as a sincere confession, expressed in typical, highly poetic language, not unlike what we meet elsewhere in the book. If so, traditional interpretation of v. 2 as eschatological, even specifically predictive of Christ's resurrection, becomes at least possible. The Targum applies it to "the days of consolation," and Calvin to the return from the Exile. Luther, however, after Tertullian and many of the fathers, saw the resurrection as the primary sense, and argued that this was Paul's "according to the Scriptures" reference in 1 Cor. 15:4. Typologically, the latter must ultimately be involved (if this is a sincere confession), but we scarcely have warrant to be more rigid. Paul's reference may not be so much to individual passages (although cf. Is. 53 and Ezek. 37) as to the judgment-salvation, death-resurrection pattern throughout the Old Testament.

Liberals once liked to seize upon Hos. 6:6 (alongside Jer. 7:21-23 and other passages) as proof positive of the true prophets' opposition to externals like cult. What further need had they of witnesses when Jesus, the greatest of the prophets, made those words his own (Matt. 9:13; 12:7)? Today, however, it is widely conceded that they were overeager. As we noted earlier, the "not" in 6a is an example of hyperbole or "dialectical negation," and is qualified by the parallel "rather than."

The following series of vivid descriptions of Ephraim's fickle faithlessness (perhaps especially Hos. 7:4, 8, 9, 11; 8:7, 12; 9:11, 14), is punctuated by a clear typological tendency, essentially the same that we met in chap. 2. Both judgment and salvation are described as a "repetition" of the circumstances of Israel's birth, that is, in later language, Israel must be "reborn." Since "laws by ten thousands" (8:12) would be futile, Israel must "return to Egypt" (8:13; 9:6; 11:5; 12:9-13), that is to the grave, to Sheol. Sometimes "Egypt" is paralleled with "Assyria" (11:5; perhaps 9:6) as a reminder that the names are used symbolically or typologically—just as in the Gentile oracles of other prophets.

In Hos. 9:10 the Exodus and wilderness sojourn are sarcastically described as eventuating only in the licentious idolatry of Baalpeor (Num. 25), typical of Israel's behavior down to the present day. Chap. 11:1 picks up the same theme, describing Israel as a headstrong child, straining to be "free" of its father's guiding hand, and 12:13 refers to Moses as a "prophet" (the like of which God could raise up again after their punishment). In spite of their fractiousness, He remains their loving father (cf. the husband metaphor in chaps. 1—3), even when as "Holy One" (cf. Isaiah) he must chastise (11:8-9). Matthew's application (2:15) of 11:1 to Jesus' return from Egypt is surely also typological in its point of departure (Jesus as "Israel reduced to one," the Son, *the* Elect One, recapitulating and consummating in His life the history of the "son," the elect people), but, as we have stressed many times, that is complementary to, not contradictory of, prophecy in the predictive sense.

Nearly all of Hos. chap. 12 appears to compare and contrast Ephraim with its ancestor, Jacob (in v. 2 also parallel with Judah, which critics, however, often regard as a late alteration). The general gist appears to be that instead of emulating the patriarch's behavior *after* his change of name and heart at Penuel (Gen. 32), they have behaved like the subethical, cheating trader (v. 7, literally "Canaan") Jacob has previously been. Critics have convinced themselves that Hosea remembers a different version of the Jacob "legend" than "JE," but it is much more presupposition than demonstrated conclusion.

Hos. 13:14 is another ancient and famous *crux*, not least because of St. Paul's famous quotation in 1 Cor. 15:55. Paul, however, cites it according to the Septuagint (as commonly) which takes it as a glorious promise, in contrast to understanding it as a threat, as most modern commentators and translators do. Context might favor the latter, but its weight is often minimal in Hosea, or one could have here "alternation of weal." Thus, the verse might depict either the Father pitying his wayward son, or Yahweh Himself using Death and Sheol as His instruments to flail the rebel mercilessly. Even in the latter case, Yahweh is plainly master of death and the grave (in contrast to Canaanite dualism and fatalism), the definitive mastery of which the Greek translation highlights more, and as realized on Easter morning.

Theology

It remains to underscore the importance of Hosea from a "Biblical theology" perspective, perhaps the greatest among the minor prophets. At any rate, Hosea looks far better in that light than he did to classical criticism. He did not readily fit into the early, rather atheological evolutionistic scheme, and so was criticized for not pursuing and developing the ethical and universalistic perspectives that Amos had allegedly pioneered. At most he was credited with making a slight "advance" in shifting the basis of religion a bit from fear to love, but, as we noted, those critics lacked the presuppositional equipment to appreciate Hosea's accent on the "resurrection" which necessarily would follow after the judgment. In recent criticism that approach is usually muted, but it is still deemed necessary to read Hosea as one of the great "sources" of especially Jeremiah and Deuteronomy, rather than tracing the Mosaic roots of all three. Hosea did not pioneer his themes, but he does often give beautiful and classical expression of them. (It is *possible,* however, that Hosea originated the metaphor of God—later Christ—as the groom of the people of God; cf. Canticles, Eph. 5, etc.)

To those with theological antennae, Hosea's more direct and more exclusive religious formulations are highly prized. Nor is it accidental that Hosea is the most frequently quoted of all the minor prophets in the New Testament (some thirty times, exceeded in frequency only by the much longer Isaiah and Psalms).

The reason, obviously, is that Hosea is one of the most overtly "evangelical" of the Old Testament books. Hosea is the major prophet of Yahweh's "love," and among the eighth-century prophets he is often compared in that respect with Amos' accent on "justice" and Isaiah's on "holiness." Sometimes Hosea is styled the "St. John of the Old Testament" (and, if so, the Book of Deuteronomy must certainly be included).

Hosea is adept in his deployment of especially two Hebrew vocables to articulate that theme. The two appear in parallelism in Hos. 6:6, but also often elsewhere. The first is the untranslatable *"chesedh,"* that unique *covenant* relationship (no universal quality or ideal), both vertically between God and man, and horizontally among covenant-brethren. Possibly "devotion" is the best rendering, but one also meets "loving-kindness" (KJV), "steadfast love," (RSV), "grace", "mercy," etc. It is the Old Testament's single closest equivalent to the New Testament's *agape.* The analogy to the marital covenant is always close at hand: the same combination of emotional attachment and volitional determination is of the essence in both cases.

The other root is *yadha,* to "know" or the gerund, *da'ath,* "knowledge" (cf. also 4:6). Much more than our English equivalent, the Hebrew term is emotional or relational as well as intellectual. Sometimes "love" is again the best single translation, and its use still today as a euphemism for sexual intimacies has its roots in the Bible. Care must be taken to maintain balance, however. Orthodoxy, no doubt, sometimes accented intellectual assent to doctrinal propositions onesidedly, but existentialism has been at least guilty in virtually reducing the term to some irrational mysticism. The problem with this word almost epitomizes the radically different epistemologies or "theories of knowledge" underlying all the other differences between liberalism and conservatism.

Hosea's stress on "knowledge" is paralleled by another motif which informs much of the book, namely "remember," although the vocable itself is not prominent. Perhaps more than any other prophet, Hosea is the prophet of *"Heilsgeschichte."* Israel's basic failure is that she does not "remember," but pursues other lovers instead. Because Israel does forget or tends to idealize the past to her advantage, Hosea recalls some rather uncomplimentary episodes of the past (Baalpeor, Jacob's youth, etc.) As often in the Bible, "remember" like "know" is far more than mere mental recollection, but includes involvement, commitment, participation. (Cf. also the *"Anamnesis"* of the Eucharist.)

Especially for the sake of Christian appropriation of Hosea's review of Israel's history, the prominent and intrinsic typology accompanying it must be underscored. By his marital history, Hosea himself had become a walking type, an internalization and "incarnation" of the inner meaning of God's way with Israel. And that way reached its *telos* and *plēroma* in Jesus of Nazareth (of which Hosea 11:1 and Matt. 2:15 are the classical exemplification), but also a way or pattern to continue individually and corporately in all who are baptized into Him. It is incorrect to make Hosea the "father of typology" as some critics do, but the truth in the assertion is Hosea's importance as a Biblical source for understanding and presenting that pivotal concept.

Finally, in all of this, however, the pivotal role which judgment or Law plays in Hosea must not be lost sight of. Again, confession of the unity of Sacred Scripture forbids us to join some critics in making Hosea the "father" of Israelite eschatology, often with the assumption that Amos preached only doom (cf. below). The central prophetic paradox of total rebirth rising out of total destruction was not *born* in the chaotic milieu of Hosea's life, but, humanly speaking, that ambiance obviously was a major catalyst in provoking one of the profoundest Biblical presentations of Law-Gospel. If we forget that Hosea proclaimed the ineluctability of Exile as unflinchingly as any other prophet, not only is the prophet himself readily caricatured into a silly sentimentalist, but we pervert his robust and profoundly evangelical message into that "other gospel" of "God accepts you as you are."

JOEL

Less is known of Joel's historical situation and personal circumstance than any other prophet. As a result, the book is a major reminder that the Bible's real concern is not history as such but with history in the sense of His-story, that is, the inner, ultimate "sacramental" meaning of events in the total horizon of God's relation to man.

About all we can say with assurance is that he was the son of one Pethuel, and that his oracles center about a locust plague affecting Jerusalem and the temple. The strongly liturgical cast of the book might suggest that he was a priest or "cultic prophet," but even that is a guess. Some regard even his name ("Yahweh is God") as a sobriquet for anonymity, but that is surely speculative! Locust plagues, of course, were a recurrent phenomenon.

Date of the Book

Where facts are lacking, theories and presuppositions rush in to fill the gap. Guesses as to Joel's date range over nearly half a millennium, through the entire history of prophecy, from one of the earliest to one of the latest. Because of its many parallels with other prophetic books, it is regarded as either the original prophetic quarry or the latest conglomerate of quotations.

A traditional viewpoint, still defended by some conservatives, makes Joel one of the earliest of the prophets, perhaps second only to Obadiah, who may be dated some twenty years earlier. Because no king is mentioned, many located Joel's ministry in the *ninth* century under the regency of the priest Jehoiada during Joash's minority after Athaliah's deposition (c. 837 ff.). That historical argument was buttressed by Joel's location in the Hebrew canon, but, as we have seen, that consideration carries little weight, especially because we know of other sequences in antiquity. A related consideration was Amos' alleged dependence on Joel: there certainly are a number of parallels, but that argument is a two-edged sword, and some argue that it was these parallels which led to Joel's placement in the canon next to Amos. (Certainly, if Joel did precede Amos, much of the extravagant praise critics have often showered on Amos for his alleged originality has to be retracted!) There are also some close parallels with Obadiah (depending on its dating), and possibly Joel 2:32 ("as the LORD has said") is quoting Obad. 17. The enemies mentioned in Joel, it is furthermore argued, are more those of the preexilic period (Philistia, Phoenicia, Egypt, Edom) than of later time (Syria, Assyria, Babylonia). Finally, among the major arguments was appeal to Joel's relatively classical style, considerably different from that of many known postexilic figures.

With the rise of historical criticism in the nineteenth century a late postexilic date became more popular, and still prevails today, though with many dissenters. (At critical hands, devaluation of its worth often also accompanied late dating, though not always.) Just how late varies, but many are prepared to situate Joel as late as the fourth century, not long before the arrival of Alexander the Great (a few even in Maccabean times). Scandinavian scholars prefer a late seventh-century date, contemporary with Josiah and the battle of Megiddo. The arguments for a later date are as inconclusive as those for an early one. Furthermore, many of them are based on developmental suppositions, and thus constitute an argument in a circle. At the same time, their applicability to

Joel cannot be dismissed out of hand either. It is only that they lose their cogency if not accompanied by a redistribution of the contents of other prophetical literature along the same lines.

The major argument for Joel's alleged lateness is the general, universal character of the references. Specific sins are not mentioned, and the "day of the LORD" arises not so much against Israel or even specific, historical enemies, as against transhistorical, eschatological ones (e.g. the "northerner" of Joel 2:20). What specific references there are (remnant, dispersion, "Israel" applied to the South, etc.) are taken to presuppose postexilic circumstances. There is no denying the observations, as such, but in a context of Biblical integrality they tell us little about date. Also the distinction between historical and transhistorical cannot be sustained, because it informs the entire Biblical viewpoint.

Related is the argument from Joel's alleged proto-apocalyptic character. The locusts, especially in chap. 2, have this coloration, and the showdown battles in the last times between *all* nations and Jerusalem of the final chapters may be so construed. Accent on the "spirit of Yahweh" was also supposed to be a case in point. However, as we have noted, "apocalyptic" is an exceedingly elusive entity to begin with, and the question of the date of its rise is bound up with critical issues (especially the date of Daniel).

Another consideration is Joel's preoccupation with cultic matters, allegedly pointing to postexilic circumstances when little else was left to Judah besides its temple and cult. That argument might carry much weight if one bought the critical reconstruction of much of the cult first becoming dominant after the Exile, but the Bible presents another picture! If Joel is the "sacramentarian" of the prophets, it is only because he champions one of its valid, intrinsic elements.

Fourth, Joel's alleged frequent quotation of early prophecy (as these supposedly were beginning to assume canonical status) is supposed to be characteristic of late prophecy. (There are some 22 parallels with 12 other books.) The Book of Zechariah demonstrates that there may be some truth to the general principle, but, apart from corroborating evidence, it is difficult to determine who was dependent on whom (cf. above on the parallels with Amos.) The argument is also undercut by indications that prophets in all ages apparently often drew on a common pool of traditional phraseology and imagery, much of it derived from the cult and/or from erstwhile mythology (and both sources seem to be much in evidence in the Book of Joel).

Finally, we may note that, as with most alleged postexilic literature, it once was fashionable in criticism to adduce linguistic evidence for lateness. Ugaritic and other philological discoveries have now all but demolished that approach, although on a much more subjective basis many still attempt to apply it to Joel. Somewhat related was the former argument that mention of trade with "Greeks" in Joel 3:6 forced a date near the Hellenistic period, but archaeology has shown that trade with the Aegean region even antedated Israel.

In sum, all we can say about the date of Joel is *Ignoramus et ignorabimus!* The book does not diminish the value and necessity of "historical criticism" (in the narrow and neutral sense), but it does deflate much of its arrogance and pretense as usually practiced, and impels us toward a truly Biblical definition of "history."

Unity and Message

In critical circles, however, the question of the date of Joel is often quite inextricable from the issue of its unity. Especially after Duhm again, it was widely held (and still often is) that Joel himself was responsible for only the first half of the book (1:2—2:27; the locust plague itself). The latter half (2:28—3:21) was supposed to have been contributed by some later apocalyptist ("Deutero-Joel"), who linked his work to the first half by interpolating "Day of Yahweh" at four points (1:15; 2:1b, 2a, 11b).

The real issue here (and by no means only in a critical context) is the relation between present and future or between historical and eschatological in the book. At one (critical) extreme the unity of the book was sometimes defended by viewing the entire book as late and apocalyptic (that is, also the locusts as mere symbols of apocalyptic terrors). The other extreme, perhaps ascendant today, softpedals the eschatological character of the book, or "demythologizes" it into no more than a symbol of ultimacy. Joel is supposed to be interested only in the everyday distress of his contemporaries; the book's eschatological perspectives are "only intended to emphasize the terribleness of the present distress and are not there for their own sake"; thus Joel exemplifies "the true character of prophecy" (Eissfeldt).

One traditional view coincides in many respects with the first critical view noted above (never questioning the book's unity and usually dating it much earlier). This is the ancient tradition (the fathers, Calvin, Young, etc.) of allegorizing Joel 1—2, or viewing it as totally predictive. Some (e.g., Hengstenberg) even wanted to align the four different types of locusts with the four world empires of Daniel.

Other conservatives (e.g., Keil) argued for more immediate, historical connection, while also emphasizing their typical, eschatological significance. This is the viewpoint defended here. It has a superficial correspondence with the second critical view above, but with a radical difference in seeing an integral, "sacramental" connection between the two levels of meaning (sometimes one level highlighted more, sometimes the other, but always both). In fact, that theological exposition of the Biblical understanding of *H*istory is at the heart of the significance of the Book of Joel. Expressed hermeneutically, *unus sensus literalis* compels us to take the locusts literally, but not for their own sake. The "one sense" is multiple, though remaining unified. These locusts are also "symbols," that is, sacramental of, proleptic of, and already participating in the final judgment—which is also literal! Every day *is* judgment day, but there also *is* a (final, eschatological) Judgment Day. Joel thus clarifies as succinctly and classically as any prophet that interpenetration of history and eschatology, of vertical and horizontal, of immanent and transcendent, the improper understanding of which lies at the very heart of most modern theological confusion.

Scandinavian scholars especially (Kapelrud, Ahlström) have defended the unity of the book and neutralized the traditional history-eschatology dichotomy by appeal to *Religionsgeschichte* and to the cult. Their precise form of presentation (a semipagan, highly "syncretistic," pre-Levitical cult) and many details are uncongenial to conservatism, but an adaptation of it may underscore the thesis just defended. Canaanite parallelism is undoubtedly exaggerated, but there is no reason to deny that many pre-Israelite elements were adapted or "baptized" into a different context by the cult as well as by the prophets. From the standpoint of Biblical theology, however, "syncretism" is then a thoroughly misleading term. Likewise, to associate the book with a putative "New Year's festival" is speculative, at best. Similarly, to label Joel a "cultic/temple prophet" (sometimes he was put forth as a prime example) either belabors the obvious, or raises more questions than it answers.

All these excrescences notwithstanding, the basic cultic orientation may help to bring into relief some of the permanent significance of the book. Liturgy by definition deals with the irruption of eternity into time, of the concentration of all of Time into the present existential and sacramental moment before God (not escape from it, as in pagan cult). If Joel writes from that perspective, one can understand why the historical particulars are less important to him, and why, *sub specie aeternitatis,* present and future telescope (as to a lesser degree they do in all prophecy). The "sacramental" perspectives of cult would also explain why fertility and other nature/creation motifs play so prominent a role in his prophecy. In both respects, ex-mythological materials may have been useful to Joel (or, more likely, already at hand in the liturgy) in expressing universal and transcendental significances, but so thoroughly grafted into another stock that technical origins are of little more than archaeological interest.

Any Bible student will recognize that such a dimension would not be radically unique to Joel; the differences would be only of degree, not kind. If no ultimate hermeneutical depreciation of history is implied, that cult-historical perspective makes Joel more readily accessible in Word and Sacrament to later generations than many other pericopes where the historical "accidents" initially get in the way and often obscure the eternal message for hasty readers.

Text and Style

Both text and style in Joel approach eschatological perfection as closely as any part of the Old Testament. Joel writes superb, smooth, classical Hebrew poetry, lyrical and graphic. Repetition, contrast, metaphors, similes abound. Chronologically, however, as we noted, nothing can be concluded on this score alone—partly because style always depends at least as much on the individual as the age in which he writes. In balance, Joel's style would favor an early date, closer to Amos (with whose style there are many similarities), when "classical Hebrew" (the dialect of Jerusalem in the united and early divided monarchy) was in its heyday. However, those who prefer a late date can cogently argue that Joel was simply a good student and imitator of the style of the "good old days," much like classical revivals at various times in the West. Presumably, it is at least in part because of his lucid style that the text of Joel is also unusually well preserved, and the few problems encountered are not serious.

Outline and Contents

The major division of the contents may be placed either at Joel 2:17 or at 2:27, depending on whether we use form or content as our major criterion. If the former, it is primarily a matter of the people's lament over the catastrophe, followed by divine oracles in answer. If the latter, the division highlights the transition from more contemporary and historical commentary to more eschatological vision. The difference is ultimately immaterial, but we shall opt for the latter, as perhaps better conveying the inner dynamic of the book itself. We must also note that the Hebrew text counts four instead of three chapters, derived by carving a special third chapter out of 2:28-32. Again nothing depends on it. That Hebrew third chapter is unusually short, but its separation does have the merit of highlighting one of the undeniable highlights of the book itself, the prophecy of Pentecost.

Joel 1:2-12 describes the (first?) invasion of the locusts. The four types of grasshoppers distinguished in v. 4 are probably only representative (Hebrew has still other words for an only too familiar pest). The description is followed by a call to repentance and fasting (vs. 13-14) directed especially to the priests. V. 15 introduces an eschatological element to the entire description of the catastrophe (vs. 16-20), describing it as the harbinger of the "day of the LORD." V. 15 is almost identical with Is. 13:6 (including an inimitable Hebrew alliteration), one of the first instances where the question of relationships inevitably arises.

The structure of Joel 2 is very similar. Again the locust plague is described, but this time in far more eschatological, even apocalyptic (v. 10) language. Its character as *a* "day of the LORD" as well as an anticipation of *the* "day" is more prominent (on 2:2 cf. the *dies irae* passage of Zeph. 1:15). The grasshoppers become even more clearly (cf. 1:6) an army of "the northerner" (2:20), mysterious, sinister, irresistible (cf. Is. 5:27-30 on the Assyrian invasion). The Hebrew poetry here is some of the most exquisite in the Bible. Much of Joel's description of the locusts in both chapters is echoed in Rev. 9, giving even sharper focus to the writer's original eschatological intent.

There follows in Joel 2:12-17 another call to repentance, parallel to 1:13-14. (For Lutherans it is especially significant as the traditional lesson for Ash Wednesday, and for the Day of Humiliation and Prayer towards the end of the church year). Here priests and cult are even more prominent than in the parallel passage, but in both the entire congregation is obviously to be involved. Otherwise, too, the passage almost suffices as a refutation of every slander of "priestly religion." God is not to be appeased, but repentance is to make His boundless grace available (v. 13, a traditional and classical summary of God's *covenant* attributes; cf. Ex. 34:6). Repentance is ultimately a matter of the heart, not merely of externals. It is all-important that sacrifice not cease, because it is God's appointed "means of grace" (parallel to Christian sacraments), yet God is not magically bound to it (v. 14's "Who knows"). The parallelism of "blessing" and "offering" in v. 14 classically summarizes the dialectical "eucharistic" and "Offertory prayer" character of Israelite sacrificial ritual: God conveys sacramental blessing through the sacrificial gifts which His grateful and sanctified people offer to Him.

In Joel 2:18-27, however, the course of chap. 2 diverges from the third part of chap. 1. Since the people respond and repent, further depiction of the catastrophe is replaced by the "great reversal": Yahweh intervenes and restores the land. The "blessing," as commonly in the Bible, is initially described immanentally and materialistically—as material and immanental as the scourge had been—, but it is an unscriptural dichotomy to drive any ultimate wedge between that and the more "spiritual" and eschatological portraits which follow. The "blessing" comes in Sacrament as well as special revelation, to body as well as soul. Redemption and "new creation" are similarly interlocked throughout prophecy.

The chapter concludes and climaxes (Joel 2:28-32), however, with explicitly eschatological prophecy of the "pouring out" of God's spirit on all flesh, just before "the great and terrible day of the LORD comes" (2:31). Its isolation as a separate third chapter in the Masoretic tradition makes it stand out still further. The remainder of the book is explicitly and heavily eschatological. In a way, parts two and three of the classical prophetic outline are collapsed into one universal vision of the defeat of the nations and the salvation of the "Israel according to the spirit," or of the "remnant" (cf. 2:32).

This pericope, of course, is the *locus classicus* of God's Spirit as the agent of the eschaton, of the time of the church and of the Third Article, fulfilling Christ's work in grace and judgment, yet with the "final curtain call" still ahead. Only in a very technical, historicistic sense will one hesitate to join in labeling Joel, "the prophet of Pentecost." In a narrowly historical, exegetical sense one will not *simply* identify the "spirit" of Joel 2:28 with the Holy Spirit, the Spirit of Christ, the third person of the Trinity, but confession of the unity of Scripture and its revelation of that fulfillment will soon override all misgivings.

Joel 2:32 also introduces the accent on Zion/Jerusalem of the rest of the book. As always in prophecy, the ultimate perspective is not political and geographical but eschatological (both vertical and horizontal), Zion (church) as the type and prolepsis of the Church Triumphant. By extension it is always also Messianic. The alleged contrast between Joel's "particularism" and Paul's "universalism" in citing the passage (Rom. 10:13) is a figment of the liberal-critical search for contradictions.

Two apocalyptic images dominate the definitive defeat of the nations in Joel 3 (Gentile oracles of a sort): the "valley of Jehoshaphat" (vs. 2 and 12) and the "valley of decision" (v. 14). There is no evident specific historical reference in either case. It is doubtful if "Jehoshaphat" is even an allusion to the Judahite king; probably we have only a pun on the meaning of the name, "Yahweh judges/saves." Phoenicia and Philistia are specified as culprits in 3:4-8, but they are probably purely exemplary and symbolic. Both here and in vs. 1-3, enslavement and dispersion of God's people are also specified as the occasion for judgment, but if any specific historical occasion is in the prophet's mind, it eludes us. Certainly, we need not think only of the Babylonian exile and its aftermath to understand them, and the context suggests that we should think *primarily* of spiritual and religious bondage. The judgment is described in less particular terms in vs. 9-17, but the difference is probably purely formal. Note in v. 10 the reversal (describing the showdown battle *before* the parousia) of Isaiah's (2:4) and Micah's (4:3) famous portrait of eschatological peace (or historically did they reverse Joel's picture—or was there a common source?).

Joel moves gradually (esp. v. 16 or 18 to the end) into a climactic portrait of the blessings due to Zion after the final battle, because of Yahweh's eternal presence there (cf. the conclusion of Ezekiel and Revelation). Vs. 16 and 18 parallel the beginning and end of Amos, respectively, and v. 18 features the same picture of the waters of life in Paradise Restored which we meet in Ezek. 47; Zech. 14; John 7; Rev. 22; etc.

Since Joel is often overlooked, or only the Pentecost pericope noted atomistically, a concluding summary note on the book's importance is in order, underscoring points we have already made. First, it is a classical statement of the eschatological component (Word) of all of history and nature.

Second, it highlights the "sacramental" component (Sacrament) of all of history and nature. Third, it features the Holy Spirit as the "Lord and Giver of life," the agent through whom, via Word and Sacrament, Law and Gospel, Zion is being established. For the Christian, of course, Christ is the implicit but ultimate subject of all three confessions.

AMOS

The Liberal Viewpoint

As we have already noted repeatedly, Amos was lionized by classical higher criticism as no other Old Testament figure. "Prophecy" in that context meant largely Amos and Jeremiah—although expurgated editions of both. Perhaps the major reason was Amos' alleged "originality"; the evolutionary theory of Israel's religion had made only "J" out to be earlier among the writings of the Old Testament, and had largely disposed of all other predecessors in any positive sense. Thus Amos became the originator of "ethical monotheism" (and its implicit universalism), supposedly replacing the preceding ritualistic henotheism (or even more primitive forms of religion). All the other reasons for Amos' early critical popularity are largely subdivisions. His stringent denunciation of ritualism and cultic abuses, understood as an attack on ritual and cult as such, was music to the ears of nineteenth-century *Schleiermacherei*. Similarly with Amos' sharp attacks on social abuses, which superficially paralleled the agenda of the "social gospel." Amos, then, was almost totally judgmental (cf. below), a perfect example of the "liberated man versus the establishment" presupposition of what it meant to be "prophetic." (Some assert that Amos was the angriest because he was the first to react against the *status quo,* but both premise and conclusion are debatable.) Finally, perhaps, since "monotheism" in the jargon of the day really meant immanental monism (the Hegelian "Idea" or the like), the Book of Amos contained a minimum of supernaturalism and an apocalyptic type of eschatology (implying that man could not solve his own ills) to embarrass the prevailing historicism.

Change in the theological atmosphere inevitably brought somewhat different assessments of Amos, but never ones in which he suffered. Form criticism shifted the main focus of interest to short, oral components in earlier times, and more conservative assessments of Israel's earlier religion (especially, of the *Heilsgeschichte* and "Biblical theology" brand) did not set Amos off in quite so bold relief over against his predecessors. Yet, a perusal of the literature indicates that the shift was more a matter of degree than of principle, and the radical winds of the sixties revealed with a vengeance how much subliminal life the old ideals still retained.

Conservatism might have overreacted, but it does not appear to have done that so much as often to evince perplexity as to what to do with Amos, especially in the absence of Messianic prophecies. Little remains of Amos' vaunted "originality" if the principles he championed were Mosiac (at least), and if he had been preceded by other prophetic figures. If Joel, Obadiah, and Jonah preceded Amos, as many conservatives still hold, he was not even the first of the "writing prophets." But apart from writing, many of Amos' points were also anticipated by Samuel, Elijah, and other prophets reported in the prophetic books (assuming, of course, that those reports are worthy of credence). Regardless of questions of Amos' precise relations with other prophets, he remains, nevertheless, a classical example of some of the major themes of preexilic prophecy, and one of the first of which we have detailed records.

Amos and "Justice"

Amos is commonly referred to as the "prophet of justice" *(mishpat),* and that accent is often compared with Isaiah's stress on holiness and Hosea's on love in two eighth-century contemporaries. In full Biblical context and then with proper definitions, that summary is unexceptional. Mischief easily begins, however, with the usual translation, "justice," which simply is no adequate equivalent for *mishpat.* Nor is the older "judgment" much better. This problem remains a parade example of the frequent impossibility of fully correct translation and of the indispensability of knowledge of the original languages. The major problem is that Amos' "justice" is inevitably heard in the modern secular and universalistic sense, as only one more species (with a little dispensable Old

Testament veneer) of a universal ideal, toward which all men of good will
will strive. To hear Biblical vocabulary in that demythologized a sense is
simply to emasculate it, and transform it into a totally different creature.

It can scarcely be stressed too much that Biblical *mishpat* (and
similarly the nearly synonymous "righteousness") is not only ethical and
"religious" but metaphysical as well. Both the definition of its contents
and contours, as well as the ability to meet its requirements in a fully God-
pleasing manner, are gifts of His covenantal grace, no matter how
superficially similar with ideals and morals elsewhere. "Justice" is *solely* a
result of God's forensic "judgments," and the response determines
whether the ultimate judgment is salvatory or damnatory. "Salvation plus
response" or "both justification and sanctification" would be better
translations, if possible.

In addition, the matter of "justice" is the focus of especially the
Lutheran concern that the two kingdoms, that is, Law and Gospel, be
properly distinguished. Amos is a major reminder that those principles
are not only dogmatic, but also hermeneutical (confessional). They
profess to be derived from Scripture's self-understanding, and, in turn,
must be employed by the exegete to grasp and expound properly that self-
understanding. Specifically, the "church" and "state" components which
were combined in the Old Testament theocracy must be carefully
distinguished in the New Testament "kingdom of grace." The "justice"
which it is the church's work to proclaim is that *vicarious* "justice" we have
in the covenant with Christ, namely the Gospel, by which alone we escape
condemnation, no matter how fine a moral code we pursue.

Amos does *not* accent that more theological aspect of the totality,
although it is by no means absent: in canonical context it is implicit
everywhere and informing everything, and becomes explicit especially in
his accent on election (especially Amos 3:2). In that light, much liberal
treatment of Amos is wrong even when it is right!

Amos does, of course, heavily accent the "state" component of the
totality, the kingdom of God's power, where His love can manifest itself
only through the rule of law. Amos emphatically does remind Christians
that they, too, still live in that kingdom of power and have responsibilities
before God there. And precisely because of their tendency to "put Amos
on the back burner," precisely because of their priority concern for the
pure Gospel, Amos always needs to be accented—especially in conservatism.

Date and Background

A medium amount of personal information about Amos has been
preserved. The superscription places him "among the shepherds of
Tekoa." Tekoa is situated some twelve miles south of Jerusalem on the

edge of the wilderness of Judea (acres of Byzantine rubble on the site today). It is noteworthy at the outset that, although a native of Judah, nearly all of his preaching is directed against the North (critics have tended to excise the few references to the South), and perhaps a good share of it was also physically delivered there too. Why his activity was so one-sidedly northern is not clear, but it makes crystal clear that the idea of "all Israel" was never abandoned, that theologically (as well as politically, the part critics tend to highlight) the South continued its claim on the North. (Also Isaiah and Micah direct selected oracles against the North while it still stands, as conversely, Hosea does toward the South.)

"Shepherds" in Amos 1:1 translates a rare Hebrew word, used elsewhere in the Bible only in 2 Kings 3:4 of King Mesha of Moab. Since the root is used, however, in Ugaritic of "cultic" personnel who had charge of the shrine's flocks, some researchers for a time grasped at this straw to make Amos also a "cultic prophet." That fad has largely passed, but Amos' own self-designation in 7:14b as a "herdsman and dresser of sycamore trees" would indicate that "shepherd" too should be taken in essentially its ordinaly sense. At most, the use of the rare word would indicate that Amos was employed on estates or plantations owned by the temple, but the information would scarcely be significant. Amos' preceding assertion (7:14a) that he was "no prophet nor a prophet's son" (which has also spawned much debate) would seem to mean that he was no *professional* prophet (perhaps member of a hereditary guild or "school"), and thus the assertion would seem to fly in the face of any suggestion that he was a "cultic prophet." Of course, when Amos continues (7:15) to describe how God called him precisely to "prophesy," it is plain that Amos is not disassociating himself from that activity in a broader, less institutionalized, sense.

We have no account of Amos' call, though the visions in Amos 7—9 are widely suspected to preserve some of that information (cf. also the "lion's roar" in 3:8). That is by no means impossible, though nowhere even hinted at in the text (cf. below). Besides the account of his clash with Amaziah, priest of Bethel, in 7:10 ff. and his apparent subsequent expulsion from the North, we may have an allusion to personal opposition in 5:10. We have no way of knowing whether the oracles in the book are in anything like chronological order, and, hence, where in his career his expulsion from the North occurred, and hence how much or what part of his ministry was actually carried out on northern soil. Neither can we guess how long a duration his activity had, but most tend to suppose that it was relatively short. There is no other personal information, and no clue to his manner of death.

Amos' rural background dare not lead to the conclusion that he was some uneducated rustic. Rural imagery is prominent enough in the book, but its language is pure and superb, classical Hebrew (possibly second only to Isaiah's). The poetic style exhibits classical simplicity, the oracles are carefully balanced, and there is a discernible unity of design throughout the book. Since even more radical critics are convinced that we have Amos' *ipsissima verba* in most of the book (even if possibly collected and arranged by someone else), this judgment on the prophet's literary abilities polishes his image even further. Perhaps again because of that clear, pleasing style, copyists had no problems with the book; at any rate, its text-critical problems are nearly negligible.

Neither are there any serious problems in dating Amos. The superscription is not doubted, even if critics, as usual, believe it to be a later editorial addition. The two essentially contemporaneous kings of the divided kingdom are specified, Uzziah of Judah and Jeroboam (II) of Israel. (Note the Messianic implications of Uzziah's mention first, something one might expect of a loyal Judahite anyway.) If we had sufficient information, the following "two years before the earthquake" might help us be even more precise. (It must have been unusually severe, because it apparently is the same one alluded to much later in Zech. 14:5, and we also now know it archaeologically from the excavations at Hazor.) A few have tried to link 8:9 with a solar eclipse known from Assyrian records to have occurred on June 15, 763 B.C., but Amos' eschatological language there is too common and too traditional to establish any connection.

In any case, there is no debate that Amos is to be located primarily in the decade 760—750, just before the middle of the eighth century. That places him just after the activity of Jonah (2 Kings 14:25) and just before the ministry of Hosea. The period is well known, both from Biblical and Assyrian records (archaeologically it is also the period of the famous Samaria ostraca). Amos' preaching is inextricably linked with the politics of the period, especially the policies of Jeroboam II. In the period after the Assyrians had prostrated Israel's old competitors, the Arameans, but were momentarily too weak to follow through against Israel, Jeroboam had regained most of the territory Israel had previously lost (as Jonah had predicted, and alluded to also in 6:13). Between them, Jeroboam and Uzziah had regained much of the former Davidic empire.

Not being forced to face the Assyrian juggernaut, the internal economy was free to flourish, at least as far as the establishment was concerned. Many obviously concluded that it must be a sure sign of God's favor and blessing and that the millennium-like "day of the LORD" (Amos 5:18 f.) must be just around the corner. The period is often aptly styled Israel's "Indian summer." But underneath Amos saw only rot, not primarily "social" and "economic," as the secularist reads it, but religious and covenantal. Hence, when everything is prospering externally, Amos is called to preach that Israel's current heresy, adding to the long series of precedents, was finally filling the cup of God's wrath to overflowing. Amos is by no means alone, but no prophet portrays the impending doom in blacker, bleaker light. Critics usually minimize the little bit of promise the book does contain, but, no doubt, it was not a time for that message.

In other respects, too, higher criticism was quite gentle with Amos; it found him too congenial to wield the scalpel as carelessly as many other places. Details we will consider in connection with contents below. In general, though, one may say that only the following portions were considered "ungenuine": (1) two or three of the initial Gentile oracles, especially the one against Judah (Amos 2:4-5; (2) the three nature-doxologies in the book (4:13; 5:8-9; and 9:5-6); and (3) the concluding promissory, even Messianic oracle (9:11-15). At one time rejection of that final oracle was virtually a litmus test for critical orthodoxy, but recent times have seen an increasing number of defections from the once solid critical phalanx. There are also a few tradition-critical concerns about the compilation of the book which we shall note.

Outline and Contents

Amos has a clear threefold outline: (1) Chaps. 1—2: Mostly "Gentile oracles" against neighboring nations, but climaxing with malediction of Israel and Judah; (2) chaps. 3—6: Various oracles against Israel's social and religious corruption; and (3) chaps 7—9: Visions, interrupted by a B-type account of the clash with Amaziah of Bethel in 7:10-17. It casts no aspersions on its genuineness to admit that the concluding eschatological, Messianic oracle (9:11-15) is a sort of appendix, albeit a climactic and theologically integral one.

Critics commonly infer from Amos' priority as a "writing prophet" that his book was also the first of the prophets to be completed in essentially its present form. Since the "Gentile oracles" here appear first, instead of in second place according to the "classical" prophetic outline, it is concluded that the shape of Amos' book had become fixed before the "classical" pattern had established itself (usually with Ezekiel, which see). While none of that appears impossible, it is also entirely speculative, and there is no good reason to abandon the traditional supposition that Amos himself was also responsible for the writing down of his oracles.

Critics also once tended to credit Amos with originating the *Gattung* of "Gentile oracles." Even the chauvinism allegedly prominent in later productions of this type seemed to be missing in Amos, not only because he climaxes with even greater condemnation of Israel but also because the

Gentiles too are indicted for their infractions of the "universal, moral law," exploitation of society, atrocities or "crimes against nature." Amos would still usually receive the pat on the back, but form criticism established to critical satisfaction that, not only did "Gentile-oracles" not originate with Amos, but were possibly the oldest type of Hebrew prophecy, presumably parallel to neighboring practices (e.g., Balaam, Num. 22—24). (More sterile debates as to whether they originated in "holy war," cultic "New Year's" context, or even were rooted in the Egyptian execration texts, need not detain us here.) More specifically, some argued that Amos was not very original here at all but simply adapted oracles originally composed at least a half-century earlier, when the countries mentioned might have been strong enough to attack Israel with impunity (which, as such, is by no means impossible).

All we can say with certainty is that, whatever their provenance, it suited Amos' purposes to place these "Gentile oracles" at the head of his collection. Theologically put, they anchor the "second use of the Law" flavor of his entire book in a universal perspective. The exordium in Amos 1:2 makes the point explicit: God's right and will to judge all is based on his status as Creator of all. However, Amos knows Him and His judgment not as some wrathful *Deus absconditus;* rather His judgment proceeds from *Zion,* where He is "incarnate" as the revealed God of the covenant. The verse also appears in Joel 3:16, which may establish nothing about the relation of the two prophets, but only that it was traditional (cultic?) language. We hear the lion's roar (imminence and inescapability) again in 3:8, where Amos applies it to the prophetic call; perhaps his shepherd experiences are also reflected.

Most scholars agree that the unity of the eight oracles in Amos 1—2 is not essentially redactional, but represents an original sermon delivered on one occasion, possibly at some religious festival when crowds were ample. (Some even associate it with Amaziah's rebuke in chap. 7; cf. also Isaiah's "Song of the Vineyard," chap. 5). Each indictment is introduced by the same formula: "For three transgressions of N, and for four, I will not revoke the punishment, because. . . ." "Not revoke" is literally, "Not let return," that is, to my heavenly judgment seat. "Three . . . four" represents a sort of (near) parallelism which we know also from outside Israel and which appears to have been especially at home in Wisdom circles. Possibly "three" represents "enough," with "four" indicating a pluperfect (when even one infraction would have been serious enough).

Most commentators also agree that Amos here artfully uses the rhetorical device known as *captatio benevolentiae.* That is, first he gains his audience's attention and goodwill by condemning other people, saving his "knockout blow" until he has them "eating out of his hand." The sequence of peoples condemned appears to resemble the gradual circling and tightening of a lasso until the noose finally tightens and settles on the major target, Israel and Judah. Especially if Amos was an unknown country preacher from the South at the time, this reconstruction is eminently plausible.

As one would expect, Amos condemns other nations only for the violations of "natural law" for which they could be held responsible, while the particularities of covenant and election became the basis for the indictments of Israel and Judah—a point of departure which continues throughout the book. Amos 2:4 specifically mentions *Torah* ("revelation" more than "law"), and vs. 9-10 summarize the Exodus.

Many critics have entertained skepticism about the authenticity of some three of these oracles, not very convincingly, however, especially to a conservative. The oracle against Tyre (Amos 1:9-10) is sometimes doubted on no better grounds than its brevity and repetition of the language of the preceding oracle. The following speech against Edom (1:11-12) is sometimes thought to presuppose the major Edomite incursions after the fall of Jerusalem in 587, but, especially in the light of Israel's nearly perennial conflict with that nation, the argument has no merit whatsoever. Especially the oracle against Judah (2:4-5) is commonly questioned because of (a) its generality, (b) Amos' usual preachment against Israel, and (c) its allegedly "deuteronomic" language. The latter argument especially illustrates how one critical hypothesis tends to be built upon another. More conservative critics think of an original oracle later expanded deuteronomistically. If one thinks of the crowd psychology sketched above, the oracle against Judah fits perfectly as the next to last before Amos' major one, Israel.

Only selected oracles or passages can be noted in the rest of the book. Some of the most famous and typical passages of Amos occur in chaps. 3—6. The fact that chaps. 3; 4; and 5 all begin with, "Hear this word," as well as the twofold "Woe" in 5:18 and 6:1, could indicate some preliminary collection of oracles according to a catchword principle. Likewise, the doxologies (4:13 and 5:8-9) could indicate liturgical conclusions at some stage of transmission (cf. below). Otherwise, however, there are no signs of deliberate order or arrangement in this section.

Amos 3:1 ff., like the preceding two oracles is directed "against the whole family which I brought up out of the land of Egypt." Since God had "known," that is, elected, and entered into a covenantal, virtually marital, relationship with only Israel and Judah, they were not only not exempt from His requirements, as apparently some imagined, but all the more accountable (3:2). The "therefore" of that verse summarizes much of the book; to whom much is given, much is required, judgment begins with the household of God (1 Peter 4:17), etc. A similar point is made throughout the book with respect to Israel's cult: what God had given to sustain must now destroy *(corruptio optimi pessima)*.

God's "secret" (Amos 3:7), that Israel is doomed, is apparently a reference to the deliberations and decision of the heavenly council where history is really made and to which the prophet has been given access, so that he can herald the message on earth (cf. 1 Kings 22; Jer. 23; etc.) The concept is essentially the same as "mystery" in later apocalyptic and New Testament parlance.

Amos 3:12 is one of Amos' notable and sarcastic caricatures of the fatuous popular "remnant" hopes (cf. 5:3). In 4:1-3, Amos, like Isaiah (3:16 ff.) does not hesitate to score also the distaff side for its idle, irresponsible luxury (endless cocktail parties; cf. Amos 6:6). It is followed (4:4-5) by famous sarcasm of Israel's officious religiosity. Therefore, "prepare to meet your God" (4:12), but not in the way envisioned!

At Amos 4:13 we meet the first of the three doxologies in the book (the second shortly in 5:8-9, the third at 9:5-6.) The theory that they reflect liturgical influences in transmission (cf. above) is plausible in this first instance (concluding the first "Hear this word" collection), but the other two cases are less explicable in that fashion. Critics tend to assume the addition was first made by the exilic or postexilic community (and futile attempts have been made to reconstruct the original hymn of which they were presumably only excerpts), but, as such, the liturgical hypothesis need not preclude Amos' authorship.

There seems to be no good reason, however, why the doxologies should not have formed an integral part of Amos' original preaching. The point made is similar to that of the exordium (Amos 1:2), arguing from universal creation to universal judgment, or from general revelation to its full impact in the light of special revelation. Much as in the Book of Job, God's inescapable justice is thus affirmed. But divine retribution, even when initially condemnatory, is ultimately to be regarded in *heilsgeschichtliche* perspective. Hence, theologically, we are probably also to read these pericopes as "doxologies of judgment" (cf. Ps. 51:6); by His judgments God teaches us true praise, and we praise Him precisely in and because of His judgments. Perhaps all this implies that a sort of "alternation of weal and woe" principle was operative in the inclusion of the doxologies.

In Amos 5:14-15 it is all-important that "good" and "evil" be heard and expounded in covenant context. The prophet does not speak of universal moral ideals (let alone situational, culturally conditioned standards) but of definitions and contents clearly revealed in Mosaic revelation. The same, of course, is true of "justice" (cf. above) and "righteousness" throughout the book. The very fact that Amos can speak in such general terms presupposes his audience's thorough theoretical familiarity with his standards. When the final Messianic oracle (9:9-15) is excised, as critics commonly do, the "it may be" of v. 15 and the assertion of 9:8 are Amos' only concessions to any hope of salvation for a remnant through and beyond the judgment.

There follows in Amos 5:18-20 one of Amos' most famous passages: his vivid deflation of mass expectations about the "day of the LORD." Arid debates about the concepts' origins (especially cult or holy war) need not deflect us, neither does the Bible give us any reason to doubt that it was about as old as Israel itself. Nevertheless, the expectation had been perverted into "cheap grace," or "Smile, God loves you," and Amos must stress most emphatically that, in their circumstances, it could mean only "darkness and not light."

One of the most famous and eloquent of all prophetic denunciations of rites apart from right living follows in Amos 5:21-24 (cf. Is. 1:10-17). Especially since it is linked with the following oracle (5:25-27) which appears to imply that sacrifice was a later Canaanite import, never observed in the wilderness, early critics were quick to seize upon especially this pericope and Jer. 7:22 ff. as major proof texts for the documentary hypothesis' point of departure, namely, that the entire Pentateuchal picture of cultic commands to Moses was a postexilic fiction, and that the prophets championed a return to the pristine, purely ethical state of affairs. Even few critics would go that far today, although retreating in various degrees. Even apart from theological appeal to Scriptural unity, it seems plain that we have here another example of prophetic hyperbole: the fathers had not offered *mere* external sacrifices in the wilderness, as they were doing.

In Amos 6:1, the "woe to those who are at ease in *Zion"* continues the accent on the special liability of the elect we noted at 3:2. Chap. 6:9-10 is one of the eeriest and most terrifying in the book. Once they had regarded God's name lightly or taken it in vain, but now they will caution against even uttering it, lest its mere mention bring a further curse upon them. Their viewpoint would still be magical, but at least the "Law" would have taught them their proper relationship to the deity. In striking pictures 6:12 equates the perversion of justice (true religion) with a perversion of creation; of course, the parallelism is not merely literary!

The question of the redaction of the Book of Amos is most complex in the final section, chaps. 7—9. One would presume that the five visions originally formed a unity, perhaps originally concluded by the third doxology in the book, 9:5-6. However, as we now have the book, for reasons entirely unknown, the visions are twice interrupted: the narrative of the conflict with Amaziah (7:10-17 after the third vision), and another series of oracles (again beginning with, "Hear this") after the fourth vision (8:4-14). One old hypothesis explains the first interruption as betraying the origination of the present Book of Amos in two parts 1:7—9:8 and 8:1—9:15, with the Amaziah pericope (7:10-17) allegedly added as an introduction to the latter part just before its unification with the first. In addition, the final doxology is unexpectedly followed by one of the most vitriolic oracles of judgment in the entire book.

As noted above, the visions are often thought to have originally constituted Amos' call. While not impossible, there is no way even to test the hypothesis. Some understand the insertion of the Amaziah pericope to imply that the visions also came as an integral part of his mission to the North, which might or might not contradict the view that they constituted a "call." In any event, while the word "sign" *('oth)* is not used in this part of the book, the visions are an excellent illustration of the common Biblical meaning of the concept. Sometimes, of course, it may imply "miracle" in the strict sense, but here the only miracle consists in the act of revelation, in God's opening the prophet's eyes to see a "sacramental" *sign*ificance or transparency of transcendental realities in everyday events and circumstances. (It does not follow that, with liberalism, we may limit all miracle to merely the subjective "miracle of faith"!) The fourth sign (Amos 8:1-3) is linguistic in root, a sort of a "pun" on the similarity (or in the northern dialect perhaps identity) of sound between the Hebrew words for "summer fruit" (especially figs) and "end" (cf. Jer. 24).

In Amos 8:9 the judgment almost begins to assume apocalyptic dimensions (the language is not only metaphorical), and in 8:11-12 the curse of divine obduration, as upon Pharaoh, is predicted: habitual disregard of God's Word will eventually make it utterly inaccessible, no matter how or where the belated search is made. Also because it is the Word which creates, makes, and sustains history, its hiddenness really is a "final judgment!"

Amos 9:2-3 is obviously the obverse of Ps. 139. Here God's omnipresence does not imply His constant care but the inescapability of His judgment. In v. 3 Amos alludes to the "serpent" which Canaanite mythology believed to inhabit the ocean depths (virtually a personification of the depths themselves). (Cf. "Leviathan" in Is. 27:1 and "Rahab" in Is. 30:7; 51:9; Ps. 89:10.) Like other originally mythological allusions in the Bible, Amos makes this reference in a purely literary way—a possibility as hypothetical as climbing up to heaven in v. 2. Above all, evil does not stand in eternal, dualistic opposition to God as in paganism but must also do the Creator's bidding.

Amos 9:7-8 is the capstone of Amos' attack on the false security Israel derived from the Exodus and election. In one sense, God had also been behind the migrations of other peoples (even the Philistines from "Caphtor," that is, Crete) to their homelands, so that Israel could lay no claim to special divine favor on that basis. But this sharpest of all attacks upon (the misunderstanding of) the very foundations of Israel's existence before God is followed (8b) by the clearest assertion in the book so far that he will "not make a full end" (to use Jeremiah's parallel phrase) but will preserve a remnant (cf. 5:15).

Is that the most Amos could ever bring himself to concede about restoration and *Heilseschatologie?* So critics have traditionally argued, once almost unanimously, although with increasing defections in recent years. The remaining verses in Amos (9:11-15) were taken to be so out of character with the rest of the book that they could not possibly have derived from Amos himself. Rather the pericope was taken as a major example of the postexilic congregation's practice of adding "euphemistic liturgical appendixes" to relieve the gloom of the preexilic preoccupation with judgment. Allegedly, 9:11-15 was especially easy to append here in order to open wide the door of hope which Amos himself (9:8) had left only slightly ajar.

More recent critical defenders of the pericope's authenticity (at least of its core) explain it to allude to the division of the kingdom after Solomon's death. Then, by predicting the North's reunification under the Davidic dynasty, the message would be of a piece with Amos' whole anti-Israel stance. Later it was allegedly amplified more theologically and eschatologically. This critical position is preferable to the first but still leaves a good deal to be desired. Indeed, the pericope teems with typical promissory language, but only an evolutionistic shuffling of the Bible's contents can deny its antiquity already in Amos' time ("in that day," "behold, the days are coming," "restore the fortunes of," "Edom" as a symbol and type of the kingdoms of this world, etc.). Neither the reference to raising up the fallen "booth of David" (a phrase unique in the Old Testament, evidently signifying humiliation), nor the promise of restoration to their land need presuppose the Babylonian Exile. The general pattern of exile was only too well known already in Amos' day, and the specific "premonition" of Israelite exile followed by return is attested already in the Pentateuch. Both the specifically Messianic (second David) expectation and its inseparability from "new creation" (v. 13) were well established components long before Amos. Amos' Judahite citizenship makes the Davidic expression of the eschatology even more credible.

One might well agree that Amos did not utter such words to the audience he excoriated throughout the rest of the book, but there plainly was a faithful "remnant" already in his day, or he may well have composed the oracle specifically as a climax for the literary fixation of his oracles in a book. In any event, the oracle is a superb Law-*Gospel* climax to the book, fulfilled in the death and resurrection of Him who did resurrect the Davidic empire and restore His people to their land in a fuller sense than it probably was ever given to Amos himself to understand. Apparently St. James first fully grasped its implications at the apostolic council (Acts 15:16-17), applying vs. 11-12 specifically to the mission to the Gentiles.

OBADIAH

Obadiah is the shortest book in the Old Testament canon (only 21 verses long) but, as St. Jerome already noted, both theologically and historically it often poses problems far out of proportion to its size. Its very brevity makes it easy to overlook (and this writer recalls that in his youth he associated the name only with a neighbor's small, white dog). In many ways its contents and problems are similar to those of Nahum.

With the proper typological hermeneutics Obadiah will be seen as not only a lovely miniature and epitome of many major prophetic themes but as a meaningful promise also for the Christian church.

In contents the book is little more than a single Gentile oracle against Edom (vs. 1-14), broadening out in the final verses (15-21) into proclamation of the eschatological great reversal, when final judgment will overtake *all* nations and Zion will be restored.

Thus the entire book is promissory to Israel. The one major prophetic motif which is missing is judgment on Israel—the precise motif criticism tends to view as constitutive of genuine prophecy. For that reason liberals have generally dealt very harshly with Obadiah, putting him down as only another rabid nationalist, a mere mouthpiece of the establishment, calling down divine judgment upon his nation's foes and assuring his people that the God who is surely on their side will eventually set all things straight. One viewpoint even attributes Obadiah's presence in the canon to its usefulness as anti-Herodian (anti-Idumean) polemic at the time of Christ.

Date and occasion of Obadiah's message are difficult to pin down (again reminding us of the non-ultimacy of the question). The prophet obviously speaks of some devastation of Jerusalem in which the Edomites were implicated. But which one? Friction, often bitter, was a constant of Israel's history, and Edom is repeatedly scored also by other prophets. There are three main possibilities, and all three have their champions. Theological viewpoint apparently plays only a minimal role in deciding.

Older conservative scholars were inclined to favor a quite early date for the book, relating it to the Philistine and Arab attack in the reign of Jehoram of Judah, c. 850 B.C. (cf. 2 Kings 8:20; 2 Chron. 21:16 ff.). That would, of course, make Obadiah the *earliest* of the "writing prophets," preceding even Joel (by the early dating of that book) by some twenty years. Except among some conservative scholars, that dating is almost entirely out of favor today. However, there is no good reason why the possibility should not be seriously entertained, particularly if critical developmental theories to the contrary are discarded. The tendency today even in critical circles to consider Gentile oracles as one of the earliest of prophetic types would make especially vs. 1-14 entirely plausible at so early a date (cf. below on the unity of the book).

Recent scholars, in contrast, have often favored a relatively late date, perhaps around 450 B.C., when various Arab tribes from the desert (the later Nabateans) began to press into historic Edomite territory east of the Arabah, and the Edomites, in turn, increasingly moved west into southern Judah (the beginning of the "Idumea" of New Testament times, whence the Herodians hailed).

The majority of scholars, however, probably prefer to think of the destruction of Jerusalem by Nebuchadnezzar in 587 B.C. as the most likely occasion for Obadiah's activity. That was Luther's preference already, and it is the one assumed here. There are various evidences of Edomite complicity in that catastrophe (Ezek. 35:10; Lam. 4:21-22; Ps. 137:7), although details are lacking. This position must concede, however, that Obadiah does not refer *explicitly* to either Jerusalem's razing or to the Babylonian captivity (the "exiles" of v. 20 might have appeared in many periods).

Two subsidiary issues are involved in the question of date: Obadiah's connections with other prophets, and the unity of the book. Many prophets (Isaiah, Ezekiel, Amos) condemn Edom in language very similar to Obadiah's. There are especially close affinities between Joel and Obadiah scattered throughout both of those two books, and it may be that Joel 2:32b is explicitly citing Obad. 17a when it adds "as the LORD has said" (or is the reference more general?). Especially significant is the close relation between Jeremiah's oracle against Edom (49:7 ff.) and Obad. 1-9. The verbal parallelism is particularly striking between Jer. 49:14-16 and Obad. 1-4, and between Jer. 49:9 and Obad. 5.

In the case of both Joel and Jeremiah only three solutions are possible: one prophet was dependent on the other, or both used a common source. Again, all three positions are defended, often, it would seem, depending as much as anything on prior decisions about the date of Obadiah's (and Joel's) activity. In general, the "common source" hypothesis would seem the most likely, with the result that little can be decided about the date of any prophet on this basis alone. There is a little clear evidence (especially in Zechariah) that quotation of earlier (now semi-canonical) prophecy was characteristic of later times, but with critical amplification the observation readily turns into an argument in a circle.

The second related issue is that of the unity of the book. Critics have sundered Obadiah at various points, but most commonly a seam is said to be detectable between v. 14 and 15. Since at this point the subject shifts from condemnation of Edom to "the day of the LORD—upon *all* nations," it is often argued that the latter part of the book is no longer the particularized prophecy of Obadiah, but a more universalized, incipiently apocalyptic addition of a later period. If such evolutionary theories are not invoked, however, the progression from particular to general is readily explainable as Obadiah's own indication of the *typical* and eschatological significance of his oracles against Edom. No doubt, as time goes on, "Edom" (like "Babylon") increasingly takes on universal significance as a symbol of "all the kingdoms of the world," but that symbolism was present to some degree in all periods. Otherwise, too, Obadiah shows many signs of theological and literary unity.

Some recent, more cultically oriented, scholars, have tried to account for a unified core of the work as an oracle on the occasion of some great, probably preexilic, festival in Jerusalem (enthronement, New Year's, covenant renewal, etc.). Obadiah's "day" was then initially the day of the festival, when Yahweh's universal reign was celebrated, the reign of the Davidic king as His vice-regent was confirmed, and prophecies of judgment upon Israel's enemies were uttered. Here Edom was the main example, but at other times it was Assyria (cf. Nahum) or the like. As we noted, some critics envision the origin of the entire "Gentile-oracle" type in such a setting. Allegedly, the cult primarily celebrated the proleptic, "sacramental" presence of these realities in the *present*. That is, some eschatological import was present initially, but Obadiah's original oracle would have been amplified in especially this respect when revamped after the Exile, possibly for use at a comparable festival in that period. While nearly all details of this reconstruction are speculative, potentially at least it is theologically much closer to the target than the more politically oriented theories of other critics.

Especially in the case of a book like Obadiah, one is aware how much the absence of real tenses in the Hebrew verb complicates the problem of dating. Like other prophets, Obadiah appears to use the "prophetic perfect" often (i.e., the future described as already past, so sure is the prophet because of his vantage point in Yahweh's throne room of the fulfillment of his oracles). Often, however, the Hebrew perfect may simply have its ordinary past-tense reference, and it is not easy to distinguish. The omnitemporality of the Hebrew "imperfect" also causes difficulties.

Both KJV and RSV translate, in effect, "you should not have" in vs. 12 ff., but a much more likely translation would seem to be, "you should/must not," depicting the prophet speaking to contemporaries.

Contents

Obadiah opens (vs. 1-4) with a prophetic announcement of imminent judgment upon Edom because of her overweening pride, which, however, like the mountain heights she inhabits, is really very vulnerable. "Rock" in v. 3 translates "Sela," also the name of the major Edomite bastion. Its Greek counterpart is "Petra," still a major tourist attraction in southern Jordan.

Vs. 5-10 stress the totality of the judgment. Thieves usually take only what is of value, but "Esau's" perfidious friends will leave nothing, just as she had devastated "Jacob" (cf. Gen. 25:29 ff.). Her "wise men," for which Edom was apparently especially renowned, are singled out: God's wisdom will bring theirs to nought (cf. 1 Cor. 1).

Vs. 11-14 detail the particulars of the indictment. "In the day of his calamity," Edom had not only not come to her brother's defense but had gleefully joined the destroyer in his plunder. One must stress, as in all Gentile oracles, that the refrain, "You should not have . . ." is not universalistic, moralistic preaching, but proceeds from the assumption of general revelation, which even the Gentiles know and for which God holds them responsible (Ps. 82, Rom. 1, etc.).

The remaining verses (15-21) are of somewhat different character, as already noted. They describe the "great reversal" on the "day of the LORD." If Obadiah is dated early, it is the first appearance of the latter phrase (cf. on Amos 5); in any event, it is specifically contrasted here with Edom's or man's "day" in the preceding verses. When God intervenes, the turning of the tables will be apparent in two respects: Mt. Zion will rule "Mt. Esau" instead of the reverse, and Edom's punishment will correspond with her crime.

Furthermore, God's judgment upon Edom will be tantamount to the destruction of all nations that have not confessed the true God. Then Israel and Judah will be able to inherit fully the patriarchal promise of land. Mt Zion will be an asylum for the remnant (v. 17), and from there "saviors" (the same word often applied to the "judges") will rule Mt. Esau. But the real victor is not Israel, but Yahweh, and the kingdom will be His (v. 21).

Many of the major prophetic types are thus aired in the little Book of Obadiah (Zion vs. Edom, justice, land, remnant, kingdom, etc.). The book is never quoted in the New Testament, but he who has the proper hermeneutical key, based on parallel Biblical citations, will experience little difficulty in transposing it into its Christological key. The book contains no Messianic prophecy in the strict sense, but, as always, Zion and Messiah, king and kingdom are correlative. The New Testament in a way begins where Obadiah left off; its "good news" is the proclamation that in Christ the kingdom *has* become the LORD's, His justice and "great reversal" have been established. Yet "Edom" is not completely vanquished, and we still pray, in effect, with Obadiah, "Thy kingdom come."

JONAH

The Book of Jonah has long been one of the most visible outposts along the liberal-conservative battle line. Strict conservatives do not hesitate to draw the line at this point, and liberals have reserved much of their arsenal of ridicule of "fundamentalist literalism" for the traditional position at this point. Whether taking Jonah factually is "literal" or "literalistic" will be determined largely by prior hermeneutical and confessional commitments.

No doubt, Jonah is an unusual member of the "Twelve." Unlike most prophetic literature, which consists primarily of ("A"-type) oracles, Jonah is almost exclusively ("B"-type) narrative *about* Jonah, except for chap. 2. Neither the book itself nor other Scripture ever asserts that Jonah himself wrote it, as tradition has tended to assume, and hence that should not be insisted upon (chap. 2 may be a partial exception; cf. below). Yet that may be only a technicality, and Jonah may have been very closely associated with its composition. (The "was" of 3:3 need not imply that Nineveh was no longer standing at composition, as some have argued.) Neither its facticity nor its verbal inspiration are directly linked with such technicalities.

Outside of the book, Jonah is mentioned elsewhere in the Old Testament only once in 2 Kings 14:25. There Jonah is described as hailing from Gath-hepher (probably some four miles north of Nazareth; modern Moslem popular piety has shrines dedicated to him in not only several places in that area but also in the regions of Joppa and Nineveh). In Kings it is reported only that Jonah had predicted the victories of Jeroboam II in restoring "the border of Israel from the entrance of Hamath as far as the Sea of the Arabah." Since Jeroboam reigned c. 786—746, that would probably give us a median date for Jonah around 775—750, making him an early contemporary of Amos. That the reports in Kings and the Book of Jonah have no contact beyond the name is scarcely surprising in and of itself; not even the names of many "writing prophets" with far larger books are so much as mentioned!

Liberal Viewpoints

To liberalism, of course, the matter looks altogether different. In some fashion or the other the book is read as a postexilic literary fiction, which merely latched on to the figure of Jonah as a bearer of its message. Why Jonah? The standard answer follows from the usual critical understanding of the purpose of the book. It is usually read as a protest document by the more liberal, universalistic wing of postexilic Yahwism, in line with "Deutero-Isaiah" and other figures, allegedly stressing God's love for all people, and directed against the dominant exclusivism and particularism of the times, represented by Ezekiel and Ezra, especially perhaps the latter's exclusion of the Samaritans and unyielding opposition to mixed marriages. Alternatively, it protested against the "legalism" of the times, which thought that God was almost mechanically bound to his pronouncements, especially of judgment. In either case, the "chauvinistic" Jonah described in 2 Kings would make a fine foil to their message, as though to say that the classical Yahweh faith contained both universalistic and particularistic impulses, or that at least the postexilic community should be broad enough to harbor both parties.

Exactly what *Gattung* Jonah should be, criticism has had a hard time deciding. At one time, the book was frequently called a "prophetic legend," and compared with the vast amount of extracanonical tales about Jonah and many other prophets. Some compared the author to a modern cartoonist, who may employ all kinds of absurd features to make his point (in the case of Jonah, its prominent supernaturalism!). In recent years, the language has probably moderated a bit, yet without substantial change in position. Some compare the work to Jewish "midrash" or "haggadah" (edifying, homiletical embroidery of a theme). Possibly "prophetic novel" would describe the current critical center of gravity as well as any term. Form critics, of course, have been assiduous in adducing "fish tales" and other alleged parallels from all over the world.

These questions of formal classification have somewhat overlapped with more functional debates whether the book should be considered something like a parable or allegory (the latter, of course, being a more extended or consistent version of the former). The question is usually answered affirmatively, but somewhat cautiously. Even critics recognized that, especially in the case of allegory, the Bible itself indicates when such a genre is being used. The big attraction of such theories, of course, is that they relieve the interpreter of all concerns about the facticity of the story.

Especially certain British scholars (Cheyne, G. A. Smith, etc.) have explained the story as an allegory. Jonah represents Israel, which has been elected (Gen. 12:3) to convert the heathen but instead runs away from its obligation. "Jonah" means "dove," with which Israel is elsewhere compared (Ps. 74:19; Hos. 7:11; 11:11), and the father's name, Amittai, may be associated with *'emeth* ("truth"), supposedly to signify Israel's commission to uphold and propagate divine truth. The cuneiform characters for *Ni-nu-a* (Nineveh) are those of a fish and a house (perhaps the fish inside a tomb). Because Israel shirked her duty in the Exile, however, she was "swallowed" by the monster, Babylon (the metaphor is used in Jer. 51:34-44), and disgorged (allowed to return) only upon repentance. Israel still remains dissatisfied that the Gentiles have not been punished and has only reluctantly resigned herself to the task.

A less popular allegorical explanation (H. Schmidt) would identify the "Nineveh" of the tale with Jerusalem, which supposedly is depicted as asking whether God's judgment on itself would be lifted if the city repented, and the answer is affirmative (cf. Ezek. 33:11 ff.).

Since most such allegorical approaches collapse when it comes to trying to work out all details, critical sentiment has tended to favor the term "parable," that is, often merely a more relaxed version of essentially the same understanding, which needs to worry about only one point of comparison. (Jonah then perhaps is comparable to the "Prodigal Son"). At most the "parable" is thought to have been elaborated with a few additional legendary or novelistic elements, presumably for mass appeal. Even from a form-critical standpoint, however, it must be noted that such a lengthy, detailed "parable" is virtually without comparison, and parables usually receive their impact from their historical verisimilitude (here the critical argument can be turned against itself).

The usual critical dating in the fifth to fourth century B.C. is also based on the above assumptions of the book's provenance and purpose (chap. 2 is a special case; cf. below). In evolutionistic light the theme of Jonah necessarily presupposed the universalistic pioneering of the great prophets and in the other direction its approach to pseudepigraphy suggested apocalyptic habits toward the end of the millennium. On no account can Jonah be dated much later than fifth-fourth century, because it is cited already in the apocryphal books of Tobit and Ecclesiasticus, each with earlier roots (and surely also eloquent testimony to canonical regard for Jonah at an early date). It was once common to attempt to buttress a late dating by pointing to certain alleged "Aramaisms" or other late expressions in the text. However, as elsewhere, evidence from Ugarit that many such "Aramaisms" were even older than Israel has made even critics very cautious about such arguments. Furthermore, there is evidence that such "Aramaic" idioms were more common in northern than in southern Canaan—and Jonah hailed from northern Galilee! In addition, just as in Amos and Obadiah, there are clear parallels with Joel (3:9 with Joel 2:14 and 4:2 with Joel 2:13), but with the same ambivalence of results.

Conservative Viewpoints

Hence, there appear to be no compelling reasons why one should question an eighth-century date for the book, except on the basis of dogmatism to the contrary. The prose is good, classical Hebrew for the most part, and the psalm (chap. 2) is even antique in flavor. Again probably for the same reason (cf. Joel and Amos) text-critical problems are trivial. The conservative would have no difficulty conceding some minor linguistic updating after presumed eighth-century composition, but the burden of proof would lie on those who believe the hypothesis needs to be resorted to.

The conservative rebuttal of nonliteral interpretations of Jonah finally rests (as in the case of the unity of Isaiah and Mosaic authorship of the Pentateuch) solely in the testimony of the New Testament and of our Lord. The two relevant texts are Matt. 12:39-41 and Luke 11:29-32. Critics commonly try to make hay out of the fact that the "sign of Jonah" is presented a bit differently in the two texts: in Luke, it is the preaching of judgment by the Son of Man, the antitype of Jonah, to the present unbelieving generation, while in Matthew the sign is the Son of Man's "three days and three nights in the heart of the earth," corresponding to the period Jonah spent "in the belly of the whale." It seems to be a specious distinction without a difference, however: it is precisely Christ's death and resurrection which seals His condemnation upon those who refuse to believe. In both cases we clearly have Christ's own explicit typology, presenting Jonah's "death and resurrection" as an anticipation and forecast of His own. (Nor, perhaps, is it significant that Jonah is the *only* prophet Jesus ever directly compares Himself to—a circumstance possibly explainable by the proximity of Jonah's home to Nazareth.) And typology, in the Biblical sense, necessarily implies historicity. It is never mere analogy or illustration, but denotes an inner continuity between the anticipation (prophecy) and the climax (fulfillment). (Cf. Jonah 1.) For those who demur that Jesus was only arguing analogically (for which any parable or other tale would serve as well as historical fact), the clinching refutation would appear to be Jesus' reference to the "men of Nineveh." He obviously regards them not only as historical figures, but as still available to "arise at the judgment with this generation and condemn it" (both Luke and Matthew!)

For most conservatives, this argument from Scripture's self-interpretation would suffice. However, as always in apologetics, the strictures of those who disagree must be answered, and so corroborative arguments are welcome. Also, as always, no one will be convinced unless he is already convinced on higher authority!

There can be little doubt that the major stumbling block to literal understanding of the book is not only an antisupernaturalist bias in general, but the rampant, repeated, and self-evident supernaturalism of the book. Perhaps there is ultimately no rejoinder to be offered but that any quantity or quality of miracle fades in comparison with the doctrine of the resurrection of the body (which, in a way, is precisely the point of our Lord's allusion!). Documented instances in modern times of men who were swallowed and regurgitated alive by whales may be comforting to some, but the Bible suggests that the fish itself may have been a special miraculous creation; certainly all the "coincidences" are miraculous. And, of course, the Bible (also Matt. 12:40) merely says "great fish" not "whale"! The fast-growing (castor bean?) plant cannot be matched by even the fastest growing varieties in tropical climates (in a way similar with the storm which subsides after Jonah has been thrown overboard, except that there we have many near analogies within the Bible).

In addition to the supernatural events which they regard as impossible, critics usually also complain about a number of others which they regard as improbable or, at best, highly imprecise. Certain answers cannot be given to all the objections, partly, no doubt, because of lack of full information, but partly because of the apparent popular—perhaps we even dare say breezy—style of historiography the author adopts, and not without a good touch of humor. Nor is that so unique; virtually none of the Bible is "history" in the modern sense. Again one observes that no one is more "literalistic" than the critics when it serves their apologetic purposes!

The major "improbability" is, of course, the core of the book: that an Israelite prophet would journey to Nineveh to begin with, let alone successfully convert the entire city. However, Elijah and Elisha not too long previously clearly illustrate prophetic activity in the neighboring areas of Tyre and Damascus. (Also other aspects of their ministries have many parallels—the miracles, the antipagan preaching, the despondency, etc.) The "Gentile oracles" in most of the prophets clearly indicate Yahweh's *claim* on all nations (cf. esp. Jer. 13) even if they were not ordinarily delivered abroad. Jonah's own reasons for reluctance to obey are not explicitly stated.

In any event, there seem to be two periods of Assyrian history, where credible points of contact can at least be made with the Biblical narrative. During the reign of Adad-Nirari III (c. 810—782), son of the famous Semiramis, there were great religious stirrings in the empire, including even one known quasi-"monotheistic" push to "put your trust in Nabu and no other god." Another possibility a little later is Ashurdan II (771—754), during whose reign two severe plagues and an earthquake (cf. Amos 1:1) are known to have wracked the populace.

It is somewhat in the nature of religious revivals but particularly in the days of *cuius regio, eius religio,* for mass conversions to occur. As also often happens in those contexts, this conversion appears to have been quite ephemeral, but that is beyond our writer's concern. The inclusion of the animals (3:7-8; 4:11; also attested by Herodotus) appears to be merely another example of the presecular homology of man and nature in both fall and restoration.

The diameter of Nineveh no longer appears so fantastic if one understands that "the great city" means something like "greater Nineveh" or the "Nineveh district" (cf. Gen. 10:12). "Kings of Nineveh" (3:6) is an unexpected expression (instead of "Assyria"); it may have been popular usage in Canaan, or we may not be fully informed.

Chapter 2: The "Sign of Jonah"

The psalm or song of Jonah in chap. 2 stands out by any reckoning, beginning with its poetic form in contrast to the prose context. In addition, it alone is couched in first instead of third person terms. In one sense, no doubt, they are Jonah's own words (formulated, no doubt, after the experience; hence a thanksgiving more than a lament), but, in another sense, we have such a typical psalmic "individual thanksgiving," in general form as well as particular phrases, that it appears likely that Jonah is also adapting, if not quoting, a psalm or hymn that was already familiar (some of its expressions are even archaic), just as believers have done in all ages, especially under stress. In fact, that would well illustrate the intent of the "I" in many psalms; their general language and figurative expressions are intended for "all sorts and conditions of men."

To say that, however, is something quite different from the ordinary critical judgment that the song is an extraneous addition. (Cf. Wellhausen's famous crack: "Seaweed does not grow in the belly of a fish.") Among other things, the symmetry of the two halves of the book is destroyed if the psalm is dropped. The psalm heaps up quite a number of traditional expressions for "death" or judgment (whatever their precise application in the experience of the worshiper): "Sheol" (v. 2), "flood," (v. 3), "deep" (v. 5), "land" (v. 6, in the archaic sense of "underworld"), "Pit" (v. 6). Vs. 4 and 7 evince that vertical typology or ultimate unity of God's "holy temple" on earth with that in heaven, which was so basic to Old Testament piety and belief. As usual, the thanksgiving is not only verbal and volitional but concretized by a formal sacrifice (v. 9).

The psalm of Jonah is also significant for giving clearest expression of the theological significance of the book, to which we now turn. The typological correspondence between Jonah and Christ (the "sign of Jonah") receives clearest expression here. Christ is shut up three days and three nights in "the belly of Sheol" (v. 1), as was Jonah. Christ is "cast out" (v. 4; forsaken, cf. Ps. 22) from God's presence, as was Jonah. But also in both cases God restores "life from the Pit" (v. 6). (Similar language in Ps. 16:10 is specifically applied to our Lord's resurrection in Acts 2:27.) As the fish was ultimately beneficent, saving Jonah's life, so death and judgment lead to eternal life. No wonder that catacomb art so prominently illustrates the resurrection from the story of Jonah.

Both this general theme as well as the specific expressions in Jonah 2 are so common in the Old Testament, however, that by extension they indicate that the typological significance of the book is not only limited to the experiences of Jonah. What Christ fulfills and gives climactic expression to is also *Israel's* history of judgment and grace, peaking in the "death and resurrection" of the Exile and Return. Thus the "sign of Jonah" is very parallel in import to the "Suffering Servant" in Isaiah. The allegorical and parabolic interpretations often brought out this wider significance of Jonah better than conservative stress on factuality, but what criticism offered with the left hand, it more than withdrew with the right. As always, the typical and theological significance of Jonah is enhanced and anchored by historicity, not detracted from.

In their own backhanded way, critics also correctly sensed two other major accents of Jonah, which need to be reformulated within conservative hermeneutics. One of these is its universal import—not liberal universal*ism* ("God loves all His children"), but the universal evangelistic thrust of the book (implied in many other books in the third part of the classical outline). It is not entirely misleading to call Jonah the "first apostle to the Gentiles," or to consider Acts 10 ff. as the sequel and continuation of the book. (Cf. Jerome's report that Cyprian was converted by reading the Book of Jonah.) Second, the book certainly is also a graphic illustration of the recurrent prophetic theme of the "contingency of prophecy": Jonah's sulking and pouting when judgment is overruled by grace because of repentance, and new members brought into the cozy club alongside those who "have borne the heat and the burden of the day," has had far more than 120,000 (4:11) emulators down through the ages!

MICAH

Micah is the fourth of the great eighth-century prophets, but often so overshadowed by the others, especially his fellow Judahite, Isaiah, that he is sometimes rightfully considered "the neglected prophet." Early critics were unable to discover much "originality" in Micah, and conservatives were sometimes interested in little beyond the Messianic prophecy of chap. 5. Some redress possibly comes in another comparison, suggesting that if Amos is the prophet of justice, Hosea of love, and Isaiah of holiness, Micah champions and synthesizes all three (cf. esp. 6:8). In any case, many inner connections between Micah and Isaiah are traceable (e.g., 4:1-4 and Is. 2:2-5; 2:1-5 and Is. 5:8 ff.; 5:9-14 and Is. 2:6 ff.).

Name and Background

The name, "Micah" means "Who is like Yahweh?" and it has often been supposed that the concluding doxology in the book (7:18 ff.) is a sort of play on the name. Some thirteen other Biblical figures also bear the name, but the major namesake of the eighth-century prophet is another great prophet a little over a century earlier, Micaiah ben Imlah (1 Kings 22). "Micaiah," of course, is simply a longer form of "Micah"; the *Kethib* of Jer. 26:18 even refers to our prophet by the longer form, but apparently the shorter version was generally preferred to minimize confusion. The Jeremiah reference is also interesting, because when a century later Micah's prediction of the destruction of Jerusalem is adduced in defense of Jeremiah's life, it is the only occasion that one canonical prophet ever explicitly refers to another one. (Because Micah 3:12 is so harsh—and so accurate—some critics question its authenticity and dismiss the Jeremiah citation as "redactional.")

About the only personal information we have on Micah (not even his father's name is mentioned) is his home in Moresheth (-gath), 1:1 and 1:14. The site is the largely unexcavated Tell-ej-Judeideh, a few miles north of Lachish, in the foothills on the edge of former Philistine territory. Commentators often seek to explain various features in Micah's preaching as reflecting his small-town background; there may be partial truth in the explanation, but one should be cautious. Those origins might help explain the feeling with which he condemns exploitation and oppression of the poor (and here comparisons with Amos may be in order). In G. A. Smith's famous words: "Pinched peasant faces peer between his words and fill the ellipses." However, we skate on very thin ice if we offer that background in explanation of his specification of Bethlehem as the birthplace of the Messiah (5:2) or of his emphatic prediction of Jerusalem's destruction (3:12; note that a number of small villages, including Micah's home, are also so singled out in 1:10-16). Particularly when some critical exegetes make Micah's (like Jeremiah's later) prophecy of the destruction of Jerusalem a contradiction of Isaiah's assurance of the "inviolability of Zion," they betray their utter lack of theological sophistication (although "Zion" and "Jerusalem" can sometimes be synonymous, as in 3:12). It is true, however, that Micah, unlike his great contemporary, evinces no interest in the political machinations of the times, and provincial origins could account for that.

As to further personal information, we can only deduce from the sarcasm of Micah 2:11 and the contrast he draws between himself and other prophets in 3:5-8 that he was no professional prophet, or at least distanced himself from most "prophetic" figures. Similarly 2:6 ff. and the acerbity of some other passages may hint at the popular opposition aroused by his preaching (perhaps still echoed a century later on Jeremiah's behalf).

There are no problems with the superscription's specification of the reigns of "Jotham, Ahaz, and Hezekiah" as the period of his ministry (the same as in Is. 1:1). Likewise, the preserved oracles support the information that his visions were "concerning Samaria and Jerusalem," that is, partly occurring before the debacle in the North. Anti-Samaria preaching seems clearest in the opening oracle, predicting its fall (Micah 1:2-7), and in 6:9-16, where "the statutes of Omri and all the works of the house of Ahab" are scored. Toward the other end of his ministry, Jer. 26 specifies that the prediction of Jerusalem's destruction, quoted there, was uttered during Hezekiah's reign.

The text of Micah alternates between excellent and desperate, again for reasons past finding out. An early example of the latter is Micah 1:10-16, although here likely reconstruction is not too difficult. In at least three instances, however (2:7-10; 6:9-12, and 7:11-12) the copyists appear to have lost the thread of the thought altogether, and the translator must resort to conjecture.

Outline

The most useful outline of Micah is probably a simple threefold one. (1) Chaps. 1—3 are prophecies of doom against Samaria, against various cities near Micah's home, and against various segments of the establishment, climaxing in the prediction of Jerusalem's devastation, cited in Jer. 26. (2) Chaps. 4—5 are prophecies of hope and restoration, almost as great a contrast as imaginable from the opening chapters. After Zion has been established as the "capital" of the world, the dispersed Israelites will be gathered, their enemies will be destroyed, the second David will come, the remnant will flourish, and Israel's religion will be purified. (3) Chaps. 6—7 are again largely prophecies of doom, but ending again in 7:7 ff. with a beautiful prayer of hope and confidence. The divine arraignment of Israel leads up to the classical summary of Biblical ethics in 6:8, followed by a condemnation of dishonesty and a lament over the nation's moral disintegration.

Thus, there is no hint in Micah of the classical tripartite prophetical outline. The other great redactional expression of judgment-salvation (Law-Gospel), namely, "alternation of weal and woe" is in clearest evidence throughout the book, however. The major "fly in the ointment" of structuring the material is Micah 2:12-13, apparently a beautiful, even Messianic prophecy of hope and restoration squarely in the middle of stout invective (chaps. 1—3). Hence, the two troublesome verses have a long history of interpretation. Some (Ibn Ezra in the Middle Ages, many critics and also not a few conservatives) have sought to solve the problem by construing the verses as a satiric quotation by Micah of the saccharine preaching of the false prophets. That would certainly suit the context, and is by no means impossible (especially since Hebrew uses no quotation marks). It certainly would highlight the superficial identity of much false prophecy with the promissory and Messianic oracles of the true prophets. (Many critics, of course, tend to reject the verses as Micanic, whatever their provenance, on the basis of the dogma that early true prophets never uttered such oracles at all.) Nevertheless, to have a false prophet quoted at such length and without clear notice seems highly exceptional, so it is best to regard the passage as the first illustration in the book of the "alternation of weal and woe" principle of editorial arrangement. (See also below.)

Because of the problem, however, other outlines of the entire book are often suggested in order to do justice to the pattern of alternating judgment and hope, which is clearly evidenced throughout. Some suggest a different tripartite outline to make the first section climax with the passage just discussed, and the other two sections similarly: chaps. 1—2, 3—5 and 6—7. Others would divide the book into only two parts, chaps. 1—5 and 6—7, but with each section evincing the alternating pattern (1—3 and 4—5; 6:1—7:7 and 7:8-20. The differences are ultimately inconsequential, especially if the interpreter senses the underlying "Law-Gospel" principle of arrangement in any event.

Critical Viewpoints

All of this suggests that Micah is prime material for tradition-critical experimentation. As already indicated, however, much of it may be neutral or even helpful, at least if Micah is the author of all of it and largely responsible for the arrangement. One effort, while speculative, has attempted to show how an oral tradition crystallized around the Messianic prophecy of 5:2. Micah 4 may plausibly be understood as collected by common reference to "Zion." There are various possible indications of preliminary collections. These might have originally concluded with promissory accent, and their subsequent cementing together might account for some of the "alternation of weal and woe" pattern of the completed book. Micah 3:1 opens curiously with "And I said," as though it might have originally introduced an autobiographical (A-type?) collection. It is followed by the imperative, "Hear," which we also meet at 1:2 and 6:1 (cf. the first alternate outline above). But it is finally difficult to say whether or not these notations are only coincidental.

Classical literary criticism was quite severe with Micah, and after an interval of considerable softening, often appears to be reverting to type. Micah 1—3 (with the likely exception of 2:12-13) has nearly always been regarded as largely genuine—but very often that was all! Nowhere did the dogma that preexilic true prophets were exclusively heralds of doom require such extensive surgery as in the case of Micah. The citation of Micah in Jer. 26 as a preacher of judgment scarcely proves that was *all* that he preached!

Micah 4—5 was once virtually as unanimously denied to Micah as chaps. 1—3 were accepted. Not only was there the problem of the preachment of promise on the lips of an eighth-century prophet, but also the stumbling block of the supernaturalist prediction in 4:10, of Babylon as both the locale of the captivity and the origin of the return. Recent criticism has tended to become more cautious: often eighth-century anti-Assyrian oracles (perhaps authentic) were much expanded and amplified in later times. The prediction of Babylon is often evaded by considering the line or the entire verse a later gloss updating an original reference to Sennacherib's invasion in the light of postexilic memories. Then chaps. 4—5 become a sort of "Deutero-Micah" (the expression is actually used).

In reply, we must remind ourselves (apart from revelatory considerations) that the general threat of restoration after judgment in case of unfaithfulness was at least as old as Deuteronomy (of course, to critics a century *later* than Micah). Even the "scandal" of the early mention of Babylon (assuming its genuineness, of course) is assuaged somewhat by the consideration that Babylon, as the ancient "mother" and religious capital of Assyria, often lent its name metonymously to the latter even in its prime (Assyria is mentioned too in 5:5). As elsewhere, there is no reason to suppose that Micah delivered such promissory oracles at the same time or even to the same audiences as the threats, but by the same token there is no reason besides dogmatism to deny them to him.

Micah 6—7 is more similar to 1—3, only somewhat milder in tone, and as a result critical rejection of these chapters has never been as assured as of 4—5. Alternative theories of their origination, however, vary widely. A radical, minority position seizes on the reference to broken walls (7:11) and other "evidence" to argue for a "Trito-Micah" penning much of the section about the time of Ezra and Nehemiah. However, the Wellhausenian supposition is probably still as typical as any, that while they might actually contain or echo genuine Micanic material, most of their contents derived from anonymous circles in the following (seventh) century. The reference to human sacrifice in 6:7 allegedly pointed to the reign of Manasseh, when the practice was supposed to have especially flourished (perhaps so, but, assuredly, not only then). The reference to the "statutes of Omri" in 6:16 was sometimes taken to be a precursor of the "deuteronomistic" refrain, "to walk in all the ways of Jeroboam the son of Nebat"—but even by critical standards that appears to be grasping at straws. Much of chap. 7 has a hymnic or psalmic quality to it, but one cannot legitimately deduce dates from such formal considerations.

Contents

The "Hear, you peoples" with which the collection of Micah's oracles opens (1:2) may well be a deliberate echoing of a characteristic phrase of Micah's great namesake, Micaiah (cf. 1 Kings 22:28). The exordium continues with a classical merger of heavenly courtroom ("witness"), heavenly temple and theophanic language (judgment rooted in God's creatorhood). "Place" (1:3), as often in the Bible, means shrine or temple, and we obviously have here again the familiar picture of the heavenly judge enthroned in the temple on Zion as well as in its vertical antitype, the heavenly temple (the whole universe).

One should note that, as repeatedly, Samaria and Jerusalem (that is, "greater Israel," the whole church) are mentioned in the same breath (1:5) even though this opening oracle is directed primarily at Samaria. In likening Samaria's prosperity to "the hire of a harlot" (1:7), Micah is broaching a motif which especially Ezekiel will later amplify at great length (chaps. 16 and 23). Chap. 1:8 might suggest an action prophecy by Micah similar to Is. 20, but it is probably only figurative.

The pericope in Micah 1:10-16 is intriguing but difficult. At least in the Hebrew it is obvious that we have a series of puns on the names of various villages near to Micah's own home, Moresheth, predicting Assyrian invasion and deportation. Many of the sites and allusions are unknown, but the major problem is the difficult state of the text at many points. Scribal incomprehension may have contributed, but perhaps the damage was also mechanical: one attractive hypothesis suggests that the right margin (the beginning of the line in Hebrew!) of an original manuscript was damaged, so that most correction should concentrate at that point. The opening "Tell it not in Gath," however, is probably a traditional, proverbial caution to silence, perhaps especially redolent of David (2 Sam. 1:20). If so, the pericope also climaxes with a Davidic allusion: his flight to Adullam (v. 15; 1 Sam. 22) will be recapitulated by his heirs. Thus the entire oracle has a sort of "anti-Messianic" import as a type of Christ's death and burial, over against the more usual Messianic oracles later in the book. (The principle, of course, applies to all the doomsaying in the prophets.)

As noted above, Micah 2:12-13 is probably best taken as an intervening promise in the otherwise exclusively judgmental opening three chapters. As the parallelism shows, the "king" here is Yahweh Himself (cf. 4:6-7) but, at least in New Testament retrospect, such oracles are also "Messianic," that is, fulfilled in Him who was Yahweh incarnate.

Besides the remnant and shepherd imagery, the pericope also contains the lovely Messianic picture of (literally) "the Breaker," that is, one who breaks through or makes a breach in a wall in order to deliver.

The denunciations of Micah 1—3 climax in the vivid prophecy of Jerusalem's razing and abandonment, still remembered and quoted a century later in Jer. 26:18. In part it contrasts sharply with, and in part it emphatically confirms what Isaiah was contemporaneously preaching about Jerusalem (cf. above). Following hard upon this oracle, however, is the greatest contrast possible: the eschatological establishment of "the mountain of the house" (both 3:12 and 4:1) "as the highest of the mountains." From a purely formal standpoint, we have at once here a superb exemplification of two major editorial principles in Biblical books, both "catchword" connection, and "alternation of weal and woe" (regardless of isagogical technicalities). By denying 4:1 ff to Micah, however, critics largely denude it of its theological impact. Chap. 4:1-3 is a special case, of course, because of its virtual identity with Is. 2:2-4 (one of the more visible alignments of the books of Isaiah and Micah). See our fuller discussion in Isaiah. Whether or not one agrees with our judgment that the most likely explanation of the parallelism of the two passages is a common source tapped by both, there is no good reason to consider it non-Micanic, as far as present context and application are concerned. Both Isaiah and Micah fit out the oracle they adapt with their own conclusions; in contrast to Isaiah 2:5's appeal to walk in the light until its final revealing, Micah (4:4) concludes with an affirmation that Israel *will* be faithful, in spite of the lingering paganism.

The theme of the eschatological turning of the tables for Zion continues to dominate in Micah 4. Also in chap. 5, sometimes the picture is that of a more gradual, pacific ascendancy of Zion (e.g., 4:1-4), while at other times it is martial and envisions Zion's forceful conquest of its enemies (e.g., 4:11-13; 5:7-9). The same alternation is common in other prophetic books too, but especially in Micah, the critical tendency to mingle historical criticism and content criticism *(Sachkritik)* is very evident. The varying forecasts tend to be attributed to the "dovish" and "hawkish" factions, between which critics distribute most of what they consider postexilic literature. And, of course, it does not take long for liberal, universalistic, often pacifistic, subjectivity to decide which passages are truly "inspired" and "normative" ideals, and which are not!

Micah 4:9-10 introduces the theme of the *dolores Messiae,* which is also articulated in 5:3, that is, the "birth-pangs of the Messianic age," the exile to "Babylon," the suffering and death which must anticipate the triumph of the Messianic "king" (4:9 thus doubly interlocks with the great Messianic prophecy of chap. 5).

The transition from Micah 4 to 5 and the beginning of the Messianic prophecy is marred by uncertainties about both translation and the proper chapter division. The English text's 5:1 is the conclusion of chap. 4 in the Masoretic tradition, but the former seems clearly preferable, because the verse obviously relates primarily to what follows. Unfortunately (and probably all too typically) it is usually ignored in the West, nonetheless, even omitted in liturgical and homiletical treatments. What is lost as a result is the judgment foil to the promise, the "Law" component of the Law-Gospel unity. That much is clear, regardless of the precise translation. The reference is obviously to the siege and humiliation of Zion and its king (Messiah), preceding his unexpected triumph. The main historical type is evidently Sennacherib's investment of Jerusalem in 701 but by extension and even more profoundly, Nebuchadnezzar's sack of the city in 587.

The RSV translation of Micah 5:1a, "walled about with a wall," follows the Septuagint and has poetic parallelism in its favor, but involves a slight—although readily explainable—change in one letter of the Hebrew text (*gdr* instead of *gdd*). KJV's "gather yourself in troops, daughter of troops" sounds like the beginning of the Messianic counterattack but is textually problematic. A third possibility is to translate, "You are gashing yourself, daughter of gashes," presumably in reference to a popular, funereal reaction to the city's crisis.

Textual and exegetical problems continue in Micah 5:2, especially the "little to be," but they need not concern us here. Some of the problems probably rise from the deliberate air of mystery and/or adaptation of archaic material, as in many Messianic texts. In a masterful *double entendre,* the Messiah's origins "from of old, from ancient days," that is, His genealogy both according to the flesh and according to the Spirit, is communicated. The "she who is in travail" of v. 3 is surely related to the "virgin" of Is. 7:14—one of the many intricate parallels between Isaiah's and Micah's eschatological prophecy. At the same time, the typological dimension opens up again: the mother is also Israel in affliction, thence also Mary, the mother of our Lord as antitype (and here a valid, Biblical Mariology), and then also via Mary and her Son, the second Israel, "holy mother church."

Even though the Messianic vision continues unabated in the following section, Micah 5:5-6, it tends to be bypassed in ordinary ecclesiastical use every bit as much as 5:1 is. Here Assyria is the type of the eschatological enemy (leading many critics to assume a possible snatch of original Micanic material). The "This [One] will be peace" of 5:5 is almost certainly alluded to in Eph. 2:14 of the end to racist and religious conflict between Jew and Gentile in Christ, but it also applies to the eschatological peace in all its dimensions. It reminds us not only of Isaiah's "Prince of Peace" theme in general, but Micah's point here is probably the same as Isaiah's incessant insistence that peace can and will come only by supernatural change, not by armaments or other human measures. Note the numerical parallelism of "seven-eight" (cf. Amos 1:3 ff., etc.). The pattern may be only traditional and formal, but the numbers may also be mildly symbolic: "seven" as sufficiency and "eight" as superabundance.

Micah 6:1 ff. is one of the major examples of the *"covenant* lawsuit" (not ordinary "controversy") in the Bible. Following ancient, pre-Israelite patterns, the divine Judge in His heavenly courtroom poetically asks nature to serve as jury in His case against Israel (cf. 1:1; Is. 1:2 ff., Hos. 4:1, 4; etc.). Instead of an indictment, however, we almost have God's self-reproach at His people's lassitude (6:3-5; hence also the pericope's use in the "Reproaches" of the Christian liturgy). The tone is almost Hoseanic, admonishing Israel to "remember" and to "know." The object of the latter, "saving acts," is almost *"Heilsgeschichte"* (minus its neo-Orthodox components), but the Hebrew is "righteousnesses," that is, acts by which God establishes His righteousness, saves and justifies. The specific events to "remember" are not immediately related to Exodus or Zion, as usual, but "what happened from Shittim to Gilgal," that is, in connection with the crossing of the Jordan, especially the orgiastic apostasy just preceding (Num. 25).

The reply comes in the *Gattung* of a cultic "entrance liturgy," rhetorically inquiring (vs. 6-7) of the conditions of entry to the sanctuary (cf. Ps. 15; 24:3-6). The contrast drawn in the answer (v. 8) is not between "priestly" and "prophetic" religion, or between interiority and ritual, but between religion with and without accompanying life and behavior (the passage was another favorite in the spiritualistic arsenal of especially early critics). Since even conservative use of v. 8 often unwittingly allows it to encourage a universalistic moralism, it cannot be stressed too much that the responses required *(tob, mishpat,* and *chesedh)* are *covenant* terms, and the usual translations "good," "justice," and "kindness" inevitably tend to demythologize and secularize. The third member of the final triad (used elsewhere only Prov. 11:2) is of less certain translation. "Humbly" is apparently not so much wrong as weak; the basic picture appears to be the Oriental one of a veiled bride walking beside her husband—modestly, circumspectly, but also confidently and committedly.

The final chapter of Micah generally has an almost apocalyptic ring to it, but it is also typical prophetic "copy," and there is no reason why it should not reflect the chaotic conditions of much of Micah's ministry. In form, 7:1-10 is basically a psalmic "individual lament," depicting a decadent, disintegrating society (that also professed to be a "church"), where mutual assault and suspicion prevail, even in one's own household. The picture merges with the general one of the "messianic labor pains," and when Jesus cites especially v. 6 (Matt. 10:21 ff., etc.), He is identifying Himself as that Messianic establisher of God's truth, whose initial societal impact, however, will be to bring "not peace, but a sword."

Instead of despair, however, the book concludes with a series of most poignant expressions of confidence in the heavenly Judge's ultimate victory and vindication of the right. Micah 7:7-20 is often considered a rather model "prophetic liturgy," that is, a discourse modeled on worship experiences, and the theory is not, as such, implausible. The closing doxology (7:18 ff.) may open with a pun on Micah's name (cf. above), but continues to characterize God's incomparability as consisting in "perfect forgiveness." The metaphor of 19b may echo the *Protevangelium* (Gen. 3:15), and that of 19c is still literally acted out in the *Tashlich* ("You will cast") ceremony of the Jewish New Year. Micah concludes where the New Testament begins (Luke 1:55, the *Benedictus)* by citing the promise "to Abraham and to his seed forever."

NAHUM

In many ways, the Book of Nahum is similar to Obadiah (which see). The similarity begins with the lack of personal information. The superscription tells us only that he was an "Elkoshite," but that helps little because of the uncertain location of Elkosh. Popular tradition rushed in to fill the gap, of course. Among the suggested locations are: (1) northern Galilee (Jerome); (2) southwestern Judah (cf. 1:15), near Micah's home; (3) Capernaum (which means, "Village of Nahum"; and (4) near Nineveh (at least his tomb is shown there), perhaps because the vividness of his description of Nineveh's fall was thought to require an eyewitness.

Date

Nahum differs radically from Obadiah, however, in the relative certainty of its date. Except for a handful of radical critics in either direction, the contents of the book virtually force a date within a half-century span. The comparison of Nineveh's impending fate to that of "No-amon" (a Hebrew name for Thebes, the upper Egyptian capital) in 663 sets an incontrovertible *terminus a quo* for dating. At the other end, Nineveh's fall in 612 sets an obvious *terminus ad quem* (and even those who do not regard it as prophecy are reluctant to date it very long after that epochal event).

Can we be more precise? Theological motives, recognized or unrecognized, play at least as much a role as historical ones in attempting to pinpoint the date further. Conservatives tend to date the book as close to 663 as possible, partly in order to highlight its predictive aspect. Liberals who prefer to replace "prophecy" with mere prescience or inspired foresight, tend to move closer to a 612 date. How much closer varies, but two favorite suggestions are 625, shortly after the death of the empire's last great ruler, Ashurbanipal, when Nineveh was first beset by the Medes, or near 612, not long before the city fell to a Medo-Babylonian coalition. Of course, those who wish to make the book, or parts of it, "prophecy after the event," or mere commentary on what is now seen as God's predetermined will, must date the book somewhat later.

How one chooses between most of these alternatives is not necessarily a theological matter, and may depend merely on how one reads the evidence. A certain rationalism probably lurks in attempts to tie the message closely to specific historical events (the historicistic reading of the prophet "speaking to his own times"). On the other hand, its specifically predictive quality is in no direct proportion to the interval between prophecy and fulfillment.

Especially Scandinavian scholars have sought to neutralize the historical question by construing the book as a liturgy (probably at New Year's) and Nahum as a "cultic prophet." Thus the real subject of the book is understood as suprahistory, with Assyria as only a current illustration or "historification" of timeless, mythical themes. Together with Obadiah, Joel, and Habakkuk, Nahum has been a favorite target of such efforts. In more extreme form, Nahum loses his personhood altogether and becomes only a symbol (the name means "comfort"), and the liturgy behind the book is construed as dramatizing a quasi-mythological, dualistic struggle between Yahweh and Tammuz, the Canaanite fertility god, or the like. Many of the images and expressions in the book are also thought to be derived from the regular liturgies of the two deities.

Of course, with specifics anything like that, the cultic hypothesis is unthinkable to a conservative. In "demythologized" form, however, the supposition may not be entirely off target, at least as a hypothesis. Composition by Nahum precludes neither heavy dependence on liturgical forms, nor cultic formation and/or use afterwards. There is an undeniable psalmic cast to much of the language, and a passage like 1:15 at least makes specific reference to liturgical acts. Above all, at least the broad outlines of such a theory are useful in reminding us that Biblical theology is concerned neither with the secularists' "history," nor with the "timeless truths" of ancient myth and modern moralism, but rather with eternity "incarnate" in Time, of present judgment and salvation as "sacramental" of final judgment and salvation, in principle already realized in Christ, but with its universal effects still ahead. So seen, the judgment on Nineveh becomes part of our history, of a piece with the judgment on our imperiousness, but also at one with the judgment visited for all upon the One on Calvary.

Nahum, then, is also at one with Obadiah in being largely a single Gentile-oracle, not against "Edom," but Nineveh (Assyria). To many critics that has sufficed to classify him a chauvinistic, nationalistic prophet, probably representative of the very "false prophets" which so exercised contemporaries like Jeremiah (cf. Hananiah in Jer. 28). A recent scholar has sought to exonerate Nahum by literary criticism: Nahum allegedly preached moral judgment, while later additions gave the book its jingoistic flavor. However, even assuming the criticism itself held up theoretically, that is no solution theologically.

The real problem with such interpretations is, indeed, theological, but even from a purely literary standpoint its biggest obstacle is chap. 1, which, as we shall see, emphasizes the justice and universality of God's action in world history. That Nahum concentrates on the application of that justice to a major scourge of God's people (as most other prophets do too) does not mean that he is insensitive to or repudiates the deserved aspect of that scourging as punishment for Israel's sins. In canonical context, the Biblically literate reader would ordinarily read even Nahum 2—3 in that broader light, but chap. 1 mandates it.

Style

It is everywhere agreed that stylistically Nahum easily heads the list of the minor prophets, excelling even Amos, and himself excelled in all Biblical literature only by Isaiah. Many of his deft, vivid, word-pictures are fully worthy of Isaiah himself. Some of their forcefulness is evident even in translation, but much is inevitably also lost. Pfeiffer calls Nahum "the last of the great classical Hebrew poets," and G. A. Smith observes that his rhythm "rumbles and rolls, leaps and flashes, like the horsemen and chariots that he describes." Similar encomiums could easily be multiplied.

What has just been said applies to chap. 1 to a much lesser degree, however. Here the style is not only more varied, but the chapter shows signs of greater adaptation or condensation of original exemplars. This may be especially evident in what appears to be the remnants of an acrostic (alphabetic) poem in the first part of the chapter. Efforts to recover the original form of the acrostic poem have proved entirely futile, and some deny the existence of such an underlying pattern altogether. However, it does appear that the letters of the Hebrew alphabet can be followed fairly accurately down to *lamedh*.

It may well be that Nahum departed much more radically from his prototypes or supplemented them much more in chap. 1 than in the following ones in order to make his theological direction unmistakably clear at the outset. Critics, of course, would often go much further and either deny the chapter to Nahum altogether, or blame its alleged deterioration on later scribes. The synthesis might be signaled already by the superscription's styling of the book as both an "oracle" *(massa')* and a "vision" *(chazon).* Some critics have attempted to relate the two terms to "genuine" and "ungenuine" portions of the book. Both terms are used so broadly of prophetic messages, however, that further inferences can scarcely be made.

Contents

In form, Nahum 1:2-11 is a magnificent hymn or psalm of praise to the majestic Yahweh, who is outraged by the evil, and now comes to "take vengeance on his adversaries." Nineveh or Assyria, the object of His wrath, is not mentioned at this point (and rarely in the text of the book as a whole), as though to remind us that the prophet's ultimate proclamation is of a theological *principle,* with constant applications in history. At the same time the later specification of Assyria as the object of judgment (2:8; 3:7, 18) as well as of Israel as the recipient of salvation (2:2, and by implication often) reminds us that the subject is not some universalistic impersonal "law," but the personal God of special revelation intervening in the specifics of *Heilsgeschichte.*

A number of ancient and classical characterizations of God (cf. Ex. 34:6-7 and 20:5-6, the latter the "close of the Commandments") dominate the first two verses of the poem. The first is God's "jealousy," of course, not arbitrary pettiness, but better "jealousness," within the Biblical context, at least a monogamously based picture of a devoted husband, who is not about to share his wife with other men, and who brooks no obstacle in establishing the probity of his relationship once and for all ("no more" in 1:12 and "never again" in 1:15). Similarly, "vengeance" *(n-q-m),* but here we have severe translation problems; the Book of Nahum is an especially clear illustration of the root's binary import: "vengeance" or "defeat" of the enemy, indeed, but, simultaneously, "rescue," "vindication," etc., of those in the proper relationship to the subject. But, third, God's unrelenting "wrath" upon the evil, a ruling principle of God's governance of the universe, but never a favorite theological theme, if applied evenhandedly, also receives classical expression. V. 3, however, exhibits the other side of the coin, God's "longsuffering," even toward the heathen in His "left-hand kingdom," but *a fortiori* to those in a covenant relationship with Him.

Vs. 3b-5 continue with a theophany, such as often begins prophetic books (esp. Amos and Micah). In creation perspective, God's particular judgments within history are readily seen as already anticipating the final judgment. His earthly temple, Zion, is not specified here as His judgment-throne, but is surely implied.

At chap. 1:12 the prophet shifts from hymnic to oracular form. Nahum 1:12-15 and the apparently parenthetical 2:2, as oracles of salvation for Judah, are the explicit obverse of the rest of the book. Hence, many critics inevitably think of a later insertion. Chap. 1:15a celebrates the foretaste of eschatological salvation evidenced by Assyria's fall in the familiar words of Is. 40:9 and 52:7 (very possibly a liturgical source was common to both prophets), and also of Acts 10:36 and Rom. 10:15, proclaiming its Christic realization. Judah's "feasts" and "vows" would constantly celebrate and sacramentally experience that fulfillment, "until He come," essentially just as the Christian counterparts.

Chaps. 2 and 3 are less specifically theological, but the refrain, "Behold, I am against you," reminds us that the context is still very much Yahweh's personal and particular retribution. In contents, they are largely variations on the same theme, a "poetic description in the most vivid language of the fall of the Assyrian capital, and a stirring expression of the relief spreading over the entire Near East, as the expectation of the fall of the hated tyrant grew." One commentator calls them "one great 'at last!' of deliverance" (which the Christian exegete must relate theologically to the church's eschatological hope).

Much further commentary, however, only gilds the lily. Among the tumble of the pictures, one might note particularly the grasshoppers of 3:17 (cf. Joel). Conservative commentators are sometimes tempted to try to match almost each individual feature of Nahum's poetry with some specific event fulfilled in Nineveh's fall (e.g., 2:6 and the known destruction of part of Nineveh's walls by a flood). While certainly not impossible, in the case of Nahum that really appears to be "literalistic," and literally "prosaic." If liberals are often guilty of reducing nearly all of Scripture's specificity to aesthetics, conservatives are easily prone to miss the very nature and spirit of genuine poetry (which is certainly no less present because of *verbal* inspiration).

The symmetry of the arrangement of Nahum 2—3 cannot be accidental. Chap. 2 follows a rhythm of: (1) *attack* (on Nineveh and its frenzied defense, vs. 1—5); (2) *capture* and destruction of the city (6-10); and (3) the *crimes* of the city (11-13). Chap. 3 repeats the pattern (vs. 1-3, 4-6, and 8-17), only reversing the second and third members in order to climax with the city's sacking. Another difference is that the immorality of Nineveh's behavior is illustrated in sexual terms in 3:4-6.

Nahum closes (3:18-19) with a sublime "epitaph of the Assyrian empire." The verses are at once an ironic elegy of the permanently fallen city and a joyful shout of relief by the nations of the world. "For upon whom has not come your unceasing evil?" It is the church's confession that Assyria's precipitous fall was anything but adventitious. One cannot but note that Nineveh's ruins were not even recognized by Alexander the Great a scant three centuries later, and so they remained until Layard dug into the tell of "Kuyunyik" in 1845, at the dawn of modern archaeology.

It may be accidental (some critics think it deliberately artificial), but the name "Nahum" superbly summarizes the book's message. God's justice means judgment on the enemy, but "comfort" to the faithful. The book thus exemplifies the role which "Gentile oracles" play in all the prophets. The point is not that God's people go scot-free, but precisely the reverse: if God so judges those whom He employs temporarily as instruments of His judgment upon His unfaithful people, how much more fearful the judgment upon His own people if they finally miss the message. But the message has to do with universal world history, with nations as well as individuals. *Die Weltgeschichte ist das Weltgericht.* In Christ that judgment is revealed most heinously, and only in the "Comforter," the Spirit of Christ, can we join the "At last" of the saints in all ages.

HABAKKUK

The Book of Habakkuk has many broad similarities with Nahum, beginning with its superscription which characterizes the work again as, in effect, both an "oracle" *(massa')* and a "vision." That is about all that the superscription tells us, and in truth, everything else about the prophet is surmise or attempted deduction from its contents.

Name and Content

The first conundrum is the prophet's name. The Septuagint gives it as "Ambakoum." It does not at all appear to be the normal Hebrew type derived from a triliteral root, usually with a theophoric affix or suffix. Luther's explanation of the name in association with the root *ch-b-q*, to grasp, embrace, etc., and thence *"Herzer"* ("heartener, comforter") is hardly philologically defensible, and is today usually abandoned. The most likely association of the name appears to be with the Akkadian name of a culinary herb, presumably current in Judah also at this time because of the massive Mesopotamian influences. (Cf. "Susanna" = lily; "Hadassah" [Esther] = myrtle, etc.)

All of this would be of no significance, except that the seeming oddity of the name always seems to attract attention. Some critical scholars have seized upon the name's apparent etymology as possible evidence of the cultic (fertility) associations of the prophet and the book. That seems farfetched, but we do have to reckon with cultic possibilities in the composition and structuring of the book again. Especially Humbert has worked out a detailed theory according to which the book originated among the cultic prophets in the Jerusalem temple in the last quarter of the seventh century. The present order of the oracles stems from a liturgical festival c. 602, awaiting Nebuchadnezzar's imminent invasion to deliver them from Jehoiakim's evil rule. Details aside, the pros and cons are again about the same in the case of Joel, Obadiah, and Nahum (which see).

If one is so inclined, it is about as easy as anywhere to detect "cultic influences" in Habakkuk. The major evidence is the psalm, replete with typical psalmic superscription, "Selah" (its only occurrence outside the psalter) and even "colophon," which constitutes the whole of Hab. 3 (cf. below). But much of chap. 1 is also a quite typical individual lament, chaps. 1 and 2 have an almost antiphonal structure, and chap. 2 concludes with what can easily be construed as a rubric or versicle.

Habakkuk himself appears to give us a little information about his inspiration (in the phenomenological sense), which does not readily accord with cultic hypotheses. If Hab. 2:1 is to be taken literally, it reports that the prophet took his stand "on the tower" to "watch until a vision" came in answer to his complaint. Does this mean that he tries to procure visionary experiences, or at least to cultivate a mental attitude in which revelations would occur? In any event, when the vision does come, he is commanded to "make it plain upon tablets, so that he may run who reads it." Possibly, the picture is that of proclamation by public display of placards (one exegete speaks of the "placarded prophet"). Second, 3:16 (unless it is part of the psalm's poetry and hence not autobiographical) may describe psychosomatic sensations in the prophet, as his prayer is answered. (A few critics think chap. 3 is misplaced, and originally *was* the vision mentioned in 2:2.)

If this information were to be pressed, it would imply more of an "ecstatic" than a "cultic" prophet, and some have tried to bend the superscription's characterization of Habakkuk as a *nabi* (the only preexilic prophet so distinguished) in that direction. Others take *nabi* here to mean more (cultic) "singer," as in Chronicles, and adduce especially the psalm in chap. 3. However, the entire discussion appears to pay few dividends.

Later legend and tradition is especially rife in the case of Habakkuk. Is it because of the peculiarity of his name, or because there was so little hard information to contravene? The only tale we need to note is that which appears in one of the apocryphal additions to Daniel (14:33-39), entitled "Bel and the Dragon." Here Habakkuk appears as one who miraculously carries pottage to, and finally rescues Daniel, after he had been cast to the lions a second time.

Whether the Qumran community was also especially fascinated with Habakkuk, or whether it is due to accidents of discovery, the *"pesher"* or pneumatic "commentary" on Hab. 1—2 is among our prize finds there. Like other Dead Sea Scrolls, it tells us much of the hermeneutical principles and exegetical techniques prevalent in the sect (often comparable to, or at least illuminating those of the New Testament), but its value to Old Testament studies is largely limited (!) to the area of textual criticism. Except for the psalm which the *pesher* does not gloss, the text-critical situation in Habakkuk is about average.

Higher Criticism and the Problem of the Book

Early criticism left Habakkuk in shambles, but that has now generally moderated. The psalm (chap. 3) was especially widely questioned on grounds of both contents and language (and the psalter was generally felt to be a postexilic product to begin with!) It was often thought to have been excerpted by a compiler from some liturgical collection, where perhaps it already possessed its present superscription linking it with Habakkuk (critics, of course, granting that about as much credence as they do the psalm superscriptions in general). Initially the absence of the psalm from the Qumran Habakkuk scroll added some fuel to the fire. However, that appeal is today widely regarded as an argument from silence, and most would probably agree with Duhm already that the psalm constitutes an integral crown and climax of the book. Duhm also defended the rest of the book against some of the exaggerated literary criticism of his day, classically against Marti, who left only seven verses in the entire book as genuine! This led even Duhm (no gentle critic himself!) to observe that "Marti treats the book just as cruelly as Yahweh will treat the ungodly, according to 3:13."

Major critical energies were often diverted to the difficult problem of the date and occasion of Habakkuk's ministry in relation to his recorded oracles. Let us first outline the first two chapters. Structurally they initially exhibit a neat balance of two laments (1:2-4 and 1:12-17) and two replies (1:5-11 and 2:1-5). Chap. 2:6-19 continues with a prophetic speech of doom, structured around five "Woes," and concludes (v. 20) with a liturgical piece. That structure led some early critics to compare the book with classical Greek dramas and even to suggest that it had been intended for dramatic performance. In more recent mutation, it has buttressed the hypothesis of a "prophetic liturgy" or the like, as we have seen.

The crucial question is who is the subject of the laments, and/or against whom are the woes of Hab. 2 directed? Conversely, who are the righteous in 1:2-4 and 1:33 ff.? Are the same people in view in all instances, or different ones? Are the evils spoken of internal (Judah's) or external (some foreign oppressor)? Habakkuk gives no specific historical references, and in the light of other prophetic analogies, the moral concerns could apply to Gentile nations as well as to Israel (or to both). There are enough variables here that quite a few combinations or alternatives are theoretically possible—and one wonders if every conceivable one has not been defended. Just about every empire in the history of the Near East from Assyria on has been suggested as playing a role. We shall make no effort to review all the theories here.

Fortunately, the frequent critical concern that Habakkuk might turn out to be another chauvinistic "prophet of salvation" (as Nahum and Obadiah are supposed to be) if his oracles are addressed only against Israel's foes, need not trouble us. At the same time we need not erect mutual exclusives; certainly in the broader canonical context, and perhaps quite specifically, the prophet's horizon will have encompassed all ungodliness, whenever it manifested itself. Also form-critical atomization of the book into a number of discrete units soon brings us to a dead end in dating efforts, and hence probably has little ultimate merit.

Early critics, typically, tended to date most of the book as late as possible. We need mention only Duhm's ingenious and influential suggestion (partly offered to correct Marti's hypercriticism; cf. above), to emend *Kasdim* (Chaldeans) in 1:6 to *kittim* (Greeks; a change of only one consonant in Hebrew), and similarly *yain* (wine) in 2:5 to *yawan* (Greece), thus enabling a date for the entire book around the time of Alexander the Great, toward the end of the fourth century. Change in critical climate has generally thrown such approaches into disfavor, and the Qumran scroll has now dealt it the *coup de grâce*. It is interesting, however, that while the Dead Sea manuscript plainly reads *kasdim* (Chaldeans), the accompanying midrashic commentary applies it to the *kittim,* by whom the Qumran community meant the Hellenistic party and/or the Seleucids (cf. Dan. 11:30, etc.)

Contents

In any event mention of the *Kasdim* or "Chaldeans" in 1:6 appears to give us our only firm anchor in dating and ultimately understanding the book. ("Chaldea" is technically southern Babylonia, but especially because the dynasty to which Nebuchadnezzar belonged in ruling the "neo-Babylonian" empire hailed from that area, it is frequently used from that time on—late seventh-century—for all of Babylonia.) Certainly, Hab. 1:5-11 is the *crux interpretum* of the entire book: decisions here largely determine those elsewhere. We can safely dismiss persistent critical misgivings that the section or the specific reference is an interpolation in an otherwise generalized context, that is, for many critics (Wellhausen, etc.), much earlier than the rest, and perhaps the only genuine part. A few have sought to interpret the reference in connection with Merodachbaladan's envoys to Hezekiah in the days of Isaiah (Is. 39; 2 Kings 20). However, most tend to associate the "Chaldeans" with the "neo-Babylonian" empire under Nebuchadnezzar in the late seventh century, and with that viewpoint we identify here.

Since the Chaldeans in Hab. 1:5-11 are plainly offered by God as an answer to the prophet's preceding lament (1:2-4), the next question is who or from what the Chaldeans are to deliver. Precisely why does the prophet's cry here, with the faithful in all ages, go up "How long"? (cf. Rev. 6:10 and repeatedly in the psalter.) Here it is difficult to decide between internal and external evil, that is between Judah under Jehoiakim (especially), or Assyrian oppression of Judah prior to the Babylonian era. Because of their inclination toward a political paradigm, critical opinion probably also inclines toward the latter alternative, but here generalization is risky. Perhaps it is more a both-and than an either-or. Our ultimate understanding of the book may be about the same in either case. The Josianic (or "deuteronomic") reformation would have made questions of "law" and "justice" (v. 4) very prominent in people's minds, whether the primary application was to international policies or to the corrupt Judahite theocracy.

Because of that "deuteronomic" formulation, and because of similar concerns elsewhere in the book (especially if the woes of chap. 2 have the same audience in mind), we cast our vote in favor of the view that Habakkuk in 1:2-4 is concerned *primarily* with *Judah's* faithlessness, but by no means excluding the problem of Assyria's tyranny. This happens also to be the oldest and traditional viewpoint among both Jewish and Christian interpreters.

If so, not only the date, but also the general character and thrust of the book begins to emerge. God's answer (1:5-11) to the first lament (1:2-4) is that He has appointed the Babylonians to execute judgment upon His people, just as He had employed the Assyrians earlier (whom now the Babylonians were also judging as well). Hence, the date for at least this part of the book will be around 605 B.C., when the battle of Carchemish made plain whose empire would succeed the Assyrians in control of most of that part of the world. The rest of the book might be a bit later, but scarcely by more than a decade or so.

Already God's answer in Hab. 1:5-11 made plain that the Babylonians, though His instruments, were themselves no more paragons of virtue and justice than the Assyrians had been. The second lament (1:12-17) apparently follows, then, some time later, after Babylonian hegemony had established itself in Judah, and their own character hit home for the prophet. It was almost a case of "from the frying pan into the fire." The moral atmosphere in Judah was certainly no better now than it had been before (at least ever since the collapse of Josiah's reform efforts), and very possibly even worse. V. 13 sums up the concern of the entire book: "Thou who art of purer eyes than to behold evil . . . , why dost thou look on faithless men, and art silent when the wicked swallows up the man more righteous than he?"

Thus the problem of the book is the problem of evil—in world history, in the church, in the human heart, the realization that every human "solution" contains the seed of its own dissolution and often only exacerbates the problem. L. Fuerbringer has aptly entitled it, *The Eternal Why,* and Habakkuk is the prophetic counterpart to the wisdom-oriented Job in Biblical consideration of this perennial problem. Pagan dualism and fatalism could (and can) always attribute the problem to other "gods" or inscrutable forces immanent in the universe, but a monotheistic belief in one, righteous, and holy God must somehow reconcile the continued power of evil with His governance—and perhaps ultimately with His very existence.

The answer to the deeper, ultimate question comes in Hab. 2:1-4. As already noted, the prophet appears to solicit it from God by external behavior, and God, in turn, commands him to publicize it by the unusual external action of publishing or placarding it, "so that he may run who reads it" (the obverse of the modern tabloid slogan). To human eyes, the fulfillment, the ultimate resolution of the problem, may seem slow, but, nevertheless, "wait for it; it will surely come, it will not delay" (v. 3). Before a final denunciation of the current embodiment of evil (Babylonia) in v. 5, there follows the most famous passage in the book in v. 4, the "justification by faith" *locus classicus* so central to St. Paul's argument in Rom. 1:17 and Gal. 3:11, and thematic of the Lutheran reformation. Habakkuk thus takes his place alongside Isaiah as the "prophet of faith" in the Old Testament.

Did St. Paul cite Habakkuk correctly, or did he bend the prophet's words to his own new meaning? Liberals often make that charge, arguing especially that the Hebrew *'emunah* does not mean "faith" in the Pauline sense of the inert hand that merely receives God's proffered and objective gift but rather denotes "faithfulness, trust," etc. It can scarcely be denied that the latter is Habakkuk's primary point (as it also was Isaiah's in comparable passages). V. 4 then only restates V. 3. God's answer is primarily (as it was to Job) to trust, to believe that God has not abdicated, that "God's mills may grind slowly, but they grind very fine." God will unfailingly see to it that all human *hybris* finally destroys itself. The posture of the faithful suppliant, then, will always be one of waiting, hoping, of sublime confidence, no matter what the catastrophe. The entire book then sounds a *sursum corda* to all of little faith. There finally is no other "answer" to the problem of evil, but the answer of faith.

However, only modern liberalism with its subjectivistic presuppositions, its reduction of faith to psychology, could understand Paul's application as any kind of a conflict with Habakkuk's. (Note also how Heb. 10:38-39 also applies Hab. 2:3-4 to the intensified "not yet" of the Christian era in a way technically more parallel to the prophet's usage.) Neither Paul nor Habakkuk nor anyone else in either testament before the Enlightenment understood subjective "faith" apart from its objective complement in "revelation." And the content of that revelation was not merely some immanentalistic "Providence" (often distinguished from pagan fatalism or determinism only by its greater optimism), but the active, aggressive labor of a personal God for the restoration of the universal "justice" and "righteousness" lost in the Fall, that is, the covenant—or "justification!" Paul thus only articulates the indispensable presupposition of Habakkuk's "trust"—the same presupposition which, to conservative confession, informs and unifies the otherwise disparate "Biblical literature" into a canon and Scripture. Paul's "faith" necessarily eventuates in "trust" as inevitably as Habakkuk's "trust" presupposes Paul's "faith" (even if the verbal articulations vary). If "faith" is thus fully and Biblically defined, there is no problem either with the alternate translation sometimes suggested for the entire verse, "He who through faith is just shall live."

At points like this one sees clearly that the liberal viewpoint not only formally loses *sola et tota Scriptura,* but often also forfeits the objective, soteriological content of "faith" as well. "Faith" becomes, then, as it also is in much of the popular mind, merely a moral quality resident in all good men, a universalistic potential of the human race which needs only to be cultivated, and only so, allegedly, can evil be "overcome." Habakkuk would have recognized that kind of "faith" no more than Paul—and both would surely have included it in their condemnations!

Hab. 2 continues (6-19) with the five woes. Again we confront the question, as in the earlier dialogue of whom the prophet is addressing. Again critics tend to opt for the more political alternative: the chapter is read as a polemic against personified Babylonia, contrasting "righteous" Judah with the "not upright" Chaldean. Often the references to "nations" and "peoples" in vs. 5, 8, 13, etc., are taken as certain evidence of that viewpoint.

These latter mentions do, indeed, establish a certain universal, international vista to the prophet's vision of God's judgment, but they by no means preclude the understanding, which we would prefer, that the major contrast is again internal—between "righteous" and apostate Judahites, or between the "remnant" or true church and the external church-state unit. Parallels with Isaiah's woe-section in 5:8 ff. and with other prophets support this alternative. Since Jehoiakim was only a satellite of the ruling power, his wicked actions might easily have merged in Habakkuk's vision with those of his masters and other "nations" and "peoples" under their control. In any event, this section is not entirely threatening either but also envisions the eschatological solution (v. 14, the same words as in the Messianic prophecy of Is. 11:9).

The little liturgical-sounding interlude or versicle at the end of Hab. 2 is in part, no doubt, transitional to chap. 3, but its significance extends much further. Precisely because "the LORD is in His holy temple," that is, also in His throne-room where history is really made, there can be no doubt about the ultimate outcome. Hence, as emphasized throughout the book, the believer's response must be "silence," that is, faithful watching and waiting. Close parallels in Zeph. 1:7 and Zech 2:13 describe Him as already bestirring Himself into action, but the import is the same. The "temple" is ultimately God's dwelling in heaven, of course, but repeated Biblical parallels remind us that God's theophany is also inseparable from the temple on Zion, where God is "incarnate" amongst His people. Neither before nor after Christ, dare God's judgments be universalized apart from the history of election.

The "psalm of Habakkuk," which constitutes chap. 3, makes perfect sense as an integral part of the work (cf. above). Since the promised destruction of the wicked in 2:2-4 never occurs, but the prophet is only instructed to believe and wait, the psalm is to be understood as describing God's definitive intervention in the cultic language appropriate to God's "holy temple." (Cf. Ps. 73, where the problem of evil is grasped only when the writer enters the sanctuary.) The divine intervention is not only subjective and psychological (in the worshiper's mind), nor is it only a poetic vision of the eschatological victory (as perhaps promised in 2:3), but use of a psalm signals that the victory is already realized and celebrated proleptically and sacramentally in the cult. God's previous salvific acts are all gathered up, recapitulated and climaxed—as well as communicated to the believer, in the sacramental action.

There is no way of telling whether Habakkuk composed the psalm, or adopted an ancient, existing one for his purposes, nor does it matter much. If the former, the psalm must be called "archaizing" (a later revival of archaic forms, a practice which seems to have been especially popular in this chaotic age, when all earthly props were collapsing) rather than "archaic." In any event, there is no question that the psalm simply swarms with philological antiquities, and since later copyists apparently often no longer understood them, textual problems also abound (cf. Ex. 15; Judges 5; 2 Sam. 22, etc.) All linguistic and isagogical considerations aside, neither is there any debate about the singular splendor and forcefulness of the poem. From a purely literary standpoint, it is one of the finest in all Hebrew poetry.

Scholarly study has demonstrated the likelihood that the psalm is composed of some four "forms" or units, each with its own background, but our concern is primarily with those four units as integral parts of the present psalm. It opens (Hab. 3:2) with the "prayer," as the superscription labels the whole piece, "In wrath remember mercy," thus summarizing the Law-Gospel context in which the entire book must finally be read. It continues (vs. 3—7) in prototypal theophanic language to describe God marching from the southeast, from Sinai (the primary theophany) across Midian to Zion, recapitulating the history of salvation in which God initially fulfilled His covenant promises. It is a classical expression of the "Exodus to Zion rhythm" which is so central to Biblical typology. Biblical worship celebrates and represents, not the "timeless" universals of paganism, but the particularities of God's "incarnational" actions in redemptive history. In Word and Sacrament the church too rehearses and celebrates the presence of the same action, finally recapitulated and consummated in Christ's greater exodus and entry into Zion to prepare a place for us.

Hab. 3:8-15 teems with ex-mythological imagery, not in contradiction of the preceding historical language, but to make plain that the interest is really in History, in the eschatological component of time. Yahweh (not Baal) has definitively (not recurrently) defeated the "rivers," the "sea," etc. all ancient representations of the demonic and chaotic in life.

Finally, vs. 16-18 bring the entire book to a serene and fitting conclusion. The archaic features of the earlier verses drop away here, but that does not mean, as many critics opine, that these lines were added secondarily to make an older psalm fit the book. In the light of God's sacramental theophany of His final judgment and redemption, the prophet acquiesces in the counsel of 2:4. "I will quietly wait. . . . Though the fig trees do not blossom, . . . yet I will rejoice in the LORD."

Though ultimately invidious in the light of the unity of Scripture, some comparison between Habakkuk and his great contemporaries, Jeremiah, Nahum, Zephaniah, and Job (very comparable, even if not given final shape in this period, as often assumed) may be fruitful. Sometimes Habakkuk is faulted for not pursuing the theme of "theodicy" as thoroughly as Job—but finally what more is there to say? The solution to the problem of evil is not ultimately intellectual or philosophical, but spiritual and relational. While Job attacks the problem in wisdom categories, those of Habakkuk are more directly related to the themes of *Heilsgeschichte,* as one would expect in a prophet, and he speaks more explicitly for all of God's people, not only for himself, but the difference is ultimately only one of idiom. Habakkuk (and Zephaniah) brings out the moral dimension of evil and its judgment more explicitly than Nahum, but only a liberal critic will sense any ultimate difference in that respect. For Jeremiah the problem of evil was internalized even more than it apparently was for Habakkuk, but one notes the common dialogic form, as both prophets intercede and mediate between church and God. Unlike most prophets, however, Habakkuk does not so much address the congregation directly, as merely share with them the struggles of his own soul. Finally, we cannot overlook Isaiah's prophecy of the "Suffering Servant," applying initially to much of the same history, but pointing most clearly of all to the full import of the establishment of God's righteousness.

ZEPHANIAH

If Micah is the "neglected prophet" among the eighth-century seers, Zephaniah surely deserves the term among those of the seventh, especially when measured against the breadth, depth, and variety of his oracles. One cannot help but wonder if both often fail to attract much interest simply because they are such epitomes of the prophetic messages of their eras.

Date and Background

We have no more personal information about the prophet than that given in the superscription. The genealogy is unusually long, going back four generations to one "Hezekiah." Inevitably, that has raised more questions than answers. On the one hand, one wonders what its purpose might have been if Zephaniah's great-great-grandfather was not the well-known king. The name "Hezekiah" does not seem to have been too common a one either. On the other hand, if that was the intent, why was not "the king" added to the name, as commonly, to remove all ambiguity? It is difficult, but not impossible, to squeeze the required number of generations into the time available, but the brief time span does suggest that Zephaniah, like Jeremiah, may have been relatively young, at least at his call. For that reason, he is occasionally referred to as the "young prophet." If he was of royal blood, his inclusion of "the king's sons" in the denunications of Zeph. 1:8 would carry extra weight.

The name of Zephaniah's father has also aroused speculation. "Cushi" would ordinarily translate as "Ethiopian," that is, better "Nubian" and perhaps even "Negro" (cf. Moses' wife, Num. 12:1). The name may imply partially black ancestry, but one can say no more.

Inevitably, there have also been those who wanted to make Zephaniah a priest. Cultic language and allusions do appear in the book (Zeph. 1:7, 9; 2:1, etc.), but not enough to prove anything. Some have also adduced the prophet's name a support for this thesis. Etymologically, at least, it probably means "Yahweh is Zaphon." Zaphon was an important Canaanite god, somewhat like the spirit of the "mountain of the gods" in Canaanite mythology, which also bore this name. The name thus appears to have polemical or apologetic significance: Yahweh really is what Zaphon only claims to be. It is argued that a priest might be more likely to bear such a name. That, however, is not only uncertain, but the etymological significance of the name may long since have fallen into desuetude. Hence, later generations usually explained the name with reference to another root: "Yahweh has hidden" (= treasured, cherished, etc.).

As to date, the superscription says only "in the days of Josiah." Since Josiah reigned over thirty years (c. 640—609), that is not exceptionally precise. Majority opinion, probably correctly, favors the period before Josiah's reformation (c. 625) when the dire religious situation described in the book seems most likely to have existed. Usually, however, the date is not put much before 625, because of possible problems with the prophet's youth (cf. above).

At one time, the hypothesis was popular that Zephaniah's ominous predictions of invasion referred to a Scythian threat. Since Herodotus' reference to such an invasion of Palestine is not substantiated by the plentitude of information on the period that we now possess, the whole idea is largely abandoned today. At any rate, the assumption has no more merit here than in the case of Jeremiah's early oracles (chaps. 1—6, which see).

Outline and Contents

Theologically, it is perhaps important that Zephaniah does *not* specify which particular historical enemy God will use as agents of His judgment. As we have stressed repeatedly, one of the major "curves" which historical-critical method has thrown us is the exaggerated attention to such questions. Nor is it valid to argue evolutionistically that only later, degenerate, and proto-apocalyptic prophecy became so general. Whether or not the specific historical agent is mentioned, prophecy's primary concerns are with the divine factor in human history as it moves toward the eschaton, no matter what the current manifestation. One of Zephaniah's major themes, "the day of the LORD," has more, not less, impact as a result, because we more readily see its reference to the very essence of time itself, since the Fall.

Zephaniah is an almost perfect exemplification of the classical tripartite prophetical outline—almost perfect, furthermore, in that each of the three chapters in the book corresponds almost precisely to one of the points in the outline. Thus we have: (1) Chap. 1 - Judgment on Judah (the day of the LORD); (2) Chap. 2:1—3:7 - Gentile oracles (judgment on foreign nations); and (3) Chap. 3:8-20 - Eschatological promise to the remnant. The transition is a bit ragged at the beginning of each chapter, but the main outline remains clear. Zeph. 2:1-3 is an appeal to Judah to repent after the preceding threat of judgment, perhaps as a way of stressing that deliverance (indicated by the following Gentile oracles) will come in no other way. After the Gentile oracles, 3:1-7 returns to the theme of Chap. 1 (judgment now specifically on the "oppressing city," Jerusalem, although some apply it to Nineveh, as Nahum would shortly), as if to lump Judah together with the foreign nations when it comes to God's righteous judgment (cf. Amos 1—2). Many critics think this arrangement is editorial and later than Zephaniah himself, but there is no reason why it need be.

Literary criticism of Zephaniah has been quite checkered and is not easy to summarize. Since the theme is judgment on Judah until 2:4, there never has been much question on that first section. However, especially earlier critics again invoked their dogma that true prophets did not preach hope in order to question much of the rest of the book. These doubts applied especially to chap. 3 with its generally hopeful outlook, and here again especially to the concluding vs. 14-20, whose jubilant, buoyant tone was thought to clash completely with the gloom of the first chapter. As usual, this material was thought to have been added as assurance to the postexilic congregation that better days yet were in store for Jerusalem.

Recent critics have been more cautious, and usually prefer to think of mere amplifications of a genuine core. They point out, rightly, that the "remnant" theme was at least as early as Amos, and the frequent use of the "prophetic perfect" in Zephaniah's eschatological oracles is no more problematic than elsewhere. Form-and tradition-critics have made their usual attempts to rediscover the allegedly original brief units of the prophet's discourse, and to demonstrate how they achieved their present combinations, but, again, and at best, with the usual moot results.

Zeph. 1:2 plunges *in medias res:* the universal judgment, the main burden of the book. The language is reminiscent of that used in Gen. 6—8 of the Deluge. As we proceed, it is plain that the prophet's primary concern is with Judah, and later, with specific foreign nations, but the juxtaposition is a good illustration of the fact that any specific nation was targeted primarily as an anticipation and exemplification of the course of cosmic history since the Fall. Judah's judgment in 587 was proleptic and typical of both Christ's death on the cross and the Great Assize.

Zeph. 1:7 introduces us to the central motif of the book, the "day of the LORD." Zephaniah is the major seventh-century representative of that theme, as Amos and Isaiah had been in the eighth. By implication, the call to "silence" indicates that Yahweh has taken His judgment seat in Zion (cf. Hab. 2:20, etc.). The battle on the last "day" is described as "the LORD's sacrifice" at Zion, only now Judah will not benefit, but will be the victim, and the heathen (Yahweh's agents) are "consecrated" to join in the sacrificial meal following.

The picture in v. 12 of Yahweh searching Jerusalem with lamps has brought superficial comparisons with Diogenes' lantern. It also explains why Zephaniah is usually depicted holding a lamp in Christian art. Especially to be ferreted out are the practical atheists who say, "The LORD will not do good, nor will He do ill."

The theme of the "day" builds to a powerful climax in Zeph. 1:14 ff. V. 15 is probably the most famous in the book: Jerome's translation *"Dies irae, dies illa"* became the opening line of Thomas of Celano's "Hymn of the Giants," "Day of Wrath, O Day of Mourning." Almost epitomizing the mood of the Middle Ages, it remained central in the Catholic requiem Mass until Vatican II and usually also appeared in Protestant hymnals. Today we face the opposite extreme: its neglect parallels the neglect of not only end of the church year themes, but much of the Old Testament (especially the prophets) as well, and ultimately neglect of themes of Law, judgment, retribution, etc., in general. Thus our "Gospel" readily becomes "another Gospel."

Critics often found reason to be concerned about the different form and meter of Zephaniah's Gentile oracles, and especially about the similarity of Zeph. 2:8-11 to Obadiah, but all of that only confirms what we have repeatedly observed, namely, that the prophets often use and adopt traditional material, especially in this type of oracle. Some have read 3:5 as the prophet's personal confession of faith in God's justice in the midst of the horrors of history, similar to those we meet in Habakkuk.

With Zeph. 3:9 begins the final portion of the book: life in the "new creation" beyond the judgment. The "pure speech" promised to all people, enabling them to worship properly (cf. Ps. 51:15) sounds like a reversal of the curse of Babel, that is a prophecy of Pentecost. Although again the prophet's primary concentration is on Israel, the restoration is plainly as universal as the judgment ("beyond the rivers of Ethiopia," v. 10).

The "remnant" theme sounds prominently in 3:11 ff. Like the pious speakers of the psalms, and like the famous description of the Messiah in

Zech. 9:9, the remnant will consist of "a people humble and lowly" (v. 12). Among the prophets, however, this motif is relatively unique to Zephaniah.

The final verses (3:14-20) are virtually an eschatological hymn, similar to those we meet in portions of Isaiah. The "King of Israel" (v. 15), "the warrior who gives victory" (v. 17), will forever dwell with His people (the primal covenant promise), will initiate the Messianic banquet "as on a day of festival" (v. 18), and in the most comprehensive phrase of all, will "restore your fortunes" (v. 20). None of the language is "Messianic" in the very narrow (second David) sense of the term, but anyone who treats Scripture holistically will recognize it as profoundly and gloriously Messianic.

The final chapter of Zephaniah may be important in another sense in the history of the prophetic proclamation of salvation. The times were so desperately wicked that the theme of restoration does not bulk large in seventh-century prophecy. In Zephaniah, however, we meet it as clearly and prominently as in the eighth-century prophets, Isaiah, Micah, and Hosea. Because he also paints the judgment in as dark a hue as any prophet, Zephaniah may well have served as a major bridge to the postexilic period and beyond, when the congregation at large first began to comprehend the persistent prophetic insistence that for the remnant, the "invisible church," judgment *was* salvation, death was glorification (John), etc. One may speculate that it was this transitional quality of the book of Zephaniah which led to its placement in the "Twelve," slightly out of order, but introductory to the three postexilic prophets.

HAGGAI

In many respects, we enter a different world with the three postexilic prophets, but one thing remains the same: our almost total lack of information about their biography or personal circumstances. They too are content to be heralds, servants of Another.

Ecclesiastical tradition tended to construe Haggai as a priest, partly because of his name ("festive one" or the like, derived from the common word for "pilgrimage festival"), but that does not necessarily follow. Not only his overriding concern to get the temple rebuilt, but his third oracle (Hag. 2:10-19) would indicate great interest in cultic matters and close contacts with the priests. If anything, however, the pericope would suggest that he was not himself one of the priests. No one knows what to make of the Septuagintal superscriptions to Ps. 137 and 144—148, linking them with Haggai and Zechariah. (Contrary to much criticism, it must be stressed that priest and prophet were no more at loggerheads with each other on principle in preexilic than in postexilic times, neither can it be asserted evolutionistically that priestly ritualism was first now being codified, canonized, and given supreme importance by the fiction of attributing it to Moses!)

The historical activity of Haggai (and Zechariah) is confirmed by independent mention twice in the Aramaic portion of Ezra (5:1; 6:14). Since neither prophet is mentioned until about 520, it is sometimes thought that they had only recently arrived in Judah together with a fresh group of exiles. There are patristic traditions that they had previously preached in the Exile itself. This may be, but it is equally possible that they had come as children with their parents nearly two decades earlier (c. 538) and witnessed the gradual drift of the community into demoralization and despair. Certainly, if many of them took the earlier prophecies of restoration literalistically, especially perhaps those of Isaiah II, the disparity with the facts at hand would have been almost too much to bear. If Hag. 2:3 indicates that he had himself seen the first temple, his old age at this time could explain why his prophetic activity was of such short duration.

One striking contrast between Haggai and the preexilic prophets is the precise dating of Haggai's oracles. Perhaps it is partially anticipated in Ezekiel, but its only real parallel is in the nearly contemporaneous oracles of the first half of Zechariah. Modern scholars would give their eyeteeth to have such precise information about earlier prophecies, but, as we have noted many times, the Bible's ultimate interest is not, as such, with time, but with God's Time, "in, with, and under" man's time.

Contents

As the text of Haggai stands, we have four of these precisely dated oracles, all in the second year of Darius (520), and covering a period of not quite four months: (1) on the first day of the sixth month (1:1); (2) on the twenty-first day of the seventh month (2:1); and (3) and (4) two oracles on the twenty-fourth day of the ninth month (2:10 and 2:20). Zechariah's ministry begins in the middle of this brief spurt of activity by Haggai, in the eighth month of that same year (Zech. 1:1), a month before Haggai's last two oracles. Ezra always mentions Haggai before Zechariah, but whether that reflects Haggai's precedence in activity or greater age, or something else, cannot be said with certainty.

Not only is all of Haggai in prose, but the style is very pedestrian (although direct and very much to the point). Critics are only too happy to add that to their other "evidences" of the drastically inferior, epigonic quality of Haggai's work (and of most of the rest of the postexilic period). From a purely literary standpoint it is undeniable, but theologically it is entirely beside the point. No doubt, it reflects the radical cultural discontinuity and trauma which the community had experienced.

It is striking that all the oracles are in the third person (in quite a contrast to the I-narrative of Zech. 1—8). That, plus the brief narrative interlude in Hag. 1:12-15, describing the initial impact and success of Haggai's preaching, would seem to suggest some other party besides Haggai as the compiler of the book in its present form. There is no reason, theological or otherwise, to reject that possibility. On the other hand, we confront this situation repeatedly in Scripture (Moses and the Pentateuch, Jonah, the biographical narratives in Jeremiah and "B"-type passages at many other points). At very least, it would seem that Haggai was intimately involved in the shaping of his book not long after the oracles had been delivered orally, because the precipitous disappearance of Zerubbabel whom he had hailed is nowhere alluded to (cf. on Zechariah).

The text of Haggai generally poses no great problems, but many see a problem at the end of chap. 1. The date given there for the beginning of building activity (twenty-fourth day of the sixth month, about a month after Haggai's initial sermon) seems to hang. The most likely explanation would seem to be stylistic infelicity. There is no text-critical support for any change. However, many critics argue that 1:15 originally introduced 2:15-19, which they think should follow now. However, that implies that the prophecies in the book have not really been transmitted in chronological order (the third speech would really be the second) and involves deletion or emendation of the "ninth" month specified in 2:18.

How do we then reconcile "ninth" in 2:18 (the same as 2:10) with "sixth" in 1:15? Perhaps the context indicates that the people had not *really* devoted themselves to the work until this time, so that for all practical purposes, the work had not progressed beyond "the day that the foundation of the LORD's temple was laid." Perhaps it is better to relate to the well-known fact that more than one foundation ritual was customarily held in antiquity for houses as well as temples, often at different stages of the construction (cf. our "ground-breaking" and "cornerstone laying"). The reference in 2:18 would then be to a second ritual occasion (cf. Ezra 3:10), perhaps coinciding with a fresh start and renewed enthusiasm. Still a third possibility is to disassociate 2:18b from 18a, and consider the reference in the latter to be to Sheshbazzar's initial work on the foundations shortly after the return in 538 (Ezra 5:16).

It is interesting that Haggai is recorded as addressing the people directly or primarily only once (1:13), when he assures them that Yahweh is with them in their resolve to proceed with the construction. The third sermon concerns the people as a whole, but the first two oracles are addressed, as such, to the two leaders who figure as prominently also in

Zechariah, namely Joshua the high priest and Zerubbabel, governor of the province (apparently successor to Sheshbazzar, although the precise relation of the two is one of the big problems of the period). The fourth oracle is an accolade to Zerubbabel alone.

The first sermon (Hag. 1:1-15) is simply an admonition to begin work on the temple, and we are told that the "remnant of the people" (1:14) followed the lead of Joshua and Zerubbabel in responding. Haggai clearly links the drouth from which they have been suffering with their priority building of their own "paneled house, while this house lies in ruins" (1:4; cf. Joel?). We know that other factors beside the drouth had contributed to the debilitation of the people and their failure to continue the construction begun by Sheshbazzar. The Samaritans (or their predecessors) and other neighbors had opposed them from the outset. Cambyses (530-522) had always been less enthusiastic than his father, Cyrus, about encouraging a measure of local autonomy, and insinuations of seditious intent by the surrounding communities certainly did not dispose him to treat Judah more favorably. It was only after Cambyses' death and after Darius had emerged as victor in the subsequent disorders that the word came to Haggai to challenge those who were still saying, "The time has not yet come to rebuild the house of the LORD" (1:2).

The second sermon (Hag. 2:1-9) consoles the "remnant of the people" (2:2; cf. 1:14) who are making invidious comparisons with Solomon's temple. Not only has the Exodus promise of God's presence not been revoked (2:4-5), but the new temple will get even more glory, because the coming Messianic age will bring the treasures of the nations to Jerusalem (cf. Isaiah III and Zech.). The language in v. 6 ff. is almost apocalyptic; but in a typical prophetic theme Haggai insists that the "unshakable Shaker" will turn the tables in some miraculous way and usher in the eschaton. The turmoil in the Persian empire after Cambyses' death may have triggered the language, but the application far surpasses human politics, as indicated by the typological, "once again," evidently harking back to the Exodus and Sinai events.

Unfortunately, the traditional Messianic epithet in Hag. 2:7, "Desire of all nations," is probably based on a mistranslation. Both context and the plural Hebrew verb indicate that the Hebrew noun also should be pointed as a plural, meaning "desirable/costly things" or "treasures" (so Septuagint also, although the traditional rendering is not altogether indefensible grammatically). In a broader sense, the picture is plainly Messianic in any case. Taken literalistically, Haggai would almost have to be accused of false prophecy and of rousing vain, utopian hopes (as many critics have done!). At most, the aid the Persian authorities eventually gave the reconstruction (Ezra 6:8-9) would count as only a preliminary fulfillment. Only when both temple and treasure were redefined (although not simply "spiritualized") in Christ would the full import of Haggai's promise appear, and Heb. 12:26 reminds us that some of their promise aspect still remains in the time of the church.

The third speech (Hag. 2:10-19) is almost an "action prophecy": the prophet inquires of the priests about a ritual matter and draws a parallel with ethics, specifically the problem at hand. The section is instructive for Biblical theology beyond its immediate exegesis: it illustrates the inseparable unity of ritual and life, external and internal in general, and it illustrates the normal and normative picture of prophet and priest standing shoulder to shoulder (when neither is unfaithful). The matter Haggai inquires about was so basic to Israelite piety that neither he nor the people could have been in any doubt about the answer. The priests predictably reply that "cleanness" (health, if you will) cannot be communicated, while the contagion of "uncleanness" can. The application (v. 14 ff.) is that the sacrifices they had continued to offer on the temple site, even while the building lay in ruins, a dead body as it were, were of no value in sanctifying the people, no matter how well-intentioned, while their own uncleanness invalidated and corrupted all that they did, the best evidence of which was their desperate poverty.

Zerubbabel and Postexilic Prophecy

The fourth and final oracle (Hag. 2:20-23), delivered on the same day as the preceding one (no problem in that!), is addressed to Zerubbabel alone. Picking up the theme of shaking the kingdoms of this world again, Haggai heaps up Messianic language and applies it to Zerubbabel, grandson of Jehoiachin. He is called "servant," "chosen" (or Elect one), and "signet ring" (representing the owner in sealing letters and documents). This promise is very similar to some in Zech. 3 and 6 (which see). It is the major *crux* of the book and of the period, at once historical, exegetical, and hermeneutical.

In critical circles it has virtually become dogma that here Haggai (seconded by Zechariah), convinced that the Messianic age was about to dawn, induced the Jews to crown Zerubbabel as king, in rebellion against Persia. Allegedly, the Persians swiftly crushed the insurrection. This should explain why Zerubbabel drops from sight and why the Persians appoint no more Davidides as governors of Judah. Of course, this also makes Haggai and Zechariah false prophets—or worse!

The best one might say of this hypothesis is that it is an argument from silence. Historically, there is evidence neither for nor against it. In all our vast lacunae of knowledge about the postexilic period, it is scarcely surprising that we happen to hear no more of Zerubbabel.

The prophetic interest in Zerubbabel does illustrate another point we have underscored, namely the concurrence of the institutions of prophecy and kingship. The first "prophet" in anything like the classical sense was Samuel (versus Saul), and after Haggai's and Zechariah's interest in Zerubbabel, prophecy in that sense drops from sight too. It is as though when there are no more visible kings to use as types of the King of kings— negatively as well as positively—prophecy has nothing to do but await the Antitype.

That is a way of getting at the critical miscarriage in connection with the Zechariah prophecies: its dismal failure is ultimately theological and hermeneutical (and never is a critic more "literalistic"). The critical treatment of the Zerubbabel oracles is not at all untypical of its understanding of also the earlier Messianic prophecies. Conversely, the conservative will also understand them as quite paradigmatic of the entire genre. Haggai (and Zechariah) indeed give Zerubbabel a hearty accolade as a worthy representative of the Messianic promise, but the full application or "fulfillment" could and would come only on another level.

The Zerubbabel problem is, in a way, only one aspect of a final one to which we must turn—the general critical disparagement of the postexilic period, particularly its prophets (and our concern here is primarily Haggai). Critical criticism has probably abated a bit in recent years, but scarcely changed in principle. Conversely, one wonders if the same attitude is not often implicit in conservative practices. In a way, if a "prophet" is to "speak to his own times," Haggai surely comes off as well as any. The common charge that Haggai marks the transition from "prophet" to "teacher" and anticipates rabbinic styles (cf. Malachi) is partly based on the slender thread of 2:20 ("to" instead of "by" Haggai) and betrays liberalism's false alternatives, not only in historical study of all Biblical prophets but in modern church life as well. The problem is, as usual, presuppositional: Haggai (like his contemporaries) was allegedly a partner to the crime of foisting sacerdotalism, ritualism, legalism, institutionalism, et al, on the community, and, even worse, of inventing Mosaic authorship for most of it.

Lack of sympathy for, or even understanding of, the importance of the temple and its rites is very much part of the problem. Haggai understood as well as the early Biblical figures that God was not bound in some mechanical, semipagan fashion to the particularities of temple and its rites. But God had bound His people to them, and if "incarnation" was no more spiritualistic and immanentalistic a concept then than it was antitypically in Christ, then intrinsic in the "scandal of particularity" is the confession that God's "glory" (cf. Hag. 1:8, 2:3) and "presence" (cf. 1:13; 2:5 etc.) was no more separable then from the concretion of the covenant in temple and sacrifice than it is today from Word and Sacrament. Haggai's repeated reference to the "remnant" (1:14; 2:2) betrays the nagging question in the background whether or not they really were the true Israel, the heirs of the promise. The prophet proclaims that those external signs, if reaffirmed and accepted, were God's ancient, sacramental assurance that the "remnant" really was the true Israel.

ZECHARIAH

Criticism quite unanimously regards only the first eight chapters of the book as "genuine." The remainder (Zech. 9—14) is often referred to as "Deutero-Zechariah." Often it in turn is divided further, and chaps. 12—14 are considered a "Trito-Zechariah." Since all of these problems are conveniently clustered in the latter part of the book, we shall reserve further consideration of them until that point.

Background and Date

As usual, we know very little about the person of Zechariah. He is mentioned in Ezra 5:1 and 6:14 alongside Haggai as playing a major role in getting the temple rebuilt. In addition, Neh. 12:16 lists him as a son of the priest Iddo who had returned from the Exile (cf. 12:4) together with Zerubbabel.

The latter reference initially appears to conflict slightly with Zech. 1:1 and 1:7 which refer to the prophet as "the son of Berechiah, the son of Iddo," that is, as Iddo's grandson. A few have suggested that "Berechiah" was erroneously introduced into the text here from Is. 8:2 where another "Zechariah the son of Jeberechiah" is mentioned. It is infinitely more likely, however, that in Neh. 12:16 the less significant Berechiah has simply been passed over, as is not uncommon in genealogies (the often flexible term, "son," is not even used). ("Berechiah" as the father of Zechariah in Matt. 23:35 is surely a scribal error for "Jehoiada" and hence irrelevant here; cf. 2 Chron. 24:20-21.)

Nehemiah's reference to Zechariah as the head of a priestly house is very instructive. We suspect that many prophets (among them the contemporary Haggai) may have been priests as well as prophets because of the convergence of priestly and prophetic interests in their books, but in the case of Zechariah, there is no doubt (cf. also Ezekiel a bit earlier). In one sense, this is less surprising in the case of the postexilic community, where the rebuilding of the "institution" was the order of the day, but, in principle, it probably is just as applicable to the preexilic period, *pace* repeated critical assumptions of a basic cleft between the two groups in the earlier periods. Neither does Zechariah's priestly descent have anything as such to do with the question of "cultic prophecy": the fact that Zechariah was of priestly lineage does not imply that his prophecy occurred at some set time or occasion within the regular cult. In fact, the evidence of the book would suggest the very opposite.

Both because of the contents of the book, and because of three precise dates after the manner of Haggai, there is no serious question about the date or circumstances of Zechariah's work. The first date (Zech. 1:1), the eighth month of the second year of Darius (that is, Oct.—Nov., 520; the day is not specified on this occasion) is roughly a month before the last recorded utterances of Haggai (2:10 ff.). (As usual, the two prophets make no mention of each other.) A second date at the beginning of the visions (Zech 1:7) is some three months later, "the twenty-fourth day of the eleventh month" (of the same year), that is, Feb.—March, 519. The third and final date in the book occurs in 7:1; the fourth day of the ninth month of the *fourth* year of Darius, that is, Dec.—Jan. 519/8, nearly two years later than the visions. Thus, in contrast to Haggai, Zechariah's recorded ministry lasts a bit longer, extending somewhat over two years. Whether or not he lived at least two years longer to witness the dedication of the temple in the sixth year of Darius cannot be stated with certainty. Ezra 6:14 is often so interpreted but remains a bit ambiguous. If so, it would have represented the achievement of a goal toward which he had bent a lion's share of his energies.

In other respects, however, Zechariah's message appears to correspond to a slightly later situation in the struggling Judahite community than Haggai's, as the slightly later dating of his oracles would lead one to expect. The intense hopes aroused by Darius' accession appear to have abated, and the prophet has the task of assuring the people that although the parousia some of them may have expected has not materialized, God's eschatological program continues undiminished. It may be true that the enigmatic figure of Zerubbabel plays a somewhat less central role in Zechariah than in Haggai, but we are too little informed on details to venture much further (cf. both below, and above on Haggai). In any case, Zechariah is able to buoy the faith of the congregation in the divine promises in the face of the disillusioning realities of continuing foreign rule, economic uncertainty, and internal apathy. By his concentration on the temple and the theology of purification or sanctification accompanying it, Zechariah played a major role, under God, in the preservation of that congregation until the parousia did in fact begin to dawn with Christ.

Contents of Chapters 1—8

The contents of the first part of the Book of Zechariah fall naturally into the three parts delineated by the three chronological notices: (1) the introductory oracle in 1:2-6; (2) the eight "night visions" in 1:7—6:15; and (3) the so-called "fasting sermon" in chaps. 7—8. The bulk of the book thus consists of visions, presented in an "apocalyptic" style midway between that of Ezekiel and Daniel.

The visions may be classified form-critically as "A-type" oracles (that is, first person report, all following the same general pattern). They are preceded and followed by "C-type" explanations, where Zechariah is sometimes referred to in the third person, like Haggai. Whether or not the latter signifies the involvement of another hand in the final development of the book is a familiar problem, and cannot be answered more certainly here than elsewhere (assuming that the theological presuppositions are equally unobjectionable in all cases). Presumably the explanations are added because of the ambiguity and frequent obscurity of the visions by themselves—this too a standard feature of the apocalyptic genre. There certainly is no justification for the opinion expressed by some critics that they reflect "corrections" by Zechariah when his original predictions were not fulfilled. Neither do we need to think with other critics of interpolations by other hands.

The difficulties are undoubtedly even greater for us than for the original audience because of allusions to little-known historical details, as well as because of a much less restrained utilization of originally mythological motifs than in earlier prophecy. The latter is characteristic of apocalyptic, apparently because that brand of paganism now posed less of a threat to the congregation. In any event, much of apocalypticism's lush imagery for the transcendental and suprahistorical has clear mythological antecedents. In the other direction, Zechariah's influence on later apocalyptic (also of the New Testament) is almost incalculable.

In addition to the explanations of the visions, other oracles appear to have been inserted (e.g., Zech. 2:6-13; 4:6b-10). Since the exact number and their extent is debated, however, it probably is abortive to think with some critics that they represent an originally independent collection of Zecharianic material. They are probably to be reckoned as merely more homiletical explanations or expansions of the surrounding visions.

A clear pattern of arrangement of the eight visions is also evident, and it is not impossible that in some sense it is partly editorial. (The date at 1:7 would appear to indicate that all the visions came in the same night, which is surely not impossible, but it may also be that further details have not been bequeathed to us.) The first and last of the visions provide a sort of framework, while the middle ones are arranged in pairs (2 and 3, 4 and 5, 6 and 7). The framework of the patrol of heavenly horsemen signifies God's universal rule and judgment.

At the same time, the two framework visions can be fitted into a certain developing patternism of all eight. Visions 1—3 especially stress the future greatness of the community; they also stress that the normally unseen messengers of God surround and protect it. Visions 4 and 5 concern the two leaders of the community, Joshua and Zerubbabel, and insure each one (and thus the congregation as a whole) of divine sanction for his position. Finally, visions 6—8 concern the lingering contamination of evil in the land and provide symbolically for its divine removal. The final vision climactically indicates God's satisfaction with the accomplishments initiated by the other visions.

Zechariah's initial sermon (1:1-6) is a rather general call to repentance, and, although precisely dated, is not connected with any known historical event of significance. However, its use of the historical lesson of the past is very significant: "Be not like your fathers, to whom the former prophets cried out" (v. 4). Again in 7:7-12 Zechariah consciously distinguishes himself from the preexilic prophets. Here not only has the history which led to the Exile become as essential a part of Israel's confessional recital of its *"Heilsgeschichte"* as the Exodus and Conquest, but we also have evidence of the emergence of a prophetic canon of Sacred Scripture, alongside the Mosaic Pentateuch.

The first vision (1:7-17) describes four horsemen on steeds of various colors, who have been patrolling the earth (cf. the "watchers" of developed angelology) and now report to the interpreting angel that "all the earth remains at rest." The disorders accompanying the rise of Darius did not signal the final, apocalyptic cataclysm, as some had evidently hoped. However, the peace on earth established by men does not mean that Yahweh has forsaken His people "these seventy years" (v. 12). Rather, while His anger still rests on the nations for inflicting more judgment on Jerusalem than He had bidden (cf. the "double" of Is. 40:2), His anger with His people has turned to compassion, and He will soon intervene to "comfort Zion and again choose Jerusalem" (v. 17).

The second vision (Zech. 1:18-21) witnesses the demolishment of the "four horns," which have scattered Judah, by "four smiths." Unlike other developments of the motifs (Dan. 7, etc.), no clear identification with specific historical forces appears to be intended. In both cases, "four" apparently signifies only the four points of the compass. *All* of the agencies which Yahweh used to buffet His people will themselves be demolished by the universal forces at Yahweh's disposal.

In the third vision (Zech. 2:1-5) two angels impress upon a man with a measuring line the futility of his attempts to measure the eschatological Jerusalem's area, because its future population will exceed all humanly measurable bounds (cf. Is. 54; Ezek. 40 ff.). The lack of visible walls need not disturb the people, because Yahweh will be "incarnate" in His "glory"

(v. 5) to protect it (cf. Ezek. 43). Here we plainly have the eschatological continuation of Isaiah's "inviolability of Zion" theme. Its fulfillment never came in any merely earthly Jerusalem, and if that were its application, Nehemiah's walling of the city not quite a century later would be a simple contradiction of the prophecy.

Before the fourth vision, an oracle intervenes (Zech. 2:6-13), appealing to the many Israelites who have stayed behind in Babylon to return from "the land of the north" (both geographical and symbolic, as usual) in order to share in the blessings of the new Jerusalem, for Yahweh is about to execute judgment upon the nations that have plundered Judah and effect the promised great reversal. The pericope climaxes (vs. 10-12) with rhapsodies redolent of Is. 40—55, and concludes with the same liturgical refrain we met in Hab. 2:20 and Zeph. 1:7; man's part is faithful silence as the final judgment, which the congregation always experiences proleptically and sacramentally in God's "holy dwelling," actually draws nigh.

Zech. 3 is devoted to the fourth vision, set in the heavenly courtroom, presided over by "the angel of the LORD." (Because of its differences from other visions, many critics regard it as a later addition, but the judgment is gratuitous. Conversely, Christians often tend to view it as climactic, because typologically it leads into vicarious satisfaction, at the very heart of the Christian faith.) Joshua, the high priest, is on trial and is clad in "filthy garments" as a visible sign of his sin (cf. Job 9:31). The prosecuting attorney is "*the* Satan," as in Job 1—2 (that is, "Satan" is not yet a proper noun, as we meet it a century later for the first time in 1 Chron. 21:1—although liberalism invariably construes the nominal shift as evidence of evolutionistic development toward "dualistic" demonology, far beyond what any Biblical evidence will bear). But plainly it is not so much the high priest who is being personally charged, as the high priest in his capacity as mediator and representative of the whole congregation ("Israel reduced to one," as sometimes also of prophets and kings). Hence the form of the Satan's rebuke in v. 2 (cited by the archangel Michael in Jude 9): "The LORD who has chosen Jerusalem rebuke you! Is not this a brand plucked from the fire?" Henceforth, by God's favor, Joshua will be clad in "rich apparel" (that is, Jerusalem's future purity and glory, her "alien righteousness," in contrast to her present humiliation and sin).

The fourth vision (Zech. 3:1-10) is an oracle to Joshua, underscoring the exaltedness of his position. Since it uses Messianic language, it bears on the entire question of the relation between Joshua and Zerubbabel and must be considered in connection with another oracle to Joshua in 6:7 ff., with the vision concerning Zerubbabel in chap. 4, as well as with the pertinent oracles in Haggai (which see). The promise to Joshua in 3:6 f.

that, if he is faithful, God will guarantee him "the right of access among those who are standing here" (i.e., to God's heavenly courtroom or council chambers, access to which the Satan apparently wished to deny him) occasions little difficulty except that we nowhere else meet the idea in connection with the high priest, although it is common enough with prophets. Christians can scarcely but see its fulfillment in Christ's permanent entry into the heavenly Holy of Holies (Heb. 10). It may be significant in that connection that v. 8 calls Joshua and his friends "men of good omen" (RSV), probably better translated "types" or living action-prophecies (cf. Is. 8:18, etc.).

But the verse continues to hail Joshua as "my servant the Branch." Criticism inclines strongly to the opinion that the language was originally intended for Zerubbabel (whose Babylonian name means, "Branch of Babylon"), but was later adapted or edited in Joshua's favor, after hopes in the former miscarried (cf. 6:9 ff.). No doubt, at least since Jer. 23:5 and 33:15, "Branch" had been Messianic currency (cf. also Is. 4:2 and 11:1), and "my servant, Branch" here could scarcely but recall "my servant, David" in the Messianic prophecies of Ezek. 34 and 37. The only question is whether it could be applied only to a royal figure.

The use of the same metaphor in Is. 53:2 indicates that its applicability was not so limited, and, in fact, the stress in both the Isaianic and Zecharianic contexts on vicarious atonement might indicate a deliberate association by Zechariah. The shift in application of the metaphor may well correspond to the heightened importance of the high priest in the postexilic community in general, as well as to the increased awareness that the true Israel, the remnant, was more church than state. One also thinks of the many intertestamental (also Qumran) hopes for a priestly *as well as* a royal Messiah, hopes which first Christianity was able to unify in one person. At any rate, there is not an iota of evidence to support critical suspicions of the passage, as it stands.

Zech 3:9, with its abrupt transition to the figure of "a single stone with seven facets," occasions grave problems for exegetes of every stripe; the application would appear to be either to the eschatological fulfillment of the significance of the stones in the high priest's vestments, or via metonymy to the temple, the rebuilding of which would also be of great typological and eschatological significance. In either case, the clear application of the "stone" to Joshua's work makes it most unlikely that "Branch" was ever intended in any fundamentally different way.

The fifth vision (Zech. 4) has many parallels with the fourth, except that it is applied to Zerubbabel. Instead of any contradiction or later adjustment, we need only assume that Zechariah's intent was to stress the harmonious operation of both Joshua and Zerubbabel toward common ends (cf. 6:13). There is even less difficulty when we see how the labors of both debouch typologically in Christ. The vision is of a seven-branched golden lampstand (not "candlestick") with seven lamps apiece (?), apparently a transfiguration of the temple menorah. Somehow it is connected to a reservoir of oil supplied by two olive trees, one on either side. Various technical questions arise but in a vision are probably beside the point.

The angel himself explains the main points of the vision. The lampstand is apparently the restored community, which ultimately receives its energy via the "two anointed [literally, "two sons of oil"] who stand by the Lord of the whole earth," that is, both Joshua and Zerubbabel, representing spiritual and temporal power. Even though it is "the day of small things" (v. 10), the church is watched over by God's seven eyes, and He will implement Zerubbabel's efforts in rebuilding the temple "not by might, nor by power, but by my Spirit" (v. 6). Vs. 7-10 are often viewed as intruding between the vision and its explanation—which in one sense they undeniably do, but who shall say that they could not, or should not?

The sixth (Zech. 5:1-4) and seventh (5:5-11) visions both symbolically describe the removal of wickedness and impurity from the land. The first envisions a huge flying scroll, explained as 'the curse that goes out over the face of the whole land," ferretting out and exterminating especially thieves and perjurers. No doubt, there are formal parallels galore in pagan music to this concept (as there are to the concepts of "blessing" and "cursing" in general), but in Biblical context, under a personal God, the parallels remain purely formal. (In the context of modern hermeneutical debates, one must also note that we have here a sort of "inscripturated Word," albeit of a negative sort; the written Word has the same power as the *viva vox* behind it; cf. also Ezek. 2:8-10).

The seventh vision (Zech. 5:5-11) is more cryptic. Zechariah sees an ephah measure (a basket holding about three-fifths of a bushel), in which is seated a woman, representing "the iniquity in all the land." Two other winged women carry the measure to "the land of Shinar," that is, Babylon, the archetypal source and center of iniquity. There the measure will be set on its base in a house especially built for it, that is, apparently put on a pedestal for worship in what, in effect, is the "temple of antichrist." Modern sensitivities often see some type of misogyny or "sexism" here, because the passage appears to make the woman the very symbol of wickedness. Even if so, however, there would appear to be enough similar masculine imagery in Scripture to more than offset it! Most likely, however, the figure is feminine merely because, in the absence of a neuter gender, abstractions in Hebrew are normally feminine; cf. Proverbs where both "wisdom" and its opposite number are presented as women.

The eighth and final vision (Zech. 6:1-8) harks back to the first one, with its view of four horsemen, who are now sent to the four corners of the earth to execute Yahweh's judgment. Emphasis is given to the one sent to the "north," that is, to Babylon, the seat and origin of evil. This final vision is proleptic of a "final judgment": the preliminary events of the preceding visions have been accomplished (Zion established, evil removed, the world at peace), and now "the kingdom is at hand."

Somewhat curiously, this main section of the book, consisting mostly of visions, is concluded by an independent oracle (Zech 6:9-15), confirming the point made by especially the fourth vision. There is a structural balance, however: the fourth vision concluded with a charge to Joshua (3:6-10), parallel to this promise to Joshua after the eighth vision. Zechariah is commanded to requisition some of the gold and silver brought by a deputation from exiles still in Babylon (undoubtedly illustrating how most of them were more eager to give financial support to the returnees than to return themselves). From it, he should fashion a crown and place it on the head of *Joshua.*

It is virtual "critical orthodoxy" to assert that the text originally read Zerubbabel, with later alteration, as in Zech. 3:8 (which see). This conclusion is supposed to be supported by various considerations: (1) the use of the term "Branch" again, as in 3:8; (2) specification of *"royal honor"* in v. 13, with "a *priest* by his throne"; and (3) the Hebrew plural, "crown*s*," in both v. 11 and 14 (although in the latter case the Hebrew verb is singular). The third argument is the only one with objective, grammatical support, but in context it seems that the plural is used either of the complex, multiple composition of the crown, or else is a sort of "plural of majesty" (possibly also a linguistic archaism). Otherwise, the passage accords completely with 3:6-10, and the two pericopes stand and fall together.

There is no objective evidence that Zerubbabel figures in this oracle at all, although similar things are said of Zerubbabel too in Zech. 4. At most, it would seem that Zechariah is going no further than Ezekiel had: correcting some of the incursions upon the primordial power and glory of the high priesthood in the days of the monarchy, but without repudiating the latter. For the immediate future, however, kingship must recede before priesthood as the major type and walking prophecy of Him who would perfectly incarnate all offices in Israel.

Zech. 7—8 appears to be an independent collection of oracles. Sometimes they are referred to as "the fasting sermon," but only 7:1-7 and 8:18-19 clearly concern that subject. It appears that into that framework, various other oracles on basic, present moral requirements and on the future great reversal have been inserted. If so, the date at 7:1, the last in the book, and nearly two years after the visions, might apply to only 7:1-7. It is noteworthy, that, unlike the visions, this oracle comes in response to a question from the people (cf. Malachi and later rabbinic *toroth* or *responsa*). Even more interestingly, it is addressed to both priests and prophets, evidently signifying their equal regard by the people. That the deputation comes from Bethel probably has no direct connection with the Samaritan question but only indicates to what an extent this widely based cult had continued at Jerusalem even while the temple lay in ruins (cf. Jer. 40:4 ff.).

The question is whether the fasts should continue (together with Zech. 8:18 ff., it is clear that four separate fasts were held, commemorating various phases of the destruction of Jerusalem). The gist of Zechariah's replies (also of the surrounding oracles in this context) is that, just as in the days of the former prophets' (7:7), whether or not they fast is not the all-important question (the fast on the Day of Atonement was the only Biblically mandated one). One might apply Luther's words on preparation for the Eucharist: "Fasting and bodily preparation is indeed a fine outward training, but . . . ." In fact, the counsel in 8:18-29 is in the same vein as Jesus' *logion* on the subject in Mark 2:18 (Luke 5:35): since the "seventy years" (7:5) is now about over, and the "Bridegroom" is at hand, "seasons of joy and gladness" (8:19) are more appropriate.

"Deutero-Zechariah"?

With Zech. 8, the "genuine" Zecharianic material in the book concludes as far as virtually unanimous critical opinion is concerned. At most, a few "genuine" snatches reworked by disciples of a putative "school" will be conceded (cf. Isaiah). In fact, the unity of even the remaining six chapters of the book is commonly denied. Since chapters nine and twelve both begin with a sort of superscription ("An Oracle"), two originally independent collections are supposed (to which, as such, the conservative need not object), and not only a "Deutero-Zechariah" but also a "Trito-Zechariah" is often spoken of. Since, in addition, the same "superscription" may appear at the beginning of Malachi, it is commonly held that originally the compilers of the prophetic canon had before them merely three collections of anonymous oracles. In order to obtain a total of *twelve* "minor prophets" (one for each tribe?), two of these compilations were attached to the end of Zechariah, and the third outfitted with the artificial name "Malachi" on the basis of one of its major formulations (Mal. 3:1, which see). As often, the best one can say of such critical speculations is that they lack even a particle of objective support. In this case, unlike the otherwise quite parallel problems of the unity of Isaiah or of the Pentateuch, there are no New Testament statements to contravene the critical theories, but, in presupposition as well as execution, they remain so inextricably linked with liberal-critical hermeneutics that the conservative can scarcely even entertain them.

In fact, in the case of Zech. 9—14, critical theory has described so many gyrations that it would often appear to be its own best refutation. The history of critical examination of the material, since it first began seriously in the eighteenth century, is so variegated that it is not even easy to summarize. At first, the predominant tendency was to date the material *preexilic* (on grounds somewhat similar to the early dating of Joel and Obadiah). Various passages in chaps. 9—11 could be read as implying the threat of Assyria and other powers against the Northern Kingdom before 722. The hope for unification of Israel and Judah (11:14) was taken to imply that Israel was still standing, and the mention of *teraphim* in 10:2 suggested the idolatries of the period. Chaps. 12—14 were dated after the fall of Samaria, but still preexilic; the "house of David" is featured prominently, the mourning at Megiddo in 12:11 was related to Josiah's death, and signs were seen of the Babylonian threat against Jerusalem. In fact, Diestel in 1875 proclaimed the preexilic hypothesis as "one of the surest results of modern criticism"(!).

Increasingly, however, the critical pendulum swung to the other extreme, and especially since Stade in 1881, the assumption of a post-Alexandrian Hellenistic date (that is, close to Daniel by critical reckoning, and one of the latest portions of the Old Testament) became the basis of most modern discussions. Now the nations of Zech. 9 were read as a list of countries overrun by Alexander, and the mention of Greece in 9:13 (considered a prophecy *post eventu*) appeared to clinch the point. The depreciation of prophecy in 13:1-5 was taken to parallel the deploring of its absence in Maccabees, and above all, the chapters' allegedly heightened apocalyptic flavor was thought to demand a relatively late date in the evolutionary scale. Comparative material from Qumran has seriously eroded this position, like other similarly late critical datings. The Hebrew style is unlike that of the Dead Sea sectarians, and there is no hint of Aramaisms.

A third, mediating critical position conceded the late date for final composition, but argued for the reuse of considerable preexilic material, "Assyria" now standing for the Seleucids, "Egypt" for the Ptolemies, etc. The conservative can warm somewhat more to this position: if the attempt at precise non-Zecharianic applications is dropped, it does at least suggest the possibility of a sort of "typological history," with earlier Gentile oracles becoming symbols or types of any and all enemies of the kingdom of God. Appeal to and reuse of earlier prophetic material does seem undeniably to have been more characteristic of later prophecy, as we have already noted in Zech. 1:4; 7:12, etc.

The most recent criticism has tended to retrench even further, sometimes even despairing of certain dating, and often defending positions which would require minimal adaptation by a conservative hermeneutics. The historical references (including "Greece" more or less on a par with Zion) require no dating later than the late sixth century, and close literary and theological parallels are noted with especially Ezekiel and "II Isaiah." The conservative cannot fail to observe that if a date in the "late sixth century" is considered defensible, we are so close to the known, dated oracles of Zechariah, at most a decade or two previously, that there seems to be no cogent reason remaining why actual Zecharianic composition should continue to be dismissed out of hand. The conservative too might concede the possibility of somewhat more or different traditioning of the material in the two sections of the book, but, by the same token, the differences simply do not appear to be of the kind or degree that would necessitate any hypothesis of dual or multiple authorship. It would be simply that the prophet's own more general oracles were collected separately, corresponding to their slightly different tone. Furthermore since we know nothing of the prophet's age, it is not unlikely that the later oracles also stem from a later period in the prophet's life. The specification of "Greece" in 4:13 could have come in almost any prophetic period, we now know, but the prophet may well have lived to witness Greece's signal victories over Persia in 490 and 480. Differences in style and content would thus both be easily accounted for.

Differences in tone and atmosphere in Zech. 9—14 there certainly are. To a certain extent a mere glance at the relatively large amount of poetry (that is, more technically oracular material) confirms this observation. At a more penetrating level, the scholar soon becomes painfully aware of it also by the relatively poorer state of the Hebrew text of this part of the book, partly for reasons unknown, partly, no doubt, because of the poetry and otherwise greater obscurity of the material.

The major difference always adduced, however, is that all the historical specifics of the first nine chapters (rebuilding of temple, Joshua and Zerubbabel, political situation under Darius I) not only now drop from sight but also are not replaced by comparable ones. Formally, one notes this in the absence of the exact dating at points in Zech. 1—8 (as in Haggai). However, we need to recall that there were questions already in the earlier chapters about whether the dates applied to all the material, and, in any event, preexilic prophecy is full of undated oracles too. Materially, the criterion for the alleged ungenuineness of Zech. 9—14 is the same specious one we have met repeatedly in our encounter with higher criticism. Allegedly, specific semipolitical targets, and the belief that Yahweh would act immanentally within history, are characteristic of genuine prophecy, whereas, when prophecy degenerates into apocalyptic, it speaks more generally (and theologically), and yearns for supernatural intervention from beyond history. It is doubtful, however, if any objective study of even the oracles which criticism generally concedes to be genuine would sustain any such a distinction, and, except with the aid of the critical scalpel and the resultant argument in a circle which redistributes most of the rest of the prophetic literature according to the same evolutionistic standard, it plainly does not have a Biblical leg to stand on. If Daniel remains dated in the sixth century, and that anchor of critical evolutionism is no longer available, its fall is even more ignominious.

Certainly, in the case of Zechariah, it can scarcely be asserted that an "otherworldly," transhistorical concern is missing in the first nine chapters, in spite of their more immediate concern with specific problems at hand. The more one is aware of the typical and typological import of even the specifically targeted sermons, the less the distance that appears to loom between them and material such as in Zech. 9—14, which speaks more directly of the eternally valid. In the structure of the entire book, the more miscellaneous and homiletical character of chaps. 7—8 may be viewed as somewhat transitional from the one part of the book to the other. The recent studies of Lamarche appear to have demonstrated a remarkable amount of symmetrical arrangement (either of exact opposites or of exact correspondence) in chaps. 9—14. While that could be attributed to someone else as well as to Zechariah, it does establish that we are not confronted merely with a miscellany of floating, "timeless" material, and we noted a very comparable symmetry in the arrangement of the eight visions.

Sometimes it is argued that there is less interest in ethics in "Deutero-Zechariah" than in his predecessor. However, except in the general terms of cleanness or purification, it can scarcely be said that specific ethical problems are an overriding concern of Zech. 1—8, nor is ethical sensitivity absent in chaps. 9—14. In fact, the presence of that concern in chaps. 12—14 is one of the few topics which distinguishes them from chaps. 9—11, alone providing any foundation for an overall outline of "Deutero-Zechariah." Whereas chaps. 9—11 concentrate on the overthrow of all powers which threaten the kingdom of God, chaps. 12—14 include the motif of the eschatological sifting of Israel herself.

Quite a few themes are common to both parts of the book, most of which cannot be enumerated here. At the most basic level, both parts enunciate God's promise to preserve the remnant and ultimately establish

His kingdom. One interest which certainly is common to both is interest in cult. The temple as such is no longer the focus in Zech. 9 ff., but Zion remains at center stage, most obviously in chap. 14. In 12:10 ff. we find "the house of Levi" and other priestly groups mentioned on a par with "the house of David," quite parallel to the equality of Joshua and Zerubbabel in Zech. 1—8 (and Haggai).

If one remains aware, as we have stressed repeatedly, that the "Zion" and "David" themes are the two sides of one coin, one readily sees the importance of the Book of Zechariah from the standpoint of Christian theology. Zechariah's accent on the priestly component of Messianism adds still another major dimension to its latent Christology. If we do not construe it negatively and evolutionistically, as critics are wont to do, the undeniable accent throughout the book on God's transcendent holiness (as already in Isaiah—and "P") and His use of angelic intermediaries may be viewed as part of the *preparatio evangelica* for the coming of the Messiah. The very accent of especially the second part of the book on *supra*history renders it even more immediately applicable to Christ, and His death and resurrection as "the only thing that ever *really* happened" (Sayers). Thus, it was really profound hermeneutics that made Zech. 9—14 one of the primary sources of early Christian *testimonia* of the Messiah. Zechariah is often known as the "Prophet of Holy Week," an accolade which is ultimately valid for the entire book but is especially evident in four prominent New Testament quotations from the last six chapters (9:9 in Matt. 21:4 f. and John 12:12-15; 11:12 f. in Matt. 27:3-10; 12:10 in John 19:37; and 13:7 in Matt. 26:31, and Mark 14:27). That ready, meaningful accessibility of Zechariah to primitive and traditional Christianity contrasts glaringly with its obscurity and problematic quality in modern "scientific" study and its wild-goose chases after precise historico-political occasion.

Contents of Zechariah 9—14

The first oracle in the second part of the book (Zech. 9:1-8) illustrates the problems we have been discussing. It may well be an ancient "Gentile oracle," originally describing an Assyrian (?) invasion from the north down to Philistia, but bypassing Jerusalem. Here, however, its application appears much more to be to *H*istory, to the eschatological judgment upon the nations attendant upon Israel's final deliverance. Thus it is introductory to the famous Messianic oracle following: the great king will come to rule over the Promised Land once the promise is eternally established.

The famous "Jubilate" of Zech. 9:9-10 is formally very reminiscent of Isaiah II, and materially parallel to many Messianic prophecies. Zion's king enters Jerusalem, not riding on a war-horse, but on an ass, and establishes a universal *"pax Ierusalemitica"* (cf. Is. 9; Ps. 46; etc.). The adjectives describing the Messiah are notoriously difficult to translate. RSV's "triumphant and victorious" can be understood correctly, but something like "justifying and saving" would better bring out the theological content. That, in addition, the Messiah is "humble" connects His victory with the motifs of Is. 53 (cf. Phil. 2). Matt. 21:5 and John 12:15 hail the beginning of the fulfillment of the prophecy in our Lord's Palm Sunday entry into Jerusalem. But in another sense it was only a beginning, as the traditional liturgical association of the pericope with Advent wishes to emphasize.

Zech. 9:11-17 gives further details of the eschatological victory. Especially vs. 11-12 appear often to be overlooked in the shadow of the preceding two verses. "Because of the blood of my covenant" (cf. ultimately the Eucharist) the "prisoner of hope" will be released from the "waterless pit." In v. 13, "Greece" appears as a major type of the competition to the kingdom of God.

With Zech. 10 we begin a sort of "flashback" to the turmoil and other circumstances preceding the Messianic triumph. A "shepherd" theme pervades especially chaps. 10—11, specifically conflict between the true and false shepherds (kings). Chaps. 10:1-2 describes "want of a shepherd" (further political and especially religious confusion) as punishment for superstitious, pagan behavior. Fertility and blessing of every sort comes only from Yahweh.

Possibly by a catchword connection, Zech. 10:3-12 moves from absence of a true Shepherd to denunciation of the present "shepherds" of God's flock. The reference is plainly primarily to foreign rulers ("Egypt" and "Assyria" in v. 10), who must release the captives "till there is no more room for them." A second Exodus occurs (v. 11), and, by implication at least, Israel will once more be united under "one shepherd." This type of oracle is very common also in preexilic prophecy, and it is possible that again we have a Zecharianic "reissue" here. In any event, its primary application is not to political circumstances at this or that period in Israel's history but to the Messiah's final eschatological release of the faithful from spiritual bondage.

Zech. 11:1-3 describes how the "shepherds" of neighboring Lebanon and Bashan will lament the destruction of their forests, symbolizing their pride and strength. By any standard, however, 11:4-17 is one of the most cryptic and elusive pericopes in the whole prophetic corpus. As a virtual hotbed for wild interpretations, it demonstrates superbly the bankruptcy of a historicizing exegesis of this entire portion of Zechariah. (Over forty sets of names, ranging over all of Israelite history, have been proposed for the three shepherds in v. 8 alone!) Were it not for Matthew's Messianic citation, we might be as much at sea as anyone: again the suprahistorical, eschatological dimension must dominate.

Apparently the *Gattung* of the pericope is the familiar prophetic one of a (tripartite) action-prophecy. After the people have been given one last chance (Zech. 11:4-6), the prophet first removes three competing shepherds and then impersonates (typifies) the "Good Shepherd" (Yahweh Himself in historical manifestation). As in Ezek. 34 and Zech. 10, He visits His flock and assumes the care of them. But when after only "one month," that is, apparently, a very brief time, the flock rejects Him, he performs a second action-prophecy by breaking the two staffs symbolic of his office. Third, he then comports himself like a "worthless shepherd," signifying God's abandonment of the congregation to Antichrist, in whatever historical manifestation. The pericope ends with a brief "woe" oracle (v. 17).

The two symbolic staffs, "Grace" and "Union," are similar to Ezekiel's two sticks in 37:15 ff. Apparently, they represent two aspects of the blessings or salvation which the populace stood to receive under the rule of the Good Shepherd: God's gracious, covenantal care for His elected flock and the healing of the schisms which rend Israel (church). The subsequent breaking of the staffs reinforces the curse, partly evidenced immediately in failure to repent, even though they "knew that it was the word of the LORD" (v. 11). When the prophet asks for his "severance pay," they contemptuously give him the "lordly price" of an ordinary slave, thirty silver shekels.

In Zech. 11:13 there appears to be no cogent reason to emend the Hebrew "potter" to "treasury," but the significance of the action remains moot. Possibly there was a proverbial expression something like our "throw it to the dogs." Alternatively, a potter may well have had space in the temple precincts for preparing or selling pots for sacrificial uses (cf. 14:20); he would represent one of the most menial services in God's house. To "throw" the money to him in God's house (that is, before God's face) would be a way of saying, "He who rejects me rejects Him who sent me." Judas' fate would capsulate the people's own rejection as a result (and in the New Testament it is the traitor himself who flings the money into the temple). The prophet's typology "became flesh" in Holy Week.

Another (in)famous problem arises in connection with this pericope: the attribution of Zech. 11:12 f. in Matt. 27:9 f. to Jeremiah instead of Zechariah. What further need have liberals of witnesses to Biblical fallibility! Awareness of the difficulty antedated higher criticism, of course. Luther, for example, notes it but dismisses it as no more important than the frequent free quotation of the Old Testament in the

New; hermeneutically, it is noteworthy that he does *not* draw liberal conclusions of errancy or of a dichotomy between Word of God and Scripture. When viewed through critical lens, the apparent discrepancy nourished the rise of hypotheses about "Deutero-Zechariah" (one, Joseph Mede, in 1653 first argued that Zech. 11 was really Jeremianic) and is still often cited as evidence of the original disunity of the book.

If both that possibility and Matthean error are disallowed, how do we explain the ascription to Jeremiah? No certain answer can be given, and various hypotheses have been offered. Most likely, Matthew means to affirm the fulfillment *both* of Zech. 11 and of Jeremiah's typological actions of buying a field and observing a potter (Jer. 18 and 19). If two prophecies have thus been conflated, it would by no means be the only time in the New Testament where only one (usually the more prominent) author is cited. If Matthew used a *testimonia* collection of Messianic prophecies, as many opine, the composite citation may have already been at hand in that form in one of his sources.

It is noteworthy that the poetic curse at the end of the pericope (Zech. 11:17) is directed against *"My* worthless shepherd"; all of God's agents of judgment, even Antichrist, rule only by divine sufferance, as all the prophets stress. Often this single verse of poetry is thought by critics to be an original unity with the "my shepherd" of 12:7-9 (the only poetry in the last three chapters in the book). In some precanonical source the hypothesis is not impossible, but, if so, the application of 12:7 to Christ in the New Testament in contrast to 11:17's reference to "Antichrist" makes it plain, that at least in Zechariah's reuse, the two shepherds have nothing in common. Furthermore, any such common source would militate strongly against the common critical distinction of a "Trito-Zechariah" beginning with chap. 12.

Apparently echoing especially Ezek. 38—39 (and possibly also a proleptic liturgical drama), Zech. 12:1-9 describes the final last-ditch attack of heathendom upon Judah and Jerusalem. According to the ancient "holy war" pattern, Yahweh will smite the attackers with sudden panic. That the outlying areas of Judah will be rescued before Jerusalem (v. 7; cf. 14:14) has led to much critical speculation about some historical friction between the two. Most likely, though, it is simply a feature of the "great reversal": those who first fell to the enemy will also be the first to be delivered.

The theme of "great reversal" continues in Zech. 12:10-14. Israel's change of heart by divine intervention will lead her to rue her rejection of the Good Shepherd. The Hebrew plainly says *"Me,* whom they have pierced," although the verse does continue in the third person. Only if one reads historicistically (searching vainly for a reference in Maccabean history, as critics usually do) and rejects the Messianic reference (John 19:37) can the arbitrary change to "him" be justified. As the text stands, it is one of the many notices in the context of the virtual identity of God and His Shepherd, "an only child" (v. 10). Vs. 12-13 stress the public nature of the lamentation, and Rev. 1:7 explicitly associates it with the Great Assize (cf. Matt. 24:30). The comparison to "Hadadrimmon in the plain of Megiddo" (v. 11) is obscure, however. Josiah's death at Megiddo (cf. 2 Chron. 35:22-25) does not appear to be involved (unless it later merged; although it would be apt—the just king as a type of the Just King), but rather some pagan rite of lamentation for the annually "dying" fertility god (cf. that for Tammuz, Ezek. 8:14). The death of this God, however, was of an entirely different order, and He would rise and live forevermore.

Zech 13:1 further describes the restoration. In Paradise Restored, the primordial river or "fountain" would cleanse from sin (cf. Gen. 2; Zech. 14:8; Ezek. 47; Ps. 46, etc.). Exegetically, there is no immediate connection with the preceding "piercing," or any direct reference to "a fountain filled with blood," but Christian poetry and typology rightfully did not hesitate to make the connection. One of the results of the cleansing will be the elimination of "the prophets and the unclean spirit" (v. 2). If anyone does claim to be a prophet, his own parents will repudiate him and "pierce him through." Prophets themselves will be ashamed of their profession, and invent excuses for the telltale scars on their backs from previous ecstatic frenzies. The context makes plain that it must be *false* prophecy that is condemned here, the blind leaders of the blind. Nevertheless, critics persist in seeing the repudiation of *all* prophecy, as postexilic sacerdotal institutionalism allegedly attempted to extinguish all spontaneity and creativity in Israel's religious life. At most, we might concede that, because the viewpoint of the passage is from the fulfillment, all prophecy is now considered superfluous and *eo ipso* false.

Conceivably continuing Zech. 11:17 (which see), in 13:7 ff. God calls upon the sword to smite "my shepherd"—and, in parallelism, "the man who stands next to me." Our Lord applies these words to Himself as God's Son in Gethsemane (Matt. 26:31; Mark 14:27). Only a "third," a remnant, of the sheep will survive the trial and be saved.

The final chapter (14) of Zechariah is an extended symbolic picture of the coming "day of the LORD," pulling together and developing virtually every Old Testament motif on the subject. Its obviously thorough eschatological perspective should be paradigmatic for the interpretation of all of Zech. 9 ff. We begin again with the final apocalyptic battle against Jerusalem. When all appears lost (v. 2), Yahweh will appear as a "man of war" (Ex. 15:3), that is, recapitulate and consummate the Exodus.

Only this time, "His feet shall stand on the Mount of Olives" (14:4), "and all the holy ones with Him" (14:5), (that is, in typological perspective, His visible, bodily return to the site of His ascension). In the convulsions of the new creation, the Mount of Olives will split in half and form a natural amphitheatre of refuge from the enemy (vs. 4-5), with Jerusalem forever towering above the newly formed, but deserted, plain around it (vs. 10-11). Darkness, cold, and frost will become unknown (v. 6), and "living waters" from Jerusalem will fructify the entire land the year round (v. 8). Yahweh's kingship, so long celebrated proleptically and sacramentally in Jerusalem, will be universally established and acknowledged (v. 9).

Continuing the Exodus reminiscences and typology, a terrible plague will come upon Jerusalem's enemies (Zech. 14:12-15) leading them to attack and annihilate one another (again in "holy war" manner). The Messianic banquet (v. 16 ff.) is not described in terms of Passover, but of Booths ("Tabernacles"). The autumnal harvest festival, also commemorating the interim before reaching the Promised Land, was an especially appropriate type of the final ingathering of all nations to their inheritance. The ceremonies of Booths probably included prayers for adequate rainfall in the forthcoming growing season, but it (that is, ultimate blessing) will be withheld from any who neglect the "Eucharist." If it is Egypt, which is not dependent upon rain, she will suffer a special plague for backsliding.

The book ends (Zech. 14:20-21) on what may appear to be an anticlimax, but it is really one of the greatest climaxes in prophecy, couched as it is in priestly conceptuality. "Holy to the LORD," in the old aeon inscribed on the high-priest's turban (Ex. 28:36), will in the new aeon of total sanctification, when the universal priesthood has been established and holiness (both physical and spiritual) again suffuses all of creation, be inscribed even on the bells of the horses' harnesses. Separate pots for sacrifice will no longer need to be sanctified, because all pots will be holy: the original unity of sacred and secular will be restored—as it has been in Christ, but also "not yet." The Christian sacraments now represent the interim, the time of the church, between fulfillment and consummation. And, finally, throughout all creation (the antitypical and eschatological "house of the LORD"), the "trader" who mixes pure and impure motive also in his worship *(simul iustus et pecator)* will give way to unalloyed, eternal hosannas to the King.

MALACHI
The Name

The first question about the Book of Malachi is whether we even know its author's name. Virtually without exception, criticism believes that the superscription (assumed to be an editorial addition, as always) mistakenly coined the name on the basis of Mal. 3:1, where God promises to send "my messenger" ("Malachi" in Hebrew; the word might also be translated, "my angel"). Presumably, the compiler identified the eschatological figure with the prophet himself, either taking it to be his personal name, or understanding it as applying to his ministry.

The critical assumption of the anonymity of Malachi usually dovetails with the hypothesis that originally "Malachi" was the third of *three* anonymous collections of prophetic material, originally all beginning only with the label "Oracle." The first two allegedly were appended to Zechariah as chaps. 9—11 and 12—14, while the third retained its independence, in order that the scroll of the minor prophets might attain the ideal total of twelve entries (see at Zech. 9). Both ideas are equally hypothetical, but each must be evaluated separately. In general, a better case can be made for the anonymity of Malachi than of Zech. 9—14.

The arguments against "Malachi" as a proper noun are both text-critical and intrinsic. For one thing, the name, "Malachi" (or its full, theophoric form, "Malachiah") is unattested elsewhere in the Old Testament and other onomastica. It is often argued that use of so singular a name would be especially unlikely in the postexilic period when the Hebrew *"mal'ak"* was increasingly becoming specialized terminology for "angel" (in contrast to any "messenger"), and at a time when angelology itself was becoming increasingly prominent.

The text-critical evidence, at best, points to ancient uncertainty on the score. The Septuagint took "malachi" in the superscription as a common noun with a *third*-person suffix, translating "by the hand of his messenger" (although it does *entitle* the book, "Malakias" or "Malachi"). The Targum likewise, but retaining a first-person suffix and identifying the author with Ezra: "by the hand of my messenger, whose name is called Ezra the scribe." Jerome, probably due to his training under rabbis, accepted the tradition of Ezrahite authorship. Other rabbinic traditions, however, fitted Malachi out with a Levitical genealogy.

To the liberal critic, the anonymity of Malachi poses no problems either historically or theologically. Historically, he believes that much of Scripture, and specifically much of prophecy, is really anonymous anyway (cf. "II Isaiah," sometimes even names such as Joel, Nahum, and Obadiah). Theologically, he tends to attribute much of it to "community inspiration," according to which tradition, in one form or the other, is constantly updating, revising, contemporizing, etc.

To the conservative, matters will not be quite so simple. Theologically, of course, he will insist that any judgment be subordinate to and compatible with special inspiration. He will note that, although the Bible rarely presses the search for contemporary occasion to the same degree that historicistic criticism does, as a minimum it generally at least indicates the name of the author, at least of entire books. The Book of Malachi undeniably bears the stamp of one individual personality, apart from what his name may have been. The conservative cannot share the wholesale skepticism of superscriptions that characterizes criticism, but he must concede that the textual variety makes Malachi a somewhat different case. Neither is there any *a priori* incompatibility between anonymity and verbal inspiration.

In sum, the balance of probability would seem to favor "Malachi" as a proper noun, but grounds are lacking to dismiss the other possibility out of hand as merely some more critical folly, as some conservatives do. In any event, following universal convention on both sides, we shall speak of "Malachi" as the personal name of the author of the last book in the "latter prophets."

Date and Context

There is far less debate when it comes to the date of the Book of Malachi. The fact that the temple has obviously been restored and the cult reinstituted makes 516 an absolute *terminum post quem*. The fact that the priests are already weary of the rituals and sloppy in their execution suggests that some time has elapsed. Reference to a raid on Edom (Mal. 1:3) helps little, because that was a recurrent event (cf. Obadiah, etc.). Likewise, with the reference to poor harvests and locust plagues (3:6-12; cf. Joel, Haggai), and the evident disillusionment at the "delay of the parousia" (2:17 ff.). Tiny Jerusalem appeared to be forgotten not only by the world but also by God, so why should they weary themselves in His service?

In general, the ritual and ethical problems confronted by Malachi are similar to those combatted by Ezra and Nehemiah in the middle of the fifth century, but it is difficult to be more precise. Probably 450 is a good median date, but some would prefer to push the date nearly half a century in either direction. The major issue is Malachi's position relative to Ezra's mission in 457 and Nehemiah's two visits in 445 and 432. We may safely discount the Targumic tradition that "malachi" *was* Ezra. Likewise, various critical hypotheses need not detain us. The question about the priority of Ezra or Nehemiah (cf. below) would not materially affect our answer, in any event. The evolutionistic assumption that some of the principles and regulations which Malachi upholds were not even known in the community before the coming of Ezra and the promulgation of "P" will find no resonance whatsoever in conservatism. In any case, that assumption is a two-edged sword: theoretically, Malachi could have anticipated the Ezrahite reforms, or he could have deplored the congregation's failure to obey them (the latter assumption often leads to an attempt to pinpoint the date between Nehemiah's two visits). Sometimes it is argued from the use in 1:8 of the usual term for a Persian satrap or "governor" *(pechah)* that Malachi could not have been active while Nehemiah was on the scene, but the term apparently could be used much more flexibly too. Thus, again, 450 appears to be as good and safe a round figure as any.

Traditionally, Malachi has been regarded as the last of the prophets, corresponding to his position in the canon. Conservatives would probably still see little reason to abandon that position, although it might be conceded that Joel and Obadiah could be a little later. Criticism, however, confidently dates much of the prophetic copy later or at least quite contemporaneously: "Trito-Isaiah," "Deutero-Trito-Zechariah," Jonah and Daniel, plus huge blocs of "later additions" in nearly all the Biblical literature.

It must be stressed, however, that even by conservative reckoning, Malachi is not the latest *book* in the Old Testament. In this respect, the arrangement of the Hebrew canon is less misleading than the familiar Western sequence. In the Masoretic tradition, the "Writings" follow the "Latter Prophets," and last of the Writings is Chronicles (which see), probably to be dated around 400, perhaps a half-century after Malachi. And it may well be that some of the other canonical books received final touching-up even after that time, although surely to a very minimal extent.

Critical appreciation of Malachi, as of most postexilic prophecy, tends to be quite grudging and niggardly. Although it will be conceded that Malachi was no mere formalist, his predominant concern with the purity and correct execution of the cult tends to be viewed as seriously compromising his prophetic integrity. Apart from theological considerations, it may be doubted if such an elitist, spiritualistic position is any more realistic today than it was in the fifth century.

On the basis of holistic Biblical principle one may argue, on the contrary, that Malachi is very typically prophetic precisely in his unification of cult and ethics, of external and internal. Malachi is thus a major exemplification of the principle that, "He who does not pray at specified times and places probably does not pray at all." One is hard put to point to anything excitingly "creative" in Malachi (although cf. some critical evolutionists below), but that is an improper hermeneutical canon to begin with.

Malachi is sometimes disparaged on another, more formal, score, viz., the stylized, dialogical pattern that pervades his book, in contrast to the more rhetorical pattern of earlier prophecy (cf. below on details; cf. also

Zech. 7). Hence, many argue that Malachi committed his ideas to writing from the outset (as most apocalypticists shortly are thought to have done). The spirit of the legalist, catechist, and scribe is supposedly beginning to quench the spirit of prophecy. "The last hour of the immediate spirit-inspired prophetic word has struck, and the hour of the synagogue lecturer has come" (Sellin). Even more pejoratively, some, who note (correctly) that Malachi's method anticipates one common among the rabbis and in the Talmud, characterize him as a "forerunner of scholastic rabbinism" or the like. Objectively, however, it is doubtful if the formal change makes any material difference whatsoever.

As to authenticity, critics have found relatively little to cavil about. Some wish to place Mal. 3:6-12 after 1:5 to provide better context. A major exegetical *crux* in the book is 1:11 (cf. below), and, not surprisingly, a few have attempted to cut the Gordian knot by declaring the passage an interpolation. Otherwise, questions of this sort are largely limited to the last three verses (4:4-6), which are widely viewed as later commentary, concluding liturgical formula, or appendix rather than an integral part of the final oracle. Typically, the editor of the Minor Prophets is thought to have sought to identify the "messenger" of 3:1 with Elijah. Believing that the age of prophecy was at an end, he sought thus to unite the Law and the Prophets (the two preceding parts of the Hebrew canon) and encourage his readers to remain faithful to the Torah until the eschatological herald announced the fulfillment of prophetic predictions. The exegesis, as such, is not bad, but the isagogical hypothesis is entirely without objective evidence.

There is no connection with the fact that the Masoretic text recognizes no chapter four. Mal. 4:1-6 in Western versions (following the Septuagint) are 3:19-24 in the Hebrew Bible. No other textual problems of note are exhibited in Malachi. The prophet's style is perhaps undistinguished, but, at worst, "prosaic" only in the purely formal sense.

Contents

The Book of Malachi is arranged in six speeches or oracles, each introduced by a standard dialectical or dialogical pattern: (1) Yahweh or the prophet first advances a thesis; (2) an antithesis, challenge, or question is uttered by the people or the priest; (3) a defense by Yahweh, sometimes in words of reproach and doom. The first three oracles (chaps. 1—2) concentrate more exclusively on current problems in the community, while the remainder of the book has a somewhat more eschatological coloration. The second, third, and fifth sermons indicate the three main abuses which concern Malachi: (1) the degeneracy and lassitude of the priesthood; (2) intermarriage with pagan women and often heartless divorce of their first partners; and (3) the congregation's remissness in payment of the sacred dues, to the detriment of especially the Levites.

The first oracle (Mal. 1:2-5) attaches to the mainstream of the Biblical message, the themes of election and covenant (the latter term is used repeatedly in the book). Proclamation of that Gospel is the only way to counter skepticism about the genuineness or value of Yahweh's love. It is the polar opposite of any and all liberal universalism of "God loves all people" or "loves the sinner, only hating the sin." Malachi's classic formulation of the "scandal of particularity" is thus also a sort of a "Gentile oracle" (the only approach to that classical prophetic usage in the book): "Jacob have I loved, but Esau have I hated."

St. Paul, too, can only cite it (Rom. 9:13) to underscore the inscrutability of the divine purpose, especially the mystery of election *("Cur alii prae aliis?")*. "Hate," of course, is a matter of God's "consequent will," not a result of deterministic double predestination, but, in proper context, there is no warrant to tone the term down. Malachi's insistence that Edom's hope of restoration is vain may well reflect some contemporary historical circumstance (cf. Obadiah), but he is not far from the general, typological use of "Edom" in many prophetic oracles.

The second speech (Mal. 1:6—2:9) reproves the priests for their neglect of the sacrificial cult, the "covenant with Levi" (2:4.8). By sacrificing inferior and ritually improper animals, they have shown themselves even worse than the Gentiles (1:11) (?). The teaching office of the faithful priest as "the messenger of the LORD of hosts" (2:7) is underscored. If they do not reform, "I will curse your blessings" (2:2). The problem of perfunctory ministers was not new in Malachi's day, nor is it in ours.

As indicated above, Mal. 1:11 is a major *crux*. As it stands, it may easily be read as an expression of sheer universalism: the fundamental validity of all sincere religious expression, regardless of understanding or intent. Not a few critics with that understanding hail the verse as a major "breakthrough" in Old Testament religious insight. That exegesis founders, however, on the explicit particularism of the context (esp., 1:2-3). Furthermore, the reference to "my name" implies, according to standard Biblical usage, *special* revelation. With the same exegesis, some critics excise it as an interpolation because of its incongruity. Others refer the verse to Jewish worship in the Diaspora, but, at best Malachi's language would then be very hyperbolic, and the language suggests sacrificial worship in the temple, not the "spiritual sacrifice" of the synagogue.

A familiar traditional and conservative understanding attempts an eschatological explanation: the future universality of the true faith (fulfilled in the New Testament) is here contrasted with the present. While that is theologically congenial enough, the Hebrew idiom (simple juxtaposition) is more naturally translated as a present (or is it something like the common "prophetic perfect"?). A recent and attractive suggestion understands it to say, in classical prophetic vein, that if *mere* sacrifice were sufficient for true worship, all religions could proffer plenty of that, and hence, by comparison, there would be nothing unique or praiseworthy about Israel's mechanistic, meritorious practices. No explanation seems fully satisfactory, and perhaps we can say only that Malachi insists on a contrast with present practices which plainly are not viewing matters from God's perspective.

The third speech (2:10-16) is Malachi's brief, but trenchant condemnation of mixed marriages, often accompanied by divorce of their first, Jewish wives (cf. Ezra and Nehemiah). Such marriages were probably often contracted for economic or other security reasons, but Malachi sees clearly the inevitable religious dimension: indifference toward the only true religion and profanation of the temple (v. 11), not to speak of breach of covenant with their first wives (v. 14 f.). It is imperative that 1:10 ("Have we not all one father?") not be yanked out of this obviously particularistic context and turned into an expression of universalism (cf. the Lord's Prayer), as liberals sometimes do. The "fatherhood of God and brotherhood of man" is a Biblical concept only within "the covenant of our fathers," that is, solely according to the order of redemption, not of creation (or general revelation). Because of its embarrassment to them, some critics would like to regard these verses as a later addition, but purely on subjective grounds.

The fourth discourse (Mal. 2:17—3:5) takes a more eschatological turn. To those who have grown skeptical that God will ever intervene in judgment, Malachi insists that Yahweh "will suddenly come to his temple," the familiar locus of theophany and judgment throughout prophecy: what was constantly proclaimed and sacramentalized in the cult will achieve its definitive, eschatological expression. In almost a paraphrase of Amos 5:20, God's coming will be "darkness and not light," yet its purpose will be purgation, not judgment (and beginning at the house of God with the priests). Although Malachi indicates that it was a common part of popular expectation ("whom you seek" and "in whom you delight"), this is the first clear appearance in Old Testament eschatology of the concept of a herald or forerunner of the heavenly monarch of the Messiah. Anticipations are obvious, however, in Is. 40:3, 9, etc., which the New Testament cites in the same breath with this passage in application to John the Baptizer. Obviously, by New Testament times, it was a major aspect of Messianic hope (cf. 4:5 and the identification of the "messenger" with "Elijah"). Self-evidently to Christians, Yahweh's climactic coming to His temple occurred in the Incarnation, the beginning of the final judgment (John 3:19), but also the ultimate implementation of all the potential of Old Testament sacrifice.

Malachi's fifth speech (3:6-12) associates the congregation's current social and economic distress to their "robbing God" by failure to bring "the full tithes." The ultimate inseparability of spiritual and material blessing is a standard part of the Bible's "sacramental" perspective.

The sixth and final homily (3:13—4:6) again picks up the complaint of 2:17 that despaired of any righteous judgment and answers it in even broader eschatological perspective than the fourth discourse had. The "scandal of particularity" becomes most scandalous at the final judgment! Those whose names are written in God's "book of remembrance" (a frequent Biblical figure, but perhaps here in eschatological perspective for the first time) will be His "special possession" on that day, fulfilling the ancient covenant formula (Ex. 19:5). For them the "sun of righteousness" will rise, perhaps not only a symbol for the triumph of light, but another expression of the "sacramental" application of God's "justification" to the realm of nature as well as of the spirit (cf. 3:6-12; Is. 45:8; Joel 2:18 ff.).

The conclusion to this homily and to Malachi (4:4-6) again recapitulates themes in the fourth speech. Perhaps it is a sort of an epilogue, but there is no need to consider it ungenuine (cf. above). The promise of the "messenger" in 3:1 is reformulated according to the typology of Elijah, the great embodiment of prophecy. "The great and terrible day of the LORD" is near, but not yet, and in the interim "the third use of the Law" remains valid (v. 4). The "generation gap" is held up as a major illustration of a deep-seated malaise which only the eschatological execution of the covenant curse can extirpate once and for all. "Curse" translates *cherem,* the anathema or sacral ban of holy war (cf. Joshua 8) here applied to the final judgment.

Synagogue rubrics direct a repetition of v. 4 after v. 6 so that the lection will not conclude with such a horrendous curse (cf. the end of Isaiah). Malachi does not conclude the Hebrew Old Testament, of course (cf. above), but Christian readers from the Septuagint on, where it does, have often been wont to draw invidious comparisons between the Old Testament's conclusion with a curse (even if provisional) and the New Testament climax in the promise, "Surely, I come quickly" (Rev. 22:20), as though that aptly characterized the contrasting Law versus Gospel orientation of the two testaments. Anyone who reflects for a moment on the respective contexts, not to speak of any serious knowledge of Biblical theology, will readily see that the contrast is not only misleading but pernicious.

The Christian community, of course, no longer awaits the arrival of "Elijah" (cf. the orthodox Jewish tradition of leaving an empty place for him at the Passover table). But, in the paradoxically continuing "not yet" of the time of the church, the ancient anathema upon the unresponsive is not only lifted but heightened. Malachi ends where Christianity is.

PART III

Introduction to the "Writings" and to Wisdom

To the third part of the canon, the Hebrew tradition merely gave the nondescript name, "Writings" *(Kethubim).* Of course, the adjective, "holy" or "sacred" is implied, and hence the Greek rendition, "Hagiographa."

To a certain extent, "Writings" means no more than "Etc." or *Et alii,* that is, a miscellany of pieces that fit neither into the Torah nor the Prophets. Beyond that we know too little about the historical circumstances of the formation of the canon to say much more. Date of composition obviously plays some role, but one must be careful to limit that criterion to final editing, because the substance of some of the pieces is obviously earlier. By any reckoning, some of the books are no later than, and sometimes earlier than, the prophetic books.

Clear liturgical influences are apparent in the case of the five *Megilloth* ("scrolls," literally) in the middle of the hagiographic canon. These five were (and are) the liturgically proper pericopes for five major Jewish festivals (the books listed in the chronological order of the festivals with which they are associated): Song of Solomon for Passover, Ruth for Weeks or Pentecost, Lamentations for *Tish'a b'Ab* (commemorating the fall of Jerusalem), Ecclesiastes for Booths (Tabernacles), and Esther for Purim. One cannot say with certainty how ancient are either the liturgical associations or the canonical positioning, but there is no reason why both should not reach far back into the Old Testament period itself. Scholars have often theorized that cultic influences played a major role in the formation of the canon in general (in a very broad sense, it undeniably did—humanly speaking), but only here can we be sure.

With its preference for topical classifications, the Septuagint (followed by nearly all modern versions) redistributed the "Writings" among two new classifications, "historical" and "poetical" books. One can scarcely say that this represented any improvement, however. There is much poetry elsewhere in the Hebrew Bible, especially in the prophets, and "history" as usual raises at least as many questions as it answers for the modern, Western mind (as "historical criticism" or "historical-critical method" drives home to us with a vengeance).

"Wisdom" is not coextensive with "Writings," of course, but at least four of the hagiographa are of "wisdom" character: Proverbs, Job, Song of Solomon, and Ecclesiastes. In addition, as we shall see, the Psalter may well have been given final form as a "Wisdom Book" (esp. Ps. 1). Neither the Masoretic nor the Septuagintal sequence manages to group all of the "wisdom" books together, however. Other criteria apparently took precedence. The Hebrew sequence of Psalms—Proverbs—Job may simply wish to highlight the Psalter, while Ecclesiastes was placed in the liturgical sequence of the Megilloth. The Septuagint appears to have rearranged the order in order to bring together the three works associated with Solomon (Proverbs, Qoheleth, Canticles), but with Psalms intervening between Job and those three.

Definition of "Wisdom"

In an "Introduction" our primary concern will be with the canonical Wisdom *literature,* but that topic cannot be considered apart from the broader questions of the nature and significance of "Wisdom." It is not easy to say even what "wisdom" means in Biblical context, partly because of its great variety of nuances, partly because there are no adequate English equivalents of the Hebrew vocabulary. The secular inroads are such that rarely even in church circles is "wisdom" heard any more in its full Biblical tonality. The root usually translated "wise" or "wisdom" is *ch-k-m.* Its major literary expression is the *mashal,* usually translated "proverb," although "parable," "allegory," etc., are also possible. In certain contexts the matter of "counsel" *(y-'-ts; 'etsah)* is also important. All these terms have a great variety of near synonyms.

What is "wisdom" then? One may venture to say that, on the objective side, and perhaps on the lowest or most elemental level, it is the "natural law," an all-embracing cosmic order, immanent in all existence, and by which everything is ruled and governed. Subjectively, it is the awareness of these universal, eternal norms, and the ordering of one's life and behavior accordingly. From observation of a cosmic order follows the advice to attune one's own life to its eternal rhythms. Such a man is "wise," in contrast to the "fool," who tries to be a law unto himself. Inevitably, each is "rewarded" according to his deserts, the idea of retribution being closely associated with that of the cosmic order. (More mainline Biblical thought expressed the same idea under the rubric of "righteousness," and its parallelism with "wisdom" summarizes much of the ultimate unity.)

Functionally, very often one could define "wisdom" then as "ability to cope"—with life in its broadest dimensions, as well as with specific tasks. In the latter context it often became synonymous with "know-how," with the specific skills needed for a trade, or with the God-given talents and experience which made it possible. By that definition, one could even say that God was most "wise," because He was supremely able to cope, because He was equal to the task of being God!

This "natural revelation" or "wisdom" was present on the same three levels which one discerns in connection with other Biblical formulations. First of all, it was evident on the anthropological or psychological level, on the level of personal behavior and ethics (the "way" or "path" of the "righteous" man). Second, it was manifest on the level of interpersonal relationships, of society, politics, and history. Third, it was also something cosmic and transcendent, evident also in the realm of nature. That is, the cosmic order could be viewed also as an ethical category— "justice" or "righteousness." Thus, if said with all due caution, one may say that wisdom was the "science" of antiquity; at very least, it did proceed somewhat inductively or on the basis of observation, and it developed lists and classifications of various sorts. Also, if said again with proper reserve, it was the "philosophy" of the ancient Near East (both in comparison and contrast with "theology"), and from the Hellenistic age on it became one of the major avenues of merger of Occident and Orient (cf. below).

The "laws" or principles involved were not perceived deterministically or fatalistically, although they could easily degenerate into that, and outside of Biblical context often did veer strongly in that direction. Rather, they represented more perimeters or outside limits, within which a considerable measure of freedom or variety was possible. As a result, some proverbs are contradictory—because life is often that way. (One thinks of the English saying: "Out of sight, out of mind" versus "Absence makes the heart grow fonder.") Sometimes, the mystery, inscrutability, and final uncontrollability of life gave rise to profound theological observations.

Sometimes "wise man" became a (quasi-) professional term, used of one who in some systematic way observed, collected, and taught the realities of existence. Thus, we often meet the "wise" as one of the four major classes of Israelite intellectual society, alongside of prophet, priest, and king. Sometimes their sociological role and teaching function seems to have been quite informal, but at other times it appears likely that we can speak of more formal "schools," or of carefully structured institutions. Elsewhere in the ancient Near East, we know of such structures in connection with both temples and courts, but in Israel we lack details until a very late period.

It probably is helpful, however, to distinguish three separate *Sitze im Leben* of Israelite wisdom activity: popular, political, and theological. Probably all three were operative in most periods, but, to a certain extent, they also correspond to three different chronological stages through which the wisdom movement passed. The earliest, and in all ages, the most elementary form of wisdom is that of *family or clan wisdom,* the common sense expressions of how to get along, that form the bedrock of any culture. In that form we meet it in virtually all the Biblical literature, and many of the literary collections undoubtedly root there. Beginning with the monarchy, and probably heavily dependent on Egyptian models, we may speak of *court wisdom,* concerned partly with the king as a guarantor of justice and "righteousness" (cf. below), but especially concerned to communicate the art and skills of statescraft, political administration, etc. Not even liberal scholarship is disposed any longer to look so skeptically on Biblical reports of Solomon as the fountainhead and patron of Biblical wisdom (although it is usually reluctant to admit his actual authorship of the Biblical pieces attributed to him; see below). In fact, with the "Solomonic Enlightment" thesis, it has sometimes swung to the opposite extreme; the term, however, is not only anachronistic, but misleading: Biblical wisdom was never so secularistic, nor the previous ages so totally "unenlightened." Third, we plainly can also speak of a *"school" or scribal wisdom,* apparently especially after the Exile, and apparently concerned more with "universal education," and often developing in a more explicitly theological and/or philosophical direction.

All of this indicates that, whatever the sociological structures, "wisdom" often came close to being synonymous with "culture"—and, in antiquity, that would be always a sacral culture as well. This must be borne in mind in reading wisdom's products, but in much recent scholarship, "wisdom" has come to be used so broadly as almost to be evacuated of all specific meaning. Sometimes "wisdom" is applied to any literature with a didactic or even humanitarian concern, especially if it is not couched in specifically revelatory language. When the term thus includes almost the whole range of human experience and aspiration, it can, indeed, be applied to (or at least its "influence" can be found in) almost all Biblical literature, but in too diffuse a sense to be very helpful.

"Wisdom" in Liberal (Critical) Perspective

To the Biblical scholar, and especially to the conservative, the major problem is how to relate "wisdom" (especially, but not only, the canonical wisdom literature) to the rest of the Biblical revelation. If one rereads the previous paragraphs, it is easy to see that very little about them is necessarily unique to Israel. The "sanctified common sense" or pragmatic and eudaemonistic moralism which first meets the eye there is indeed well-nigh universal, give or take a few cultural accidents. One fears that all too often it describes only too well what passes for "religion" or even "Christianity" for the man on the street. It becomes much more pernicious when even many faithful Bible readers read the wisdom literature from that perspective and are only confirmed in work-righteousness and quasi-paganism as a result. Perhaps nowhere is the proper hermeneutics as indispensable as in the case of wisdom!

There is clear record within the Bible, especially in the prophets, of clashes with "wisdom." Sometimes the term may then be used in a very general sense (much like St. Paul's "wisdom of the world," 1 Cor. 1:20 ff.), but nonetheless it illustrates how readily wisdom could become the bearer of an outlook on life that could not coexist with the Mosaic revelation. Many liberals are willing to leave it at that, and view wisdom as a fundamentally alien insertion into the Biblical corpus. At best, this might tell us something about "civic righteousness" or life in God's "left-hand kingdom," but it is not only no structural part of God's positive revelation, but allegedly urges salvation by merit as well. If it were only a matter of the "wisdom" which we often meet scattered throughout the rest of the Bible, the conservative might come to terms with aspects of such a viewpoint. But since it also involves the *canonical* wisdom literature, it necessarily clashes with the dogmas of verbal inspiration and of the unity of Scripture. Nowhere is the difference between liberal and conservative hermeneutics more obvious than in their usual assessments of Biblical wisdom literature. (The Old Testament problem here can be readily compared with that of James in the New Testament, often referred to as a New Testament wisdom book, or viewed as an unassimilated bit of primitive "Jewish Christianity.")

Because of the liberal prejudice, wisdom, at least until very recently, has always been very much a stepchild of historical-critical study, even at its most positive. Wellhausen almost completely ignored the wisdom books, clearly regarding them as late and secondary. Duhm developed this assumption more specifically in the light of evolutionary principles in a way that virtually became a tenet of "critical orthodoxy." The wise men were regarded as largely postexilic heirs of the prophets, who applied the latter's lofty ethical ideals to the mundane circumstances of everyday life. Two major aspects of prophetic theology were thought to have been especially championed: belief in the certainty of retribution for the wicked and hostility toward the cult. Often the wisdom movement was read as a general protest movement against the provincialities and rigidities of postexilic Judah, not only against the cult but against its orthodoxism in general, and often against the entire historically oriented traditions of mainstream Israel. The disillusionment of the "wise" with "revelation in history," which had led only to disaster and exile, allegedly led them to search for more universal and "timeless" religious values.

With basically those same assumptions, one can at least understand why even "Biblical theology," while perhaps accentuating the positive a bit more, generally gave wisdom about the widest possible berth. Wisdom with its accent on universal ontology simply did not fit into categories of "revelation in history," or of "Heilsgeschichte," especially as often narrowly interpreted to exalt "redemption" at the expense of "creation" and "nature."

Form Criticism

In the meantime, form criticism tended to undercut such assumptions, but it was a long time in making itself felt. Because of its general lack of interest in "relevance," however, it contributed nothing, at best, to a better theological appreciation of the material. However, the observation of the extent to which Amenemope exhibited a "social conscience" and stressed individual responsibility within a moral society played a large role in undermining the old liberal edifice according to which the Israelite prophets had first discovered "ethical monotheism," on which the morality of the sages was allegedly dependent. On the contrary, it now began to appear that the reverse was true: the prophets were often dependent on the sages!

Form criticism also highlighted the antiquity of at least the elements of the wisdom literature, and, in addition, began to note the many comparable types of material increasingly uncovered by archaeology, especially in Egypt and Mesopotamia. On the basis of those parallels, Gunkel and others postulated a traditional class of wise men in Israel very similar to that of her neighbors.

As usual, however, form criticism often substituted its own brand of evolutionism for that of the literary critics, and only very slowly has it yielded to the weight of increasing evidence to the contrary. Gunkel's assumption, as usual, was that brevity was a sign of antiquity, with extended discourses developing only much later. Second, theological reflection, especially religious individualism, was supposed to signal lateness. All kinds of extra-Biblical evidence, however, has forced the virtually complete abandonment of both of these dogmas (cf. on Proverbs). Most critics would agree today that no particular form is limited to any one period or to any type of wise man. Particularly as concerns the personification of wisdom, we now have many examples from high antiquity (cf. esp. Prov. 8).

Form criticism has probably made more of a contribution in delineation of the wisdom forms or *Gattungen* themselves, and the recent surge of interest in wisdom has devoted vast energies to the question. As usual, much of the result appears to be the belaboring of the obvious, and intense terminological debates mar the entire discussion. Perhaps some half a dozen categories, however, are commonly considered to be especially characteristic of the wise, although often utilized under other auspices as well.

Most basic, of course, is the *mashal* or "proverb" itself, in simplest form a simple observation without any imperative or admonition, and often characterized by poetic features such as paronomasia, assonance, alliteration, rhyme, puns, or synonymy (sometimes apparently associating the intrinsic "order" of language itself with "order" in its broader reaches). Other types are more common outside the Book of Proverbs: riddles (*chidah;* cf. Judges 14:10 ff.); fables and allegories (Judges 9:8-15; 2 Sam. 12:1-4; 2 Kings 14:9; Prov. 5:15-23; Eccl. 12:1-6; often in Ezekiel; cf. on Solomon in 1 Kings 4:32-34); hymns and prayers (especially in the Psalter, but cf. Job 5:9-16; and 28; Prov. 8); the dialogue or *Streitgespräch* (esp. Job); the "confession" or autobiographical narrative (esp. Ecclesiastes).

Extra-Biblical "Wisdom"

Whether one attributes the insight to form criticism or not, there is no denying the many phenomenal parallels to Biblical wisdom in other ancient Near Eastern cultures, probably more so than in any other area of Biblical studies. Neither the formal similarities nor the material or theological differences should be minimized, although both often are.

The profound differences are perhaps summarized as well as anywhere in the fact that it is about as hard to find real synonyms to "wisdom" in Akkadian as it is in English. The Mesopotamian equivalents signify skill in especially magic and incantation, a concern conspicuous by its absence in the Biblical collections. Both Mesopotamian and Egyptian discussions often take place in an atmosphere of fatalism or resignation to unalterable destiny. The extra-Biblical examples are equally pragmatic in dominant concern (admonitions to marital fidelity and warnings against indiscretions with women are prominent themes in both cultures), but especially Egyptian collections often exhibit an amoral "how to get ahead at all costs" or "it doesn't matter what you know but who you know" sort of cynicism.

The more philosophical Egyptian concept of *ma'at,* however, has many similarities to Biblical "wisdom" and may well have been one of the raw materials adapted by Israel under God in articulation of its own position. Both terms articulated the idea of a basic *Weltordnung* undergirding both cosmos and society (ethics) and, hence, both may be translated "order, truth, rightness, righteousness," etc. But the profound differences also emerge in that Egyptian *ma'at* was itself usually understood as another god rather than one aspect of a personal Creator's revelation.

For a useful and representative listing of parallels, see Pritchard and the commentaries. Only a few examples, besides the many collections of aphorisms, can be noted here. The striking parallelism of Prov. 22:17—23:11 (which see) with the Egyptian "Teaching of Amen-em-ope" cannot be dismissed with the wave of a hand. Certain similarities of Ps. 104 with the "Hymn to the Sun" of Egypt's heretic-monotheist Pharaoh Ikhnaton have often been noted. From all periods (and not only late ones) we find expressions of disillusionment or skepticism about facile dogmas, superficially comparable to Job and Qoheleth: the Egyptian "Song of the Harper" and "Dialogue of a Man with His Soul"; and the "Babylonian theodicy" and *"Ludlul bel nemeqi* [Let me praise the lord of wisdom]" from Mesopotamia.

Worthy of special attention are the novelistic "Sayings of Ahikar," perhaps originating in Assyria in the eighth century but circulated in various recensions throughout the ancient Near East. Originally perhaps a maligned chancellor under Sennacherib, Ahikar is presented as the "counselor" and "father" of all Assyria. An Aramaic version was found among the ruins of the Jewish mercenaries of Elephantine (fifth century B.C.), and in the apocryphal Book of Tobit Ahikar appears as Tobit's nephew. In the late Old Testament period the book sometimes achieved quasi-canonical status (Charles includes it among the pseudepigrapha), and echoes of it are found in the church fathers, Talmud, and Koran.

Strangely enough, we do not so far have any real "wisdom literature" from Israel's immediate neighbors, although the Bible itself makes frequent mention of it. The mysterious East, and perhaps especially Edom and/or north Arabia, seems to have had a special reputation for wisdom (possibly the "Massa" of Prov. 30 and 31), but we lack details, and some scholars have developed hypotheses of influence on Israel from those quarters far beyond the evidence. Thus 1 Kings 4:30 describes Solomon's wisdom as surpassing "the wisdom of all the people of the east, and all the wisdom of Egypt." The next verse describes him as "wiser than Ethan the Ezrahite, and Heman, Calcol, and Darda, the sons of Mahol," all names which we can associate with the indigenous Canaanite culture of the area. The "Daniel" whose proverbial wisdom is said in Ezek. 28:3 (which see) to have been exceeded by the king of Tyre may well be the same as the king who figures prominently in one of the three great Ugaritic epics. Otherwise, the large number of lexical, syntactical, and stylistic "Ugaritisms" which are evident in the Book of Proverbs (even by a minimal, non-Dahoodian reading) establish the cultural continuity, on that level at least, of Canaanite and Israelite wisdom expression.

Besides Ahikar (above) the important deuterocanonical (canonical to Catholicism) exemplars of wisdom must be noted. Some of them may be quoted or at least alluded to in the New Testament (cf. also James as a New Testament wisdom book, often posing theological problems very similar to those of its Old Testament counterparts). Ecclesiasticus or Sirach (c. 200 B.C.) is quite comparable to Proverbs, while the pseudepigraphic "Wisdom of Solomon" (c. 100 B.C.) contains longer compositions and sometimes shows marked Hellenistic influence. Wisdom influence is also very apparent in portions of Tobit, Baruch, and 1 Esdras (the tale of the contest between the court pages won by Zerubbabel).

Except for these late and mostly post-canonical products which evince strong theological influence, one can readily understand how the radical sixties could resonate so readily to the wisdom literature. In contrast to the oblivion in which it had languished during the reign of "Biblical theology," wisdom was now so highly exalted that it put much of the rest of Scripture in the shade. Read by itself in isolation from total canonical context (that is, without Scripture providing its own basic hermeneutical paradigms), wisdom can easily be heard as championing essentially the same type of universalistic, humanistic, immanentalistic, this-worldly "no distinction between sacred and secular" type of religion so dear to the heart of "let the world write the church's agenda" liberalism. One liberal study of wisdom from that ethos trumpeted the title, *In Man We Trust* (Brueggemann).

On the surface, the appeal is not to revelation, to God's love, but to man's reason or common sense. The great Biblical themes of the election of Israel, Sinaitic covenant, Exodus and conquest, promises about the people and the land, sacrifice and temple, are almost totally absent, as is most of the semi-technical vocabulary employed elsewhere in the Bible to present them. The theme of "kingship" is not developed in the light of Nathan's oracle to David but is more a matter of etiquette or protocol before royalty anywhere, anytime. "Sin" is not a matter of fundamental fallenness and rebelliousness, but of atomistic infractions of a code of conduct. The particular name of Israel's God, "Yahweh," appears often enough but in so casual a way that one can easily substitute "God" or "deity" of almost any sort. Similarly, the expression, "fear of God/Yahweh" (Hebrew idiom for "religion") as someone has said, *can*

THE WORD BECOMING FLESH

easily be read as saying, in effect, only that "a little religion never hurt anyone."

Conservative Understanding of "Wisdom"

Needless to say, such constructions are utterly incompatible with conservative convictions. How do we, then, confront these problems and approach wisdom in full canonical context? Perhaps the first thing to stress is the difference between an *explicit* theological statement and one which is assumed or implicit. Formally, much of wisdom literature is of the latter type, but if Scripture is ultimately one, it must be understood and interpreted in the light of not only the more explicit wisdom statements, but of all of Scripture, of the "canonical context." The real subject of wisdom is not (any) man but Israelite (covenant, Christian) man. Its "humanism" is Biblical (Israelite, Christian) humanism. Its "universalism" involves, indeed, God's claim on all the universe, but one realized and realizable only in His gracious covenant. Its *Sitz im Leben* is the daily life of people who confessed Yahweh as Creator, Judge, and Redeemer. Its accent on "retribution" and "reward" was an assertion of faith, based on revelation, not some naive deduction from experience. "Sacred and secular" are not distinguished because everything is sacral! The very assumption of an underlying moral order belies any real secularism.

Outside of the covenant or faith, God's universal claim can only be of that of the Law (second use), confronting and condemning all until they convert. At most in a positive way, then, the proverbs will only indicate certain "moral principles" which also the believer will be concerned to inculcate in the "kingdom on the left hand." Wisdom is understood and applied in its full and true intent only within the covenant, where the full content of God's revelation is proclaimed and accepted. Because both "wisdom" and "righteousness" assume a universal moral order, it becomes helpful to subsume the former under the latter: that order (of salvation or new creation) is available only through God's gracious gift of an alien righteousness (justification by faith). Sacramentally, one says that it is baptism which bridges and unites the *heilsgeschichtlich* and existential aspects of the Christian life.

In a word, the main dogmatic category for properly approaching wisdom is "third use of the Law." It represents an alternate mode of expression and type of approach to the illustration of faithful living found in the "legal" sections of the Pentateuch, and thoroughly harmonious and compatible with it. It concentrates on those aspects of living which the believer shares with all men, and where the motivations or any uniqueness will often be unapparent to men. Believers are certainly not less concerned about the ordinary, everyday concerns of living than unbelievers.

"Sanctified" common sense is not less commonsensical as a result! "Wisdom" deals with life where it is actually lived by all people, with the "trivia" of existence, where if the believer is not faithful, he certainly will be nowhere, with intangibles to which neither legal prescription nor prophetic broadsides easily speak.

Proverbs and maxims dealing with such concerns have a great deal of commonality among all ages and all peoples—precisely because the problems of basic living are much the same, regardless of religion, culture, historical epoch, etc. Hence, one need not be surprised that Biblical wisdom shows phenomenal parallels with its cultural neighbors. As always, it is not a matter of "borrowing" in either direction (the question itself is misconceived) but of a cultural continuum. And the differences are infinitely greater than the surface similarities, because the same principles have been transplanted into an entirely different context. The real and ultimate "uniqueness" of Biblical (and Christian) ethics is not in external behavior patterns (respectable citizens of goodwill usually agree on these to a large extent) but in the theological context, motivations, or goals. One may compare the modern Christian adaptation or "baptism" of many modern proverbs: "A stitch in time saves nine," "A watched pot never boils," etc., almost *ad infinitum*. The Christian faith is not compromised thereby, nor is the universal validity of such sayings, properly understood, called into question. Rather, faith insists that their real and ultimate "wisdom" is released and established only in the proper relation to God in Christ. In that new context, as someone has said, former enemies make good apostles.

It may be helpful to compare such wisdom to "general revelation" or to the "order of creation." Of course, as Biblical documents they are verbally inspired, that is, represent "special revelation," as much as the rest of Scripture. But the topic or aspect of life to which they point is "general revelation" or "natural revelation/law." Although written in all men's hearts, it not only conceals but condemns until special revelation makes all things new. The same things are no longer the same. After conversion, the Christian continues to grow and learn in many respects and from any source, but confessing that the real Source of "secular" knowledge is the same as that vouchsafed in Scripture. God's self-conscious creature (and *a fortiori* the redeemed one) is no passive robot, but one who actively seeks his place in the world of his Creator *(fides quaerens intellectum)*. As one made in God's image, this search is part of his quest for God's will in his life, and believing that all truth is ultimately one because its ultimate author is One, he utilizes all relevant sources, whatever their earthly mediation. All knowledge is not revealed in Scripture, but all knowledge becomes "wisdom" *coram Deo* only when ultimately subordinated to, tested, and evaluated in the light of Scripture. In a sense, then, wisdom provides a sampling or exemplars of how the believer confronts the valid aspects of this world's wisdom and employs it *ad maiorem Dei gloriam.* Now, proleptically, he has at his disposal all the blessings of creation before the Fall and is intended to exercise the best possible stewardship. "All things are yours." (To the trained Christian this theology is jejune, but it is obvious that its functional application to Biblical wisdom has all but slipped through our fingers.)

Only if one keeps this theological context in mind will one of the major problems in Biblical wisdom be comprehended theologically in a satisfactory way. That is the problem of the apparently naive, if not deterministic, black-and-white contrast between the "two ways," that of the "righteous" and of the "wicked" (classically in Ps. 1; a variety of synonyms are also employed). Liberals denounce the "work-righteousness" allegedly implied, and universalists reject any scheme of "retribution" or "reward" which does not finally exculpate virtually everyone. Usually Job and Ecclesiastes are read as a protest against the rigidity of this dogmatic wisdom orthodoxy, classically represented in Proverbs.

However, it seems unthinkable that anyone, let alone a "wise" man, could really believe that life was that simple. The ancients surely knew and experienced as well as we that virtue is not always rewarded, nor vice invariably requited, that the "good guys" are by no means automatically the richest, happiest, or most successful. Such a literalistic reading would appear to collapse under the weight of its intrinsic nonsensicality.

One may make amends simply by inserting an "ultimately" before the stark black-and-white assertions. As usual, however, the nature of that ultimacy is not clearly spelled out in the wisdom texts themselves, but must be supplied from the total canonical context. Wisdom's own axiology would highlight primarily the vertical, existential aspect of man before God, always under God's searchlight (cf. Ps. 139). *Every* day is judgment day. Man is always at the crossroads. His situation is always poised between life and death, order and chaos (the explicit polarities of wisdom throughout). Every choice and activity of his, even the most trivial, is fraught with ultimate consequences. Each thrusts ultimately in one direction or the other; *sub specie aeternitatis,* there is no middle ground.

It surely is no accident that this dialectic, so central in Biblical wisdom, plays only a very peripheral role in the wisdom of Egypt and Mesopotamia. If the Biblical formulations can be attributed, liberal-fashion, to "experience" at all, it is the experience of *faith,* based on revelation and knowledge of Yahweh, not simple empiricism (which, as we saw, never yields such results).

Although the formulation is different, it is no trick to amalgamate such assertions with those of mainstream Biblical expression: blessing and curse, covenant and promise, etc. Since the ultimate subject, then, is a personal Creator and Redeemer, the resultant "doctrine of retribution" is no longer some ineluctable pagan "nemesis" or Greek *moira* (fate, destiny). Since the "righteousness" or "wickedness" is no longer simply a matter of personal merit and deserts, but of whether or not in the light of God's promises and covenant, one has been found guilty or innocent before the heavenly court, the believer can and does always appeal to a vicarious righteousness to contravene what otherwise is a sure "law of condemnation." Here, the ultimate unity of the concepts of "wisdom" and "righteousness" enable us to bring the entire matter within the forensic rubric of "justification by faith."

It follows, then, that the ultimacy of wisdom's assertions must include the horizontal (eschatological) as well as the vertical dimension, in line with the main thrust of *Heilsgeschichte.* Only "the Day" will finally reveal the eternal disjunction of the "two ways." We cannot enter here into the question of how much of this futuristic eschatology (*eternal* life vs. *eternal* punishment) is already present in the Old Testament. Liberals usually reject it out of hand, and while conservatives may accent it prematurely, wisdom's accent on ultimacies will be a major part of the argumentation that such a theology was, at very least, *implicit* throughout mainline Old Testament thought, and often surfaced also in a more explicit way. (Cf. below on the psalter and Dahood's theories.) It is no accident that many of those most explicit assertions appear in wisdom contexts (e.g., Ps. 49; 73), and many other wisdom texts are open to it (e.g., Ps. 1; 139). In one sense, the full nature of that ultimacy could not be revealed until the ultimate act itself, the resurrection of our Lord. As always, the faithful exegete will be careful to distinguish the degrees of explicitness in revelation of that ultimacy (i.e., he will not "read in" alien meanings), but the far greater danger today is that he will fail to "read out" of these texts their full Christological import.

Development of Wisdom as a Theological Idiom

One can develop a certain typology of degrees of theological explicitness in Biblical wisdom. However, it is important to stress again that this *logical* "development" in no way corresponds to any *chronological* evolution, although there is no doubt that use of a more explicit theological idiom, or even employment of wisdom categories as a major idiom of theological discourse became more common in later (probably mostly *post*-canonical) times. Regardless of the idiom or degree of explicitness, however, the fundamental theological relationships remain the same.

At the simplest level, as we said, we have simply a concatenation of sayings, where theological context is almost completely taken for granted. At more popular levels (then as now) that was probably always the case, but even many wisdom *literati* apparently did not concern themselves with explication of theoretical theological associations—not out of antagonism or even indifference, but, we should insist, as a sort of "division of labor." There was no point in all circles rehearsing the same thing in the same way (one might also compare the special idiom employed by the priesthood and the cult, with its many external differences from both prophet and wise man).

Possibly, one may distinguish a second "level" when "Yahweh" instead of "Elohim" becomes the explicit subject of sentences, or when "the fear of Elohim/Yahweh" becomes an organizing principle. There is no need for cynicism about the real and genuinely Biblical content of such simple assertions. Even apart from theological axioms, one may argue that they *can* with perfect ease be heard and read in the light of all that the Law and the Prophets reveal about the nature of Yahweh and man's relation to Him.

Two further and all-important stages of explicit theologization apparently proceeded somewhat simultaneously. One ultimately became more important for Christianity, one for Judaism. To no little extent one can pinpoint the dividing of the ways of these two post-Yahwistic religions according to which of the two motifs became the more central. The two are: (1) accent on wisdom as ultimately a Person, an epistemology of a heavenly figure of wisdom dwelling in the midst of and informing all earthly manifestations; and (2) *explicit* identification of wisdom with "Word," Torah, or Proverbs with the Pentateuch—of general with special revelation, if you will.

In one sense, it is ironic that both of these developments find most explicit expression in literature written *after* the close of the Old Testament canon, in certain apocryphal books. In spite of their literary, apocryphal context, those developments retain great importance, both for illuminating the less explicit, earlier canonical literature, and as a bridge to and background for the New Testament (and the Talmud). Possibly the earliest text in the series is the final verse of Job 28 where the real source and content of wisdom, otherwise ultimately inaccessible to man, is identified as the "fear of the LORD." Already implicit here is a motif to which especially Ecclesiastes gives classical expression: the *limits* of man's "wisdom" and of man's ability to master and govern his own life, that is, the marking off of areas of life which belong to Yahweh alone. Very explicit, and very important, however, is the canonical Prov. 8 (which see), where wisdom identifies herself as the "first of God's acts," hence as one pre-existing the creation of the universe, and furthermore as God's daily delight and master workman in the labor of creation. In spite of semantic debates, we are justified in describing wisdom here as a divine "hypostasis" (a semi-independent manifestation—the same term later employed in Greek theology to denote a "person" of the Trinity). At any rate, it is more than merely a "personification" of wisdom, the more preliminary (but ultimately the same) formulation which we meet in the earlier chapters of Proverbs. Partly because "wisdom" is feminine in Hebrew, it is presented as a female figure ("Lady Wisdom") in contrast to the "loose/strange woman" of the earlier chapters.

Third in sequence is the apocryphal Ecclus. (Sir.) 24 (esp. v. 23), stressing the identity of wisdom and Torah. Although its source is "the mouth of the Most High," *she* is somewhat available to all men, albeit only in inchoate form. She took root like a tree especially in Zion, where she invites all to eat and drink from her—which, however, will only incite greater thirst or hunger.

Finally, Wisdom 7 develops the theme. Here in semi-Hellenistic form, her immanence in all souls and easy access to all men is stressed. As "a pure emanation of the glory of the Almighty," she orders all things well, especially in teaching the four cardinal virtues: self-control, prudence, justice, courage.

The mysteries of canonization cannot always be fully explained, but, humanly speaking, the strong admixture of Greek, semi-pagan thought in the "Wisdom of Solomon" readily explains why that book remains outside the canon, in spite of its important role as preparation for the doctrine of the incarnation. Somewhat similarly in Sirach, increasing clarity about Wisdom was accompanied by increasingly Judaistic (in contrast to Yahwistic or Old Testament) concepts and formulations.

As we said, the theme in this development of wisdom formulation that became most important for Christianity (and hence also for Christian understanding and exposition) was the accent on the *personal* element in wisdom. God is indeed immanent in all creation, but (and ultimately more significantly) is also transcendent to it, and hence a genuine "Creator" (and ultimately, "Redeemer," both terms implying a personal being). "Nature" cannot be the result of impersonal, evolutionistic process, but stems from and is upheld by the personal Word of a personal God. To the believer, "nature" becomes a transparency of, a window into, God's eternal, eschatological design. Natural "law" cannot finally be eternal, immutable principles but must be expressions of His *personal* will.

"Retribution," "reward," etc., cannot be forced into ineluctable, legalistic straitjackets but are overruled by His personal offer of redemption.

The affirmation that this revelation came to fruition in the incarnation lies at the very heart of the Christian understanding of "Biblical theology." It is no accident that much of the "high Christology" of the New Testament is couched in wisdom terms. Christ is that *"Hagia Sophia"* incarnate, in whom the "new creation" is realized (and the "mysticism" of the Eastern church has generally found the theme easier to retain and appropriate than the West; cf. the repeated refrain, "Wisdom!" in the traditional Byzantine liturgy). Two New Testament pericopes are especially significant in this connection: Colossians with its cosmic Christology, and John (esp. chap. 1), where the Logos concept both is heir to the explicit merger of general and special revelation we have just discussed, and can make contact with the vast amount of comparable Greek thought about the immanental Logos, world-reason, or divine "logic" in all creation. The same wisdom themes continue in New Testament pneumatology: the Spirit of Christ transmits and contemporizes the personal energy of Wisdom Incarnate, of the "Word *Become Flesh.*"

This proclamation of Christ as the fulfillment of the Wisdom promises is not only a datum of New Testament theology in the narrow sense, however. It also casts its shadow backwards and becomes determinative of the Old Testament component of Biblical theology as well. Following the New Testament lead, "wisdom" is a major category for articulating Christ's pre-existence in the Old Testament, and becomes a sort of magnet for the Old Testament's own various articulations of the subject (e.g., "the angel of the LORD"). Lutherans especially might well recall in this connection that Christ's "real presence" in the Old Testament congregation was one of Luther's major means for educing the Christian content of the Old Testament as a full partner with the New, in fact as well as name. Hermeneutically, here as elsewhere, we do not "read into" the Old Testament something that is not intrinsically there, but, rather, with the New Testament, we "read out" of the Old Testament, or make patent its full latent meaning in the light of Christ.

The second prong of the explicit theologization of wisdom (besides stress on its personal character) was its *explicit* identification with the Word, with Torah, with the mainstream of special revelation or *Heilsgeschichte.* Much of the development of classical Judaism out of Old Testament Yahwism follows this path. As wisdom merges with Torah, the wisdom-teacher increasingly becomes a "scribe," the expounder of Scripture, and his authority will be enhanced as the synagogue gradually overtakes and replaces the temple. At the very same time, many wisdom techniques and idioms continue to be employed by the rabbis and are gathered in the Talmud (classically in the *Pirqe Aboth*, an early collection of rabbinical proverbs). Under these auspices, wisdom presses not toward the "orthodoxy" of Christianity, but toward the "orthopraxis" or accent on "halakah" characteristic of Judaism to the present day.

One must be careful about drawing mutual exclusives between the two directions, however. Judaism did not completely deny the personal aspect of wisdom, but obviously did not accept its Christological application. Just as obviously, however, Christianity did not reject the identification of wisdom with Word: not only were the two parts of Scripture at one in Christ, but both creation and redemption achieved their *pleroma* in the incarnation and resurrection. The unity continues to find expression in the three simultaneous meanings of "Word" in Christian theology: the person of the incarnate Christ, the Gospel about Him, and the Scriptures which define those terms.

Finally, we should not overlook the central role which these issues play in the higher criticism of the New Testament. To one degree or the other, liberal criticism has always tended toward the view that the "historical Jesus" (or the view held about him in "Palestinian Christianity") was basically only a noted teaching rabbi in the post-wisdom tradition that was so common at the time. And indeed there is truth in the portrait which we often overlook, including many wisdom echoes in the parables and even some explicit notices in the Synoptics (e.g., Matt. 11:19; Luke 11:49). But we cannot follow further hypotheses that very little, if any, of the alleged "high Christology" of post-resurrection explications of the "Christ of faith" root in Jesus Himself, but should rather represent the Hellenistic input of Gentile Christianity, or, at best, the allegedly alien ideas of a subcanonical apocalypticism.

The Writings

PSALMS

It is almost redundant to underscore the importance of the Psalter, whether in contemporary life or in the history of the church (or the synagogue—or the temple preceding both), whether in public worship or in private devotion. Anyone who is not already aware of this circumstance certainly testifies to existence on the fringes of, if not outside of, the community of faith. Of course, the different communities employ them differently. Over against the monastic use highlighted in the Middle Ages, Reformed reaction exalted psalm paraphrases over "human" hymnody, while Lutheran use centered on liturgical survivals (Introits, Graduals). The general Protestant accent on individual piety tended to encourage more private use of the Psalter, but as the original anchorage in church and cult often lessened, the private use lost its urgency too—a process of secularization which we have not yet learned how to reverse.

At best, we may lament the fact that often the Psalter is virtually the *only* still familiar portion of the Old Testament (and sometimes only Ps. 23 or a few similar snippets). The frequent practice of printing the psalms as an appendix to editions of the New Testament encourages the tacit *de facto* assumption that little else in the Old is really very relevant. Indeed, psalms may validly be viewed as an Old Testament in miniature, or as a distillation of its entire message. But consistently used in isolation, they aid and abet the crime of our age, the docetic divorce of faith and spirituality from history and the totality of Scripture. Because of its sublimity, isagogical questions about the Psalter readily seem like the dissection of a flower, the intrusion of "science" and reason into the realm of the spirit, but precisely for that reason there is no better place to take up arms against the grave dangers of such "great shame and vice" as fideism, aestheticism, and psychologism.

In the Hebrew canon, the Psalter commands pride of place at the head of the *Kethubim* or hagiographical (third) portion of the canon, and, as a result in later Hebrew literature and in the New Testament (Luke 24:44) "Psalms" is sometimes shorthand for all the "Writings."

Nature of Hebrew Poetry

The more topical, Western reordering made the Psalter the first of the "poetic" books. The Masoretes or their predecessors had already recognized the psalms (together with Job and Proverbs—but only these three) as poetry, and hence had furnished them with a somewhat different punctuation-cantillation system than used elsewhere. Since that system could not be reproduced in translation, the Septuagint's reclassification was, no doubt, a happy means of continuing the implicit advice to shift gears because of the different, poetic nature of the literature. However, until relatively modern times it seems to have escaped attention that far more of the Old Testament is couched in poetic idiom than either of these ancient traditions recognized (especially nearly all of the prophets, and thus—as bears constant emphasis—some 50 percent of the entire Old Testament, and perhaps some 80 percent of those portions in most frequent theological and liturgical use). The typographical distinction between poetry and prose must be reckoned as one of the major pluses in most modern translations, whatever other merits or demerits they may have.

Not all aspects of Hebrew poetry are understood or agreed upon yet, by any means, and this is not the place for any full treatment of the subject. Most details apply to all Biblical poetry, but a discussion is especially apropos in the case of the Psalter, because of the intrinsic "beauty of holiness" (e.g., Ps. 29:2; 96:9), that is, the virtual inseparability of aesthetics from worship. There is, of course, such a thing as "aestheticism," a secular worship of beauty for its own sake, but our major battles are surely on the opposite front.

Fortunately, the one feature which is agreed upon (it is also common in other ancient Near Eastern literature) is also the only one which is really accessible to the reader who is limited to translations, namely "parallelism (of members)." It is a feature which is quite obvious, once pointed out, but since it is not characteristic of Western poetry, it *must* be pointed out! Rhyme is, as such, almost totally absent, but the lavish use of assonance and alliteration (repetition of vowels and consonants, respectively) sometimes has a similar effect.

Basically, "parallelism" is of only two types, synonymous and antithetic. In the first type, the second (or third) "member" of the line (also sometimes called a colon or a stich) repeats essentially the same thought in different words (cf. Ps. 1:5), whereas "antithetical" parallelism states the opposite or reverse (cf. Ps. 1:6). The exegetical significance of this feature, especially when there are uncertainties or difficulties, should be obvious, but needs to be emphasized. For the same reason, wherever a psalm exhibits one or the other of these two types of parallelism, its antiphonal recitation in public worship should be by *half*-verse, according to the sense, not whole verse by whole verse.

Many manuals, in addition, speak of a third type of parallelism, often styled "synthetic," "formal" or "constructive," but since the parallels are strictly in form rather than thought (cf. Ps. 2:6), it is debatable whether it should still be regarded as "parallelism." Its problematic nature is further indicated by the many subdivisions which are often suggested. Perhaps only one need detain us, what is sometimes called a "stairlike" structure, a repetition of a part of a line with varying additions (e.g., Ps. 92:9, exhibiting an *abc-abd-efg* pattern, which was also familiar at Ugarit).

In addition to parallelism, most (not all) scholars agree that Hebrew poetry was metrical or rhythmical, but no consensus obtains about details. Early scholars often worked with the analogy of the fairly rigid rules of classical Greek and Latin poetry ("quantitative"), but that is today almost unanimously regarded as beside the point. A "caesura" or divide between the two (or three) members is usually evident, but it is not clear how the beats on either side should be counted (if at all). A common solution is to count only the accented or stressed syllables, yielding a sort of "free chant" or "sprung rhythm." The most common scheme (as also at Ugarit) appears to be a 3:3 bicolon or distich (a two-membered line with three beats or stresses apiece), although tricola (tristichs) and even quatrains appear, and sometimes with two or (less frequently) four beats per member. (Assuming the basic correctness of this approach, attention should be called to the "Grail Psalter," the metrical translation of Fr. Joseph Gelineau, which strives to reproduce in English the cadence of the original—also furnished with helpful captions indicating the traditional Christian understanding of the psalms.)

The entire question is complicated by text-critical issues. Especially if and when the ancient patterns fell into desuetude, it is entirely plausible that copyists easily made mistakes or altered in accordance with new idioms, but great caution is imperative. As indicated by the frequent *"mcs" (metri causa* = for the sake of meter) emendations suggested in the Kittel text, early critics were often quite subjective and arbitrary in reconstructing poetic lines according to whim. Greater reserve is common today, but the underlying problems are still with us. Only the specialist is directly involved at this point, but it remains a classical example of the ultimate indivorceability of form and content.

Third, in addition to parallelism and meter, it seems undeniable that Hebrew poetry also had some sense of stanza or strophic structure. Since, unlike classical patterns again, it appears to have operated quite flexibly, its presence is often easily transferable to translations. Besides arrangements according to topic, we may see evidence of it in the use of certain refrains (e.g., "The LORD of hosts is with us . . ." of Ps. 46, where it probably also originally occurred after v. 3, at the end of the first strophe). The enigmatic "Selah" (see below) may have been preceded by refrains (cf. Ps. 46 again), and thus may be further evidence of "strophes." At times acrostic (alphabetic) structures (e.g., Ps. 119) also give us a sort of stanza arrangement.

Pronunciation and Numbering

Certain other "bookkeeping" matters also require our initial attention. This writer has long been accustomed to beginning psalms lectures with an attempt to correct one of the most egregious mispronunciations frequently associated with matters Biblical: the "l" in "psalm" is *silent*—as in virtually all other similarly spelled English words, palm balm, calm, etc.). In "psalter," however, the liquid sound is again heard.

There is also the pesky problem of the varying numbering systems, both of some of the psalms themselves as well as of verses within them. (We, of course, employ here the system common in English, Protestant Bibles.) In this case, not only the Hebraist is involved (as he is also with many similar variations elsewhere in the Bible), but the variations reach even into translations into modern languages. Differences in versification arise from different attitudes toward the superscriptions: in Hebrew, German, and other Bibles they are usually (unless very short) counted as verse 1 (if long, occasionally even as two verses), whereas in English they are not counted at all. Different numbers for the psalms themselves arise from different combinations, going back to the Septuagint, but via the Vulgate still often current in Catholic Bibles and derivative literature. Since Ps. 9 and 10 are combined, while 147 is divided into two, the result is that throughout most of the Psalter the Catholic number is one lower than that familiar to most Protestants (e.g., our Ps. 23 is Ps. 22). (LXX also combines our Pss. 114 and 115, but then promptly divides 116 into two, so that further displacement in numbering is only temporary.)

Psalms Outside the Psalter

Both numbering systems total 150, which for unknown reasons (humanly speaking) apparently became fixed very early as the canonical maximum. LXX, however, preserves a "Ps. 151," superscribed, "A genuine, though supernumerary, Psalm of David, composed when he engaged Goliath in single combat." Two more psalms are appended in many Nestorian Syriac manuscripts, and Hebrew originals of all three, plus three additional psalms (six in all) are attested at Qumran (not to be confused with the community's own compositions, the "*Hodayot*"). Whether we have here psalms which were really "deuterocanonical" in some circles, or simply the attraction of other liturgical favorites to a closed canonical collection, is a matter of considerable debate. Qumran also attests to a different sequence of psalms in some cases. Especially since the synagogue lectionary had 153 Torah readings, strenuous attempts have been made to discern some cycle of liturgical accompaniments by the 150 psalms but with no sure results.

In any case, we must be aware that the rest of the canonical Scriptures itself preserves many psalms which, humanly speaking, might just as easily have been included in the Psalter (although in some cases it is debatable whether they are really "psalms" nor not). Often called "psalms" are Hannah's prayer (1 Sam. 2:1-10), Hezekiah's thanksgiving (Is. 38:10-20), Jonah's prayer in the fish (2:3-10), and the "Psalm of Habakkuk" (chap. 3). Ps. 18 is reproduced almost precisely in 2 Sam. 22, and in Chronicles we find many psalms (or parts of them, sometimes in different combinations) quoted in connection with historical events. But there is little reason why a number of other pieces should not be so classified as well: e.g., the "Song of the Sea" in Ex. 15, the "Song of Moses" (Deut. 32), etc.

Special attention must be called to two genuine psalms at the beginning of the New Testament, Mary's Magnificat (Luke 1:46-55) and Zechariah's Benedictus (Luke 1:68-79). The former, of course, is in many ways only a recension of Hannah's prayer (cf. above), and neither piece contains anything explicitly or overtly "New Testamentish" about it. The fact that both songs are, nevertheless, widely used in Christian worship forms a sort of paradigm, not only of the ease with which the psalms are, in fact, likewise employed, but also of the hermeneutical principles that must ultimately be spelled out if Christian use of the psalms is to be distinguished from that of the synagogue or of "religion in general."

Some of the difficulty in determining whether religious poetry is psalmic or not is betrayed in the varying titles of the canonical collection. The Hebrew *tehillim*, "praises" (the artificial masculine plural apparently indicates a special, canonical collection of praises) applies technically to the many laments and other non-laudatory types only in a very broad sense. The conclusion of Book II (Ps. 72:20; cf. below) indicates that "prayers" may have been used at some earlier stage, but that too is not immediately applicable to all the specimens included. Hence, possibly the Greek tradition, from which our own usage is derived, made the wisest choice: *psalmoi* (Luke 20:42; Acts 1:20) technically derived from only one of the various superscriptions (*mizmor;* cf. below), but since it means literally "song/hymn," especially one sung to the accompaniment of a *psalterion* or stringed instrument, it has very broad applicability. *Psalterion* (psalter), which appears at the head of some Greek manuscripts, refers to the stringed instrument accompanying *psalmoi* or songs, but in practice it came to mean any "collection of songs" and so virtually merged with the other term.

The principles of selection are never specified, but (humanly speaking) we probably do not go too far astray if we think analogously to the production of our best hymnbooks today. Among the mensurable factors would be: applicability to "all sorts and conditions of men," suitability for public worship, aesthetic and poetic distinction, theological acceptability, etc. As far as we know, the selection did not take place "once upon a time," but, like the canonical process in general, was a product of the Spirit's guidance over a considerable period (this to be distinguished, of course, from the inspiration of the songs to begin with).

Development

It is evident, in any event, that our Psalter is a collection of earlier collections. These coincide in part with the division of the Psalter into five "books," apparently at the very end of its literary history, and also certainly in artificial imitation of the five books of Moses. Possibly there was also by this time a liturgical assocation of thirty psalms with each of the books in the Pentateuch (cf. above on the canonical total of 150); at any rate, liturgical motives of some sort are plainly evidenced by the fact that each of the five books ends with a doxology (cf. Christian liturgical usage). Some think that Book I took shape first, and so on, but the evidence for a chronological order, corresponding to the numbers of the books, is, at best, ambiguous (see below). Otherwise, however, these divisions have no clear historical or exegetical value.

Book I = Pss. 1—41, with 41:13 as its doxology. Book II = Pss. 42—72, ending in 72:18-19 with its doxology, but followed in 72:20 with: "The prayers of David, the son of Jesse, are ended," apparently the conclusion of a preliminary collection. Book III is briefer, Pss. 73—89, with 89:52 again being doxological. Book IV = Pss. 90—106, with concluding doxology in 106:48. Book V comprises the rest of the Psalter, Pss. 107—150; in this case, the entire final psalm serves as doxology, apparently not only for the last book, but for the entire Psalter as well (doxology of the entire creation). Except possibly for Ps. 150, it is entirely possible that the doxologies were added only at this final stage of the Psalter's history; if so, the charism of special inspiration must likewise be extended, but there is no reason why it cannot or should not be.

Of these five "books," only Book I appears to coincide closely with a preliminary collection. With the exception of Pss. 1—2 (cf. below), 10, and 33, all have the superscription "A Psalm of David" (cf. below). For that reason, it is sometimes referred to as the "Davidic Psalter." Regardless of isagogical conclusions otherwise, it is often also presumed to be the earliest collection (although equally early individual psalms plainly appear elsewhere). Otherwise, the contents are quite miscellaneous, and there is no evident special principle of collection and arrangement. The absence of a "Davidic" superscription to Ps. 2 is surprising, especially considering its contents. There is evidence in the Talmud and New Testament (the Western text of Acts 13:33), however, that it was originally Ps. 1. If so, its superscription may have dropped off when Ps. 1 began to precede it (perhaps specifically as an introduction to the entire Psalter; cf. below), especially if initially the two psalms were linked as one (as may be indicated by the macarisms, "Blessed . . . ," which would serve as an "inclusion" for the united composition).

Book I has another significant characteristic, especially in comparison with Book II (and most of Book III as well, which may well indicate that these latter two were together a second preliminary collection; see below). Book I generally prefers the divine name "Yahweh," whereas in Pss. 42—83 the preference is for "Elohim." In fact, the proportions are almost exactly the same in both cases, the preferred name exceeding the other by a ratio of 85—15 percent (the preferred name nearly always appearing in the first colon or stich of the line). On its face, this could scarcely be accidental, and its deliberateness is surely clinched by the doublets, Ps. 14 = 53 and 40:13-17 = 70, with only trivial variations except for the different names for God.

As a result, Book 1 is often referred to also as the "Yahwistic Psalter" and Books II—III as the "Elohistic Psalter." Critics naturally have a hard time not relating this phenomenon to the alleged "J" and "E" sources of the Pentateuch, and hence sometimes theorize that these two collections in the Psalter also took shape in the South and the North, where "Yahweh" and "Elohim," respectively, were supposedly preferred (cf. on the Pentateuch). Unfortunately, there is not a shred of objective evidence supporting that supposed preference. Other scholars think that the "substitution" of Elohim in Pss. 42—83 reflects the aversion of late postexilic piety to utter the Tetragrammaton. This hypothesis is at least possible, but there is no evidence that it was the determinative factor here. Certainly, Books II—III do not lack for archaic psalms. All we can say with certainty is that different traditional poetic preferences for the divine name are reflected in the two collections, but that hard evidence is lacking for the reasons (if, indeed, any others are necessary).

There is ample evidence, however, that at least three different earlier cultic collections lie behind our present "Elohistic Psalter" (Books II—III). Pss. 50 and 73—83 are "Asaph psalms," probably a reference to an ancient and senior guild of temple singers and cymbalists. (Cf. the considerable information on Asaph in Chronicles: 1 Chron. 15:17; 16:4-5; 2 Chron. 29:30 specifically describes him as a "seer" and author of psalms alongside David.) Similarly, we have "Korah psalms" in 42—49, and again in 84—85 and 87—88 as increments at the end of Book III (cf. 1 Chron. 6:22). Third, we again have "Davidic" psalms in 51—65 and 68—70; there is no telling how or why they were separated from those in Book I. Ps. 72 is a lone "Psalm of Solomon" (cf. 127), but it concludes with a conclusion noting the end of "the prayers of David" (the latter, as we saw, possibly added when the schematism of the five books was imposed). One must also note that Pss. 84—89 are again "Yahwistic," suggesting that they may have been added after the major Yahwistic and Elohistic collections had been combined. All of this cumulates to indicate how complex the process of formation of this part of the Psalter was, a process which we are able to recover only very tenuously.

Books IV and V (Pss. 90—150) betray little evidence of the circumstances of their collection. It seems to be generally agreed that most of their contents are somewhat later than in the first three books; at least in this respect there appears to be truth in the supposition that the order of the five books corresponds to the chronological order of their collection (cf. above). Some very early psalms are, however, imbedded in also these two books, e.g., Ps. 90, attributed to Moses (possibly, then, the earliest in the entire Psalter), and 122; 124; 131; 133; 138—145, which again are "Davidic."

Liturgical associations are also much more obvious in these final two books. As we shall note below, some critical theories propose very precise cultic associations for almost the entire Psalter, but, on the whole, those hypotheses would probably apply more readily to Books I—III. Since the cultic associations of Books IV—V are more with what is known of later Judaism, the critical instinct is to date both these psalms and their liturgical associations to a later period—at least that of the second temple. However, there appears to be no good reason why these traditions could not also have been current in the first temple.

Pss. 120—134 have the superscription, "A Song of Ascents / Degrees." Mishnaic tradition has it that the Levites of the second temple sang them one per step, on the climb up to the court of men in the temple. Sometimes these are also considered "pilgrim songs," the "ascents" allegedly referring to stages in the pilgrimage up to Mt. Zion at especially the three great pilgrimage festivals. Only Ps. 122, however, gives clear internal indication of any such original association.

The "Hallelujah Psalms" (104—106; 111—113; 115—117; 135; and 146—150, so called, of course, because of the prominence of that refrain, "Praise Yahweh," are sometimes thought to have originally been a separate collection. Jewish liturgical tradition also knows a number of psalms in Book V as "Hallel psalms" ("song of praise"), but the antiquity of the usage is indeterminate. The ordinary Hallel, Pss. 113—118, is often also known as the "Egyptian Hallel" because of its close association with Passover, although it is also used at the other two major festivals and at Hanukkah. At Passover, Pss. 113—114 are traditionally sung before the meal (the latter a sort of poetic meditation on the Exodus), and Pss. 115—118 after it; the latter may well constitute the "hymn" sung by our Lord after the Last Supper and before Gethsemane (Matt. 26:30; Mark 14:26). At least in later times Pss. 119—136 (the latter with the refrain, "for His *chesedh* endures forever") were often known as the "Great Hallel" (in distinction from the ordinary one).

Also in the latter two books we note doublets or repetitions of psalms or parts of them which appeared in the earlier books: 108:1-5 = 57:7-11 and 108:6-13 = 60:5-12. In this connection, we should also note the many partial parallels and different combinations of parts of psalms, which occur throughout Chronicles. (E.g., at 1 Chron. 16:8 ff. we have a song of praise at David's bringing of the ark to Jerusalem, composed of 105:1-15; 96:1-13; and 106:47-48.) Likewise in 2 Chron. 6—7 Solomon includes Ps. 132 in his prayer, and the people respond with the refrain from 136. Like the different combinations in the Septuagint, this probably witnesses to the great fluidity, already in very early times, of many psalmic components, at least in actual liturgical usage.

The Superscriptions

Some of the superscriptions have already been mentioned, and some space must be devoted to the question in general, surely one of the knottiest in the entire study of the psalter. The Middle Ages and even the Reformation attached all sorts of mystical significance to the superscriptions, e.g., the "Sheminith" (eighth?) of Ps. 6, and the "Hind of Dawn" of Ps. 22. At the other extreme, much modern scholarship has tended to discount their antiquity or value (or both) almost entirely. A consistent—if extreme—instance of such cutting of the "Gordian knot" is offered by the *New English Bible,* which does not even deign to include them in its translation. Most versions continue simply to transliterate most of them, apparently as safe a procedure as any because translations and interpretations of them in modern times continue to vary about as much as in antiquity. Extreme skepticism is unwarranted, however, not only because we find comparable elements in Sumerian, Akkadian, and Ugaritic compositions, but also because of the weight the New Testament places on some of them (e.g., Mark 12:35 ff; Acts 2:29 ff.). In fact, the only justification for reserve is text-critical. Leupold, however, greatly overstates the case in asserting that "the fact that they do not belong to the text every student of Hebrew has long known" (he continues to argue that they represent a generally reliable tradition nonetheless). The fact is that the ancient versions (especially Septuagint and Peshitta) do frequently vary significantly in this respect from the Hebrew textual tradition. MT contains some 34 "orphans" (as those lacking superscriptions are sometimes known), while LXX has only two and the Peshitta differs from both. The variation is not enough that one has cause to be *a priori* suspicious of the antiquity and reliability of all the superscriptions, but enough so that it is apparent that the tradition varied widely, apparently being open to expansion, so that in given cases one may indeed query whether it really was part of the original, inspired text. (Cf. Archer's admission, p. 441, that "we cannot maintain the inerrancy of the Hebrew psalm titles as such.")

There are many types of superscriptions, of course. Some simply describe the type of composition. In some cases the description appears to be quite nontechnical, as with *shir* (song), *mizmor* ("psalm," at least originally implying stringed accompaniment; cf. above), *tehillah* (praise) and *tephillah* (prayer). Perhaps of the same type, but more technical (and certainly more obscure) are *maskil* (presumably related to the wisdom root meaning "teach; be prudent/successful"; translated "psalm" in 47:7), *miktam* (Pss. 16; 56—60) and *shiggaion* (Ps. 7; Hab. 3; cf. Akkadian *shegu*—"lamentation").

Others appear to be the names of melodies (probably better "modes") according to which the psalms were to be chanted. The "Sheminith" (apparently: "eighth") of Ps. 6 would appear to belong here, as also "Lilies" (sometimes in various combinations; Pss. 45, 60, 69, 80); "The Dove on Far-off Terebinths" (Ps. 56); and especially "The Hind of Dawn" of Ps. 22; since "Dawn" (*Shachar* = Aurora) is a well-known deity at Ugarit, it is possible that we have evidence here of the Canaanite roots of temple music. If these explanations are at all correct, they are comparable to the names of tunes appearing in most modern hymnals, which are usually just as enigmatic to the uninitiated (e.g., "Toplady" and "Redhead #77," two common settings of "Rock of Ages").

Some of the superscriptions are almost certainly musical directions, roughly comparable to our "allegro," "forte," etc. This would seem to be the import of *"neginoth"* in Pss. 4; 6; 54; 55; 61; 67; 76, apparently specifying accompaniment with "stringed instruments." And two of the most common of the superscriptions are apparently of this type. Fifty-five times (mostly in the first three books) we meet *lammenatseach,* apparently a Piel participle. The Chronicler applies the term to various overseers or superintendents of temple construction, but also to the musical director or "choirmaster," and hence its nearly universal rendition in English. Since it frequently stands by itself in superscriptions, however, without any indication of specific directions "to the choir-master," many scholars postulate the existence of an older major Psalter known as the "Director's Collection" or the like, parallel to the Asaphic, Korahite, and Davidic collections. Rather curiously, the Septuagint and Targum relate the word to one of the Biblical expressions for "duration, eternity" and translate it *eis to telos.* Whether they understood that in some eschatological sense, or simply took it to mean something like "full rendering" is not clear. Some Akkadian and Egyptian hymns end with a notation, "to the end," but whether that influenced later tradition, and, if so, whether it provides any clue to the original meaning of the Hebrew phrase is also unknown.

"Selah" is surely the most (in)famous of the superscriptional material in the Psalter. It occurs 71 times in 39 psalms, mostly in books I—III, plus three occurrences in Hab. 3. While its total omission (as in *NEB*) is scarcely justifiable, it is probably advisable to pass over it in public recitation of the psalms, as suggested by RSV's italics. Where it is recited, as frequently in some Sunday schools, it appears to be commonly misconstrued as a quasi-synonym of "Hallelujah!" But that supposition is not demonstrably more arbitrary than the scores of the other suggestions, both ancient and modern. In grammatical form, the best explanation appears to be an imperative of the verb to "lift up, exalt." Thus the word is commonly taken to signal something like an increase in the volume of either the choir or of the musical accompaniment. Presumably, the Septuagint's *diapsalma* is related to this understanding; it implies an interlude or refrain of some sort, and since "selah" seems generally to occur at the close of a strophe (cf. above), probably a majority of also modern scholarship is inclined to concur. However, another widely attested ancient explanation also has its modern defenders, namely some association of the word with the idea of eternity (thus Jerome's *semper* and Kraus' *per omnia saecula saeculorum*).

In addition to the number of superscriptions apparently having musical reference, a number of others plainly specify the "proper" liturgical occasion for their use in temple worship. (Mowinckel and other cultically oriented scholars [see below] have attempted liturgical ex-planations for virtually *all* superscriptions.) Since most of these superscriptions have reference to the *"tamid,"* that is, to the psalms accompanying the daily morning and evening sacrifices in the temple, most critics are especially certain that this type must be of late second temple origination. That, of course, follows from the critical dogmas of discontinuity between first and second temple and of the lateness of P, but if one ascribes such matters to the Mosaic revelation, no good reason remains to question their high antiquity—in some cases conceivably even rooting in tabernacle services antedating David. Ps. 92 is prescribed for the Sabbath; similar rubrics for other days of the week are found only in the versions, but that does not prove their lateness (Ps. 24 for Sunday, 93 for Wednesday, and 81 for Thursday). Ps. 30 is characterized as "a song at the dedication of the temple," but, tantalizingly, we are not told *which* temple. Perhaps in this classification also belongs the *hazkir* of Pss. 38 and 70, possibly to be related to the *'azkarah* (the portion of the grain offering which was burned), but the root is also used in broader senses of "praise, commemorate, call upon."

Superscriptions, Date, and Authorship of the Psalms

However, far and away, the most important of the psalmic superscriptions are those which apparently indicate authorship, and of these, of course, those mentioning David are both the most frequent and the most significant. Often, of course (fourteen times, to be exact), additional notations specify the occasion on which David penned the psalm. Almost needless to say, critical scholarship regards these, especially the latter, as historically worthless, and representing only late haggadic or midrashic fancy. We have already mentioned the textual variation which justifies some reserve about whether all of these superscriptions are really part of the inspired text, but nowhere are objective grounds to be found for dismissing them out of hand, and it seems very difficult to envision circumstances under which anyone could (or would wish to) add such fictional embellishments to psalmody which would already have been universally recognized as canonical.

Besides the discrepancies between MT and LXX, a major argument against the validity of the superscriptional specifications of historical occasion has always been their alleged lack of correspondence with the circumstances presupposed in the psalms themselves. The cultic approach to the psalms, as we shall note below, has gone even further and denied the validity of such biographical or historical interest altogether. Some who disapprove of the cultic approach have argued that the "Davidic" superscriptions were added at a late date specifically to deculticize and "historicize" the psalms, thus facilitating the later focus on the author's inner life. It appears, however, that criticism here posits false alternatives.

Literal Davidic composition on the occasions indicated precludes neither
an individual's adaptation and employment of earlier, traditional forms,
nor the use of those poems afterwards in more general worship
circumstances, and no longer necessarily related directly to the occasion for
composition. On both counts one can readily venture parallels with
modern hymns. Often we offer both praise and thanksgiving for specific
occasions in words that are about as traditional and inspecific as possible
(whether the piece is technically new or not), and our ordinary use of hymns
proceeds quite independently of circumstances of composition. (If the
latter are known at all, we are generally quite content to leave the matter to
the hymnologists and their handbooks.)

Herewith, however, the entire question of the date of the psalms, and
specifically the likelihood of any literally Davidic compositions, is
broached. The two questions are not entirely identical, of course, but do
run parallel to a great extent. Let us first consider the *le-dawid*
superscription itself. Its traditional translations "of David" (already in
LXX, which has 15 more of them than MT) reflects the nearly unanimous
supposition that it implied authorship, of course. The *le* was traditionally
classified as a *"lamedh* of authorship"; in Hab. 3:1 it almost certainly has
that signification, and we are now happy to have such a usage attested
outside the Bible. But the extra-Biblical evidence is ambiguous: there are
also times, for example in the Ugaritic epics, where *le-X* must refer to the
subject, not the author of the composition (e.g., *le-Baal, le-Keret,* etc.).
Furthermore, even minimal knowledge of Hebrew will tell one that *le* is
capable of a tremendous variety of meanings. The Ugaritic usage may
also suggest ascription, yielding a translation something like "dedicated to
X." Another popular alternative understands the entire phrase as
meaning something like "David*ic*," that is, following his example or
tradition, and in this way many scholars think of a "Davidic Psalter" as
one of the preliminary collections (alongside the Choirmaster's, Asaphic,
Korahite ones) underlying the canonical collection. Finally, we may note
that it once was popular to argue on the basis of Hurrian usage in the
Mari tablets that *dawidum* was originally a common noun meaning no
more than "ruler" or "prince," for example, and that in the superscription
it originally meant no more than "belonging to the royal ritual," "under
crown sponsorship," or the like (cf. "Caesar"). Thus Mowinckel (see
below) could argue that the superscription meant only "for the use of the
david [the monarch]" who happened to occupy the throne at the time. But,
at best, a generous amount of conjecture is involved here, as seems to be
increasingly recognized. (Others have interpreted "Dawid" as a throne
name, replacing the original name, Elhanan, at accession; (see at 2 Sam.
21:18 ff.)

How can we decide? As usual, mere philology will not give us a definitive answer. Perhaps the safest rule of thumb would be to invoke the ancient maxim, *In dubito, pro traditio.* As far as the conservative is concerned, we have sufficient independent attestation of David's musical proclivities and authorship of specific psalms from both the New Testament and elsewhere in the Old Testament, that the superscriptions themselves might theoretically be regarded as dispensable for establishing Davidic authorship of at least some psalms. And even if on textual grounds (cf. above) we do not follow all the superscriptions slavishly, they still contain sufficient testimony to confirm the case further. This does not preclude the possibility that in some instances the *le* does not (also?) have one or the other of the alternative meanings mentioned above, but we lack the wherewithal to be certain. What is ruled out of court is the common critical supposition that the entire tradition of Davidic authorship is a late, fanciful deduction from traditions such as 1 Sam. 16; 2 Sam. 1 and 3; Amos 6:5; e.g., describing David as a skillful singer, not to speak of "midrashes" such as 1 Chron. 22—29 which describe David's reorganization of temple worship, especially its choral aspects. (Very similar considerations would apply to the other proper names in the superscriptions: Korah, Asaph, Solomon, Moses, for instance—and perhaps also additional ones in the LXX; cf. 2 Chron. 29:30 which seems to evidence "Davidic" and "Asaphic" collections of psalmody in the time of Hezekiah.)

Besides general evolutionistic considerations, the other critical arguments against Davidic authorship of some of the psalms apparently attributed to him are quite easily checkmated. A negative consideration advanced is the apparent frequent reference to the "temple" as already built (e.g., Pss. 5; 27; 68; 69), but a brief concordance study will soon establish that not only "temple," but synonyms like "house of the LORD" or "tent" were often used very flexibly and interchangeably (cf. also 1 Sam. 1:9, where the tabernacle at Shiloh is referred to as a *hekal* or "temple"). Second, it is also frequently objected that Davidic psalms sometimes (e.g., 20; 21; 72; 110) refer to the king in the second person, but ample extra-Biblical as well as Biblical parallels (especially Moses in the Pentateuch) to this usage emasculate the objection, all the more so if, as seems likely, David spoke not only of his person, but also of his (Messianic) office.

While critics still generally discount Davidic authorship of specific psalms, they are rarely any longer so doctrinaire about denying the possibility of much earlier (at least preexilic and monarchical) psalmic composition, in general. Change in critical climate accounts for some of the shift, but the ultimate reasons are probably largely archaeological.

Linguistic arguments for post-Davidic origin from alleged Aramaisms in certain psalms simply no longer hold water in the light of Ugaritic evidence. From both ends of the time-line has come evidence, not only enhancing the likelihood of earlier date, but virtually rendering impossible so late a date as classical criticism originally championed. "Hymnbook of the *second* temple" had once been the great critical slogan. Pfeiffer called it the "great manifesto of the Pious" in the postexilic era (largely presumed to be a flowering of the prophets' pioneering of individual and "spiritual" religion). Duhm was by no means atypical in desiring to date the majority of the psalms in the Maccabean period. Critical reaction to such attitudes were already rampant before the Qumran discoveries, but the vast distance between the canonical psalms and the *Hodayot,* or psalms of praise composed on the shores of the Dead Sea in the century or two before Christ, dropped the previous dogma with a single shot, as it were. Today one could scarcely find a single scholar who would defend such positions.

Ugarit was the major, but not the sole, source of evidence from the other direction. "Psalms" of one sort or the other we now have from almost all over the ancient Fertile Crescent. Egypt produced some as early as the pyramid age (Old Kingdom), and the rough parallels between Ps. 104 and Akhenaton's hymn to the sun disk are especially often noted. Moses' schooling in this culture makes plausible the Biblical ascription to him of not only Ps. 90, but also the extra-Psalter pieces of Ex. 15 and Deut. 32—33 (in all cases we probably have to concede some linguistic updating, however). Mesopotamia offers psalms already in Sumerian times, and the repertory grows extensive as we come down in time. The many laments as well as praises to Marduk, chief god of Babylon, are especially noteworthy. As usual in such matters, the parallelism should not be overstated, but the point here is of a cultural milieu in which psalmic composition was commonplace millennia before David.

Canaan has so far yielded very few "psalms" as such, but it is both geographically and chronologically so much closer that its evidence is much more weighty. From Amarna we have only a few possible psalm-fragments, and the Ugaritic literature is largely epic rather than psalmic in nature, but the parallels in vocabulary, phraseology and prosody are little short of phenomenal, and we are still a long way from digesting them fully. Some psalms so teem with archaisms that there would be little difficulty in defending a *pre-*Davidic date, nor is there anything unlikely about David's availing himself of structures and even phrases already at hand. Theological "uniqueness," whether empirically evident or not, by no means implies absolute external uniqueness!

Among the psalms which are especially archaic in form are 18 (= 2

Sam. 22) and 68, but many others are subject to illumination on the basis of Ugaritic studies. The retention of archaisms by the ancient scribes, even when they were no longer understood, is impressive testimony to the almost frantic care with which the ancient texts were preserved and handed down. In other cases, the texts appear to have been modernized linguistically in the course of transmission before being fixed (cf. the argument that the "Davidic" psalms exhibit a great variety of styles and linguistic periods). Even when linguistic parallels are few, Ugarit often illuminates the meaning of words or concepts (as an example, the "gods" or angels of the heavenly council in Ps. 82, who have been unfaithful in their charges over earthly kingdoms; cf. John 10:31 ff.). Ps. 29 is often cited as an example of a psalm that may have, humanly speaking, undergone little revision in Israelitization other than the substitution of "Yahweh" for "Baal"; there is no way to test such a supposition one way or the other, but there is nothing impossible (also theologically) or even improbable about it, and such a procedure would certainly have had massive apologetic and polemical force: Yahweh, not Baal-Hadad, is the only true "storm God," and it is Him alone whom men and angels are to glorify.

For detailed illustration of such archaeological-philological illumination we must, of course, defer to the commentaries. Comparison will, however, soon establish considerable variation among the commentators in assessment and employment of the new material. Some scholars are simply too exclusively oriented toward philosophy, theology, or various anthropological-cultic reconstructions even to be very knowledgeable in this rather specialized field. In America the "Albright school" has generally taken the lead in investigating and urging the importance of these discoveries—and not only in the psalms.

Here too, however, there are excesses, evident especially in the controversial work of Dahood in the *Anchor Bible* commentary, and one even hears coinages such as "Dahoodianism." If Dahood's contributions had appeared in a more technical series, one might easily understand many of them as "trial balloons," as a part of the vital hypothesis-verification process of any true scholarship. However, the publication of his work in a relatively popular series suggests to the reader that his proposals are commonly accepted in the scholarly world, when that is, in fact, anything but the case. Hence, the danger is that "the baby will be thrown out with the bath water," and the valid aspects of Dahood's work dismissed out of hand as well as the excrescences. Dahood's problem is that he is a maximalist: he applies his various possibilities whenever theoretically possible, employing very little self-criticism, and thus leaving it to others to sift and choose.

Dahood's procedures are virtually impossible to discuss without a good knowledge of the Hebrew language, and, in any case, cannot be reproduced here. They involve possibilities such as: forgotten meanings of some archaic Hebrew vocabulary more in line with the Ugaritic lexicon; different meanings of prepositions such as *l, b, min,* etc; possibilities of incorrect word divisions by copyists; various enclitic particles; different understandings of the Hebrew verbal system, including archaic forms, and the like.

The conscientious exegete should at least acquaint himself with the possibilities Dahood raises, all the more so since similar investigations are likely to accelerate throughout the Old Testament, especially its poetic portions. For the moment, he will often have to defer to the specialist, and probably wait until much more of a consensus emerges. Biblical poetry, especially the Psalter, is far more than mere misunderstood vestiges of Ugaritic literature (an impression Dahood might easily leave), but if and when Dahood offers possibilities for better comprehension of passages which have scarcely been comprehended at all heretofore, we certainly should not "pass by on the other side." Albright has gone on record as asserting that even if only ten percent of Dahood's suggestions ultimately pass muster, he will have made a greater contribution to psalms study than any other modern scholar.

Text

Some of Dahood's suggestions could be classified as text-critical, but, on the whole, his work must be distinguished from text-criticism in the conventional sense. In the latter respect, the same principles apply to the Psalter as to the rest of the Old Testament, of course. As a glance at the critical apparatus in the Kittel Hebrew Bible will demonstrate, however, the textual condition of individual psalms varies widely all the way from virtually perfect to very obscure (corrupt?). Nor are the reasons for the variations any clearer than in the case of similar variations elsewhere in the Old Testament; sometimes apparent textual corruptions can be attributed to a linguistically more archaic original, which later copyists would more readily misunderstand, but many other unknown variables were obviously involved as well.

Perhaps the only unique thing worth mentioning in the textual history of the Psalter is the *three* separate Latin translations made by St. Jerome (attesting, of course, to the importance and popularity of the psalms). At the bidding of one of the popes, Jerome first attempted only a revision of an older Latin translation—the so-called "Roman Psalter," because it has still been used in modern times at St. Peter's in Rome (partly, no doubt, out of conservative resistance to any more thorough revision or retranslation). Later Jerome undertook a more thorough revision, based on the Hexapla; this is the so-called "Gallican Psalter" (because first adopted by Gregory of Tours), and of major importance because it is the translation preserved in most editions of the Vulgate, and hence the basis of most Roman Catholic usage until Vatican II. These first two efforts of Jerome were based primarily on the Greek—hence, important as witnesses to the history of the Greek text, but twice removed from the Hebrew original. That defect Jerome corrected by his third and most thoroughgoing revision, based on the *"hebraica veritas"* itself, and completed during his sojourn at Bethlehem with the assistance of rabbinical scholars. To text-critical scholars this is, of course, the most important of Jerome's three versions, but the very familiarity of the masses with older versions of the Psalter prevented it from receiving the same acceptance eventually accorded to his translations from the Hebrew of other Biblical books.

Form Criticism

But we have gotten ahead of our story. Our point of departure had been the extent to which archaeological discoveries had enabled critics to date much of the Psalter in earlier (preexilic) times. In that light, the conservative can only ask what hinders him from going a little further and conceding literal Davidic involvement in their composition and production. Nevertheless, it probably is safe to say that today nearly everyone, liberal or conservative, would be able to agree in at least general terms that the psalms derive from nearly every period of Israel's history, from David (or before) down to the Persian period (fifth century?), when the Psalter must have assumed essentially its final and present form (of course, the date of the completed collection must postdate the latest individual composition).

In the meantime, however, newer developments in especially critical scholarship have attempted a sort of "end run" around the entire question of date, authorship, and historical circumstances of psalms composition. Anyone even superficially acquainted with the course of Biblical criticism will readily surmise that the new factor was "form criticism," and, indeed, perhaps nowhere in all of Biblical studies has it been more influential than in the Psalter. The Psalter was one of the concentrations of Gunkel himself, often known as the "father of form criticism." Even the conservative stands to profit from some aspects of his work, and under no responsible circumstances is it possible to ignore it.

In balance, one may say that form criticism has had more positive results in the case of the Psalter than in many other areas of Biblical scholarship, and that for three reasons: (1) its skepticism about, or even evading of, the question of historicity did not as readily apply to the psalms, which are not "historical" documents in quite the ordinary sense;

(2) its search for small, discrete units behind the later combinations often had atomistic, centrifugal results elsewhere, but in the case of the Psalter the units were generally relatively small to begin with; and (3) its accent on cultic backgrounds was more immediately germane to devotional literature like the psalms than in many other instances.

In a way it was ironic that, in spite of its usual thoroughgoing reaction to tradition, early higher criticsm had agreed in principle with tradition that the psalms were to be approached primarily as expressions of personal and individual piety. Tradition, of course, thought primarily of David, while the critics envisioned poets of a much later era, but essentially the same questions were posed in both cases. These were basically the author's historical situation and his inner, psychological feelings, both often thought to reflect national and political circumstances.

Form criticism, beginning shortly before the turn of the century, vigorously combatted such presuppositions. As elsewhere, the primary concern in psalms research now became the *pre*-literary *Sitz im Leben* (sociological setting) of the piece, presumed to be primarily a matter of group, and often cultic, rather than individual activity. Reduction to writing was commonly considered the *end* of a long process of primarily oral transmission, and often even a sign of decadence and atrophy of the living culture that had originally nourished it. From the standpoint of tradition, one fortunate spin-off of this new accent was a renewed willingness to date the psalms, or at least their roots, in a much earlier period (offset, however, by a different type of "evolutionism" which has died slowly in form-critical circles, namely dogmas to the effect that (a) "shorter" and (b) "purer" (unmixed) types had to be earlier—both of which assumptions have now been contradicted archaeologically many times).

The general openness to earlier provenance of many psalms coincided with the increasing testimony of archaeology (sketched above), itself one of the major stimuli of the entire form-critical endeavor. To a certain extent, the earlier critics could not be faulted for failing to use evidence which was not yet available, but increasingly it became apparent that they had no interest in heeding it wherever it did not coincide with conclusions they had reached on other *a priori* grounds.

Besides archaeology, there was also input from or overlap with various other new movements. New anthropological theories interacted with archaeological discoveries in various ways, and increasing knowledge of neighboring religions developed into a full-blown *religionsgeschichtliche Schule,* sometimes even going overboard into a "pan-Babylonian school" (trying to explain nearly everything Biblical according to Babylonian analogies). And not the least of the new influences (perhaps in some respects foundational to them all) was a revival of romanticism with its aesthetic and "spiritual" (with a small "s") sensitivities.

Gunkel himself still apparently had his feet in the old era sufficiently that, at least initially, he viewed the psalms as late, more "spiritual," individual derivatives of earlier, cultic piety. (The prejudice, shared by many others, was that cultic affairs are somehow intrinsically much less "spiritual" and genuine; often the word "spiritual" is used as a virtual catchword in Protestant scholarship with that kind of overtone.) But as the movement gained momentum, others (esp. Mowinckel; see below) stressed insistently that the psalms were originally cultic pieces from the period of the first temple, and Gunkel too increasingly went along with that viewpoint. It still remains, however, one of the major open and unresolved questions in contemporary psalms research.

At any rate, the older questions of individual authorship and accompanying personal, historical circumstances were now often dismissed as irrelevant—whether David or someone else, it made no difference. Cult, it was argued, is concerned with the "timeless," or at least with what is true for all time, and the psalms were considered to have been written initially with that perspective in view. And "cult" implies public, group, community activity, in which the individual is to submerge himself. Many psalms were assumed to have been written like many of our liturgies, leaving only a blank for the individual's name to be inserted (cf. our baptismal or nuptial rituals). Even if we did know which individual composed the material, the argument went, it would be beside the point. Thus, the "historicism" attending the older approach would be overcome: the modern reader would no longer have to go back and search out what was "relevant" in some ancient worthy's experience, but, apart from antique idioms, the material would speak to "all sorts and conditions of men" in all times.

(The conservative will recognize accents here to which he may readily assent, and which often correspond to his actual use of the Psalter, but he will not approve of eliminating individual devotion from the Psalter's production altogether. We noted above that literal, Davidic authorship and more communal use need not be pitted against one another; cf. again below on the cult. One must also stress the actual cultic context to which the psalms themselves repeatedly allude, namely the sacrificial cult of especially Leviticus, which together with Chronicles, remains indispensable collateral reading to the Psalter.)

A closely related issue has been the debate about the import of the "I" of the psalms. Is it really an individual who speaks (as Gunkel himself preferred), or is it the group speaking in the collective singular (cf. the Christian creeds)? A variant of the latter alternative made the king the original speaker as the "corporate personality," the soul of his people, with "democratization" of the material (that is, making it available to "everyman" for "private" use) only later, after the collapse of the monarchy. Both extremes have been defended in the history of scholarship, and probably something like a consensus obtains today that both extremes are to be avoided. The excessive individualism of especially liberal Protestantism is now widely seen as modern cultural imperialism upon the ancient texts, but at the same time, both Biblical and extra-Biblical evidence from antiquity make plain that private worship services were not uncommon in antiquity either, and that psalms were used also in such settings. One can scarcely help but note the great preponderance of individual over communal psalms of all types, at least in terms of surface expression, but the use of Ps. 30, technically an individual thanksgiving, for the (community's) dedication of the temple probably well illustrates how easily the two categories merged. In fact, if one renounces the evolutionistic assumption that individual worth, piety, and faith surfaced only in later times at the behest of prophetic preaching, one would almost *a priori* have to insist that group and individual piety coexisted throughout the Old Testament, essentially as they do in Christendom today, and that as a result "I" and "we" overlap and interchange with equal ease.

In general, however, Gunkel's approach has found such near-universal acceptance in virtually all camps that we can do no better than consider and evaluate the major *Gattungen* individually. As in form criticism generally, there are logomachies galore, and skirmishes over nomenclature still flourish, most of which we need not take note of here. Only Westermann's reclassification has had much impact, partly because of his concentration on strictly form-critical questions (*The Praise of God in the Psalms*), partly because of his rejection of a cultic point of departure. In essence, Westermann reduces all categories to two, psalms of lamentation *(Bittpsalmen)* and psalms of praise *(Lobpsalmen)*. The latter is really a merger of Gunkel's "hymns" and "thanksgivings," but Westermann himself promptly subdivides them into (a) "declarative" (recalling one definite act of salvation) and (b) "descriptive" (celebrating Yahweh's majesty and power in general) types.

Besides a host of "minor" (less frequent) genres, Gunkel himself originally proposed four major ones: hymns, individual laments, individual thanksgivings, and communal laments. Eventually, as a result of pressure from co-workers, he added a fifth, the "royal" psalms. That issue highlights a problem which haunts Gunkel's whole scheme, namely, the interplay of the formal and the material. As we have noted throughout this book, if "form" criticism had really contented itself with the relatively neutral and objective questions of form and structure, it would have been an entirely different story. "Content," of course, is a thoroughly valid consideration too, and ultimately it cannot be hermetically sealed off from considerations of form, but in critical milieu the former is far more vulnerable to vagary and subjectivity. In the four *Gattungen* he initially recognized, certain formal or structural characteristics were fairly demonstrable, but in the royal and some of the minor types hardly at all. The conservative generally has little difficulty appreciating and appropriating the purely formal analysis, but, all too often, all kinds of reservations must be registered when judgments are not limited to formal grounds.

Hymns

One of the most helpful (and innocuous) classifications made by Gunkel was "hymn." As *Sitz im Leben,* Gunkel postulated joyous occasions when the people assembled at the sanctuary to praise God. As long as the individual is not excluded from the picture, it is impossible to take exception to such a construction, belonging to the very bedrock of the concept of "worship," as it does. Hence, neither is one very surprised, nor does it prove very much, when it is mentioned that externally there is relatively little that is "unique" about this genre: parallels can be found all over the ancient Near East, especially Babylonia, praising the god(s) for goodness and presumed favors (although neither is one surprised to note that very often the flavor is one of flattery in order to make the deity yield to personal desires). Individual laments are a fairly distinguishable type, but "communal laments" (which Gunkel classified as a minor form) merge almost imperceptibly with the hymns, one of the weaknesses of the system.

In form, the hymn tends to have a clear fourfold pattern: (1) an introductory call to praise, usually a plural imperative (often "Hallelujah" = "Praise ye the LORD," or "Praise/bless, my soul . . . ," which may well recur as a refrain); occasionally we meet the cohortative ("Let me/us sing" etc.); (2) the reason for the praise, commonly a *ki*-clause ("for," sometimes simply *ki tob* = for He is good, or expressed in Hebrew by means of the "hymnic participle," usually rendered into English by a relative clause, e.g., 103:3 ff.); (3) the corpus, body or main part of the praise; and sometimes (4) a renewed call to praise, often in the same words as at the beginning.

Most hymns tend to have a very universal flavor, and hence are easily subject to universal*istic* abuse. They often envision all peoples, even all of nature, joining in the praise and celebrating the climax of God's judgment and salvation. The proper understanding is not some "anonymous Christianity," but a very particularistic "antecedent will" of God *available* to all who believe, offered fully, if proleptically, in the cultic "now" (cf. below) and straining toward the final judgment.

Christian worship has little difficulty in appropriating this part of the Psalter, but certain assumptions are made, and if it is to be genuinely Christian worship, these cannot be allowed to become entirely self-evident and unconscious. When he uses them, the Christian assumes not only the unity of Scripture in promise and fulfillment, but the unity of the Godhead as the common subject of both testaments. The "LORD" or Yahweh of the Old Testament is also the "God and Father of our Lord and Savior Jesus Christ," whom the Holy Spirit makes our God in Word and Sacrament. The nature and attributes of this God and His works of creation, redemption, and sanctification are essentially the same, but these have also been more fully revealed in the new covenant. The acts of God for which the psalms praise Him are also part of the history of our salvation, but they are accessible to us only via Christ, and to them we add the climactic acts of God on Good Friday and Easter. In a way, to make such points is to belabor the obvious, but they dare not remain so "obvious" that we tacitly encourage "religion in general" or worship of "Providence." In certain contexts it is also important to distinguish the church's use of the psalms from that of the synagogue (properly understood, in continuity as well as discontinuity).

In a sense, these considerations apply to Christian use of all the psalms, but they do apply, and the necessity for their explicit application is perhaps most immediate in the case of the hymns. Hence, perhaps this is the place to underscore a liturgical usage which summarizes much of what is assumed in Christian use of the Psalter, although it too must be explained if it is to communicate. We refer to the tradition of *always* concluding public recitation of a psalm with the Gloria Patri (after which the antiphon, summarizing the psalm's message, is repeated). The Gloria Patri is a symbolic way of stressing that the psalms (like the rest of the Old Testament) are not Christianized by "reading into" them some alien meaning, by doing violence to their literary and historical integrity, but by "extending" their literal sense, "reading out" of them together with the New Testament their fulfilled and antitypical meaning in Christ and the Holy Spirit. And also worthy of all acceptance is the liturgical custom of bowing one's head in acknowledgment of and devotion to the saving mystery confessed as the Gloria Patri is recited or chanted.

"Hymn" is so comprehensive a word, however, that one is not surprised that Gunkel found it necessary to subdivide this *Gattung*. Most of the subdivisions, however, are determined according to subject matter or content, not form. Many times that signals nothing necessarily objectionable, but much critical arbitrariness has also seized upon this point of entry.

Besides "general" hymns, one major subdivision is "Hymns of Zion," praising the holy city of God's election, the place where His "name" or "glory" is "incarnate." Examples include Pss. 46; 48; 76; and 87. As throughout the Old Testament, Zion is the complement of king/Messiah, and a basic type of the Christian church. Ex-mythological imagery is freely used to express the promise that "the gates of hell shall not prevail against her." The ease with which the church (at least until the modern era) understood herself as heir to these promises is aptly illustrated by Luther's use of Ps. 46 as point of departure for "A Mighty Fortress."

One customarily also speaks of "history" and "nature" hymns. Aspects of these elements are present in nearly all psalms, of course, but are especially prominent in certain ones, justifying a separate classification. The titles are nearly self-explanatory: "nature" hymns (e.g., Pss 19a, 29, 103, 104, 147—150) praise God especially in His capacity as a "nature God," that is, Creator and Preserver of "nature." The implicit apologetic against modern evolutionism is essentially the same as against ancient Baalism (no real "creation" or "Creator" in either), and, hence, it needs repeatedly to be made explicit as well. "History" hymns (e.g., Pss. 78; 105; 106; 114), recounting God's salvific work, are more self-evidently "unique," but even here the mere immanentalism plus subjective "interpretation" or "inference" of even some of the best of modern historical criticism must often be explicitly combated.

Finally, we may note the subdivision commonly referred to in modern scholarship as the "enthronement" hymns (e.g., Pss. 47; 93; 96—99). It is to be noted that in usual parlance the "enthronement" in question is that of Yahweh, not the earthly monarch. Their obverse, then, is the "royal psalms" with the elect king as their subject; there is no ultimate reason why these should not be called "hymns" as well, but, as noted, they are usually considered a distinct *Gattung*. As the name indicates, the "enthronement" psalms celebrate Yahweh's kingship over all the earth, and what follows from it, His "judgment" over all the earth. They are characterized by the refrain, "Yahweh rules." The universal and eschatological dimension seems very prominent. Yet because of Mowinckel's theories, few parts of the Psalter have attracted as much attention as these psalms. Suffice it to say at this point that the basic issue is whether these psalms describe an eternal state of affairs, or whether they celebrate a real enthronement in some sense. As we shall argue below, that is probably a false alternative, but it does raise questions about the aptness of the label "enthronement."

Laments and Thanksgivings

Of the major *Gattungen,* we may turn next to the laments and the thanksgivings. Gunkel, of course, counted individual and communal laments as two discrete types, but, as noted, except in external form and/or *Sitz im Leben,* the two are not always distinguishable. Structurally, the thanksgivings are very similar to the laments, and often we find the two types united in a single psalm (e.g., Ps. 22; cf. below). Gunkel himself compared the two types to the halves of a shell. "Communal thanksgivings" are very rare (Gunkel counted only two: Pss. 84 and 122), and, as noted, they merge with hymns.

There are many more individual than communal thanksgivings. These include Pss. 30; 32; 34; 116; and outside the Psalter, the psalm of Hezekiah (Is. 38:10-20) and the psalm of Jonah (2:3-10). But in the individual as well as in the communal categories, the number of laments far outweighs the number of thanksgivings. Should we attach any significance to that fact? There may well be truth to the explanation sometimes offered that the proportion corresponds to our disposition much more readily to petition than to thank God. If so, the Psalter does not intend to sanctify that failing but represents part of God's condescension and accommodation to our sinful need. At the same time the imbalance may also reflect a more lively sense of sin among the Old Testament pious than is common among us, and thus be part of the divine attempt to correct an imbalance which is really in our own sinful imagination. Similarly, one might offer as an historical explanation the very difficult lot of the people of God in the Old Testament, which we should then also understand theologically as exemplary of the divine administration of the Law, without which a truly evangelical thanksgiving will never flourish either.

The individual laments are numerically the most common of all (perhaps some forty in all), and thus form the backbone of the Psalter. A few of them are among the best known in the Psalter, namely the seven "penitential" psalms (6; 32; 38; 51; 102; 130; 143). The Eastern church also counts seven of them, but with a somewhat different listing. That, however, well illustrates how the entire *Gattung* might just as well be labeled "penitential," nomenclature which would at least better expose their theological gravamen than "lament." On the other hand, the careful reader cannot help but note how relatively little *explicit* "penitence" one encounters in the Psalter; no doubt, we are to understand the very descriptions of distress (punishment for sin) as implicit admissions of guilt.

The fact that Ps. 32 is today usually classified a "thanksgiving" rather than a "lament" also well illustrates the extent to which those two types are the obverse of one another, and sometimes almost interchangeable. In fact, one noteworthy motif sometimes encountered in the laments is the "doxology of judgment" (perhaps best and classically illustrated in Ps. 51:4), the profound recognition that the faithful often thank God in most heartfelt and spontaneous fashion in the very midst of lamentation as they experience His "Law" or judgment.

Formally, laments and thanksgivings are characterized by some half-dozen elements. However, the inspired poets were no slaves to any inherited structure; there is no fixed order, and certain elements may be omitted completely (or at least the degree of attention devoted to each may vary widely from psalm to psalm).

They commonly begin with a vocative or invocation, "O, Yahweh," or the like (cf. hymns which are regularly introduced by an imperative). The actual plea or petition for help, usually in imperative form ("help, save, have mercy, wake up!") may follow immediately, be delayed, or be repeated at various points. Sometimes the vocative is accompanied by honorific epithets of various sorts, often "reminding" Yahweh of His promises or performances of deliverance in the past, and sometimes "chiding" Him for His delay or apparent lethargy in responding similarly in the present. The modern reader often comments on what appears to Him as near-irreverence, if not flippancy, at these points, but undoubtedly we have witnessed here not only a certain covenant "intimacy" with the Father, but also a "boldness and confidence" (Luther) which holds God to His promises and will not let go without a blessing (cf. Gen. 32).

Sooner or later, in greater or lesser detail, one meets the description of the distress or the calamity, which forms the body of these psalms. At first blush, one is easily surprised to note that the misfortune is often depicted at greater length and in more harrowing detail in the thanksgivings than in the laments. It would seem that part of the explanation is pyschological: it is common experience that it is easier to relate woes after they are past and relieved than while one is in their throes. Possibly there is also a literary desire to construct an ample foil for the thanksgiving and praise which is the real subject of these psalms.

In the case of the communal laments, there is usually little difficulty in approximating the *Sitz im Leben* (cf. Pss. 36; 44; 74; 77; 79; 80; 83). It is invasion, exile, famine, etc. which imperils the entire people and brings them or their representatives to the sanctuary in fasting, supplication, etc. The book of Joel probably illustrates the situation, and the historical books preserve other instances.

It is different with the individual laments, however. Here the problem, one of the major ones in psalms exegesis, is to determine precisely what the problem was, and there is extensive literature on the subject. On the one hand, there is great variety in the descriptions, but on the other hand, also much sameness and even monotony (and the boredom which the casual, half-hearted reader of the Psalter often experiences usually centers here). and hence there is the question of whether they are intended to be taken literally.

On the surface the reader meets descriptions of what appears to be sickness, imminent death, false accusation, imprisonment, fiendish enemies, or the like. A highly figurative, but also obviously rather stylized, language often punctuates these descriptions: attack by troops, menace of wild beasts, "many waters" engulfing the worshiper, parched lips, and body wracked with pain.

What shall we make of it all? If the ordinary reader sometimes naively takes it all as a clinical report, critics have certainly often been guilty of a gross literalism too, usually by picking out one type of figure and trying to force all the others into that one mold. Critics who wished to deny or minimize the individual element often tried to interpret all the "enemies" as political and national (Birkeland, for example, explained them all as "foreigners"), but, at best, many instances simply will not be forced into such a straitjacket. The early and more radical Mowinckel read the "workers of iniquity" as evil magicians or sorcerers who had cursed the worshiper with sickness, and the psalms as incantations to neutralize or reverse their spells! H. Schmidt overstressed the aspect of unjust accusation, and tried to read as many of these psalms as possible as prayerful protestations of innocence, perhaps accompanying some kind of ordeal (cf. Num. 5:11-31). Others, too, have stressed the judicial aspect of these psalms, most bizarrely Delekat, who tries to construe them as graffiti scribbled on the temple wall by refugees, who in "incubation sleep" receive dreams, oracles, or the like!

Some of these theories obviously view the preexilic temple as semipagan, and are their own refutation. But many of them contain elements of truth. If the idea of "justice" at the temple is pursued in its Biblical fullness, it will also be brought into connection with the concept of "justification." The "enemies" and "false accusers" will not only be empirical, but transhistorical and metaphysical. The "many waters" motif probably has ultimate roots in mythological depictions of chaos, a chaos here described as invading and nearly overwhelming the order God has graciously implanted in the believer's soul.

And then we probably have the major clue to understand the variety of descriptions with their many metaphors. One might say they represent a classical case of the necessity to interpret *both* literally and non-literalistically. The descriptions are not simply to be allegorized into

"spiritual" ciphers: as long as Israel was also a state (and by no means
entirely absent even in Christian experience today) overt enemies, unjust
accusations, etc. were not that uncommon (and here the applicability of
some of these psalms to David comes into focus, as the superscriptions
indicate). Certainly sickness and death remain the common lot of
mankind. The vast variety of circumstances is deliberate in order to speak
to "all sorts and conditions of men." The wide applicability of these
psalms is part of their power even when approached as great literature,
and all the more so when viewed as inspired Scripture.

At the same time, their meaning and significance is not exhausted in
that literal applicability. Their *typical* sense must also be stressed—which,
one suspects, the pious throughout the ages have usually sensed almost
instinctively. Even empirically, they intend to apply to all sorts of
unfortunate circumstances which are not explicitly mentioned. But they
also point toward something far deeper than any individual's diagnosable
ills, whatever their nature and variety. Above all one must not forget, that
the subject is not primarily the ills of *any* one person anywhere, but, first
and foremost, those of the covenant man, of the man before *Deus
revelatus,* man who is at least partly capable of grasping the real depths of
his woes (cf. rather similarly on the wisdom literature). Their topic is
"anthropological" in the *theological* sense of that term. They intend to
point man beyond all superficial diagnoses of his empirical ills, real
though they be, to the ultimate problem of alienation from God, of
original sin, etc. God Himself through the Law must supply the right
question before the right answer of the Gospel has an audience.

And if one thus defines "typical" in its Biblical sense one must also say
"typological," that is, must also be aware of the promissory, eschatological context of the covenant. Furthermore, if one has not
divorced typology and prediction, one begins to comprehend the
Messianic character of these psalms. Many of them are explicitly cited in
the New Testament as fulfilled in Christ (e.g., Pss. 22, 69, 109), but that
citation appears to be, in part, illustrative of what applies on the whole to
the entire genre. The Christian church confesses that Christ is the only
one who can or who has plumbed the depths of the primal suffering of
which these psalms ultimately speak, but whose experience of it was also
undeserved and hence of vicarious and redemptive significance for those
who join themselves to Him. Only He can fully pray these psalms in all
their fullness, and only in covenant with Him can the faithful, Old
Testament as well as New, pray them validly. Even more profoundly, we
insist that via Baptism it is Christ, the last Adam, the "new Israel," who
prays these psalms in us and for us before the throne of the Father. And
because of His victory, we know that we do not pray them in vain.

This "Righteous Sufferer," whom we recognize to be ultimately none other than our Lord, is one of the two major figures of the Psalter, the other being the king of the royal psalms, who, of course is ultimately a Messianic figure too (cf. below). One line of cultic interpretation would, as we have noted, identify these two figures; allegedly, it was originally the king who prayed the laments in his capacity as "corporate personality" or "Israel reduced to one," and only later were they supposedly "democratized" and made available to all the faithful. Such a construction is, in a sense, attractive from the standpoint of Messianic interpretation, but, on other grounds, it is too speculative and too beholden to other very questionable reconstructions for one to embrace it, except perhaps as an outside possibility. And, even if, as most still presume, the sociological circumstances of the "righteous sufferer" were ordinarily different from those of the "king," the New Testament still gives us ample warrant to make the same ultimate typological and predictive application to Christ in both cases.

The sufferer in the psalms does not always plead innocent, however. Partly on the basis of Egyptian analogies, scholarship has grown accustomed to speaking of two types of confessions: (a) the "negative confession" in which the worshiper denies his guilt and asks God's justice on His enemies (the type of which we have just been speaking), and (b) the "positive confession," where the speaker concedes his culpability and implores God's forgiveness. The latter are especially known as "confessional" or "penitential" psalms (cf. above). One will not simplistically identify the latter type with Christ in the same way as the former, but it remains profoundly true that the latter cannot be validly prayed outside of the covenant either, that is, apart from an imputed righteousness and in unity with its Giver *(Christus et pro nobis et in nobis)*.

The "Self-Righteous" and Imprecatory Psalms

For many readers, who read the psalms as only great religious literature and forget its true theological *Gattung,* two severe theological problems often arise in this connection, whence nonconservatives are often not at all reluctant to excise, in effect, what they regard as unworthy religious sentiments, sub-Christian and incompatible with the New Testament and the Gospel. These problems surface especially in the "negative confession" where the "righteous sufferer" speaks, and if their liberal interpretation were correct, one could, indeed, regard them as little more than ancient products, only part way along the evolutionary road toward mankind's highest ideals in his never complete quest for and perception of "God," and certainly no longer "Scripture" for us.

Both problems appear side by side in Ps. 139:19-24, and we may well take it as our major exemplar of both. Ps. 139 is usually classified as a "wisdom psalm," and it probably is no accident that we confront the problem in such an ambience that concentrated on problems of ultimate destinies, retributions, etc. (cf. both below on that genre and above on the wisdom corpus in general).

The first problem is that of alleged "*self*-righteousness." And so, indeed, it often easily appears on the surface, not only in Ps. 139:23-24, but also in the protestations of Job, in the facile distinctions of Ps. 1, etc. How easy it is for the ordinary reader to hear such expressions as simply self-congratulation for mere external respectability, or for the critical theologian to contrast such sentiments with the profound hamartiology of St. Paul, among others. Hermeneutical presuppositions will again determine the final answer: if the one Author of Scripture does not contradict Himself, those liberal understandings cannot possibly be correct. Hence, in the light of the covenant and "imputed righteousness" framework of all of Scripture, orthodoxy naturally hears such words as the forgiven and justified sinner's boasting and glorying solely in Christ. It may well also be true that the speaker is not empirically guilty as accused, but the real point transcends all empiricism. It may—undoubtedly was— true that many in the Old Testament *mis*understood and *mis*applied such words, as many still do in the new covenant (and correction of such Biblical misunderstandings should be high on the pastor's and teacher's agenda), but that is ultimately beside the point.

The second and more grievous problem is that of the cursing (imprecatory or minatory) psalms. How can one "hate them with perfect hatred" (Ps. 139:22), not to speak of the almost incredible, blood-curdling curses which sometimes escape the psalmist's lips (perhaps especially Pss. 35; 58; 69; 83; 109; 137, 149)? How is such apparently sheer spite and unrelieved hatred compatible with Jesus' prayer on the cross, or the gospel of "Love your enemies" in general? For many liberals the problem appears not only in the overtly imprecatory psalms, but it jars and obtrudes whenever "enemies" are mentioned negatively, even in otherwise tranquil contexts, such as Ps. 23:5. Outside of confessional and evangelical contexts, such passages (perhaps alongside "holy war" concepts and the prophet's "Gentile oracles," which see) serve nearly universally as parade examples of the inferior morality of the Old Testament, which has not yet discovered the full implication of universal love. Even in relatively conservative contexts, the liturgical rubric is often unfortunately observed, which eliminates these psalms from considera- tion for public worship (and "selected psalms" virtually never includes them).

Problems within the canon, however, are never solved by creating a

canon within the canon, not even a *de facto* one. And only the canon, as
usual, can provide the definitive solution. Only a minute part of the
explanation can rest on cultural differences, but, for what it is worth, it
seems true that the ancient (like the modern) Orient indulged in coarse,
hyperbolic language of this sort more readily than we (cf. even Luther in
more modern times very often), and parallels can be found in the
literature of Israel's neighbors. Much more to the point, however, is the
realization, which one stresses repeatedly throughout the Old Testament,
that Israel was "church" and state combined. This, of course, meant that
Israel's political (and very concrete) enemies were normally also God's
enemies. And likewise with individual imprecations, which dare not be
read as effusions of personal spleen, but in solidarity with the entire
covenant people and its destiny under God. The real subject of these
psalms is not individuals or nations whom one should love or pray for as
an absolute alternative, but (of a piece with the stylized, typical language
of the Psalter in general) archetypes of the "demonic," of that primal evil
which always and everywhere opposes God, His work, and His people,
ultimately of course, the Antichrist or Satan who indwells the wicked
instead of Christ (and since we remain *simul peccator,* indwells also us).
Also this typology is constantly assuming empirical form, but the deeper
realization is that no human power will ultimately exorcise it. A major
Biblical application of this antichristological typology occurs in the
citations of Ps. 109 as fulfilled in the person and activities of Judas
Iscariot (cf. similarly "Edom" and "Babylon" on the ecclesiastical plane).

And in this connection one must not hesitate to underscore how un-
Biblical spiritualisms and sentimentalizations of the Gospel have
complicated the problem for many marginal Christians. One thinks of the
"God hates sin, but loves the sinner" Manichaeanism, intended, no doubt,
to articulate God's universal *offer* of forgiveness, but, if pursued
consistently, implying falsely that there really is an abstract "evil" apart
from embodiment in evil people, as though God really saves or damns
only "souls," not people, as though God is really satisfied with mere good
behavior and does not want the whole being, etc. Possibly even more
serious is the "other Gospel" which seems not to know that the "wrath of
God" is structurally just as prominent and indispensable a part of New
Testament theology as of Old, and that the cross is a maximal expression
of God's wrath upon evil *people* (beginning with His own Son) just as much
as it is of His love. Indeed, there is no warrant in these psalms for *human*
vengeance, individual or corporate, least of all in the name of religion, as,
no doubt, there always have been those who so misconstrued these
pericopes. Vengeance is God's alone, of course (Rom. 12:19), but
wickedness that refuses to be forgiven can only be destroyed, and in so far

as the Christ who took all of God's vengeance upon Himself dwells in us, we not only can but must join Him in both prayer and labor for the final "judgment," which will at once spell extirpation of all evil and final triumph of the original, paradisiacal order.

We return to consideration of the form-critical structure of the laments and thanksgivings. The structural elements considered thus far just about suffice for the laments, but, as already noted, the two *Gattungen* tend to merge into one. Not only does a psalm of thanksgiving frequently follow immediately upon the lament, but, even if not, the laments often close with a feature which Gunkel aptly called "Certainty of Hearing." In his view, this feature eventually became independent of the lament, giving rise to a separate, minor *Gattung,* which Gunkel labeled "Psalms of Confidence" (most famously Ps. 23; but also 4; 11; 16; 27:1-6; 62; 131). There is no way at all to test Gunkel's hypothesis (and one notes that it is more of a material than a formal criterion), but neither is there anything intrinsically objectionable about it. In any case, it gives occasion to emphasize the necessary theological context of these beautiful psalms, which is easily overlooked. Particularly in the case of Ps. 23, it should be almost an obsession to depaganize the piece: it does not reflect the indomitable human spirit, even in the face of death, but is loaded with very particularistic *heilsgeschichtliche* vocabulary, celebrating the *covenant* man's repose *after* the demands of the Law have been vicariously met.

The suddenness with which a psalm of thanksgiving often follows the lament without transition has often seemed very puzzling. Begrich's hypothesis seems most plausible and has won nearly universal acceptance: in the original cultic situation, Begrich proposed, there intervened after the lament and before the thanksgiving, a priestly *Heilsorakel* ("oracle of salvation"—or "formula of absolution," one is almost tempted to paraphrase), assuring the worshiper that his prayer has been favorably heard and answered. Ps. 22:21b may even preserve evidence of such a ritual in the otherwise incomprehensible "thou hast answered me" at the point of transition from lament to thanksgiving. Begrich and others went on to theorize that the prophets often modeled their eschatological oracles of salvation (especially evident in Is. 40—55) on this familiar worship circumstance, and, again, although the hypothesis is beyond testing, it has the ring of plausibility about it.

In other respects, from data within the psalmic thanksgivings themselves, as well as by historical reports elsewhere in the Old Testament, the cultic setting of this *Gattung* is often as obvious and undeniable as anywhere (cf. below). As clearly evidenced in Ps. 22:25 ff., the worshiper often publicly acknowledges his deliverance before the congregation, and often also announces the payment of his vow, which, in part, includes a sacrifice. And it is no accident that Old Testament vocabulary uses the same word, *todah,* to denote both thankoffering and thanksgiving psalm (the word is also etymologically related to the "praise" words). We see again the usual Old Testament pattern of sacrifice and prayer as normally inseparable complements (cf. Ps. 141:2, the familiar Vespers versicle); in this case too, the usual practice appears to have been to recite the thanksgiving prayer either before or during the presentation of their offering.

Minor Types

Before we proceed with the fifth major *Gattung,* the royal psalms, let us consider other minor types which have not yet been discussed. "Pilgrimage Songs" are plainly among these. As already noted, the relation of this type to the later (?) "Psalms of Ascent" (120—134) is uncertain, but, of those, only Ps. 122 gives clear internal indications of originally having such associations. Ps. 84 with its longing for Zion plainly belongs in this category, and there are allusions elsewhere to such pilgrimages (Pss. 87; 121; 126; cf. Is. 2:3 = Micah 4:2).

Closely related are the processional hymns, or "entrance liturgies," as they are often called, in which pilgrims or other worshipers ritually inquire about the conditions for admission into the sanctuary and receive symbolic catechetical instruction. We have two clear examples, Pss. 15 and 24, esp. vs. 3-6 of the latter, although 48; 68; and 132 are also possibilities. Modern theory has often postulated the ark, representing Yahweh, as the "King of glory" at the head of the procession, which while speculative, is not beyond the realm of probability (cf. 2 Sam. 6; 1 Chron. 15). At any rate, allusions in other psalms (42:5; 55:15; 118:19-20) make it plain that processions played a prominent role in Old Testament worship.

Gunkel himself preferred to speak of "Torah liturgies," that is, occasions when the priest gave instruction *(torah),* especially on cultic procedures. At least outside of the Psalter, he thought he could discern other types of liturgies, e.g., "oracular" ones (priestly guidance in times of crisis, as when a king leaves for battle), and "prophetic" ones, concerned with typical prophetic themes. Gunkel himself thought of prophets attached to shrines (an insight blown out of all proportion by the later rage for "cultic prophecy"), but he found most evidence in what he regarded as later, freer imitations by the canonical prophets or by the traditors who collected their oracles (e.g., Is. 12; 33). Subsequent opinion has often agreed substantially with Gunkel also in this area, but "liturgy" is so broad and often amorphous a term that it is difficult to get one's hands on it. The accent does, however, reflect the great, and generally wholesome accent, which form criticism succeeded in putting on Israel's public worship as not only the major *Sitz im Leben* of most of the psalms, but also with great influence on the rest of Israel's life and literature.

Last but not least among the minor categories, we must include the wisdom psalms. Although not great in number (some eight or nine), they require more than passing attention, if for no other reason, because Ps. 1 plainly bids us approach the entire Psalter as, in some sense, a "wisdom book." Initially, that tends to be less help than hindrance for us, because of our grave difficulties with "wisdom" in general (cf. the discussion in that chapter), and Ps. 1 certainly illustrates many of them (the apparent moralism, if not works-righteousness, the facile division of mankind into "two ways," etc.).

Suffice it to say here that "wisdom" deals with ultimates, with the entire created order, accessible in part after the Fall to reason and experience in "general revelation," but ultimately available and testable only within "special revelation" (Bible and Gospel, if you will). Wisdom literature tends to *assume* that theological background, and to express itself in more universal language; at least two wisdom psalms (127 and 133) answer to that description, and humanly speaking, could just as well have appeared in the Book of Proverbs. Other wisdom products, however, show greater signs of explicit theological reflection, and exhibit greater use of mainline Biblical vocabulary. The bulk of the psalmic specimens are of that character (1; 37; 49; 73; 112; 119; 128; and perhaps 139). Echoes of wisdom language or procedures are apparent also in other psalms (e.g., 78:1-2; 34:12; 62:12), and, above all, as Ps. 1 probably intends to remind us, it is possible to consider the entire Psalter a wisdom book because it deals with the same ultimate issues of life and death, of suffering and retribution, etc.

All of this raises the question whether form criticism's native penchant for "atomization by classification" has not been most unfortunately effective in the case of wisdom and specifically the wisdom psalms. Of course, we can ultimately insist that theologically wisdom must be read in canonical context as an integral tessera in the entire mosaic of revelation, but, even apart from dogmatic grounds, we must insist that wisdom, for all its uniqueness of expression, was in no sense an alien element in ancient Israel.

In addition to the general hermeneutical problems, the issue arises in the Psalter especially in connection with the *Sitz im Kultus* assumed for most of it. Unfortunately, the usual critical portrait of the sage has been that of the solipsistic intellectual, not only ahistoric and humanistic, but also acultic if not anticultic, and hence the general tendency has been to assume that wisdom influences like Ps. 1 could have infiltrated the Psalter only at a very late date, after the intelligentsia had allegedly emancipated themselves from temple and cult in favor of their private academies. Or it is argued that Ps. 1, representing a later stage of the tradition-history of the entire psalter, wants to steer *us* away from its earlier cultic moorings into a more privatistic study of and meditation on its contents (Childs).

However, the Bible itself fails to sustain such a dichotomy, and recent research into both Biblical and extra-Biblical wisdom (Perdue) supports the thesis that the "wise" were by no means so uninterested, let alone hostile, to matters cultic. This authorizes no fancy theory or cultic use of the wisdom psalms, but it does enable us to view their presence in the Psalter as another reflection of the totality of Israel's religious life, cultic and public as well as private, which characterizes the Psalter as a whole.

Royal (Messianic) Psalms

We have saved the "best wine," the royal psalms, till last, because they form a natural capstone to the Psalter in the eyes of both tradition and of much modern scholarship ("royal" and "Messianic," of course, being substantially synonymous). As noted above, Gunkel did not initially consider this a major *Gattung,* and, certainly, from the standpoint of formal criteria alone, he should have "stuck to his guns," because no clear structure is discernible. At the same time, however, the material importance of the royal psalms almost justifies a separate *Gattung,* because, as we have noted, the king (alongside the righteous sufferer; cf. above) is undeniably one of the two major personages in the Psalter.

Gunkel himself pursued the matter little further than attempting to determine the various *Sitze im Leben* of the psalms of this type: a king's enthronement (2; 101; 110), anniversary of the enthronement (21; 72), anniversary of the Davidic dynasty and its sanctuary on Zion (132), a royal wedding (45), the king's departure for war (20; 144:1-11), celebration of the king's victorious return (18 = 2 Sam. 22), etc. Of course, there has been no lack of critical debate about many specifics of those associations, but in broad thrust there is no doubt about the general assent. Neither has there been much critical concern about the relatively "secular" nature of the contexts, as the above captions indicate.

Inevitably, however, the question of the compatibility of such an exegesis with traditional and New Testament Messianic interpretation presses to the fore. It is to be noted that Gunkel views these psalms as expressed by or about one of Israel's monarchs on some specific historical occasion, not as idealizations (let alone predictions) of some future regent. On both sides there are those who would deny the possibility of any compatibility of the two views (historical and eschatological or Messianic), but we defend their ultimate unity (both are aspects of the "one, literal sense") on the basis of the ultimate unity of prediction and typology and/or of history and prophecy/suprahistory/eschatology.

The royal psalms are to be read in the light of especially 2 Sam. 7, Nathan's pivotal Messianic prophecy of perpetuity to the Davidic dynasty, specializing and extending to it the same covenant which was the fundament of Israel's entire existence. If with some critics we do not dismiss the grandiose language of these psalms as merely the traditional, fulsome bombast of ancient Near Eastern "court style," it soon becomes apparent that their primary subject is not any empirical king, but the *office* of kingship under the promise. But "office" is an abstraction; the terms of the promise were partly "fulfilled," that is, exemplified and objectified again and again in Israel's kings (potentially even by those who were externally unfaithful to it), but the very incompleteness of that application always reminded that that partial fulfillment was also a prophecy and type of Another who would fully and finally incarnate and establish its terms in an eternal kingdom. Nor is this something "read in"; the Old Testament context alone suffices to defend the viewpoint that the ultimate, eschatological and Messianic import was part of the speaker's original vista and intent.

The nations indeed conspired against the LORD and His anointed (Ps. 2:1-2) throughout Israel's history, but that very real history was of a piece with the ultimately cosmic battle of the kingdoms of this world against God's kingdom (about as central a Biblical motif as can be found). In reply, God reiterated the Nathanic decree (2:7) and made their enemies a footstool (110:1), but not apart from Christ's definitive victory. Precisely because the Israelite kingdom was a microcosm of the eternal kingdom, the Israelite king could lay claim to the "ends of the earth" (2:8), but the reality was available to them essentially only as it still is to us—in Word and Sacrament (that is, even after Christ's advent, but before the consummation, we continue to pray these words in an eschatological vein not totally different from ancient Israel's). Israel's kings apparently exercised authority over the regular, Aaronic priesthood, thus possessing a special priesthood "after the order of Melchizedek" (110:4), but the full potential of that ultimately eschatological order could not emerge until great David's greater Son occupied his throne (the Book of Hebrews). Israel's king was indeed God's "son," "begotten" (adopted) in the unique covenant relation as a sort of "incarnation" of the sonship of all of Israel by virtue of election, but that had no more ultimate meaning then than our sonship has for us except by Baptism (election and covenant) into Him who is the only-begotten Son in an utterly unique and ontological sense.

Perhaps most climactically of all in Ps. 45:6, the king is addressed as *elohim* (God). In surrounding paganism that might well have been taken more literally, but in Israel it must have had a more derivative meaning as language of deity does elsewhere (cf. "gods" = "angels," etc.). Thus, on one level of meaning RSV's rendering "divine" is justified, but on another—the climactic eschatological level—it could only apply to the Messiah (Heb. 1:8-9).

Thus, as we have stressed so often, Messianic and Christological interpretation of the royal psalms (cf. especially the "dynastic oracles" of the prophets) does not require us to divorce ourselves from the realities of Israel's history any more than it does from our own. But it does require us to define the word "history" in the Bible's own sacramental and eschatological sense, precisely what the "historical-critical" method is unable to do. It is not less than history, but more than mere history, and in Christ the history of Israel's monarchy is also part of the history of *our* salvation. We will not "read into" the ancient texts a consciousness of all the details of the fulfillment, but in our secular culture we will remain painfully aware that the front on which we must amass our major forces is that of the inability to "read out" of them their full prophetic and typological, Christological, and eschatological significance. We will not succumb to the "intentionalist fallacy" of arguing that the ancient words could have no meaning beyond that intended and fully understood by the ancient human authors (presuming we can ever ascertain it), but we will also not hesitate to accept the intention of the ultimate Author, as He has revealed it to us in further Scripture. Possibly, it was easier for the older dogmaticians to cite passages such as these as proof texts or for preachers to use them as texts, but we need desperately to expend the effort merely to regain the *ability* to do so! Obviously, the relevance of much of the entire Old Testament as *Scripture and Gospel* is simultaneously at stake.

Cultic Understanding of the Psalms

As noted above, a new element was injected into critical discussion by the accent on cult by many of Gunkel's successors, and its impact centered on the meaning of the royal (and enthronement) psalms. The fervor has abated somewhat, but the issue is still very much alive. While Gunkel had recognized the ultimate setting of most psalms in the cult, he had held that most pieces in our present Psalter came from a later stage when the connection with the "formalistic" cult had been broken, and a more "spiritual" piety was being expressed. The motives for the new accent were more *religionsgeschichtliche* and anthropological than they were strictly form critical, but the lines between the various fields always had been rather indistinct.

The precise reconstructions varied (cf. below), but all of them held in common that most of the royal and enthronement psalms (to use central

examples) were originally neither historical nor eschatological-Messianic
in primary import, but liturgical texts in a periodic, dramatic ceremony
which may have even mimed the events spoken of, thus "actualizing" or
"contemporizing" them for the present audience. Our concern at the
moment is not the details of the reconstructions but the validity of the
approach in general, especially from an orthodox or confessionally
Lutheran standpoint. We cannot consider all aspects of the question here,
but a few important distinctions can and must be made.

For one thing, pagan and Biblical conceptions of the nature of cultus
must be distinguished, something which many critical researchers have
failed to do. In pagan cult one can really speak of "repetition" of some
essentially "time*less*" order *(illud tempus);* in fact, the action of the cult
has magical force, in some real sense "priming" the cosmic process,
actually "enthroning" the gods anew, *causing* "creation" to happen yet
another time, and simultaneously reaffirming the "divine kingship" of the
earthly viceroy of the gods, and therewith upholding and maintaining the
political order and ensuring military success throughout at least the
coming year. The Babylonian cult of Marduk, peaking at the *akitu* or
New Year's celebration, was undeniably of this sort, and it was the major
model Mowinckel and others used to reconstruct the preexilic Israelite
cult. Allegedly, Yahweh too was *made* king each year and the
enthronement psalms were its liturgy, but simultaneously the quasi-
metaphysical "sonship" of the Davidide ruler was also reestablished, the
monster of chaos (Tiamat, Leviathan, Rahab) in both creation and
history was subdued for another year, the coming of ample rains and
other signs of life and fertility assured, and so on.

Obviously, in such a milieu one cannot speak of "eschatology," and
hence not really of history, of election and covenant, or of other Biblical
concepts dependent on the assumption of one, personal God. In
that sense, the magical objectivism *(opus operatum)* of pagan cult, like
mythology in general, is the absolute antipode of all that makes Biblical
and Christian faith "tick."

Hence, it is understandable that many Christian scholars overreacted.
For all of their differences otherwise, both liberal and "evangelical"
scholars could often offer as an only alternative some version of
subjectivism or fideism, according to which there might, at most, be
"symbols" or "symbolic actions," but all final validation inhering in the
willing assent of the believing subject. And there tended to be a lingering
suspicion of even that much "ritualism" or "cult" as a relic of paganism
(or of "Catholicism"), with a distinct preference for purely verbal or
intellectual constructs.

We argue that historic Lutheranism offers a Biblical *via media* between the objectivism of paganism and the subjectivism of most modern post-Kantian thought. We label it "sacramental," rather than "sacramenta*lism*" because of the frequent pejorative connotations of the noun (indicating a relapse into magical objectivism). (When Mowinckel himself was once asked by more conservative Lutherans whether his Lutheran upbringing had in any way influenced his cultic theories, he replied negatively!) In this view, there is real objective power in connection with the true cult of "Word and Sacrament" (for either salvation or damnation; cf. *manducatio indignorum)* whether the worshiper knows it and confesses it or not, but there can be no positive benefit for him apart from his conscious, subjective faith and appropriation.

This at least opens up the theological possibility that psalmic texts may well have been originally of a liturgical nature, components of a ceremony. Yet no magical power inhered in either them or the dramatic ceremonies they acompanied. Rather, they are to be understood as aspects of the "Word," extensions of the "sermon," and sometimes even specifically as counterparts of the "Words of Institution," transmuting the external elements into means of grace. On the whole, the "elements" in this case would be the accompanying sacrifices, which, as we have seen, were essentially sacramental in signification, and to which the psalmic texts often allude. Critical theory, unfortunately, rarely made much of the sacrifices in this connection, and the lack is one of the major indications of the minimal extent to which their theories were often informed by the Bible itself (cf. our stress on Leviticus and Chronicles as indispensable complements of the Psalter).

If the psalms, especially the royal and enthronement types, were liturgical texts, how were they also prophetic or predictive? Here it is imperative that false alternatives be avoided. All too often, scholars have asked us to choose between historical, cultic (existential) and eschatological alternatives, when in reality it is a matter of all three at once! One must maintain the historical element, not only in faithfulness to the Biblical texts themselves, but in principle in order to avoid the docetic, ahistorical timelessness that defines mythological cult. But the historical by itself yields only an ancient datum, the "values" or "relevance" of which the modern reader must recover for himself as best he can ("historicism").

Properly ("sacramentally") understood the cultic accent simultaneously stresses that the actual ancient history is also "represented," that is, made present and actualized "for me," as though I were a contemporary (*anamnesis;* "remembrance"), and, of course, both "Word" and "Sacrament" combine in this respect as vehicles of the Holy Spirit. This "updating" occurs not only intellectually, "spiritually," and verbally, but also physically, "sacramentally," with reference to the "whole man." It is not *only* the matter of the lone individual's personal relation to God, but anchors conversion and the entire Christian experience solidly in the means of grace, in the church, and ultimately then in real incarnational history as well. The "today" of Ps. 95:7b ff. (redolent of especially Deuteronomy) is one of the most explicit psalmic expressions of this representation or contemporization, but it seems to be implicit throughout. Presumably, the ancient texts in their context repeatedly performed this contemporizing function in ancient Israel and continue in Christ to perform it for us. Compare our "Christ is risen today" of our Easter celebrations, neither annulling its historicity, nor simply affirming Christ's presence in our hearts, but celebrating the work of the Spirit in Word and Sacrament in bringing Christ out of the remoteness of ancient history. Here one also sees how "typology" and "sacrament" are largely equivalent terms, the former having primarily B.C. applicability, the latter A.D.

But the reference was simultaneously to the future, as well as to past and present. Precisely because Biblical "history" is a teleological concept, it always includes and points forward to the goal and climax. In terms of the royal psalms, that means "Messianic," and even for us it means the "Until He come," the final, consummative establishment of the kingdom of God. Yet, there is always the "now" alongside the "not yet"; to faith both Word and Sacrament always proleptically offer the totality of what is promised or typified. And parallel to all three tense dimensions, one must not forget the vertical, the supernatural, the incarnational; only in the denouement, in the new creation, will vertical and horizontal totally coincide as they did in Paradise at the beginning.

Mowinckel especially threw this type of question into relief by his denial of *any* eschatology to preexilic cult. His position was really the result of a mutation of the old Wellhausen evolutionism, partly reaffirming the dogma that eschatology was a late import into Israelite thought, partly the continued assumption that preexilic Israelite religion centering in the first temple was still semipagan (now fueled by many history-of-religions analogies). Mowinckel's great theme was: *Vom Erlebnis zur Hoffnung* ("from [cultic] experience to hope"), that is, only after the collapse of the Israelite monarchy with its mythological superstructure did the disillusioned Jews transfer to some future fulfillment what previously they believed they had *received* annually in the cult. That position, of course, assumes that Israel's preexilic cult was essentially pagan ("eschatology" being of the essence of Biblical uniqueness) and, in that form, is totally unacceptable to orthodoxy. But if one defines the *Erlebnis* in sacramental instead of mythological terms, it contains a partial truth: prophetic eschatology is, indeed, often very dependent upon cultic constructs, and what the prophets are saying is that the promises which, in a sense, repeatedly were "fulfilled" in the present to the eyes of faith in worship, would ultimately be fulfilled openly, empirically, Christologically, in the eyes of all the heathen.

Important a contribution to the full understanding of the psalms as cultic research potentially is in general terms, when it comes to specific theories one can and must sit very loose. Certain aspects must be rejected *a priori* on the grounds of incompatibility with the analogy of Scripture, while many others, at worst, merely exceed the evidence.

Mention must be made of some five influential cultic reconstructions. We mention first the most radical one, which, fortunately, was always recognized as such, and today commands little more than historical interest itself. This was the position of the Swedish "Uppsala school," especially Engnell. It postulated a "New Year's festival" in Israel, with only minimal differences from its alleged Babylonian prototype, including even a mimed "death and resurrection" of the king representing the deity, and a *hieros gamos* ("sacral mating") between king and prostitute to insure fertility throughout all realms. No doubt, if anything of this sort ever transpired in Israel, it was about as pagan as could possibly be! The most one might concede is that it possibly illustrates some of what went on in the darkest days of apostasy in the divided monarchy, some of which the Book of Kings does not blush to recount itself, but, in no way, could it ever have been normative for Yahwistic and Biblical faith!

Other reconstructions too tended to date their festivals in the autumn at New Year's, but without quite the accent on that idea as such. Vast energies have been devoted to the debate of this issue, including whether ancient Israel even celebrated New Year's at this time of the year (cf. above). On that score, as such, there seems little reasonable doubt, but it remains remarkable that the Biblical texts never make much of it—and, certainly, far less than later and modern Judaism do with *Rosh Hashshanah*. Even less is there any hint of a "New Year's *Festival*," and the rejoinder that postexilic reformers suppressed it is, at best, an argument from silence. Both Ugaritic and Biblical (Deut. 30:10) evidence suggests, at most, a seven-year rather than an annual cycle of autumnal observances. This major "Achilles heel" does not invalidate the entire cultic approach, but it is a major factor in calling into question much of the detail of the proposed reconstructions, dependent, as they often are for their details, far more on extra-Biblical evidence.

Perhaps most akin to the Swedish Uppsala theory was the British "myth and ritual" school (especially S. H. Hooke). Although it grew increasingly conservative in the course of time, it, too, scarcely exists any longer as a recognizably independent "school," and hence it does not serve our purposes to detail its theories. It will suffice to point out that "myth and ritual" was used here in a theoretically neutral sense of "story of the liturgy and liturgy"—a "story" which, as such, might be either true or false, either historical or mythological (cf. "Word and Sacrament" or "prophecy and typology").

Somewhat more "conservative" (and increasingly so in later years) than either the Swedes or the British, was the Norwegian Mowinckel, and, no doubt, his theories have been the most influential of all. With proper adaptation, and at least as a catalyst, his *The Psalms in Israel's Worship* still makes very worthwhile reading. Although he also located the major festival on a putative Israelite New Year's, he preferred to describe it as primarily an "enthronement festival," using the enthronement psalms (some 43 of which he so classified) as his key texts. The liturgical cry, "Yahweh *has become* king" (through the cultic *Geschehen*) was the key to his reconstruction, and other elements followed in its wake: recreation, reestablishment of the monarchy, mimetic battle, etc. And it is to be noted that Mowinckel also included in the "representations" of the festival specifically Biblical and historical events or themes such as the exodus, election, and covenant, although they played a relatively minor role (cf. below). Nevertheless, even in his later, more conservative years, Mowinckel never quite succeeds in anchoring his theory sufficiently in actual history. But the practiced student can often easily make satisfactory adjustments: Israel's "kingship" was not "divine" in the pagan sense, but its rituals celebrated the constant coming of God's kingdom, anchored in the *history* of election and promise, to the faithful at worship (as similarly ourselves; cf. the Second Petition). Similarly, God was not really "enthroned" by any liturgical action, but His eternal reign, tied to Messianic promise and fulfillment, ever and again came into Israel's midst through "Word and Sacrament."

The other two reconstructions came from Germany. Of course, the national provenance is of no moment, as such, but one is naive to think that nationalistic rivalries play no role in academic competitions such as this. German scholarship, on the whole, remained very cool to the entire cultic approach, and one of its leaders, Martin Noth, vigorously combatted it. The resistance partly reflects the continued popularity of a more classical Wellhausenianism in its German homeland, and the fact that the newer and rival ideas stemmed from the *Ausland* did little to endear them!

Kraus' "royal Zion festival" was a far more Biblical and historical-based version of some of the same motifs, but it never won many adherents, and little of his work has ever been translated into English. As the name indicates, Kraus postulated two principal motifs, the election of David and his dynasty and the concomitant election of Jerusalem or Zion as his seat. Kraus too thought of a processional to Zion with the ark (Ps. 132 as its hymn) and of a sort of reenactment of the founding of the Davidic dynasty. Mythological motifs were, however, thoroughly secondary and illustrative, and the celebration of Yahweh's "enthronement" was not really "cultic" at all but a mere commemoration of *historical* manifestations of Yahweh's power, especially in the deliverance from Babylon. (Kraus also construed the enthronement psalms as dependent upon "Deutero-Isaiah's" prophecies, a direction of influence with which few would concur, including conservatives who think of "Isaiah of Jerusalem.") Kraus does thus highlight one of the Bible's own "primary symbols," the election of David and Zion (alongside exodus, conquest, and exile). There is a clear break here with all mythological cyclicism, but if one can still speak of a "cultic" theory at all, it appears to be only in a thoroughly nonsacramental, low-church, Protestant sense of the term.

The fifth major cultic hypothesis was the "covenant festival" of A. Weiser. Many of the same types of judgments would apply here as in the case of Kraus, but, at least in America, he has been far more influential. Part of the reason, no doubt, lay in the Reformed background of much established American Biblical scholarship to which the theme of "covenant" was intrinsically rather attractive. Furthermore, Weiser's pursuit of the covenant theme in the Psalter often coincided with the vast amount of interest in covenantalism in the "Biblical theology" movement in general (especially Eichrodt), and more particularly with the "covenant renewal festival," allegedly centering at Shechem and underlying many Biblical narratives, as Alt, von Rad, Mendenhall, and many others tried to work them out. To Protestants of this persuasion, Weiser's "covenant festival," with its accents, in effect, on the kerygma, the sermon, on call to commitment, was an attractive alternative to the more "Catholic" or "sacramental" versions of Mowinckel and others. (Better examples of the role of presuppositions, sometimes barely recognized, on critical theory could scarcely be found!)

Noting the prominence of Yahweh's self-revelation in some liturgical texts (Pss. 18; 50; 81; etc.), Weiser made "theophany" his point of departure: via some cultic dramatization or the other, Yahweh "shone forth" in the midst of the annual cultic assembly in essentially the same way as He had originally at Sinai, when the covenant was first sealed with Israel. Other central features in Weiser's scheme fan out from this central act of revelation: recapitulation of Yahweh's deeds in history (cf. Ps. 78), proclamation (possibly by a "covenant mediator" representing Moses) of apodictic commandments representing Yahweh's will (cf. Ps. 81), and a ceremony of covenant renewal or profession of renewed commitment.

Weiser added a number of other minor themes, which, it should be noted, are very close to Mowinckel's major ones—on the whole, a good summary of the greater Biblical verisimilitude of Weiser's proposals. Among these were: the celebration of Yahweh's kingship and creative power (Pss. 47; 104); His universal judgment over all peoples (Pss. 68; 82; 99); enthronement of the Judean king (Pss. 2; 45), and others.

All in all, the conservative will probably rate Weiser's commentary as one of the best out of critical circles. The reason will not be out of any favoritism for a "covenant festival" (which one might take or leave), but because, as he strains to relate nearly every psalmic motif to that festival, he also relates them to covenant theology, by any standard a central Biblical theme. And most of the individual themes themselves which Weiser highlights can, indeed, be deduced from the Biblical material, regardless of any cultic hypothesis.

Theology of the Psalter Today

Except possibly for a rather undefined, universalistic sense of "celebration," the mood of the sixties did not encourage cultivation of cultic interests, certainly not those of ancient Israel. In fact, the Psalter was far from its center of gravity in general. In the seventies, efforts have been made to pick up the pieces, but, as in Biblical studies in general, there is no clear indication of the direction in which the critical study of the Psalter is heading.

No matter what its gyrations otherwise, on one point liberalism, if it retained any theological interests at all, has been consistent, namely, its view of the Psalter as not so much "revelation" as "response to revelation." Of course, the "revelation" in question is the liberal's understanding of the term as "encounter," "interpretation of historical process," etc., and the conservative cannot fully respond until revelation is also defined in propositional terms. If the latter were not denied, one could agree up to a point. From a purely human standpoint, the praises of the Psalter certainly do exemplify the response of the faithful in all ages, and, for all the chronological and geographical distance between us and the first responders, it is impossible that they should or ever can vary materially. But as elsewhere in Scripture, that human component cannot be allowed to cancel out special inspiration.

If one hears the psalms as God's very Word, then, of course, one finds there a magnificent summary of Biblical theology (Luther called it a "Bible in miniature"), and expressed in such incomparable terms that it really is a gilding of the lily to attempt any "theology of the Psalter." That being so, it obviously intends not to make the rest of the Old Testament superfluous, as often appears to happen in practice, but by epitomizing it to trailblaze the way for its full appreciation. The day of the breviary with its schedule of reading the entire Psalter through each month or even each week is momentarily in eclipse, as is probably any comparable discipline within Protestantism, and what happened with the Psalter is undoubtedly only a repetition on smaller scale of what has happened with the entire Bible.

The Psalter itself contains the ingredients for a reversal of fields. Its continued use in Christendom provides a convenient point of departure for rethinking the entire issue of the unity of Scripture, specifically of recovering the entire "older testament." In contrast to one-sided liberal accent on "response," the diligent reader will soon discover that, like the whole Bible, its real subject is not man, his devotion, inspiration, or experience, but God as He still creates, elects, redeems, sanctifies, reigns, reveals, judges. And perhaps even in contrast to one-sided conservative accent on "theology" and doctrine, its insistent poetry and doxology is a salutary reminder that its horizons must extend far, far beyond what the saints below can ever grasp, even now merging vertically and "mystically" with the angelic liturgy and pressing on eschatologically to "respond" forever—"together with angels and archangels and all the company of heaven."

PROVERBS

(See the introduction to the wisdom movement, above. The Book of Proverbs is the major Biblical specimen of mainstream wisdom activity, Job, Ecclesiastes, and Canticles being somewhat derivative or marginal. Our concern here is primarily with the isagogics of the *book,* not the cultural-theological movement it represents.)

Development

No doubt, the Book of Proverbs is a collection of collections, even though it is no longer possible to say with certainty how many there were. Perhaps the more ultimate issue is their relation to Solomon. As we noted above, higher criticism is generally no longer quite so skeptical of the Israelite origins of official, professional wisdom in connection with Solomon as it once was. However it still entertains grave doubts about any but the most distant Solomonic connection with the Book of Proverbs—although these have moderated somewhat too.

There seems to be no good reason for such reserve, however, neither culturally nor Biblically. The precise wisdom topics which 1 Kings 5:9-14 credits to Solomon (trees, beasts, birds, reptiles, fish) cannot easily be collated with the contents of Proverbs, but the two are probably not commensurable to begin with. Our most direct evidence for Solomonic involvement in the Book of Proverbs is found in the book's various superscriptions, but even these indicate that we cannot be simplistic about the matter. Both at Prov. 1:1 and 10:1 we have "the proverbs of Solomon." This most likely means that technically the superscription of 1:1 applies only to chaps. 1—9, not the entire book; the possibility cannot be precluded, however, that it was placed at the head of the book at the end of its editorial history and intended to apply to the entire unit. A third superscription appears at 25:1. "These are the proverbs of Solomon which the men of Hezekiah king of Judah copied." The relatively rare Hebrew verb may leave room for some redactional activity, but would suggest indeed quite faithful "copying." In addition, there are the superscriptions to chaps. 30 and 31, each associated with "Massa" in some way (cf. below), but plainly *not* attributed to Solomon.

Are there other preliminary collections in the book besides those with the five headings? Beginning at Prov. 22:17, there is a discernible change of style, and since in the Septuagint we do meet the heading, "Words of the Wise," at this point, and because of the parallels with the Egyptian "Teaching of Amenemope," nearly all scholars agree that a new subcollection begins here (the superscription apparently having fallen out of the Hebrew textual tradition at some point). This would give us at least six previous collections, but it may be that some of them should be further divided. If the "These also are the sayings of the wise" of 24:23 is not a superscription, it does at least suggest a transition or the incorporation of material from another source, possibly a seventh. Also the final two chapters may be a composite of four different chapters (see below on the Septuagint). Other scholars, of couse, dissect the book still further, but it seems safe to say that we have at least six or seven earlier "books of proverbs" behind the canonical Proverbs. Each collection has some of its own characteristic vocabulary, and there is some evidence of influence or dependence of some of them on others.

The Septuagint probably also preserves evidence, at least towards the end of the book, of an earlier period when some sequences in the book were still a bit fluid. Various additions and omissions appear throughout, but the order remains the same until 24:22, when the Septuagint inserts part of the "Words of Agur" (30:1-10), followed by 24:23-24. Next comes the rest of chap. 30 (11-33), followed by the first part of chap. 31 (1-9). Following this are chaps. 25—29 (the Hezekianic collection), and the book concludes with the panegyric on a good wife, like the Hebrew. As usual it is hard to say whether the Septuagintal variation represents a deliberate departure from the "Masoretic" one, but more likely it reproduces an alternate *Hebrew* textual tradition preceding translation.

As noted, there are a number of other variations between the Greek and Hebrew texts of Proverbs, including some material not found in the Hebrew at all. Thus the textual situation is not unlike that we meet in a number of other books, and Qumran probably teaches us that we must take both the Greek and the Hebrew versions seriously.

Thus, the Biblical evidence itself requires the acceptance of strong Solomonic input into most of our canonical collection, but with varying degrees of further transmissional adaptation (all of it remaining under the rubric of special inspiration, of course). Is it possible to determine the date of the fixation of the various collections after leaving their common Solomonic fount? Generally, it is much easier simply to distinguish them (form criticism proper) than it is to arrange them in chronological order. From a purely formal standpoint, it is relatively easy to distinguish some three types of collection: (1) simple concatenation of sayings; (2) arrangement of a number of maxims according to some principle; and (3) longer didactic poems.

Early "form criticism" (a misnomer then) tried to force this logical sequence into an evolutionary straitjacket. Just as in the study of prophecy, it was assumed that simple, brief utterances must be early, with developed, complex ones a sure sign of lateness (and probably also of degeneracy). By that criterion, Prov. 10:1—22:16 was confidently declared the earliest part of the book, and 1—9 the latest (also because of its explicit theologization), with the rest of the material fitted somewhere in between. Archaeological evidence to the contrary from all over the ancient Near East would seem to have knocked that assumption into a "cocked hat," but its influence still lingers. At any rate, there certainly is no objective, external evidence why we should not expect long as well as short wisdom compositions in *any* period!

The early critical viewpoint would concede at most only a few preexilic "roots," and tended to date most of the composition as well as collection of the work in the fifth to third centuries. In contrast, today even liberal scholarship would minimize the degree of postexilic activity, and it is well aware of even *pre*-Solomonic roots of much of the material. Beyond this, little can be said with certainty, except that there would appear to be no good reason why even the final form of the book need be dated much later than the time of the copyists of Hezekiah.

Contents

Even if no isagogical conclusions can be drawn from it, it is convenient to proceed according to the formal criterion of stylistic complexity. First to be considered, them, is Prov. 10:1—22:16, entitled, "The Proverbs of Solomon" (missing in the Septuagint). There is little to be said about them in a general way, other than that we have some 375 examples of simple "sentential wisdom," unrelated and unreflective sayings simply strung together according to no overarching scheme. In chaps. 10—15 especially they tend to be antithetical in form. Only occasionally may one discern use of a content or catchword principle of arrangement, e.g., a few concerned with the "king" in 16:12-15. The existence of the monarchy is also presupposed in 21:1 and 22:11, and there is no reason why Solomon should not be considered the immediate example. Both the everyday practicality of their contents and the classical poetic parallelism usually exhibited (essentially typical of popular sayings of any time or place) suggest roots in "folk-wisdom." Nevertheless, some one-seventh of them have at least indirect reference to "Yahweh," making plain that we err if we try to read them on a purely philological level, divorced from the total canonical context of covenant and *Heilsgeschichte.*

Not much more can be said of the Hezekianic collection in Prov. 25—29. If the superscription at 25:1 means that its contents were first reduced to writing in the time of Hezekiah, it certainly is testimony to the faithfulness and accuracy of the preceding oral tradition. Frequent mention of the king attests to the Solomonic roots of this material. Recent studies have even suggested Egyptian roots for some of it, possibly going back to the twelfth dynasty (early second millennium). But the greater editorial activity of the "men of Hezekiah" over the collectors of 10:1—22:16 is evident in the increased grouping of sayings (e.g., fools in 26:3-12; sluggards in 26:13-16; troublemakers in 26:17-28), a greater use of multiple-line sayings, and less antithetical parallelism (except in chap. 28). Since chaps. 28—29 are more like 10:1—22:16, some have thought of two subcollections involved here too. Some have found significance in the fact that there are 137 proverbs in this collection, while the numerical value of the letters in the Hebrew for "Hezekiah" is 136. This is by no means impossible, because we now know that this "play" with numbers (and sometimes the attachment of all kinds of mystical symbolisms to them) was by no means a late, but a very early Oriental interest.

The collection in Prov. 22:17 ff., however, raises more questions. Not only is the literary structure somewhat more complex (mostly two-or three-verse exhortations with the second or third verse giving the reasons for, or consequences of, good or bad action) but there is the matter of the phenomenal parallelism (see commentaries for details) of much of the section with the "Teaching of Amenemope" (an Egyptian sage who lived sometime in the latter half of the second millennium B.C., thus well before Solomon). Some conservative scholars have been loathe to concede any kind of dependence (forgetting about the radical theological transference in any event), and some critics have thought simplistically of Israelite dependence, often editing the Hebrew severely according to the Egyptian and forgetting the relative freedom with which such material is often transmitted under any circumstances. In spite of efforts to the contrary, there appears to be no reasonable doubt about the technical Egyptian priority, but the ultimate relation of the Egyptian and Biblical contexts is much more complicated. Sometimes the contacts are almost verbatim, while at other points the variation is considerable, and perhaps we should reckon with a common source for both. Especially after 24:22 the divergence may be greater still and, as noted above, may be a subsidiary collection altogether. (Some possible Amenemope parallels have been noted in other parts of the Book of Proverbs too.)

The clearest indication of some internal relation of the two may appear at Prov. 22:20. The Hebrew is at best difficult, but, as elsewhere, seems to be clarified when read alongside its Egyptian counterpart. Most likely, RSV's "thirty sayings" is correct, corresponding to the thirty "houses" or chapters of Amenemope. Without too much difficulty (although some demur), it appears possible to count thirty such discrete sayings in the Hebrew, concluding at 24:22 (cf. above).

Although chaps. 1—9 are clearly the capstone of the complete Proverbs, let us consider first the final two chapters, comprising a sort of double appendix. Perhaps it was originally four appendixes; we noted above the different distribution of the material in the Septuagint. And this is only the beginning of conundrums on the proper translation and interpretation of at least aspects of these chapters.

If "Massa" in both Prov. 30:1 and 31:1 is correctly rendered as a proper noun (the Masoretic pointing is otherwise in both instances), the reference would appear to be to a north Arabian tribe mentioned elsewhere, and indicating a non-Israelite source for these chapters. That interpretation might parallel other Biblical references to "Edomite" wisdom, especially if one could argue, as some have, from the similarity of Job 38:3-38 (whose roots are often sought in the same area) to 30:4 (both in form and vocabulary). On the other hand, *massa* is also a standard Hebrew word for "oracle" (common in the prophets), and that rendition is possible in both cases.

We have no lead on either Agur or Lemuel from any other source, either Biblical or extra-Biblical. The latter was often traditionally taken as a *nom de plume* for Solomon, describing him as "toward/dedicated to God" or the like. The Vulgate does the same at 30:1 with "Agur." The Septuagint apparently recognizes no proper names in any of the four cases, indicating at least one ancient tradition of translation.

Esp. Prov. 30:1b is virtual gibberish as it stands. We cannot survey all possibilities, but there is much to be said for the recent suggestion that it was originally the beginning of the confession continuing in vs. 2-3 (apparently Aramaic, but later not understood as such). Vs. 2-3 may be simply the writer's disarming confession of his innate stupidity compared with "the Holy One." How we proceed depends on how we construe v. 4. It may be the beginning of an orthodox reply (as in the formally parallel Job 38) emphasizing the contrast. On the other hand, if they are still Agur's words, they may be read as the climax of an expression of skepticism or even agnosticism which began at 1b: since no one has ever visited God and returned to report what he found, all speculation about God lacks empirical basis. Then the orthodox reply would begin at v. 5. If so interpreted, the opening verses form a sort of a dialogue as in Job, or a debate with oneself as in Ecclesiastes (especially if the speaker is a king, as is likely) with Agur possibly playing the role of "devil's advocate." Conceivably, even some well-known words of foreign skepticism are quoted here in order to be refuted.

How far Agur's words go is also debated, but from v. 7 on we appear to have a different type of material. Vs. 7-9 are the first of the numerical sayings in the chapter, followed by five more in vs. 15-33. This type of numerical parallelism (in Prov. 6:16-19 and often also found in prophetic poetry) was once considered a late development, but we now know from Ras Shamra that it was an ancient and favorite device of poets. Many other lexicographical affinities with Ugaritic literature are especially evident in this section. The prominence of zoological subjects would suggest possible Solomonic connections also in this chapter (cf. 1 Kings 4:33).

Prov. 31:1-9 is the only example in the book of a type which is very common in extra-Biblical literature: vocational wisdom or career instruction for a young prince or potential king. Hence, the Aramaisms of the section pointing to extra-Israelite provenance may not be accidental. However, in no other known case is it the *mother* who gives the instruction, as here. The contents of the instruction, however, are relatively commonplace as wisdom goes: warnings against loose women and excessive drink, a reminder to attend to social justice, etc.

The final portion of Proverbs (31:10-31) is really an independent poem, the famous acrostic on "a good wife," following upon the previous example of a mother's ideal activity (although it also concludes in the Septuagint, where the sequences are different). Acrostics, too, were once considered a sign of late artificiality, but no one informed would be caught defending that viewpoint any longer. Its completely practical and unromantic perspective views the wife primarily as a prudent manager of her household, making the pericope of dubious applicability to the sentimentalities of "Mother's Day" in another culture. Nevertheless, it is a testimonial to the dignity and status of women in Israelite homes and hence also the importance of the family, as also in their Jewish and Christian successors. Especially with its final accent on the fear of the LORD over the ephemerality of beauty (v. 30), it makes a fitting end to a book which has had so much to say about contentious and immoral women.

Women also play a prominent role in the structure of the first collection of the book, Prov. 1—9. By any other standard, these chapters are the capstone of the entire canonical collection, but apparently positioned first to orient and set the tone for the less explicitly theological material following. Both because of its stylistic and theological development, this collection was once unanimously regarded as the latest section of the entire book. The first feature is perhaps most evident in chap. 2, which is virtually all one long sentence, and the latter climaxes, of course, in the hypostatization of wisdom in chap. 8.

The tendency to date this opening collection late dies hard, but it is increasingly difficult to maintain. Increasingly, it appears that the part of Proverbs which was once dogmatically thought to be the latest is the easiest to defend as early and literally Solomonic! Especially Kayatz from the critical side has recently marshaled massive arguments for quite literal Solomonic authorship on the basis of Egyptian exemplars, especially the parallels between the speeches of the Egyptian divinized *ma'at* concept (cf. above) and the personification of wisdom in this section. Other scholars stress the Canaanite affinities of the section, although there are still those who see it taking shape much later, some still professing to find evidences of Greek influence.

The preface or prologue (Prov. 1:2-7, a single, unbroken sentence) has many formal parallels, and much of the favorite vocabulary of wisdom is clustered here. Between the prologue and the first of the discourses stands the well-known theme of Yahwistic wisdom (1:7). Since it also appears in essence near the end of the collection at 9:10, we may have a species of literary "inclusion" (cf. also 15:33; Job 28:28; and Ps. 111:10). "Beginning," of course, implies not only starting point, but also controlling principle—hermeneutical or epistemological assumption, if you will. Luther well summarizes its obverse: "Educate a devil, and all you have is an educated devil."

In Prov. 1:20-33 we meet the first of many passages where wisdom is personified. This literary feature climaxes in chap. 8 where wisdom has ceased to be a mere personification and become a full-fledged hypostasis or "incarnation" of the deity. At the same time the hypostatization probably indicates the full import of also the earlier passages where formally wisdom was only personified. Both this viewpoint and the terminology of "hypostasis" are hotly contested by many critical scholars, however. Also noteworthy is the plural form of the Hebrew for "wisdom" in 1:20 and a few other passages; either it is an archaic, Phoenician form, or it is a construction (also ancient) analogous to the "plural of majesty" in "Elohim." Wisdom is here presented as stationing herself in the market, inviting busy men to follow. If the picture is not simply literary, it may reflect the actual behavoir of some wisdom teachers, although it sounds more like what we know of some prophets.

Prov. 2:16-19 provide the first of the many warnings against the "loose woman," in apparent contrast to "Lady Wisdom." So also Prov. 5; 6:20-35; 7; and 9:13-18—so prominently that the contrast almost structures all of chaps. 1—9. Two parallel terms are used in the Hebrew, literally the "strange (woman)" and the "foreign/unfamiliar (one)." Both expressions are ambiguous and have occasioned much debate. The explanation that the antithesis is foreign cult or religion, not promiscuity or adultery as such, seems at best one-sided. Not only were the competing Canaanite religions usually of a fertility type, but warnings against affairs with especially foreign women are also present in ancient Egyptian sapiental literature. It may well be that both paganism, especially its fertility rites, and adultery are simultaneously condemned, especially when we note that the outcome of all such liaisons is often described as "death" (e.g., 2:18—19), a way outside of Yahweh's order of life which can ultimately lead only to utter ruin.

Two short poems (Prov. 3:13-18 and 19-20) briefly interrupt the series of didactic addresses. The first one begins and ends with the common wisdom concern (cf. also Ps. 1) with "happiness" (ultimately coalescing with "blessedness," but with wisdom approaching the subject anthropocentrically or from below, as usually). Also significant is the comparison in v. 18 of wisdom with "a tree of life" (also in 11:30; 13:12 and 15:4). The figure has all kinds of parallels in ancient Near Eastern mythology and glyptic art. In Biblical context, however, there is no reason to doubt that it was ultimately nourished by the narrative of Gen. 2—3 (cf. also its use in many Biblical eschatological contexts). The second poem (vs. 19-20) is virtually a little hymn to God the Creator and is especially significant in anticipating the fuller account of wisdom's role in creation in 8:22-31; hence, we may well consider it in the hypostatic sense already here.

Prov. 1—9 begin to move to their climax in chap. 7, as chaps. 7 and 8 in succession offer the major expressions in canonical wisdom of the two aspects of increasingly explicit theological articulation (cf. above). Although in form chap. 7 continues the theme of the rivalry between Lady

Wisdom and the loose woman, the former ("general revelation") is here plainly identified with Torah or "special revelation." The very word "torah" is used in v. 2, and v. 3 appears to be a reference to the use of phylacteries (cf. Deut. 6:8).

By all accounts, Prov. 8, esp. vs. 22-31, is the acme of the Book of Proverbs. The chapter has a clear internal structural unity of three strophes (1-11, 12-21, 22-31) of 22 lines apiece (the number of letters in the Hebrew alphabet). The entire chapter provides the sharpest possible contrast to the frank portrait of the brazen seductress in chap. 7. Especially in the second and third strophes, the first-person personal and possessive pronouns become so prominent that we have a sort of "self-adulation" by wisdom (cf. some of Jesus' discourses in especially John). What wisdom really has to offer is herself—all that really and internally bestows life upon mankind. The third and climactic strophe (vs. 22-36) relates to the preceding by giving a metaphysical or theological explanation for wisdom's empirical superiority. It traces the horizons of wisdom and morality beyond the "phenomenal" into the "noumenal" world, and locates them ultimately in a primordial and cosmic order, the order of creation.

Exegetical debate about vs. 22-36 has long focused on two words, the root *qanah* in v. 22 and *'amon* in v. 30. But the debate is also a hermeneutical one. We have almost forgotten that esp. v. 22 was one of the major foci of the Christological debates of the early church. In so doing, the fathers were merely following the lead of the New Testament, which makes great use of the language and conceptuality of this passage on the primacy of wisdom to describe the primacy (pre-existence, divinity) of Christ (John 1; 1 Cor. 1:24, 30; Col. 1:15-17; 2:3; Heb. 1:3; Rev. 4:11; 22:13). Arian adoptionism appealed to the Septuagint's translation of *qanah* as "created" as a major argument against the Athanasian *homoousios* doctrine of Christ's eternal deity, which they supported by the translation "constituted." For conservatives who still refuse to divorce Old and New Testament, the matter dare not be decided only on a philological basis, as liberals attempt (as usual without definitive results). As here, hermeneutics will often not dictate one precise translation, but the philological option chosen must be demonstrably compatible.

Usually *qanah* in the Old Testament means "get, acquire" and hence often "possess" (a favored translation already in antiquity). In a few passages, however, especially archaic ones (such as Prov. 8 may well be) it denotes "create." Superficially, we now know it well in that sense in Ugaritic literature, especially of Asherah, the Canaanite "creatress of the gods"—except that "creation" in the strict sense is impossible in a mythological context (cf. Gen. 1), so that "procreate" would be more apropos. Apparently the word meant to "get" or "possess" in ways that varied with the context. "Beget" might be a good translation, both compatible with Christology and not reading into the context more specificity than is certainly there.

Other words in the context assume enlarged significance in the light of Christological fulfillment. The very next word in Prov. 8:22 may mean either first in sequence ("beginning") or first in importance (cf. 1:7); the two often coexist, but the parallel with "first" here and the "before" of v. 25 tip the scales toward the priority of the former. Vs. 23-25 continue the birth metaphor, while the "set up" of 23a may imply a royal installation (the same word in Ps. 2:6), thus facilitating the Messianic application.

The second major *crux* is the *'amon* of Prov. 8:30. The two main alternatives are (1) "master workman/foreman," etc., and (2) "little child/ward/nursling," etc. The former has the support of most of the ancient versions and is the most congenial to Christology, but the latter is not without ancient attestation and fits both the birth metaphors of vs. 24-25 and the following context of vs. 30b-31.

In spite of difficulties with details, Prov. 8 remains the major Messianic text of canonical wisdom literature, or, more strictly, its major Christological typology. In greatest possible contrast with the early church (and the New Testament), even conservative Christendom today sometimes appears to have lost the thread of its thought and, therewith, theological entree to virtually the entire wisdom corpus.

After Prov. 8, chap. 9 easily appears anticlimactic. Some critics think of disarrangement of materials, but probably we should view it as recapitulative of much of the contents of this entire collection (chaps. 1—9) and thence of the entire book. The "seven pillars" of wisdom's house (v. 1) has engendered all types of debate and speculation; in some sense it probably implies completeness, that is the cosmic extent of her invitation. In full Scriptural context, it is ultimately not only proper, but necessary, to interpret esp. vs. 1-6 as an invitation to the "Messianic banquet" or Eucharist (cf. Is. 55), a fitting climax to *all* of Proverbs indeed. It stands in explicit contrast to the rival "feast of fools," an initiation banquet to hell itself, with which the chapter ends.

JOB

Few will disagree with Luther's assessment that Job is "magnificent and sublime as no other book of Scripture." Neither will many dispute the judgment that it is also one of the most difficult, one of the most widely commented on, but also least agreed upon. Commentaries tend to get bogged down in a myriad of small problems, especially linguistic ones, and the ordinary reader is discouraged by a highly poetic and seemingly diffuse dialogue in an unfamiliar idiom. Summaries of its "meaning" or

"message" often seem to vary as widely as conceivable. Both he who
forgets that the work is of the wisdom genre and he who tries to read it
out of its canonical context forfeit major keys to its comprehension.

Authorship

The book itself gives no clear indication of who wrote it, when, or
where. Its wisdom classification suggests some wisdom teacher as author,
but that is not very definite. The wide range of allusions suggests that he
was widely traveled and well educated, but that also makes it difficult to
pin him down to any particular locale. It may be helpful to assert that the
"real Job is the author of the book," that is, that there may be a strong
autobiographical element to it (although it is probably as common in
critical circles to stress a reflection of corporate, rather than of individual
suffering). There are Talmudic and Syriac traditions of Mosaic
authorship (and hence in the Peshitta Job follows directly after the
Pentateuch), but they seem worthy of no credence whatsoever, except
possibly as an indication of the antiquity of the composition. We are in no
position to improve upon the counsel of St. Gregory, who while the
barbarians were pounding on the gates of Rome, insisted that the
important thing was to affirm that the Holy Spirit was the real author of
the book.

Historicity

Before one pursues other isagogical questions, perhaps the basic issue
of the book's historicity should be addressed. No other Scripture bears on
the matter, with the possible exception of the allusion to the
"steadfastness of Job" in James 5:11, but since the nature of the reference
is not typological (unlike, for example, Jesus' references to Jonah), its
force would stand, theoretically, even if the referent were fictive.
Nevertheless, the canon of "one, literal sense," and the absence of any
internal indications of figurative significance would surely point
massively in the direction of historicity, as tradition and conservatives
have virtually always assumed (although there are exceptions in the
Talmud and in rabbinic exegesis).

Critical exegesis, not surprisingly, usually assumes the precise
opposite just as self-evidently. Not the least of the reasons is the book's
supernaturalistic framework! The prose prologue and epilogue are often
referred to as the "legend," which the later poet simply used as a
springboard and drawing card for his own writing. At very most, some
small historical core might be conceded because of the apparent antiquity
of the name (see below).

Conservatives, too, are usually disposed to make a slight concession of
another sort, due to the book's unique character. The dialogues are

couched in such a highly artistic and poetic form that it is hard to view them as any kind of exact transcription of actual conversations. Hence, we probably must assume a fair amount of creative literary development of the original exchanges by the author in order to better elucidate their theological significance. Such a concession need militate against neither the basic historicity of the book's report, nor against the special inspiration of the book as we have it (cf. below on textual problems).

Date and Setting of the Narrative

When we ask about date and place, then, we must distinguish between the events themselves and the actual literary composition of the work. No events are mentioned which can be synchronized with any other known history. There are, however, many indications of the high antiquity of the narrative. One of the main ones is the name itself, "Job," or in Hebrew, *Iyob.* Although we know it also from later Arabic sources, it appears as early as c. 2000 in an Egyptian Execration Text in the mimated form of *'ybm,* and thereafter frequently in the second millennium (Amarna, Alalakh, Mari). The other names in the book are also appropriate for a second millennium milieu. This is the general period of the Biblical patriarchs, of course.

The references in Ezek. 14:14 and 20 (which see) to "Noah, Daniel, and Job" as paragons of righteousness also point in the same direction. About the antiquity of Noah, there is no question, and although some conservatives still think the "Daniel" referred to is the canonical figure, it seems much more likely that it is another ancient worthy (so also the reference in Ezek. 28:3 to the king of Tyre or his archetype as "wiser than Daniel"). If so, the fourteenth-century Ugaritic legends (garbled derivatives of earlier history) of a Dan'el would indirectly indicate the antiquity of Job too. Within the texts themselves, the experiences of a King Keret more closely resemble Job's than do Dan'el's.

Certain other possible parallels to the Biblical Job in ancient Near Eastern literature may point in the same direction, although these are generally as notoriously difficult to date (and may well rest on even earlier materials) as the Biblical specimen, and the putative parallelism may be only coincidental. If anything, most of them might indicate the antiquity of the "Job" literary tradition more than of the events themselves. The so-called "Babylonian Job" apparently dates from the latter half of the second millennium and contains harrowing descriptions of an affliction comparable to Job's, but the differences are equally profound, and formally it begins where the Biblical Job leaves off, with *thanksgiving* for recovery from illness (hence its real title, *Ludlul Bel Nemeqi,* "I Will Praise the Lord of Wisdom," that is, Marduk).

Much older, and in some ways formally much more parallel, is an ancient Sumerian tract, describing how a sufferer cajoles his personal god (cf. Job's "umpire," "witness," etc., below) to pity and release him; in a mechanical and almost deterministic sense there is a recognition that all suffering is a result of "sin," but without the profound moral earnestness and even questioning of divine justice, which we find in Job. There is also a so-called "Babylonian Theodicy" an acrostic from about 1,000 (sometimes compared also with Ecclesiastes), which in dialogue or debate form similarly laments the fact that the gods made men sinful (!) but makes no attempt to solve the problem.

Probably even more coincidental are the Egyptian "parallels," "The Protests of the Eloquent Peasant," from the early second millennium, "The Dispute over Suicide," from the late third millennium, and others. Although it fits the modern, existentialist temper well, neither is there any real affinity between Job and the Greek Prometheus (Lindblom on esp. Job 29—31); unlike Aeschylus' famous poem or the Faust of German literature, the Book of Job does not end on a note of defiant challenge to God (although some critics have argued that it originally did).

The various striking parallels in individual detail, as well as the general homology of theme with the Biblical Job, if not simply a coincidence of universal human experience, are all readily explainable as due to the common background of much ancient Near Eastern wisdom literature, not excluding the Biblical (cf. above). At the same time, perhaps nowhere is the extent to which Israel "baptized" its human heritage more obvious than in the case of Job, which emerges as really without extra-Biblical parallel at all. The main point at the moment, however, is the high antiquity of nearly all of the "parallels" cited, enhancing the likelihood that the Biblical exemplar can be similarly dated. If the literary roots of the work are that ancient, the likelihood that the events behind it are as old or older is also increased.

Possibly the strongest evidence for an ancient date is internal. It has long been noted that the work has a clear "patriarchal" flavor to it, both sociologically and religiously. The "extended family" type of social organization points in that direction, as does the offering of sacrifice by the head of the family rather than by an official priesthood. Likewise the rarity of the Tetragrammaton in the book and the preference for the generic terms "Elohim" or the singular, "Eloah"; and even more so for the epithet "Shaddai" (usually translated "Almighty"), which occurs in Job almost twice as often as in all the rest of the Old Testament together. (The general picture on usage of names of God thus coincides remarkably with what we find in Genesis.) Another bit of evidence is the mention of the *qesitah* as a unit of currency, otherwise attested only in Gen. 33:19 and Joshua 24:32.

Some of the evidence adduced above for antiquity might just as well point toward an extra-Israelite (or marginally Israelite) locale for the book's original setting and/or composition. Precisely where, however, depends on the location of the land of "Uz," from which Job in 1:1 is said to hail. Most modern scholars have placed it to Israel's southwest, probably somewhere between Edom and northern Arabia. A few have gone so far as to argue that the book represents an example of Edomite wisdom, but there is no way even to test such an hypothesis, and, at best, it exceeds the evidence. Geographical proximity to Edom might be supported by the apparent placement of Uz in that area in Jer. 25:20 and Lam. 4:21, as well as by the inclusion of Job in 1:3 as among "the people of the east." His vulnerability to raids by "Sabeans" and "Chaldeans" (1:15 and 17) could point in the same direction, although it is more ambiguous. The Psalm of Habakkuk appears to associate the denominative *Eloah* for the deity with Teman, another region in this same general area, whence came Job's "friend," Eliphaz (cf. also Elihu's origins in "Buz," again apparently in this area). In a postscript the LXX plainly situates Uz "in the regions of Idumea and Arabia," but this is apparently connected with its highly questionable (although not impossible) identification of the person of Job with the Jobab, king of Edom, mentioned in Gen. 36:33.

However, some features in the book do not seem to agree with such a southern location of "Uz." A few scholars have tried to locate it much farther north (near Antioch or Palmyra, even northern Mesopotamia), but the Hauran, south of Damascus, or perhaps northern Gilead is much more likely. Josephus, as well as both Christian and Moslem traditions, can be adduced in support of this location. The indications of extensive farmlands in chap. 1 especially might point to more populous areas such as these. The animals of Job 40—41, as well as other references to reeds or papyrus (cf. 8:11 and 40:21), also suggest better watered areas, possibly even swamps or river mouths. Sarna has recently stumped for a Canaanite wisdom setting, but specific parallels again are wanting.

Language

Job's geographical location, however, can scarcely be investigated apart from consideration of the language of the book, although, as noted above, the latter may speak only to the question of literary composition. In any event, the language of the book poses every bit as currently insuperable and hence highly debated a problem as those of its date and location. Job contains the largest number of *hapax legomena* of any Old Testament book (about 100 of them), and, as a cursory check of nearly any Hebrew lexicon will demonstrate, it often uses otherwise familiar words in unusual senses. Albright once even estimated that as much as 45 percent of the book's vocabulary is of less than certain meaning. The problems are morphological and syntactic as well as lexical. Sometimes they may be textual as well (see below), although critics today are generally much more hesitant to seek that way out than they once were. A certain affinity with Ps. 139 (also probably a wisdom product) has long been noted, but we know little of its provenance either. Rarely is the gist entirely obscure, but surety about the precise nuances quite regularly eludes us, as the extensive discussions in the commentaries often make plain.

Neither is there any agreement about what accounts for this circumstance. An Edomite dialect has often been suggested, but, again, we know too little of that language to check the hypothesis out. The Ras Shamra discoveries have enabled satisfactory explanation of many linguistic features (see especially Pope's commentary), as well as enhancing the likelihood of ancient composition. Nevertheless, as a whole, the style of the work is not very close to that of the Ugaritic epics, and hence the talk is more of "northwest Semitic" or of Phoenician of the Amarna period. The problem is that the more we seek an explanation in that direction, the less contact we can maintain with the "sons of the east" (unless the locale of the events and of the book's composition are disparate). Hence, perhaps a sort of compromise, the Hauran or northern Transjordan comes into consideration again, as an area whose dialect might well show influence from many directions. The latter explanation has in its favor its easier ability to account for the apparently strong Aramaic coloration of the Hebrew of Job, especially (perhaps) in the Elihu speeches (a major example is the preference of -in over -im as the masculine plural ending).

Because none of these hypotheses account for everything, however, some have attempted the explanation that Job is translation Hebrew, but still reflecting many features of the mother tongue. Aramaic and Arabic have been major candidates. The Israeli scholar, Tur-Sinai, has tried to demonstrate the former, arguing that much of the original Aramaic did not need to be translated because the translation was made at a time when Aramaic itself was becoming increasingly familiar to the entire ancient Near East. Guillaume (pursuing a suggestion made already by Ibn Ezra in the Middle Ages) has argued just as strongly for an Arabic original, and has tried to buttress his proposal by a very ingenious theory about the circumstances of the book's composition (the aftermath of Nabonidus' invasion of Tema.) These explanations, however, have not convinced very many scholars either, so we end up with the same question mark with which we began.

Date of Composition

Can we, then, reach any conclusions at all about the date of the book's composition (prescinding for the moment from the question of the date of the events themselves)? Here one must cast a wider net for evidence, but the yield is still insufficient to establish any more of a consensus than on the previous questions. No doubt, partly because it is of the "wisdom" genre, Job makes clear reference to neither historical events nor particular theological formulations in a way which will facilitate dating. Some four different periods still have their defenders: (1) that of the patriarchs; (2) of Solomon; (3) of the late monarchy; and (4) during or after the Exile.

Nineteenth-century critics tended to favor a seventh-century origin, and many thought especially of the long reign of Manasseh, when evil and suffering should have flourished. At least one critic tried to date the work as late as the second century on the grounds that Job 15:20 ff. referred to Alexander Jannaeus. A fifth- or sixth-century date, however, is probably the critical center of gravity, although the grounds for the opinion vary.

Far and away the preponderance of the modern, especially critical opinion prefers the third or fourth alternative. A wide contemporary understanding views the book as reflecting the trauma of the Babylonian Exile, possibly even as a "parable" of the righteous nation in affliction. Allegedly, exilic and postexilic experiences had thrown classical wisdom with its facile belief in a cosmic order and reward or retribution, depending upon response, into a grave crisis. If so, it is very strange that no clear reflection of that catastrophe is evident in the book. Some critics thought that the book was influenced by Jeremiah's laments (so particularly Steinmueller) and, in turn, itself influenced "Deutero-Isaiah," perhaps especially his portrait of the Suffering Servant. The conservative, of course, cannot accept the latter part of the statement, because he believes that Isaiah himself wrote also chaps. 40—66 of his book in the *eighth* century, and he finds it gratifying that even so radical a critic as R. H. Pfeiffer has made a strong case for the priority of Job over "Deutero-Isaiah."

Many other arguments for so late a date appear to depend on similar evolutionistic arguments in a circle. These appeal to its allegedly "advanced" theology, especially with respect to its wrestling with the problem of suffering, as though monotheism were not present in Israel earlier, or as though Israel or humanity had never confronted that issue earlier. As long as almost the entire wisdom movement in Israel was thought to be a postexilic phenomenon, it almost followed necessarily that Job had to be composed somewhere in that context. It still is widely assumed that Job (like Ecclesiastes, allegedly to an ever greater degree) is largely protest against the allegedly mechanical and legalistic "deuteronomic" doctrines of reward and punishment—but, if Deuteronomy is Mosaic and if the "legalism" is a figment of critical imagination, that argument loses all cogency, at least as a criterion for dating. Similarly with the fact that the problem of suffering is dealt with on an individual instead of simply corporate terms: although the Exile undoubtedly did highlight individual predicaments and accountability, there is ample evidence, both within and without the Bible, that it was anything but a *novum* in the seventh century or later (cf. on Jeremiah and Ezekiel).

Closely related is the argument that although already thinking individualistically, Job witnesses to a time before personal immortality was accepted in Israel (cf. on Job 19). That entire issue cannot be discussed here, but there is ample evidence also of that belief in Israel as well as in its environs in the earliest times, although it undeniably became more prominent in later periods. If we may turn the tables and argue from parallels, the great interest Egyptian wisdom evinces in the maintenance of the mortuary cult at least establishes the possible affinity of ancient wisdom with hope of immortality.

Especially the appearance of *"the* Satan" in the prologue has encouraged some critics to posit Persian influence on the book, and date it as late as the fifth or even fourth century. Allegedly, the use of the definite article with "Satan" should align Job with a similar usage in Zech. 3, but a little before the anarthrous usage in 1 Chron. 21. We lack evidence to challenge that bit of neat evolutionism directly, but the prologue's general picture of the heavenly courtroom appears in the earliest Biblical strata by any reckoning (cf. Gen. 6; Deut. 32 and 33; 1 Kings 22; and repeatedly in the prophets). In fact the appearance of the comparable pagan idea of the "assembly of the gods" already in second millennium texts in both Canaan and Mesopotamia establishes the likelihood that the Biblical "mutant" of this picture in the prologue of Job was as ancient as many other features of the book.

Hence, in sum, although there is no reason why conservatives need to reject the possibility of an exilic or postexilic date for the present form of the Book of Job (and some of them do not reject it), the majority probably favor a somewhat earlier date. Part of the reason, no doubt, is that conservatives put greater store by the historicity of the book's narrative and favor a lesser interval between the events and their narration. The possibility of a late recension of an essentially earlier work must also be considered, but easily one only confounds confusion by such speculations.

So how much earlier should we go in search of a most likely date? In both Jewish and Christian circles it once was common to think of an actual patriarchal date of composition (e.g., Eusebius). At least in its essence, we are still in no position to dismiss that possibility, but we still know too little of the language and other aspects of the culture of that period even to test this alternative thoroughly.

Already Gregory of Nazianzus in the fourth century A. D. suggested the age of Solomon as the most likely period of composition; he was seconded by Luther, and probably the majority of modern conservative scholars would concur, as do we. (So, e.g., Keil, Delitzsch, Young, Unger, and Andersen, the latter suggesting in addition a final, normative form by the time of Josiah, and in an Israelite, i.e., northern Gilead, rather than a Judean ambience.) The preference for this period pivots on the traditional association of Solomon with wisdom in general. The cosmopolitan atmosphere of the Book of Job well fits that period, as does also the scholarly "leisure" presumably necessary to produce a work of this sort.

Nevertheless, it must be conceded that the final word has by no means been spoken on this question, and there is no prospect of a definitive answer until or unless we benefit from a windfall of information far beyond what we presently possess. Fortunately, not only is this sort of isagogical question not a theological issue, but the wisdom milieu of the book (with its primary concern with universals) also makes it less germane to the understanding of this work than of many others.

Literary Classification

If the Book of Job was not written at essentially the same time as the events and dialogues it narrates, it can scarcely be a simple transcript, as we noted above. Inevitably, then, the "form-critical" question (in its proper and neutral sense) arises as to the genre of material we have. Delitzsch was apparently the first in modern times to address that question, and his suggestion, following Theodore of Mopsuestia in the fourth century, was that the book was a "drama" (which would not need to imply any basic historical inaccuracy). Some have followed Delitzsch, but generally that particular answer meets with little favor today, because drama (at least in any precise sense) appears never to have penetrated the ancient Near East. Attempts at comparisons with other types of classical literatures, tragedies, epics, even Plato's dialogues, have generally proved no more convincing, although points of contact can be established with nearly all of them. Hence, taken as a whole, it appears best to admit with many scholars that from a literary standpoint the work is *sui generis*. That, of course, is simply another way of saying what is virtually never challenged, namely, that from a literary standpoint alone, Job is one of the unique masterpieces of world literature.

Modern form criticism has probably been more interested in the classification of the individual components of the book. In this respect it is virtually an anthology of all Old Testament types, with ample parallels also outside of Israel. The sapiental character of the prologue is evident in its terminology: Job as "blameless and upright" (cf. below), who "feared God and turned away from evil"; his wife as one of the "foolish women," etc. The casting of the entire book into the form of a didactic narrative also appears to be of wisdom inspiration. Wisdom themes are obvious also in Job's refusal to speak rashly, the emphasis on the efficacy of Job's prayer (42:7-9), and, of course, "retribution." Many parts of the poetic section of the book can be explained as a sort of dramatization of the genre of the "individual lament." This helps explain the many affinities with the Psalter that are so evident at points. Much of the book has an obvious legal or forensic tone, as Job, in effect, accuses God of breach of contract. Hence, courtroom analogies may explain much, and if we accent the ultimate unity of law and wisdom, one may even think of the "covenant lawsuit" form, so often employed by the prophets. Job's great "negative confession" (plea of innocence) in chap. 31 has prominent parallels in both Egyptian and Babylonian literature. Those cultures also provide many examples of the *Streitgespräch* or disputation which many see as a likely formal analogy to the book; these usually were structured along the lines of: (a) mythological introduction, (b) debate between two friends; and (c) divine resolution of the issue. It seems plausible that some wisdom disputational material has been used in Job, but the further appropriateness of the parallel is itself hotly disputed.

Outline and Unity

The outline of the Book of Job is unusually distinct. (See below for further comment on details.) Chaps. 1—2 form what is commonly referred to as the "prose prologue," relating the familiar account of how Job is deprived of virtually all his earthly possessions in order to test the Satan's suspicion that Job's virtue is only calculated to curry divine favor. Until the epilogue in 42:7 ff., the rest or body of the book is couched in poetry. First come the three cycles or "rounds" of speeches (3—14, 15—21 and 22—27), in which the three "friends," Eliphaz, Bildad, and Zophar, accuse Job with increasing acridity, and he even more spiritedly defends himself. Chap. 28 appears to be an interlude (cf. below)—a magnificent meditation on the inscrutability of divine wisdom. In the monologue of chaps. 29—31 Job concludes his own defense and challenges God a final time to defend Himself. Before God replies, there intervene the Elihu speeches. The climactic dialogue, finally between Job and God Himself, appears in doublet form: God speaks in 38:1—40:2, and Job repents in 40:3-5, followed by a second divine discourse in 40:6—41:26 and a second submission in 42:1-6. The book closes with a brief prose epilogue (matching the prologue in which the three friends are reprimanded, while Job is commended and restored.

This well-rounded structure should constitute strong prima facie evidence for the unity of the entire book. Inevitably, however, critics are rarely satisfied with that, and hence usually challenge the "genuineness" of many parts of the book and/or posit a complicated tradition-history before it achieved its present and final form. Inevitably also, those judgments are often bound up with interpretative viewpoints. Conservatives would have few difficulties with such speculations if it were *only* a matter of hypotheses about the *pre*canonical stage of the book, particularly if only one author were involved, but rarely is the procedure so innocent.

First of all, it is almost universally argued in critical circles that the original "Job" consisted basically of the present prologue and epilogue (chaps. 1—2 and 42:7-17). Generally (following Duhm and Wellhausen) this is thought to have been an old folktale, on to which the later poet grafted his lofty lucubrations. Commonly, it is supposed that the original tale had nothing at all to do with the problem of unmerited suffering, but that the poet deliberately chose a traditional figure of unassailable uprightness in order better to attack the orthodox doctrine of retribution. The most immediate objection, namely that this "framework" (as it is often called) is scarcely a complete story by itself and that the epilogue even assumes some dialogue with the friends which the prologue had not mentioned, is usually countered by the assertion that the original folkloristic core was simply dropped by the poet when he substituted his own "dialogs." *Mutatis mutandis,* it is not unthinkable to the conservative that the author of the present Job might have proceeded in such a fashion, but such procedure need not militate against the unity of the work, in fact may be a powerful argument for it.

At the same time, there is no reason why the same author should not have *composed* in both prose and poetry (this obvious difference in form usually being adduced as the major evidence to the contrary). Certainly, no great literary figure would have any difficulty in switching back and forth between the two types (and, obviously, the poetry contains a great number of subtypes, as we have noted). Most of the difference in the vocabulary of the prose and poetic sections is a simple corollary of the two different idioms, and, conversely, some scholars have also demonstrated a goodly number of linguistic affinities linking the two sections. Furthermore, it appears to be a common Biblical pattern to cast especially speeches into poetry (so commonly in the Biblical histories), and even when they are presently in prose form many scholars think they can detect an original poetic substratum. The same thing can be asserted of much extra-Biblical literature in the ancient Orient; in fact, almost precise parallels to Job's poetry within a prose framework can be cited (e.g., the Egyptian, "Tale of the Eloquent Peasant," and the obverse in the Babylonian Code of Hammurabi).

Critics also claim to have sniffed out a number of inconsistencies or contradictions between the prose framework and the poetic body of the book. Thus it is often pointed out that "the Satan" who figures so prominently in the prologue never reappears after chap. 2; this objection, however, appears to overlook the point of the unified work, namely, that the reader should know the supernatural occasion for Job's misfortunes, which, as always, is hidden from the eyes of the human participants. Somewhat similarly, some scholars profess to miss Job's termagant wife after chap. 2, but one can only ask how else Job might have obtained children again, as the epilogue tells us he did! Different "answers" to the problem of suffering appear in different parts of the book, but this surely *is* part of the unified work's intent (cf. below).

It has long been noted that the Tetragrammaton predominates in the prose portions of the book, in contrast to the preference for not only "El" and "Elohim," but also the rarer "Eloah" and "Shaddai" in the poetry. Most of such variation can readily be attributed, however, to artistic choice in the two different idioms. It must be noted, however, that the distribution is not exclusive in either direction; we meet "Elohim" at times in Job 1—2, and "Yahweh" in 19:9; 28:28; and in chaps. 38—43. The use of "Shaddai" appears to be associated especially with the patriarchal age (cf. on Genesis), and may well reflect a patriarchal substratum to the poetry (fully as ancient as the prose), regardless of when it was composed in its present form. (Usage also suggests that "Shaddai" may have been especially associated with divine judgment, either blessing or cursing, and, if so, one perceives a further reason why this title is so prominent in the dialogue; cf. esp. 27:2.) The singular use of the singular form, "Eloah," cannot be so readily explained, but we lack context to construe it, as some do, as indicative of an extra-Israelite provenance of the work (cf. above).

Perhaps more profoundly, the difference in Job's temper in the prologue and the dialogue is often pointed to. It must be admitted that, at first blush, the traditional portrait of Job as "patient" and submissive appears to apply only to the prologue, whereas in the dialogue he appears querulous, defiant, and rebellious. The problem is probably more in the common one-sidedness of the depiction of Job as "patient" than in the narrative itself, because the radical change in Job's mood seems amply explained by his sudden deprivation; silence or resignation in its face would have signaled pagan fatalism (often apparent in extra-Israelite "wisdom") rather than the attitudes nurtured by Biblical revelation.

Similarly, it is often objected that the "materialistic" solution of the epilogue is at variance with the "spiritual" sublimity of the poems, or, stated differently, that the almost *deus ex machina* manner in which the epilogue illustrates the orthodox dogma of a *quid pro quo* retribution clashes with the sustained concern of the dialogue to demolish it. No doubt, this concern penetrates to the very heart of the meaning and interpretation of the entire book, if assumed to be a unity. Suffice it to say here that, in our conviction, the epilogue offers not so much a "solution" as a simple conclusion, furthermore that much of the point of the entire book is to assert that the much maligned "orthodox dogma of retribution" is not so much wrong as inadequate as a total explanation of the phenomenon of evil and suffering, especially if it is applied in a mechanical, legalistic fashion.

In the view of many tradition-critics the first and major poetic supplementation of the framework consisted in the dialogue (Job 3—31), and (apart from a host of minutiae) their essential unity has never been seriously questioned. The only serious problem here arises in the third cycle of speeches (chaps. 22—27), where the Bildad speech is curiously short (only five verses, 25:1-6), the expected Zophar speech does not materialize at all, and, above all, Job in an extraordinarily long speech (26—31), often appears to endorse the friends' viewpoint which he had been repudiating all along (24:18-24; 26:5-14; 27:13-23). Since Job's speech here is most similar to Bildad's usual line, many critics assume that, among other things, one of his speeches was deliberately transferred to Job by later editors or traditionists in order to neutralize Job's apparent attacks upon orthodoxy by confusing the issue. Commentators have proposed many reconstructions of the presumed original of these chapters especially in order to try to recover the "lost" speech of Zophar (cf. Snaith's study), but no consensus has emerged.

It would appear, however, that liberalism's own antipathy to the "orthodox dogma of retribution" is the major problem here, as a result of which virtually the entire book is evaluated on that, too narrow a basis. It seems entirely plausible to suppose that the progressive shortening of the speeches and final omission of Zophar's altogether is a deliberate device to signal that the three friends have run out of steam, and simply have nothing more to say. Neither need Job be understood as contradicting himself, if it is not dogmatically assumed that he cannot endorse the traditional dogma of retribution at all. Without entering into exegetical minutiae, it may be asserted that in these chapters Job, indeed, affirms the divine visitation upon evildoers every bit as stoutly as the friends have done hitherto. What he does, however, is to deny just as stoutly that the principle is applicable in his case, and, furthermore, he appears to suggest that its most immediate applicability might be to his own tormentors (possibly even quoting their own words against themselves). Not only is this, then, thoroughly congruent with Job's position in general, but it also neatly forecasts the book's own denouement in the epilogue.

The common critical assumption that the first major stage in poetic expansion of the prose framework consisted of the dialogues usually puts great weight on Job 31:40b ("The words of Job are ended"). There is no good reason why that sentence cannot be construed differently, but, if those critics are correct, it would mean that at this stage of the book, God was not represented as speaking at all, but simply intervened in the epilogue to express His favorable verdict on behalf of Job (42:7a must then be elided as redactional). Because someone was uncomfortable with the idea that God Himself never participated in the debate, it is sometimes thought that the next major addition to the book consisted essentially of the Yahweh speeches in chaps. 38:1—42:6. Many, however, feel that this interpolation radically altered the character of the entire book, because of the obvious fact that God seems to be entirely oblivious to the terms on which Job had demanded a hearing. And, no doubt, in the interpretation of these speeches, we either have an alien element in the book, one of many "solutions" to the problem of human suffering offered by the various circles who contributed to it, or we have a major key to the interpretation of the entire corpus. Since we believe the latter to be the case, further exposition of the Yahweh speeches is best reserved until below.

Higher criticism often does not rest with this, however, and the Yahweh speeches themselves (whether or not they are regarded as later additions on the whole) often come under the knife. Many are disturbed by the fact that we have *two* speeches by God (Job 38:1—40:2 and 40:6—41:34), each followed by a speech of submission or "repentance" by Job (40:3-5 and 42:1-6). Instead of being an example of a "doublet," however (cf. frequently in Pentateuchal source criticism), the typical Oriental expansiveness that we now know well also from extra-Biblical literature, and/or repetition for the sake of emphasis, will suffice to explain the repetition. Possibly (although we think unlikely; cf. below) Job's response to Yahweh's first speech is to be understood as *only* a submission or grudging resignation to destiny, with genuine repentance not forthcoming until after another lecture. It is also possible (but also in our view, unlikely) that the first speech was concerned to answer Job's challenge to God's authority, while the second went further in eliciting a retraction also of Job's charge of divine injustice.

Some critics also express doubts about the two long discourses on the monsters Behemoth (Job 40:15-24) and Leviathan (chap. 41), either judging them redundant and tedious, or simply viewing them as intrusive. Other critics, however, rightly regard them as climactic compositions in the context, "knockout blows," if you will, which finally elicit Job's definitive capitulation.

Critics who reject the monster-speeches usually consider them to be independent compositions which were later fitted into their present context quite carelessly and inappropriately. A much wider critical consensus consigns chap. 28, the magnificent poem on the inscrutability of divine wisdom, to the same fate. Some view it merely as an independent piece by the same author, others as stemming from a different hand altogether. It is commonly argued that its theme anticipates God's speeches, almost rendering them anticlimactic, and that such dispassionate, philosophical talk ill accords with the more frenzied tone of Job's surrounding speech.

More than one line of defense is possible. Any interpretation will ultimately be of a piece with the solution chosen for the other problems surrounding the third cycle of dialogue (cf. above). If chap. 27 is understood as Job's turning of the tables on his own accusers (they, not he, are liable to retribution), chap. 28 may be taken as its sequel and conclusion: man is capable of phenomenal wisdom (as they themselves had demonstrated by telling part of the truth) indeed, but when it comes to ultimate issues, man must defer to the Creator (as they have not). Others, however, while viewing the poem as "genuine" do not take it, as intended, to be Job's own speech (remember that Hebrew has no quotation marks). Rather, it is understood as the author's own commentary, a sort of "coda" (Andersen) between the main dialogue and Job's concluding oration. As such by showing their necessity, it indeed anticipates, as on a sort of first plateau, the Yahweh speeches and the point of the entire book.

One final major section of the book, the authenticity of which is often called into question, is the Elihu speeches (Job 32—37). Scholarly opinion, however, varies widely, both on this main question, as well as on the various supporting arguments. Commonly, however, the theory is advanced that, unlike Job 28 and the monster-speeches, this disquisition was deliberately composed as a later addition to the book by someone who was disquieted by what he took to be Job's blasphemous accusations against God, and thus essayed a sort of theodicy. More mildly, others view "Elihu" as the author's third draft, as his own thought progressed.

A major argument against genuineness is the lack of any mention of Elihu, either before or after. It is especially pointed out that Elihu does not even share in the three friends' reprobation in the epilogue, although he seconds many of their arguments. However, the fact that, unlike the earlier dialogues, Elihu's discourses (probably four in all) teem with allusions and quotations from virtually all parts of the earlier chapters suggest strongly that he had been present throughout, just as 32:2-4 asserts, even if unmentioned. If so, the apparent pomposity and turgidity of his speeches can be viewed in better light as a human appraisal of the dialogues before Yahweh appears with the definitive verdict. Thus, even though Elihu claims to have the definitive solution to the dialogue, he really remains only an interested bystander and is more fittingly ignored by God than rebuked. Some critics also amass arguments for the alleged stylistic and theological inferiority of Elihu's discourses, but these are canceled out by counterarguments from other critics. Elihu does have his own contribution to make (see below), and even the allegedly greater Aramaic cast of his language appears to be a subjective judgment (or, if true, there is no reason why it might not reflect actual historical circumstance and/or be part of the author's endeavor to endow Elihu with individuality).

Text Criticism

Not unrelated to the tradition-critical problem of the book is the much more palpable text-critical one. Of course, because of the singularity of its language (cf. above) it is scarcely surprising that Job has more than its share of textual problems of the more ordinary sort. The variations in all the versions (see especially Dhorme's commentary) as well as the perplexities often evinced by the Masoretes testify to the antiquity of the problem, and rarely is the modern scholar in a position to do more than add one more opinion to the series. However, in addition, Job is one of those books where the LXX often differs quite radically from MT, mostly in the direction of greater brevity, although sometimes apparently displaying considerable freedom. LXX is some 400 lines or one-sixth shorter than MT, resulting in a text-critical problem similar to, although not quite so severe as, that in Jeremiah (which see). As usual, nothing that can really be called substantial is at stake, and in the light of present evidence there is simply no way of knowing for sure whether the autograph was abbreviated in the Masoretic tradition or abbreviated in the Septuagintal one. All other things being equal, the usual functional presumption is that of Masoretic superiority, and it is interesting to note that assumption already apparent in Origen's *Hexapla,* where portions of the Hebrew text missing in the Septuagint were supplied from Theodotion's translation.

Striking new evidence on the question has recently come from Qumran, where two fragments of a Targum on the Book of Job have been found, dating to the time of Christ (and thus the earliest Targum known). While in general it appears to support MT, there are other times when it favors LXX, and sometimes goes its own way. Thus, it renders a very mixed verdict and, at this stage of our knowledge at least, really does not help at all in reaching a solution. It must also be noted that the Targum supports the evidence of all the ancient texts on the order of Job 24—31, so that, at best, any putative dislocations there would have had to arise at a far earlier date.

Contents

We now turn to a survey and investigation of highlights of the book as it stands. More must not be read into the characterization of Job as "blameless and upright" (Job 1:1; 1:8) than is intended. The words do not signify absolute moral perfection but are simply the type of empirical observation characteristic of wisdom. The immediate context, however, also suggests a broader context, *coram Deo,* in which the meaning, "forgiven, justified" would not be totally wrong, although we can hardly expect wisdom to use the more technical theological language.

The real setting of the book is described in Job 1:6 ff., in the heavenly throneroom or courtroom where God rules in conjunction with the "sons of God," later known as "angels" (the terminology changes, the basic concept does not, *pace* many evolutionistic critics). This is the same setting in which the prophets often receive their calls or other oracles (cf. esp. 1 Kings 22), and we meet it often elsewhere in Scripture.

Technically, no doubt, "the satan" here is a title, not a personal name, but it is little more than a technicality: the difference from the later "Satan" is, quite literally, only nominal! The name means "adversary" or perhaps "prosecuting attorney," and the picture here plainly is not simply that of an upholder of justice, but of an officious and ambitious barrister who is always searching for excuses to display his legal talents. The fact that God questions "the satan" may indicate that, although he plainly was not barred, his presence among the "sons of God" was not as regular as most commentators assume.

In a way, then, the real debate or contest in the book is between God and Satan. The issue is the profoundly Biblical one whether or not God is served for His own sake, out of sheer gratitude and loyalty, or whether, as in Satan's opinion, every man has his price. "God, indeed, tempts no one," but plainly in the prologue God permits a testing of Job, and in a sense even initiates it (Job 1:8), and this is surely *part* of the message of the book. Therewith the stage is set for the entire book, although it is not given to man to know the precise supernatural dimensions of his suffering. There is more to be said about the "mystery of iniquity," of course, which the book proceeds to do at some length, but nothing can be said profitably apart from this dimension of transcendence.

Job's sublime benediction at the conclusion of the first test (1:21) in many ways anticipates the book's conclusion; it is not to be read as mere resignation or fatalism. Technically, no doubt, it has verbal roots in widespread comparisons between the mother's womb and "Mother Earth" or *magna mater* (microcosm and macrocosm), but such mythological background is obviously no longer functional here (cf. Ps. 139:13; Ecclus. 40:1). The rest of the book teems with familiar ex-mythological imagery (cf. Pope).

The disease with which Job is afflicted in Satan's second and more drastic test cannot be precisely identified. The Hebrew *shechin* is always used of skin diseases, but we cannot be more definite. Earlier commentators usually thought of a type of leprosy, while moderns have preferred boils or smallpox. The question is not important, except for the disproportionate amount of attention it has sometimes attracted.

In 2:9 Job's wife (traditionally known as "Dinah") makes her only appearance. She is scarcely the ideal "helpmeet for him," but she does obviously again become the mother of his children in the restoration at the end of the book. The book itself makes no more of her behavior, but her exemplification of Eve's primordial role as temptress did not escape ancient commentators, sometimes spilling over into virtual misogyny. Thus, to the question why Satan spared Job's wife, Chrysostom answered that it was because she was "the devil's best scourge." Similarly, Augustine's *diaboli adjutrix* and Calvin's *organum Satani*. Apparently only more modern commentators have attempted to excuse her shrewishness as a reflex of love for her husband.

The "Dialogues"

We shall make no attempt to summarize the sequence of the dialogues. In fact, it probably is misleading to attempt to do so, at least if one thinks in any strict terms of a "dialogue," or, even more so, of a "debate." Although Job and the three friends alternate in speaking, they really do not "answer" each other and often do not even appear to be speaking to each other. In fact, "answer" regularly in Job follows Hebraic idiom (and thence often reflected also in the New Testament) in implying not so much response to conversation as the beginning of discourse, regardless of the context. We probably understand them best if we assume that the speakers do *not* primarily seek to convince each other, but *us,* that is the unseen audience of listeners or readers (and perhaps in a more ultimate sense, God Himself). It may be, as some commentators propose, that the ancient Oriental genre of "contest literature" is technically our most helpful analogy. In modern terms, one might better think of an oratory contest than of a "debate." The prize goes to him who makes the best speech, not to him who has best rebutted an opponent. Each speech, then, must be considered primarily as a self-contained unit, with only minimal direct relation to those preceding and following. Evidently, the tone becomes more acrimonious as the "dialogue" ensues, but even that judgment may follow from the false assumption of a "debate."

Neither is it really possible to sustain any clear-cut distinction between the individual themes of the three friends. Indeed, in a sense, the "orthodox dogma of retribution" underlies all that they say (Job's plight *must* be a result of something he has done), but that alone is too narrow a summary, and by overemphasis on it, critics betray their own distaste for "orthodoxy" and an overhasty attempt to fit Job into some evolutionistic scheme. (Von Rad is doubtless correct in characterizing it as really a "dogma of interpreters.") Eliphaz, the "dean" of the group, gives classical and beautiful expression to it at times (e.g., Job 4:12 ff; 5:17 ff., 22:21 ff.).

All of them also counsel the conventional cultic remedy, to "seek" God (e.g., 5:8, 8:5) in prayer, especially lament, after which the priest would normally declare divine absolution ("righteousness"), and the suppliant would further respond in a psalm and sacrifice of thanksgiving in fulfillment of the vow made in connection with the lament.

In the course of their "lectures" on the problem of evil and suffering, they expound virtually every "solution" there is: (a) that "confession is good for the soul," even if one is aware of no particular sins, for no one is perfect; (b) the disciplinary and probationary value of suffering; (c) its frequently temporary and sometimes only apparent character; (d) its inevitability ("Into each life some rain must fall"); (e) its necessarily mysterious and inscrutable character—and probably many more. Every reader will recognize in their speeches not only universal, human "wisdom" on the subject, but many accents which the Bible or "special revelation" affirms elsewhere in more specifically theological dimension.

Hence, it is important to stress that the friends can virtually never be faulted for what they say *per se*. In fact, the book no doubt wishes to reaffirm the truth of what they say—as far as it goes. Taken out of context, their arguments are often more cogent than Job's, and if it were simply a matter of a human panel of judges, they would probably win over Job hands down. They are ultimately faulted because unmindful of what the reader knows on the basis of the prologue they have virtually made God a prisoner of His own "law," have transmuted orthodoxy into orthodox*ism*, and forgotten that the ultimate verdict between man and God is a relational one, finally transcending laws and codes altogether.

Similar considerations are necessary to understand Job's part of the "dialogue." Like anyone in the throes of deep distress, Job is not concerned to challenge any dogma or theory of suffering, but to make sense out of his own experience in the light of what he knew on the basis of revelation.

(As in most wisdom literature, the detailed contents of that revelation receive little expression, but one is bound to misunderstand the book without the presupposition.) Since he also knows that no *quid pro quo* concept of retribution can explain his plight, he demands a "friendly God" again (Luther). God has not only become *absconditus,* but the enemy. With a *rational* God like Yahweh, one could not even take refuge in some unknown, unconscious sins. Neither can Job proclaim his own innocence, that is, "justify himself," but a forensic pronouncement from on high is mandatory. The issue is that of "Yahweh *pro me*" (von Rad). Since God does not respond in good faith to Job's confession according to His word, He accuses God of being an arbitrary, malicious despot. Since he currently experiences God as an enemy, even a brutish and monstrous one, his outcries, sometimes approaching the blasphemous, are understandable, even if not exemplary. (No doubt, to a certain extent they represent an Oriental tradition, ancient as well as modern, of venting emotions which tend to be frowned on in Western cultures.) From a literary standpoint alone, some incomparably beautiful meditations on the desirability of the peace and repose of death appear. Thus Job 3:16-19 (after a lament very similar to some of Jeremiah's); chap. 7 (with parallels in Ps. 8); and perhaps especially chap. 14 (cf. below). One should note that Job never decries either the material losses of chap. 1 or the sickness of chap. 2, but concerns himself throughout exclusively with the real issue, his relationship with God.

Job's "Redeemer"

As Job fights his way "out of the depths" and strives to regain his spiritual equilibrium, it is widely recognized that his famous "I know that my Redeemer lives" declamation of 19:25 ff. is one of the high points. What is not so well known and widely overlooked is the fact that that passage is only a climactic expression of a motif which surfaces at least three other times in the book. We first meet the theme with the *mokhiach* of 9:33 (often translated "umpire"). Job has been depicting God as virtually a big bully, before whom he never stands a chance. Even if he should take God to court, it would mean only another display of "might makes right" procedure. (Note the ex-mythological imagery used to describe God's superior power: trampling the back of the defeated sea-god Yam (Job 9:8; cf. 7:12) and overwhelming "the helpers of Rahab" (9:13; cf. 26:12; Ps. 89:11; and Is. 51:9). Hence, all Job can hope for is an "umpire," a neutral "mediator" (so LXX translates the word) who will "lay his hand upon us both," and reestablish fair play. It is not clear from the text whether Job already longs for such a figure (most of the versions translate as a precative), or whether the idea merely flits into Job's consciousness, only to be dropped at this point as fatuous (so MT).

It is not unthinkable that already here Job has in mind some idea like the "personal angel" of later thought; at any rate, in ancient polytheistic contexts the formally comparable idea is widespread of a "personal god" for each man, who acts as his advocate in the council of the gods, especially when the great gods were too busy to attend to the affairs of individuals. Possibly then "umpire" is too weak a translation; AV's archaic "daysman" does at least remind us of the forensic context, which will be clearer in some parallel passages. It is overinterpretation to regard the passage as simply a prophecy of Christ's intercession, as some have, but, as usual, our temptations are far greater toward underinterpretation.

Job does not pick up this idea again until 16:18-22, but chap. 14 is important in the sequence of his thought. For the first time the idea of a solution beyond the grave appears to enter Job's thinking, an idea which will not be developed further until the famous passage of chap. 19. Most of the chapter is a general meditation on the brevity of human life; since it is so, why doesn't God simply "bug off" and allow man to enjoy the few days he has (v. 6)? But beginning with v. 13, Job has a sudden thought and begins to speak personally. What if he could be "hidden" (not dead, but given respite and asylum) from God's fury until His apparent tantrum was over? Then, when God called, he would "answer," i.e., perhaps be resurrected and returned to earth for a fair trial. But (vs. 18 ff.) it is too much to hope for at the moment; man passes on and decays like everything else. In v. 12, when Job had rejected the idea the first time, he had used three Hebrew terms which were at least pregnant with the idea of resurrection, and at least in later times they often came to signify just that.

In Job 16:18-22 the idea of life after death is muted, but now Job returns to the ideas adumbrated in chap. 9. Even though God and his "miserable comforters" (16:2) have ganged up against him, he will not give up. Even if God is about to do him in, he prays that his blood will remain unburied in order to continue to cry to heaven for justice and vindication (cf. e.g., Gen. 4:10; Is. 26:21; Ezek. 24:7-8). But to do any good, someone must be in heaven to hear his cry and plead his case. And now for the first time Job no longer speaks hypothetically, but, at least momentarily, is sure that "even now, behold, my witness is in heaven" (v. 19).

Who is this "witness" ('edh) or "he that vouches for me" (shahed)? Probably the majority of commentators understand it to be God Himself, that is, that Job here appeals, as it were, "to God against God," to the God of justice and forgiveness, as he knows the true God must really be, against the apparent ogre of a God he is presently experiencing. This understanding is by no means impossible, but both the immediate context and the parallel pericopes seem to make a third party more likely. Since God in this context is still the accuser and executioner, the "witness" here, like the "umpire" of chap. 9, is more likely an intercessor or intermediary, who will plead with God like "a man with his neighbor" (v. 21).

In 17:1-3 Job appears to have lost his certainty and slipped back into the "slough of despond"; the passage is not totally clear, but Job seems to say that since he has no witness to his surety in the heavenly court, he prays that God Himself may relent and "lay down a pledge" for him. The Christian knows that only the risen Christ fulfills this hope, but how clearly Job himself saw is hard to say. In any event, he plainly has taken a step further in the direction of the certain conviction and profound declaration of 19:25-27.

After another bitter complaint about his treatment at the hands of God and man alike, Job's spirit begins to rise again in 19:23. This time Job evinces no doubts whatsoever, and articulates his hope in terms of a *goel,* who surely is roughly comparable to the *mokhiach* ("umpire") and *'edh* ("witness") of the preceding passages. The traditional rendition of *goel* as "Redeemer" is not so much wrong as premature. The basic reference of *goel* is to a kinsman who is obliged to "redeem" his less fortunate relatives from slavery, or at least their property from foreclosure (classically illustrated on that more "secular" plane by Boaz in the Book of Ruth). On the first level, Job here appears to do no more than adapt the idea to his situation before God in the celestial courtroom, and something like "vindicator," "champion," "defense attorney" (perhaps explicitly over against Satan as "prosecuting attorney") is acceptable translation. As in chap. 16, it is theoretically possible that Job is merely thinking of God Himself, but to us it seems much more likely again that a third party is in mind (although in the light of the fulfillment the difference narrows in the God-Man, Christ).

In the rest of the Old Testament, there is no doubt that the *goel* image is often applied in a broader sense to God's "redemption" of his people, particularly in the Exodus. If Job were not wisdom literature with its characteristic reluctance to tie in explicitly with mainstream Biblical themes and usages, the exegete would be much less reluctant to hear *goel* in that broader sense also in this context. Nevertheless, ultimately the conservative will not hesitate to hear the word also here in its broader canonical context of *tota Scriptura,* where there is no doubt about its ultimate applicability only to Christ, our "Advocate" (e.g., 1 John 2:1), who "was raised for our *justification*" (Rom. 4:25).

In many other textual and exegetical details, this pericope is notoriously difficult, and we can note only a couple points. It is possible that, instead of the adverbial "at last" in v. 25b, we should understand a noun in parallelism with *goel* and render, "as the Last (One)," "back-up man," "guarantor," or the like. Whatever the precise force here, the root often has eschatological significance in the Old Testament (cf. the two parallel expressions in 16:19). The same word for "stand" is used as in 14:12; thus, it may be used in a resurrection sense here, although the word may, as such, imply no more than a witness' or attorney's rising to testify in court.

Life after death is, however, undeniably prominent in these verses. Three times Job confidently asserts that *he* shall see God "and not another" (i.e., perhaps now reconciled, and no longer as an enemy). The only real issue is whether Job's language implies a resurrection of the *body* or a more "spiritual" beholding of God (possibly in the intermediate state). The decision turns especially on the meaning of the Hebrew preposition *min* with "flesh," whether it is private ("without, apart from") or implies source ("from"). It is impossible to settle the matter definitively, but mention in the context of "skin," "eyes," and "heart" (literally "kidneys") would seem to favor the interpretation that Job thinks of his future, vindicated existence in bodily terms. In any event, the pericope remains one of the peaks of the book, and the Christian will not hesitate to "fill" it with all the fuller meaning of the fulfillment. Such an affirmation does not contradict Job's earlier oration on the inevitability and finality of death (in one sense, an incontrovertible fact of human experience), but it does insist that that is not all there is and that the ultimate resolution of life's problems lies in an otherworldly context.

Some also object that, if the traditional understanding is correct, it is strange that it is never alluded to again in the book. The objection, however, appears again to misunderstand the book's primary purpose to be to give theoretical answers rather than to orient everything toward the proper relation to God. It may well also be true, as many commentators think they discern, that the remainder of Job's discourses have a much calmer and more dispassionate tone, and that Job is able to turn the friend's arguments against themselves. If so, the genuineness of chap. 28, even on Job's lips would be easier to understand (cf. both above and below), and it may be no accident that the "dialogue" winds down and sputters out hereafter (Zophar not even giving his expected third speech in the third cycle).

Before we proceed seriatim, however, we should note that Job's idea of a(n) "umpire-witness-mediator" appears at least once more in the book, this time on the lips of the enigmatic Elihu in 33:23. There are many uncertainties about the interpretation of the pericope, 33:19-33, but it appears that Elihu is picking up and attempting to modify Job's own earlier references to some heavenly champion. In reply to Job's complaints about the silence of God, Elihu argues that God has various ways of communicating with man—but primarily in order to discipline him, and thus evoke repentance. Among those ways is the possibility of "an angel, a mediator" *(melits),* who cannot be expected simply to exonerate Job, but who may convince God that the guilty one has suffered enough, and thus encourage the man's repentance. (We cannot enter into the debate about the more precise identification of this *melits,* whether he is a "redeemer figure" in the heavenly council [Irwin], a cultic mediator in the sanctuary, e.g., Is. 43:26, or what.) Elihu states all this only conditionally, and even then is several notches below Job's own declarations. Nevertheless, he does pinpoint once again a critical problem in the book, the "communications gap" between God and man, and the need for an intercessor who will be enough like God to speak to Him, but also enough like man to speak for him. It is not yet the "fullness of time," and the book of Job carries the theme no further, but in retrospect we recognize here too part of the *praeparatio evangelica.*

Chapter 28

Regardless of how one construes Job 28 in the context of the entire book (cf. above), the power and importance of this great paean of wisdom is universally recognized. After illustrating with the example of a miner the great "wisdom" man does possess (vs. 1-11), the poem proceeds to stress the inaccessibility of ultimate wisdom, not only to man, but to everything else in the created universe. Only "God understands the way to it" (v. 23), illustrated in language redolent of Is. 40:12 ff., and indeed anticipatory of God's theophany in Job 38 ff. Then in vs. 27-28 the poem ends in a swift, two-part climax. In v. 27, "wisdom" is virtually personified (if not hypostatized), and four verbs are used to describe its employment as God's "right-hand man": God "saw" it (apparently as it came into view at the creation); He "declared" it (perhaps to be His official representative); He "established" it, and, finally, "searched it out" (perhaps, after testing, gave it full authority). Both the conception and the language are very similar to Prov. 8 (which see)—in fact, almost a miniature of it. If one recalls the profound Christological import of Prov. 8, the significance of Job 28 comes into focus also. Liberal handbooks often posit an evolutionary sequence in the hypostatization of wisdom, beginning with Job 28 and continuing through Prov. 8 into the apocryphal Ecclus. 24 and Wisdom 7. If that "evolution" is conceived as an "evolution outward" rather than "upward," that scheme may even be acceptable in a chronological sense, and, in any event, the logical sequence is undeniable.

For a variety of reasons, partly because they regard it as anticlimactic, partly because of the new introduction, "And he said to man," critics quite unanimously regard v. 28 as a later addition, presumably by some pious scribe who wished to stress that wisdom was not entirely unavailable to man. However, one can just as easily formulate that positively and understand the verse as a description of "special revelation" after the previous verse's accent on natural revelation: as Creator, God indeed reserves cosmological (speculative) wisdom for Himself, but He does reveal religious and ethical (practical) wisdom to man. With typical wisdom economy of line, that revealed wisdom is here summarized under two headings: (1) "the fear of the Lord" (the only time 'adonai is used in the book), that is true religion or faith; and (2) "to depart from evil," its counterpart in sanctified living. Of course, these two aspects of wisdom are not ultimately disparate at all but find an eschatological unity in the Incarnate One.

Whether chap. 28 are Job's own words or the author's observations at this juncture, it thus seems entirely in accord with the movement of the book. The intimation, at least, in v. 27 of incarnate wisdom is ultimately homologous with Job's convictions about a "mediator" (chap. 19, e.g.), and, even apart from that, it is about as close as the book ever comes to a "solution." When all is said and done, there is little left for man but to confess God's wisdom and to get on with life in the light of the wisdom God has vouchsafed to him. He cannot penetrate the mystery reserved for God alone, but by grace he can and must be faithful to what has been committed to him. What is thus affirmed in chap. 28 is very similar to the wisdom summaries we meet, for example, in Prov. 1:7; 9:10; Ps. 110:10, and perhaps most immediately, in the conclusion to Ecclesiastes (12:13). The formulation is that of "wisdom orthodoxy," be it noted, which Job does not repudiate, but in context, does reformulate. He has not refuted the argument of the friends, but transcended it in the light of revelation, and in that confidence he can proceed. In a sense, God seems to be "priming" or preparing Job for His own theophany shortly.

Chapters 29—37

As had happened before, however, Job is not able to maintain the same high level of confidence, and we have somewhat of a relapse in chaps. 29—31, Job's final speech or peroration (sometimes inappropriately also referred to as a "soliloquy"). After contrasting his former felicity (chap. 29) with his present plight (chap. 30), Job moves in chap. 31 into a solemn and climactic abjuration of all offenses that might have caused his change of circumstances. The form is the well-known one in antiquity, also outside the Bible (most famously in the Egyptian *Book of Dead*) of the "negative confession," in which specific sins are denied, while asking God to intervene in punishment if the suppliant is lying. Chaps. 29 and 31 form superb summaries of the ethical standards inculcated by Yahwistic wisdom in general.

Job's oaths of clearance come to a climax in vs. 35-37, one of the book's major junctures. He follows the legal procedure of signing a document (cf. 19:23), thus validating the potential self-imprecations of the preceding verses. Now if only Shaddai would deign to answer him with His own indictment! A "hearing" from God is really all he had asked for all along, and, should that ever happen, to the end Job remains confident of acquittal, and of the possibility once again to behave "like a prince."

God does answer Job finally—in chaps. 38 ff., but first intervene the four speeches of Elihu. On that score alone, one can at least understand why most critics regard them as intrusive (cf. above). It is not entirely true, however, as often charged, that Elihu has nothing to add to what the three older friends (32:4) had asserted. We have already noted his apparent partial acceptance of Job's "mediator" idea, and although it is not absent in the earlier speeches, Elihu places great accent on the educative and disciplinary value of suffering. By apparently challenging the friend's rigidity in assuming that all misfortune is punishment for personal sin, he prepares the way for God's speeches and much of the point of the entire book. Yet by his very grandiloquent cocksureness, the brash young man backhandedly underscores one of the book's major points: "flesh and blood," even when quasi-"orthodox," must be converted, not merely convinced.

What is usually reckoned as Elihu's fourth speech (Job 36—37) really divides into two. The first (36:1-21) is a superb, sensitive summary of the wisdom "orthodoxy" of the friends, and in the proper context beyond reproach. The remainder of Elihu's oration, however, is plainly transitional to Yahweh's intervention in chaps. 38 ff. Apparently, as the very thunderstorm out of which God speaks begins to rise, Elihu marvels at the spectacle (cf. e.g., Ps. 29), cites metereological phenomena as a demonstration of God's greatness, and in 37:14 ff. even "softens up" Job, as it were, for the impending theophany by addressing to him some of the same kind of ironical, rhetorical questions which we hear shortly from Yahweh's own lips.

Yahweh's "Answer" and the Message of the Book

When Yahweh finally does respond to Job's repeated requests—even demands—for a hearing, what He says is about as big a surprise as anything in the book. Readers have always been nonplussed by the fact that God seems entirely oblivious to the terms on which Job had demanded a hearing. There is neither bill of indictment nor acquittal, and

God does not seem to give a fig about "the orthodox dogma of retribution." That surely suggests that most readers have asked the wrong questions, or that our problems with the book are easily as irrelevant to the answer as the problems Job and his friends thought they saw. If we insist that the prologue-epilogue and the body of the work are an intended unity, it surely is no accident that God never reveals to Job the ultimate reason for his trauma, namely the challenge from "the Satan." Thus, the divine speeches should not be searched for *the* answer to the problem of suffering, as is often done—although, of course, in a broader sense they are a major part of the "answer." The book is not a "theodicy," at least not in any Western, philosophical sense of the term as a treatise leading by rational argument to a conclusion. God's "answer" to Job or the "dialogue" between the two is as oblique as we have already noted the "dialogue" between Job and his friends to be; again it is more to the point to understand Yahweh as addressing primarily the entire audience of readers or hearers.

What is that point? Let us first summarize the contents of the remainder of the book. Plainly there are two speeches by Yahweh (38:1—40:2 and 40:6—41:34), each followed by a submission by Job, but in terms of function or purpose, it seems impossible to distinguish the two. Sometimes it is suggested that because Job had challenged both God's power and justice, the first and second speeches should meet those two objections, respectively. However, very little in the difference of contents of the two speeches seems to correspond to that distinction, unless one puts great weight on 40:8-14 (cf. below). On the whole, however, at least at first reading, it would seem that Job had questioned God's justice rather than His power, while God's reply underscores His power and hardly speaks at all to the question of His justice or moral government of human affairs.

The first speech consists almost totally of a series of ironical questions—like "Do you know?" "Were you there?" "Can you too?"—all intended to put the smallness of man in bold relief before the Creator. In 38:1-38 we have a review of inanimate nature, followed in 38:39—39:30 by a summary of the wonders of animate nature. (The chapter division is not the happiest at either the beginning or the end of this second part of the first speech.)

Yahweh's first speech ends with a repetition (40:1-2) of the challenge with which it began (38:1-2), and Job's submission is just as brief (40:3-5). As noted, critics have great difficulty with this brief exchange, partly because of its brevity, and a frequent solution is to regard the entire second divine speech as a later addition. If we reject that "solution," it still is not easy to decide precisely what the dynamics of the book are at this point. Is Job's submission here insufficient, possibly even insincere or covertly still defiant, so that another sermon is required to finish the task? Job's second submission (42:1-6) is a bit longer, but scarcely different qualitatively. Perhaps it is best to assume that we have here only a pause, governed more by literary or artistic than by contextual considerations (cf. earlier).

After a repetition of the challenge (Job 40:6-9), Yahweh's second speech again divides into two parts, although the first portion is very short. In the first (40:10-14), Job is ironically invited to "play God" by defeating all the forces of evil in the world. Only in these verses, at least at first reading (cf. below), does God appear to be dealing with the moral issues Job has raised, and the "answer" is very similar to what both Job and the friends have already asserted in their own ways: justice must be left to God. It is conceivable, though scarcely self-evident, that the positioning of these verses between the nature poems fore and aft is intended to signal their centrality and importance in the total "answer." In any event, their connection with the context must be seen as an integral one: as always in Scripture, God's ability to redeem is based on His ability to create—and recreate, and "redemption" is finally cosmological as well as anthropological. It is one of wisdom's bedrock emphases that the same order of "righteousness" is intended to pervade all realms of existence.

Most of the second speech is constituted by two long "monster speeches," on "Behemoth" (40:15-24) and "Leviathan" (chap. 41). These two formidable creatures, both the work of God's hands (like Job; cf. 40:15), are described at great length, again in the form of rhetorical questions (the latter especially in the case of Leviathan). Can Job enter into conflict with and subdue them? And if not, how does he ever expect to be able to stand before God?

Who are these beasts? The literature on the question is immense. "Behemoth" is simply the plural of the Hebrew word for "beast" or "cattle," apparently used here (40:15) and perhaps elsewhere (cf. Ps. 73:22; Is. 30:6) as an "intensive plural" for a specific beast of great size and strength ("*the* beast *par excellence*"). In this plural form, the word is never used with the definite article, suggesting that it is also a proper name (as at least it is usually rendered here). If so, which beast is it? Early commentators usually thought of the "elephant." Modern interpreters have inclined toward "hippopotamus," although mention of the "lotus" in vs. 21-22 has seemed to point toward Egypt, causing some to prefer "crocodile." If so, however, "Jordan" in v. 23 is troublesome, and, if not emended away, appears to point definitively toward a Palestinian habitat. Pope has recently marshaled many arguments in favor of identifying the beast with the "bullock" or "water buffalo." Does it really matter? In one sense, not very much, especially if the intent is only to describe some huge earthly beast, that is, with no typical or supernatural import. That major issue cannot be settled with reference to "Behemoth" alone, apart from consideration of the following "Leviathan" (chap. 41).

The name of the second beast, "Leviathan," much more readily suggests supernatural or typical import. (Liberal commentaries will commonly use the adjective, "mythological": there is no doubt about the name's mythological connections outside the Bible, but the adjective is scarcely defensible in a canonical context; as elsewhere, it may be heard neutrally, but with difficulty, and hence is best avoided.) In Canaanite mythology, "Leviathan" (Lotan) is well known as the name of a seven-headed sea-serpent (?), more or less personifying the ocean itself, which was defeated by Baal at the "creation," a defeat which must annually be repeated ritually if creation is not to revert to chaos. With demythologiz-ed import, it is used in Is. 27:1 and Ps. 104:26 (cf. Amos 9:3) as a picturesque depiction of the monstrous forces of evil which Yahweh has defeated and neutralized. Apparently "Rahab" ("Arrogance") was a name or epithet for the same monster, and is used in the Bible in the same way, with special reference to Egypt (Is. 30:7; 51:9; Ps. 87:4; 89:11; this name must not be confused with that of the Jericho prostitute in Joshua 2, which is spelled differently in Hebrew).

It is to be noted that in that ex-mythological, picturesque sense, both "Leviathan" and "Rahab" are mentioned earlier in the book, "Leviathan" in 3:8, and "Rahab" in 9:13 and 26:12 (in 7:12 an unnamed "sea monster" is also alluded to).

The big question (parallel to that of "Behemoth" above) is whether "Leviathan" has essentially that same metaphorical force here, or whether it refers to some natural denizen of our planet. That there is *some* natural reference seems undeniable, but commentators are no more unanimous in identifying it than they are "Behemoth." Most prefer "crocodile," although there are other identifications (especially "whale," particularly if Behemoth is interpreted as a crocodile). There is ample evidence for the presence of crocodiles in Palestinian waters in Biblical times, so no Egyptian setting need be sought here either. Crocodiles are mentioned nowhere else in the Bible, so that we have no way of knowing whether "leviathan" was the everyday designation of that beast, or whether the anarthrous usage (like "behemoth") again indicates a proper noun and more transcendental import.

That returns us to the major exegetical issue surrounding both "Behemoth" and "Leviathan": are they natural or supernatural (typical, "mythological") creatures? Possibly the majority of interpreters incline toward the former alternative, in which case God's argument in this second part of the second speech is essentially the same as in the first speech (at most, with only a difference in degree or intensity, because of the monstrosity of the beasts and their detailed description). We think the matter is not quite so simple, however. But neither should we opt for *solely* the other alternative, that is, we should not erect false alternatives.

We believe that natural beasts (whatever their precise identification) are partly in view and are part of Yahweh's argument. At the same time, we believe that the natural beasts are also and simultaneously take-offs for transcendental or supernatural significances. The evidences of this, we believe, are many. The very language describing the beasts often is otherworldly (e.g., esp., 41:18-21), although poetic metaphors are inevitably ambiguous in that regard. The natural animals were sometimes captured and killed, while the poems describe these monsters as too powerful and ferocious for man to master. Especially if the names are to be capitalized (as proper names), it seems likely that we are dealing with personifications of more than natural genera or typologies. Particularly in the case of the second beast, Leviathan, then, it seems difficult to avoid hearing some of the same ex-mythological, transcendental, and cosmological significance the name has elsewhere in Biblical usage (cf. above). In the Bible "Leviathan" commonly symbolizes and summarizes the object of God's eschatological victory, but in the holism of Biblical thought one can readily move from the eschatological to the protological (creation) and/or to the existential (present).

In post-Biblical literature (Enoch 60 and IV Ezra 6) we meet Behemoth as well as Leviathan in eschatological contexts. The general picture of a god commissioning an animal—and specifically a bull—to fight a man is common enough in ancient mythology. In any event, whatever decision we reach with regard to Leviathan in this respect will surely have to apply equally to Behemoth. The briefer description of Behemoth is generally also more restrained than that of Leviathan, but 40:19a appears to establish a transcendental significance for Behemoth as well. His depiction as "the first of the works of God" is identical with the description of hypostatic wisdom in Prov. 8:22. Its precise application here is moot; "first" might mean simply "most powerful" (cf. 41:33-34 on Leviathan) or possibly refer to the first of the animals created on the fifth day. However, we would suggest that its poetic signification here is somehow connected with the primordial creation of (who shortly became) Satan and the evil angels.

That is, the very monstrosity of the earthly animals (again no matter what their precise identification) should remind the audience of the monstrosity of evil. To the original audience perhaps the very names would suggest the association—"Leviathan" because of its embarrassment of mythological associations, and "Behemoth" possibly more etymologically, that is, "beastliness" incarnate, as it were, the embodiment of all that is brutish in this world, of "might makes right" ideologies. Both beasts would then represent diabolical power—and, ultimately, the Diabolos or Satan himself. (Compare the use of the dragon symbol for Satan in Revelation.)

If this interpretation is correct, the hiatus often seen between the first and second parts of God's second speech is removed, and we see clearly how the second speech as a whole moves beyond the first to a powerful climax. God does not *merely* continue to impress upon Job his inability to master natural forces, as in the first poem, but proceeds to stress that he is even more impotent in the face of transcendental evil, of "spiritual hosts of wickedness in the heavenly places" (Eph. 6:12). The Behemoth and Leviathan poems thus illustrate and objectify the proud forces of evil mentioned in the first part of the second speech (40:10-14). Only God's "justification" enables and maintains justice, in cosmological and eschatological aspects as much as in anthropological and ethical ones. Both in the context of the Book of Job and of wisdom accents in general, the immediate accent is probably existential (the principles' applicability to Job's—and to man's—circumstances), but it is also characteristic of wisdom to stress a *natural* order, and nowhere is that better illustrated than in these two superb poems in the Book of Job.

In 42:1-6 Job "recants" a second time, but, as noted above, there is no evident difference from the first submission (40:3-5). One noteworthy difference, however, is that twice Job appears to quote God's own initial question (42:3a = 38:2 and 42:4 = 38:3b). A few critics inevitably have thought of textual disorder, but the more likely inference is that the questions are still echoing through Job's mind, and he repeats them before his own responses in order to acknowledge their validity.

The book hastens to its conclusion in the brief prose epilogue (42:7-17). Repentance and its objectification in sacrifice are required of Eliphaz (the oldest and hence representative of the three friends), as it is not of Job, "for you have not spoken of me what is right, as my servant Job has" (v. 8). How then can these things be, considering the friends' stout defense of God's probity and justice versus Job's sometimes almost blasphemous outcries against God? It certainly need not imply the fundamental incongruity between the prose and poetry of the book, as critics commonly construe it. Of course, the friends erred in their mechanical correlation of sin and suffering, in their virtual equation of faith with intellectual assent, in their failure to realize that "orthodoxy" is existential and relational as well as propositional, that the "answer" to evil and suffering is beyond mere translation into rational argument.

But how does Job get off so scot-free? It bears emphasis that God in His speeches never demands anything like a conversion or even "repentance" of Job. (The Hebrew word used of Job in 42:6 is not the ordinary one for man's repentance but rather signifies a more general change of mind, relenting, regretting. In context, this should mean, among other things, that Job vindicates God's confidence in him over against the Satan's sneers: he does worship God from the perspective of disinterested piety, neither expecting reward nor complaining when external rewards do not ensue.) Throughout the book Job is never required to renounce his stubborn claim that his suffering was underserved. His often bitter complaints are not only tolerated by God, but we are surely given to understand that such a stance can be the *proper* one for the person who takes God and His Word seriously (in contrast to any supine resignation or fatalism). Job's main problem all along had been God's silence, and now the mere fact that He is speaking again is (in the context) sufficient. "Any topic will do for a satisfying conversation between friends. It is each other they are enjoying" (Andersen).

Neither should the "materialistic" conclusion of Job pose a problem in the holism of all Biblical thought for anyone acquainted with the unity of the material and the spiritual. As noted already, wisdom in particular was prone to use a nature or creation base to discuss spiritual realities, and, also in this context, (cf. below) the unity extends all the way to the indissolubility of "immortality of the soul" and "resurrection of the *body*." It is probably no accident that "restored the fortunes" in 42:10 translates the Hebrew phrase commonly applied also to the ultimate, eschatological turning of the tables in God's final victory.

Job's material possessions are doubled, not to highlight materialism or Job's virtues but to underscore the magnitude of the "reward of grace." Andersen is doubtless correct in styling it "a kind of resurrection in flesh"—"not just a personal and hidden reconciliation with God in the secret of his soul, but also visible, material, historical, in terms of his life as a man." As tradition has always taken it, the text probably intimates even more of resurrection thought in that the number of Job's children is *not* doubled, presumably because they were never really lost to him (although in honesty one must note the strange Hebrew numeral in v. 13 which might mean "twice seven," that is fourteen sons—although the number of daughters certainly remains the same). A Septuagint addition to the book explicitly extends the thought to Job himself: "It is written that he will rise again with those whom the Lord raises up." Certainly together with 19:25 ff. (which see) this is part of the book's horizon, but precisely how clearly it was given to the author of Job to see in this respect is hard to say, and both speculative extremes should be avoided.

Other wisdom pieces (e.g., Pss. 49; 73; 139; Dan. 12) reinforce explicit resurrection intent in the epilogue of Job; apparently wisdom reflection on the problem of innocent suffering was one of God's major means in nourishing and preparing for His final resolution of the problem of evil in the resurrection of His Son. "Even in the New Testament we have not gone substantially beyond Job. The knowledge of a blessed immortality in the next life assuages suffering in this world, but it does not solve the problem of God's justice. The only real progress is the cross—itself a mystery, which is, as it were, a continuation of Job's sufferings" (Murphy).

In conclusion, perhaps it needs to be stressed that many of the problems inherent in the proper understanding of wisdom literature in canonical context in general meet us with double vengeance in Job, not so much because of the special problems of the book, but because its fame and undisputed literary power and beauty attract so many readers. Hence, possibly nowhere is the overarching hermeneutical canon of "Scripture interprets itself" more important than in Job, in order to fill out and make explicit what in typical wisdom fashion is articulated only very minimally or obliquely, at least as compared with mainline Biblical expressions. Job is *not* "everyman" or some universal "biography of the soul" (to say that is only to affirm that it is great literature); one may say, however, that it is every covenanted man (in the Biblical sense), every *Christian* person.

In real liberalism the purely humanistic aspect of Job's experience will tend to be accented, and, indeed, properly understood, wisdom always has a strong "humanistic" flavor. Always present in modern times somewhat, this slant became very prominent in the 1960s. One classical expression of it from a slightly earlier period was Archibald MacLeish's *J.B.* Here there are no divine "songs in the night" (35:10), only *man's* "unquenchable spirit" in the face of evil, only a human reaction to the problem of evil without faith in a loving God. "God" speaks, as it were, but merely as a manifestation of an impersonal power, a personification of the will to love in the universe ("When we love, the Gospel happens"; "It is in man's love that God exists and triumphs.")

Much less virulent, but ultimately just as much a caricature of the book, was neo-Orthodoxy's one-sided existentialist reading of the book, a viewpoint still widely represented in the commentary literature, (again, no doubt, a partial truth here, in that there is a strong "existentialist" strain in Biblical wisdom). One writer in that tradition describes the message of Job as "justification by faith"—a summary that orthodoxy might finally find very congenial, if properly defined, but, in his context, the phrase appears to have more in common with the popular misunderstanding of the words than with Pauline and Reformation theology.

The same judgment must be made on many similar summaries of the book's message: Man does not even know how to answer the right questions, let alone find the answers to his ultimate metaphysical problems. God will not allow Himself to be questioned but reveals Himself only as the Questioner. The only truth about God is the truth of God. It is said that a man will drown unless he believes that God intends him to swim. Human dialogue (Job and friends) and monologue (the way of the mystic, of religious psychology, of "human potential") must give way to divine-human dialogue (a neo-Orthodox rendition of the book's outline). The list of such summaries could be extended almost indefinitely, and probably none will be found entirely without merit.

Their very variety and at least partial validity are ample testimony to the protean character of the Book of Job. Not that Job can be stretched to fit everyone's taste (although it can hardly be denied that that happens too), but they underscore the message that although God does not give all the answers, He does give the Answer (that is, Himself, as revealed in all of Scripture and in His Son). The problem of evil and suffering is greater than all the answers; the sum is more than the total of the parts. From man's perspective there often will be no more of an "answer" than there was to Job; to reason the "irrational" aspect will always bulk large.

Neither does Job give any "answer" to the problem, but he points to the cosmic order which only God knows and controls. At this point one must be familiar especially with wisdom ideology and conceptuality in order to fully comprehend Job. The cosmic order of creation which God's speech depicts so forcefully is the same as the ethical and psychological orders; from the "wisdom," "justice," and "righteousness" apparent (ultimately only to the believer) in the former, he infers it, applies it, *believes* it also in the latter realms. The point of the book is *not* that one must forsake all belief in a just and rationally ordered universe and take refuge in some irrational world of "faith" (as many liberal commentators aver); it is not a matter of things contrary to reason, but of matters above and beyond the human ken. This differs from the fatalism and legalism of pagan wisdom, ancient and modern, ultimately only in that a personal and just deity stand behind it. The friends were perfectly correct in stressing the order of the universe; they were, however, very deficient in their perception of the Creator of that order. "It was not that this man sinned, or his parents, but that the works of God might be made manifest in him" (John 9:3).

There is a God who cares, and the heavens declare it. "Under the high notes of cosmic transcendance, a *de profundis* of God's own agony may be heard," climactically on Good Friday, and into which we have all been baptized. "An evil and adulterous generation seeks for a sign; but no sign shall be given to it except the sign of the prophet Jonah" (Matt. 12:39).

SONG OF SOLOMON (CANTICLES)

In the Hebrew canon, this work heads the subgrouping of the five Megilloth because of its traditional liturgical association with the feast of Passover, the most preeminent occasion in the Jewish calendar. The rest of the Megilloth then follow in the chronological order of the festival with which they are associated. With the greatest of the festivals was associated what was regarded as one of the greatest of Biblical lyrics, the Song of Solomon. To most modern readers, that evaluation appears to be, at best, an overcorrection of the monumental problems and challenges associated with the book. At very least, however, it does throw into bold relief the very low regard or at best supreme puzzlement in which the book is usually held today, in practice at least, often scarcely less so by conservatives than by liberals. The Septuagint's placement of the book after Ecclesiastes (followed by all western versions) loses sight of the Passover association, of course, but the book remains both philologically and theologically problematic.

Canticles and "Wisdom"

It is debatable whether or not the book is really to be classified together with "wisdom literature." Because it is not explicitly didactic, it is often held that it can be included only for want of any better classification, or that the association with "wisdom" arose only because of its traditional ascription to Solomon. At most, many will concede only that wisdom circles arranged and/or transmitted the material as one aspect of their general "humanistic" concern.

We would argue, however, for a much more integral connection. On the very surface, it is obvious that themes of love, sex, and marriage play a very prominent role in Proverbs too. This is true both on the level of repeated moral instruction in those areas, as well as in the metaphysical metaphors of "Lady Wisdom" versus the "loose woman" which structure especially Prov. 1—9. Sometimes the similarity extends to the very vocabulary employed to discuss the subject (e.g., the "cistern" and "running water" of Prov. 5:15-19 with the "fountain sealed" of Cant. 4:12). One also notes the absence of the Tetragrammaton in Canticles, as in many proverbs. An explicitly proverbial quality is not entirely absent in Canticles, most obviously in 8:6-8, and, otherwise, it is most unlikely that the book has no ultimate didactic intent (although this is bound up with the entire question of the book's nature and purpose).

Furthermore, Canticles' themes fit squarely in the center of those which occupied wisdom in general. If one's major topic is "nature," or better, "creation," as wisdom's was, sexuality is bound to occupy a prominent place. If one's sweep is universal, considering what in one sense applies to all men everywhere, the mystery of human love and of sexual attraction will not be overlooked. No one knew better than wisdom that sex is one of the great levelers of mankind, no matter what else may divide them, "male and female created He them." One does not need to be Freudian to recognize that little is done in life without some reference to sexuality, and most of life's ultimate questions cannot be posed without consideration of its origin and transcendental significance. (One may also note the wisdomlike introduction to Ps. 45, which is probably ultimately quite parallel to the Song of Solomon.)

There also appear to be ancient Near Eastern parallels, as with other Wisdom literature. This seems especially true of certain Egyptian love lyrics (which would also suit a Solomonic milieu). The parallels are not exact (and may be coincidental), but a general similarity of atmosphere, situations, and favored metaphors seems evident. Three specifics are noteworthy: (1) the many allusions to nature, a parallelism of the awakening of love and sexual urges in humanity to the awakening of nature in spring; (2) the address of the lovers as "brother" and "sister" (although this is still common in the Orient); and (3) the theme of lovesickness in the absence of the object of one's affections. More controversial are alleged parallels between Canticles and mythological fertility rites (cf. below).

Titles and Authorship

At least three titles of the book are current. In Masoretic Bibles, the title (or superscription) of the book is simply "Song of Songs," that is, the ordinary, Hebrew superlative idiom (cf. "vanity of vanities" in Ecclesiastes) which might be translated, "The best/highest/greatest song," "*The* Song *par excellence*," etc. Cf. Luther's rendition, *Hohelied*. The very title, no doubt, reflects the book's supreme theological appreciation. Traditionally, it was often also understood as specifically the "best" of Solomon's songs in comparison with the total of 1,005 that 1 Kings 4:32 reports he composed.

Both the Septuagint and the Vulgate translated the Hebrew title literally. From the latter's *Canticum Canticorum* is derived the English "Canticles," especially common still in Roman Catholic circles. We adopt it as our favored designation simply because of its brevity and convenience.

The third title of the book, and the one most common in English-speaking Protestantism, is derived from v. 1 of the book. It repeats the title, "Song of Songs," and then adds, "which is Solomon's." At least, that is the ordinary translation, implying the traditional understanding that Solomonic authorship is being asserted. On the purely translational level, the problem is the same as in many of the psalmic superscriptions (which see). The Hebrew *lamedh* may imply authorship, and it may not. Linguistically, it may also be a formula of dedication, imply genre of material ("Solomonic"), or other things. Unless with liberals one regards the attribution of authorship to Solomon as simply a late and fanciful tradition, how one translates the phrase in v. 1 will be bound up with his disposition of the question of authorship in general. And therewith the first of many grievous issues in the interpretation of Canticles is joined.

As indicated, liberal criticism almost unanimously rejects anything literally Solomonic about the work. The late ascription is supposed to have arisen partly because of his renown as a composer of songs (1 Kings 4:32), partly because of his large harem (700 wives and 300 concubines, according to 1 Kings 11:3, which assuredly would both make him a great lover and require the greatest of "wisdom"), partly in an attempt to justify the work's popularity and ultimately to "baptize" and canonize it. The favored critical dating of the book is probably fifth to third century, that is, among the latest in the canon. Others, however, think of a late preexilic date, perhaps around 600. Many are willing to concede earlier roots (perhaps even in paganism, cf. below), but that is no longer the issue of "authorship."

The conservative must concede that the evidence supporting Solomonic authorship is tenuous. Assuming that the rest of the theological house is in order, undue significance should not be attached to what will then be a purely exegetical or isagogical question (not one of Scripture's veracity, but of what it can certainly be established to say). The six explicit references to "Solomon" in the book (Cant. 1:1, 5; 3:7, 11; 8:11, 12) do not unambiguously imply authorship and may be readily understood as historical references to a prototypal figure. Three additional references to an unnamed king (1:4, 12; 7:6) are even more ambivalent. Unlike Isaiah or the Pentateuch, no other Scriptural passages speak to the issue. (In fact, the Song of Solomon is not quoted at all, or evidently not even alluded to in the New Testament—a fact to which, however, no further significance should be attached, as though its canonicity were in question.)

Nevertheless, the conservative will not lightly disregard the un-animous Christian tradition of Solomonic authorship until modern times. (The Talmud, as it does in other connections, speaks of Hezekiah, but it is unclear what that should mean—if it deserves credence to begin with.) Entirely without any theological apriorism, a cogent philological

case can still be made for the traditional opinion, but, as usual, mere
philology or history cannot carry us beyond the realm of probabilities.
Let us first, however, consider some of the major critical objections.

Apart from general evolutionistic proclivities, probably the major
animadversion is linguistic. The case is similar to that of Ecclesiastes
(which see), though probably not as strong. In both books the classical
relative pronoun *'asher* is replaced by *she-*. There is no doubt that this
may signal late (proto-Mishnaic) Hebrew, but, on the other hand, its
appearance at many other points in the Hebrew Bible (even in the archaic
Judges 5) makes dogmatisim very unwise. Some of the other postclassical
syntactical features found in Qoheleth do not appear in Canticles,
possibly, however, because it is poetry instead of prose.

The allegation of "Aramaisms" in the book nowhere carries the weight
it once did, since Ugarit has demonstrated their presence in the language of
the area even in Mosaic times. At least two words (including *pardes* in
4:13, that is, "paradise," originally signifying an enclosed park or
nobleman's private preserve; the word also appears in Eccl. 2:5 and Neh.
2:8) are commonly argued to betray Greek influence. However, the same
roots also appear in Sanskrit, the influence of which the widespread
Solomonic trade contacts make not at all implausible. The many exotic
plants and products mentioned in the book probably witness to the same
mercantile associations, although many skeptics adduce their mention as
additional evidence of a much later provenance for the work.

Assuming the work is Solomonic, there is no reason why we should
exclude the possiblity of later linguistic restatement, but neither is there
clear reason why we need to resort to any such hypothesis. A much more
attractive explanation of the book's linguistic eccentricity suggests a
northern or Galilean dialect. Our knowledge of the subject is scanty, but
various evidences make the variations intelligible in that light. Solomon
himself was a thorough product of the Jerusalem court, the home of
classical Hebrew, but if the girl being wooed hailed from the North, use of
a court poet skilled in that dialect would not be unusual. At any rate, one
interpretation of "Shulammite" (twice in 6:13) understands it as a
reference to Shunem (in the Esdraelon plain), and the LXX translitera-
tion *Sounamitis* would support that view. (Other interpretations include
construing it as an artificial feminine construct parallel to "Shlomo"
[Solomon], or as a derivative from *shalem,* thus "perfect one" or the like.)

Certain other geographical references in the book could support the
hypothesis of a northern *Sitz im Leben* for the work (Lebanon, Hermon,
Carmel, Tirzah), but others are southern (Engedi, Heshbon, Jerusalem),
plus not a few of uncertain location. In Cant. 6:4 the beloved's beauty is
compared to both Jerusalem and Tirzah, and much is often made of the

latter reference. Conceivably, it is no more than a play on the name's possible meaning ("pleasing, charming"), but if the reference is topographical, as seems likely, it represents a major stroke in favor of very early, if not Solomonic, origin. Since Tirzah was an early capital of the northern kingdom, its favorable mention (like other northern references) seems unlikely at a time after the Disruption (922), either preexilic or postexilic, and it may be noteworthy that Samaria, Tirzah's successor as capital, is nowhere mentioned in the poem. The indiscriminate references to all parts of the land, and the absence of even a hint of knowledge of later circumscriptions of territory would strongly suggest at least origin in the period of the United Monarchy. Also in favor of Solomonic authorship would be the book's great interest in the fauna and flora of the land, consonant with the notice in 1 Kings 4:33. Not only the several references to royalty, but the general aura of regal opulence and luxury, while certainly not decisive, are strongly suggestive of the Solomonic court.

One ancient tradition associated Canticles with Solomon's youth, when passion would have been strong; Proverbs with his more pensive middle age; and Ecclesiastes with his crabbed and cynical old age. While we can be sure of nothing of the sort, not even of Solomonic authorship (cf. above), we have seen, nevertheless, that there is ample reason why we need not allow the "assured opinion" of higher criticism to stampede us into hasty abandonment of a traditional posture.

A few other observations about the book's text and style are in order before we proceed. Text-critically, there is little to comment on, because the Greek and Latin versions are almost slavishly close. Partially this answers to the high theological regard in which the work was apparently early held, but one also surmises that translators and copyists had little difficulty staying awake when dealing with such subject-matter! At the same time, translational difficulties abound to the present day, partly because there are so many unique terms (many probably representing archaic survivals from an early period, some fifty of them *hapax legomena,)* partly also because of hermeneutical uncertainty about the precise milieu.

Most agree that the poem is ultimately popular or folk poetry, not a learned composition, although that implies no artistic inferiority. The concreteness, even earthiness of the imagery, suggests the farmer's or peasant's close feeling for the countryside, and an urban suitor might readily adopt the idiom. Both the rural context and the Oriental culture may help account for some of the sexual and physiological candor of the poem (sometimes concealed by euphemisms in translation). Israelite sensitivities were properly shocked and outraged by the nudity of Greek art and the Hellenistic gymnasium, but verbal descriptions tended to be earthier and franker than are generally considered good taste in the Occident. Cultural feelings about taste and issues of basic morality should not be confused, however. Some similes are simply alien to our experience, e.g., the maiden's comparison to "a mare of Pharaoh's chariots" (Cant. 1:9), or her hair to "a flock of goats moving down the slopes of Gilead" (4:1). All of this magnifies the exegetical task, of course, but it is also a salutary reminder that the Holy Scriptures are no "timeless" revelation but very much bound to particularities of time and space, and any interpretative attempt to evade them is ultimately fraudulent.

History of Interpretation

A far more nightmarish problem than authorship, however, is the hermeneutical one, the question of the nature and meaning of the book in the Biblical canon. (Delitzsch once flatly called it "the most obscure book of the Old Testament.") Not surprisingly, the history of the book's interpretation is tortuous, and we may best proceed by recounting it and evaluating the alternatives as we go along. Much of this history is adumbrated in the disputes about the book's canonicity at the council of Jamnia in A.D. 90. At that time, there obviously were misgivings about the book's surface secularity, if not eroticism, and it was even reported that some of its lyrics were being sung in local taverns!

Sometimes it is asserted that Canticles survived the attacks upon its canonicity only because of its ascription to Solomon. One doubts, however, if such superficiality may fairly be attributed to ancient scholars, Jewish or Christian. Much more to the point was the appeal to the allegorical method of interpretation in its defense. The superorthodox Rabbi Akibah took the lead in defense of the book, asserting that those who understood it in secular vein would be excluded from the resurrection. His defense of it was characterized by superlative statements such as: "The world itself is not worth the day on which this book was given to Israel, for all the Writings are holy, but the Song of songs is the Holy of Holies." And Akibah obviously carried the day, because, as we have seen, that superlative evaluation of the book is obviously reflected in its association with the major Jewish festival of Passover, an association which we know from the Mishnah antedates the destruction of the temple. A few grumbles about the book also surface a little later in the Mishnah, but for all practical purposes the matter was settled until the rise of modern criticism (also for Christianity; cf. below).

What kind of history of interpretation may have preceded Jamnia is a matter of critical speculation. As usual, Jamnia did not canonize books for the first time (or even formally "close the canon") but simply fielded challenges to certain "antilegomena." It is hard to imagine how Canticles might even have achieved *de facto* canonical status in the first place apart from some understanding like Akibah's, and it at least strongly suggests that that had been its intended meaning in Israel from the outset. Of course, there are those who assume that the work first achieved national popularity on a more secular basis, with spiritual rationalization following secondarily, but that is simply to assert some hypothesis or the other.

The situation is not substantially different in the history of Christian exegesis. Canticles is included without apparent question in the earliest canonical lists. The only major exception appears to be Theodore of Mopsuestia (†428) of the more literal and historical minded school of Antioch. The details of his exegesis are lacking, but apparently he interpreted the book at least in part as referring to Solomon's love for Pharaoh's daughter. Whether he rejected all spiritual meaning or possibly even its inspiration seems unlikely, but we do not know for sure. At any rate, in Constantinople (553) the fifth ecumenical council emphatically rejected that opinion as "offensive to Christian ears." In Reformation times Calvin denounced Castellio, and the Inquisition condemned Luis de Leon for similar positions.

There is no doubt that, on all sides, even after the Reformation, the allegorical approach (or something very similar to it; cf. below) held virtually unchallenged sway. In the early church Origen is perhaps the most dexterous of the allegorists, and not even the historically minded Jerome veered in other directions. In the Middle Ages Bernard of Clairvaux (whose commentary is still in print) stands out, like many other medieval mystics, applying the book especially to the individual soul. Its intense popularity was enhanced by a frequent Mariological twist, and/or the facility with which cloistral "brides of Christ" could sublimate its sentiments. The "allegory" perhaps tended to be a bit more restrained after the Reformation and the hermeneutical theory accented the literal more, but important commentaries such as those of Spurgeon, Hengstenberg, and Keil did not differ significantly in ultimate result. Cocceius was even able to interpret the book as a history of the church, climaxing in the Reformation. The headings of the Authorized Version clinched the triumph of "allegorical" exegesis of the book in the English-speaking world.

Thus, there is no reasonable doubt that at least some sort of spiritual-allegorical approach is the oldest: describing God's love for His people in terms of human love. The general approach would be anything but unusual within the canon. Especially the negative imagery of adultery or "whoring after other gods" is apparent already in the Pentateuch, especially Deuteronomy, and is prominent in the prophets, especially Hosea, Jeremiah, and Ezekiel. Ps. 45, depicting on the surface a royal marriage, is a very parallel pericope. (Many of these appear to have northern roots or associations, which might be related to Canticles' possible own northern context.) In the New Testament the parallel "bride of Christ" metaphor is developed especially in Eph. 5. To any attempt to justify any spiritual exegesis of Canticles on the basis of those parallels, it is commonly objected that there the allegory or metaphor is clearly indicated, whereas in the text of Canticles itself there is no such thing. The objection is not without force, but at very least the parallels do suggest a "climate" in which a similar understanding of Canticles could develop and/or flourish.

As we will argue below, while the allegorical interpretation is preferable to many modern alternatives, it, nevertheless, has fatal weaknesses. This assumes that the term "allegorical" is being strictly used; very often, especially in Catholicism, it is used in a more general sense of nearly any type of spiritual interpretation. If used strictly, however, the method is objectionable in various ways. Every single detail must represent something else, and it is no little trick to work out all such correspondences in a coherent way. In principle, the "spiritual" meaning has no intrinsic connection either with the text or with the history of which it speaks. In practice, this means sheer arbitrariness and subjectivity in interpretation, of which there is no better illustration than the vagaries of the history of Canticle's exposition.

In addition to variations in that history already mentioned, it may be instructive to note a few more. Already the Targum took the book as a historical allegory of Yahweh's dealings with Israel from the Exodus to the return from the Exile, and it was followed in this not only by various Jewish interpreters, but also by the great medieval Christian exegete, Nicholas of Lyra, and even by a few modern interpreters. For example, one "anthological" approach understands the text as a highly sophisticated compilation of midrashic allusions to other Biblical texts, especially from the prophets, and thus the entire book offers a "prophetic" interpretation of God's relationship to Israel. Not totally unrelated is traditional Catholic Mariological exegesis (reflected in various references in the traditional liturgies of Marian festivals): Mary, representing Israel and the Old Testament typological matrix of Christianity, concurs in Christ's accomplishment of the mystical union between God and man. An amusing illustration from Protestant circles recalls Spurgeon's uncertainty whether Cant. 6:13 ("Return, O Shulammite") represented Christ's call to the backsliding church or the siren call of lapsed Christians to the faithful to join them in their apostasy—a dilemma Spurgeon resolved by preaching two sermons on the text!

Modern Interpretations

Modern opinion especially since about 1800, conservative as well as liberal, has moved massively and almost unanimously away from allegory, at least in any strict sense of the term. As often, however, it was easier to reject the traditional stance than it was to agree on a replacement, and the division was by no means always along liberal-conservative lines. Nineteenth-century thought inclined strongly toward a *dramatic* instead of an allegorical interpretation, but there was no agreement on whether there were two or three main characters (and in either case a chorus of "daughters of Jerusalem" or the like was often added, after Greek analogies). The two-character version received classical exposition at the hands of the conservative Lutheran exegete, Franz Delitzsch. Solomon, pictured as a shepherd, meets the Shulammite maiden during a royal tour of the North and, being physically attracted, brings her to Jerusalem to marry her; but he comes to love her truly before he wins her for his wife. Many details in the work, however, resist this construction: Solomon as a shepherd, the final scene in the girl's home village, etc.

More popular generally was the three-character dramatic hypothesis, often referred to as the "shepherd hypothesis." Ewald in the nineteenth century was its first major champion, but many have followed him, at least in general principle. In this reading, the book becomes a sort of a prototype of the "eternal triangle." Solomon is no longer the shepherd (thus avoiding a major difficulty of the preceding version), but the villain of the piece. Solomon either abducts the girl to his harem or makes advances in the guise of a shepherd. However, the girl refuses to be swayed by promises of a luxurious life and remains faithful to her fiance, a shepherd in her hometown of Shunem. Eventually, Solomon is impressed by the purity of the love of the rustic pair and allows the two to marry. (Especially this version easily lent itself to further allegory: Solomon stands for the world, while the girl represents the "bride of Christ," who refuses to be seduced from her spouse, and there would even be a certain historical aptness, in that Israel as a nation first encountered the allurements of the world in the reign of Solomon.)

However, the dramatic interpretation in any version suffers from almost as many detriments as the allegorical, and it finds very few defenders any longer. In another form, some recent cultic interpretations have followed quasi-dramatic lines, but they are even more speculative. There certainly is no more internal indication in the text of drama than of allegory. The closest we come is a possible dialogue, but mere dialogue does not constitute drama. (Gender differences, of course, are clearly indicated in the Hebrew, and already the ancient codex Sinaiticus seeks to identify the speakers in marginal notations, as do some modern versions, e.g., B = bride, G = groom, and D = daughters of Jerusalem.) Instead of the conflict necessary for real drama, the expressions of love appear to remain on essentially the same level throughout; we have more the expression of a mood than dramatic action. The "stage instructions" that would have to be added for a drama embroil interpreters in further subjectivities. Above all, in the light of archaeological evidence, it appears that the dramatic form never really caught on at all in the Orient. And, hermeneutically, it is almost as hard to see how mere dramas of such a sort would ever come to be viewed as Holy Writ as it is in the case of the even more "literal" and secular interpretations which soon followed.

Subsequent historical-critical attempts probably agree on little more than rejection of all the above interpretations. Increasingly any unity of the entire book is abandoned in favor of the view that it only contains a miscellany of discrete love poems—but there is no agreement at all on how many of these. Most guesses probably range between five and thirty. (Recent "rhetorical criticism" may be challenging this diachronic excess too; if repetitions are any signal of unity, however, Canticles is certainly not missing them—in fact, perhaps is second only to Ecclesiastes in the whole Bible in this respect.) In addition, "literal" exposition of the Song has increasingly come to be virtually synonymous with "erotic," and many even speak of an "erotic hypothesis."

Comparative studies have led many to view the work as specifically a collection of popular, earthy wedding songs. One of the first hypotheses along these lines grew out of observations of wedding customs in modern Syria in 1873 by the Prussian consul in Damascus, one J. G. Wetzstein. He observed a "King's Week" during which the bride and groom reigned as "king" and "queen," often sitting at a special table while songs were sung in honor of especially the bride. These songs (of the so-called *wasf* type) were stylized descriptions of the charms, physical and otherwise, of the beloved, enumerated often from head to foot or in reverse order. Possibly Solomon and the Shunamite, Abishag, became prototypes of the marriage rites in later communities, accounting for those names in the book. Wetzstein even thought he could discern echoes in Canticles of a "sword dance" performed by the bride (cf. 6:13—7:6), of a procession in which a threshing sledge served as a palanquin for the bride (cf. 3:6-11), etc. Both the language and the festivities of the Syrians were often rather uninhibited.

Wetzstein's thesis is still influential but not nearly as much so as formerly. The "parallels" are often moot (e.g., the girl is never styled a "queen") and apply, at best, to only a small number of songs. In addition, Syria and Canaan were not identical cultures in antiquity, and the relevance of modern customs to Biblical times is even more questionable. Hence, the modern critical disposition is probably to view the poems more as general love songs than as specifically wedding songs. The conservative might concede the possibility of some of the precanonical meaning or the Solomonic point of departure being exposed by such an hypothesis, but scarcely anything very significant for the exegesis of the book in its canonical context.

Many recent comparative studies have favored a cult-mythological or liturgical interpretation, according to which the poem(s) did not originally refer to human love at all, but to that of the gods. Usually the "sacred marriage" of Ishtar and Tammuz is thought of, represented by a "king" and a sacral prostitute in the earthly ritual. That is, we should have, then, part of the liturgy of a pre-Israelite cult and part of its fertility ritual, possibly in connection with the autumnal festival. Only later and secondarily was the rite allegedly "democratized" and applied to ordinary weddings. To make it acceptable in Yahwistic circles, it was perhaps "historified" by reference to Solomon and then eventually allegorized into the "marriage" of Yahweh and Israel. Many even try to pinpoint the time of the beginnings of Yahwistic acceptance as the syncretistic reign of Manasseh, when the vassal state of Judah would have been especially vulnerable to pagan influences.

This approach probably continues to grow, although most scholars are still cautious. The parallels are easily exaggerated and are certainly not self-evident in the text. The poem itself speaks only of the quite ordinary love of man and woman, not of the "cosmic fertilization" of pagan cult. At most, it is conceivable that this hypothesis has uncovered some of the ultimate elements of the canonical text, possibly even adapted deliberately with apologetic and polemic intent. Even the later association with Passover might be a riposte to the use of comparable texts in pagan liturgies. If the pagan parallels and associations were nearly as close as many of these researchers allege, however, on any orthodox reading of the history of Israel's religion it is virtually impossible to see how the songs could ever have been regarded as even fit candidates for "baptism."

Especially in the radical 1960s a literalistic (that is, the opposite extreme of allegorism) approach to the book was pressed in directions that were avowedly, sometimes even militantly, erotic. As marriage became a "bourgeois" institution, the association of the songs with weddings came to be regarded as too tame. Instead they were regarded as songs simply sung in praise of sexual passion, frankly erotic, and candidly impatient of consummation, regardless of societal conventions and formalities. The only "spiritual" or "religious" meaning was allegedly that of sexuality and eroticism—of course, as great gifts of "God" to be "celebrated." Certain passages in the book were pointed to as allegedly even celebrating the ecstasies of premarital sex (Cant. 3:1-4; 5:3; 8:1 f.), although there was no unanimity on how far the erotic interpretation was to be carried in individual cases. Obviously, then, the songs would not only be wedding songs, but would be quite inappropriate for such an occasion!

In a sense, the conservative will probably regard such a reading as scarcely worth refutation. At very least, it does illustrate a sort of *ne plus ultra* of "treating the Bible like any other book." Very often it is highly debatable if the imagery is really all that erotic to begin with; often it would seem that such interpretations tell us much more about the interpreters than about the text! Yet, at least on the first level of meaning, it does contain an element of truth which cannot simply be dismissed. Already Cant. 1:2-4 strikes the note of desire for union that runs throughout. In chap. 3 the girl *dreams* that her beloved is in bed with her, but in her "mother's house" (v. 4)—scarcely the place for "affairs." Again in chap. 5, she *dreams* that her lover is rattling the latch of her door, but finds no one when she rises, and when she again ventures into the street to look for him, the watchmen take her for a loiterer and administer a beating! In chap. 8 she *wishes* that her lover were really her brother, who might enter her chambers without arousing suspicion and gossip.

But is not all this part of the verisimilitude of the poem? To long for and dream of the consummation, even to broach the eternal question, "Why wait?" is part of the *reality* of the world of romance and courtship and is not quite tantamount to jumping the gun. Likewise with other features of the songs: the "make-believe" fantasies, the sense of *Einmaligkeit* (once-for-all, utterly unique quality), as if nothing else in the world mattered or even existed besides their love, the element of teasing between lovers, the complaints that the way of true love is difficult, etc. Neither are such sentiments unworthy of bearing some further spiritual significance, unless one is Manichaean in orientation. Erotic love is not synonymous with illicit love.

Conservative Interpretation

Conservative thought, too, has moved in the direction of a more literal interpretation of Canticles (as at least one element of the whole) in the last century, but usually with an ultimately radically different hermeneutic from liberal versions. A few conservatives such as Young even wish to limit its meaning to the "literal" one of expressing the beauty of monogamous love over against various degeneracies or perversions, ancient as well as modern. Its expression of the "monogamous ideal" (present even though polygamy and divorce were allowed) might remind the reader of God's love for lost humanity, but that was not really part of the textual meaning. Such an interpretation of the book is not far removed from various nonerotic readings by critics, who find it to be only a lyrical expression of the essential rightness of the man-woman relationship. In a way, it is characteristic of "historical-critical" method, *at best,* that more cannot be found in the text!

Most conservatives, however, are not satisified to leave it at that. Unless "canon" is understood only in a historical (non-normative) sense, some further spiritual meaning seems imperative; certainly to deny it would fly in the face of ecclesiastical disapprobations throughout the centuries. As usual, especially in wisdom precincts, a purely philological exegesis seems only to scrape the surface. If the message of the book were no more than that, it is hard to see (humanly speaking) how the book would ever have been received into the canon, all the more so since the theme is expressed so much more clearly and less obliquely many other times in Scripture.

Nevertheless, if we really are renouncing allegory with its *divorce* of literal and spiritual meanings, there must be a historical and literal baseline for all subsequent meaning. There is no time and age (and certainly not ours) when a host of aberrations in the area of sex and marriage do not have to be countered by wholesome examples and instruction to the contrary. "Natural revelation" teaches a good deal of this (even when it is flouted), and "special revelation" confirms, establishes, and enables in an ultimately different context (cf. above on this relation in "wisdom literature" in general). Treatment of women as "sex-objects," sometimes accompanied by an overt misogynism, was as widespread at times in the Biblical world as it is in ours. That "marriage is honorable in all, and the bed undefiled" (Heb. 13:4); that the human body is indeed, God's creation and not something to be ashamed of, as such; that sex is not intrinsically "dirty" nor the subject too "secular" to be of concern to the "religious"; that conjugal play, even eroticism, in that context, is not *per se* objectionable—while the world stands, the time will never come when the *church* will not have to make such points. If such were not the case, human love certainly would not be a fit symbol of divine love. Conversely, stress on a spiritual meaning alongside does not lessen, but enhances the message of the rightness of human love in proper context.

Sometimes it is most regrettable that by simple default, however, it is left to the humanists to urge such themes over against an unbiblical puritanism and prudery. Having stressed that, however, we do well to remember that we again live in a hedonistic age which does not care to hear of original sin or of how especially in this area, *Corruptio optimi pessima.* The truly Biblical churchman needs to take care that he does not overcorrect ancient failings or lingering suspicions in a few corners that sex may really be "dirty" after all, and thus confront the enemy on a front where his major forces are not currently massed. Instead he only seconds with a little "spiritual" veneer the world's agenda, and thus plays into the enemy's hands by contributing to the secularization of the church.

Thus, if the Book of Canticles, like its subject, sex and marriage, has *more* than merely a "literal" meaning, how shall we express the relationship? There is no agreement among conservatives on terminology, and much of the difference is only terminological. Whatever language is used, the *unity* of the various levels of meaning must be accented. It will not be a matter of a multiple or even a double sense, but of various aspects of the *unus sensus literalis.* In fact, this point should already be made of the Reformation's understanding of the book. For all of the surface similarity with medieval exegesis, hermeneutically and theoretically the Reformer's Christological interpretation was fundamentally different. Modern historicists and literalists often lump both together as "allegory," but that represents an alien critique from the opposite end of the spectrum. The Reformation principle might be styled "theological literal": the spiritual or theological meaning *was* the literal meaning, not some hidden, second sense under or behind it. It may sometimes appear to us that our ancestors did not always stress the historical component of that same literal sense as much as seems desiderative in our culture (although our problems are usually at the opposite extreme), but we will want to take care not to make a break in principle with their hermeneutics.

Many conservatives speak of a "parabolic" interpretation of the book, stressing the existence of only one *tertium* (God's love in terms of man's) in contrast to allegory's compulsion to squeeze significance out of every detail. Others speak of a "didactic-moral" intent as part of the literal sense. Still others prefer the term, "typical" or "typological" usually accenting some historical incident in Solomon's life as underlying the poem, and stressing the parallelism with prophetic use of the marriage analogy for the covenant. Cf. also Solomon as a type elsewhere in Scripture (2 Sam. 7:12-17; 23:1-7; Ps. 72; Matt. 12:42). Of the three, we would prefer the latter but would attempt to refine it still further. In line with terminology used throughout this book, we would prefer to accent a "vertical typological" and a "sacramental" meaning. Like wisdom literature in general, Canticles stresses the eternal, existential moment before God, and the historical, eschatological connections with *Heilsgeschichte* must be supplied by the reader under the assumption that the Holy Spirit, the ultimate Author of all the books, must have included that perspective in canonical context. The adjective "sacramental" will stress both the indispensability of the elements (a literal, historical aspect), as well as the fact that a certain *double-entendre* is built in, not read in. To the believer, human love is both an echo of divine love and a transparency of another order of perfect love. Finally, all of nature will be typical and sacramental of the new creation—the antipode of any platonic spiritualism. Nature too shares in the redemption, now proleptically and sacramentally, then eschatologically. Canticles' use at the Jewish Passover even suggests typologically its use at the Christian Easter (whose themes encompass nature). As Eph. 5 and Rev. 22 teach us, in Christ we see all this most clearly, all the while still awaiting the consummation.

Outline

We have said nothing about the book's outline or thrust on the purely philological level, and if allegory is not returning via the back door, that question cannot be ducked. It will be evident by now that it is impossible even to attempt a summary of the book's contents without committing oneself to a theory about the interpretation of the book. Except in very broad terms, the wherewithal to attempt the latter very definitively still seems to elude us. And, in a certain sense, if we proceed hermeneutically along "parabolic" or "sacramental" lines, the same general import will be defensible, even with quite a variety (not all, however) of philological points of departure.

This would even be true if there were no more internal unity to the work than a series of songs on the same general theme. That issue is not necessarily theological, but an explicitly religious view nearly always inclines toward at least some minimal unity. The repetition of certain verses (e.g., Cant. 2:6-9 and 8:3 f.) and of situations (3:1-5 and 5:2-8) would seem to point in that direction, as perhaps the very pattern of speech and response throughout the book.

We submit one very common outline, which itself, however, is often construed quite differently by different commentators. Delitzsch thought of six acts in a drama, whereas a common, recent construction sees a series of five poems, expressing the growth of love, each one of which exhibits a rhythm of tension and repose (mutual search of the lovers for each other, ending in the repose of mutual possession), with the final union and repose in a sixth poem (8:4-7). I. 1:2—2:7. The mutual affection and yearning of the lovers. 1:2-4 may be a sort of introduction, and in 2:3-7, they may actually meet. II. 2:8—3:5. The bride is invited to the fields; in the evening they return to their homes, but the bride is not at ease until she again finds her beloved (at least in her dreams). III. 3:6—

5:1. "Solomon" arrives with all the pomp of a royal pageant; he is enraptured by the girl's charm, and rejoices in her company. Delitzsch thinks of a climax in an actual marriage. IV. 5:2—6:2(9). The bridegroom comes unexpectedly while the bride is in bed (or, at least, she thinks he does), but when she rises to welcome him, he has vanished. She ventures outside in search of him, but the night watchmen rudely send her back to her quarters. 5:10-16 describes the groom, and many continue this section with a balancing praise of the bride's beauty in 6:4-9. Delitzsch's dramatic interpretation understands the section as "Love scorned, but won again." V. 6:3(10)—8:4. Mutual praises of the other's beauty; especially the groom's admiration of the bride. In 7:10—8:4, the bride declares her unanswering attachment to her lover. VI. 8:5-14. The lovers are inseparably united, and declare the unquenchability of their affection. Vs. 8-14 may be an appendix, and some scholars seek the easy way out by regarding them as later additions.

The last word on Canticles appears to be as eschatological as the divine love toward which it points. At least one sympathizes with the old rabbinical rule that no one under thirty years of age should read the book!

RUTH

The position of the Book of Ruth in the Hebrew canon as the second of the Megilloth is obviously determined by the chronological sequence of the liturgical festivals for which these works were proper (beginning with Canticles for Passover). The connection with *Shabu'oth* (Feast of Weeks; Pentecost) in this case is quite extrinsic, however, apparently based primarily on the notice of Ruth 1:22 that Naomi and Ruth returned to Bethlehem "at the beginning of barley harvest." That being the case, the Septuagint's relocation of the book, followed by most modern versions, is in this instance probably a net gain. The relocation, influenced by more Western and probably also more secular notions of "history," to a niche after Judges was determined by the opening words (1:1) dating the narrative "in the days when the judges ruled."

A careful reader will note even in English translation—and it is much more obvious in the original Hebrew—that the Book of Ruth derives from a different "school" of historiography than the surrounding material, particulary Judges (or most of it). Higher criticism usually formulates the difference in terms of the non-"deuteronomic" character of Ruth. If it is possible to use the term "deuteronomic" neutrally, or better, to connect it with a *Mosaic* Deuteronomy, it is perhaps as handy a summary as any.

The above generalizations have to be qualified, however, with respect to the last chapters of Judges (19—21) where the "deuteronomic" impress is far less evident than in other parts of the book (which see). Since those chapters may possess certain linguistic features in common with Ruth, while their portraits of life in that period are almost antipodal, it is possible that the Septuagint preserves some more original connection anterior to Ruth's placement among the Megilloth. When one recalls that the books of Samuel also have a non-"deuteronomic" character (different again from Ruth's, however), one is reminded how tenuous Noth's "deuteronomic history" hypothesis is, and how little we really know of how these "historical" books took shape.

Historicity and Purpose

All of this raises the question of the nature of the Book of Ruth, particularly its historicity. As usual, one can on philological grounds argue only for the plausibility or possibility of the story; ultimately, of course, we would also invoke criteria of theological hermeneutics. As the book stands, there certainly is nothing to suggest that the author did not intend to relate an episode of premonarchical history (not even any supernaturalism to upset the liberal-minded), and not much to suggest that his purposes extended far beyond that. The concluding genealogy (assuming its genuineness; cf. below) must indicate that there was some interest to relate the genealogy of David. (The very fact that David's ancestress is described as a Moabitess, is a major argument for the book's historicity, as is often pointed out.) To attribute any profound further "purposes" to him requires reading between the lines of his straightforward narrative, and such inferences will probably be bound up with basic presuppositions about the nature of the book.

It is plausible, however, to assume that a subsidiary purpose may have been to counteract one-sidedly dark portraits of the quality of life in the period of the Judges (as in Judges 19—21) and then also to suggest examples of right living under the covenant, of piety and fidelity, of home life and family solidarity for all times. There is no indication that he particularly wants to stress it (*pace* the critics; cf. below), but, in a way, it was all the more significant to see those ideal qualities exemplified in a foreigner, and indirectly, at least, the point is surely made that the covenant was not limited by national, political, or racial boundaries. These various purposes probably overlap and are all to be related to the book's theological stance (see below).

Almost to a man, however, critics find such explanations, at best, deficient. Not many are prepared to pronounce the book entirely devoid of historical worth, but most entertain reservations to one degree or the other. Form critics then inevitably debate about what to label it. Some would say "popular legend" or the like, but perhaps most common is the designation, *Novelle,* a somewhat broader and perhaps slightly more positive term (as concerns historicity) than the English cognate, "novel," but mostly just suggesting some well-wrought, relatively brief artistic product. Perhaps the translation "historical novel" conveys its force as well as any, at least in application to the Book of Ruth. If so, there is still the question of the relation between the adjective and the noun, and different critics answer it differently. The general lines of the answer, however, seem to be that the private-life aspects of the story are fictional (although why this family should not retain a memory of its background remains unclear), while there may well be a genuine memory of temporary migration from Judah to Moab in time of famine. The tradition of David's partial Moabite ancestry will often also be conceded.

The latter poses various historical problems on which we can barely touch: it would explain why David sent his parents to Moab for safekeeping while he was a fugitive from Saul (1 Sam. 22:3-4), but it makes even more puzzling David's unusually harsh treatment (perhaps half of them massacred) of the conquered Moabites later on as he is building his empire (2 Sam. 8; presumably some treachery must have been perpetrated, of which we are not informed).

A novelistic or legendary understanding of the book is often accompanied by an attempt to interpret the names in the book as symbolic. Like most names, especially in Hebrew, those in the Book of Ruth do undeniably have a meaning (although often debatable when it comes to specifics), but that is a far cry from establishing that they were contrived for the story-teller's purposes. Their historicity is at least strongly suggested by the fact that their types, if not the actual names, are all well attested in ancient onomastica.

Linguistically, the meaning of "Ruth" is the most difficult of all to establish. The translation, "(female) companion" is satisfying to proponents of a novelistic theory, but scientifically "unlikely in the extreme" (Campbell). Not much more firmly based are derivations from two other roots, yielding meanings such as "attractive" (from *ra'ah,* to see) or "refreshing" *(rwh).* The symbolists like to associate "Orpah" with the Hebrew for "neck" and interpret it as "stiff-necked, stubborn, disloyal," or the like, allegedly symbolizing her willingness to leave Naomi and return home, but every indication is that that association is equally fanciful. Similarly, the association of "Boaz" with "strength" is only one of various possibilities. "Mahlon" and "Chilion" have been interpreted as "sickness" and "failing," respectively, but also without any good foundation; the latter name is attested at Ugarit, and both are good Late Bronze types, but we have no real clue to their meaning. The most common Biblical *type* of name, of course, is "Elimelech," probably meaning, "The King [Yahweh] is my God." But the only name for which we have any warrant in the book itself for making anything of is "Naomi," meaning "delightful/pleasant," on which the bearer herself puns in 1:20, suggesting that she be called "Mara" ("Bitter") instead.

Various fruitless efforts have been made to trace the prehistory or earlier stages of the book. Perhaps best known is Myers' attempt to demonstrate an early poetic stage of the story (possibly a nursery tale), but it is very doubtful if he has established any aspect of his case.

In the critical understanding, what should the purpose of this *Novelle* have been? Of course, various answers have been offered. Especially early form critics, typically minimizing or ignoring the question of historicity, tended to view the book as only a "novel" in the popular sense, that is, intending little more than to entertain and satisfy the audience. Among other things, however, it is difficult to understand the inclusion of such a pointless story in the canon.

An eccentric offshoot of form criticism was the effort by a few to expound the book as a Bethlehem "cult-legend." The names in the book were related to the fertility cult (e.g., Ruth a sacral prostitute), much was made of Ruth's nocturnal visit to Boaz at the threshing floor (cf. below), and appeal was even made to St. Jerome's report of a fertility cult at Bethlehem in his day (the Adonis of his time allegedly a successor to the god Lachmu after whom Bethlehem was named). It is a pleasure to report that not even many critics have ever taken this hypothesis very seriously.

Far and away the majority of critics, however, have followed Wellhausen's lead in interpreting the book as an exilic, or, more likely postexilic (probably fifth century), political tract, representing, like Jonah (which see), the "liberal" or universalistic party of the day, heirs of "Deutero-Isaiah," who were making propaganda against especially the particularistic and anti-mixed marriage policies of Ezra and Nehemiah. Nationalistic or even jingoistic positions as allegedly represented also by Esther (which see) and, later, by Judith, would also have been in their sights.

For all of its popularity, however, this hypothesis seems unusually vulnerable, as also some dissenting critics have been quick to point out. For one thing, it tends to stand or fall with a fifth-century date (see below). Similarly, it almost necessarily implies that the book is largely (if not totally) fictional—and it is a good illustration of higher criticism's general tendency not only to look for tensions and conflicts within Scripture but also to read as much of Scripture through a political lens as it possibly can. Third, the story simply does not read as though it has a chip on its shoulder: Orpah is not condemned for returning "to her people and to her gods" (Ruth 1:15), and Ruth's stated reasons for not doing likewise are—from a theological viewpoint—not formulated very satisfyingly (1:16-17; see below). Finally, Ruth's case scarcely parallels the problem of mixed marriages with non-Yahwists that the book is supposedly polemicizing against: Ruth, in contrast, becomes a proselyte and adopts the religion of Israel. Deut. 23:3, which stringently commands that "No Ammonite or Moabite shall enter the assembly of the LORD, even to the tenth generation," is often cited as an example of the kind of attitude that Ruth opposes, but there is no reason why female proselytes should not have been thought of as an exception from the beginning (cf. Deut. 21:10 ff. and rules regarding marriage to women captured in war).

Because of all these difficulties with the "orthodox" critical position, some scholars today tend to back away from the polemical or propagandistic aspect of the Wellhausenian posture and simply describe the book as "universalist" in its attitude. That, however, leaves the question of its purpose (and date) entirely up in the air, but, properly construed, the conservative would have no necessary difficulty with such a designation.

A final theory holds that the Book of Ruth has primarily a legal or humanitarian concern that relatives look after childless widows. The proposed social reform was developed in terms of one or both of two ancient Israelite customs, the levirate obligation (of a brother-in-law to have children by his deceased brother's widow, if he had died childless) and the ge'ullah ("redemption"; the obligation of the go'el or nearest of kin to "redeem" the person or property of destitute relatives from foreclosure; cf. below). There are many versions of this theory, corresponding to the fact that, by any reckoning, we encounter in this connection one of the major interpretative conundrums in the entire book. Some think the purpose was simply to revive or enforce the moribund levirate custom, while others think there was also an intent to expand it and perhaps bring it into connection with the law of "redemption." A problem then immediately arises with respect to the levirate legislation of Deut. 25:5 ff., which exhibits significant differences from those described in Ruth (cf. below). Inevitably, the question of the relative date of the two pericopes also enters the discussion. Suffice it to say here that the very lack of precision on these points (e.g., neither Boaz nor the other kinsman was brother to Ruth's former husband, Mahlon, and thus no "levir" in the sense of Deut. 25) and makes it rather less than obvious that the writer had any such purposes in mind.

Date and Authorship

What can be said about the date and authorship of the book? The

Talmudic ascription to Samuel (like the surrounding two books) can safely be dismissed as "unscientific," but no more plausible suggestion seems ever to have been made. Ruth is *one* of the books in the Bible where the conservative can agree with the liberal on the anonymity of the book (as an exception, rather than the rule, however).

Date is also difficult to pin down. The usual critical conclusion, as we have already noted, is fifth century, allegedly in opposition to the policies of Ezra and Nehemiah, although minor variations on that theme have suggested alternatives a century in either direction. Besides that presumed historico-political occasion, other arguments are also adduced, but just as debatably. The book's presence in the hagiographical canon certainly does not betoken lateness of composition; especially the five Megilloth were all brought together in this position out of liturgical motives, regardless of date. The argument that the concluding genealogy (if allowed to be "genuine") must be of about the same period as the Pentateuchal "P," with all of its genealogical interests (assumed, of course, to be postexilic) would not be very conclusive even if the existence of such a postexilic document were conceded. Equally an argument in a circle is the appeal to Ruth's allegedly "learned, antiquarian" interest (cf. esp., Ruth 4:7) in the obsolete customs of the levirate and *ge'ullah:* unless with the critics we assume that the writer must have been familiar with both the levirate legislation of a *seventh*-century Deuteronomy and the "redemption" laws of an exilic "Holiness Code" (Lev. 25:25 and 27:9-33), the book could be markedly earlier and still deal with an "antiquarian" usage.

That leaves us with only one other defense of so late a date: the alleged Aramaisms and other supposed linguistic indications of lateness. Since the discovery of "Aramaisms" in pre-Israelite Canaanite texts, however, most of that "evidence" has evaporated. Both that and the other linguistic problems are too technical to detail here (see the commentaries, on this point, especially Campbell), but dialectical variation, perhaps reflecting provincial speech around Bethlehem, seems better to explain the speech idiosyncracies of the book than any hypothesis of late composition. Whatever the explanation of these relatively few peculiarities, it must be stressed that they are exceptional. In general, the language and style of the Book of Ruth is pure, classical Hebrew, on a par with Samuel and palpably different from what we encounter in indisputably late material, e.g., Esther, Chronicles, or Nehemiah (Driver). While it is conceivable then, as some have argued, that the language is artificially "archaistic," not genuinely archaic or classical, the preponderance of evidence is overwhelmingly in the opposite direction.

If one says "classical Hebrew," he implies a date perhaps as early as the United Monarchy itself, and scarcely later than the middle of the Divided Monarchy (thus perhaps 900—700 B.C.). Since David is mentioned by name in the genealogy (assuming its origination with the rest of the book), the book can scarcely antedate his reign. Perhaps it is even to be dated sometime within his reign, as many conservatives hold, because no subsequent kings are mentioned, not even the renowned Solomon. That does not necessarily follow, however, since "David" would suffice to establish the lineage of the entire dynasty, and Messianic interests might even have made it desirable to stop with his name. Really, it is not possible to be any more precise, though Campbell's cautious suggestion deserves condemnation, namely, that the book's interest in right judgment and care for the unfortunate bespeaks final fixation of Solomonic roots in connection with Jehoshaphat's judicial reforms in the second quarter of the ninth century.

Contents and Theology

The story of Ruth is too well known to justify recounting it here. Hence, we may limit ourselves to only a few specific difficulties or high-points, leading into a broader consideration of the book's theological significance. One of the first matters to require attention is the real import of Ruth's oft-quoted speech in 1:16-17, expressing her resolve to accompany Naomi. One should take care neither to read into Ruth's words more than is actually said, nor fail to hear them in total context. As usual in the Old Testament, the cultural and the religious, the political and the theological, are intertwined. Ruth gives little surface expression to the latter, expressing herself rather in terms of personal and familial loyalty. These elements are not to be eliminated in contemporary application, of course, yet one has only "person-centered" human values if that is all that comes through. Ruth's "conversion" is nowhere narrated, yet the context gives ample clues that she speaks out of covenantal, *heilsgeschichtliche* convictions, and these must be highlighted: the use of *"Yahweh"* in Ruth's oath (the only time in the book on Ruth's lips), the use of "loaded" theological terms in the context, such as God's "visiting" *(pqd)* His people (1:6), or His "kindness" *(chesedh,* 1:8 e.g.,). Similar vocabulary is artfully used throughout the book, but it is rarely apparent in English translation (see the commentaries).

Second, there is the questionable matter of Ruth's clandestine visit to Boaz at the threshing floor (chap. 3). At Naomi's instigation, it is plain that the purpose of the visit is to prod Boaz into exercising his role as "redeemer" *(go'el),* as Ruth explicitly calls him when he awakens (3:9; RSV: "next of kin"). Both Biblical parallels (Ezek. 16:8; Deut. 22:30;

27:20) and modern Arabic custom make plain that Ruth's request to Boaz to spread his "skirt" (literally, "wing" i.e., corner of a garment) over her meant a request for marriage; that was the specific way Boaz should function as "redeemer" (cf. below), somewhat in fulfillment of his own prayer in 2:12. In other phrases in the context the sexual *double entendre* is probably even more obvious in the Hebrew than in translation: words such as "lie," "know," and especially in this context, "feet"—which can, in Hebrew idiom, be a euphemism, but which like the other words, can also be taken at face value, and obviously must be here. Perhaps the possibility of sexual hanky-panky or the temptation to premature coitus is highlighted as much as it is precisely to stress that this is *not* the response of covenanted people who live within the context of *chesedh*. It is surely no accident that Boaz praises Ruth (3:10) for that very quality, as he agrees to pursue the matter promptly.

Behind all of this, however, and central to the book's plot and significance, is the idea of "redemption," both its theological significance and the historico-exegetical question it raises. The latter are basically twofold: (1) apparent differences between the levirate law here and in Deut. 25 especially in the use of the sandal (Ruth 4:7-8 versus Deut. 25:9); and (2) the combination of the levirate marriage and redemption responsibilities here, attested nowhere else in the Bible. If both the levirate and the redemption laws (Deut. 25 and Lev. 27) are Mosaic, two contradictory critical theories about the date and purpose of the book are precluded: (a) that Ruth must be *later* than the latest of the two laws, that is, postexilic because Lev. 27 is judged to be exilic (part of the Holiness Code); and (b) that Ruth (like Gen. 38, narrating the birth of Boaz's ancestor, Perez; cf. Ruth 4:12, 18) is *earlier* than Deuteronomy (assumed to be a seventh-century product) because it supposedly witnesses to an earlier period when someone other than a brother-in-law could function as levir, but when the levir, whoever he was, had greater obligation than Deuteronomy later allowed.

If, however, we reject those critically based hypotheses (and all dating speculations built on them), it is not possible to offer a certain alternative. Levirate laws were widely known in Israel's environment but also differed widely in detail, and we must reckon with the possibility of provincial variation in the Book of Ruth. Furthermore, even if one ascribes all the Pentateuchal "codes" to Moses, it is plain that the various collections, taken individually, are each incomplete and often only illustrative. Hence, it may well be that the combination of levirate and redemption responsibilities evidenced in Ruth may have been more common than our paucity of sources would indicate. Likewise, the assumption by a more distant relative of the levirate responsibility when a woman had no brothers-in-law, as Ruth did not, may or may not have been regular practice. And since "redemption" was concerned with persons as well as property, bringing it into connection with *marriage* of persons may not have been that unusual a step either. The differences in the shoe symbolisms of Deut. 25:9 and Ruth 4:7-8 (the latter text bristles with problems of its own) are so great that it is reasonable to assume that they refer to entirely different situations and are not to be compared at all.

Whatever the sociological particularities, Boaz plainly does exercise his obligations as both levir and redeemer. The marriage blessing of Ruth 4:11-12 is prominently represented in later Jewish and Christian nuptial ceremonies. Both it and the book's concluding genealogy (4:18-22) anchor in Boaz's ancestor, Perez, Judah's child by Tamar (Gen. 38), by marriage into which line Ruth becomes an ancestress of David and an inner participant in the Messianic promises to which it was heir. Its fulfillment is heralded by incorporation into the genealogy of Matt. 1 at the head of the New Testament, ending with "Joseph, the husband of Mary, of whom Jesus was born, who is called Christ."

A longer version of the genealogy also appears in 1 Chron. 2, on which (or a common ancestor of both) many critics think it is dependent, especially if it is construed as a later addition. Stylistically, it is, indeed an "appendix" to the book, but functionally it is better regarded as climactic in integrating private history into the mainstream of *Heilsgeschichte*. Its style (especially the use of *toledoth* or "generations") is like that of "P" in Genesis, but if "P" is Moses, we have not an argument for lateness or ungenuineness, but possible evidence of a deliberate attempt by the author to pick up earlier genealogical threads. Part of the argument for its ungenuineness is lack of mention of Ruth in other Old Testament genealogies of David—but mothers are often omitted (Boaz is not), and especially if Ruth is an early composition, her specific inclusion would be unnecessary. Furthermore, the fact that Obed is reckoned as Boaz's instead of Elimelech's son need not contradict the levirate concern of the book that the firstborn continue his family, because custom may well have regarded the offspring of a levirate union to be the son of both his "legal" and his actual father.

It is because the genealogy sets the narrative in its broader redemptive context that the book's featuring "redemption" is so significant (the verb, *ga'al,* is used twenty times in the four chapters). The Book of Ruth is the Bible's major exemplification of the "sociological" foundation of the more theological and technically more metaphorical use of the concept of "redemption," and that background needs to be stressed for full understanding of the theological expression. The first point of extension of the metaphor is the perception of God as Israel's relative via the covenant, and thence as helper of the helpless, the defender of the defenseless. (Cf. also Job's "redeemer" in Job 19:25, which see; after Naomi makes a veritably Jobian indictment of God's covenant faithfulness in 1:14 ff., also this book proceeds to demonstrate how God's "justice" is vindicated.) The "redeemer's" concern is not only for persons in an interior, psychological sense, but also for their property, land, or inheritance, thus bringing into the orbit another major Biblical-theological complex. The Old Testament's theological application of the metaphor centers, of course, on the Exodus (Ex. 15:13), but it is developed especially in Is. 40—55 in typological application to the "exodus" from Babylon. Because of Boaz's "redemption" of Ruth, and their union, the ultimately antitypical exodus becomes possible in *the* Redeemer *par excellence*. More detailed word study would also have to point out that in New Testament usage "redeem" has been enriched by merger with the companion concept of "ransom" (Old Testament *padah*).

Thus, there is legitimacy in the common evangelical practice of regarding Boaz in his capacity as "redeemer" as a type of the Redeemer. But the Book of Ruth also often seems to be illustrative of excesses in the use of that method. It scarcely follows that Ruth typifies the "bride of Christ," and, except perhaps in homiletic application, other elaborate parallels between Boaz and Christ's mediatorial work soon go out of bounds. In any event, it must be clear that in the Old Testament it is Yahweh who is Israel's *Go'el,* and all human agencies are only His representatives.

Perhaps it is also fruitful to read Ruth, in the light of especially the genealogy, as "Messianic history," that is, noting from the book that the levirate and *go'el* institutions, concerned as they were with preserving family name, seed, and inheritance, found their ultimate fulfillment in Christ and His kingdom.

Properly construed, these more traditional accents are thoroughly compatible with the stress in more recent literature (especially Hals) that in Ruth God does not act in supernatural and miraculous, but in immanental and "providential" manner. The validity of this insight is not canceled by the fact that at some liberal hands a hidden agenda accompanies it, namely, the judgment that we have here, perhaps like the "Court History" of 2 Sam. 9 ff., a firstfruit of the "Solomonic Enlightenment's" breakthrough into genuine historiography and the only paradigm of God's presence and activity which is still acceptable in our modern, secular age. In an orthodox hermeneutical framework, however, Ruth does classically illustrate how, even within the covenant, God normally operates "in, with, and under" ordinarily human decisions (in both grace and judgment), which are always, therefore, fraught with eternal and eschatological significance. We noted above some of the covenant vocabulary that must not be overlooked in the book's exposition; in that context, the horizontal dimension on which the book concentrates will not subtract from, but rather enhance the view *sub specie aeternitatis.*

LAMENTATIONS

The usual Hebrew name for this book, following the ancient Oriental pattern evidenced also in other Biblical books, is simply its opening word, the exclamation, *'ekah* ("How"). It was apparently a standard opening word for a dirge over a fallen city (cf. Is. 1:21, also addressed to Jerusalem prophetically). In the Hebrew text, its special character is also highlighted metrically: not only in 1:1, but also at the beginning of chaps. 2 and 4 it stands in extrametrical position at the beginning of the poem (anacrusis).

Exactly when the work began to be called "Lamentations" is not clear. The Babylonian Talmud and other early Jewish writings do so refer to it (Hebrew: *qinoth).* It is not unlikely that the Septuagint was dependent on such an early Hebrew tradition in labeling the book *threnoi,* and thence the *Liber Threnorum* of the Vulgate and most subsequent translations (cf. our general term, "threnody").

Authorship

Equally ancient and widespread (though not univocal) is the tradition of Jeremianic authorship. The Talmud can be cited again, and most of the ancient versions witness to it, if not in their titles, then in a brief prologue, Only the Peshitta of the ancient versions includes it in the title, as do also most of the English versions we are familiar with. The Vulgate, however, prefixes to the first chapter: *Id est lamentationes Jeremiae prophetae;* and the Septuagint (at least some recensions) even more expansively: "And it came to pass after Israel had gone into captivity, and Jerusalem was laid waste, that Jeremiah sat weeping and composed this lament over Jerusalem and said," (a prologue which stylistically suggests a Hebrew orginal). The traditional association of Jeremiah with Lamentations undoubtedly accounts for much of that prophet's unfortunate characterization as the "weeping prophet," an epithet which really does not apply in any event.

Obviously it was this traditional ascription to Jeremiah that caused the Septuagint to sandwich Lamentations between Jeremiah and Ezekiel, a sequence which is still followed almost universally in the West. In the Hebrew canon, of course, Lamentations appears in the third or hagiographical division, specifically amongst the Megilloth or scrolls proper for liturgical reading on Jewish festivals (and not, be it noted, because of lateness of composition; cf. on Daniel). In this case the liturgical association is most obvious and apropos—with *Tish'ah b'Ab* (the ninth day of the fifth month, Ab, on the Hebrew calendar, falling in late July or early August on the Gregorian calendar), commemorating not only the fall of Jerusalem to Nebuchadnezzar on that date (so 2 Kings 25:8-9, although Jer. 52:12 says the "tenth," apparently referring to a different phase of it), but also the capitulation to Titus in A. D. 70 and the fall of Betar (Bar Kochba's redoubt) in A. D. 135, all traditionally on the same date.

How far back the association of the Book of Lamentations with the liturgical commemoration of the events it depicts may go cannot be ascertained. The commentaries of Kraus and Weiser attempt to establish an originally cultic *Sitz im Leben* for the poems, but their efforts, each differing markedly from the other, while not totally unattractive, are too speculative to command credence in any detail. However, the reference in Jer. 41:5 to public mourning shortly after the catastrophe and the debates about fasts related to the commemoration mentioned in Zech. 7:3-5 and 8:19 (which see) make it not at all unlikely that the usage roots already in the exilic or early postexilic periods. Christian liturgical use of the book also began very early in the Christian era, but associated with the last three days of Holy Week (especially in the Reproaches of the Tenebrae service) via typological interpretation (cf. below), and quite unrelated to position in the canon or to isagogical issues of authorship.

More attention has often been devoted to the question of authorship than it deserves (especially in comparison with the book's message and importance). We have seen that a strong *traditional* case for Jeremianic authorship can be made, but technically it is not possible to go further. Since nearly everyone agrees that the work was produced in the *time* of Jeremiah and almost certainly by an eyewitness or participant in the tragedy, the difference between the various traditions is, quite literally, only nominal. True to form, liberals quite unanimously break with tradition and think of some other poet besides Jeremiah, and one can scarcely but suspect that some of the hidden (perhaps even to themselves) agenda here is the critical predilection for anonymity, and preference for an impersonal product of "tradition" or the community over a longer period of time. Conservatives still generally tend to support the tradition, but at least informed conservatives all recognize that it is a matter of tradition, not of doctrine, because the variety in the superscriptions (even when these are not questioned, as critics regularly do) eliminates the possibility of defending the tradition on the basis of a verbally inspired text. All in all, however, in our judgment, the traditional association with Jeremiah remains the hypothesis with the fewest difficulties.

Critics commonly surmise that the faulty ascription to Jeremiah arose from a careless reading of 2 Chron. 35:25, which reports that the prophet wrote a lament for Josiah which were "written in the Laments," and "all the singing men and singing women have spoken of Josiah in their laments to this day." Indeed, Josephus does seem to identify a dirge over Josiah which was extant in his day with Lam. 4 (and in later times especially 4:20 was often thought to refer to Josiah, rather than to Zedekiah or Jehoiachin, as it apparently must) but, in general, there is no warrant for assuming that all precritical scholars were such dullards. *If* the tradition is incorrect, a much more likely explanation for the association would be the well-known popular tendency to cluster nearly all compositions and exploits around a few famous heroes. If, on the other hand, the tradition of Jeremianic authorship is correct, it still can scarcely be the composition of which the Chronicler speaks, because the subject of the canonical book is obviously a fallen city, not a king.

Apart from the tradition, neither the arguments pro nor con are conclusive. There are numerous and striking affinities between some of the laments in the book of Jeremiah and those in Lamentations (e.g., the phrase, "daughter of" occurring about twenty times in each book, and "eyes flowing with tears" in Lam. 1:16; 2:11 and Jer. 9:1, 18). The calamities lamented are attributed to the same causes in both books (national sin, faithless priests and prophets, the perfidy of allies in whom vain hope had been placed etc.), although it must be conceded that these similarities are too common in Biblical thought to establish any definite connection. Furthermore, in spite of formal differences among the five poems (cf. below) there is no doubt that the same mood pervades all of them.

On the other hand, there are also numerous divergencies from Jeremiah's undisputed laments (or "confessions"), some of which can be better paralleled with other books, especially some of the laments in the Psalter. The style is generally more elaborate than Jeremiah's, and especially chaps. 2 and 4 are more like Ezekiel. Not all of the so-called divergencies stand up, however. For example, one must dismiss as ultimately simplistic the frequent critical assertion that Lam. 3:59 ff., with its petition for God's judgment upon the wickedness of the Babylonians, conflicts with Jeremiah's consistent insistence that Babylon was God's own chosen instrument to effect His wrath upon Israel; Jeremiah's own oracles against Babylon, as e.g., in 25:12 and chaps. 50—51, would suffice to refute the charge, let alone more general knowledge of prophetic theology in its totality. Similarly, Lam. 4:17 does not contradict Jeremiah's opposition to placing any hope in deliverance from Egypt, but simply records the fact that most of the populace did, in fact, entertain such vain hopes.

Such straining of gnats aside, there is no reason at all why a poet of Jeremiah's calibre might not have composed a book like Lamentations, often employing variations which are not evidenced in the collection of · his oracles. We know of no one else of such literary or theological stature among those left behind after the deportation to Babylon, but the possibility is not thereby precluded. One can readily agree with most critics in the supposition that the book derives from among those who were left behind in Palestine after the deportation. However, it is scarcely impossible, as such, that someone in exile penned the lines, either while the memory was still fresh in his mind, or, conceivably, even by someone who was not a participant or eyewitness (one recalls Ezekiel as an example of an exile who was phenomenally conversant with developments in Judah). Jeremiah remained in Judah long enough before Johanan kidnapped him to Egypt that Lamentations might plausibly stem from that interval. If, however, we are to think of some other author, the book is of even more interest as possibly our only direct evidence of the mood and mentality of those whom Nebuzaradan had spared from deportation.

Unity and Form of the Poems

Quite a number of critics are convinced that the five poems in the book do not stem from a single hand, and considerable energy has been expended in attempts to establish the order and various circumstances in which they were originally written. Some have sought to associate some of the poems (especially chap. 1; so Rudolph) with the 597 instead of the 587 deportation, and suggestions as late as Maccabean times have been made. A common suggestion is that chaps. 2 and 4 are the work of an eyewitness, to which were later added the laments of chaps. 1 and 3 and the prayer of chap. 5 (the last three perhaps from about 540, in the depths of the Exile). However, the great variety of these conjectures and their lack of common acceptance remain their best refutation.

Attention must also be given to the form-critical question of possible Mesopotamian influence on the *Gattung* of the Biblical Lamentations. In ancient Sumer this was a cultic genre, and one over the destruction of Ur is especially noteworthy for its sometimes striking parallels. The neo-Babylonian period was also noted for its threnodies over fallen cities, and influence from this quarter is even more plausible. Destruction of cities was certainly a common enough occurrence in the ancient Near East, and the event was normally attributed to the wrath of the god(s). Hence, it is not impossible that ancient literary conventions were at hand for commemorating such castastrophes and that our author availed himself of some of them. Nevertheless, the even greater differences in theology and often detail, as well as the fact that some of the "parallels" are found also in entirely different genres, seem to indicate that whatever connection there is (if any), is more a matter of broad cultural continuum than of any direct influence.

A more substantial form-critical issue arises from the more individual expression of the poems at points. Especially Lam. 3 is often regarded as an "individual lament" in contrast to the more communal or national reference of the other songs, and hence is often considered a later, independent composition, originally having nothing to do with the destruction of Jerusalem. The "I" is also much in evidence in the clearly communal lament of chap. 1, however, indicating how easily the singular and plural forms of expression were interchangeable. Hence, it appears much more likely that the difference is purely formal, a matter of variation purely for the sake of variety. Perhaps via the device of "corporate personality," the city is simply personified more directly at points, or the author more directly identifies himself with, and speaks in the name of, his beloved city at some points than at others. Typical form-critical logomachies also surface in some debates about the correct classification of some of the other poems, especially in the question whether they are to be reckoned as communal laments, or are more dependent on the traditional forms of the funeral dirge and/or "lament over a ruined sanctuary" (Kraus).

Lam. 3 appears to have attracted a disproportionate amount of critical "wrath" also in other respects. Various theories about the alleged development of the chapter in two or more stages into its present acrostic form have been proposed, but it does not serve our purposes to attempt to delineate or refute them in any detail. Archer, however, makes the very telling observation that one type of dissection is not suggested, even though it would correspond to a common critical criterion for distinguishing "genuine" material from alleged later additions in other Biblical books, especially the prophets: the opening and closing sections of the chapter are quite typical lament, while the middle verses (19-39), almost alone in the entire book, give nearly classical expression to the Biblical theme of hope and trust in God's overarching grace and mercy (cf. below).

In a sense, it is also a "form-critical" observation that all five of the poems are "alphabetic" in some sense (itself a major argument for unity of composition). The first four poems are also quite strictly "acrostic," although the acrostic principle is applied in different ways (something which is quite evident in the Hebrew text). Lam. 1 and 2 exhibit the simplest type of acrostic: each verse (with the curious exceptions of 1:7 and 2:19) consists of three lines, but only the first line begins with the requisite letter of the Hebrew alphabet. The general pattern is the same in chap. 4, except that there are only two lines per verse. The acrostic pattern in chap. 3 is more complicated: each verse again is composed of three lines, but *each* of those three lines begins with the same letter of the alphabet. As noted, chap. 5 is the only poem not structured acrostically, but it too is at least "alphabetizing" in that it contains twenty-two verses, almost certainly one for each letter of the Hebrew alphabet. (Cf. similarly Pss. 33; 38; and 103; Lam. 5 also displays other structural differences from the rest of the poems; cf. below).

Acrostics, of course, are by no means unknown or even rare in the Bible outside of Lamentations (cf. esp. Ps. 119). They are also known in both ancient Egypt and Mesopotamia, thus demolishing an earlier critical supposition that they evidenced late and degenerate formalism. Certainly in the case of Lamentations the use of what initially appears to be so cumbersome and constricting a device has not cramped the writer's style, because on the literary power and beauty of the book there is no dispute. However, the use of the form throughout virtually an entire book does throw into bold relief the question of why it was employed at all. To that question, however, there is no clear answer, unless (humanly speaking) perhaps simple variety, personal taste, or an opportunity for the poet to display his skills. Whatever truth there may be to the hypothesis that the form roots in primitive magic and mysticism, it can be no more than irrelevant prehistory as far as Biblical usage is concerned. Some have suggested that so "controlled" a form commended itself to the author as an aid to keeping under control the almost overpowering emotions of those who first recited the poems. There may also be truth in the suggestion that the form was sometimes intended to convey the idea of comprehensiveness, of covering everything relevant "from A to Z," and would then here perhaps intend to effect a complete catharsis of the trauma (Gottwald) and/or to suggest that "Israel had sinned from aleph to tau." It would also make a composition easier to memorize, but there is no reason why that concern should have become so paramount on only certain occasions.

A quite unique problem (that is with the possible exceptions of Prov. 31 and Ps. 34) arises in the acrostics of chaps. 2—4, in that in these three chapters the Hebrew letter *pe* precedes *ayin*, just the reverse of the normal alphabetic order (which is followed in chap. 1). There is no convincing explanation for this oddity. Magical "explanations" are again, at best, beside the point, and an odd suggestion that the order of these letters had not yet been fixed at this time seems to be demolished by the discovery of the usual sequence in Ugarit, nearly a millennium before Lamentations.

The Book of Lamentations was also the major springboard for Budde's thesis that there was a special meter in Hebrew poetry for laments, which he named *Qinah,* the Hebrew word for "lament." The name has stuck, even though everyone agrees that some modifications of Budde's hypothesis are in order, and some have abandoned it altogether (partly because of widely varying suppositions about the nature of Hebrew poetry to begin with, an issue into which we cannot enter here). So-called *Qinah* meter has a 3:2 beat, and thus has an uneven or "limping" character, supposedly evocative of the brokenness in spirit of the lamentation itself, "a rhythm that always dies away" as Budde characterized it. There may be some truth to Budde's association of this meter with lamentation, but only partially so. Even within the Book of Lamentations, while it remains the dominant metric pattern, many others also occur, and chap. 5 consists entirely of 3:3 bicola. Outside of the book, too, it sometimes is not employed in elegiac contexts (most egregiously in David's lament for Saul and Jonathan in 2 Sam. 1), and, conversely, at other times it is employed where there is no hint of lament (e.g., Is. 40:9 ff.; Cant. 1:9-11, etc.)

Contents

Beyond the observations already made, it is all but impossible to limn significant differences among the five songs (let alone faithfully reduce their poetic impact to prose in any fashion). A few varying lines of thought may cautiously be suggested, however. In Lam. 1 the desolation and misery of Jerusalem is described especially in contrast to her past glories and 1:1 well epitomizes the entire book. Sometimes the personified city itself speaks, and particularly in the famous, poignant cry of 1:12 (cf. below) laments the indifference of those who observe her plight. Even though the author is well aware that the judgment was fully deserved, he concludes (1:22) with a petition for divine retribution also upon the agents of that judgment.

Lam. 2 especially underlines that the catastrophe was a result of Yahweh's anger; nevertheless, the only hope of deliverance lies in contrition and supplication to Him. The chapter also contains some particularly vivid depictions of the horrors of the city's siege and fall (cf. 4:19 ff.). The "terrors on every side" of 2:22 is especially redolent of Jeremiah, and the theme of the taunts of the passersby in 2:15 is a familiar refrain in many prophets.

Except for its first person singular formulation (cf. above), Lam. 3 repeats the same themes: the "wormwood and the gall" (v. 19) of God's apparent enmity, the desideration of repentance (esp. vs. 40-42), and prayer for requital upon the enemy (vs. 64-66). As noted above, chap. 3 is most distinguished within the book by its lengthy articulation of the theme of consolation in God's "antecedent will" of mercy, the conviction that judgment represents only the disciplinary aspect of His *chesedh* or "steadfast love," etc. (vs. 19-39).

Lam. 4, with its vivid, harrowing depictions of the debacle, is similar to chap. 2, but the final two verses again take comfort in the thought of the future reversal of fortunes, when the cup will pass to "Edom" and "Uz" (cf. Job). Chapter 5 has a particularly precatory tone to it: Yahweh should "remember" and not forget forever. Zion's desolation reminds the faithful of Yahweh's eternal reign (v. 19), but the time is not yet, and the book ends with a poignantly plaintive query: "Or hast thou utterly rejected us? Art thou exceedingly angry with us?" (Synagogue rubrics direct the rereading of v. 21 after v. 22 so that the lection ends on a positive note).

Theology

The theological significance of Lamentations is considerable, both on the immediately historical level, and also in broader typological perspective in the light of also the New Testament (the two, of course, are ultimately one). The reader must have a more thorough appreciation of the theological significance of the land as Israel's "inheritance," and of Zion and particularly of the temple located there, than the average Protestant possesses, in order to begin to empathize with the writer and his contemporaries. How could the God of the covenant allow to fall into the hands of infidels the "sacrament" and seal of His eternal covenant and promise, the seat of the son of David whom 4:20 calls "the breath of our nostrils, the LORD's anointed"? Was He impotent? Had His promises failed? Did He no longer care? Was there any prospect of future deliverance? Of return of the exiles? Would justice ever be meted out to their tormentors? What was the point of such suffering? In the latter respect Lamentations can certainly be compared somewhat with Job and Habakkuk, although more readily with the latter than the former, both because of the prophetic (instead of wisdom) articulations common to the two, and because the two also consider the subject in primarily national instead of individual terms.

The pain is still so great that the immediate need almost appears more to be to "get it out" and articulate it rather than to theorize about its meaning. However, it is far more than just psychological catharsis; it is obviously also confession of *sin*. Gottwald's thesis that the key to the book lies in the tension between historical reality and "deuteronomic" theology of reward and retribution, is much too narrowly (and critically) formulated, but not entirely off the mark. For all of the bitterness of the moment, Lamentations never questions either God's justice or His love. There is no attempt to evade or alibi their own responsibility, but if God is faithful, there must also be a future under Him and His Word, and especially in chap. 3 the writer's stubborn confidence in the God of the covenant swells to fervent exclamation of hope in His unfailing goodness.

Thus, Lamentations represents a major (if not perhaps a first) appropriation of the consistent Biblical and especially prophetic preachment of the meaning of judgment, of God's wrath, and of the "remnant." The deeper meaning of the disaster was a major exemplification of God's *sub contrario* method of leading His people to repentance, of the indissolubility of judgment and salvation, of Law and Gospel, and thus in total Biblical context a major expression of the "death and resurrection" of Jerusalem as a type of Good Friday and Easter. (Over against all brands of "political theology" let it be stressed that the antitype is the *church,* not any modern nation or political entity which should be moved by the book to "national repentance" or the like!) In the commentary literature, especially Knight develops the typological significance of Lamentations as describing "the crucifixion of God's adopted Son, Israel," and he styles the book "the Easter eve of the human soul," for in it the believer, though crushed by God's judgments, remains confident of restoration and resurrection.

Via Christ, the church sees itself as the heir of the Old Testament people of God, recapitulating and fulfilling the rhythms of its experience before God in the time of the consummation, and into that History all have been baptized. The church's appropriation of the book and of the history it describes thus differs only superficially from that of Judaism on the "Ninth of Ab": it not only confesses the destruction of Jerusalem as part of its history, but it sees the *pleroma* of that history in God's judgment upon all mankind in Christ, yet also with a final judgment still to come. One would think especially in this connection of Jesus' own repeated comparison (and typology) of His death with the destruction of the temple. The typological significance of Lamentations is thus very close to that of the Book of Jonah.

Much of the vocabulary of Lamentations has entered into the warp and woof of Christian meditation on the cross, and it is not to be dismissed as mere literary accommodation. It is doubtful if Lamentations is ever directly cited in the New Testament, but it is one of those cases where subsequent liturgical and homiletical usage was profoundly faithful to the spirit and intent of the New Testament. Major examples would include: "Is it nothing to you, all you who pass by?" (1:12); "they hiss and wag their heads" (2:15; cf. Ps. 22:7); and the "wormwood and the gall" of 3:19.

The loss of this entree to Lamentations in most recent church history is only symptomatic of developments across the board with respect to the Old Testament. One part of the book is still perhaps relatively familiar (the beautiful words of hope in 3:19 ff.), but their near exclusive use, or at least use apart from the context, suggests as strongly as anything how dire the danger is that our "Gospel" is becoming sentimentalized and universalized into "another Gospel." Lamentations can play a major role in holding before us the magnitude of God's righteous wrath, apart from which there is little need for "Gospel."

ECCLESIASTES (QOHELETH)

The isagogical and exegetical problems which one meets here have many similarities with those in Canticles (which compare), although the character and contents of the two books otherwise differ drastically (on the surface, a melancholy skepticism versus a lush eroticism). Both are probably to be classed as wisdom literature (which see), although both somewhat marginally. The Solomonic authorship of both is widely rejected, and in both cases the rest of Scripture or the New Testament does not speak to the issue (in fact never quotes or clearly alludes to either at all). The canonicity of both was under fire at Jamnia, but both survived (in the case of Ecclesiastes, the school of Hillel winning out over the more conservative school of Shammai). In both cases, however, many of the same questions have risen to a crescendo in modern times, especially in the glare of historical-critical skepticism. Perhaps partly in compensation, both were early assigned as proper lections for a major Jewish liturgical festival, Ecclesiastes for Succoth (Booths or "Tabernacles"), obviously as a sort of a *Memento Mori* damper on the excesses often associated with that autumnal vintage festival.

The Title

Specific problems with the book begin with its Hebrew title, "Qoheleth," obviously based on the superscription (1:1), "The words of Qoheleth, the son of David, king in Jerusalem." The form, "Qoheleth," apparently the *feminine* singular of a Qal active participle, appears nowhere else in the Bible besides its seven occurrences in this book. The feminine form is usually understood as a species of abstraction for which Hebrew ordinarily employs that gender, in this case an office, function, or a title, and there are parallels to that usage. However, with one exception (7:27) a masculine predicate follows, presumably because the office was always filled by a man. Strictly speaking, then, the word is not a proper noun. Since, however, it is only once (12:8) used with the definite article, it appears that the author of the book himself used the title as a virtual *nom de plume*. Thus, it is an appropriate designation for both the author and the work, and especially as more attention has come to be paid to the apocrypha in recent years, "Qoheleth" is often preferred over

"Ecclesiastes" to avoid confusion with "Ecclesiasticus" (Sirach).

There are also misgivings, however, about the Greek translation, "Ecclesiastes," and its English equivalent "Preacher." "Qoheleth" is probably etymologically related to the noun, *"qahal,"* which means "assembly" or "convocation," of almost any sort, including, indeed, "cultic assembly," "congregation," or "church." If the latter were the reference, the translation "Preacher" would probably not be a bad translation. However, the author speaks in a wisdom rather than a liturgical context, and his message is more "philosophical" than homiletical. Theologically, we will want to insist that the difference is not ultimate, but, sociologically, it is considerable, and we cannot ignore the latter.

Possibly, however, there is also great exegetical significance in the fact that the author describes himself as a speaker in a public *wisdom* assembly. He may thus indicate that he is not addressing initiates in "wisdom," that is, those who comprehend its full theological dimensions, but rather those of the "outer court," the general public whose "wisdom" is still largely that of this world. This audience he meets on its own terms, terms which he largely demolishes ("vanity of vanities") in order to prepare them for a higher and truer wisdom (cf. below).

Authorship and Date

Who was the author of the book? Was "Solomon," in effect, as much a *nom de plume* as "Qoheleth"? The name, "Solomon," is never explicitly used, but is clearly implied in the "son of David, king of Jerusalem" in the superscription (1:1) and similarly in 1:12 and 2:9. Various other allusions in the book plainly point in the same direction: the author's "great wisdom" (1:16), massive wealth and many servants (2:4-8), etc. Until modern times, there was only a minimal question about it. It probably was assumed at Jamnia, although we debate the frequent contention that the successful defense of the book's canonicity was largely based on that ascription; we suspect, that, as in the early church, "apostolicity" was not quite so purely a nominal matter as that! (In fact, the Tosefta clearly questions the book's canonicity, while assuming Solomonic authorship.) The sequence of books in the Septuagint witnesses to it: Proverbs, Ecclesiastes, and Song of Solomon, ascribed to Solomon, following the Davidic psalter, as son follows father.

On the other hand, the Talmud preserves considerable evidence of Jewish misgivings about the work (both authorship and canonicity), even in post-Mishnaic times. St. Jerome reports Jews in his day who wish the book had not survived. Luther complains about the great difficulty of the work, but apparently did not regard it as an antilegomenon (and his commentary may well be one of his little known classics). In the case of authorship, however, he departed from tradition. In his preface, Luther avers only that "this book was certainly not written or set down by King Solomon with his own hand. Instead, scholars put together what others had heard from Solomon's lips," and he cites 12:11 as evidence. But in his *Table Talk* he is much more radical and anticipates much modern critical opinion: "Solomon himself did not write the Book of Ecclesiastes, but it was produced by Sirach at the time of the Maccabees.—It is a sort of Talmud, compiled from many books, probably from the library of King Ptolemy Euergetes of Egypt."

Not surprisingly, then, not only does modern critical judgment reject Solomonic authorship virtually unanimously, but the vast majority of conservative scholarly opinion agrees (Hengstenberg, Delitzsch, Young, Leupold, Harrison, Pfeiffer, etc.). Estimates of the precise date, however, range over almost the entire postexilic period. Some early critical attempts to place its composition late in the second century appear to be contradicted by its apparent familiarity to the author of Sirach, and the discovery of fragments of the book at Qumran give that position the *coup de grace*. Possibly a majority of critics still cling to a third century date, but the trend appears to be toward a somewhat earlier period.

The major argument for postexilic date is linguistic. The situation is similar to that in Canticles (which see), but stronger. No one who knows both classical and Mishnaic Hebrew will dispute the judgment that Qoheleth's affinities are more with the latter, often in syntax as well as in vocabulary. Delitzsch is often quoted to the effect that if Ecclesiastes is really Solomonic, the Hebrew language had no history, and he amasses some 96 words, etc., found elsewhere only in undeniably postexilic literature. Among the late words cited are *she-* instead of *'asher* as the relative pronoun, *pardes* (park or "paradise"; cf. in Canticles), *zeman* (time), *kasher* (correct or "kosher"), etc. Syntactically, one notes the frequent use of the personal pronoun as a copula, the rare use of the *waw-*consecutive, etc.

The linguistic argument, however, is a very ambivalent one, and archaeological discoveries in the past century have seriously weakened it. The "Aramaic" cast of the language no longer carries much weight in the light of evidence at Ugarit that these were ancient western Semitic elements also on the Mediterranean littoral. Albright, Dahood, and others have launched weighty arguments in favor of heavy Phoenician-Canaanite influence on the book's diction; while they themselves think of early postexilic provenance of the work, the arguments are also amenable to Solomonic application and/or to northern origins, possibly because that was the dialect in which discourses of that sort were ordinarily couched at the time. Neither is the evidence for lateness as unambiguous

as it is often purported to be (see Archer); at best, we simply lack
sufficient Hebrew literature to construct with confidence any certain chart
of the development of the language in different times and areas beyond
the broadest generalities. As in the case of Canticles, Sanskrit (due to
Solomon's extensive trade contacts with the East) might explain what is
often understood as Greek influence. Furthermore, the possibility is by no
means precluded that an essentially Solomonic text was later updated
linguistically (a revision of Chaucer or even Shakespeare into modern
English is a frequent and apt comparison).

The occasion for such a recension in late times (if such it is) might be
the similarity of later challenges to Yahwism under especially Greek
influence to those current in earlier times. At very least, such a reissue of a
newly topical work is as plausible as the once popular opinion that the
writer of Ecclesiastes was himself heavily indebted to Stoic, Epicurean, or
other Greek philosophic thought. For example, the "nothing new under
the sun" refrain of especially the opening chapter (1:2-11) is not
inappropriate as a summary of much Greek thought (cf. Heraclitus'
famous "All is flux"), but it is also a classical summary of the "myth of the
eternal return," of the cyclicism which was apparently characteristic of
paganism from time immemorial.

Instead of adducing alleged Greek influence, a more common
comparative argument for lateness today appeals to allegedly parallel
developments in wisdom circles elsewhere in the ancient Near East.
Ecclesiastes is widely understood as part of a late revolt against "wisdom
orthodoxy," especially its allegedly rigid doctrine of reward and
retribution for good or evil. There is no doubt that wisdom all over the
ancient Near East entered into a crisis in late Old Testament times, but
not clearly for any further reason than the general cultural dissipation of
the times in connection with the breakup of the old Semitic empires and
Alexander's program of Hellenization. On the other hand, we have
evidences of periods of disillusionment (and even the entertaining of
suicide) in both Egypt and Mesopotamia from much earlier periods (the
"Song of the Harper." the "Dispute over Suicide," the "Pessimistic
Dialogue Between Master and Servant," even themes underlying the
ancient and famous Gilgamesh epic). In general, one is surely justified in
arguing that such moods are so recurrent, both individually and
culturally, that a chronological case based on such parallels is extremely
weak.

Another type of anti-Solomonic argument adduces alleged
anachronisms or other internal evidences which supposedly militate
against the traditional connection. The claim in 1:16 to have acquired
more wisdom than "all who were over Jerusalem before me" has always

aroused suspicion, but the statement does not specify kings, and Jerusalem was certainly an ancient city in Solomon's time. Similarly, in Eccl. 1:12 the Hebrew perfect *hayithi* might just as easily be translated, "I have *become* king" as RSV's "have been." Various times in the book (e.g., 4:13; 10:17) an objective or even critical viewpoint is adopted toward kingship, but if Solomon (or anyone else) wished to speak in traditional wisdom vein, that is exactly what one would expect (cf. many parallels in Proverbs). Neither is there any reason why Solomon should have been incapable of the idiom, nor why he should only have been an apologist for his own reign. Finally, it is often argued that the book evinces very difficult economic and social circumstances (e.g., 1:2-11; 3:1-15; 4:1-3; 7:1), such as would fit much of the postexilic period, but scarcely Solomonic prosperity. However, it would seem again that the wisdom idiom is being forgotten: the movement speaks to circumstances that recur constantly in human experience, and there is nothing in Qoheleth which cannot easily be read in that way.

In sum, what shall we say on the issue of authorship? As we noted, not only liberals but also most conservative commentators are persuaded that the work is not Solomonic, and one does not lightly disregard such a preponderance of opinion, especially when it does not root in liberal dogmas which he cannot share. On the other hand, we have noted that all the arguments against the traditional position can at least be parried, if not refuted. Especially if one is ready to concede the possibility of later linguistic recension, little remains which hinders the assumption of literal Solomonic production.

At the same time, one does not appear justified in making the matter a confessional issue—assuming that only the isagogical issue is at stake. At any rate, a long and distinguished line of conservative interpreters, beginning with Luther, have been unwilling to do so. Possibly the biggest general issue opened is that of "pseudepigraphy." Conservatives have probably often become more sensitive and defensive about the issue than they need to be, because of the abandon with which liberals often assume that later traditors impersonated and spoke in the name of their forbears, and because of the mischief they have worked by appealing to the concept especially in the case of apocalyptic literature such as Daniel (which see). Of course, the very term, *"pseud*epigraphy," is readily objectionable, implying, as it often does, something less than forthrightness and uprightness. However, the use of pen names or sobriquets is as old as literature itself. Given the right conditions, it does not necessarily imply any deceit, nor that anyone is, in fact, deceived, and there would appear to be no *a priori* reason why the Holy Spirit could not have utilized such a universal idiom (perhaps especially in the case of wisdom with its universal horizons). In any event, Ecclesiastes can scarcely be "pseudepigraphy" of the usual type, or else the author would have followed the normal pattern of actually styling himself "Solomon" (as well as "Qoheleth"). It is thus at least possible (and we are discussing only possibilities!) that "son of David" in 1:1 is used with some of the flexibility that "son" often has in Hebraic usage.

A much more weighty (and difficult) issue than authorship is that of the message and purpose of the work. (When it came to this subject, the precritical church had little hesitation; in contrast to the book's virtual *de facto* exclusion from the canon in modern times the church fathers and Reformers produced many (still useful) commentaries and preached countless sermons on it!) One of the puzzling characteristics of the work is its frequent alternation of viewpoint, from what at least appears to be rank agnosticism to very traditional, orthodox-sounding assertions—and back again. Already the rabbis were concerned about what appeared to be "contradictions." Some commentators have attempted the explanation that we have reflected here the vacillation in the author's own mind, his dialogue with himself as he struggled (barely successfully) to staunch the rising tide of skepticism about traditional values.

At one time, it was popular in critical circles to seek a literary solution to the problem. This took various forms, but a frequent common denominator was to postulate a double revision of Qoheleth's own work: (1) by a *chakham* or wisdom editor, who sought to neutralize Qoheleth's strictures on the wisdom movement itself by stressing the merits of wisdom as a way of life; and (2) by a *chasidh,* or orthodox pietist who tried to render harmless various heresies in the work by interpolating it with passages stressing divine judgment and urging reverence toward God on the part of the reader. Among the passages commonly suspected are: 2:25; 3:15b, 17; 5:6b, 19; 7:18b, 29; 8:5; 9:7b; 11:9b; 12:1a, 13-14. However, the fact that the critics themselves could not agree on the alleged history of the book's formation, plus the absence of any kind of linguistic evidence that the suspect passages were interpolations, has made this approach today a less-favored one, and even many critics are prepared to defend the book's essential unity. But the phenomenon that gave rise to these hypotheses still cries out for an explanation (cf. below). Let us first attempt a survey of the book's contents.

Contents

As with most wisdom literature, it is generally agreed that it is difficult, if not impossible, to discern any clear-cut plan or structure in the work. Many portions of it read like the simple "sentential wisdom" which characterizes Proverbs. Form-critically, the work is a "confession" in the form of an autobiographical narrative (the wise man sharing his experience and reflection), to which we have many ancient Egyptian parallels (especially by kings; cf. also Prov. 4:3-9 and 24:30-34). Thus we often get a nearly "stream of consciousness" flavor, and the frequent comparison with Pascal's *Pensées* is appropriate.

Eccl. 1:1-11 may reasonably be called a prologue to the work, enunciating a major theme of the work that, from a certain perspective at least, man's life is devoid of meaning and ultimate satisfaction. History is as much a closed cycle as nature. Two of the book's famous slogans or refrains appear here already: (1) life as a "vanity of vanities" (repeated 31 times in the book) that is, the Hebrew superlative of a word that means literally "breath," that is, ephemerality, fruitlessness, pointlessness; and (2) "nothing new under the sun," repeated some 25 times to underscore the universal monotony of the cycle of human existence.

Eccl. 1:12—2:26 read like illustrations of the theme. No matter what it is that men take solace or seek escape in, learning, labor, riches, pleasure, sex, or justice, all ultimately disappoint. First wisdom's own pretensions are deflated (1:12-18); it is nothing but "vanity and feeding on wind" (v. 14; repeated six more times in the book). Chap. 2:1-11 includes pleasure and work in the indictment. Life in its totality is pointless (2:12-17); the wise have a clear temporal advantage over the foolish, but ultimately both will be equally forgotten. Even vanity itself is vain (2:18-23)! There is no future in being cynical either; there is no knowing what will come of anyone's efforts after death. The best one can do (2:24-26) is enjoy what God has given him, which is more to the wise than to the sinner, but it too is "vanity."

Eccl. 3 is one of the book's more famous chapters. The monotonous repetition of nature (chap. 1) has its counterpart in the fixed patterns of human life, "a time" for everything. In fourteen antitheses, Qoheleth delineates the predetermined poles between which man, willy-nilly, lives out his whole life "under the sun," from womb to tomb. The agony of it is summarized in v. 11: God "has put eternity into man's mind," but the creature is finite. He has time, but not Time. He knows that God has appointed a time for everything, but the meaning of Time itself is beyond his discovery.

Eccl. 3:16—4:16: Even justice on earth is approximate, and one cannot evade it by waiting for the final judgment. The more immediate experience is that of death, and there is no evidence ("Who knows," v. 21) that man is any better off then than animals. In many respects, the dead are better off than the living—and better than both, those who were never born.

Eccl. 5—11 appear to be Qoheleth's own wisdom collection,

anticipated somewhat already by 4:5-12. Hence in both form and content these chapters differ somewhat from the preceding, in part merely in their more miscellaneous character. (Some prefer to delay the major transition until chap. 7.)

Eccl. 5 is the major internal refutation of the common perception that Qoheleth is a cynical determinist who has all but lost his faith. In fact, in especially the first half of the chapter almost more attention is given to cult and to formal religion than in all of Proverbs and Job together. In fact, Qoheleth's admonition to "guard your steps when you go to the house of God" sounds more like the prophet than the typical wise man.

Again and again Qoheleth drives home points already made, especially the conclusion that, in the light of the inscrutability of existence, the Creator's major gift is the relative enjoyment of one's work, family, and companions; at least it will keep his mind off his predicament (cf. 5:18-20; 8:15; 9:7-10, the latter phenomenally parallel to the advice which the barmaid, Siduri, gives to Gilgamesh in the course of his fruitless quest for immortality).

Eccl. 9 contains two oft-quoted phrases, which summarize much of the book: (1) "A living dog is better than a dead lion" (v. 4); and (2) "The race is not to the swift, . . . but time and chance happen to all" (v. 11).

Most famous of all probably is the book's climax and conclusion in chap. 12. On all sides it is agreed that, at least as far as "the Bible as literature" is concerned, it ranks with the very best. There is some question about the aptness of the chapter division; the idea or introduction to it begins already at 11:8. At 12:1 the "Creator" is introduced, but otherwise there is no transition at that point; cf. 11:9b. (Partly because the term is not used elsewhere in Qoheleth, many critics needlessly seek to emend it or regard it as interpolative; the idea, however, is part of the book's bedrock, as in wisdom generally.)

Eccl. 12:2-7 can probably be called an allegory—in fact, two of them which intertwine and are not always kept distinct: (1) the brooding, ominous approach of a storm; and (2) a decaying old mansion, the parts of which stand for parts of the human body. The point of the superbly beautiful pericope is the inexorable advance of old age and of its concomitant decrepitude, as life winds down, "and the spirit returns to God who gave it" (v. 7). Thus, both life and the book come full circle: "vanity of vanities, says the Preacher; all is vanity" (v. 8). But let us not forget that the passage also recapitulates the entire book in placing the whole under the rubric of "Remember" (11:8 and 12:1), *before* it is too late.

Eccl. 12:9-14 constitute a sort of double epilogue to the book, and critics widely regard them as later additions. Vs. 9-10 speak of Qoheleth in the third instead of the usual first person, and apparently summarize much of his career (and probably that of many others of the "Wise" as well). Instead of the words of a doting disciple, one can read them as a sort of modest colophon by the master himself.

Vs. 11-14, and especially 13-14, typify and summarize the portions of the book which many regard as interpolative, if not contradictory. But if we renounce all jaundice, and let them speak their piece, they really do reveal the "end of the matter" (v. 13), that is our major key to what this otherwise most enigmatic work is all about. When all is said and done, to "fear God" is not only the beginning, but the end of wisdom. Since true wisdom comes only from the "one Shepherd" (v. 11), that is, God Himself, "anything more than this comes from evil" (Matt. 5:37; cf. v. 12).

Message of the Book

If the entire book is read in that light (together with similar comments inextricably interspersed throughout), it comes off as anything but the exemplar of virtual determinism, fatalism, cynicism, hedonism, etc., it is often taken to be, and which has often led to questions about its very canonicity. In their haste to read the book as a protest against orthodoxy and a contradiction of much that Yahwism held dear, one suspects that many liberals are simply looking into the mirror. Yet if taken out of its evolutionistic context and read in full canonical context, there is much partial truth in the liberal construction.

It was not only in postexilic times that wisdom needed to be reminded of its limits. "Under the sun" this too was one of the universals with which wisdom had to deal, and Ecclesiastes is by no means the only place in the wisdom corpus where we meet the theme. Neither Solomon's age, nor the Hellenistic period, nor our own are times when the limits of empiricism, of reason, of science, must not be stressed. Ecclesiastes has been styled the "border guard" who forbids "wisdom" to try to cross the divinely ordained frontier to take possession of the "tree of life" itself. Nor is this only true of the unchurched; even those who profess to view general revelation in the light of special revelation, the so-called "religious people are prone to settle down comfortably in their faith, supposing that they possess the answer to life's questions under their hats." Their facile dogmatic formulae become virtually magical incantations by which they all but imprison the Creator in His own "laws." Orthodoxy is God's gift, but "orthodox*ism*" spells reversion to paganism.

The problem often comes to a head in connection with the hope of everlasting life (and *a fortiori* in the New Testament when its dimensions are even more fully revealed). On the one hand, it is the very glory of special revelation, but who will deny that there is truth in Marxist charges that it can be the "opiate of the masses," a hope for "pie in the sky" that turns religion into only a branch of self-interest and insensitizes its adherents to the "horror of history," to life as it is. Qoheleth can be read as rejecting life after death altogether (often, critics think, because he is conservatively reacting against a novel idea in Yahwism), and others have grasped at straws like 9:5 and 12:7 to reject any personal "immortality of the soul" or to defend a "soul-sleep" in the interim before the parousia

Read in full context, however, Qoheleth appears to be saying no more than that neither on an empirical or a revelatory basis does man have any warrant to evade the responsibilities of the time in which God has placed him. Like wisdom in general, the primary accent is on a vertical, existential *carpe diem;* one must "remember" now, *before* it is too late. The recurrent refrain of God's "judgment" is oriented primarily towards the decisions of this life, but, at very least, it is open to greater ultimacy, and Qoheleth is very aware that, once death comes, the judgment is irreversible. There is certainly nothing here which contradicts other Scripture, but the exegete must invoke "Scripture interprets Scripture" to expound its full impact.

Qoheleth's main point, however, remains to polemicize against any claim, under whatever auspices, to be able to discern God's ultimate purposes, even to venture beyond the sure word of revelation to any *de facto* replacement of faith with reason. Christ is the Answer, but He does not give all the answers. Qoheleth is not disillusioned, but *un*illusioned; not a cynic, but a realist. Even less is he any sort of crypto-atheist; God is obviously fundamental to his whole outlook. His "metaphysics" is still the traditional one (that is a personal God, not "process"). God in *His* omnipotent and omniscient wisdom does have the answers, but He does not reveal them all to man (cf. Job). He is *Deus absconditus*—not the inscrutable *moira* (Fate) of Greek cynicism, but sovereign, transcendent Creator, who does not react, but acts in unconditional freedom. To the unbeliever He forever remains only hidden (in spite of "general revelation"), and even to the believer the mystery is revealed only to the eyes of faith. God has given man his "portion," but the whole, Time itself, He retains in His own hand.

In wisdom (general as well as special) man may catch a glimpse of God's own absolute freedom, but the more he begins to grasp for it (rather than receiving it in grace), the more it eludes him. (And certainly our generation should have learned that neither science nor reason leads either to absolute certainty or to absolute freedom; rather absolute freedom, like absolute power, corrupts absolutely, and the greatest intellectual may turn out to be the silliest monster.) And even if all else fails, finally death unfailingly convinces man of his utter finitude (Eccl. 12).

Thus, we understand the bulk of Qoheleth to be one of the Bible's own major preachments of the *Law*—the second use, *usus elenchthicus*. It presents a clear, cold picture of man's life without the covenant relationship with God. Hence, as someone has said, to have assimilated Ecclesiastes and no other book in the Bible would imply having advanced further towards the truth than most men do, because God's first way with men is the way of the *via negativa*. This would be especially true of the unbeliever, but in another sense scarcely less true of the believer as *simul peccator*. Who must not admit resonating to many of Qoheleth's sentiments? For example, Qoheleth's statements in 1:2 ff. on the circularity of nature are indisputably true as such; the ultimate question is how one understands or interprets them, whether as the totality of reality or as evidences of God's covenant with nature (Gen. 8:22 ff.). Similarly, with later statements on the unprovability of life after death; empirically more cannot be said, but the question is whether or not more can be said at all. He who never questions, never doubts, is either a liar, or unacquainted with revelation. There is truth to Bonhoeffer's treatment of the book as a manual on how to overcome doubt.

Not, of course, that positive and corrective statements are absent in the book. They are rather brief, formulaic and undeveloped, but we have consistently noted that as characteristic of the entire wisdom genre (cf. above). In that context, there is no more reason for reading them as superficial and half-hearted in the case of Qoheleth than of Proverbs and Job.

And if read in full canonical context, the book has far more to say. Delitzsch's characterization of the book as the "quintessence of piety" is far closer to the mark than Heine's "quintessence of skepticism." Hertzberg's "one of the most startling Messianic prophecies of the Old Testament" is hyperbolic and plays with words but is not totally off target. Following Zimmerli, we agree that Qoheleth teaches us that wisdom overcomes "vanity" and gains the fullness of life (its own limits as well as its divinely ordained fulfillment) only when it dares believe that the Creator is also the God who gave Himself to Israel, encountered it in wrath and judgment, but also redeemed it—in Jesus Christ.

ESTHER

In the Hebrew canon, Esther concludes the subcollection of the five festival Megilloth, following a chronological order that begins with Passover (with Canticles as its lection). In none of the five instances is the connection more intrinsic than in the case of Esther, actually narrating, as it does, the origin of the feast of Purim, usually occurring toward the end of February or the beginning of March on the Western calendar.

As usual, "historical" interests took precedence in the Greek world, and the Septuagint removed the book to its familiar position after Ezra and Nehemiah, that is, the last of the "historical books." Although the type of historiography employed in Esther differs markedly from that of some of the earlier "histories" (see below), the new association was not bad, because, at least according to the most likely datings, the events of Esther fall between those recorded in the sixth and seventh chapters of Ezra (the latter recounting Ezra's expedition to Jerusalem in 458, sixteen years after the initial Purim, apparently in 474).

Historicity

Is the book "historical"? There certainly is nothing in the book (not even "miracles" in the strict sense) to suggest that it is not, and to the conservative mind that pretty well settles the matter. Inevitably, however, that emphatically is not the case for the liberal, and, much as in the case of Ruth, one meets an entire spectrum of critical views about its historicity. The doubts concern not only the narrative itself but also the originality of the connection with the feast of Purim. The marks of normal Hebrew history-writing, both the "and it came to pass" at the beginning and the bibliographical reference at the close (Esther 10:2) to "the Chronicles of the kings of Media and Persia" are often dismissed as mere artifices by the writer, especially since the "Chronicles" mentioned have never been found. To those so inclined, many other skepticisms come very easily, because of our paucity of information about the fifth century B.C., specifically of the Persian empire in that period and the role of the far Eastern Jewish diaspora in it.

Because, however, whenever we can test them, the author does display a phenomenal knowledge of Persian customs, and because numerous Persian loanwords occur in the book, it will usually be conceded that his "local color" is authentic, but often not much more. Many scholars regard the book as a "historical novel," although generally with much less of a historical element than Ruth, and perhaps more like the apocryphal tales of Tobit and Judith. As usual, archaeology cannot glibly be said to "prove" the story true (we have no evidence yet of any general Jewish persecution in this period) but its evidence has been consistently supportive of facticity.

We need first to consider some of the major historical problems in the book. Our discussion proceeds with the usual assumption that King "Ahasuerus" is Xerxes I (486—465 B.C.). (The original Persian and Hebrew forms of the names are much closer than appears in our translations.) Confusion of names was ancient, however, because the Septuagint consistently has Artaxerxes. Also a minority of modern scholars has attempted to identify Ahasuerus with Artaxerxes II (404—358; see also on Ezra 4:6 and Dan. 9:1), but the historical problems of the book are only compounded by situating it a century later.

If the identification with Xerxes is correct, a very plausible synchronism between the book and well-known world history presents itself, and the puzzling gap in the book between his third year (Esther 1:3) and his seventh (2:16) is readily explained. The great banquet thrown by the king in his third year (483) would correspond to preparations made for the attempted naval invasion of Greece, which came to grief in the famous debacle at Salamis in 480. Herodotus reports that thereafter Xerxes sought escape in his harem, which is readily compatible with Esther's selection in the seventh year (479).

It is sometimes argued that the book's portrait of Xerxes as weak, dissolute, and capricious, conflicts with other depictions of him as a very able and resolute general and king. However, Xerxes would scarcely be the only example in history where a man's private life differed drastically from his public image, or where a valorous warrior or king sought solace in women—and not only after defeats! Certainly, the book's general picture of Oriental court and harem intrigue rings true. (It is probably somewhat inaccurate or anachronistic to describe Xerxes' demand of his wife as a request for a "striptease," as is sometimes done, but, obviously, Vashti is supposed to display herself to the assembly, and, understandably, she is less than eager to oblige.)

Some critics have charged the author of Esther with poor historical memory because, at superficial reading, he appears in 2:6 to imply that Mordecai had been among the first of Nebuchadnezzar's deportees over a century earlier in 597. The difficulty readily dissolves, however, if we take Kish (Mordecai's great-grandfather) instead of Mordecai as the antecedent of the relative pronoun at the beginning of the verse.

One still unsolvable problem concerns the name of Xerxes' queen. Instead of the Biblical "Vashti," Herodotus calls her "Amestris," the daughter of a Persian general, who had long been married to the king (two of their sons joined the campaign against Greece), and he makes no mention of any "Esther." However, Herodotus is scarcely the most reliable of historians himself, and at least one aspect of his characterization of "Amestris" may correspond to "Vashti," namely, her reputation as a cruel and calculating woman, a cause of concern to the king himself. In addition, there is the possibility of dual names, and, above all, if we but recall that it was a polygamous society, the difficulty will scarcely be insurmountable.

Herodotus also reports that a Persian king was supposed to choose his wife from one of seven noble families (cf. Esther 1:14), and, if so, Esther, a Jewess, would have been ineligible. Of course, Mordecai and Esther do not broadcast her background, but laws of that sort are easily evaded anyway, especially by a despot who regards himself above the law. Esther was also breaking Jewish law by marrying an uncircumcised unbeliever, and this too the author reports without overt comment. All of this is undoubtedly related to the book's theological perspective; cf. below.

Herodotus' report that the Persian empire was divided into twenty "satrapies" is often also urged against the book's opening statement (1:1) that Ahasuerus ruled over 127 "provinces." However, there is no reason to assume that the two terms are commensurate ("province" is probably a subdivision), and other evidence indicates that the number of administrative units in the Persian empire was not constant. Earlier Assyrian records mention an "Agag" as the name of one of the districts in the later Persian empire, thereby lending historicity to "Haman the Agagite" (not a descendant of the Amalekite king, Agag, as Jewish tradition sometimes supposed, nor his symbolic counterpart, as critics who view the book as fiction have sometimes argued).

One earlier critical objection is now clearly seen to be hypercritical, namely that "Pur" (and thence the name of the festival, "Purim") did not really mean "lot," as it is explained in Esther 3:7 and 9:24. Now, however, archaeology has presented us with Assyrian texts as early as the early second millennium, which use both the noun *puru* and a cognate verb in the requisite sense. Haman's use of dice to determine a date for the extermination of the Jews was vividly illustrated by the uncovering of large numbers of them in the excavations at Susa.

Critical skepticism also once questioned whether a Jew could have risen as high in the Persian administration as Mordecai did, even succeeding Haman in his position as grand vizier, second only to the king, after he had exposed Haman's plot against the Jews (chaps. 7—8). However, in perhaps our greatest archaeological coup of all in connection with the book, we now have a cuneiform tablet from near Babylon which mentions one "Marduka" as a high official at the court of Susa already during the early years of Xerxes (and possibly even under his predecessor, Darius I). Even many critics concede the identification with Mordecai, and, if so, we have major external testimony toward the historicity of the entire book, and not only of this detail.

In the subsequent reigns of Artaxerxes I and Darius II we have archaeological evidence of many Jews holding important posts (among them Nehemiah, cupbearer to Artaxerxes I), some of them even governors of administrative districts. It has plausibly been suggested that this increasing Jewish prominence in the empire may have stemmed from Mordecai's example and influence, beginning perhaps with the "fear of Mordecai" (9:3) which caused all the officials of the empire to cooperate with him in reversing the intended pogrom.

Many other skepticisms about the book's historicity appear under the rubric of alleged "implausibility" rather than outright denial. However, neither knowledge of Persian attitudes toward human life nor of human nature make it less than credible that Haman might have plotted a massive massacre of many Jews because of his hatred of Mordecai, nor that a Persian king might have assented to such a scheme (Esther 3:7 ff.). Questions are raised especially about the total of more than 75,000 of their enemies whom the Jews are reported to have slain in a single day (9:16 and context). Given the size of the empire and the careful preparations made (8:9 ff.), however, the figure is scarcely unthinkable. At the same time, it is conceivable that we have some of the same hyperbolic numerical symbolism we meet in other Biblical books (Harrison). The Septuagint reports a mere (!) 15,000 slain; in any event, such massacres are by no means unparalleled in ancient Oriental history.

If the book is not historical (or minimally so), what, according to the critics, was the author's purpose in writing? Answers again vary, depending partly on opinions about its date. At most extreme, some hold that the writer had little in mind besides entertainment, and harem tales such as those found in *A Thousand and One Nights* are adduced as analogies. Often pointed to are such twists as Vashti's refusal to display her beauty, the common fear that her stubbornness may undermine male supremacy in homes throughout the empire (Esther 1:16 ff.), Haman's outrage at Mordecai's refusal to do obeisance to him (3:2 ff.), the way he is forced to signally honor Mordecai when he expects to be so honored himself (chap. 6), the king's suspicion that Haman is about to rape Esther as he pleads for his life (7:8), the outsized gallows (75 feet high), which Haman erects for Mordecai (5:14), only to be hanged on them himself (7:9-10)—in a way, the entire plot of the story with its ironies, intrigues, sudden reversals, and happy ending. No doubt, all the elements of popular storytelling are here, but if that proves anything, it is only that "truth is stranger than fiction." In a certain minimal sense, such narrative ability need in no way conflict with historicity and need not be debated. Certainly, on the purely literary level there is little debate about the author's skillful artistry, making the book an artistic masterpiece, quite apart from more ultimate judgments about it.

Form critics have attempted to isolate original components of the story, and often suggest that it was woven out of three originally independent tales, perhaps from a Jewish midrashic source: Vashti's insubordination, conflict between two courtiers, and Esther's rise and role in saving her people. Scholarship's recent obsession with wisdom literature had led to the suggestion (Talmon) that in final recension the book was supposed to illustrate that movement's tenets (much as many critics suggest for the Joseph stories in Genesis, or the "legends" in the first part of Daniel). There may be a grain of truth here, however, related to the book's theological idiom (cf. below).

At any rate, the latter suggestion is superior to the hypothesis of mythological origins (later "historified" at Jewish hands), which until recently was often quite popular in some critical circles. Originally, the myth should have described the rivalry of the chief gods of Babylon and Elam (an early counterpart of Persia), eventuating in Babylon's political ascendancy over its eastern neighbor. Much was made of the names of the principle characters: "Mordecai" should be a derivative of "Marduk," head of the Babylonian pantheon; "Esther" is supposedly derived from "Ishtar," the popular Mesopotamian goddess of love (and even Esther's Hebrew name, "Hadassah," is explained on the basis of the Akkadian word for "bride," a frequent Ishtar epithet); Haman should represent Humman, the chief Elamite deity, Vashti the Elamite goddess Mashti, and so on.

As noted above, archaeological verification of a historical "Mordecai" in Xerxes' court has dealt a deathblow to a mythological theory, and it now appears that its only contact with reality was the mythology of the name "Mordecai." Not surprisingly, "Mordecai" was a quite common name in the neo-Babylonian period. Its presence is scarcely surprising in the successor Persian kingdom, especially among Jews who had migrated there from Babylon, as is explicitly stated in this instance (Esther 2:5-6). In fact, in Ezra 2:2 another "Mordecai" is mentioned, one of the leaders of the returning exiles, together with Zerubbabel (which is itself almost certainly a Babylonian name meaning "seed of Babylon"). The adoption of such foreign names by the Exile scarcely even signifies assimilation, and certainly no necessary syncretism or apostasy from the ancestral faith.

Derivation of the name "Esther" from "Ishtar" is not impossible, but much more likely it represents the same Indo-European word as the English "star." Esther's original Hebrew name "Hadassah" (Esther 2:7) is almost certainly a feminine form of the common Hebrew word for "myrtle." "Esther" was perhaps substituted to conceal her Jewish identity (cf. 2:10), or it may have been a royal name given her at her coronation.

Esther and Purim

By any reckoning, one of the purposes of the Book of Esther, as it presently stands, is to explain the origin and background of the festival of Purim. The only question is whether the connection is integral and original or not, and almost predictably, the usual critical reply is negative. In this context, the book is often characterized as the "festival legend" of Purim or the like, history allegedly rising from custom, not custom from history. It is often opined that the main concern was to sanction a festival which was not commanded in the Torah, but the apparent ease with which Hanukkah and the Ninth of Ab were accepted belies that explanation.

Some of the arguments against an original connection are textual, but it appears to be largely a case of argument in a circle. There are relatively few text-critical problems about the *Hebrew* text of Esther (cf. below). (One oddity worth mentioning, however, is the writing of the names of the ten sons of Haman in the Masoretic text of Esther 9:7-9 in a perpendicular column, because of ancient haggadah that they were hanged over one another.) The major exception in many critical eyes are 9:20—10:3, which are widely regarded as spurious, on the basis of alleged inconsistencies or contradictions, especially in supposedly ignoring the different length of time the festival was observed by rural and urban Jews (9:16-19), and supposed linguistic and stylistic differences. The arguments, however, are at best indecisive (see the commentaries, especially Anderson). The *entire* ninth chapter begins to shift from the main narrative to issues of law and cult, although "Purim" does not, as such, come to the fore until 9:20 ff. The explanation of the word in vs. 24-26 was anticipated as early as 3:7 when Haman first cast the *pur* or lot, an incident which is "so organically related to the narrative as a whole that it cannot be removed without the most drastic textual surgery" (although many critics do just that).

Until archaeological verification of the book's explanation of the word *pur* as "lot," many other etymologies were proposed in connection with the putative origins of the feast itself, but these are themselves of no more than archaeological interest today. Demonstration that it is a Semitic (Babylonian) word (like "Mordecai" and perhaps "Esther") encouraged speculation that the festival was originally domiciled there. Sometimes that hypothesis merged with the theory of mythological origin (cf. above), but not necessarily so. More recently, a Persian origin of the festival has been gaining critical support, however. Many seek echoes of a disturbance in earlier Persian history, namely Gaumata's rebellion against Cambyses before the accession of Darius I (cf. Haggai and Zechariah), a rebellion which was quashed through harem help and ended in a great massacre of the plotters, and which was commemorated for a time in a popular feast. Others prefer to think of a Persian new year festival which allegedly the Jews adapted. Whatever its origins, since it was already so popular, so the argument goes, official sanction and justification was given to it by associating it with the preexisting tale of Esther and Mordecai, and eventually it was also fitted out with the new name, "Purim" based on that legend. Also encouraging this type of speculation has been the relatively "secular" character of both the book (see below) and of the festival in traditional Jewish observance. However, the best refutation of all these hypotheses in contradiction of the book's own testimony remains the inability of any of them to establish themselves on anything more than a speculative basis.

If, however, the book's account of the festival's origins are not impugned, there may be secondary truth in the last observation. It is quite possible that the Jewish commemoration of Purim more or less coincided with some Persian festival, some of whose popular observances came to be mingled with it. Many parallels to that kind of thing can be adduced in both Judaism and Christianity (one thinks, among others, of "Santa Claus," or Easter eggs). In later times, certainly, the rather "Halloween" type of popular Jewish observance of Purim was encouraged by the fact that it tended to coincide, at least in Europe, with Christian (?) pre-Lenten "carnival" and Mardi Gras merriment. (Cf. rabbinical dicta that "On Purim anything is allowed," or that drinking could continue until it was no longer possible to distinguish "Cursed be Haman" and "Cursed be Mordecai"!)

Date and Authorship

What can be said about the date and authorship of the book itself (as distinguished from the veracity of the account)? As to authorship, Esther is undeniably another of those (relatively rare) instances where conservatives must agree with liberals on the anonymity of the writing. Many ancient and even some more recent commentators have attributed the book to Mordecai on the basis of Esther 9:20 and perhaps also 9:32. While not impossible, the verses do not say that, and the most one could safely infer from them would be that Mordecai's writings and royal records were among the unknown author's sources (cf. 10:2).

Agreement is not so easy to reach on date of composition. A Maccabean date was once widely defended among critics, especially by those who doubted both the narrative itself and any relation with Purim, but this view is no longer so popular. The idea then tended to be that Haman was Antiochus Epiphanes in disguise, and that the story was fabricated in order to bolster Jewish courage in the dark days of Syrian persecution (quite parallel to the critical view of Daniel, which see). It is true that Sirach (c. 200) does not mention the book (but neither does he Ezra or Daniel), that the festival is not referred to earlier than 2 Macc. 15:36 (where it is called the "Day of Mordecai"), and also that Josephus provides the first-known quotation of the book. However, these are all arguments from silence, and may, at most, witness only to the length of time (not necessarily any resistance) that it took for a book and festival originating in the eastern Diaspora to reach the centers of Judaism in Palestine and gain common acceptance.

Even critical opinion increasingly inclines toward the view that at least early editions of the book must root in the Persian period, before Alexander's invasion. Not only is there the absence of Greek influence, but the large amount of Hebrew prose from Qumran (Esther not among it) is plainly of a different character. The Hebrew of Esther probably finds its closest Biblical parallel in Chronicles (which see), usually dated around 400, except that the vocabulary of Esther reflects distinct Persian influence. There is also the matter of the author's uncanny acquaintance with Persian customs. It is also valid to adduce the accord between the author's description of Xerxes' palace at Susa and the reports of the archaeologist who excavated it (Dieulafoy). Since it was destroyed by fire in the reign of Artaxerxes I, some thirty years later, details of its structure would scarcely be remembered much longer. If we add to all that the conservative assumption of historicity, we get a very strong case for Persian origin, possibly even by a contemporary living in Susa or its environs, and perhaps not too long after Xerxes' death in 465. Dates later than the turn of the century would be increasingly hard to defend, although it is impossible to be more precise.

Theological Significance

All of the above questions and problems with respect to the Book of Esther pale in comparison, however, with the issue of its theological significance and canonicity. Difficulties of this sort have attended the book almost from the outset, and certainly have not been lessened by modern historical-critical perspectives. Esther is the only Old Testament book not represented at Qumran, and although this is conceivably an accident of discovery, it seems more likely that the sectarian community rejected the book, especially since there are other indications of the group's Eastern affinities, which should have made them even more favorably disposed toward it. One can only guess at their reasons for spurning it, but we tend to assume that they were similar to later ones: its minimal religiosity, the absence of mention of the name of God, Esther's disobedience to the Torah by marrying an infidel, etc.

There is no indication, however, that the book's canonicity was in dispute at Jamnia, and hence it cannot accurately be included among the "antilegomena." Josephus obviously regarded it as canonical, yet the Talmud plainly preserves evidence of later rabbis who denied that the book "defiled the hands" (was holy or canonical). Among the Jewish masses, the book has always been extremely popular, not only because of the lighthearted celebration accompanying Purim (cf. above), but also because of its strongly nationalistic character (see below). To this day, it is customary for worshipers to participate vocally in the contemporization of the story as it is read in Purim synagogue services, expressing rage at mention of Haman's name, repeating after the reader accounts of Jewish victories, etc. The common critical wisdom is that the rabbis may have been reluctant to canonize a book which showed contempt for Gentiles and might thus provoke further anti-Semitism (if they did not object to its very contents), but that they were finally forced into embracing it by popular pressure. Humanly speaking, this is not impossible, but it is purely hypothetical. It is undeniable, however, that waxing persecution of the Jews at the hands of Christendom made it all the easier for them to identify with it and view it as ever more precious. Hence, it is at least understandable that Maimonides in the Middle Ages would say that in the days of the Messiah only Esther and the Torah would survive, and there were even rabbis to be found who ranked it above the Law and the Prophets.

The additions to the Hebrew text in the Septuagint are surely also indirect evidence of the book's popularity. The Greek text adds some 107 verses not found in the Hebrew, and all indications are that they never were Hebrew but were composed in Greek and probably added to the Septuagint after its initial translation. Just when is uncertain, but Josephus was plainly acquainted with at least some of them. (In Protestant circles they are regarded as apocryphal, and hence (following Jerome's precedent) collected separately under that heading, but they often make little sense apart from their original context.) Some of the additions are simply rhetorical or even fanciful embellishments of the more terse original (e.g., a dream by Mordecai, and its interpretation—an explanation of the feast), but many of them plainly have the purpose to amend the "secular" character of the original (e.g., prayers by both Esther and Mordecai), and the name of God, so conspicuous by its absence in the Hebrew text, is now conspicuously intoned. When we say "Septuagint," we mean as usual the "B" or Vaticanus text, but it is to be noted that Alexandrinus is probably a separate translation of the Hebrew (probably based on a separate Hebrew text to begin with; cf. Moore), surely further testimony to the book's popularity.

In early Christendom, Esther was apparently not nearly so popular as in Jewry, but assertions of its rejection there often appear to be exaggerated. Nothing can be concluded from the New Testament's failure to allude to it. The church fathers refer to it rarely, but this may be partly due to the fact that Purim found no counterpart in Christian calendars, that is, the book did not readily lend itself to typological exposition. Many Christian canonical lists in the East omit Esther, while in the West it was nearly always included (because it knew of the religious additions in the Septuagint, while the East did not?), but all overt objections appear to have been silenced by the council of Carthage in 397. When Esther is referred to, it is often in close association with Judith (with its very similar theme, deliverance of Jews through a beautiful and brave woman), which was also widely regarded as canonical.

No doubt, however, the same increasingly bad blood between Jews and Christians which enhanced its popularity among the former served as a damper upon its popularity among the latter. It is hard to disassociate Luther's unfortunate comments from this context: "I am so hostile to the book [2 Maccabees] and to Esther that I wish they did not exist at all; for they judaize too much, and have much heathen perverseness." It is to be noted, however, that the words come from Luther's *Table Talk,* and like many other of his *obiter dicta* in that dubious context, it is often less than clear how seriously he meant them himself. In any case, it is surely not insignificant that Luther never acted upon these offhand remarks by attempting to expunge Esther from the canon.

If, then, we defend the book's inspiration and canonicity, how do we answer the objections raised against it? (It is another classical case where presuppositions will tell much of the story.) The criticisms of the book are basically reducible to two: (1) Apart from fasting (Esther 4:1-3), it appears to be devoid of distinctively religious practices or concepts. The conception of Judaism is more ethnic and nationalistic than theological. It could even be considered anthropocentric, because the name of God is not mentioned even once, as well as prayer, worship, Jerusalem, temple, etc. (2) The book not only describes the Jews' wholesale slaughter of their enemies in retaliation for the designs on their own lives but appears to exult in and encourage such behavior. On both counts (particularism and vengeance), it is easy to draw superficial contrasts with the spirit of Christianity, but more profound reflection can, at very least, suggest viable alternatives.

There is no one, certain explanation for the absence of the name of God and other matters religious in the book, however. The suggestion that it was simply too dangerous to worship Yahweh openly in those days or mention His name is at best speculative, and would seem to be contradicted both by evidence of Jewish ascendancy in the Persian empire in the wake of Mordecai's triumph (cf. above) and by the Book of Ezra. Another commonly offered explanation thinks of the book's composition in the context of the secular character of the observance of Purim: the author allegedly avoided formal and conventional religious terminology to forestall the possibility of even accidental blasphemy or irreverence toward Jewish sanctities by the revelers. So understood, the absence of religious references would be a sign of profound reverence, not the opposite. This is not impossible, but it seems superficial, and if later Jewish practices are any indication, the liturgical use of the book in worship (even if punctuated by congregational involvement; cf. above) was carefully distinguished from the subsequent revelry.

Young's explanation, followed by other conservatives, seems just as farfetched. He argues that the *name* of the covenant God was no longer associated with the Jews in Persia because, although Providence would still watch over them, they were no longer in the "theocratic line" or in the Land of Promise from which the promised salvation was to come to the world. Unfortunately, there is not a glimmer of either internal or external evidence to support the hypothesis that such a usage was ever extant.

The only defensible explanation in our judgment is simply that this was the idiom in which the author (under inspiration) elected to write. Except for the statistical anomaly of the total absence of the word "God," its idiom is not as different from other portions of Scripture as may appear at first blush. The occasional attempt in connection with the recent "wisdom" craze to classify it under that rubric is too narrow, and the hidden agenda of exalting immanentalism over "supernaturalism" that often accompanies it is entirely unacceptable. Nevertheless, there is truth in those expressions. Esther is very similar to units such as the Joseph narratives, Ruth, David's Court History, etc., where God acts in no overt way, but only hidden "in, with, and under" the fumbles and foibles of mankind, the sum of their actions, whether laudable or reprehensible.

Of course, we understand that this represents no conflicting theology nor mere literary variation, but corresponds factually to God's manner of operation at the time. What looks like pure coincidence in the book is really personal, divine guidance, and deliverance. The "natural" circumstances it deals with are really supernatural. The very absence of explicit mention of God in the book can be construed as a testimony to His sovereign rule at all times, even when men do not intone His name. "He that keepeth Israel shall neither slumber nor sleep" (Ps. 121:4).

The viewpoint is essentially the same as that of the prophets' predictions of divine use of historical agents such as Assyria and

Babylonia to chasten His faithless people. The prophetic parallel can fruitfully be pressed further: the "great reversal" of the fortunes of God's people in Persia which the Book of Esther records can (and must in canonical context) be seen as one historical manifestation of the eschatological quality and ultimate goal of all of history which the prophets constantly proclaim. Furthermore, the analogy of Scripture assures us that the moralistic criteria by which Esther is often faulted are as invalid here as elsewhere. It would be just as invalid to try to alibi for Esther's entry into a harem or for the Jewish vengefulness on moralistic grounds. Nowhere is the Bible to be read as "a book of lessons designed to make men morally better" (Anderson), but rather as the revelation of how God made both human "wisdom" and folly work together for His transcendent good, climaxing in Christ.

Thus, when explicitly "religious" additions were made to the Greek version of Esther, it was surely no case of blatant revision of a secular-minded work, but simply an articulation of the tacit understanding and use of the work all along. In spite of all the frivolous frills, Judaism has always found real religious meaning in the story, partly expressed by the tradition of using the feast as an occasion for distribution of alms and presents, made by pious worshipers with religious intentions (see also below).

"Providence" is the term commonly used to describe the author's theological perspective, and we may accept it, provided we do not simply subsume the book under the rubric of "general revelation." Of course, from the divine perspective, the kingdoms on the right and the left are ultimately one, but Esther must ultimately be read as part of the history of *election,* as part of God's special governance for His *chosen* people. Many of these issues come to a head or can be illustrated in one well-known and pivotal verse, namely Esther 4:14, Mordecai's admonition to Esther: "Who knows whether you have not come to the kingdom for such a time as this?" The above caveat surely applies fortissimo to its common use as a sermon text for special occasions when it often fails to be expounded in the light of the "scandal of particularity" and is used to proclaim "providence" rather than the Gospel.

The same verse probably even constitutes an exception to the oft-repeated statement that the author of Esther avoids reference to God. It is very doubtful that Mordecai is simply telling Esther that, if she fails to do her part, deliverance will come to the Jews "from another quarter" (RSV), that is, through some other individual or via some other political agency (although even that would surely suggest "providence"). The Hebrew word here is "place" *(maqom),* and it is far more likely that the traditional exegesis is correct which understands the word as the same reverent circumlocution for the divine name which we know well from only slightly later Jewish literature (cf. similarly "heaven" in Matthew's "kingdom of heaven").

This interpretation is reinforced by Esther's request in v. 16 that all Jewry in Susa "hold a fast on my behalf." We need to recall that fasting was normally accompanied by prayer (of course, to the one, true, *personal* God). (We also understand then why the LXX interpolates at this point prayers by both Mordecai and Esther.) In that light, neither will Esther's, "If I perish, I perish" be misread as merely human pluck, let alone fatalism. In fact, the entire book and the festival based on it must be read as polemic against that quasi-superstitious dependence on "chance" or "luck" for which "providence" is often only a euphemism: Haman casts "lots" (Purim) to set a date for the extermination of the Jews, but a personal God, not the roll of the dice or other happenstance, determines "destinies," and Haman never lives to see his "lucky day" (Baldwin).

Christian misgivings about the Book of Esther have often also fastened on the alleged "nationalism" of the book, or its apparently primarily ethnic approach to the concept of the "people of God." Mindfulness of the "canonical context," as sketched above, will ameliorate some of the problem, but at this point a common Christian difficulty with the Old Testament is met head on: the people of God under the old covenant *was* constituted as state (that is, political and/or cultural or ethnic entity) as well as "church." Historically, there is no abstract "stateness" but only particular states, and in the Old Testament this inevitably and properly merges with the particularity that follows from election ("How odd of God to choose the Jews!"). To be sure, the Book of Esther illustrates how easily sinful men may add to the valid particularism of election an oppressive, even vengeful *apartheid* and separatism which is not of God. However, it does not approve or commend such excesses, and before Christians carp, they had better take a look at their own pathetic record in this department. Such behavior in a way is even less defensible when committed in the time of the fulfillment by the church with its supranational, universal calling. "He that is without sin among you, let him cast the first stone" (John 8:7).

The sometimes less than ideal deportment of the modern state of Israel in this respect demonstrates how Jewry still can transgress when the tables are turned and it, for a change, is the majority and the establishment. Yet there is no denying that in the broad sweep of history, and especially since the edict of Milan, Jews have been vastly more sinned against than sinning. Hence, it really requires little empathy to grasp why Jews have found it so easy to identify with Esther and enter into its commemoration with gusto. The virtual "genocide" which Haman plotted is thoroughly typical of the perennial fate of the Jews, and nowhere more diabolically paralleled than in the Nazi holocaust of our own day. In many ways, Esther is a classical case study in anti-Semitism, a hydra-headed monster that we have not yet learned how to exorcise. Typically, it is triggered by the stubborn Jewish refusal to syncretize and assimilate, which orthodoxy, above all, should be able to appreciate. The "banality of evil" also in this respect is seen in the fact that it is not initially nourished by any spontaneous racism but rather by the ambitions and jealousies of a few demagogues, who generally have little difficulty in rousing the bureaucratic apparatus and a scapegoat-seeking mob to rally to their demented cause. And all too often the church has not only not cursed the darkness, but, if not by irresponsible talk of Jewish "deicide," has often at least tacitly shuttered the light by allowing the Gospel of the *fulfillment* of Judaism to degenerate into anti-Judaism, even into raw anti-Semitism.

On the more positive side, however, the book's account of God's providential intervention is also typical of "the eternal miracle of Jewish survival." And the miracle has continued for two millennia of the "common era." Thus, the Book of Esther takes its place in the canon alongside especially Rom. 9—11 as a testimony to God's continuing purposes for His ancient olive tree. If Paul interprets Paul, we will not be able with the liberals to abjure Jewish evangelism, but we will reverently own the mystery (Rom. 11:25 ff.), and not leave other expressions of regard for our brethren to liberals, not even by default.

So far, we have used the word, "typical," in the common illustrative sense, but, if applied with due reserve, it also has validity in the stricter, typological sense. Perhaps it is pressing things too far, as some Christian tradition has done, to view Esther's voluntary going to the king as a freewill offering, a way of the cross foreshadowing the crucifixion. But the New Testament proclamation of the church as the spiritual Israel, as legitimate heirs of the covenant promises, founds a sounder typology. Something is seriously wrong in Christendom when it too cannot identify with the struggle for spiritual (not only institutional) survival of which Esther speaks; "woe to you, when all men speak well of you" (Luke 6:26). But then as now, the enemies are really God's enemies, and the "great reversal" which Esther records (cf. above) enshrines the eternal promise, also to us, that the gates of hell shall not prevail.

DANIEL

It is safe to say that virtually all problems of Biblical study "come home to roost" in connection with the Book of Daniel. We encounter not only nearly all the standard problems here—and those often in heightened form—but quite a few relatively unique ones as well.

Perhaps nowhere has the impact of "higher criticism" been so great or so startling as here, and it is no accident that on both sides Daniel regularly takes its place as a litmus test for either orthodoxy or "critical orthodoxy" (alongside Jonah, unity of Isaiah, and Mosaicity of the Pentateuch).

In addition, conservatism itself is sharply divided on the proper interpretation of many key portions of the book between millennial (mostly premillennial and dispensationalist) and amillennial outlooks. (The same cleavage appears, of course, at other points in the Old Testament, especially in the latter portions of Ezekiel and Zechariah, but scarcely to the same degree or with the same cruciality as here.) Hence, perhaps nowhere is the explication of a proper hermeneutics so vital as in the case of Daniel.

Our problems begin with the proper definition and understanding of "apocalyptic," as Daniel is nearly always classified, and of which genre it is regularly cited as the major Old Testament exemplar. In some literature "apocalyptic" and "eschatological" are used as virtual synonyms, in which case both are usually regarded as more optimistic, postexilic developments to be distinguished from the earlier and genuinely prophetic accent on judgment. (Sometimes, a third term, "Messianic," is used in essentially the same sense.) More often, however, "apocalyptic" or "apocalyptic eschatology" is contrasted with the "eschatology" of the prophets, the latter allegedly more sober, immanentalistic and this-worldly in contrast to otherworldly and supernaturalistic apocalyptic (see below).

Evaluation of Apocalyptic

The jockeying about definitions is often only a symptom of underlying aversion to the subject matter itself. Klaus Koch has well captured the dynamics of the problem in the title of his recent study of the history of critical investigation of the subject: *Ratlos vor der Apokalyptik* (freely, "Thoroughly puzzled by apocalyptic," but in the official translation insipidly rendered, "The Rediscovery of Apocalyptic"). The ultimate issue is theological, of course, and it provides a parade example of the "hermeneutical circle." The characteristic liberal distaste for the subject roots, it is safe to say, in the fact that apocalyptic highlights (at least by implication) just about everything that liberalism prefers not to highlight: supernaturalism, original sin, *sola gratia* instead of human cooperation, predictive prophecy, verbal inspiration, particularism, final judgment, bodily resurrection, etc. That same list of qualities explains, at least in part, why apocalyptic plays so central a role in orthodoxy. Käsemann's oft-quoted dictum, "apocalyptic . . . was the mother of all Christian theology," is a gross exaggeration, of course, but by no means entirely off target (see below).

As in so many other areas of Biblical study, Wellhausen forms the major watershed, and he continues to cast a long shadow over contemporary thought on the subject. Wellhausen's point of departure in this respect was the assumption of a fundamental hiatus between the "prophetic spirit" of preexilic Israelite religion and the "Judaism" of the postexilic period, the legalism, supernaturalism, and particularism of which allegedly stifled prophetism. The apocalyptists were put down as "epigones," inferior imitators of the great prophets, who partly in response to the trauma of the Exile and its aftermath and partly in dependence on Iranian and Zoroastrian "dualism" (cf. below), developed prophetic ideas in an unfortunate and regressive manner. While the prophets allegedly had anticipated "salvation *in* history" (that is in continuity with the present and with man's full cooperation), the disillusioned, pessimistic apocalyptists preached a utopian "salvation *from* history," that is, sudden divine intervention and transformation from on high.

Such a view was not without profound implications for the understanding of the nature of the unity of the testaments or for the interpretation of the New Testament. The standard Wellhausenian view of such matters is often referred to as the "prophetic connection theory." That is, Jesus and the preexilic prophets should be directly connected; for all practical purposes, one might skip over the half a millennium between the Exile and Christ, as having produced nothing of theological merit—or worse. (So pervasive was this prejudice in Germany that scholarly research in the area all but ceased throughout much of the first half of the twentieth century.) A usual corollary was an understanding of the "historical Jesus" as a great ethical teacher, the last and greatest of the prophets, and the "Christ of faith" (the apocalyptic Son of Man, incarnate and resurrected) as largely a kerygmatic construct of the primitive church.

A minority of critics went further, not only regarding apocalyptic as a deformed, degenerate offspring of prophecy, but denying the relationship altogether. Hölscher found apocalypticism's parentage in wisdom instead—a view we might dismiss as a curiosity had von Rad not revived it and lent his immense prestige to it in our own generation. Although von Rad, unlike many of his predecessors, concedes a certain importance to apocalyptic (thus making his work in this area as rewarding reading as elsewhere), that importance is for him ultimately as negative and "epigonic" as in classical criticism. And not even von Rad could convince most scholars of the wisdom roots of apocalyptic; few would view apocalyptic as any more hermetically sealed off from wisdom than other movements (e.g., Dan. 12:3), but that does not establish paternity; and, above all, wisdom's minimal eschatological interests (at least in any explicit way) are about at the farthest possible remove from apocalyptic.

Not that there were no efforts within criticism to assess apocalyptic more positively, but, for the most part, they never seemed able to carry the day. In fact, Charles, one of the most important names in English-language study of the subject, disagreed with majority criticism on two cardinal points: he related prophecy and apocalyptic more organically and positively than most, and he resisted the popular hypothesis of Zoroastrian influence. Also Gunkel and his form-critical colleagues must be mentioned as suggesting more positive alternatives. In line with his usual probing into preliterary roots, Gunkel, Hölscher, and others stressed both the antiquity and the meaningfulness of many of the symbols and motifs popular in apocalypticism. Gunkel recognized that the "mythical" enemies of apocalyptic were to be identified with those threatening the community, and the account of their defeat was a promise of the triumph of the enemies of the people of God (although he continued to maintain the usual critical position of the late composition of the book in its present form).

Somewhat parallel to these more positive treatments of apocalyptic's roots and heyday were rejections of the "prophetic connection theory" and emphases on Jesus' *dependence* on apocalyptic, best known, of course, from the work of Albert Schweitzer. For the most part, however, this thrust resulted only in what Koch labels "agonized attempts to save Jesus from apocalyptic" on the part of most New Testament scholarship down to the present day. As noted above, Käsemann has highlighted the importance of apocalyptic for New Testament studies, but he continues to attribute this accent to the early *church,* not to Jesus Himself. The Pannenberg school, of course, disputes that, but it suffices here only to accent the centrality of the apocalyptic question to virtually all modern discussions of Christology and eschatology.

How shall the confessional theologian react to all this discussion, proceeding from his axioms of special inspiration, unity of Scripture, and the like? Perhaps above all, he will want to stress a prophetic-apocalyptic-Jesus continuity. Continuity does not imply identity (there are developments and adaptations along the way), but continuity nonetheless, and of a positive sort. Apocalyptic certainly highlights certain themes found already in classical prophecy (and, inchoately, even earlier), especially conflict motifs, the hopelessness of the human predicament apart from divine intervention, etc. It certainly also vastly expanded the repertory of imagery in the rococo directions so characteristic of apocalyptic, but even here prophetic antecedents are often not lacking. Furthermore, in making such points, the conservative will want to stress the extent to which critical dissections of the prophetic literature nourish the critical dogma of prophetic-apocalyptic disjunction. Passages in the prophetic books which stress themes or use language considered "apocalyptic" are regularly declared "ungenuine" and later additions; hence, of course, with such materials eliminated from consideration, the critical notion of the genuinely "prophetic" is also easily upheld. A better—and more fateful—example of critical argumentation in a circle can hardly be found!

Date and Definition of "Apocalyptic"

Questions of the date and definition of "apocalyptic" are inevitably also at stake. Obviously, if the more apocalyptic passages in the prophetic corpus cannot blithely be declared ungenuine, it is not so easy to pontificate about the lateness of apocalyptic as criticism normally does. This, of course, has a very direct bearing on the question of the date of Daniel. If some of the proto-apocalyptic sections of prophecy (perhaps especially Joel 3—4, Is. 24—27, Ezek. 38—39 and Zech. 9—14) stem from some time well into the postexilic period, the critical assumption of a still later date for more developed apocalyptic literature like Daniel is very difficult to counter. We, of course, possess a fair number of extracanonical apocalyptic works (Enoch, 4 Ezra or 2 Esdras, etc.), which formally have much in common with Daniel, and which are usually dated in a period around the turn of the testaments, commencing with Daniel itself. However, many examples could surely be found in world literature of "sleepers," of styles of writing which literarily were ahead of their time, and whose lead was not widely followed until a much later era.

But the question of the very definition of "apocalyptic" is involved. Form critically (in the neutral sense) "apocalyptic" is sufficiently distinguished in degree, even if not in kind, from earlier prophecy by the veritable jungle of baroque, even bizarre, imagery in which it often immerses itself (including the degree to which it indulges in the symbolic use of numbers) that a separate category or *Gattung* by that name is eminently justifiable. At the same time, the underlying continuities also imply that the two categories will often overlap, and the best terminology will be a matter of debate. Even within criticism there is no complete consensus on the meaning of the term. We do well to remember that etymologically *apokalypsis* simply means "revelation," and that the specialization of the term for a special style of writing is a very modern development.

Partly because of their circular argumentation, critical literature commonly attributes to the "apocalyptic" genre a number of unique characteristics, to which the conservative can only assent with reservations. For example, it is commonly asserted that, whereas the classical prophet was primarily a man of the spoken word, the apocalyptist was not only primarily a writer, but perhaps his "visions" were no longer even actually seen. His almost exclusive use of prose instead of the poetry in which prophetic oracles were often couched was supposed to confirm the point. It seems very doubtful, however, that we know enough of the phenomenology of either prophetic or apocalyptic inspiration or of the transmission and writing down of their messages to make any such assertions.

Similarly, it is stated that while the classical prophet, speaking in public, was known, "apocalyptic" is nearly synonymous with "anonymous" or even "pseudonymous." At the least, this assertion often again exceeds the evidence, or appears to generalize unjustifiably. In the case of Daniel (cf. below), the conservative will want to distinguish between canonical and extracanonical specimens of the literature. Much of the latter, no doubt, did place its words in the mouth of some ancient worthy. Even here, however, the label "pseudo-" appears to inject unnecessary moral issues into the discussion. If use of a pen name or sobriquet is not accompanied by utter anonymity, that is, without any intent of pulling the wool over anyone's eyes, there is no intrinsic problem, of course (cf. on Canticles and Qoheleth).

Unfortunately, however, criticism generally assumes that the device was motivated by an attempt to lend greater authority to the books, to conceal the author's identity from hostile authorities, or the like. If any attempt is made to defend the action, it will probably be a hypothetical appeal (unsupported by extra-Biblical evidence) that the conventions of the time were such that no one would ever have construed such behavior as fraudulent. (Cf. also Russell's appeal to "corporate personality," according to which the writer should simply have operated as a spokesman of the entire people.) It must also be noted that for criticism the problem is only a matter of degree, considering the vast amount of Biblical material which is attributed to faceless "community inspiration," even though internally ascribed to some figure in antiquity (much of the Torah to Moses, psalms to David, wisdom to Solomon, and a host of prophetic material to the various prophets).

Ethical questions are no less in the critical assumption that the apocalyptist was not really predicting the future, but simply encouraging his contemporaries under the guise of the predictions of an ancient figure. Again the conservative will want to make a sharp distinction between canonical and extracanonical, and, of course, at this point he will detect the fundamental issue of differing presuppositions anent supernatural prediction of the future. Neither does it follow that genuine predictions are irrelevant to the present.

Closely related is the critical description of apocalypticism's view of time and history as "dualistic." No doubt, apocalyptic has a sharply honed sense of the distinction between the present age or aeon and the future or coming one, the two set apart, of course, by history's climactic act of divine intervention, the "final judgment." Except possibly for accent, however, it is doubtful if this theme differs at all from the prophetic *cantus firmus* of the "great reversal"—particularly, if the critical scalpel has not excised all of the latter pericopes as later additions! As noted above, criticism usually intends by this language to contrast the alleged escapism and utopianism of apocalyptic with the "sober, realistic" immanentalism and confidence in human potential of their heroes, the prophets.

The term "dualism" is not totally objectionable, but careful distinctions are imperative. When especially earlier critics were convinced that apocalyptic was beholden to the genuine Zoroastrian dualism of light and darkness (Ormazd and Ahriman), it was easy to assume also that it exhibited the same feature, and thus conflicted fundamentally with the "monism" of genuine prophetism (the critical version of Biblical "monotheism"; see on the prophets). But this spurious contrast between early "Yahwism" and postexilic "Judaism" does at least suggest the valid difference between pagan and Biblical "dualism." The latter is perhaps best illustrated by the contrast between light and darkness in especially Isaiah (cf. John in the New Testament). In a way, it is no real dualism at all, at least if one means by that the eternal, ontological, metaphysical alternation of good and evil forces, that is, the cyclicism that stands at the very heart of pagan mythology. Such an ideology, of course, clashes frontally with Biblical assumptions of the eternity of only one personal and omnipotent Creator. In this context, evil enters the picture only with the primordial rebellions of Satan and man, and it maintains power only by the sufferance of the Almighty. It is one of apocalyptic's central proclamations that the Evil One and all his works have in principle already been judged, and that the time is but short before his final elimination—but, of course, the idea was anything but alien to earlier Biblical writers, either! Sometimes adjectives like "ethical," "soteriological," or the like are placed in front of this genuinely and centrally Biblical "dualism" in order to set it off from the metaphysical or cosmological species of paganism.

Often the apocalyptic interest in God's definitive management of time and history expresses itself in terms of well-defined dispensations or kingdoms (especially the four of Daniel; see below). Here too, however, we recognize no more than a sharpening of the general Biblical sense of time *sub specie aeternitatis.* In a sense, God's battle with evil leading up to the end goes on incessantly, but, at least to creatures of space and time, there will be an inevitable periodicity about it, certain occasions when the movement is especially evident. The perspective of *world* history (not only Israel's), indeed of judgment upon the *cosmos* (not only history) and hence of "new *creation*" in prospect, is certainly more prominent here than in prophecy, but again it is a matter of degree, not of kind. One may speak of "dispensations" in this connection if he wishes, but the language does not justify the millennialistic caricature which often monopolizes the terminology. Since the eschatological victory is not only future but present and "existential," the Lutheran dogmatic language of the "two kingdoms" and/or of "Law-Gospel" is faithful, however, to the theme's application to the already-not-yet situation of the church and the baptized believer.

Critics often refer further to the apocalyptic outlook as "deterministic," and, at least in any strict sense, this is scarcely acceptable at all. If it were, of course, we would again probably have "dualism" and paganism on our hands. Indeed, apocalyptic expresses in no uncertain terms the basic Biblical hope that the one transcendent Deity is firmly in control and calls all the final shots, but there is no indication that "free will" (as it appears, at least, to fallen man) is denied here any more than elsewhere. "Foreknowledge" and even "predestination" would be more accurate terms than the fatalism implied by "determinism." "Man proposes and God disposes" would summarize Pentateuchal and "deuteronomic" historiography as well as apocalyptic. The critical caricatures in this connection, of course, are of a piece with its universalistically inspired difficulties with themes of retributive justice at many points in the canon (cf. especially wisdom).

In connection with all of this, critical literature also regularly makes a great point of apocalyptic's heightened stress on God's transcendence and the alleged compensatory theme of intermediary beings to bridge the gap—specifically the development of elaborate angelic hierarchies and a corresponding development in demonology. If this is loosened from its usual evolutionistic and history-of-religions associations, one may concede a certain partial truth here. The motifs are certainly somewhat more prominent, and proper names begin to appear (Satan, Michael, Gabriel, etc), but one would be reluctant to concede much more of a "cumulative revelation" here. Certainly, the angelology of Daniel differs little, if any, from that of Ezekiel and Zechariah, and, in fact, the similarity is a major argument against dating Daniel so much later, as critics do. (One must also note that the same critical evolutionism is involved in the isolation of the "P" source of the Pentateuch and its attribution to postexilic times.)

Belief in a final, bodily resurrection in connection with the final judgment is regularly hailed by critics as one of apocalyptic's major developments. It was, allegedly, only another aspect of its despair in historical possibilities and tendency to sit back and wait for God to make everything right again. It was the ultimate eschatologization and application to each individual of the old dogma of retribution. "The blood of the martyrs was the seed of resurrection-faith," as it is sometimes put. Again we have a partial truth here, but also typical critical exaggeration of the contrasts. Critics are often loathe to concede any type of Old Testament belief in life after death except for perhaps the most shadowy type of existence in Sheol, and with that presupposition give a minimalistic misreading to passages which, at very least, are capable of more positive interpretations. (Cf. also the debate between the Sadducees and the Pharisees on the subject.) Possibly the distinction between "immortality" and "resurrection" summarizes much of the difference between what is at least explicitly stated in the earlier and later texts, but the conservative would be very much concerned to accent the continuities as well. But, no doubt, the theme is much more central in apocalyptic than earlier, and, properly understood, we undeniably have here a major factor in "cumulative revelation," as well as a major aspect of divine preparation of the seedbed for receptivity to the Gospel of our Lord's resurrection (to radical critics, of course, the latter only a crucial expression of the preaching and expectation of the historical Jesus).

"Son of Man"

Finally, there is the "Son of Man," whom, formally at least, we meet for the first time in Dan. 7. The vast critical literature on the origins and history of this concept (not to speak of the debate among New Testament scholars whether or to what extent Jesus understood Himself in those terms) cannot even be surveyed here (and probably not all that much will be lost either). In the Old Testament, much of the discussion has turned on the question of whether the Son of Man is an individual or a collective (representing Israel, "the saint of the most high") figure. In spite of the critical predilection for the latter, the individual interpretation is surely the primary intent of Dan. 7. The common critical appeal to Dan. 7:18, 27 does not contradict this; the Kingdom is, indeed, given to both the Son of Man and the saints, but that scarcely adds up to identity. But there are aspects of truth to the collective understanding. The "Son of Man," following basic Hebrew idiom, is also *Man* (cf. its use in this sense in the contemporaneous Ezekiel), the only true man (not only Israel reduced to one), the last and eschatological Adam (cf. Rom. 5), come to redeem mankind from the Beast and to restore him to his original, created glory. But first and foremost, the figure is obviously also divine, a transcendent and preexistent heavenly being who is thus in a position to effect such a change in mankind's status.

Possibly there are also overtones in the Son of Man portraiture of the "first king" (cf. Ezek. 28 and Gen. 2) figure, now revealed to establish His eternal kingdom upon earth (Dan. 7:14). But the motif is muted, and in general the Son of Man complex employs other symbols than the royal ones of Messianism (in the narrow sense). Nevertheless, the figure is ultimately as "Messianic" as can be, as the New Testament makes plain (the identification perhaps facilitated, humanly speaking, by their explicit identification in the pseudepigraphical book of Enoch). As even radical criticism recognizes in its perverse way, there is little doubt that "Son of Man" was designed by the Holy Spirit as a major magnet around which New Testament Christology (and that of our Lord Himself) crystallized, and to which the other component parts of Old Testament prophecy were attracted (eschatological prophet, priest, and king, as well as Suffering Servant).

This "Son of Man" capstone to all of apocalyptic's relative novelties thus well summarizes the pivotal hermeneutical significance which apocalyptic plays in a unified and genuine "Biblical theology." For anyone who confesses "Scripture as its own interpreter," apocalyptic plays a sort of telephone-switchboard role in both directions. On the one hand, the conservative will agree, in part at least, with the historical-critical accent on apocalyptic as a major funnel by which major Old Testament themes and prophecies are focused upon the New Testament, and thus provide it with one of its major forms of expression. The traffic, however, moves also in the other direction, the direction which the higher critic usually discounts, but which for our present purposes is even more important. Indeed, apocalyptic in a sense "reinterprets" prophecy, but that means that it is also incumbent upon the conservative exegete to interpret prophecy in that same light. Likewise, precisely because the New Testament to a large extent finds access (if you will) to the Old Testament through apocalyptic, it also serves as the conservative's major key to the proper understanding and exposition of the older covenant. Unlike "precritical" exegesis, even the conservative will be concerned to distinguish more carefully than was once done between the stages of the total revelatory history, but, unlike the critics, he will be even more exercised to maintain and demonstrate the essential unity of those stages, both the major stages of prophecy and fulfillment in general, and also the various subdivisions of each. Even within conservatism, one has here the legitimate and salutary difference between Biblical and dogmatic theology. Orthodox exegesis will not be "historical-critical" (imposing alien categories upon Scripture), but "historical-grammatical" (interpreting the history on the basis of the grammar of the inspired text.) In short, he will distinguish, but not divorce.

Historicity

Let us now turn to the isagogical problems of the Book of Daniel itself. In a way they almost reduce themselves to one: whether the book was written by a historical Daniel in the Babylonian exile, or whether it is a pseudepigraph written to buoy the hopes of victims of Seleucid persecution somewhere between the beginning of Seleucid persecution in 167 and Judas Maccabeus' rededication of the temple in 164. Taking the book itself literally, it is quite easy for the conservative to answer that basic isagogical question with the first option. In addition, of course, we have the clinching testimony of our Lord, who in Matt. 24:15 refers to "the abomination of desolation, spoken of through Daniel the prophet." The preposition *dia* makes it plain that Christ is thinking of a person by that name (and of the "abomination" as an eschatological type, beginning to be fulfilled in connection with His own life and work). Since liberal introductions commonly try to amass evidence refuting this traditional position, conservative ones almost perforce take the shape of meeting and answering those objections.

Purpose

The purpose of the book is also then very much in debate. As it stands, the book has the dual intent of comforting those in the "fiery furnace" of the Babylonian exile, as well as assuring them that present tribulations and deliverances are the vestibule to and prefigurements (types, prophecies) of events at the end of historical time. Not only will the Exile itself not be permanent, but eventually all earthly kingdoms (specifically those in closer prospect) will pass away, and God's eternal kingdom be established. Times may well get even worse, but this portends, not God's failure, but the imminence of His final triumph.

Criticism relocates the locus of that message in the Maccabean struggles of the second century B.C., and often (not quite always) loses sight of its further typological significance—or regards that as only a subsequent "reinterpretation" by the later Christian community when it found itself in similar straits. That is, the more historicistic interpreters are able to make little more of the book than an ancient political tract from which, at most, the modern reader might extract a few examples of piety. Form criticism with its greater sensitivity to the "mythic" significance of apocalyptic symbols, rarely itself pursued the matter of relevance beyond pointing out deeper historical meaning at the time of composition. It remained for political radicals fomenting "apocalyptic" happenings in especially the 1960s, to exploit those symbols in a genuinely "timeless" way—in essential harmony with a mythological understanding, and with a purely symbolic, analogizing way of treating Scripture, but incompatible with genuinely Biblical typology and prophecy.

Authorship

As to authorship, it is true that the Book of Daniel contains no heading or other explicit statement about the book's provenance. Yet literal Danielic authorship is plainly the implication of the text, as of the New Testament, and the situation is not significantly different in that respect from Moses' authorship of the Pentateuch written largely in the third person. At times Daniel speaks in the first person and asserts that visions were vouchsafed to him (e.g., 7:4 ff., 8:1 ff; 9:2 ff.), and presuming that the book is a unity, it is easy to assume that he also wrote the rest of the book, including the narratives about himself in the first part. Both the narratives and the visions are independently arranged in chronological order, but the fact that the visions commence before the narratives end also attests to unity of composition. It is true that we apparently know nothing else of the man besides the information contained in the book, but that certainly is not without Biblical precedent either.

Conservatives are generally inclined to argue that the Daniel mentioned in Ezek. 14:14, 20 and 28:3 is identical with the author of the Biblical book, that is, that Ezekiel is referring to his renowned contemporary. As we have already noted in connection with those passages, however, the parallelism with the very much more ancient personages of Noah and Job makes that position seem very unlikely to us. We judge rather that Ezekiel's reference is to some equally ancient figure of which we know nothing else except perhaps the garbled Ugaritic legends about Dan'el. Liberals usually assume that it is precisely that ancient legendary figure to which the unknown author of Daniel attributed his "visions" as a pseudepigraphon. Even on liberal premises that seems rather unusual, because even the noncanonical pseudepigrapha usually appeal to figures occupying a much more central and well-known position in Biblical history than this ancient Daniel then would.

Unity

As is their wont, critics often question unity of authorship by any hand. At best, in this connection, disproportionate effort is devoted to the search for sources and to reconstruction of stages of transmission. That orginally mythological imagery assumes a sort of second life in apocalyptic (in substantial continuity with classical prophecy) has long been recognized and need occasion no problem for the conservative if properly construed. The use of both Aramaic and Hebrew in the book raises inevitable questions which will be considered below. In addition, many critics argue for a much earlier origin (third century or possibly even earlier) of the "legends" in the first part of the book than of the visions in the latter. The former are often supposed to have originally circulated independently in the eastern Jewish diaspora, and to evince, on the whole, a much more moderate and tolerant attitude toward Gentiles than the nakedly hostile visions composed in Maccabean times to counter Seleucid tyranny. Some think of only an oral form of the earlier "legends" while others think in terms of written sources, but it is obvious that the conservative cannot tune in at all to such a debate on liberal premises.

The original independence of the various "legends" is supposed to be demonstrated by the fact that in each one Nebuchadnezzar converts and legitimatizes Judaism, while in each succeeding story he reappears as an intolerant and vainglorious heathen. To this we can only answer that superficial and repeated "conversions" are no novelty in our day either! (Sometimes it is argued that other evidence shows the Babylonians and Persians to have been too benign masters, specifically of the Israelites, for the tales to have any historical basis in fact, but we scarcely have evidence to argue that there were no exceptions, and the "conversions" may even help explain the relatively civil treatment apparently accorded the exiles in general.)

Internal Evidence for Date

As to date, however, the book itself gives us considerable data. It opens with a reference to "the third year of the reign of Jehoiakim" (Dan. 1:1), that is, probably 605, when, it is reported, Daniel was deported to Babylon after an investment of Jerusalem by Nebuchadnezzar. The latest internal reference is apparently to the "third year of Cyrus" (10:1; cf. below on "Darius the Mede"), that is, perhaps 547 or thereabouts, depending on the point of reference in Cyrus' career. How long afterwards the book itself was composed we cannot tell, but probably not too much later.

Critics, however, find bones to pick with virtually every early chronological reference in the book. Allegedly, the author's historical memory is so imprecise and garbled that he must have written long after the events of the Babylonian and Persian periods themselves. As they read the book, the author becomes reasonably precise and accurate only when he approaches his "predictions" of the second-century Maccabean events of which he was a contemporary (Dan. 7:1 ff; 8:14; 11:21-39). When he actually does attempt to predict the future, especially in 11:40—12:4, he betrays himself again by gross inaccuracies. There surely is a moral somewhere in the fact that almost precisely the same construction was placed on the book by Porphyry, a neo-Platonist philospher and anti-Christian polemicist of the third century A.D., charges which were answered already by Jerome in his famous and still useful commentary on Daniel (recently translated into English by Archer). We must postpone discussion of these allegations until the survey of contents below, after we have first answered critical objections to a literal reading of the book.

These objections begin with the opening verse, specifically its reference to a Babylonian deportation in Jehoiakim's third year. Not only was the historicity of the events itself once nearly universally denied, but a discrepancy was noted with the assertion of Jer. 46:2 that Nebuchadnez-zar's first year (when such a deportation would have to have occurred) was Jehoiakim's *fourth,* not third. The discrepancy is probably easily explained by the different methods of reckoning a king's first year in Judah and Babylon (cf. on the chronology of the divided monarchy). The event itself, a Babylonian invasion under Nebuchadnezzar (apparently the first of four) in connection with his consolidation of power after the defeat of Egypt at Carchemish in 605, is plainly chronicled also in 2 Kings 24:1 ff. and 2 Chron. 36:5 ff. Typically, however, critics were not convinced until archaeological (*extra*-Biblical) discoveries in the 1950s (the "Babylonian Chronicle") confirmed at least the basic outline (though critical doubts remain about details).

Another critical *cause celèbre* in connection with Daniel (now largely demolished) has been the references to Belshazzar in 5:11 as a "son" of Nebuchadnezzar and in 7:1 (cf. 5:30) as a "king" of Babylon, when, it was once objected, he was neither. Only in a very technical sense do the objections hold, however, and it is widely accepted today, even in critical circles, that we have nothing more serious here than use of popular idioms (which seem to be characteristic of Daniel in general). "Son" in the generic sense of "descendant" or "successor" is widely attested in the ancient Near East, and "king" is readily understandable in the popular sense of regent or *de facto* king. We now know that technically Belshazzar was a son of one Nabonidus, one of Nebuchadnezzar's successors as the result of a plot. Belshazzar served as regent in Babylon during his father's long and frequent absences at the oasis of Teman in northern Arabia, a neglect of his duties which contributed to the populace's hailing of Cyrus' conquest as really a deliverance.

Much more intractable, however, are the problems occasioned by the repeated references in the book to a "Darius the Mede." For critics this is probably the parade example of the writer's gross historical confusion. In

Dan. 5:31 he appears as the successor to Belshazzar, after the fall of Babylon, where we would expect Cyrus. In 6:28 (RSV) Cyrus appears to succeed Darius, but in 9:1 Darius is described as the son of "Ahasuerus," who otherwise is Xerxes (see on Ezra and Esther). Yet the well-known sequence of Persian rulers is: Cyrus, Cambyses, Darius (Hystapes), Xerxes. Above all, it is pointed out, Darius Hystapes was no Mede, but a Persian, a successor to Cyrus who had annexed Media to create the "Medo-Persian" empire.

No absolutely definitive solution to this conundrum is yet at hand. Yet, as usual, a more positive reading of the passages in question is at least possible, and most conservatives follow the solution proposed by Whitcomb and tentatively seconded by Albright. Considerable evidence is marshaled to identify "Darius the Mede" with a Gobryas or Gubaru, who was one of Cyrus' main lieutenants in the capture of Babylon and its subsequent administration (thus the Hophal, "was *made* king" of 9:1, a strange idiom for Cyrus himself, and evidently using "king" again in a popular sense). "Darius" here may be understood as royal title of honor, comparable to "Caesar" or "Augustus," and Gobryas may well have assumed it especially in Cyrus' absence. Then 6:28 can be read to equate the rules of Darius and Cyrus, rather than asserting a succession. Gobryas may actually have been a Mede, for we know that Medes figured prominently in the capture of Babylon, but possibly the term was another honorific, perhaps singling out that part of the dual name of the empire (Medo-Persian) because of fond memories of the ancient alliance of Babylonia and Media against Assyria. Who this "Ahasuerus" may have been (Darius' father in 9:1) we have no clue, only that he cannot have been Xerxes, who, of course, lived much later. Perhaps again the Oriental love for a plethora of royal titles is involved.

Other conservatives (especially Wiseman), however, prefer to deploy some of this data toward an identification of "Darius the Mede" with none other than Cyrus the Great himself. "Darius" may still be regarded as honorific, but we know that Cyrus was actually related to the Medes through his mother, and did bear the title, "king of the Medes." "Made king" of 9:1 then would imply God as the agent, and in 9:28 "Darius" and "Cyrus" would simply be equated. In addition, we know that Cyrus was about sixty years old when he conquered Babylon (5:31), but "Ahasuerus" as his father is no more readily explainable than for Gobryas. Still others have sought to identify "Darius the Mede" with Cambyses, Cyrus' son who for a time served as coregent with his father. Obviously, we still await further discoveries in order to arrive at a definitive identification of "Darius the Mede."

Even humanly speaking, it seems very unlikely that a writer would

THE WORD BECOMING FLESH

have been as deficient in relatively recent historical knowledge as critics assume him to have been, or that his work would have achieved any lasting popularity or authority (let alone canonicity), if it were so deficient.

For most critics, the book's presumed error about Darius' being a Mede is only a symptom of its confusion about the Medes in general. Here a basic interpretative issue throughout the book is broached, namely the identification of the four kingdoms in both chap. 2 and chaps. 7 ff. In order to defend the work as applying primarily to the presumed author's own Greek (Seleucid and Maccabean) period, critics are forced to argue that the four empires are Babylonia, Media, Persia, and Greece. But then, of course, they are able to object that there was no independent Median empire between the fall of Babylon and Cyrus' rule (Media as an independent entity, of course, having flourished as a sort of early contemporary of the neo-Babylonian empire, preceding Cyrus' meteoric rise). To the conservative this view looks again like a classical case of circular argumentation, with the critics only making further trouble for themselves by their misidentification of the four kingdoms. If Scripture interprets Scripture, the fourth empire must be the Roman one at the time of Christ, and the three preceding ones accordingly will be Babylonia, Medo-Persia, and Greece. A *combined* Medo-Persian empire following Cyrus' capture of Babylon fits the historical facts perfectly, of course. Internal evidence outside of the visions indicates that the writer thought of a *combined* Medo-Persian entity, namely the giving of Belshazzar's kingdom to the "Medes *and* Persians" (5:28) and Darius' concern with the "law of Medes *and* Persians" (6:8, 12). Further evidence supporting this identification is included in the survey of contents below.

Still another famous and related charge of error to the author of Daniel is his use of "Chaldean." The term is used in a double sense in the book. Its use in an ethnic sense occasions no problems. The "neo-Babylonian" dynasty to which Nebuchadnezzar belonged was really a "Chaldean" one, originally of a tribe or province of southern Babylonia (just north of the Persian Gulf), but because of its dominance at this time often used synonymously with "Babylonian" (e.g., Dan. 1:4; 3:8; 5:30; 9:1; cf. Is. 13:19; 3:14; 48:14, 20; Ezek. 23:22).

However, Daniel also uses "Chaldean" in a more restricted sense of "wise men," "intelligentsia," "astrologers," or at least some subdivision of these circles. Since this usage is not confirmed by inscriptional evidence and is found nowhere else in the Old Testament, critics are quick to conclude that its use in that sense here is anachronistic, that idiom allegedly not having arisen until much later when the genuine ethnic sense of "Chaldean" had been forgotten. In reply, conservatives are at least able to get Herodotus in their corner; writing c. 450 B.C. (closer to the traditional than to the critical dating of the book) the Greek historian uses "Chaldean" in the same dual sense as the Bible. Not surprisingly, the ruling Chaldean dynasty had apparently quickly put its own men into all positions of authority and influence in Babylon. This would, of course, include much of the priesthood (cf. 3:8), wisdom circles and astrologers (2:2 ff; 4:7 ff; 5:7 ff). It has been objected that Daniel would never have been initiated into such an elite caste (let alone made its head), but assuming that this did not involve becoming a pagan priest (something the text nowhere intimates; 2:48), there are no grounds for such an assertion. (It should also be noted that Herodotus also supports the account of Dan. 5 that Babylon was conquered during a feast, without the inhabitants of the city even knowing that it was taking place.)

Yet another argument in a circle for late composition of the book adduces the concern of Daniel and his companions in 1:8 ff. for "kosher" food laws and the attendant "separatism" which it evinces. If "P" (specifically here Lev. 3:17; 6:26; 17:10-14; and 19:26), had not even been composed by Babylonian times, such a concern would indeed be anachronistic. It would be strange, however, if the Hebrews, almost alone among ancient peoples, had no such ritual concerns at all in connection with food, and there is evidence also outside the Pentateuch that such "separatism" antedated the Exile (Amos 7:17; Hos. 9:3 f.). Furthermore, that is scarcely the only concern at this point. Apparently Daniel and his friends also decline to "defile themselves" because, as was common, the food had been consecrated to idols and eating it involved *de facto* participation in a pagan sacrificial rite (cf. Ex. 34:15; 1 Cor. 8, etc.).

A final major missile in the critical arsenal of alleged internal evidence against Daniel's historical credibility, i.e., against the likelihood of its composition in a period at all contemporary to the events it records, has to do with the story of Nebuchadnezzar's madness in chap. 4 (apparently technically a condition known as "boanthropy" in which the afflicted imagines himself to be a cow or a bull). The argument again was the lack of extra-Biblical evidence corroborating the tale. On three counts, however, the critical argument appears to be inaccurate. Independently from the Bible, we have three ancient notices which appear to point in the same direction: Josephus' preservation of a report by the Babylonian priest, Berossus, that Nebuchadnezzar was "ill" prior to his death; Eusebius' report of another early tradition about strange behavior by the king toward the end of his life; and, third, an inscription from Nebuchadnezzar himself confessing a strange interlude of four years when he did not engage in his usual activities.

Critics had long suspected that the tale had originally been told about

Nabonidus, the "nature boy" with his extended absences at the oasis in Tema. Unlike Nebuchadnezzar, Nabonidus was despised by his subjects, fertile soil for the growth of such a derogatory legend. Supposedly, the tale was transferred to the well-known Nebuchadnezzar centuries later when virtually all memory of Nabonidus had faded. When in 1955 from Qumran Cave IV a "Prayer of Nabonidus" came to light, it was widely hailed in liberal circles as confirmation of the long-standing critical intuition. In it Nabonidus, "king of Assyria and Babylonia" *(sic!)*, reports that he suffered from a "serious inflammation" for seven years, but when he prayed and confessed his sins, a Jewish priest of the Exile came and explained matters to him. Especially in the light of other evidence possibly linking the Qumran community with groups that had returned relatively recently from Babylonia to Palestine, it was now argued that we had evidence for the original Babylonian substratum of chap. 4. Memories of Nabonidus would survive in Palestine even less easily than in his native Babylonia, and when they disappeared, the fascinating story was attached to the famous name of Nebuchadnezzar instead.

However, what's good for the goose is good for the gander! Entirely apart from the preference we would accord the canonical version on dogmatic grounds, it seems fair to subject the Qumran tale to the same treatment given Dan. 4 at critical hands. We certainly have no other evidence of Nabonidus' madness, and his description as king of both Assyria and Babylonia scarcely encourages confidence in the document's reliability. It is just as easy to suppose that Nebuchadnezzar's experience was popularly transferred to the contemned Nabonidus as vice versa. In the light of the other apocryphal legends which were attracted to Daniel (see below), it is quite plausible that Nabonidus' prayer is another. In fact, the differences in the two stories are great enough that it is not self-evident that they have any relationship at all to begin with! Since the Qumran version is undocumented anywhere else, it is even possible that it was first composed in Maccabean times.

External Evidence

In addition to all of these pseudo-arguments from internal evidence against the antiquity and genuineness of Daniel, critics are also full of external objections to the traditional viewpoint. (Evolutionistic arguments based on the alleged lateness of Daniel's theological viewpoint have been considered above in connection with apocalyptic in general.) One of the more curious of these is the appeal to the fact that Daniel is not included in the middle or prophetic section of the Hebrew canon (where it was first placed by the Septuagint), but rather appears in the third or hagiographical division *(Kethubhim)*. Critical circularity of argument is again involved here because of the penchant to assign a late date to so many of the other hagiographical works, but a good case can be made for the antiquity of many of these (cf. on Ruth, Job, Psalms, or Proverbs). At any rate, it is abundantly clear that canonical position is not directly related to date of composition. Josephus' assertion that the third part of the canon contained only four books (evidently psalms and the wisdom books), all hymnic and preceptive, may even suggest that Daniel was transferred to the *Kethubhim* at a late stage in its solidification. If so, the reason may be related to the traditional explanation for Daniel's failure to be included among the prophets, namely, that he possessed the prophetic gift but not the prophetic office. Not only was his office primarily a political or administrative one, but a large portion of his book has externally a narrative and visionary (apocalyptic) character rather than a prophetic one in the ordinary sense.

A related argument pointed to the omission of Daniel in Ecclesiasticus' catalogue of famous Israelites (chap. 44). Since ben Sirach wrote around 180 B.C., that should prove that Daniel had not yet been composed at that time. However, the Sirach list is not exhaustive, the other most notable omission probably being Ezra (which see). This argument, however, has not only been neutralized but far outweighed by the new evidence from Qumran (two Hebrew manuscripts from cave XI, plus fragments from others, including one commentary which refers to "Daniel the prophet" like Matt. 24:15), which attest not only to Daniel's popularity but to its canonical status only a very short time after critics would date the work. Such things rarely spring up overnight, and thus we have indirect, but strong evidence at the very least of regard for, if not composition of the work, at least as far back as the third century (with the likelihood then of still earlier roots). If the pseudepigraphic 1 Enoch 14:18-22 (probably written not later than 150 B.C.) quotes Dan. 7:9-10, as seems likely, we have further evidence of Daniel's early use as Scripture— too early if it had first been written scarcely a decade previously. Other marginally canonical works of the same period also allude to Daniel and his book (1 Macc. 2:59 ff; Baruch 1:15—3:3, Sibylline Oracles III, 397 ff.). Harrison has a good point when he points to critical inconsistency in clinging to a Maccabean date of Daniel while abandoning it in the case of the Psalter on essentially the same grounds.

Linguistic arguments have also traditionally been mounted against a sixth-century date of Daniel, but more recent discoveries have greatly blunted the force of these. Daniel is written in both Hebrew and Aramaic (the latter in the older literature often referred to as "Chaldee," because it begins at 2:4 with a speech of the "Chaldeans"). In addition, a number of Persian loanwords appear throughout, and in the Aramaic section there are three words of Greek origin (a number of others once thought to be Greek have turned out not to be). The three Greek words in 3:5 are all names of musical instruments, a type which is always easily diffused beyond the country of origin (cf. our piano or viola), especially in the days of Greek and Persian confrontations in which our book is set. We cannot presently document those Greek musical terms elsewhere earlier than the time of Plato in the fourth century, but that scarcely proves their previous nonexistence. At most we might think of minimal updating here of Oriental equivalents, especially since the instruments themselves appear to be of Mesopotamian origin. In any event, the presence of only *three* Greek words in the book is strong evidence against Maccabean origin, after well over a century of Hellenistic influence in Palestine. The Persian terms really pose no problem, because Daniel himself served at least a number of years under Persian rule, and the book probably took final shape in that period.

The major linguistic debates have always raged around the Aramaic of Daniel. Older critics were wont to argue that the book could scarcely have been written in Babylon because it exhibited a western instead of an eastern dialect of Aramaic, but that argument has been quietly abandoned. There now seems to be no doubt that the type of language is "Imperial Aramaic" *(Reichsaramäisch),* for a long time the *lingua franca* of almost the entire Near East. Its existence can be documented almost throughout the Biblical period, but it became especially prominent in the Persian empire during the reign of Darius I (522 ff.).

The Aramaic of Daniel closely resembles that of Ezra (which see) and of the Elephantine papyri, both of the latter part of the fifth century. These slightly later parallels certainly do not veto the possibility of the actual composition of the Aramaic of Daniel in the sixth century; at most we might have to reckon with a subsequent modernization of Daniel's original Aramaic dialect (as in the case of the other Biblical books, and no theological problem, if properly understood). This conclusion is, if anything, confirmed by the discovery of the Aramaic literature at Qumran, especially the Genesis Apocryphon (perhaps composed as early as the third century), which exhibits many and striking traits different and indisputably later than the language of Daniel.

Essentially the same situation obtains in the Hebrew portions of Daniel. The language is similar to that found in other Biblical literature of the exilic and early postexilic periods (Ezekiel, Haggai, Ezra, Chronicles), but differs markedly from that of Ecclesiasticus, written only shortly before the critical date for Daniel. As noted above, the Hebrew of Daniel contains a number of Persian administrative terms, where we would expect to see Greek influence if the book were written nearly two centuries after Alexander's conquests.

It has been argued that the very existence of a sizable chunk of Aramaic in Daniel should testify to late composition, when the Hebrew language was moribund. The Aramaic sections of Ezra as well as the Aramaizing Hebrew of Nehemiah, both much earlier than the critical date for Daniel, should suffice to refute that thesis. Not only did Aramaic often supplant Hebrew very early on, in educated circles even well before the Exile (2 Kings 18:26 ff. = Is. 36:11 ff.), and, no doubt, especially in the East, but the evidence now is that the nationalistic and religious movement spearheaded by the Hasidim and Maccabees was accompanied by a revival of the Hebrew tongue.

Why Daniel is written partly in Hebrew, partly in Aramaic, and what the relation is between the two portions are questions which have never been answered to everyone's satisfaction. The question is, of course, related to that of the original unity of the book (see above). The situation is somewhat similar to that in Ezra (which see). As at Ezra 4:28, Aramaic begins in Daniel in the middle of a verse (2:4) with a speech of the "Chaldeans" to the king, but continues on long beyond that speech until the end of chap. 7. Even more puzzling is the fact that the Aramaic thus straddles the two obvious divisions of the book according to contents, the narratives in chaps. 1—6 and the visions in 7—12.

All kinds of hypotheses have been proposed to explain this curious situation. Many critical discussions, of course, are colored by isagogical presuppositions which we cannot share. It once was widely assumed that the book originally must have been composed entirely in one language or the other, but no one could agree which one. Charles' suggestion has been influential in liberal circles, to wit, that Aramaic was the original language, and that the first and last four chapters were rendered into Hebrew to facilitate the book's acceptance into the canon. That supposition, however, is no more supportable by evidence than another, which proposes that parts of the original Hebrew were lost and later supplied from an Aramaic translation.

Recent theorizing has preferred to assume that the employment of two languages was original and deliberate. Rowley's rather complicated hypothesis (assuming a Maccabean date) has attracted many followers: the author of the Book of Daniel employed already extant Aramaic materials for chaps. 2—6, and later added chap. 7, also in Aramaic, all of it to encourage the Aramaic-speaking masses to resist Antiochene oppression; whereas the author himself composed the visions in Hebrew, here addressing a wider and more sophisticated audience, and added the Hebrew introduction of chap. 1 when he was ready to issue the entire work. Similar is the suggestion that "safe" parts of the book, which would not get the author into trouble with the authorities, were written in the Aramaic vernacular, while the more inflammatory sections, inciting Antiochus Epiphanes' overthrow, were couched in the lesser known Hebrew (with an innocuous first chapter added to throw the suspicious off guard). Not totally dissimilar (except for date and hermeneutics) is the theory popular in some conservative quarters to the effect that the portion of the book relating especially to the Gentiles, forecasting their judgment and defeat, was written in Aramaic which might be accessible to them, while the sections proclaiming hope and salvation for God's people were put into Hebrew. A little concentration, however, soon uncovers debatable points, if not outright flaws, in all these proposals, and the simple truth is that we do not know.

One might suspect the bilingual character of Daniel to be connected somehow with the relatively unique and tortured text-critical status of the book, but there is no evidence that this is the case. (Whatever it proves, we must note, however, that the Qumran manuscripts attest to the transition from Aramaic back to Hebrew at the beginning of chap. 8.) If the Maccabean date of Daniel were correct, it would mean, as some critics crow, that the Qumran manuscripts of Daniel probably bring us within a half-century of the autographs, closer even than some papyrus copies of John in the New Testament, and closer by far than in the case of any other Old Testament book. That very novelty should arouse legitimate suspicions, and, unfortunately, we must agree that they are only too well founded!

Text Criticism

For whatever reason, the Septuagint differs radically from the Masoretic text, more so than in the case of any other Old Testament book. The deviations are not so prominent in Dan. 1—3 and 7—12, which agree reasonably well with MT except for the apocryphal additaments (see below). In chaps. 4—6, however, the difference is at times almost drastic, characterized by periphrasis and many textual expansions. As to a lesser degree at other points in the Bible, the relationship to the traditional Hebrew text is obviously more complicated than any type of mere literary dependence. The Septuagint is plainly based on another line of textual tradition, and one which we now sometimes (only sometimes) find supported by the Hebrew manuscripts of Daniel at Qumran. Some critics think that the "Prayer of Nabonidus" (cf. above), discovered at Qumran is related to the LXX variations, at least in chap. 4, but there appears to be no firm evidence of that. Others also profess to find the LXX text an "actualization" of MT, that is, interpreting Daniel's visions more clearly in the light of Maccabean controversies, but one suspects that the wish is the father of the thought.

These deviations were so many and serious that the early church apparently repudiated it and substituted the more literal translation of Theodotion. As a result the original LXX translation was all but forgotten until modern times. For a long time it was known only at something like third hand: through Paul of Tella's sixth-century Syriac translation of Origen's Hexapla, and later through the discovery of a tenth-century rendering of the Hexaplaric version, the "Codex Chisianus." The Chester Beatty papyri gave us about one-third of a much better text, and now, with the help of Qumran discoveries, a good share of it can be reconstructed.

Theodotion's text, the one used by most of the church fathers (apparently as early as Clement of Rome in the first century) is by no means identical with MT either (it too includes the apocryphal additions) but far closer to it than LXX. Sometimes Qumran readings support Theodotion too, indicating that he had access to a Hebrew text type much closer to MT than that underlying LXX. However, since we encounter "Theodotionic" readings in authors who lived earlier than Theodotion, it may be that he did not translate directly from the Hebrew but merely revised some earlier version. A recent theory even argues that what has been thought to be Theodotion's text is really that of Symmachus (another early minor Greek translation of the Old Testament). Obviously, text critics still have much to learn about early textual history, but one important thing is clear nonetheless: the obvious primacy and authority accorded the *hebraica veritas,* as St. Jerome would later style it.

Jerome's remarks, in the preface to his commentary to Daniel, are in the context both of praising the church for having preferred Theodotion over the unreliable LXX, and of dismissing some of Porphyry's arguments against Daniel because they were based on the apocryphal additions. Nevertheless, Jerome included the apocryphal additions in his commentary, as he had in the Vulgate translation. Partly for that reason, and partly because of their great popularity in the early church, where they were often quoted as Scripture, they are of too great importance to pass by here.

Apocryphal Additions

Three apocryphal additions to Daniel are usually counted, but five different compositions are really involved. There is considerable variation in the ancient versions as to the place of their insertion in the canonical text, but that of the Vulgate is the most familiar. Unlike the apocryphal additions to Esther, these do not appear to be deliberate expansions of the original text, but in all likelihood had circulated independently before

becoming attached to Daniel. Only one of the three has a good claim to
have been originally composed in Hebrew, but the matter is debated. The
date of their composition is likewise very difficult to determine, but the
second century B.C. (Maccabean period) seems to be the clear critical
consensus, and in this case there is no reason for the conservative to
dissent. All may well have oral antecedents of indeterminate age. Critics
commonly place the apocryphal tales on the same plane as those which
found their way into the canonical text, but obviously one's whole
understanding of "canon" is involved there.

After Dan. 3:24 of the canonical text we meet the first of the three
additions, really two originally independent ones combined editorially:
"The Prayer of Azariah" (vs. 26-45) and "The Song of the Three Young
Men" (vs. 52-90). The literary context of both is that of the fiery furnace
(where, it is apparently assumed, all three would naturally spend their
time in prayer and praise), but neither piece internally makes any mention
of that context. The first, here ascribed to Abednego (Azariah's better
known pagan name), confesses the people's sins and asks for deliverance.
A prose interlude (vs. 46-51) relates how the angel of the Lord joined the
three in answer to Abednego's prayer, after which all three are described
as joining in the second piece, much the better known of the two. English
tradition, unfortunately, often knows it as "The Song of the Three Holy
Children" (the last a misleading term used in a religious, not a
chronological sense, as in "children of Israel"). Much better is its liturgical
name after its opening Latin words, the *Benedicite (Omnia Opera)*. It
makes no mention of the fiery furnace either, but is simply a liturgical
invitation to all of creation to "bless the Lord," a repeated refrain perhaps
modeled after Ps. 136. Since it really is a psalm, many Greek codices
appended it to copies of the Psalter, and it has traditionally played a
prominent role in all the liturgical churches (including the first of the
"canticles" offered on p. 120 of *The Lutheran Hymnal*).

Easily the most popular of the apocryphal additions to Daniel is the
story of Susanna, appended to the book as chap. 13 in the Vulgate, but
appearing at the beginning of the book in Theodotion. The two also have
somewhat different versions of the story. The LXX speaks of two elderly
Jewish judges in Babylon who often held court at the estate of rich
Joakim. Yielding to their lust for his beautiful, but also chaste and pious,
wife, Susanna, they attempted rape. When she refused to submit, they
accused her of adultery, and at the subsequent trial, she would have been
condemned to death had Daniel not been inspired to intervene and
expose the judges' villainy. (Theodotion speaks of young Jews and
attempted seduction, plus other variations.)

Certain Greek puns make it likely that the work was originally composed in Greek, but already Origen sought for Hebrew originals (partly to defend its canonicity), and the question is still moot. The story's popularity in the early and medieval churches can scarcely be exaggerated, as is evident from Christian art as early as the catacombs. It was frequently given a typological interpretation, Susanna representing the church, and so on. Many modern scholars, even less appropriately, speak of it as a "detective story." Most likely we simply have a widespread type of morality tale which also attached itself to the figure of Daniel.

Finally, (Vulgate, chap. 14), we have "Bel and the Dragon," really two separate tales, as the title suggests. In the first, another "detective story," Daniel proves to Cyrus, who has asked Daniel to worship his god, that the god does not eat, as the king argues, and thus cannot be alive. Daniel obtains his proof by sprinkling fine ashes on the sanctuary floor and the next morning pointing out the tracks of the priests who had come to retrieve the food offered to the idol. "Bel" is simply an alternate spelling of "Baal," meaning "Lord," here obviously applied to the chief Babylonian deity, Marduk.

In the sequel, it is a dragon which Daniel is supposed to worship. When he proves its finitude by feeding it a concoction which causes it to explode, the enraged populace throws Daniel into a lions' den (apparently a second time). God intervenes by miraculously transporting the prophet Habakkuk from Palestine to feed Daniel, and when, after a week, the king finds Daniel still alive, his enemies are fed to the beasts instead. Both of these stories were obviously told to ridicule paganism, and in the latter case we obviously have some connection with the ancient "dragon of chaos" motif of mythology, which, as we have seen, also the Bible and especially apocalpytic often adapted secondarily (cf. Is. 27:1; Ps. 74:14; Rev. 12:9; etc., and the very popular medieval tales about St. George).

Outline and Contents

Now let us turn to a few details of the canonical text. In outline it easily divides itself into: (1) Chaps. 1—6, Narratives ("Legends" to most critics) of Daniel and his companions, related in the third person singular; and (2) Chaps. 7—12, Visions of Daniel, interpreted by angels, but narrated in the first person singular (Daniel himself). The stories of the first part are probably among the most familiar in the Bible—superficially at least. The danger is grave, however, that in Sunday school contexts they become bearers of the rankest moralism, and at inept hands their heavily supernatural character may even contribute to that. Theologically, they well illustrate that the only two alternatives really are moralism or Biblical eschatology (Law-Gospel). They also demonstrate that apocalyptic is most "relevant" because it deals with ultimates, and the nature of

THE WORD BECOMING FLESH

Dan. 1:6 first introduces us to the Hebrew names of the four captive youths of the tribe of Judah (whence the Messiah!) who have been selected for special training in Nebuchadnezzar's court. While Daniel's original name is familiar, those of the friends are not: Hananiah, Mishael, and Azariah (cf. the apocryphal prayer of the latter, above). Daniel is given the Babylonian name, Belteshazzar (not to be confused with Belshazzar in chap. 5), apparently meaning "May Bel protect his life" (cf. 4:8). His three friends are renamed Shadrach, Meshach, and Abednego. There are still questions about the original Akkadian form of all these names. Names often assume different forms in other languages (e.g. Louis and Ludwig), and there may also be some deliberate defacement of the names of pagan deities, a common practice. In the case of Abednego, it was once assumed to be a late second-century corruption of Abednebo ("servant of Nebo/Nabu, a major neo-Babylonian deity), but the Biblical name is now known from the fifth-century Elephantine Papyri. The special skill and wisdom granted all of them because they scrupled to eat Babylonian food (see above) sets the stage for especially the next five chapters.

Daniel's first test (chap. 2) comes in the interpretation of the king's forgotten dream of the great image made out of four different substances. (The beginning of the Aramaic section of the book with the Chaldeans' reply to the king in v. 4 is signaled by the addition of "in Aramaic" in the original text.) A stone, "cut without hands," which hits the image's feet (made of mixed iron and clay) and demolishes it, becomes a great mountain and fills the whole earth. The main import of the dream is easy enough: the familiar and basic apocalyptic (and Biblical) theme of the triumph of the kingdom of God over the kingdoms of this world. The big question—and in a way *the* problem of the book—is the identification of the four kingdoms represented. Essentially the same pattern is repeated four other times in the book, in chaps. 7 and 8 under the imagery of beasts and in chaps. 9 and 11 unfiguratively (see both there and above). In the progressively poorer composition of the image from the head down, we see the standard apocalyptic (and Biblical) theme of the progressive deterioration of world history as the end approaches; it needs to be accented over against all liberal and secular meliorism and optimism about human contributions toward the coming "kingdom of God."

In Dan. 2:18 we meet for the first time the Aramaic term *raz,* especially prominent in this chapter, as in apocalyptic in general. Its common translation, "mystery," evacuates much of its meaning: somewhat like its Hebrew counterpart, *sod,* and especially like the New Testament *musterion,* it refers to the "eternal counsel of God" as deliberated in the heavenly council of the King of kings (cf. chap. 7), which is now revealed to the faithful so that they may perceive and believe the "sacramental" import of history. When the "mystery" is first revealed to Daniel, we must note the beautiful prayer of thanksgiving with which he responds (vs. 20-23), the first of many such in the book and also very typical of the flavor of most apocalyptic literature.

The familiar story of the three men in the fiery furnace (Dan. 3) is quite universally among critics taken to be, first of all, an allegory of Antiochus Epiphanes' new Hellenistic order, requiring syncretistic conformity under pain of death, and then also an allegory of any kind of "fiery furnace" of affliction, oppression, etc. Such an unacceptable interpretation well illustrates the difference between allegory and typology in general: the fact that we insist both on the historicity of the event and the necessity of its unification with the history of Jesus Christ, does not imply less, but infinitely more, meaning. The frequent use of the pericope as an Old Testament lesson for Easter well summarizes the point. Over against both the critical judgment that apocalyptic is escapist, and the tendency of the masses to confuse religion with conformity to the prevailing social code, the narrative accents that faith has to do with ultimate meaning, not escape. The fourth person who joins the three confessors is described as "like a son of the gods" (v. 25), that is, in a frequent Old Testament idiom for the subject, like what was later known as an "angel."

Some aspects of Nebuchadnezzar's temporary insanity (Dan. 4) have already been discussed above. It is introduced by a "flashback" to one of the king's dreams (this time remembered), the fulfillment of which had led to this humiliation. The central subject of the dream, a "world tree" at the center of the earth, reaching up to heaven and representing a vast empire, appears in various other Biblical contexts in one form or the other: Ezek. 17 and 31, the mustard seed parable of Matt. 13, and probably, in a sense, the trees of Paradise. (Cf. similarly the "world mountain" as a depiction of Paradise, as in the great stone of Dan. 2:35; cf. Is. 2:2; and 11:9.) The "watcher, a holy one" (v. 23), who orders the tree to be hewn down, represents a certain type of angel; such classification probably reflects the increased revelatory accent on that subject in postexilic times (cf. above). The "great reversal" of judgment comes upon the king's overweening boast in v. 30, on its face, or "historically," true enough, but in the context obviously to be understood as implying pretensions of deity. The critical assumption that the story was told in ridicule of Antiochus II, known as "Epiphanes" (claiming to be an "epiphany" of a god) but popularly punned as Antiochus "Epimanes" (a maniac), may be true enough of later *application.*

At Belshazzar's feast (Dan. 5), when Nabonidus' coregent (cf. above) commits the blasphemy of using the sacred temple vessels from Jerusalem for his pagan banquet, there appears the "handwriting on the wall' (becoming a stock English phrase), presaging the fall of the Babylonian empire (as well as of the Semitic hegemony which had generally prevailed in the ancient Near East since Sumerian times in the third millennium).

The form and meaning of the Aramaic words inscribed on the wall has occasioned much discussion. Precisely why the crowd could not read them is not explained, but (if it was any ordinary script at all) it may have been some type of cuneiform ideogram, the meanings of which are apparent only to the instructed. In any case, there is some question as to the precise form of the lapidary inscription. "Mene" is repeated in none of the ancient versions, nor does Daniel make anything of it in his interpretation, but there is no problem in understanding it as a repetition for the sake of emphasis. The third word, "Peres," often appears in the interpretation (v. 28) as "Upharsin"; grammatically, it is simply an Aramaic plural preceded by the conjunction, but many scholars, including conservatives, believe the plural form really to be a scribal error (cf. below); if so, the RSV is correct in simply repeating "Peres."

Daniel plainly interprets all three words as Aramaic passive (Peal) participles of the roots meaning "number," "weigh," and "divide," and there certainly is no grammatical problem in that. (If one knows that "t" often appears in Aramaic cognates for Hebrew "sh," the middle word will readily be recognized as equivalent to "shekel," a unit of value which was always "weighed" until coinage began toward the end of the Old Testament era.)

In recent times, however, it has become very popular in critical circles to second-guess the text by repointing the Aramaic consonants as originally names of Babylonian weights, the maneh (cf. Ezek. 45:12 and Ezra 2:69), the tekel or shekel, and the peras or half-maneh (Culver suggests comparing our "pound, ounce, half a pound"). The idea should be that of the decreasing value of contemporary rulers (cf. the image of chap. 2), Nebuchadnezzar, Nabonidus or Belshazzar (insignificant), and now the Persians. Daniel's interpretation then would amount to a play on the names of the weights, and in the third instance a double play, not only "divided" but also "Persia" (which possibly some scribe "improved" by pluralizing into "Persians"). One hesitates simply to reject so ingenious a suggestion, but the best we can really do is point out that there is no evidence of it in the text. There may be a partial exception in the possibly punning reference to Persia in v. 28. Although the Medes are mentioned here as partners, the pun would underscore the historical fact of the dominance of the Persians in the alliance (i.e., that no separate Median kingdom is envisioned!).

The circumstance in Dan. 6, which differs from previous narratives and which leads "Darius the Mede" (cf. above) to cast Daniel to the lions, is the demand that the king himself be worshiped as deity. This type of thing, of course, was common in antiquity, and again we need not think of Antiochus "Epiphanes" to find historical context for the narrative. If it really were deity speaking, it would be logical that the decree was unalterable (vs. 8 and 12), and a Greek historian, Diodorus, reports such an assumption in the case of the later Darius III (cf. also Esther 1:19; 8:8). One suspects, moreover, that here the Biblical writer intends a little humor or even sarcasm, because God's intervention soon causes the king to back off from his purported immutability. The "great reversal" becomes especially evident when the plotters become the victims of their own plot (cf. Haman and Mordecai).

In 6:10 we note Daniel's custom of kneeling and praying three times daily, facing Jerusalem. Critics often argue that the custom of orientation toward Jerusalem had not begun so early, but 1 Kings 8:33 ff. indicates that it began even earlier—at the dedication of Solomon's temple (cf. Ps. 5:7; 28:2). The custom of praying thrice daily (cf. Ps. 55:17) passed over into the early church. Daniel's claim in v. 22 to have been found "blameless" by God must not be understood meritoriously (cf. similarly on Noah and Job), but rather of having been found "innocent." The primary reference is to the king's charge of disloyalty, but in full Biblical context we will not hesitate to regard it as one instance of the broader verdict of "not guilty" by virtue of the covenant (justification).

Chapters 7—8

With chap. 7 we begin the second and more strictly apocalyptic portion of the Book of Daniel, visions in contrast to narratives (although the visions too are set within a narrative framework, now in the first instead of the third person). As noted above, the language division does not correspond to the structural transition, Aramaic continuing yet throughout this chapter. (On that basis, some would make chap. 7 the conclusion of the first part of the book, but this seems forced and artificial). In a way, that is unfortunate because it renders inaccessible in the original, even to those whose Hebrew is still in good repair, a chapter which is not only the *pièce de résistance* of the book, but one of the key chapters of the entire Scriptures, the "Son of Man" prophecy.

The overall structure of the vision is of four beasts, described in Dan. 7:1-14 and interpreted in vs. 15-28, although functionally the two halves overlap. The interpreter of the vision (a standard apocalyptic feature; cf.

Ezekiel and Zechariah) is not identified here but surely is the same angel Gabriel who interprets throughout the remainder of the book. The overall theme is the conflict between the Creator and Chaos, the latter here exemplified and personified under the symbols of the beasts, and of the "great sea" from which all emerge. The latter is an ancient (ultimately mythological) symbol of chaos, of the demonic (cf. Is. 51:10; Rev. 17:8; 21:1). It often signifies nations in tumult (in their fallen state manifestations of primordial chaos), and here there is probably also accent on their nondivine, even diabolic nature.

The four beasts here are essentially coterminous with the four metals of the image in Dan. 2, and their respective identifications will again be determined by basic isagogical and hermeneutical presuppositions. The conservative position identifies the lion with eagle's wings with Babylon; the bear with the Medo-Persian empire; the leopard with the Greek or Macedonian (Alexander, the four wings and heads probably representing the division of his empire into four parts after his death—major evidence of the correctness of this identification); and the fourth, which almost defied description, with the Roman. The latter had ten horns (kingdoms) followed by a little horn with "eyes like the eyes of a man, and a mouth speaking great things" (cf. Rev. 17). With these final features, the going really gets rough, and understandings differ drastically.

Liberals, who identify the fourth beast with Greece (the Seleucids), understand the little horn with a big mouth again to be Antiochus Epiphanes. Part of their case is based on the alleged identification of the little horn here in Dan. 7 with the little horn of chap. 8:9 ff. Since the latter is explicitly described as rising from Greece (8:23), it is argued that the same must be true in chap. 7. It is also protested that we know of no ten kingdoms following the Roman empire, if that is the signification of the fourth beast.

Conservatives counter that it is no easier to find ten kingdoms following the Seleucids (and certainly reject the implication of historical error, which, of course, does not trouble liberals). The detailed descriptions of the little horns in the two chapters differ so significantly (as do also the fourth beast and the he-goat of chap. 8) that it is hard to see how any identification can be maintained. At most, Antiochus might be identified with the little horn as a sort of anticipatory manifestation or type of a conflict which has yet to peak; cf. below.

Beyond this, however, the conservative ranks are split into millennial and amillennial viewpoints, and that fat is in the fire for the remainder of the book. (Only the premillennial and dispensationalist brand of chiliasm seems prominent enough to merit any of our attention here, and even its ranks are fractured many ways.) Dispensationalists take the ten kingdoms literalistically as referring either to empires following the Roman (but still generally considered "Roman"—and the number of attempted identifications are legion), or to a revived Roman empire (a ten kingdom period) after Christ's return. The little horn tends to be identified with some satanic figure within that span of time.

The traditional conservative, amillennial (and Lutheran) position, in contrast, understands the number ten as simply a symbol of completeness, that is, an indefinite number between Rome's demise and the rise of the little horn. The latter is to be identified with the Antichrist, primarily in his final manifestation, but not necessarily excluding his many anticipatory embodiments throughout history. (Thus the little horn of chap. 8 which does signify Antiochus may be understood in a typological relationship to the antitype, the little horn, in this chapter.)

That we really have ultimately to do with a *final* judgment scene is made plain in the climactic theophany of Dan. 7:9 ff. (all of Rev. 4—20 can be read as an elaboration of vs. 9-14 here). The "Ancient of Days" ("advanced in years," as we might say, that is, God, depicted as a venerable judge) calls the heavenly court (cf. Ps. 82; Deut. 33:2; and Job 1—2) to order, and countless multitudes stand in silent awe as "the books were opened." Eternal dominion is given to "one like a son of man" who comes "with the clouds of heaven." He is not a personification of the saints (as liberals generally hold), although He gives the kingdom to them (vs. 18, 27). Christ plainly had this prophecy in mind in applying its language to Himself (Matt. 25:31, etc.) and, properly understood, He shares His kingdom already with the church militant (and not only with Jews in a restored Israel, as in dispensationalism). In contrast to the beasts, rising from the sea, Christ *is* true humanity, restoring to man his birthright of dominion over the beasts (Gen. 1:2-6; 2:19 ff.), in contrast to the bestiality which has invaded his soul (and the entire cosmos) since the Fall.

Even while his judgment is in progress, the little horn continues to speak "great words" (Dan. 7:11); he "prevails" over the saints until the very end (v. 21; no myth of evolutionary progress toward an "Omega point" here!); and he is given "a time, two times, and half a time" (v. 25, cf. Dan. 12:7; Rev. 12:14). With the latter phrase another exegetical crux ensues. Liberals attempt to relate it to the three-year period (in which the author of the book really is to be placed) between Antiochus' desecration of the temple and its rededication (Hanukkah). But there is no indication that "time" means "year," and how do we account for the extra half-year? By this interpretation the writer would also mistakenly have supposed that the Messianic era would commence immediately thereafter. Millennialists too wish to translate "day," and equate the period with the last half of the seventieth "year-week," the period of the great tribulation of Dan. 9:27 (which see). The analogy of Scripture, however, argues that such precise timetables were not on the writer's mind. The expression, "time," is deliberately indeterminate. "Two times" indicates that toward the end the little horn's power will double. Then, however, instead of four more times giving a total of seven, indicating completeness, we have "half a time," indicating his sudden end at the final assize. The final act in the cosmic drama is the everlasting and universal kingdom of the Son of Man and His saints.

With Daniel's second vision in chap. 8, that of the ram and the he-goat, the Hebrew language resumes. Some think there is some integral relation to the change of contents, but we doubt it (cf. above). The relationship of chaps. 8 to 7 is comparable to that of Gen. 2 to 1; we have a more narrow focus after the broad canvas preceding. Chap. 8 concentrates more on the equivalents of the second and third beasts of the preceding vision, that is on the penultimate period of the "not yet" in which the saints must be tried and tested before the end. Both the earlier and the eschatological periods are less in view, although especially the latter resumes prominence shortly. (In contrast both to liberals, who have little but disdain for such material, and to millennialists, who often leave the impression that this and the remaining chapters of the book are the very heartbeat of Scripture, it is to be feared that many Lutherans overcorrect by ignoring these pericopes and their rich kerygmatic content altogether.)

Dan. 8 is dated two years later than chap. 7, and its visionary setting (cf. Ezek. 8) is in Susa, the chief capital of the Persian empire (the setting also of Esther) at the "river" Ulai, the classical Eulaeus, a major artificial canal. The ram plainly represents the Persian empire, and its two horns of unequal height its Median and Persian components—the latter being dominant. (Here we have another major internal refutation of the critical notion that the book thinks of two separate Median and Persian kingdoms!) Its conquests are checked by the meteoric rise "without touching the ground" (v. 5) of a he-goat, plainly signifying Alexander the Great. When the he-goat magnifies himself, he is broken into four horns (v. 8; the four "Diadochi" who inherit Alexander's empire; cf. chap. 11). Out of one of them (Seleucus) grows a "little horn," *not* identical with the little horn of chap. 7 (although possibly typical of it), but here plainly Antiochus Epiphanes. His conquests extend even to "the glorious land" (v. 9) that is, Canaan (cf. Jer. 3:19; Dan. 11:16, 41), and include even "some of the host of heaven" (v. 10), apparently here the true believers, reckoned as the earthly part of the hosts/armies of Yahweh, the "LORD of hosts." The imagery of the stars underlies "host," to whom the faithful are here compared (cf. Dan. 12:3; Rev. 12:4). And more (vs. 11-12): he even challenges "the Prince of the host" that is, God Himself (not Onias, the illegitimate high priest in Maccabean times; the parallel "Prince of princes" in v. 25 is less ambiguous); and the *"tamid,"* that is, the "perpetual" morning and evening sacrifices of the temple, is brought to a halt.

So far we have unusually clear symbolical prediction, and the difficulties are relatively minimal. A major crux in the entire book arises, however, in Dan. 8:13 ff., when in answer to one "holy one's" (angel's) question, "How long?" (cf. Is. 6:11; Hab. 1:2; repeatedly in the Psalter; Rev. 6:10, etc.), another replies "2,300 evenings and mornings." "Evening and morning" may here be used in the same sense as in Gen. 1 and elsewhere, that is, for a whole day, and then the reply would imply only 1,150 days. The majority of commentators, however, appear to understand the idiom as essentially synonymous with "days and nights," thus 2,300 days. In either case, it is not easy to find an application in Maccabean history. We know that the temple was reconsecrated in 165 B.C., and if that is our anchor, it means that the period in question would begin either in 168 or 171 B.C., but neither date is totally satisfactory. The former alternative (three instead of six years) is sometimes related to the three "times" of 7:25 (which see), interpreted as meaning three and a half years, but both that exegesis of 7:25 and that kind of parallelism of chaps. 7 and 8 are debatable—and, at best, we have half a year to spare! If, then, precise numerical calculation is out of order (as it generally *is* in apocalyptic), a better symbolism might be derived by converting 2,300 (the second alternative above) into six years and 110 days, perhaps implying less than a full period of divine judgment—so transitory would the evil appear and so easily annihilated from the divine perspective.

A symbolic understanding of the number also facilitates a broader understanding of the import of the entire vision. As we stressed, Dan. 8, in contrast to 7, concentrates more on the historical tribulations of the people of God during the period of the third world empire, that is, the Macedonian or Seleucid. Yet the eschatological is surely not totally out of sight. Especially the references to the "end" and to the "indignation" (cf. 11:36) in vs. 17 and 19 appear to indicate as much (Some millennialists wish to make these phrases entirely eschatological, and some amillennialists react by denying all eschatological implication, but both stances seem extreme.) In the Biblical view, history is always typical of metahistory and of eschatology (even if the details elude us); just as the little horn (Antiochus) of chap. 8 appears to have some typological relation to the little horn of chap. 7 (Antichrist), so we should read here not only predictions of Maccabean history (suffering, but ultimate deliverance), but also intimations of the church's experience in the time of *the* end. It, of course, is as characteristic of apocalyptic as of classical prophecy to mingle what will be fulfilled sooner and later in one prospect.

Gabriel's concluding instruction (8:26) that Daniel "seal up the vision" (cf. 9:24;12:4; Rev. 22:10) may illustrate the point. The Biblical expression does not imply to hide or conceal, but rather to preserve or keep intact. Part of the reason would appear to be so that the encouragement and promise contained in the vision would be available when the people of God needed it, not only under Antiochus (when it might more easily be remembered), but also in the time of the "*great* tribulation" (Matt. 24:21, e.g.). The text is not so explicit, but we may well suppose that the angel's command implied the "inscripturation" of the revelation, eventuating in our present *Book* of Daniel. (The common critical explanation that such phrases were included by the contemporaneous, pseudonymous author to explain why they had never heard of such prophecies until the present, does not require refutation.)

Chapter 9 (The "Seventy Weeks")

Dan. 9 is best known for containing the famous prophecy of the "seventy weeks." Hence, both millennialist overemphasis on the chapter and (one fears) amillennialist recoil from it may lead to overlooking one of the devotional gems of the Bible, Daniel's beautiful and exemplary prayer in vs. 3-20 (a good two-thirds of the entire chapter). The prayer was at "vespers" or "the time of the evening sacrifice" (v. 21; cf. 6:10), even though Daniel was miles away from the temple where the accompanying "objectified prayer" of the sacrifice was being offered. Many critics regard the prayer as a secondary interpolation because its penitential tone is not supposed to fit the present context very well. However, the objection is surely superficial; the occasion is contemplation of "the desolations of Jerusalem" (v. 2). The prayer certainly is a remarkable confession of sin and petition for God's *sola gratia,* contrasting God's righteousness with man's "confusion of faces" (shame or disgrace, v. 7; Is. 59 has a very similar tone; cf. also Ezra 9 and Neh. 9). V. 11 makes explicit reference to "the curse and oath which are written in the law of Moses" (Lev. 26:14-25; Deut. 28:15-68, etc; cf. 2 Kings 22) as the cause for the people's present tragic circumstances. V. 19 is sometimes called the *Kyrie eleison* of the Old Testament, and the entire prayer's impact upon both Jewish and Christian liturgies, especially confessional services, has been considerable.

Daniel's prayer had been occasioned, to begin with, by his discovery or rediscovery of Jeremiah's prophecy that the duration of the Exile must be seventy years (9:2). The text refers to Daniel's study in "the books." It seems likely that the phrase implies *sacred* books, and thus has some kind of canonical connotations. However, it does not follow, as liberals like to argue in order to defend a late date for the book, that a *closed* canon is implied. Indeed, we see Daniel here as a typical postexilic student of *earlier* Scripture. His attitude toward earlier prophecy (Jeremiah is the only book specifically in question) is clearly documentable in Zechariah (1:2 ff.), writing only a little later, and probably also at many other points in the Biblical literature of roughly this same period.

The first year of Darius the Mede (9:1) is probably also the first year of Cyrus in Babylon (cf. above), that is, 538. The hope engendered by Cyrus' rise apparently led the prophet to search the "Scriptures" for light on the further duration of the Exile. Daniel's initial understanding of Jeremiah's prophecy of the "seventy years" (Jer. 25:11-12; 29:10) had apparently been on its first level of meaning, that is, with reference to the Babylonian exile in which he and his people still languished. However, the precise import of even that first level of meaning is not altogether certain. In a general way at least it fits more than one period of seventy years, and part of its significance was symbolical to begin with (10 X 7, both symbols of completeness). Hence, when Gabriel appears to Daniel to give him "wisdom and understanding" (v. 22) of a further symbolical significance of the "seventy years," it is in no fundamental discontinuity with the phrase's first level of meaning. We may fruitfully employ the label "typological" again to summarize the relation between the two levels of meaning: Israel's historical seventy-year captivity in Babylon is a type of or implicitly predictive of suprahistory, of future experiences of the people of God. The people will again have to pass through great trials before a corresponding deliverance comes to pass.

All interpreters will agree in such general terms to the futuristic import of the angel's reinterpretation, but beyond that lowest common denominator the paths diverge drastically. Montgomery *(ICC)* refers to Dan. 9:24-27 as the "dismal swamp of Old Testament criticism." St. Jerome already knew of nine interpretations, all of them basically Messianic, and finally he leaves it "to the reader's judgment as to whose explanation ought to be followed." The number has certainly not diminished since. Exegesis and translation always being as inseparable as they are, even the ordinary reader can easily track the different interpretations in the widely varying English translations. On the exegetical front the basic issues involve not only the manner of calculating the weeks, but also of determining both the *terminus a quo* and *ad quem* of the "seventy" (i.e., on the second level of meaning as much as on the first level). But, of course, the big questions, as always, are hermeneutical or presuppositional, and the exegetical decisions are largely determined by these.

The first issue the interpreter confronts is the proper translation of the numerical designation at the beginning of v. 24. Literally, the Hebrew simply says "seventy sevens," or seventy of some unit or period of seven. The word itself often means "week (seven days)," as in "Feast of Weeks," but then its plural is usually feminine. The use of a masculine plural here appears to indicate, according to good Hebrew idiom, that the word is not employed in that ordinary sense. What non-ordinary sense is then intended? A very ancient and still very common understanding is "hebdomad," that is, a "year-week" or "week of years," that is seven years (the entire period then being 70 X 7 or 490 years). Many extra-Biblical parallels to that usage can be cited (cf. also Sabbath and sabbatical year), but there is no direct correspondence anywhere in the Bible itself. The other alternative (and the one ultimately defended here) is "heptad," that is, some indeterminate "sevenness." (In Dan. 10:2, 3, an expression of time, "days," is added, but let it be noted that there is no such specification here— neither "weeks" nor "weeks of years"!)

The latter option goes with a general understanding of Daniel's numerology as broadly symbolic of God's definitive completion of His program within time. The accent is on the redemptive dynamic of the text, not "times and seasons" as such. Such is precisely the thrust of the bulk of v. 24, introducing the entire pericope. First three negative purposes are specified, then three positive ones. All have an eschatological and ultimately Messianic flavor. The three negative ones all have to do with the definitive removal of sin, specifically including "atonement." The positive counterparts are summarized in terms of justification by faith ("everlasting righteousness"), "sealing up the vision and prophecy" (their surcease because of their final realization), and "to anoint a most holy place" (of more disputed meaning, but apparently either the Anointed One himself, or some temple, either historical [Zerubbabel's or its Maccabean cleansing] or eschatological, that is, God's permanent tabernacling with men as in Rev. 21:22, taking "anoint" in a more figurative sense).

If we begin the pericope with the assumption of "hebdomads," these purposes will not be denied, of course, but far greater weight will be placed upon precise dates, specifically the *terminus a quo* as well as *ad quem* of the seventy week-years and of its subdivisions. The text itself in v. 25 proceeds to speak of a *terminus a quo,* namely "from the going forth of the word to restore and build Jerusalem," but chronological applications of the phrase vary drastically according to overall understandings. The use of the same idiom in v. 23 seems to establish that God, not any earthly authority is the speaker of the word, although many scour the evidence for some human decree or the other. Even with God as subject, we still have to ask about the time of its impingement upon human affairs. We can only mention here the three major identifications and their major champions: (1) 587 B.C. when Jerusalem was destroyed (liberals); (2) 538, Cyrus' edict (most conservatives, and our choice); and (3) 445, Artaxerxes' permission for Nehemiah to rebuild the city (dispensationalists).

We jolt from *crux* to *crux*. The *terminus ad quem* of this period is stated as "the coming of an anointed one, a prince," that is, apparently one who has both priestly and princely (royal) characteristics. Absence of the definite article is noteworthy, probably because the accent here is on his qualities. Most naturally think of the Messiah, but critics have no lack of other suggestions: the high priest Joshua (presumed to have assumed Zerubbabel's royal claims), Cyrus (called "anointed" in Is. 45:1), and Onias III (legitimate priest in Maccabean times).

The next and closely related problem is first of all simply the exegetical and translational one of what extent of time the text asserts for this period. Both alternatives involve unusual Hebrew syntax. The issue resolves itself initially into a question of proper punctuation. (Remember that the earliest known punctuation, the Masoretic accents, is already centuries later than and no intrinsic part of the inspired consonantal text; furthermore, it inevitably reflects the exegetical preferences of the punctuators.) The Masoretic *athnach* plainly means to separate the first period of "seven weeks" from the following "sixty-two weeks" (so also RSV). The other alternative is to join the two and translate "seven weeks and sixty-two weeks," that is, a total of sixty-nine weeks. Within conservatism at least, the punctuational alternatives convert into the interpretational question of whether or not the *second* coming of Christ is within purview at this point. Naturally, one's decision here will determine understandings in the following lines too. The question is whether the "troubled time" in which the city is to be rebuilt is the postexilic period, the time of Christ, or the era of the church.

V. 26 predicts some catastrophic period "after" the "sixty two" (probably all sixty-nine?) weeks in which both the anointed one will be "cut off" (cf. Is. 53:8) and "have nothing," and the city will be destroyed by "the people of the prince." The clear implication would seem to be that these events, like those of v. 27, occur *within* the seventieth week, but the ambiguity of the text at this point is seized upon by premillennialists who argue for a "gap" or "parenthesis" before the final week (see below). The destructive prince can scarcely be identical with the anointed prince of the previous verse. Identifications vary from the Seleucid deposition of Onias and capture of Jerusalem, to the Roman crucifixion of Christ and destruction of the city, to eschatological events perpetrated by the

Antichrist. He is described as "he who is to come," evidently a back reference to chaps. 7 and 8, but we noted the same variety of interpretations there. Reference to a "flood" may imply a typology of the Exodus and the Pharaoh, one of the major early portents of Antichrist.

It is clear that v. 27 speaks of the final (seventieth) week, but one must immediately inquire about the antecedent of "he" at the beginning of v. 27, and thus probably the subject of the entire verse. The most natural reply would seem to be the evil "prince" who has just been featured in v. 26 (whoever he is), but others prefer to refer it to the Messiah and the "covenant of grace" (Reformed terminology). Whatever the identification, he "makes a strong covenant" (evil men, of course, make covenants as well as the righteous!). The Hebrew, which literally says that he shall cause *a* covenant to be strong or to prevail, seems to imply that it is not a new covenant, but the confirmation and implementation of one already in existence. The "many," with which the covenant is made, could imply the redeemed according to a specialized usage (cf. Is. 53:11; Dan. 12:2; Matt. 20:28), but (as it seems likely here) the reference might also be to the insensate "masses." Similarly, the cessation of sacrifices could call to mind Antiochus or the Antichrist (a negative sense of the phrase), or it might imply Christ's positive fulfillment of them.

The final third of this final verse of the pericope is certainly as problematic as the rest. Its subject, "one who makes desolate," or "the desolator" (two parallel Hebrew forms) is plainly to be viewed negatively (hence, synonymous with the "prince" of v. 26 and with the first part of v. 27, if all of those clauses are also construed negatively). He comes on "the wing of abominations," that is, apparently in consort with detestable idolatries, but all types of fantastic interpretations have been attempted. The language here plainly anticipates the "abomination of desolation" of 11:31 and 12:11 (which see; cf. 8:13), but here the subject is the one who perpetrates the outrage rather than the act or the object itself.

The pericope ends on the positive note of a "decreed end" which will certainly overtake the desolator. The reference is obviously to the "eternal counsel of God," but, most significantly, nothing is made of the *time* of that end, that is, of the *terminus ad quem* of the entire prophecy. Gallons of ink would have been saved, had more attention been paid to this major hermeneutical indication within the text itself of the general, symbolic significance of all of its temporal reference.

To conclude a discussion, which is already too long except for the disproportionate attention paid to this pericope throughout the history of exegesis, let us attempt to summarize the four major understandings of the passage in its entirety (remembering that further variations in detail are literally legion). The four positions may be labeled: (1) the liberal-critical; (2) the dispensationalist-premillennial or parenthesis interpretation; (3) the traditional or Messianic; and (4) the typical-Messianic or Christian church view.

Critics, of course, understand the passage only as *vaticinium post eventu,* "prophecy" after the event. The *terminus a quo* of the pseudonymous writer's calculations is taken to be 587, the destruction of Jerusalem, and reckoning seventy "hebdomads" or 490 years, the *terminus ad quem* is the writer's own Maccabean era. The first seven hebdomads should bring us down to Cyrus' edict in 538, and the following sixty-two (434 years) to Onias' deposition by Jason in 175 and murder by Menelaus in 171. (Since those dates are too high by some seventy years, it is usually assumed that the writer either erred or was dependent upon some inaccurate tradition.) The halfway point of the final week-year (seven years) in which the writer himself lived was thought to have been reached with Antiochus' proscription of temple worship in 167. The only genuine prediction in the entire pericope, then, is that only three and one-half years remain until the eschaton, but, of course, the author was mistaken in that guess too! Modern critics since Eichhorn have virtually elevated this interpretation into an "orthodoxy," but, in many respects, it was anticipated by much Jewish exegesis. A few conservative exegetes (Delitzsch, von Hofmann) attempt to combine it with or subsume it under the "typical-Messianic" approach, and, indeed if Scripture interprets Scripture, its only possible modicum of truth would be in understanding the Maccabean traumas as an anticipatory miniature of future redemptive history (a connection which is probably in evidence elsewhere in the book; cf. on alternative [4]).

Light-years more "conservative," but probably just as wide of the mark, is the dispensationalist-premillennial reconstruction, sometimes referred to as the "gap" or "parenthesis" view after Ironside's famous work (cf. *The Scofield Reference Bible*). These interpreters also calculate with "hebdomads," but the *terminus a quo* is usually Nehemiah's coming in 445 to begin the rebuilding of Jerusalem. When that is accomplished in the first seven hebdomads, the second period of sixty-two begins immediately, bringing us down to the period of Christ's ministry (and some with mathematical precision would even specify Palm Sunday). But now comes the catch! The promises of v. 24 were not fulfilled at Christ's first coming, and the seventieth week-year does not follow immediately upon the sixty-ninth. Rather, because of sins, there intervenes the great "parenthesis" or long "gap" of the "church age," not revealed to the prophets, and now having lasted nearly two thousand years. Only at the end of the present age when Christ returns does the prophetic clock start up again. As the final hebdomad begins, the faithful will be caught up into heaven in the "rapture," while on earth a great neo-Roman leader, the "prince" of v. 26, will appear. At first he will pretend to be a friend of the Jews (the "many"), will make a covenant with them, and entice them back to their land (modern Israel). In return for their allegiance, he will allow them to rebuild the temple and reinstitute the sacrificial cult (cf. Ezek. 40—48). In the middle of the seventieth "week," however, he will suddenly break his covenant with them and demand that Jewish worship cease. The "great tribulation" will ensue until the end of the final hebdomad, when Christ will return with His saints to reign for a millennium upon earth.

Even to conservative, confessional Lutherans this genuinely "fundamentalistic" outlook is generally as unfamiliar and eccentric-sounding as it is close to the center of piety for many Christians who share the same formal principle of interpreting Scripture. Perhaps the best that can be said for it is that it is both Christocentric and eschatological in its own way, but functionally it is to be feared that it diverts attention to a literalistic preoccupation with details that finally clashes with the New Testament's own interpretation of the prophecies in question. What is here labeled "parenthetical," Christ's church on earth, is very close to the heart and core of what the New Testament proclaims as the fulfillment.

In sharp contrast to that brand of conservatism is a third understanding of the "seventy weeks" prophecy, probably the oldest of all, at least within Christendom (St. Augustine and most of the church fathers), and still held by very many conservatives (Hengstenberg, Pusey, and Young, e.g.). It may be labeled "Messianic" in the direct and traditional sense of the term, that is, the promises of v. 24 were fulfilled at Christ's first advent. It too tends to think in terms of "hebdomads," but tends to sit somewhat more loosely on the numbers than the preceding two approaches. It usually prefers 538 (Cyrus' edict) as the *terminus a quo,* and notes two uneven segments of time as foretold in v. 25. V. 26 (with no "gap" or "parenthesis") prophesies Christ's death, as well as the Roman destruction under Titus of Jerusalem and the temple, while v. 27 foresees the cessation of the Levitical sacrifices as a result of His death in the middle of the seventieth "week." The destruction of the temple will continue until the end at God's good time.

There is still a fourth interpretation, also conservative, which has no hermeneutical bones to pick with the traditional Messianic understanding (what genuine conservative could?), but which differs with it exegetically to a considerable extent. It tries to accommodate some modern historical sensitivities without compromise of conservative principle. Christ remains central, but it extends the Christological principle both backward (typology) and forward (ecclesiology). Thus its two most common designations, either "typical-Messianic" or "Christian church interpretation." Apparently Kliefoth in 1868 was the first to work out this position; Keil and Leupold are among those who agree in principle.

Of all the interpretations, it is the least interested in numerology: it breaks completely with the "hebdomad" assumption, and thinks only in terms of "heptads," that is, purely symbolical numbers, seven, or multiples of it. Its *terminus a quo* is again 538 (the end of the Exile), but the *terminus ad quem* is the second more than the first coming. In thus making reference to the whole course of the kingdom of God (of indefinite length) from Daniel's own time down to the parousia, the prophecy of the "seven weeks" is understood as essentially parallel to those of chaps. 2 and 7. The first seven "weeks" or heptads extend until the first coming of Christ (the "anointed Prince"). Then follow "sixty-two" heptads (that is a much longer period, but still of indeterminate length), during which time, even though it remains "troubled," "Jerusalem" shall be restored and rebuilt, that is, the Gospel preached, sinners converted, and the elect saved. In the first "half" of the final "week," however (vs. 26-27), Christ and His church will lose virtually all their previous external influence and prestige (the "world come of age"?). (Cf. the usual apocalyptic picture of increasingly rampant evil as the end approaches.) In place of Christ and His church, a wicked prince, really a "desolator," the Antichrist, an antitype of Antiochus Epiphanes, will destroy "the city and the sanctuary" (the visible church), proscribe all true worship, and forcibly make a covenant of terror with the masses ("many"). But his end is also "decreed," and (by implication at least) in the final "half" of the final period God's eternal purposes will finally and eternally be consummated.

Chapters 10—12

For all of the attention often devoted to it, one might think chap. 9 was the consummation and climax of the Book of Daniel. There remain three chapters, of course, but the division is really artificial and possibly even disruptive. (The dates at 11:1 and 12:1 do not signal new oracles, as is the pattern elsewhere in the book.) The central "Vision of the Last Days" constitutes chap. 11, chap. 10 being introductory and chap. 12 a conclusion. Although formally the entire unit is a vision, most of it takes the form of verbal instruction on future history by the heavenly visitor. The contents are largely only an expansion of more sketchy previous prophecies, especially chap. 12 with its details of the consummation.

Daniel has been feasting for three weeks in the third year of Cyrus (10:1-2), perhaps in sorrow that, in spite of the return of some of the exiles (whom Daniel had not joined, for reasons which we do not know), the work of rebuilding the temple had now been halted (Ezra 4:4-5). On the

banks of the Tigris he receives a vision of an angelic figure, the precise
identity of which has long been debated. Because of similarities in the
portrait here with both Ezekiel's (chap. 1) and John's visions (Rev. 1:12-
20), and because of the exalted standing he appears to have in Dan. 12,
very many have seen here a theophany of the preincarnate Christ, the
"angel of the LORD," or the Logos. Perhaps the most damaging contrary
argument is that Michael has to come to help him in v. 13. Hence, others
prefer to identify the figure simply with Gabriel, who has been Daniel's
guide and interpreter all along.

Almost in passing (10:10—11:1), we catch a fascinating glimpse of
suprahistory, summarizing much of the apocalyptic (and Biblical) view of
"history." The heavenly figure assures Daniel that his prayers had been
heard from the outset, but he has been preoccupied for twenty-one days
with fighting "the prince of the kingdom of Persia," and could only come
now that "Michael, one of the chief princes" had come to his aid (vs. 12-
13). He can remain with Daniel only a short time before he has to return
to fight with "the prince of Persia; and when I am through with him, lo,
the prince of Greece will come" (v. 20). (This, then, leads into the more
detailed preview of history in 11:2 ff.).

"Prince" scarcely refers to any earthly king or leader, but to his
celestial counterpart, to a patron or guardian "angel." (Here "prince"
translates the Hebrew *sar,* not *nagid* as in chap. 9.) Every nation or group
(yes, every individual) has one of these (cf. Rev. 1:20 ff.; Matt. 18:10). In
paganism these were usually chief gods (often little more than a
personification of the "soul" or "spirit" of the nation, but in the Bible they
are "demoted" to (what at least would later be known as) "angels."
Originally, God had installed these patrons over the nations, but they had
rebelled and become "evil angels" (cf. Ps. 82). Israel too has such a
patron, but one loyal to Yahweh, of course. He probably appears
anonymously already in Joshua 5:14 ff., and here his name is revealed.
Chief prince probably means "archangel," as he is called in Jude 9.
However, in the case of His chosen people, God did not merely delegate
authority but also remained in personal charge (Deut. 32:8; 33:2 f; cf.
Dan. 8:25, where God is called "prince of princes"). In Dan. 12:1 and Rev.
12:7 we meet Michael as leader of God's armies in the final, eschatological
battle, of which his earlier engagements are only preludes. This is the
Biblical view of "history"; things are really decided "in the heavenly places"
(Eph. 6:12), where the faithful would never stand a chance, were not
"those who are with us more than those who are with them" (2 Kings
6:16).

In 11:2 ff. (a poor chapter division) the heavenly guide proceeds to
expound to Daniel "what is inscribed in the book of truth" (10:21), not the

Book of Daniel itself, as such, but (probably figuratively) the history that God has predetermined (cf. Dan. 12:1; Mal. 3:16; Ps. 139:16; Rev. 5:1; cf. above on apocalyptic "determinism"). The interpretative difficulties of chap. 11 are perhaps less concentrated than in 9:24-27, but scarcely less in any other sense, and here too there is a long history of interpretation. On its surface, however, chap. 11 is somewhat unique in its unusual emphasis on detail, concentrating especially on the conflict between the Ptolemies and the Seleucids. Since the text plainly purports to be prediction, that means that the conflict between orthodox supernaturalists and the critics is unusually acute here. For the orthodox the chapter is a climactic example of predictive prophecy, while to the critical mind it clinches their interpretation of the book as "prophecy after the event," that is, a quasi-theological Maccabean political tract written to bolster the morale of loyal Jews in those dark days. Modern critical attitudes were anticipated almost precisely already in the third century by the anti-Christian philosopher, Porphyry, and Jerome's great commentary on Daniel, written largely to answer him, sets forth the main lines of traditional, orthodox understanding until the present day.

Naturally, the radically different hermeneutics results in radically different readings of details. The understandings diverge especially in the latter part of the chapter, where the correspondence with known, empirical history is not nearly as close as at the beginning. For critics it has all but become dogma that the contrast between the first thirty-nine verses of the chapter and the remainder enables us to pinpoint almost precisely when the pseudonymous author of Daniel actually lived. Until v. 40 (bringing us up to Antiochus' desecration of the temple) he had allegedly been recounting known and past history under the guise of prophecy and had been reasonably accurate. When in vs. 40 ff. he tries his hand at genuine prediction, however, he fails miserably.

That route, of course is out of the question for a believer in verbal inspiration, but even within the conservative camp the routes again divide. Here the problem will be formulated in terms of the interpenetration of history and suprahistory, of the overlap of near and distant eschatology (the former often a type of the latter), and specifically of the degree of simultaneity of depiction of Antiochus and Antichrist. (That type of thing is common in prophecy, especially apocalyptic, and we have noted it before in Daniel, but chap. 11 then becomes a parade example of the species.) There is no problem in the first part of the chapter; the subject is almost exclusively thisworldly history, and the presence of a few gaps is no problem except for a few critics who are looking for trouble.

The question is at what point suprahistory or eschatology enters the picture and perhaps takes over completely. Three different answers have been given to the question, both in antiquity and in modern times. Jerome and many of the fathers found a double reference already in v. 21 as soon as Antiochus is introduced, that is, simultaneously serving as a type of Antichrist. Very few expositors today appear to make the transition so early; beginning with Luther (applying it to the papacy) and for most contemporary conservative scholars, the divide comes with v. 36. Since the portrait no longer seems to fit Antiochus very well (see below), it is felt that from here on we either have direct prophecy of the Antichrist, or at least that the typical element is much more prominent. Critics, as noted above, usually see the major break (from veiled history to prediction) at v. 40, and conservatives would agree to the extent that from here on there is no doubt that the concern is purely eschatological.

Given conservative presuppositions, perhaps we should not have to choose too sharply between these three options. The difficulty in choosing probably reflects the extent to which postexilic and Maccabean history serves as a foil and a type, a "sacrament" of eschatological history throughout the book (the same principle in broader application operative throughout Scripture). The three options represent a difference in degree more than in kind, as the historical type gradually fades before the suprahistorical antitype. Otherwise the conservative might be embarrassed to try to explain why the book and especially this chapter spends as much time on Maccabean history and events leading up to it as it does; it is precisely because that crisis was such a lucid transparency or miniature, yes, a type, of future tribulations of the church, partly in connection with Christ's first advent, but especially of the last days of all human history. In the apocalyptic sections of the gospels (Matt. 24, etc.) it is similarly impossible to disentangle Titus' investment of Jerusalem and the end of the world, as has always been recognized. There is also a "typology" in a more existential sense: the monotonous similarity of virtually all history with that in Daniel ("wars and rumors of wars," the general "horror of history") teaches the faithful to discern the "signs of the times" also in their contemporary history.

Let us look at a few details. Dan. 11:2-4 moves very summarily through subsequent Persian history and the rise and fall of "a mighty king" (Alexander) to quite detailed prediction of the conflict between the "south" and the "north" (Ptolemies and Seleucids) in vs. 5 ff., where the vision's real interests begin. Vs. 10-19 feature Antiochus III ("the Great"), but in v. 21, as we saw, Antiochus IV is introduced, not as "Epiphanes," but as a "contemptible person."

A disproportionate amount of attention (at least through 11:35) is devoted to the latter, probably out of both historical and suprahistorical (typological) motives (see above). Two of his campaigns against Egypt are described, and then the intervention of "ships of Kittim" (v. 30; cf. Num. 24:24), technically Cyprus, but used of various points west, here no doubt Rome (a frequent usage also at Qumran). When Roman intervention frustrated Antiochus' ambition to conquer Egypt, he vented his rage on Palestine (v. 30b), including the temple and its services (v. 31). The succeeding verses summarize the compromise and apostasy of many, as well as the cruel persecution, even martyrdom, of those who refused. The "little help" which the latter will receive (v. 34) probably alludes to Judas Maccabaeus, not implying, as critics often opine, that the writer belonged to a different political party, or that he is "hedging his bet" on that prominent family, but rather pointing to the inability of the Maccabees to effect any permanent solution to the people's problems, something reserved for God alone.

Of special interest in this section is the first appearance in v. 31 of the phrase "abomination of desolation" (although anticipated in 8:13 and 9:27, and reappearing in 12:11). The Hebrew more literally says, "desolating abomination," or "the abomination which appalls" (probably both objective and subjective aspects implied at once). There is little debate that its first (historical) level of meaning is to the altar (and perhaps also an image) of Zeus Olympius erected in the temple. In Hebrew that deity was identified with Baal Shamaim ("lord of heaven"; the title of the ancient Canaanite storm-god, Hadad). In mockery the letters of "Baal" were exchanged with others (by "Athbash") to form the Hebrew word for "abomination," and the second element was altered simply by substituting different vowels with the same Hebrew consonants. No doubt, it is to this passage (and 12:11) to which our Lord refers in Matt. 24:15 (= Mark 13:14) as the sign which should warn the disciples to flee Jerusalem. Its precise typological application is not so certain there, and we can only note that again the events of A.D. 70 and of the eschaton are plainly telescoped.

At Dan. 11:36 ff., as we noted, the historical portraiture of Antiochus begins to recede markedly before typological and eschatological history of Antichrist, if the former does not drop out of sight altogether. The major indication of the shift is the description of a consummate evil exceeding anything perpetrated even by Antiochus. Certainly, the events predicted here cannot be related very easily to known history (critics are generally willing to settle for simple hyperbole). Furthermore, 2 Thess. 2:4 ff., speaking of Antichrist, specifically echoes the language here. (There are also various dispensationalist interpretations, usually placing the figure in the middle of the seventieth week of Dan. 9.)

Beginning with Dan. 11:40, nearly everyone agrees that the focus is (almost?) exclusively eschatological. Critics, however, usually regard it as

THE WORD BECOMING FLESH

false prophecy, because, they say, Antiochus did not meet his end in the manner depicted. Conservatives, of course, will not disagree, as such, but insist that the subject is now the Antichrist, specifically the fierce conflict in which he will engage at the end of the present age (probably a variant on the common eschatological theme of the attack of the nations upon Jerusalem). The "time of the end" (v. 40) is not completely unambiguous by itself, but surely is in the present context. The symbolic and eschatological content of the entire section (vs. 40-45) is well indicated by the mention of Edom, Moab and Ammon in v. 41; these ancient and proverbial enemies of Israel, who are often referred to typologically already in earlier Scripture (esp. the "Gentile oracles," which see), no longer existed, as such, in the second century B.C. Typology is also evident in the mention of Antichrist's invasion of "the glorious land" (v. 41); cf. 8:9; 11:11, 16, in two of which cases Antiochus is the subject. Likewise also with the "glorious holy mountain" (v. 45), obviously Jerusalem or Zion, which Antichrist will assail just before his sudden and ignominious end. All of this accords well with other prophecies symbolically locating "Armageddon" (Rev. 16:16) at or near Jerusalem (cf. Ezek. 39:4; Joel 3; or Zech. 14), and also, as usual, Antichrist's overthrow comes just when his victory appears certain.

Dan. 12, concluding the vision, shows that the reference to victory in 11:45 was anticipatory. But the chapter division is probably faulty again; 12:1-4 really belongs with 11:40-45 (note the parallel "time"), and clinches the eschatological reference of the latter. (Or, if we need still more evidence, we have none other than our Lord's use of 12:1 in Matt. 24:21-22, v. 2 in John 5:28-29, and of v. 3 in Matt. 13:43. Critics either face the same abrupt transition here which they refused to concede at 11:40, or—more commonly—simply think the writer was mistaken in supposing that the parousia would come shortly after Antiochus' imminent overthrow.)

Michael reappears (cf. 10:13 ff.), this time to lead the eschatological battle, "a time of trouble, such as never has been" (cf. Rev. 12:7). This assurance that "your people will be delivered, every one whose name shall be found written in the book" (cf. the "book of truth" in 10:21; here perhaps more a "book of life," but probably metaphorical for God's eternal counsel—and ultimately Jesus Christ Himself). Nor is the assurance limited to those who are still alive at Michael's victory; it extends also to the righteous dead (v. 2; cf. 1 Thess. 4:13 ff.).

This beautiful text has occasioned far more debate than seems necessary. The immediate accent, no doubt, is upon those who had lost their lives in the apocalyptic battle, but that by no means excludes reference to the general resurrection (a type of extension from exegetical particularity which is often—and validly—found in dogmatical proof-texting). By that kind of extension, "many" might simply imply "all," but it seems more natural to take it in the semitechnical sense of "*the* many," that is, all the elect, etc. (cf. at 9:27). Cf. our Lord's substitution of "all" when he quotes this verse in John 5:28-29. Premillennialists with their usual legerdemain commonly refer this passage to the "first resurrection" (cf. Rev. 20:5), but we are convinced that Scripture really knows nothing of that.

Even more misguided, of course, are critics who force the verse into their evolutionistic grid: the passage allegedly marks an "advance" beyond the few others in the Old Testament which touch on the subject by speaking of a resurrection of the wicked as well as of the righteous, but the "many" should indicate that no general resurrection is yet in view. The verse is, no doubt, one of the clearest and most explicit in the entire Old Testament on the topic, but the continuity is far greater than critical spectacles will permit their wearers to see.

V. 3 adds a note on the eternal beatitude of those who rise to everlasting life. They are described as "wise"—in the full Biblical sense of the term (cf. on "wisdom"), i.e., essentially synonymous with knowing and believing God's Word, the Gospel, and ordering one's life accordingly. But as the parallelism with "turn many to righteousness" indicates, the accent really is on those who *make* others "wise," that is, lead them to faith.

V. 4 concludes the major scene in the vision. "Seal," as at 8:26, does not mean to conceal, but to preserve, protect, etc., until the time of maximal applicability (cf. v. 9; see Rev. 5 ff.; 22:10, etc.). Critics tend to view it as originally an ending to the entire book, with the remaining verses representing two or three later supplements or epilogues. History would not stand still, and since the parousia was delayed, a few "corrective" footnotes were added to attempt to answer the question, "How long?" (v. 6). By their reading, vs. 5-10 make an unsuccessful stab at deciphering the prophecy of 7:25. Vs. 11 and 12 are thought to represent rejections of that supplement and attempt to answer the question with more mathematical precision, but there is no agreement as to what the annotator's original intent may have been, unless they were simply idle glosses and sheer guesses.

The text (vs. 5 ff.) certainly does address itself to the question, "How long?" but in a new phase of Daniel's vision, it is raised either by one of the two angels whom Daniel now sees and overhears (so MT), or by Daniel himself (so LXX, Vulgate, and as v. 8 seems to indicate). (We should not overlook the use of the Hebrew word for the "Nile," translated simply "stream," in vs. 5-7, evidently in antitypical reminiscence of the first Exodus.) The answer comes in a solemn asseveration (raising both hands instead of one as in ordinary oaths, cf. Rev. 10:5-7), reaffirming the promise of 7:25 ("a time, two times, and half a time"). The numerical symbolism is, no doubt, the same: the power of evil will wax greatly, but then it will suddenly wane and soon disappear. Daniel (certainly the questioner in v. 8) still does not understand, but is given to understand that the stance of the faithful is to cease further inquiry into the matter and go their way (be about their daily business). (What if more exegetes took this verse as their major hermeneutical key to all the numbers in the book?) V. 10 somewhat paraphrases vs. 2-3 (cf. Rev. 22:11); the "wise," and only they will understand, but only in God's good time.

Vs. 11-12 are problematic by any reckoning, but they are also God's Word. In different language, however, they appear merely to reaffirm the final, climactic message of the book. Renewed reference to the "abomination of desolation" and to the proscription of the sacrificial cult, seems clearly to bring us back to the outrages of Antiochus Epiphanes, but surely again as typological of the onslaughts of Antichrist (as we noted especially in chap. 11).

Again we must insist that the two numbers, 1,290 and 1,335, are symbolical. They certainly fit nothing known in Antiochus' history and even less the attempt of dispensational literalists to relate them somehow to the "seventieth week." We can really only guess as to their import. The first, 1,290 days, is about a month more than three and one-half years. Possibly, "days" is substituted for "times" (v. 7) to stress the bearability of the affliction, as meted out in God's wisdom, when taken one day at a time. Similarly, the extra month may signify an outwaiting of the time of tribulation. Then, the second number, 1,335, adding 45 more days, would say that after only a short additional period, final and eternal bliss would come. Or the first number refers to the most severe phase of the persecution, only a little more than half of the entire "week" (under Antiochus and Antichrist), and the latter to "the whole period of opposition to God's kingdom unto the consummation" (Young). But "blessed is he" who subordinates such questions to the promise itself, the Gospel!

The beautiful ending of the Book of Daniel makes the same point; one's comfort and hope in no way depends on knowing the answer to such questions. Vs. 2-3 and 9 are repeated on a more personal note: "Go your way [mind your God-appointed business and let God be God] till the end." The "rest" is plainly that of the grave in the "intermediate state" (but no hint of "soul sleep"). In spite of intervening death; the promise and predestination are sure of final resurrection glory "in your allotted place."

Daniel is not the latest book in the Old Testament canon, as critics hold, but in important respects it is indeed the closest to the Word

Become Flesh. Its final "calm note of immeasurable joy" stands out all the more against the backdrop of a book that has known so much conflict and well summarizes the real message of Biblical apocalyptic. As Keil concludes his commentary, "Well shall it be for us if in the end of our days we too are able to depart hence with such consolation of hope."

EZRA AND NEHEMIAH
Unity of the Two Books

These two books virtually have to be treated isagogically as one, not only on literary grounds but also because of the historical overlap in the careers of the two men. There are also close literary connections with Chronicles, not only because of possibly common authorship (see below) but also for the obvious reason that the conclusion of 2 Chron. 36 (vs. 22-23) is identical with the beginning of Ezra (1:1-3a). The common subject is the decree of Cyrus, and the fact that in Chronicles it is broken off in the middle of a sentence probably indicates that at some point in transmission the two were united. (That, however, by no means demonstrates common authorship.)

Since Ezra-Nehemiah is the chronological sequel to Chronicles, it probably originally followed it, an order to which the Septuagint returned and with which we are now familiar. Presumably, the original order was reversed and Chronicles placed after Ezra-Nehemiah when the hagiographical canon was being assembled. The idea apparently was thus to conclude the canon with a book that chronicled the entire sacred history (as St. Jerome described Chronicles), and perhaps Cyrus' decree was let stand, even though repetitious, in order to close the canonical collection on an optimistic note (cf. on Chronicles).

It is often assumed that Ezra and Nehemiah were *originally* one composition, but this is doubtful. The most that can be said with certainty is that they were united very soon. Ecclesiasticus (c. 200 B.C.) probably knew only a single work, as seems to follow from its mention of Nehemiah, but not Ezra in its praise of famous men. Josephus and the earliest Christian writers (including the great LXX uncials) present the same picture. In the Masoretic tradition the unity is firmly established, as evidenced not only in the lack of any space between the two, but also in the concluding comments and statistics which are only given at the end of Nehemiah for both books (the division was only secondarily introduced shortly before the Reformation).

Evidence that the two books were originally discrete compositions is probably provided both by the appearance of a superscription in Neh. 1:1 and, in Masoretic texts, by a marginal notice, "Nehemiah," perhaps witnessing to a memory of their original independence (which led Luther to abandon Vulgate usage [cf. below] and label the second book, "Nehemiah," as most since him have done). Also indicative of originally independent circulation is the duplication of the list of returning exiles in Ezra 2 and Neh. 7:6-70. If so, the two were early combined because of their obvious continuity. Young may also have a point in suggesting that another motive was to obtain a total number of canonical books equal to the number of letters in the Hebrew alphabet (22).

Relation to Esdras

In the Septuagint, the united Ezra-Nehemiah appears as "Esdras B" ("Esdras" being simply a Greek version of "Ezra"). The canonical "Esdras B" is thus distinguished from "Esdras A," a work considered apocryphal by Protestantism, but at least "deuterocanonical" by Catholicism (see below). Herewith, however, begins an almost nightmarish variation in terminology. Although Jerome had earlier recognized Ezra-Nehemiah as a unity, in the Vulgate he divided them, labeling Ezra "Esdras I" and Nehemiah "Esdras II," a usage which still prevails in much of Catholicism. The (divided) canonical works having been placed first, the "deuterocanonical" (apocryphal) "Esdras A" of LXX now became "Esdras III" in the Vulgate. "Esdras A" always remained just that (the apocryphal work) in the LXX, but at some point Jerome's division of Ezra and Nehemiah was introduced there too, and now "Esdras B" often came to refer to only Ezra (not both books, as originally), while "Esdras C" was introduced to designate Nehemiah.

As though all this were not enough, we have to reckon in addition with a late first-century A. D. pseudepigraphical apocalypse named after Ezra (Esdras). It was extremely popular in the early church but ultimately excluded from the canon. However, Jerome retained it as an appendix to the Vulgate, placing it after the New Testament together with the "Prayer of Manasseh" (see 2 Chron. 33). In the LXX it is referred to simply as the "Esdras Apocalypse" or "Esdras the Prophet," but in the Vulgate it became "Esdras IV."

Enter finally the English (Protestant) versions. Since the titles "Ezra" and "Nehemiah" were now firmly established, the apocryphal book became "First Esdras," essentially like the LXX's "Esdras A" rather than Jerome's "Esdras III." Then the apocalyptic work became "II Esdras"— although often also referred to as "IV Ezra" or the "Ezra Apocalypse" (with Vulgate and Septuagint respectively)!

Perhaps the following table will help:

English (Protestant)	Vulgate (RC)	Septuagint
I Esdras (apocryphal)	III Esdras	Esdras A

Ezra	I Esdras	Esdras B (sometimes = Ezra-Nehemiah)
Nehemiah	II Esdras	(Esdras C)
II Esdras (sometimes "IV Ezra" or "Ezra Apocalypse")	IV Esdras	Esdras the Prophet (or "Apocalypse").

The apocryphal I/III Esdras requires further comment. To a certain extent, one can say that, externally considered, it is simply an alternate recension or textual tradition of the canonical Ezra-Nehemiah, not differing much more than the LXX as a whole sometimes differs from MT (perhaps especially Judges and Kings). It almost appears as if the Western tradition, when confronted with two Greek versions of Ezra-Nehemiah, compromised by accepting both! Although the canonical text is generally superior, there are points where the alternate version is very helpful for text-critical purposes.

However, there are also significant differences in content. The apocryphal work appears to be much more exclusively interested in the history of the temple and Israelite cult, as perhaps evidenced also by its omission of Nehemiah's "memoirs" (Neh. 1—7), thus possibly also evincing greater affinity with Chronicles. Possibly this is also why I Esdras appears to be a torso, beginning with the middle of Josiah's reign (his Passover—a version of 2 Chron. 35—36) and ending in the middle of a sentence (Neh. 8:13a).

Consonant with its interest in Zerubbabel's rebuilding of the temple, it includes one long and significant pericope not found elsewhere: the "Tale of the Three Guardsmen." It purports to explain how it was that Darius was reminded of his earlier promise to support the rebuilding of the temple, namely because Zerubbabel had won a debate concerning the strongest thing in the world. The champions of "wine" and "king" had lost to Zerubbabel's "Women are strongest, but truth is victor over all things"!

Aramaic Portions of Ezra

Note should be taken of the presence in Ezra of two sizable portions written in Aramaic: 4:8—6:18 and 7:12-26. (The only real parallel elsewhere in the Bible is Dan. 2—7.) It was once widely argued that the type of Aramaic employed required a fairly late date of composition, but archaeological discoveries, especially the Elephantine Papyri from fifth-century Egypt, have long since demolished that skepticism. It plainly was the usual "imperial Aramaic" of the time, the lingua franca of the Persian empire. Thus, it is understandable that Aramaic commences at 4:8 with a letter sent to Artaxerxes, but it is not clear why the Aramaic then continues for a time (cf. below and on Daniel).

Even the Hebrew of Ezra betrays increasing Aramaic influence, but nowhere so prominently as in Nehemiah's memoirs, where the language is still technically Hebrew, but the underlying syntax and speech patterns appear to be quite thoroughly Aramaic. (Of course, Aramaic increasingly displaced Hebrew in everyday speech, Hebrew being retained largely as a liturgical language, but recent discoveries underscore that we must not overstate its demise. Especially in the stricter and more nationalistic sects from Maccabean times on and in the time of Christ, Hebrew plainly continued to flourish until at least A.D. 200.)

Outline and Contents

The basic outline of Ezra-Nehemiah is very simple. In Ezra 1—6 we have the account of the return from Exile and the restoration of the temple. The remainder describes the labors of the two great reformers who arrive from Persia to lead the restoration. Ezra 7—10 describes Ezra's religious reforms, while Neh. 1—7 contains that leader's autobiographical account of his labors in rebuilding the city walls. Neh. 8—13 reports on both figures, especially Ezra's reading of the "Book of the Law."

In more detail: the Book of Ezra opens (1:1-4) with Cyrus' edict in 538, permitting the exiles who wished to return. An alternate (Aramaic) version of it appears again in 6:3-5 (see also below on "sources"). We now know that this action was only one instance of Cyrus' more enlightened policy toward minorities and displaced elements in his empire, but that need not contradict the reported formulation of his edict in terms of acknowledgement of Yahweh as the "God of Israel." Even though it is evident from various sources that only relatively few of the exiles took advantage of the opportunity, Ezra concentrates on those who did. 1:5-10 details Cyrus' largesse to the returnees under Sheshbazzar (v. 11; cf. below), especially in returning the captured vessels of the temple. Ezra 2 (essentially the same as Neh. 7) contains lists and totals of those who returned together with Zerubbabel (v. 2) and others. Chap. 3 describes the prompt erection of the altar and the laying of the foundations, together with the reinstitution of many ceremonies.

Ezra 4 relates the adamant opposition to the new initiative on the part of "the people of the land—even until the reign of Darius king of Persia" (vs. 5-6). We do not hear of Darius (522—486) again until the closing verse of the chapter, bringing the narrative back to the point at which v. 3 had left it. We know that the temple was completed and dedicated during his reign (515); but the intervening verses of the chapter speak of opposition both under "Ahasuerus" (v. 6), that is, Xerxes (486—465; cf. on Esther) and under Artaxerxes (465—424), to whom a letter was addressed (vs. 7 ff., beginning an Aramaic section of the book), and to which he replied, putting a stop to temple labors (vs. 17-23).

Unless our own knowledge of Persian history in this period is as deficient and confused as many critics think the author's must have been at this point (sometimes used in defense of late composition), it is imperative that we recognize vs. 6-23 as a parenthesis in the main narrative, illustrating the initial opposition under Cyrus and Darius with similar behavior under also the two subsequent monarchs—and it is to be noted that the parenthesis speaks of the rebuilding of the *city,* no longer the temple. Since Ezra himself probably returned with a group under Artaxerxes (cf. v. 12), it is understandable why the correspondence at that time is recorded in detail. Possibly we can detect here some originally discrete source (cf. below) concerned with the history of opposition to the building of the walls, which was excerpted quite intact. In any case, we have here momentarily a *topical* rather than a chronological order. The type of historiography appears more abrupt than we are accustomed to (although there are New Testament analogies too), but the problem was undoubtedly not nearly so great for those who still knew the basic history of the times only too well.

Ezra 5 (now back firmly in the reign of Darius) describes how the prophets Haggai and Zechariah, after fifteen years of stagnation, manage to get things moving again. Naturally, the prophecies of these two men are required collateral reading here; as we have noted repeatedly, it is unusual to find any of the prophets mentioned outside of their own books. Renewed protests cause Darius to determine that Cyrus had indeed legitimated the endeavor, and so he himself gives the green light to proceed (6:1 ff.). (Cyrus' edict is cited here in a slightly different version than its Hebrew parallel in 1:2-4; cf. below on "sources.") Finally, in 6:15, the structure is completed and rededicated (vs. 16-17). At v. 19 (describing the subsequent celebration of Passover and Unleavened Bread) the narrative abruptly reverts to the Hebrew language.

Ezra himself first enters the scene in chaps. 7 ff., returning in the seventh year of Artaxerxes (v. 7), that is, 458, some fifty-eight years after the events mentioned in chap. 6. During this time the events narrated in the Book of Esther had transpired; possibly the activities of Malachi (which see) are to be dated this early also.

Ezra 7:12-26 is again in Aramaic, not surprisingly because it gives the text of Artaxerxes' letter to Ezra, commissioning and facilitating his return. There is no reason to be suspicious of the Yahwistic tone of the letter (see also on Cyrus' edict in chap. 1). It is plausible to suppose that Esther's and Mordecai's triumph had disposed the king favorably toward Ezra. Furthermore, "scribe" in the Persian context meant that Ezra originally held a post something like "Secretary of State for Jewish

Affairs," and was probably in a position to draft the letter himself in a way most suitable for his purposes.

The abrupt appearance of the first person singular in Ezra 7:27 ff. (as Hebrew also resumes) indicates that here we have the commencement of Ezra's own memoirs, which continue through chap. 9. In chap. 8's lists of those who returned with Ezra and description of preparations for departure, what stands out is the poor response by the Levites (vs. 15 ff.; cf. also 2:40-42), perhaps because of their inferior status of long-standing. Levites were important for Ezra's religious mission, however, and eventually a few are persuaded to join his party. Also interesting is Ezra's refusal to accept an armed escort, because it might signal lack of faith in God (vs. 22-23). Nehemiah later (2:9b) had no such compunctions!

The remainder of the Book of Ezra (chaps. 9—10) concerns the acute problem of mixed marriages, which is called to his attention shortly after his return (cf. Neh. 13:23-28 and Mal. 2). Ezra initially is "appalled," and his prayer and confession in response (9:9-15) is one of three great prayers in later Biblical literature, alongside another of Ezra's in Neh. 9:6-38 and Daniel's (9:4-19). The danger was that their laxity would bring a recurrence of God's judgment, as in the Exile from which they had just been delivered. Chap. 10 (describing the rectification of the problem and concluding with a list of the priestly guilty) is again in third-person form, but it seems likely that it too was derived from Ezra's personal memoirs.

Nehemiah—Contents

The Book of Nehemiah also begins in first-person vein with that leader's very distinctive memoirs. They clearly continue through chap. 7 and probably also constitute most of chaps. 9—13. The "twentieth year of King Artaxerxes" (2:1; cf. 1:1) is 445, but the precise problem in Judah which Hanani reports (1:2) and which leads to Nehemiah's resolve to journey there is not absolutely clear. Apparently, Ezra's religious reforms had inspired the populace also to tackle the rebuilding of Jerusalem's walls, but this led to renewed accusations from neighbors (Ezra 4:7 ff.). Evidently at the mercy of his advisors, the same king who thirteen years earlier had encouraged Ezra's mission now prohibits further construction in Judah. Apparently it is this decree, which, after fortifying himself with prayer (1:4-11), Nehemiah successfully risks asking Artaxerxes to reverse (2:1-10). Undoubtedly, Nehemiah's own highly responsible position as the king's cupbearer (usually a eunuch, charged with preventing poisoning of the royal wines) helped in obtaining a favorable response.

Almost immediately upon arrival in Jerusalem, Nehemiah undertakes a surreptitious night inspection of the walls to survey the problem (2:11-16). In 2:19 we are introduced to Nehemiah's archenemies, all of which have received archaeological illumination: Sanballat, governor of Samaria, mentioned in the Elephantine Papyri; Tobiah the Ammonite, member of the Tobiad dynasty, whose family tomb and other remains are still to be found in Jordan; and Geshem the Arab, known from inscriptions as a powerful king of Kedar in north Arabia.

Chaps. 3—7 reveal Nehemiah as very much God's man for the hour. Perfectly prepared by his background for all the machinations and intrigues of his enemies (including, be it noted even the hiring of a false prophet, Shemaiah, and a prophetess, Noadiah, and evidently others against him; 6:10-14), he is more than their match and is able to complete the difficult task in the surprisingly short time of 52 days (16:15). Kenyon's recent excavations indicate that Nehemiah's wall was probably built on the eastern crest of Ophel, because the ancient terraces *(millo')* on the eastern slope had collapsed after the 587 destruction and were no longer reparable. Chap. 5, describing some of Nehemiah's social and economic reforms, is often considered a parenthetical insertion from a later period, especially because of the supposed difficulty of holding a "great assembly" (v. 7); the desperate need to buoy the people's morale, however, might well have moved Nehemiah not to delay with such measures.

Upon completion of the walls, Nehemiah begins to consider the task of repopulating the city; to insure purity of Jewish genealogy, he uses a register of those who had returned under Zerubbabel (7:5-73a; the list is virtually identicial with that in Ezra 2). The completion of the task is recorded in chap. 11; one-tenth of the population is finally moved to Jerusalem.

There intervenes in Neh. 8—10 one of the high points of the Old Testament, the great covenant-renewal ceremony of the now secure and reconstituted congregation. The account is in the third person again, perhaps (like Ezra 10) excerpted and adapted from Ezra's memoirs, but the explicit mention of Nehemiah's presence and participation (8:9) is not to be overlooked. The pericope really begins with 7:73b, dating it in the seventh month (cf. 8:2), that is the feast of Booths (Tabernacles), the revival of which is described in 8:13-18. The reading of "the book of the law of Moses" (no doubt the Pentateuch; see below) is probably also to be understood in connection with the feast, according to the stipulation of Deut. 31:9-13.

After a three-week interval (9:1, the 24th day), the people gather again for a day of public confession (not the Day of Atonement, which falls on the tenth day, but the absence of its mention certainly does not demonstrate its nonexistence at this time, as some critics argue). The ceremony is led by Ezra in one of the great prayers of the Old Testament (vs. 6 ff.), largely a recital of God's mighty acts of grace and judgment

throughout Israel's history (cf. below). This is followed up in chap. 10 by
a list of signatories to the covenant and a detailing of its salient features.
Many scholars think it strange that the day of confession in chap. 9
should follow so soon after a festival of joy. The argument seems
superficial, but probably a majority prefer to relocate the chapter after
Ezra 10 with its concern about mixed marriages, which, it is thought,
would also explain the three-day delay.

After more lists, Neh. 12:27 continues with the dedication of the
rebuilt wall, and the ceremonies, especially the processions, accompanying
it. No date is given, but presumably the interval was not great. Perhaps it
is significant, however, that the covenant-renewal ceremony was given
priority. The "I" of 12:31 and the rest of the book indicates that we surely
have Nehemiah's memoirs again. Many argue, however, that the third
person references in 12:26 and 47 to the "days of Nehemiah" indicate later
completion by someone else, perhaps after Nehemiah's death. However,
the phrase may simply be parallel to other "days of N" in the immediate
contexts; perhaps we also have here a clue to the puzzling alternation of
first and third person idioms throughout Ezra—Nehemiah.

The dedication ceremonies climax in the implementation of the law of
Deut. 23:3-5, excluding heathen from the congregation (13:1-3), as had
earlier been covenanted (10:20). The book concludes with other reforms
of Nehemiah. None of them are precisely dated, but perhaps all relate to
problems he encountered during his second trip to Jerusalem (after at
least a year back in Artaxerxes' service), beginning in 432 (13:6). The
spirituality of the populace as a whole certainly had not improved in the
meantime! Eliashib, the priest, had even installed Tobiah, one of
Nehemiah's archenemies, in a temple chamber (Neh. 13:4-9) and the
families had intermarried (v. 28)—problems Nehemiah solves with his
usual dispatch. The old problem of mixed marriages was in general still
far from solved (vs. 23-27). Problems of Levitical support (10-14) and of
sabbath infractions (15-22) were also decisively dealt with. The book ends
abruptly with a repetition of Nehemiah's prayer (see below): "Remember
me, O my God, for good."

Date and Authorship of Completed Work

Who put Ezra-Nehemiah into final shape, and when? Ezra's and
Nehemiah's own words are quoted at length, but the fair amount of third-
person narrative raises the question whether one of them also completed
the entire work. It is just as predictable that tradition assumed precisely
that, as that criticism has tended to doubt it. Dogmatism in either direction
is impossible, but tradition certainly cannot be said to have been
disproved, and still remains as likely an alternative as any (that is, at least

someone of Ezra's own generation and closely associated with him). The earliest and perhaps still most likely tradition had the book written by Ezra (together with most of Chronicles) but completed by Nehemiah. Alternatives that Ezra himself incorporated the Nehemiah materials in his final edition, or that Nehemiah appended his entire book to the completed Ezra do not make for a fundamentally different picture. II Maccabees preserves a tradition of Nehemiah's extensive library, which, if true, may have a bearing on the question. As noted earlier, the Elephantine materials have removed all reason to doubt a fifth-century date of at least the Aramaic sections of Ezra, and the large number of Persian words throughout adds to the case.

The question is complicated by that of the relation of Ezra-Nehemiah to Chronicles (which see). Traditionally the "Chronicler" was identified with Ezra. Also some modern, critical scholars have defended the equation. More often, however, it is agreed that Chronicles and Ezra-Nehemiah have common authorship, but not necessarily by Ezra. (The Nehemiah memoirs are always a special case and are often held to have been appended secondarily at a later time.) That, of course, leaves the question of the date of both wide open. Recently, serious objections have been mounted against that assumption of common authorship (alleged stylistic, linguistic, and conceptual differences), and the pendulum has swung in the direction of either leaving Chronicles out of the picture altogether, or of positing a multilayered process in the development of both blocs (Cross). It appears to be another case where philological arguments (at least until we have vastly more hard data) can only end in a draw, and where by default alone, tradition looks as good as ever. (But even if Ezra is declared the winner, there is still the question of *his* date, to which we return below.)

Most of the arguments once adduced for a late third-century date (or later) for Ezra-Nehemiah (and also Chronicles, if they are the same work) have been quietly abandoned in recent years, but a couple of them still merit attention. One concerns the mention of a "Jaddua" in Neh. 12:11 and 22. If this were the same Jaddua whom Josephus reports as high priest when Alexander the Great entered Jerusalem in 332, we certainly would have evidence of a later hand. At most, however, it might indicate no more than some later, secondary updating of the lists. More likely, however, Josephus has telescoped several generations, and the Jaddua of Alexander's time was not the son of Johanan mentioned by Nehemiah but his grandson. From the Elephantine letters we know Johanan (grandson of the Eliashib mentioned in Neh. 3:1 and 13:4-9, 28) to have been high priest in the last decade of the century. Thus his son, Jaddua, could easily have been of age and in office by 400, and there is no insuperable problem in assuming that Nehemiah lived that long. (The discussion is rendered extremely difficult by the fact that, like "Jaddua," so many of the names of this period are family names or at least repeat themselves in succeeding generations.)

Archaeology has disposed of two other erstwhile arguments for lateness. Mention of (Greek) drachmas or darics in Neh. 7:71 is no longer taken as evidence of post-Alexandrian composition, because of the now demonstrated use of the standard at Elephantine as well as in the Persian period at Beth-zur (a short distance south of Jerusalem). Similarly, the title, "king of Persia" (Ezra 1:1) or reference to "Darius the Persian" (Neh. 12:22) is no longer a stumbling block because of ample parallels from antiquity.

Sources

It seems quite obvious—and certainly need not surprise us—that the author of Ezra-Nehemiah (whoever he was) used sources. Considerable scholarly energy has been invested in the attempt to delineate these precisely. No complete unanimity has emerged, but some of them seem quite obvious and are worthy of note. The two major ones are the two great autobiographical passages, the "memoirs" of both Ezra and Nehemiah. The precise extent of both is often debated, but their existence usually assumed (although a few regard them as compositions of the "Chronicler" or someone else). Ezra's apparently comprise at least the bulk of chaps. 7—9 where we have the first person used. More precise boundaries can scarcely be fixed because of their stylistic indistinguishability from the surrounding third-person narratives about Ezra, which, however, may well stem from Ezra too.

Nehemiah's memoirs are more distinctive, possibly because they were not subjected to as much editorial activity (Ezra's respect for his colleague's diary?). They are quite unanimously found in Neh. 1—7, and probably constitute at least the bulk of chaps. 9—13 as well. Their repeated refrain, "Remember me—O God" or the like (5:19; 13:14, 22, 31) has led to the plausible suggestion that they were modeled somewhat after the memorial inscriptions common in the ancient Near East—not merely memorials for men, but a sort of votive thankoffering to a deity (cf. below).

Besides these two memoirs, the third major bloc of material in Ezra-Nehemiah is the Sheshbazzar-Zerubbabel section of Ezra 1—6. All three blocs appear to depend heavily on three types of material: lists, letters, and official documents of various sorts. The most striking list is that of the expatriates who returned with Zerubbabel, which is duplicated almost verbatim in Ezra 2 and Neh. 7. Ezra 8:1-14 details family heads who returned with Ezra, and Neh. 12:1-26 lists priests and Levites from

Zerubbabel's to Nehemiah's time. Ezra 10:18-24 records those who face "excommunication" because of marriage to foreign women. Neh. 9:38—10:27 is a roster of the signatories to Nehemiah's covenant, as 3:1-32 is of those who had participated in the rebuilding of the walls.

The letters quoted are largely exchanges between the opponents of the new Jewish community and the Persian court—all in Aramaic, like the connecting passages, hence perhaps first brought together in some intermediate Aramaic source. These include the exchange with Artaxerxes in Ezra 4:8-22, and with Darius in 5:17—6:12.

Included in the latter is Darius' citation of Cyrus' "Edict of Restoration" of 538. It constitutes the major example of the third type of source, namely, official documents. As noted above, besides its citation here in Aramaic, we also meet it in a different Hebrew version (perhaps better: *Gattung*) at the beginning of the book (Ezra 1:2-4). For a long time the authenticity of the latter was widely questioned on the grounds of the differences in both tone and subject matter. However, Bickerman has apparently succeeded in convincing even many critics that most of the variations are due to the different settings and audiences. The matter-of-fact Aramaic document appears to be a typical *dikrona* (Hebrew *zikkaron*), that is, a memorandum of the king's oral decision filed in the royal archives, while the Hebrew version takes the form of an oral proclamation of the king's edict by a herald, town crier, or the like in the audience's own language. The genuineness of also the latter is supported by its formal parallelism with Artaxerxes' letter to Ezra in 7:12-26 (in Aramaic).

All three of the main blocs in Ezra-Nehemiah not only utilize the same three types of material but may also display a similarity of literary structure, by which the components are linked together, especially in certain summary notations (e.g., Ezra 6:13-14 and Neh. 12:26) and repetitive resumptions (e.g., Ezra 6:22b and Neh. 11:1). That type of overall structural unity need not imply free composition, of course, but it probably betrays the hand of the author of the book as it stands, whether Ezra himself or another.

Critical Reconstruction

Matters become far more subjective, however, when such criteria are employed to attempt a hypothetical reconstruction of the "actual" sequence of the historical events. As noted above, the use of a source summarizing various oppositions to the rebuilding of the walls may explain the unchronological order caused by the insertion of the parenthetical section, 4:6-23. The major gap of some sixty years between Ezra 6 and 7 (that is, between the time of Zerubbabel, Zechariah, etc., and the coming of Ezra himself) could be attributed, humanly speaking, to the lack of a good source covering that period, but it can just as easily be construed as evidence of essentially contemporary authorship (no need to rehearse recent and familiar history, especially when not germane to one's purpose).

These criteria are sometimes combined with presumed historical difficulties to support extensive rearrangement of the entire Biblical account of Ezra's career. There are quite a variety of these, but a widely followed one (more or less) suggests this as the proper order: (1) Ezra 7—8 (Ezra's coming); (2) Neh. 8 (reading of the Torah); (3) Ezra 9—10 (resolution of the problem of mixed marriages); and (4) Neh. 9—10 (the great confessional and covenant-renewal ceremony). The problem this rearrangement wishes to solve is the tardiness with which Ezra appears to tackle the problems for which he came. As the narratives stand, he appears to have done nothing for four months after arrival (7:7 versus 10:9), and then addressed himself to marital problems only when they are called to his attention. Above all, not until thirteen or more years later (Neh. 8:2) does he read the Torah and lead covenant renewal. According to the suggested reconstruction, Ezra's entire "revival" is accomplished within a year of his arrival in Jerusalem.

No doubt, the proposal is very neat—too neat! From a literary standpoint one must look askance at such cavalier treatment of a text, and from a historical viewpoint, one can at least suggest an alternate interpretation. Spiritual movements take time to blossom, and there is no reason why Ezra should not have followed the ancient maxim to "make haste slowly." One may also ask whether Ezra's great convocation was even possible before Nehemiah had arrived and restored security.

Furthermore, this literary reconstruction is almost necessarily mated with the further hypothesis that some editor artificially—and mistakenly—inserted the account of Nehemiah's arrival and building of the walls (Neh. 1—7) before chap. 8. Thus, both memoirs were allegedly split up: Ezra 9—10 from Neh. 8 (the two are connected in the apocryphal I Esdras), and the two parts of Nehemiah's diary (1—7 and 11:1 ff.). The editor supposedly did this, either because of the mention of Nehemiah at 8:9 and 10:1 (usually assumed to be later glosses or additions, as also at 12:26 and 12:47, which would mean that Nehemiah himself never mentions Ezra), and/or because he mistakenly thought that Nehemiah was present at the great covenant renewal events of Neh. 8—10.

Ezra—Nehemiah Sequence

But with that the fat is in the fire with respect to *the* problem of Ezra-Nehemiah, before which all others pale in comparison, namely, the actual *historical* sequence of Ezra and Nehemiah. We can broach here only a few salient aspects of the issue; for further details the reader is referred to the commentaries, larger introductions, or to the fine summary in Bright's *History*.

About Nehemiah's dates there is no longer any serious debate, and his career forms a fixed point in the discussions. The Elephantine texts, written in the last decade of the fifth century, prove that the "Artaxerxes" whom Nehemiah served was Artaxerxes I (465—424). Thus Nehemiah must have first arrived in Judah in 445 (the king's twentieth year) and returned to Persia in 433 after a term of twelve years as governor (Neh. 13:6). But after apparently only one year in Ecbatana, he returns in 432 for a second term of office of uncertain duration.

The questions all arise about Ezra's relation to Nehemiah. There are three main alternatives. The traditional view assumes that the Artaxerxes associated with Ezra is also Artaxerxes I, as is the case of Nehemiah. Then, the date of Ezra's arrival in that monarch's "seventh year" (Ezra 7:7) can easily be fixed as 458, thirteen years *before* Nehemiah. Two other positions are widely held, however. The most common alternative identifies the Artaxerxes of the Ezra narrative with Artaxerxes II (404—358), not bringing Ezra on the scene until 397, well *after* Nehemiah's activity. This construction caught on rapidly among critical scholars after van Hoonacker, a Belgian Catholic, first proposed it in 1880, and it still has many defenders. A third suggestion relates with tradition to Artaxerxes I, but also proceeds on the assumption of a scribal error in the date given in Ezra 7:7, namely, that it originally read "*thirty*-seventh" instead of "seventh," yielding a date of 428 for Ezra's advent, sometime in the middle of Nehemiah's second term in office. (Early on, Wellhausen had suggested "*twenty*-seventh," but it appears to have no defenders today.)

How shall the conservative react to this debate? Certainly, the third alternative cannot be dismissed out of hand, pivoting as it does on a nondoctrinal *text*-critical point (and one which on a hypothetical basis is readily explainable). That point, however, is gravely weakened (though not demolished, not turned into a doctrinal issue) by the total lack of any objective support for the hypothesis in any extant textual witness. However, one does note with satisfaction that in this alternative Ezra and Nehemiah do remain partial contemporaries, as the Bible plainly indicates. At the same time it answers one common concern about the traditional sequence, namely, how Ezra's spiritual reforms would have been possible before Nehemiah had provided physical security (cf. below). Defenders of this theory sometimes even suggest that Nehemiah arranged for Ezra's coming in order to complement and complete his own labors.

The proposal to postpone Ezra's arrival until the reign of Artaxerxes II is obviously radical, no matter from what viewpoint one views it. Textually, it involves considerable surgery in order to eliminate the names of both Ezra and Nehemiah wherever according to the theory they should not appear. Theologically, of course, it assumes that the Biblical writer was thoroughly confused. Historically, probably the most telling argument against it derives from Elephantine again. The Passover Papyrus indicates that already in 419 the cultic affairs of Jews in the Diaspora were being regulated by the Persian king via Jerusalem, and Ezra 7:25 indicates that Ezra's appointment for just such duties was the first of its kind.

That brings us back to the traditional view that Ezra arrived in 458, thirteen years before Nehemiah. None of the many objections tendered against this position are conclusive, and other possibilities can usually be suggested. That Ezra shows no concern about security may indicate only that the neighbors saw purely religious reform as little of a threat; "security" from them became necessary only after construction of the city walls began (cf. Ezra 4:7-23). The charge that, according to the traditional view, Ezra must have failed, is unfounded, because the problems involved (mixed marriages, economic abuses) are recurrent ones under any circumstances. Why Ezra waited thirteen years before promulgating the Torah cannot be answered with certainty, but it is possible that Nehemiah's extra push first made so grand a ceremony seem feasible. Another sticky point is the mention of a "wall" in Ezra 9:9, well before Nehemiah is on the scene; however the usual Hebrew word for "wall" is not used, and RSV may well be correct in taking it to be figurative for "protection." Also, who can say why Ezra and Nehemiah make virtually no mention of each other? The problem certainly is not unique in Biblical literature (cf., e.g., on the prophets). And so it goes with numerous other commonly lodged "objections."

Above all, it appears that external—specifically, archaeological—evidence is increasingly not only taking us out of the realm of supposition and hypothesis but also weighing in on the side of tradition. Elephantine, as we noted, had been helpful all along, and now our control of the era is further enhanced by the Wadi Daliyeh Samaritan Papyri and some sixth-century bullae which mention some of Zerubbabel's immediate family who were connected with Jewish governors who succeeded him. In sum, although the 428 alternative date for Ezra's possible arrival cannot be dogmatically discounted, and although the traditional 458 date suffers from various disabilities (presumably because of the paucity of our information about the period), the latter is still a position which the conservative need have no misgivings about retaining.

Among the many other historical problems of this period, mention must be made of one more, namely the relation between Sheshbazzar (Ezra 1:8; 5:14-16) and Zerubbabel. On the latter we are reasonably well informed (except for the mysterious end of his career), but the problem arises because about the same activities are attributed to both. Both are of royal descent, both lead exiles back, both lay foundations of the second temple, both are governors of the province of Judah, etc. It has even been proposed that they are two names of the same person, and, of course, critics are not lacking who simply suppose that the "Chronicler" (or whoever the author was) got things all mixed up. Suffice it to say here that the most likely explanation appears to be that Sheshbazzar is the same as the "Shenazzar" of 1 Chron. 3:18, that is, the son of Jehoiachin and uncle of Zerubbabel, that both he and Zerubbabel led groups of returning exiles, and that Sheshbazzar's career as governor of Judah as well as his efforts at rebuilding the temple were short-lived, soon being replaced by Zerubbabel, who far overshadows him.

Importance of Ezra and Nehemiah

For all of the remaining problems, the importance of Ezra-Nehemiah as a historical source can scarcely be exaggerated. For all practical purposes, our knowledge of the fifth-century Judahite community is almost completely dependent on their testimony. And were it not for their record, our acquaintance with fifth-century Judaism would scarcely be any greater than with the fourth and third centuries—which often barely exceeds zero. We know that the community was in existence, but precious little more.

However, for even that little bit, the paramount significance of the two figures, Ezra and Nehemiah, cannot be overstated. Humanly speaking, it seems certain, that, except for their labors, the little community of repatriates would surely have gone under, or at least merged syn-cretistically with their neighbors. Hopes of another Davidide physically occupying the throne had apparently died with Zerubbabel, or at least postponed to some eschatological infinity. Prophets there obviously still were (cf. above on Neh. 6:10-14), but it was no longer their hour—as, for the most part it had not been since the demise of dynastic hopes (cf. also Zech. 13:2-6). The transition to a "theocratic" or hierocratic form of government appropriate to the times until the "fullness of time" did not come easily.

Apparently the credit goes equally to both Ezra and Nehemiah. Their cooperation remains a classical example of the necessary interpenetration of the material and the spiritual in God's earthly kingdom—and not only in the Old Testament when "church" and "state" are in principle still united. Without Nehemiah's heroic and draconian measures, Ezra's labors of covenant renewal could scarcely ever have come to fruition, except perhaps for a tiny clique. And without Ezra's religious measures, Nehemiah's administrative reforms would have remained purely external and legal—and probably also very temporary, as indicated by the relapse during his brief return to Persia (13:6 ff.).

Nehemiah thus fully deserves his reputation as one of the great laymen of the Bible, accomplishing what often only laymen can. His repeated petitions that God "remember" his accomplishments suggest that perhaps he also illustrates the inexperience of many laymen at articulating their faith in a way entirely satisfactory to the clergy. (However, that problem recedes if we recall that the "form" employed was a standard votive one in the Near East [cf. above], and it can be understood in a theologically acceptable manner.) But, if so, he is also a reminder, especially standing alongside Ezra, that faith and even Orthodoxy are not simply to be equated with theological fluency, ideal though that is.

Until, within the last century or so, it fell as a casualty to historical criticism (which usually disparaged this period) and/or to simple Biblical illiteracy, there had traditionally been considerable exegetical and homiletical interest in Nehemiah (and Ezra), considering him a model of faith in adversity. Such treatments ran the grave risk of simple moralism, but, properly executed, they deserve resuscitation.

In spite of Nehemiah's importance, however, Ezra usually dominates the limelight, and, from a theological or ecclesiastical viewpoint, for good reason. Ezra's role in the "history of religion" is almost incalculable, even from the most detached standpoint. As is sometimes said of Moses, if he did not exist, we should have to invent him! (In both cases, the maxim is surely applicable: committees are not responsible for great developments!) His occasionally semi-legendary depiction as a "second Moses" is only mildly objectionable: if Moses was Israel's founder (humanly speaking), Ezra was, indeed, as he is often styled, the "father of Judaism." With such an accolade, however, relationships with both the preceding and the following periods must be made clear.

With their evolutionistic premises, liberals have devoted vast energies to the identification of the "law of your God" (Ezra 7:14 and 25) on which Ezra based his reform. It will not take conservatives long to conclude that there is no reason under the sun why it should not simply be identified with the Pentateuch (or some working adaptation of it), which, after all, had been in existence for nearly a millennium. It probably is increasingly true that critics will concede the ("substantial") completion of the evolution of the Pentateuch by Ezra's time (in which process he is often thought to have played a key role). There are still many, however, who would postpone its completion, and identify Ezra's code with P (often also thought to be taking final shape about this time), with D, or with some other collection of laws, now unidentifiable. All of these hypotheses have myriad variations, but we regard it as not worth our while to devote further time to what we regard as a nonissue.

In the other chronological direction, Ezra's role vis-á-vis "Judaism" must also be understood correctly. As we have stressed repeatedly, the "Yahwism" of the Old Testament must not be confused with the "Judaism" of later times that supplements and interprets the Old Testament in the light of an alleged oral Mosaic tradition, collected in the Talmud. One may quibble about precisely when the paths part: no doubt, Ezra sets the stage for developments that will lead into Judaism, but he himself still stands squarely *within* the Old Testament, that is, within Yahwism. It was obviously his intent simply to be *faithful* to the Mosaic past, to show his people that the monarchical interim was, in a sense, a dispensable addition to the primordial revelation. Any self-conscious sense of a closed canon, of a need for hermeneutical rules to adapt it to an entirely different era (of "Judaism") cannot be picked up until the labors of Hillel and Shammai in the century before Christ. And by the same token, one must be very diffident about speaking of "Jews" in the Old Testament: technically, the term originates first in this period (a linguistic development from "Judahite," that is, a citizen of the tiny Persian province of "Judah" clustered around Jerusalem), but it was yet many a moon before the term assumed the associations and overtones which it inevitably has to the modern ear.

The term "Judaism" also runs the risk of pejorative misunderstanding of a quasi-racist sort. Obviously, if "Jews" would simply assimilate to the majority culture, the problem would disappear—as it did for the vast majority of their compatriots in antiquity, the "ten lost tribes," the Babylonian exiles who failed to return, etc. However, that only throws into relief what for many modern, and especially for liberal, readers is the major stumbling block of these narratives: the "loveless" exclusivism and particularism which they exhibit. For "tolerant" universalists, Ezra and Nehemiah are nearly models of everything "religion" should not be. Via higher criticism, even the Bible's particularistic teaching is neutralized, because it is regarded as almost totally absent in earlier periods and purely the relativistic result of the insecurities of this era. And the extent to which Christians often join the chorus of criticism is surely an accurate gauge of alienation from their own "scandal of particularity," centering on the cross.

Ironically, and even externally, it appears that, except for Ezra's and Nehemiah's strict measures, there would have been nothing left to criticize.

Even if the community had survived the Persians, they would scarcely have been prepared for the onslaughts of Hellenism soon to come in Alexander's wake, not to speak of persecutions of the Maccabean era. Ezra and Nehemiah plainly were convinced that the prophets were right: pagan influences had to be ruthlessly expunged, compromise would be fatal. It was a time of necessary retrenchment, of withdrawal to the center for survival. Not only within subsequent Judaism, but also often in church history (our own age certainly being no exception), that are times when sheer survival is a maximal achievement. But religious communities as well as individuals are congenitally forgetful: God must ever and again apply His Law (second use) in order that the faithful grasp the necessary application of the Gospel in obedience to the law (third use).

Ezra's paramount religio-historical significance can be summarized in two areas, as a "scribe," and with respect to the canon. In Ezra, we undoubtedly witness the beginning of a momentous shift in the linguistic field of the word *sopher* or "scribe." Originally, the term applied to any "secretary" or amanuensis (e.g., Baruch to Jeremiah), but particularly of a government post at the head of an administrative division (cf. 2 Kings 12:11; 25:19). In Ezra's case, it doubtless translated into something like, "Secretary of State for Jewish affairs," and Ezra's mission to Jerusalem must have been essentially an implementation of his office's major responsibility. Given the circumstances, however, that is, the intrinsic importance of teaching and expounding the Mosaic revelation, Ezra virtually becomes an incarnation of the term's shift to the meaning of "exegete," "Bible interpreter" etc. (Jer. 8:8 may well indicate, however, that the usage was not totally new in Ezra's time.) "Wisdom" (which see) traditions apparently became ever more explicitly wedded to the "special revelation" of the Torah at about the same time (note their equation in Ezra 7:25), further enhancing the relevance of the "scribe" to the details of daily living. Only as the interpretations began to move beyond mere exposition of the Word itself, did "scribe" begin to assume (at least from the Christian standpoint) some of the negative coloration which it has in the New Testament, trends which would be continued and amplified in subsequent rabbinism, and constituting normative "Judaism" down to the present day.

Ezra apparently even deserves much of the credit for enabling Judaism to survive the destruction of the second temple in A.D. 70. Perhaps more than he himself realized, the *de facto* result of his reforms seems to have been to strip the priesthood increasingly of major religious and intellectual leadership, leaving in their hands only the conduct of the temple ritual. Instead, spiritual leadership increasingly shifted to a nonhereditary, more "democratic" community of "scribes" or Biblical scholars, whose element was the synagogue (whatever its technical origins) and the school. The Diaspora, of course, had long been bereft of the temple for all practical purposes, and when Judaism was deprived of it once and for all in A.D. 70, the community was able to pick up the pieces almost without losing a stride.

Ezra's traditional association with the closing of the Old Testament canon has even more direct significance for Christianity. There is no way to test directly the accuracy of the tradition (and, in any event, only the human, historical aspects of canonization can be "tested" anyway), but there is no reason why the conservative should not grant it essential credence. Certainly, humanly speaking, there is no better figure with which to associate the closing of the canon: a universalistic faith can draw on congenial, "inspired" thoughts from any source, but a particularistic, propositional faith has "special inspiration" as its necessary corollary. The liberal, of course, will date at least Daniel and probably quite a few hagiographa to a later period, but the conservative must disagree. If Ezra is the author of Chronicles (which see), as tradition has assumed, even that apparently latest contribution to the Old Testament canon can be included. In any event, it would seem that any changes to even the third division of the Hebrew canon after about Ezra's time must have been very minimal and nominal. (This also implies that the much-touted council of Jamnia in A.D. 90 did not "fix" any canon, as one often reads, but simply reaffirmed what had long been held, devoting explicit attention, as also certain Christian councils would later, only to a few disputed "antilegomena" on the periphery of the canon.)

The famous legend in II (IV) Esdras, in its own way, makes an excellent summation of the difference, at least as concerns canon, between Yahwism and Judaism, and then also between Judaism and Christianity. In the seventh and last vision of the book, Ezra expresses concern that after his death the people will be left without teacher or law. In response, Ezra is given a wonderful drink in a cup and inspired to dictate continuously for forty days to five scribes a total of ninety-four books. Twenty-four of them—obviously the canonical books of the Old Testament—are to be published, while the remaining seventy are to be hidden ("apocrypha") and reserved for the "wise." The legend is obviously an *apologia* for apocalyptic works like II Esdras itself; although orthodox Judaism preferred to attribute its extracanonical authority to material allegedly given orally to Moses and transmitted in the same manner, in both cases we have a clear-cut demarcation of the canonical boundaries themselves, which was (and still is) the parting of also many other ways.

Precisely as canon, however, it is important that conservative Christendom be able to relate also to Ezra-Nehemiah, not only as

important historical and religious background, nor even as a source of
excellent models of constancy in adversity, but also typologically as part
of the *church's* history. If the church *is* "Israel," then Ezra, alongside
Moses, is not only a type of the great Lawgiver, Christ, but the entire era
becomes a prefigurement of the era of the church of Christ: a time of
fulfillment, of the "new covenant," but also a time of waiting, of
developing appropriate structures for the interim, of maintaining at all
costs faithfulness to the revealed Word. Particularly orthodoxy and
confessionalism need to exalt Ezra as a major "compatriot" of the
church's continued "Old Testamentness" and his role as "pedagogue" and
keeper of the promises. Only as it faithfully fulfills that centripetal
function can it properly discharge its centrifugal and universal mission,
which distinguishes it from Ezra.

Particular notice should be given to the two great prayers of Ezra in
these books, Ezra 9 and Neh. 9, especially the latter. Both serve as major
refutations of any misunderstanding of Ezra's work as sterile "legalism,"
"biblicism," etc. Critics often regard them as two recensions of the same
prayer, which is unlikely, although like many prayers (especially uttered
by the same person), they undeniably have elements in common. The
settings are different, although in a way merely the positive and negative
sides of the same coin: the context of Ezra 9 is the confrontation with the
problem of mixed marriages, while Neh. 9 forms a major part of the great
ceremony of covenant renewal, the climax of Ezra's labors. From a
theological viewpoint, it is one of the Bible's classical statements of
Heilsgeschichte, of the "theology of recital," of the prevenience of the
Gospel of the "mighty acts of God" to man's responding "covenant
renewal," (and the value of all those formulations is not diminished by
their association with neo-Orthodoxy or academic "Biblical theology"). To
its list, the church will only want to add those of the New Testament
fulfillment, climaxing in Christ.

Likewise, from a liturgical viewpoint, we have here one of the noblest
liturgical formulae in the Old Testament. It is only technically
anachronistic to label it a "Eucharistic prayer," and as a matter of fact it has
served as a model for many such prayers in the history of the Christian
cultus (not to speak of its influence on synagogal worship). It centers in
"remembrance" *(anamnesis),* that is, the verbal and sacramental
contemporization or "representation" of past acts of Law and Gospel as
the basis of present repentance and covenant renewal, as well as of future
hope. Revival of the prayer's role today might aid also the present
generation in "remembrance" of their Old Testament patrimony.

The doxological tone of Neh. 9 is very redolent of Chronicles, but
critics often seek to drive a wedge between its accents and Chronicles, or

between the accents of both and the sacrificial cult of P. Indeed, we have here accent on the classical soteriological archetypes (Exodus, wilderness, conquest) rather than Chronicles' concentration on David and the office of the prophet. Or, if those are not pitted critically against each other, critics often highlight the lack of mention of sacrifice in connection with the ceremony (as somewhat also in Chronicles), as though its point were to denigrate temple services in favor of the synaxis or "service of the Word" of the emerging synagogue—and of Protestantism. Particularly confessional Lutheranism has the resources to retain the great canonical synthesis of all these accents, and hence to grasp Ezra's prayer in its full tonality.

CHRONICLES

Chronicles concludes the hagiographical canon of the Hebrew Bible, and therewith the Old Testament itself in the traditional Masoretic ordering. The arrangement is at least as old as the New Testament: when Jesus (Matt. 23:35 = Luke 11:51) calls down upon the hypocrites of His day "all the righteous blood shed on earth, from the blood of innocent Abel to the blood of Zechariah," it obviously is a way of saying "from Genesis to Chronicles" (2 Chron. 24:20 ff.), that is, the entire Scriptures of the time.

The fact that its conclusion (2 Chron. 36:22-23), citing Cyrus' edict of restoration, is identical with the beginning of Ezra (1:1-3a) has often led to the suspicion, not only that the two were originally a single work but also that originally Ezra-Nehemiah (which see) followed Chronicles in chronological sequence. If so, one inevitably asks why the order was reversed, and the only apparent answer seems to be that it was felt appropriate to conclude the canon with a survey or "chronicle" of the entire canonical history. Conclusion with Cyrus' decree would have been preferred, in spite of its overlap with Ezra, in order to close both book and canon on a promissory, even eschatological note (cf. similarly the conclusion of Kings).

Title

Both its canonical position and its unfortunate name may have contributed to its relative neglect and oblivion, apparently all through history, at least in comparison with the other historical books in the Bible, especially Kings. Our "Chronicles" is a fairly accurate rendition of the Hebrew *(Sepher) dibhre hayammim,* literally "(The book of) the words/events of the days/times past." The antiquity of the Masoretic title cannot be ascertained, but because it appears in the titles of various other "chronicles" which the canonical Chronicles cites as sources (see below), it may well have gone with the book from the outset.

St. Jerome first suggested (though he did not use it in the Vulgate) the translation, "Chronicles," by which the West generally knows the book. Perhaps in Hebrew culture the phrase had connotations more nearly like our "history," but certainly "chronicles" is entirely misleading, especially if contrasted with "history," such as in Kings. "Chronicles," implying, as it does, a mere annal or objective record of events without any principle of selection or further purpose in writing, applies to the Biblical book, if at all, only in the case of the exclusively genealogical first nine chapters. "History," by contrast, connotes a purposive selection and presentation of materials, and by that criterion there is perhaps no book in the Bible where the term (minus its Western suggestion of secularity!) is more fitting. Chronicles must be recognized as the third major historiographic effort of the Old Testament, alongside both the "deuteronomistic" (cf. above on the term) history in Samuel-Kings, running quite parallel, and the pre-Davidic history of especially the Pentateuch (which Chronicles also parallels, at least formally, in its initial genealogies).

The Septuagint introduced changes in both name and canonical position. Instead of "Chronicles," it ventured "Paralipomenon" (a designation, via the Vulgate, still current in Catholicism). It translates as "things omitted/passed over" that is, in Samuel and Kings. If anything, that designation is even less appropriate than "Chronicles," and the misunderstanding it entails did nothing to enhance the importance of the work. (The Septuagintal division of the book into I and II has become universal, however, even being introduced into Hebrew editions shortly before the Reformation.) The more topical relocation of the work after Kings probably led to the impression that it was merely a retelling of the same events—and hence presumably of secondary importance!

Date and Authorship

Who wrote the book and when? Strictly speaking, of course, the work is anonymous, and hence its unknown author is conventionally referred to as "the Chronicler." Traditionally, he was identified with Ezra (which see), and some modern critics have agreed (although in those circles, be it noted, the date of Ezra himself is often disputed). Sometimes scholars go further and posit Chronicles-Ezra-Nehemiah as originally one huge single work (cf. above). If we must guess (and we must), Ezra (and then a date for Chronicles of c. 430) still remains as plausible a candidate as any. Comparative studies on the language and theology of Ezra vs. Chronicles remain inconclusive, if not contradictory (see on Ezra). Many who purport to deny any connection make the mistake of including Nehemiah in their statistics, whereas there should be little doubt that his distinctive memoirs have independent (surely autobiographical) origin. Certainly the apparent purpose of Chronicles seems thoroughly consonant with Ezra's religious program: to establish the self-understanding of the postexilic community as essentially a religious entity, revolving around the two divine institutions of the temple and the Davidic dynasty (see below). Perhaps above all, Ezra the Levite seems a natural for explaining the prominent levitical interests of the book. However, there are also enough differences that one does well not to press the point.

The book, as we saw, concludes with Cyrus' Edict of Restoration in 538 B.C., and, at the outside, it cannot be earlier than that. Critics, however, have been more inclined to search out (exaggerate?) the latest events in the book and date it accordingly. On that basis, at least until recently, most scholars located the work of the Chronicler in the Greek period, that is, sometime after Alexander's victories in 333 ff. B.C. The main arguments were linguistic and genealogical, but both are very fragile. Genealogical lists often omit generations (cf. Matt. 1), but without corroboration it is hard to be certain.

Two genealogies are often adduced as evidence of so late a date. The one is that of the high priest, Jaddua, in Neh. 12:23; see our discussion there, but in any case the relevance of that appeal is dependent upon the assumption that the "Chronicler" is also responsible for Ezra-Nehemiah. The other is the list of the descendants of Zerubbabel apparently to the sixth generation in 1 Chron. 3:19-24. If we average twenty years per generation, 520 (Zerubbabel) minus 120 (20 X 6) gives us a date of 400— not bad, unless one wants to insist on Ezrahite authorship. Young, however, mounts a plausible argument that the passage in question covers only *two* generations, down to Pelatiah and Jesaiah in v. 21a, while 21b does not directly continue the line but inserts the names of four other Davidide families *contemporary* with those two, possibly their brothers. Others interpret the evidence to imply *four* generations. Either of these alternatives would yield a date compatible with Ezrahite authorship (c. 480 or 440). Alternatively, the fact that the Septuagint (followed by Vulgate and Peshitta) extends the genealogy to *eleven* generations, indicates how easily such lists could be updated. That makes the debate a text-critical one but also demonstrates how spongy the entire argument is.

(We disregard here the argument of some critics that *all* the genealogies in 1 Chron. 1—9 are interpolations, which, of course, would make the debate even more irrelevant. Generally, only the genealogies and the cultic details of 1 Chron. 23—27 are subject to that type of critical skepticism. On the whole, the LXX does not manifest major departures from MT.)

The other traditional type of argument in favor of late date was based on the supposed presence of Greek loanwords—but, again, in Ezra-Nehemiah more than in Chronicles itself. However, since Albright's demonstration that the words in question were Persian, not Greek, critical opinion has gravitated increasingly toward a 400 B.C. date. Recently, however, voices have even been heard (Freedman, Newsome; cf. Welch earlier) defending a late *sixth* century date, and, of course, divorcing Chronicles from Ezra-Nehemiah. The argument is that only in that period can we document all three of Chronicles' major interests (prophecy, kingship and cult), but, at best, it is an argument from silence, especially when something is made of the absence of the first two motifs in Ezra-Nehemiah. As we shall see, the Chronicler is undeniably very interested in prophecy, and this interpretation would make his work the historical expression of the conceptual world articulated by the postexilic prophets, Haggai and Zechariah.

Also affecting the question is Chronicles' possible anti-Samaritan animus. Evidence increasingly indicates that the schism did not become final until John Hyrcanus' destruction of the Samaritan temple in the second century B.C., but in other respects that was only the capstone of a friction which went back to the Exile itself, and hence we have no handhold here either. Critics often argue further for lateness on the grounds of the Chronicler's alleged historical unreliability, but we shall not even honor the point (see below). Surely, the great variety of viewpoints is another reminder of how much less attention the Bible devotes to such isagogical questions than higher criticism—though not so little as many "practical" readers!

Sources

Whoever he was, the "Chronicler" mentions many of his sources, and there are evidently others besides. Some twenty of these appear to be mentioned by name, although it seems that sometimes the same source is cited under a slightly different title. We have the "Book of the Kings of Judah and Israel," but "Words," "Kingdoms," or only "Israel" are substituted at times. We twice meet a "midrash" of kings (2 Chron. 13:22 and 24:27)—surely not in the later rabbinical sense of the term (edifying homiletical embroidery), but apparently with a more neutral meaning of "study, account, commentary" or the like. In addition the "Words" of a large number of prophets are cited (Shemaiah, Iddo, Jehu, *et al.*), consonant with one of Chronicles' overriding interests. If we, unlike many critics, have confidence in Chronicles' veracity, the supposition probably also follows that these works had all survived the Exile—surely no impossibility or even improbability.

In addition to all these extracanonical sources, however, it seems clear that the Chronicler's major source was a canonical one, Samuel-Kings or its equivalent. How direct the relationship was cannot be said with certainty, but the frequently verbatim parallels preclude mere coincidence. If Kings (which see) was not finished until the early Exile and Chronicles was written shortly after the Exile, the chronological gap between the two is not great at all.

Outline and Comparison with Kings

The basic outline of Chronicles is very simple. 1 Chron. 1—9, as noted, is pure genealogy, from Adam to David. The remainder of 1 Chron. (10—29) is devoted to David; chaps. 22—29 are almost exclusively concerned with David's contributions to temple worship. 2 Chron. 1—9 considers Solomon (2—7 again devoted to temple matters), and chaps. 10—36 continue with the history of Judah through the edict of Cyrus.

Inevitably, one compares the contents of Chronicles with Kings, also in any attempt to understand the purposes and principles behind the Chroniclers' selections, omissions, and additions. Already the bare outline reveals some of Chronicles' idiosyncrasies with respect to the earlier history. With the exception of the death of Saul (1 Chron. 10:1-14), the pre-Davidic history is covered only skeletally in the genealogies. Similarly, the entire history of the northern kingdom, Israel, is omitted, except when passing mention is unavoidable (including even the Elijah and Elisha narratives). There are even great gaps in the account of David's reign, especially between Saul's death and the capture of Jerusalem, and again in the lack of anything parallel to the "Court History" (2 Sam. 7—1 Kings 2).

There are also countless additions, small and large. For example, the list of David's heroes in 1 Chron. 11:10-47 is much expanded over that of 2 Sam. 23:8-39. The Chronicler lingers lovingly, as it were, on the account of David's bringing the ark to Jerusalem in 1 Chron. 15—16, considerably beyond the details given in 2 Sam. 6. In general, it is safe to predict that we will find expansions in Chronicles whenever the temple, priests and/or Levites are involved. Additional information is included about the prophets Samuel, Gad, Nathan, Ahijah, Shemaiah, Hanani, Jehu, and even Elijah, and we hear of a number of prophets who are not named elsewhere: Asaph, Heman, Jeduthun (on these three, cf. the Psalter), Iddo, Jehaziel, Eliezer, and two prophets named Oded. Some of the Chronicler's additions to political and military history are even more famous (or infamous to critical skeptics): Pharaoh Shishak's invasion of Judah under Rehoboam; Asa's confrontation with Zerah the Ethiopian; Jehoshaphat's judicial reforms; Uzziah's ambitious military and mercantile enterprises; Hezekiah's reformation; Manasseh's repentance; Josiah's great national Passover, and many more. (If Ezra-Nehemiah is part of the same corpus, that major addition will also have to be included in the list.)

In addition, the same narrative is often nuanced differently, depending on the point the Chronicler wanted to make. One of the most famous of these is the attribution of David's prideful census to "Satan" in 1 Chron. 21:1, in contrast to "the anger of the LORD" in 2 Sam. 24:1. For evolutionists, the shift has always been major evidence of later and more sophisticated theological reflection about God in relation to evil, allegedly moving in the direction of the more dualistic demonology of later times. The difference, however, is only apparent; even though technically the *name* "Satan" may not have been specialized for the purpose until later, the Bible nowhere knows of any evil which God does not at least permit, so that in an ultimate sense it must also be ascribed to him (cf. on Job 1— 2 and Zech. 3), and, furthermore, the "logic" of a personal God also requires a personal expression of transcendent evil, whatever his name. (Further illustrations of Chronicles' different nuancing must either be deferred to the commentaries, or will be included in the discussion of his theology below.)

Why the variations? Lembke has demonstrated that some of the answer may at times be textual: some of his omissions are also absent in LXX, and it is possible that the Chronicler followed a Hebrew text of the same type from which the LXX was translated. Otherwise, we obtain a much more positive result than critics usually offer if we assume that the Chronicler assumed that his readers were familiar or had access to the "deuteronomic" history, and hence avoided unnecessary duplication. This should be most obvious in the case of the initial genealogies: the basic narrative was familiar enough, and the postexilic community needed only formulaic assurance that it and its leaders stood on the bedrock of God's creative and elective grace (cf. below). The Chronicler's purpose was not to compete with or supplant the "Primary History" of Genesis—Kings, but to supplement it, or, even better, to shed alternate light on the same history in the light of new needs and interests. Thus, perhaps it is better to assume that the entire history of the Northern Kingdom is omitted, not so much because of political and religious enmity, or because the Chronicler thought that the embarrassing data would go away if he but ignored it, but rather simply because he had nothing further to add to the existing tableau. Failures in Judah and God's judgments upon them are by no means suppressed, but neither are they highlighted because of the Chronicler's purpose to encourage depressed Israel with an example of what God wished to do with and for His people if they did not rebel. Then we can also understand why he makes extensive additions to the David and Solomon narratives because of cultic interests, while other narratives in Samuel and Kings are severely cut.

Many of the additions seem to be intended simply to balance the existing picture with data not previously incorporated. Like the genealogies, these often seem intended to exemplify Israel as the true "church" of God, to demonstrate the legitimacy of its temple services and religious institutions. The public, corporate concern of the variations seems established by the fact that nearly *everything* of the private lives of David and Solomon is omitted, not only what might possibly besmirch their reputation (as critics often construe it), but also episodes which might have contributed to an idealized portrait. By such principles of selection and control (essentially no different than any other writer), the Chronicler seeks not to falsify history, but simply to demonstrate how God achieved the objectives which he had ordained for His people—even in the externally rather inglorious circumstances of the moment. Read by itself, Chronicles does not give a complete, balanced picture, but neither does Kings (nor in the sense of the modern myth of objectivity did either one try to), but that does not render either one false, unless we seek to measure it by alien criteria.

Historical Reliability

In the light of all this, little surprise that the historical reliability of Chronicles has often been questioned! We find such questioning even in the Talmud, although the book's canonicity is never known to have been at issue. Earlier higher criticism tended almost automatically to challenge the reliability of nearly every statement which was not taken bodily from Samuel or Kings and to view the entire work as simply late Levitical propaganda, allegedly describing what *should* have happened rather than what did. At most, it was conceded to be a useful compend of practices and their rationalizations at the time of composition, perhaps especially valuable as a witness to the forces that shaped Judaism, but devoid of merit as a historical source for the earlier periods they purported to depict. Pfeiffer's verdict would probably be quite typical: he labels the book, "the first apology of Judaism," and writes of its author that he is "utterly devoid of historical sense and even of a genuine curiosity about the actual events and the culture of Judah." Even Soggin recently (1976) writes that in Chronicles, in contrast to the deuteronomic history, "we may say that the theological theory existed first and that the facts came second and were often forcibly made to fit it."

One often cited example is Chronicle's classification of Samuel as a Levite (1 Chron. 6:28 ff.) in alleged contradiction of his description as an Ephraimite in 1 Sam. 1:1. Most likely, however, it is a case of a Levite living in Ephraimite territory (cf. a similar case in Judges 17:7). Alternatively, Samuel could have been "adopted" as a Levite, although it is debated whether this was possible. In any event, were it invention, we would surely expect more to have been made of it.

On the whole, however, in recent times, such consummate skepticism has abated slightly. It is conceded that the Chronicler must have had access to many ancient sources, to which, in any event, he was far closer than any modern historian. Where archaeology had been able to make a judgment, it has tended to be favorable. For example, the aqueduct and water system which Hezekiah built for Jerusalem (2 Chron. 32:30), and the border fortresses built at various times (2 Chron. 11:5-10; 16:1-6) are all now known. The truth of the account of Manasseh's rebellion against his Assyrian overlords, deportation and imprisonment, but also prayer and repentance leading to his subsequent release and restoration (2 Chron. 33:11-13), cannot yet be demonstrated in extra-Biblical sources, but surely only hypercriticism would deny the possibility of Manasseh's complicity (together with Egypt) in a four-year revolt against Ashur-banipal by his brother, Shamash-shum-ukin, in Babylon. (Perhaps the incident is omitted in Kings because it occurred too late in Manasseh's reign to leave any lasting impression.)

Much of the skepticism about Chronicles has to do with its allegedly inflated numbers. Critics, however, appear to have inflated the problem themselves. Of the some twenty instances of differing figures in Chronicles and Samuel-Kings, in only about a third of the cases is the higher figure found in Chronicles. Probably simple textual corruption (especially easy in the case of numbers) accounts for the vast majority of the discrepancies. At times, however, we may also have to reckon with the possibility of the same symbolic or hyperbolic use of numbers which we occasionally encounter elsewhere in the Scriptures, given in the first instance to an Oriental milieu that was more accustomed to such usages then we are.

Theological Historiography

All of these adjustments or rejoinders to the earlier skepticism still leave untouched what is doubtless the underlying stumbling block, namely the book's unabashedly supernaturalistic historiography, about at the furthest possible remove from that which arrogates to itself the label, "scientific." The *skandalon* has been eased only slightly by the recent demise of the myth of presuppositionlessness, and by the renewed realization that Samuel-Kings certainly is not positivistic history either. The difference is only in degree, not at all in kind, from all the rest of the "histories" in the Bible. It is easy to ridicule or caricature Chronicles' historiography when it is no longer comprehended, that is, when it is forgotten that the author is more concerned with writing a metaphysic of history or History rather then mere history—although the two are ultimately conjunctive, of course.

In Chronicles, vitually everything is the result of direct divine intervention. In utter contrast to the modern immanentalistic preference for "Providence," God's relation to history in Chronicles is so extremely close that liberals sometimes style it "manipulative." All history thus becomes "miraculous." Because God is on their side, the outcome of Israel's battles is "predestined" in advance; the significant activity of men seems almost to be limited to prayers and hymns. A good example is Jehoshaphat's battle against Moab and Ammon (2 Chron. 20). After a prayer and encouragement from the inspired Jahaziel, Jehoshaphat fields an "army" in the form of a temple choir chanting psalms in the wilderness. "And when they began to sing and praise, the LORD set an ambush against the men—destroying them utterly" (vs. 22-23). Somehow "Mount Seir" (Edom) enters the picture, so that "they all helped to destroy one another."

Now, indeed, if the Chronicler intended that as an *empirical* description of the battle, we have a few difficulties. If one remembers the conventions of "holy war," however, particularly the liturgical aspects of it (attaching to another of the Chronicler's major interests), even the empirical difficulties diminish. Undoubtedly, there was much more to it, but also unbelievers could see that, and, hence, to the Chronicler there was no point in belaboring it. What was supremely important was what only the eye of faith could see, the eternal and eschatological dimensions of the battle which transcended time and space.

In its own way, "apocalyptic" literature consistently makes the same point. Particularly, orthodox Christians who propound such a concept of the ultimacies of history should have little difficulty in appreciating Chronicles' consistent application of it. One is reminded of Dorothy Sayers' profound dictum: "The resurrection is the only thing that ever *really* happened!"

One consistent application of the above accent in Chronicles' theology of history appears in the rigorous presentation of divine reward or retribution. The viewpoint again is standard throughout Scripture, especially in the "deuteronomic" and wisdom corpuses (cf. Ps. 1). In Chronicles, retribution comes with a promptness and almost mathematical proportion that would indeed contradict experience if it were really to be taken as *simply* an experiential account. But as we stressed in connection with wisdom literature (which see), in total canonical context we must understand an "ultimately," if not an "eschatologically" before such assertions. Only by direct inspiration, of course, can any man assert precisely how the divine laws of reward and retribution have been applied in this life. (Some critics suppose that the Chronicler's stress on terrestial retribution implies a resistance to or rejection of the "newer" doctrines of reward or punishment in an afterlife, but there certainly is no hint of such an antithesis in the book, and it is obviously a problem of the evolutionists' own making.) One good example of this accent in Chronicles is its added explanation for Josiah's tragic defeat and death at Megiddo; it was because "he did not listen to the words of Necho from the mouth of God [the Pharaoh who attempted to dissuade him], but joined battle in the plain of Megiddo" (2 Chron. 35:22).

Another prominent accent in Chronicles' theology is "ecclesiology," specifically the concern for the legitimacy of the community. No doubt, the meanness of external circumstance at the time of writing accounts for some of this stress, but theologically it attaches to the pivotal doctrines of election and covenant, to the whole sense of a teleological history. Especially in such circumstances is it necessary to confess: "I *believe* one, holy, catholic, and apostolic church." The Jerusalem community, he stresses, was certainly the legitimate heir of the ancient promises, the true "visible church," the "new Israel," the remnant, the holy seed—*a* fulfillment, even if not *the* fulfillment. In a day of small things (Zech. 4:10), the Chronicler boldly proclaims that the entire history of mankind from Adam onward had taken place for the sake of this small community within the vast Persian empire. Only in the light of the history of election could the ontological and eschatological significance of the community be properly understood and expounded. Its religion was the only true one on earth, and its temple was mankind's true religious center, the sole earthly abode of the sole deity.

Both the particularism and the universalism of Chronicles should be stressed, and in proper (the normal Biblical) relationship. Especially when Chronicles is linked with Ezra-Nehemiah, critics are wont to accent only the exclusivism and interpret the omission of the history of the Northern Kingdom in that light (cf. above). More recently, the tendency has grown to read the book as a sort of a compromise of the warring separatistic and universalistic parties which had allegedly wracked postexilic history (allegedly spearheaded by Ezekiel and "Deutero-Isaiah," respectively). Such a politicizing interpretation and critical tendency to maximize conflict must be rejected, of course, but backhandedly it does give renewed attention to Chronicles' universal sensitivities. Like the prophets, he envisions a reunited Davidic kingdom with its capital at Jerusalem. Some 41 times he speaks of "all Israel" (cf. Deuteronomy), and 24 times of "the whole congregation of Israel." He misses no opportunity to speak of "evangelistic" missions to the seceded tribes, and delights in reporting occasions when Northerners did come to Jerusalem (e.g., 1 Chron. 13:2; 2 Chron. 30:10 ff.; 34:9).

Elsewhere it appears that even Gentiles are welcome in the temple precincts as long as they come in reverent acknowledgment of Yahweh's sovereignty (e.g., the duplication of that portion of Solomon's dedicatory prayer, 2 Chron. 6:32-33 = 1 Kings 8:41-43). All of this, of course, is thoroughly in accord with the "missiology" of the Old Testament as a whole.

A final bit of evidence that the Chronicler was not quite the fanatic he is often made out to be comes in his reproduction of the original names of Ishbosheth (Ishbaal; 1 Chron. 8:33; 9:39) and Mephibosheth (Meribaal, 1 Chron. 8:34) before their alteration, as in Samuel, to expunge the "Baal" element.

A sort of *analogia entis* existed between God and His followers on earth. His own holiness had to be reflected, physically as well as spiritually in their own being, if the disastrous experience of the Exile was not to be repeated. Their absolute moral standards as well as flawless execution of the cult were prerequisites (properly understood!) for divine blessing.

Inevitably, the concern for legitimacy centered on the community's leaders, specifically the hierarchy or the Levitical priesthood, not only the Zadokite high priest, but also the lesser clergy, the Levites (cf. below). If God's grace and holiness is to be mediated to his people, it must be through duly authorized and "ordained" personnel. Hence, of course, the genealogical interest, demonstrating the unbroken "apostolic succession" of the priestly orders back not only to Moses and Aaron, but also to Levi, the son of Israel. This picture, too, is no different than the Pentateuch's; here too the Chronicler is no innovator but is simply concerned that they be faithful to the ancient revelation, as befitted their exalted calling and status. The New Testament Christian does not relate to this sacerdotal picture quite as readily as to others, but unless he has completely spiritualized the concepts of church and ministry, *mutatis mutandis* they still speak powerfully to the church in the world until the end of time.

In this light, it is all the more significant that "institutional" concerns have by no means eclipsed the "charismatic" in Chronicles. On the contrary, in some respects Chronicles is the most "Spirit-filled" book in the Scriptures, precisely because all opposition between spirit and form, physical and spiritual, is almost determinedly transcended. In Chronicles, the Spirit speaks through virtually any agency, even through a pagan king such as Pharaoh Necho, as we noted above. Prophecy is "cultic," but equally noncultic, it matters little. Particularly in Chronicles we meet that usage wherein the chant and psalmody of the levitical choirs is sometimes characterized as "prophecy," no doubt partly because of external similarities at times (and possibly also common roots) but ultimately in recognition that "all these are inspired by one and the same Spirit" (1 Cor. 12:11). It is precisely because true worship, even the most formal and ritualistic, is so Spiritual, that worship in Chronicles has such an obviously celebrative and joyful atmosphere (cf. below). There is no better refutation in all of Scripture than Chronicles to the earlier critical dogma and prejudice (which still lingers) to the effect that the "prophetic religion of the heart" had no room for the "sterile rubricalism" of the priesthood, or vice versa.

The same Spirit thus inspires not only priest, but king and prophet as well. David, in prophetic manner, himself receives the divine word (1 Chron. 28:19 even reports his receiving temple plans "in *writing* from the hand of the LORD," doubtless parallel to Moses' inspired blueprint for the tabernacle; Ex. 25:9). Likewise, David's successors, at least the faithful ones, are favored with direct revelation, which they pass on to others, thus assuming the prophetic role. This general picture, of course, is not unique to Chronicles either, but nowhere so highlighted as by him.

Naturally, of course, it is the prophets themselves who are the most common mouthpiece of the Spirit. We noted above the statistical evidence for the great prominence accorded this accent in Chronicles. Especially accented is the role of the prophet as advisor to the (Davidide) king. In fact, one may wonder if Chronicles has not departed entirely from any formal or sociological sense of the word "prophet," using it totally in its basal Biblical sense of *any* bearer of divine revelation. Many of these prophets are also Levites, but apart from Chronicles' general interest in that group, no particular significance seems to attach to the fact.

In fact, the Chronicler does much of his own teaching through extensive quotation of prophetic sermons, oracles, and prayers throughout the book. The characteristic prophetic accent on the need for prayer and repentance thus receives due stress, as well as the consequent summons to faith and action. Attention must be called to a celebrated analysis of "The Levitical Sermon in I and II Chronicles" by von Rad (cf. Dodd's study of apostolic preaching in the New Testament). In his study of this *Gattung,* von Rad notes at least three elements which usually appear, at least in part: (1) quotation of an ancient source, often prophetic, i.e., a text; (2) application of the theological principle of that quotation to some aspect of Israel's past, i.e., "Gospel" as manifested in one of God's mighty acts; and (3) application of the text to the present, usually a call to faith and action. Of course, von Rad tends to think of the "Levitical sermon" as largely a literary artifice of the Chronicler, but, if taken at face value, we have here a very important entrée to a much neglected subject, the preaching of the Old Testament.

The Chronicler's effort to stimulate the rebuilding of the theocracy may be pictured as an ellipse focusing on two interrelated divine institutions, temple (with priesthood) and Davidic monarchy (in the holy city, Zion). David is the key figure throughout (again a concern with legitimacy here), but let us first explore Chronicles' overriding accent on liturgy or cultus. We have already stressed that only liberal, hyper-Protestant prejudice will misunderstand this as mere rubricalism, aestheticism, archaism, or what not. Rather, at its heart is the accent that in inner essence Israel was a "church," a worshiping community, a liturgical assembly. *All* of life is to be *leitourgia,* worship, service (one word serves for both the broader and narrower senses of the term in Hebrew as well as in English). This idea, of course, underlay the priestly materials of the Pentateuch too (which see), and the prophets had underscored it mightily, but the political concerns of the monarchy often distracted from this center and fostered false notions of the nature of the "kingdom." No doubt, by this accent the Chronicler is partly motivated to assist the postexilic community in its adjustment from a politically independent society to a religious community without political possibilities. Now that Israel's political glory was a thing of the past, it must be underscored anew that the true vocation of the chosen people was to offer God the homage of an undefiled cult in the Jerusalem temple. Not national and worldly glory, but religious zeal would have to be the source of Israelite greatness and strength from here on. Israel's hope dare not be placed in military strength or political acumen but solely in fidelity to the covenant.

The sad miscarriages of the Maccabean era vividly illustrate how difficult it was for the old Israel to learn this lesson—and, of course, from a Christian standpoint, she *could* not—has not yet—learned it fully except by eschatological rebirth into a "new Israel." The Christian inevitably finds an important part of the *preparatio evangelica* here, but, if honest, he will also be reminded how difficult it has been also for the "new Israel" on earth to be faithful to the calling, and how much less excusable its failures. Not that conservatism's record is lily-white by any means, but the conservative cannot but view much of liberalism's "political theology" as a conscious repudiation of the Chronicler's point.

Cultic Themes

In Chronicles' delineation of the cult, three themes stand out: (1) temple and ark; (2) Levites; and (3) choral chant or temple music. Critics are usually quick to suspect tension, if not outright opposition, to P in these accents. If we transpose the objection to the "Mosaic Pentateuch," one may concede half-truth in the observation. But it is assuredly another instance of the Chronicler's supplementation or addition to the existing picture rather than ideological conflict. In fact, in 2 Chron. 23—26, describing the organization and duties of the Levites, it is stressed that David, realizing that the temple would require more levitical services than the tabernacle, had not only expanded their numbers, but had also lowered the age of eligibility for service from thirty to twenty (here, of course, a major refutation of the critical assumption that "P" represents a simple retrojection of postexilic practices).

We noted earlier that much of P, especially Leviticus, is to be read as a handbook of rubrics specifically for priests, and, similarly, we may well see Chronicles as an exposition of the Levitical viewpoint. Cf. the genealogy of Levi in 1 Chron. 6, where the Levites are listed before the priests, or the more frequent criticisms of the priests than the Levites throughout the book. Humanly speaking, there is no reason why the Chronicler here should not be betraying some of his own personal interests and involvements. The theory is very plausible which suggests that he himself was a Levitical member of the temple choirs. It seems less likely to us that the Levites are stressed because of their record of unfaithfulness at times (cf. Ezek. 44:10 ff.), or because of their poor response to the call to return from Babylon (cf. Ezra 8:15 ff.). Part of the motivation may have been the recurring problem, as old as Deuteronomy, of the neglect of the tithes and offerings for the sustenance of the Levites (cf. Neh. 13:10 ff.).

Even though the Chronicler's heart appears to be more with the Levites, there is never any suggestion of breaching the traditional distinction between them and the priests, or of evading the priestly supervision of Levitical work (the vast variety of which, in addition to singing and preaching, is amply documented in the book). In fact, sometimes the Chronicler seems more concerned to safeguard the priestly position than the "Deuteronomist" had been, e.g., Uzziah's punishment for daring to offer incense (2 Chron. 26:16 ff.); or the description of David's sons simply as "chiefs" (1 Chron. 18:17) instead of as "priests" as in 2 Sam. 8:18. Similarly, the traditional sacrifices according to the Mosaic rubrics receive ample mention, but, this being a priestly province, the subject is not highlighted. And it is surely perverse (and a blatant contradiction of the evolutionism underlying Wellhausen's whole theory) to suggest that Chronicles accents celebration so much because he disagrees with the hamartiology underlying the sacrificial cult (cf. 1 Chron. 21:7, 17; 2 Chron. 19:10, etc.)!

Inevitably, the temple receives considerable accent, and not only because it was about the only rallying point the postexilic community had. Much of the relevant material in Kings is reproduced (e.g., much of 2 Chron. 2—9 = 1 Kings 5 ff.) but much is also added; e.g., David's preparations for building the temple and charge to Solomon (1 Chron. 22; perhaps in a coregency, during a rally or period of strength, in spite of the senility reported in 1 Kings 2). However, the Chronicler is at pains to stress that the angel of the LORD had specified Araunah's threshing floor as the site of the temple (1 Chron. 21), and that David received heavenly plans for the temple just as Moses once had for the tabernacle (1 Chron. 22:1; 28:19). As in 1 Kings 8 great accent is put on Yahweh's abiding "real presence" in the temple, not only the center of their present life but also typifying and pointing toward the visible, eschatological return of the LORD to His "temple," the new creation, on the coming Day of salvation. God's presence is expressed more often in terms of His "name" associated especially with Deuteronomy, than in terms of His "glory," as the priests apparently preferred to articulate it. In a way, this eternal "incarnational" presence of God amongst His people in implementation of the basic covenant promise often receives more stress than the *heilsgeschichtliche* theme of (isolated) mighty acts of God in the past such as the Exodus, etc., which are little mentioned.

The "ark of the covenant", that is, the "'incarnation' of the covenant," the center of the temple as the center of God's presence, and hence also a major symbol of the unity of all the tribes of Israel, inevitably is also highlighted, and apparently also because it was the Levites' sole prerogative to carry it, as is explicitly stressed in 1 Chron. 15:2. The entire section, 1 Chron. 13—17, describing David's bringing of the ark from the house of Obededom to Jerusalem, is considerably expanded over the parallel pericope in 2 Sam. 6—7, primarily by detailing the Levites' role in the preparations for the move, as well as in the actual procession. It cannot be proved from the Chronicles description of the event any more than from that in Samuel, that a similar procession involving the ark was a recurrent liturgical occasion as many scholars have hypothesized (cf. Ps. 24, 132, etc.) However, the great detail with which the Chronicler records the event suggests that his interest was not only historical.

The role of the Levites as liturgical singers and musicians is also introduced in connection with the procession of the ark to Jerusalem (1 Chron. 15:16 ff; cf. 1 Chron. 6:31-48). This service becomes a permanent part of the temple liturgy, and in 1 Chron. 25 the families and courses of the choristers are detailed. There it is plain that they are given an honor beyond that of the ordinary Levite (cf. Luther and his high regard for music in the service of God). (We discount much critical skepticism which holds the cultic and genealogical details of 1 Chron. 23—27 to be a later addition or expansion of 1 Chron. 6.) The liturgical functions of the Levites are characteristically listed in this order (2 Chron. 18:14): "to sing praise, and to minister before the priests, as the duty of every day required."

The Chronicler discloses an exact and detailed knowledge of the musical parts of the typical temple service, especially of its vocal aspects, but not neglecting the instrumental. This is an aspect of Israel's worship, of which we would know next to nothing, were it not for Chronicles (except possibly for the much later Mishnaic descriptions) and in most handbooks the sacrifical aspect still receives disproportionate attention. There is no reason at all why Chronicles' celebrative tone should be pitted against the more penitential one of P; they are two sides of one coin, and together they express the *Simchath Torah* (Rejoicing in the Law) which is native to Old Testament theology. Attention should be called especially to an often overlooked pericope (1 Chron. 29), where the Eucharistic theme is explicitly associated with sacrifice. The occasion is Solomon's second anointing (v. 22), and after the presentation of the tribes' freewill offerings, David expresses himself in language echoed repeatedly in the Offertories and Eucharistic prayers of Christendom: "For all things come of thee, and of thine own have we given thee" (v. 14b).

Our only other Biblical source for this aspect of Israelite worship is, of course, the Psalter. Even more than Leviticus, Chronicles should be absolutely indispensable collateral reading with the psalms, at least if one aspires to hear them in anything like their original *Sitz im Leben*. The Chronicler himself quotes the text of many of the psalms sung by the Levites on various occasions, most of which are essentially parallel to some in the psalter (although usually in varying combinations, suggesting considerable freedom in their actual use). It is these praises especially which give the whole cultic theology of Chronicles its distinctive note of supreme joy and thanksgiving. As von Rad once perceptively observed in the context of critical skepticism and negativism: "But with it all we must always ask whether a theology which saw Israel's existence in the eyes of Yahweh as so strongly conditioned by praise could have strayed so very far from the proper road."

One notes parallels also with the superscriptions of the psalms: the word commonly translated "chief musician," and the singers' guilds, Heman, Ethan, and especially Asaph (who is singularly accented, and to which guild hence some suppose that the Chronicler himself belonged). Unfortunately, not even Chronicles gives us enough information to decipher much from the superscriptions, but he is major, independent testimony to their antiquity and accuracy. (Over against critical skepticism, they largely stand or fall together!)

Time was when Chronicles' descriptions of the temple services was hooted out of court by critics, particularly if they were supposed to preserve any accurate memory of what transpired in the *first* (Solomon's instead of Zerubbabel's) temple. Archaeology cannot yet *prove* the contrary, but it has at least pulled the rug out from under any *a priori* skepticism about the possibility of the temple choirs having been David's literal achievement. Canaan had a reputation for music long before the Israelites invaded, and even the names of the guilds suggest Canaanite backgrounds (Heman, Ethan; the later styled an "Ezrahite" in 1 Kings 5:11 and Ps. 88:1; 89:1, that is an "autochthonous" native of the land). One recalls that we now also have ample ancient parallels for the texts of many psalms and for the sacrificial rites at which they were employed, both once as widely questioned as the music.

Davidism (Messianism)

However, the pinnacle of the Chronicler's edifice, or the other focus of his ellipse (alongside temple and its cult) is "Davidism." The perpetuity of David's house and the functioning of the temple are uttered in one breath, as it were. The entire work could be subtitled something like, "The History of the Davidic Dynasty, the Recipient of a Divine Promise." Undoubtedly, this theme too is related to the book's didactic intent of giving the people of his day new courage and purpose, but how? Two things stand out in Chronicles' treatment of the subject: (1) his accent on David instead of Moses; and (2) the fact that he writes at a time when the throne is vacant, with little prospect of any Davidide ever being able to occupy it again.

One must again resist the critical temptation to see any semi-polemic intent on the Chronicler's part to downplay Moses or the Torah as "priestly." As a matter of fact, both "Moses" and "Torah" are mentioned more frequently in Chronicles than in Samuel-Kings (31 versus 12 and 47 versus 14 times, respectively). Not only with respect to cult (cf. above), but in general the Torah obviously remains the official standard by which the people orders its life (e.g., Jehoshaphat's instruction in 2 Chron. 17:9; Josiah's reformation in 2 Chron. 34; and Ezra's and Nehemiah's labors, if that is to be included). In 2 Chron. 31 Hezekiah enjoins the people to be faithful in giving "the portion due to the priests and the Levites, that they might give themselves to the law of the LORD" (v. 4). And so on.

Chronicles is no more anti-Moses than P is anti-David (the latter, of course, because it long precedes David, not, as the critics would have it, a hierocratic replacement for the defunct monarchy). Possibly, Moses receives less accent because the proto-Samaritans also appealed to him, as they could not to David, but that is speculation. Rather, it is surely primarily another instance of Chronicles' supplementation of other Scripture; after all, the "deuteronomistic history" had had even less to say of Moses, and its monarchical accent was somewhat unfocused. David does not so much replace Moses, as stand on his shoulders. As in all of Biblical theology, the covenant with David does not abrogate but extends and applies the ancient oaths. The Chronicler does not repristinate to any one idealized segment of history, but relates to its totality, as it had accumulated.

Hence, since Moses was in a sense "accessible," historically as well as theologically, only via what transpired under David, it is thoroughly understandable that Chronicles, aiming at the life of the entire nation and not only its clergy, focuses on David rather than Moses as the great agent of God's purposes for Israel. In a sense, the whole covenantal relation of God to man is concretized in the man David and what God accomplished through him. It is no contradiction of the above to stress that sometimes David almost appears as a "second Moses," receiving from God's hands the pattern of the temple as Moses had of the tabernacle, and that David is even empowered to make adjustments in ritual and architectural detail, as new circumstances required (cf. above).

In another sense, however, there is a "back to Moses" aspect in the Chronicler's presentation of David, because he now presides over more of a community of faith or a "church" than a state, with its political and military preoccupations. And this gives us our transition to the other thing which must constantly be read between the lines in Chronicles, namely the awareness that, as he writes, except for the liturgical trappings, all the glories of the Davidic empire are as ancient history as the stories of Moses.

What is the point of it? Surely not just royalist nostalgia, or an archivist's ("chronicler's") love of the past for its own sake! The Chronicler's orientation is surely to the present and the future more than to the past. The critical wisdom has generally been that the Chronicler lacks eschatology, but, at best, this is superficial. Sometimes he is even declared guilty of "realized eschatology," of holding that God's theocratic plan has already been actuated, with no further fulfillment to be expected; at best, that is a half-truth, seeing only the undeniable "now" of Chronicles' kerygma apart from its constantly implied "not yet."

The Chronicler evokes memories of presently unrealizable glories partly in order to stress that the ancient dynastic promises are not forgotten in these ignominious days, nor is God powerless to fulfill them. If Israel will only remain resolutely faithful, she will yet experience even greater glories. The covenant promises to David may be in momentary abeyance, but in God's good time, a "greater than David" will surely rise from among them. One may quibble about the appropriateness of the term "messianic" to describe Chronicle's depictions, but that is surely the import, even though the technical language is not used and the hope is not couched in the futuristic language of the prophets. David is, in a sense, superior to Moses precisely because in him originated the kingdom which still has a lawful claim to rule and which is destined to Messianic transfiguration.

Stinespring has popularized a Bultmannian analogy between the early church's eschatological expectation allegedly centering on a "Jesus of Faith" (in contrast to the actual "Jesus of History") and the Chronicler's futuristic hopes expressed in his portraiture of a "David of Faith" in contrast to the historical David. The Christological analogy is itself without foundation, of course, but if we divest the formulation of its implications of untruth on the Chronicler's part, we may accept it as an unfortunate way of expressing with respect to David what we accented earlier in general, namely that the author is writing History, not history, the sacramental and metaphysical meaning of history in the light of election, not merely a journalistic account of current events. The Chronicler's David already anticipates in many ways his Antitype, and the coming of the eternal, eschatological kingdom into the present should embolden and hearten those who wait.

But the Chronicler's messianic hope is neither escapism nor triumphalism, any more than the rest of Biblical eschatology. As we stressed earlier, so in his portrait of David, while the positive of God's promises is stressed, the possiblity of human rebellion turning it into judgment is never forgotten. Here that note is especially evident in Chronicles' reproduction (1 Chron. 17) of Nathan's great oracle to David in 2 Sam. 7. Both chapters highlight the absolute and irrevocable terms of the Davidic covenant, of course, but both of them also include a condition based on the faithfulness and obedience of the reigning king. Both historians are well aware of the disastrous consequences of disobedience, and both proclaim the overruling grace of God and ultimate fulfillment of His Word, no matter what man's folly (yes, even through it, as sealed on the cross).

Likewise, the Chronicler's messianic concentration should not imply any narrowing of a broader *Heilsgeschichte* perspective. As usual, however, the Chronicler can deal with that formulaically and leave it to the rest of Scripture to fill out the details. The genealogies of 1 Chron. 1—9 not only point a finger at the physical descendants of David among them as a sign and guarantee that David's counterpart will one day take up residence in their midst in the flesh, but they also provide a messianic, eschatological signature to the entire book in the light of God's universal purposes since Adam.

How clearly in detail the Chronicler saw we know no more than of any of the worthies of the Old Testament. But especially in total canonical context we assuredly do not go astray if we press the point that Chronicles' interest in the kingdom of the first David is also an interest in the new David and the new, eschatological kingdom that will arise in God's good time. The stupendous victories of the Davidides over all foes are portents of and participations in the church militant's final eschatological triumph. Gold and silver already flow to Jerusalem in an eschatological way (cf. Is. 60 ff., Hag. 2:6-9, etc.). The sumptuous banquets are surely Messianic (and Eucharistic) in their proportions (cf. Is. 25). Above all, in the most intimate relation possible with the restoration of the house of David stands the typology of the temple and its worship. The earthly temple, with its foundations in eternity, where God Himself is already "incarnate," constantly beacons toward that city without a temple where the dwelling of God is forever with men. And the supernal music which reverberates throughout the book is a prolepsis of and partaking in the new song of a new age.

On second thought, perhaps Chronicles was chosen to conclude the canon of the old covenant, both because of its profound realization that "all theology is doxology," and also because of its magnificent forward thrust toward the new and eternal covenant in great David's greater Son.

INDEXES

Erich B. Allwardt and David A. Lumpp

TOPICAL INDEX

Funeral dirge 170
Fungus 83

G (*Grundschrift*) 38, 45
Galilee 106
Gattungsforschung 24
Genealogy 34, 52, 53, 65, 66, 507, 511,
      512, 514, 515, 603, 618, 619, 621,
      622, 623, 627, 631-632
Generations 53, 65, 66
Genesis Apocryphon 568
Gentile 345, 383, 561, 570, 627
   oracles *see* Oracles, Gentile
George, St. 573
Gerizim 39, 94, 95, 103
   and Ebal 96
Gezer 281
Gibberish
   in Hosea 290
   in Proverbs 452-453
Gibeon 105, 106, 109, 110, 118
Gideon 94, 118-119, 129, 293
Gilgal 47, 106, 109
   etymology of 105
Gilgamesh epic 528, 532
Glory of God 53, 78, 79, 85, 197, 209,
      210, 217, 227, 266, 268, 269, 270,
      279, 281, 360, 364, 631
Glossolalia 125, 172
Gnosticism 264
God passim
   as change 160
   as idea 159
   as personal 71
   as sitting 79
   glory of *see* Glory of God
   indwelling of 79
   of the fathers 52
   wrath of 85
Gog 278
Golden age of Solomon 91
Goliath 128, 132
Gomer, meaning of 287
Gospel 62 and passim
   defining 19
   other 434, 525
   see also Law-Gospel
Governor 381
Greece 175
Greek

in Chronicles 619-620
in Daniel 568
in Ezra-Nehemiah 619
influence 454, 494, 528
trade 301
transmission 154
version of Canticles 495

H (Holiness code) 56, 60, 75, 83-84,
      261, 265
   see also Holiness code
Habakkuk, the name 342
Hadad (Baal) 129, 593
Haggai
   in Ezra 601
   person of 355-356
Hagiographa 387, 405, 511, 516, 566,
      597, 615, 617
Hagiography, medieval 143
Hallel psalms 412
Hamartiology 433, 630
Hammurabi 67
   code of 468
Hananiah, rabbi 264
Hannah, song of 124, 408
Hansen's disease 83
Hanukkah 412, 579
Hapax legomena 461, 495
Harper, Song of the 394, 528
Hasidim 569
Hazor 106, 110, 281, 310
Heathen *see* Pagan
Hebdomad 584, 587, 588, 589
Hebrew language 60
   classical 303, 325
   in Ecclesiastes 527
   in Ezra 600
   of Esther 543
   of Samuel 133
   verb tenses in 320-321
Hebron 42
Hedonism 533
Hegelian waltz or dialectic 159
Heifer, red 88
Heilseschatologie 317
Heilsgeschichte 28, 30, 66, 107, 137,
      199, 207, 220, 224, 297, 307, 314,
      336, 340, 351, 364, 392, 399, 402,
      435, 451, 504, 512, 514, 616, 631,
      635

INDEX OF AUTHORS

(Ancient and Modern)

INDEX OF SCRIPTURE PASSAGES

2:5-6   540
2:6   537
2:7   540
2:10   540
2:16   537
3:2 ff.   539
3:7 ff.   539
3:7   538, 541
4:1-3   545
4:14   547
4:16   548
5:14   539
6   539
7—8   538
7:8   539
7:9-10   539
8:8   577
8:9 ff.   539
9   541
9:3   539
9:7-9   541
9:16-19   541
9:16   539
9:20 ff.   541
9:20—10:3   541
9:20   542
9:24-26   541
9:24   538
9:32   542
10:2   536, 542

JOB   23, 217, 314, 347,
350, 351, 388, 393, 394,
398, 405, 433, 448, 453,
457-491, 523, 532, 534,
535, 567, 579
Outline   466-477
Contents   473-491
1—2   365, 467, 468, 473-
474, 622
1   476
1:1   461
1:3   461
1:15   461
1:17   461
2   468, 476
3—37   474-482
3—31   469
3:8   485
5:9-16   393
7:12   476, 485
8:11   461
9   477, 478
9:8   476
9:13   476, 485

9:31   365
9:33   476
14   477
14:12   479
15:20 ff.   463
16   478
16:2   477
16:18-22   477
16:19   479
16:21   478
17:1-3   478
19   464, 476-480, 481
19:9   468
19:23   482
19:25 ff.   488
19:25   488, 515
22—27   469
24—31   473
24:18-24   469
25:1-6   469
26—31   469
26:5-14   469
26:12   485
27   471
27:2   468
27:13-23   469
28   393, 471, 479, 480-
481
28:28   400, 454, 468
29—37   481-482
29—31   460
31   466
31:40b   470
32—37   471
32:2-4   472
33:19-33   479
33:23   479
35:10   489
38 ff.   480, 482
38—43   468
38:1—42:6   470
38—42   482-491
38:1—40:2   470
38   453
38:3-38   452
40—41   461
40:3-5   470
40:6—41:34   470
40:15-24   470
40:21   461
41   470
42:1-6   470
42:7-17   467
42:7-9   466
42:7a   470

PSALMS (Psalter)   23, 81,
87, 102, 114, 124, 190,
199, 206, 214, 222, 231,
245, 265, 297, 343, 344,
346, 354, 388, 393, 399,
466, 518, 526, 554, 567,
581, 632
1—41   409
1—2   410
1   100, 388, 433, 437,
438, 455, 625
1:5   406
1:6   406
2   410, 438, 447
2:1-2   439
2:6   406, 457
2:7   218, 398, 399, 439
2:8   439
4   413, 435
5   417
5:7   577
6   412, 413, 428
7   413
8   476
9   407
10   407, 410
11   435
14   410
15   336, 346
16   413, 435
16:10   328
18   132, 408, 418, 438,
446
20   417, 438
21   417, 438
22   327, 413, 428, 431
22:7   524
22:21b   435
22:25 ff.   435
23   248, 404, 407, 435
23:5   433
24   415, 631
24:3-6   336, 436
27   417
27:1-6   435
28:2   577
29   419, 427, 482
29:2   405
30   415, 424, 428
32   428
33   410, 521
34   428, 521
34:12   437
35   433
36   429